# Microsoft® Office 2008 for Mac® Bible

# Microsoft® Office 2008 for Mac® Bible

**Sherry Kinkoph Gunter**
**with Jennifer Ackerman Kettell and**
**Greg Kettell**

WILEY

Wiley Publishing, Inc.

Microsoft® Office 2008 for Mac® Bible

Published by
**Wiley Publishing, Inc.**
10475 Crosspoint Boulevard
Indianapolis, IN 46256
www.wiley.com

Copyright © 2009 by Wiley Publishing, Inc., Indianapolis, Indiana

Published simultaneously in Canada

ISBN: 978-0-470-38315-5

Manufactured in the United States of America

10 9 8 7 6 5 4 3 2 1

For general information on our other products and services or to obtain technical support, please contact our Customer Care Department within the U.S. at (877) 762-2974, outside the U.S. at (317) 572-3993 or fax (317) 572-4002.

**Library of Congress Control Number: 2009924126**

**Trademarks:** Wiley, the Wiley logo, and related trade dress are trademarks or registered trademarks of John Wiley & Sons, Inc. and/or its affiliates, in the United States and other countries, and may not be used without written permission. Microsoft is a registered trademark of Microsoft Corporation in the United States and/or other countries. Mac is a registered trademark of Apple Computer. All other trademarks are the property of their respective owners. Wiley Publishing, Inc., is not associated with any product or vendor mentioned in this book.

Wiley also publishes its books in a variety of electronic formats. Some content that appears in print may not be available in electronic books.

# About the Authors

**Sherry Kinkoph Gunter** has written and edited oodles of books over the past 16 years, covering a variety of computer topics, including Microsoft Office programs, digital photography, and Web applications. Her recent titles include *Teach Yourself VISUALLY Microsoft Office 2007* and *Teach Yourself VISUALLY Flash CS3*. Sherry's ongoing quest is to help users of all levels master the ever-changing computer technologies. No matter how many times the software manufacturers throw out a new version or upgrade, Sherry vows to be there to make sense of it all and help computer users get the most out of their machines. Sherry currently resides in a swamp in the wilds of central Indiana with a lovable ogre and a menagerie of interesting creatures, including an iMac.

**Jennifer and Greg Kettell** have written and contributed to dozens of books about software applications, Web design, and graphics. Their most recent title is *Microsoft Windows Home Server Bible*. Jenn and Greg have lived all over the United States, but currently call upstate New York home. They share their abode with two children, a dog, three cats, and a bearded dragon, only some of which are housebroken.

# Credits

**Associate Acquisitions Editor**
Aaron Black

**Project Editor**
Martin V. Minner

**Technical Editor**
Geoff Coryell

**Copy Editor**
Gwenette Gaddis

**Editorial Manager**
Robyn Siesky

**Business Manager**
Amy Knies

**Senior Marketing Manager**
Sandy Smith

**Vice President and Executive Group Publisher**
Richard Swadley

**Vice President and Executive Publisher**
Barry Pruett

**Project Coordinators**
Patrick Redmond
Erin Smith

**Graphics and Production Specialists**
Andrea Hornberger
Jennifer Mayberry
Melissa K. Smith
Ronald Terry

**Quality Control Technician**
John Greenough

**Proofreading**
Toni Settle

**Indexing**
Infodex Indexing Services, Inc.

# Preface

You can always count on a few things in life—death and taxes. I daresay we can add another thing to the list—software upgrades. As computer technology advances, so does the need for faster, stronger, newer, and more improved software. As computer users, we're often divided on how we feel regarding software upgrades. On one hand, we're excited to see what new bells and whistles the software developers have added, anxious to see if they've improved the speed and performance, or eager to see if they've added the feature we've long been waiting for. Yet on the other hand, we're frustrated with upgrades, annoyed about having to reinstall a program, and miffed with having to learn our way around a new program, especially if they've made radical changes to how it looks and how it works. Are we being unreasonable with our dual feelings on upgrades? Not really. It's perfectly normal.

Computers have always carried with them the promise to make our lives easier, and on many levels they have. After we manage to make it past the hump of learning a new program or upgrade, they generally do turn out to be very helpful in the tasks we perform at home and at work. Isn't that what we really want anyway—to get our work done? Oh, sure, sometimes that "work" may look much more like "play," but you get the point. Down deep, we know the energy we expend learning a new program is worth it in the end, as long as we see results. We're still entitled to be a little frustrated with the process of learning to use upgraded software, but that's where a book like this can help smooth out the process.

Often, we're thrown into the chore of learning how to use software without much guidance. Software products don't come with manuals anymore, and the built-in Help systems are notoriously skimpy on real help. That's why you need a book like this—a tome that covers all the ins and outs, explains how to perform all the tasks from A to Z, acts as a reference point when we're stuck on a tool or feature, and basically makes sense of it all. You'll find plenty of information about how to use all the Microsoft Office 2008 for Mac programs in this book, and perhaps the process of learning to use the upgraded software will be a little less frustrating and a little more productive.

## What's in This Book?

The book is divided into eight parts. Here's what you can expect to find in each part:

- **Part I:** The first part of the book covers the fundamentals of installing the software and finding out what improvements have been made since the last release. If you're new to the Office suite, you find a chapter in this section to help you learn program basics, such as opening and exiting programs, working with program windows, and using suite-wide features like menus and toolbars. You can find a chapter on how to utilize the Help system if you ever need it.

- **Part II:** This section of the book covers how to use Microsoft Word 2008. Chapters in this part show you how to navigate the program window, how to start creating documents, and how to improve their appearance with formatting. You also learn how to add tables, utilize citation and proofing tools, and share documents with others utilizing the tracking and reviewing features. Learn how to use Word's new Publishing Layout view to create professional-looking publications.

- **Part III:** The third part of the book shows you how to use Excel 2008. You'll learn how to create formulas, apply functions, build worksheets and workbooks, add charts and graphs, and make your data look professional. Find out how to protect workbooks with passwords, work with Excel's database tools, and define print areas.

- **Part IV:** Learn all about Microsoft's presentation program, PowerPoint, in this section of the book. You gain important knowledge on how to create slide shows, add text and graphics, customize transition effects, add sound or narration, and turn it all into a powerful presentation. You also learn how to use the Presenter tools when giving a presentation.

- **Part V:** This section of the book covers how to use Entourage 2008, a personal information manager for keeping track of daily tasks like schedules, contacts, e-mail, and projects. You learn how to set up your e-mail account, send and receive e-mail, schedule appointments and events, build an address book, organize to-do lists and notes, and manage projects.

- **Part VI:** If your edition of Office 2008 includes the Expression Media software, this section of the book shows you how to use this valuable software to catalog and manage all the digital media files on your computer. Learn how to import digital media, create catalogs, apply filters, and export media.

- **Part VII:** This section of the book covers graphics, Web content, and Microsoft Messenger. Learn how to use clip art, photos, SmartArt, and other graphic elements throughout the Office programs. You also find out how to create Web content using the Office applications. Lastly, you learn how to use Microsoft Messenger to chat online.

- **Part VIII:** This final section of the book shows you how to coordinate and customize the various programs to suit the way you work. You learn how to use the Projects Gallery and Scrapbook features and how to customize the individual programs. You also learn a little about using AppleScripts to help speed up common tasks.

That's just the tip of the proverbial iceberg when it comes to coverage. By the end of the book, you should be extremely acquainted with the Office 2008 suite of programs and know how to use them to get your work—or play—done.

# Who Should Read This Book?

This book is for anyone who uses the Microsoft Office 2008 for Mac programs and wants to learn them proficiently or just have a handy reference when needed. Whether you're new to Office or a long-time user, this book can help you navigate the ins and outs of the upgraded software. It covers everything from basic startup tasks to more complex features like creating mass mailings or making use of the Excel database and analytical tools. You also find information to help you customize the Office suite to suit the way you work.

# How to Use This Book

You do not necessarily need to read this book from one end to the other; rather you can jump into finding out the information you want to know directly if you want. However, if you're new to Office, starting at the beginning and working your way through will help you learn and build on important tools and features for each program. The book is written progressively, which means each section builds on the basics of using a program and then progresses into more complex features.

The book also will come in handy as a reference guide to keep around for refreshing your memory about certain procedures or tasks, or as a tool for looking up new features you tackle.

# Acknowledgments

Special thanks go out to Executive Publisher Barry Pruett and Laura Sinise for allowing me the opportunity to tackle this exciting project; to project editor Martin V. Minner for his dedication and patience in shepherding this project from start to finish; to copy editor Gwenette Gaddis for ensuring that all the i's were dotted and t's were crossed; to technical editor Geoff Coryell for skillfully checking each step and offering valuable input along the way; and finally to the production team at Wiley for their talents in creating such a monumental book. Lastly, extra special thanks to my own Shrek, Matty Gunter, for keeping the swamp shack running while I concentrated on this project.

*—Sherry Kinkoph Gunter*

We wish to thank Laura Sinise, Martin V. Minner, and the rest of the editorial team at Wiley for their guidance and support. Thank you to Sherry Kinkoph Gunter for the opportunity to work together. Special thanks to our family and friends for everything.

*—Jennifer and Greg Kettell*

# Contents at a Glance

# Contents

# Contents

# Contents

# Contents

## Contents

## Part IV: Presenting with PowerPoint     535

### Chapter 19: PowerPoint Basics . . . . . . . . . . . . . . . . . . . . . . . . . 537

# Contents

# Contents

# Contents

# Part I

# Getting to Know Office 2008

# Chapter 1

# Introducing the New Office

How exciting is this? You've just purchased the latest version of Microsoft Office 2008 for Mac, and you can't wait to jump in and see what you can do! Now what? Turns out, this software package is huge and maybe a little daunting because it features myriad improvements to the overall appearance and functionality of the individual programs. How do you begin learning your away around? That's where this book can help. Whether you're simply upgrading from a previous version of Office for Mac, or you're a brand-new user starting with Office for the first time, this book can assist you as you encounter brand-new program features or old tried-and-true techniques. It can even show you some new tricks to make your work easier than ever before.

This chapter gives you an overview of the Office 2008 programs, what to expect as you open each one, and what to look out for regarding new features and tools. You'll learn all the ways you can use the programs to accomplish your work at home or at the office. So what are you waiting for? Jump in!

## IN THIS CHAPTER

**Microsoft Office suite explained**

**Office history in a nutshell**

**New and improved features to learn**

## What Is Office 2008?

At its very core, Microsoft Office 2008 for Mac is a suite of programs you can use for a variety of situations and projects, at home and at work. Whether you need a word processor to type a letter, a spreadsheet program to juggle number data, a presentation program to create slide show presentations, or a personal information manager to track your schedule and send e-mail, you can find it all in Office 2008 for Mac.

Here are just a few things you can do with Office 2008 for Mac:

- Create reports for work or school
- Track and balance a home budget

3

- Log sales figures for an entire department of employees and create productivity charts
- Build slide show presentations for work or school
- E-mail friends, family, and colleagues
- Keep an inventory of home items
- Organize and track a large inventory of products for a company
- Create a flyer or handout
- Present a marketing plan
- Schedule important appointments and calendar dates
- Organize a to-do list for a work project or a home shopping list for the grocery store
- Analyze numerical data and build powerful formulas for manipulating numbers
- Create a Web page

Perhaps this small list is enough to whet your appetite. This tiny list is just the tip of the Office iceberg; I can't begin to list the many things you can do with the programs, and chances are good that you'll find some new things to do with the programs after you've familiarized yourself with each one and set out to use them to get your work done. After all, isn't that why we use computers anyway—to get our work done and to make life easier? Sadly, when it comes to software, the word "easy" isn't necessarily the best adjective for describing anything related to computers. It's certainly not always easy to navigate complex programs and figure out how or where to find the command you need to accomplish a task. Rest assured, after you learn a thing or two about the Office programs, you will indeed find it easier to venture out and create your own list of things to do with your computer. First things first, though.

What is Office 2008 exactly? The four main programs of the suite include Word 2008, Excel 2008, PowerPoint 2008, and Entourage 2008. If you purchased Office 2008 for Mac at the store or online, one of the first things you probably had to figure out was which "flavor" to buy. Office 2008 for Mac comes in three versions for purchase: Office 2008 for Mac (the Standard Edition), Office 2008 for Mac Home and Student Edition, and Office 2008 for Mac Special Media Edition. All three versions include Word, Excel, PowerPoint, and Entourage. All three also include Messenger for Mac, a free instant-messaging application.

At the lower price end of the spectrum, the Mac Home and Student edition sticks with just the basics: the four main programs, plus Messenger for Mac. The middle price point edition, simply named Office 2008 for Mac, adds Microsoft Exchange Server support and Automator Actions for workflows. At the top end of the price spectrum, the Mac Special Media Edition adds Microsoft Exchange Server support, Automator Actions, and Microsoft Expression Media, a digital asset management program you can use to catalog and organize all the digital media on your computer, such as photo files and video clips. This book covers Office 2008 for Mac Special Media Edition, just to cover the full gamut.

Let's look at each of the main programs individually so you can see what you're up against.

## Word 2008

Microsoft Word 2008 is a word-processing program. Figure 1.1 shows you what the Word program window looks like. As its name implies, you use the program to work with words—typing and editing documents. Use Word to create letters, reports, manuscripts, thesis papers, memos, brochures, newsletters, and so on. Word can handle all your text-related projects. However, Word doesn't end with words: You can use it to create media-rich documents with graphics, themes, tables, and more. The new page-layout feature lets you build complex graphical documents. Learn more about using Word in Part II, "Working with Word."

## Excel 2008

Microsoft Excel 2008 is a spreadsheet program, which is a fancy way of saying its purpose is handling and crunching numbers. You can use the program to organize number data, create formulas for manipulating the number data, turn number data into exciting charts and graphs, and so on. Excel is perfect for building and tracking inventories, whipping up financial reports, presenting sales reports, figuring out budgets and loans—basically anything related to number juggling. Figure 1.2 shows the Excel program window. Learn more about using Excel in Part III, "Using Excel."

**FIGURE 1.1**

Microsoft Word 2008

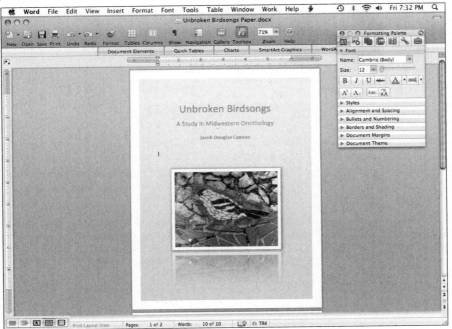

**FIGURE 1.2**

Microsoft Excel 2008

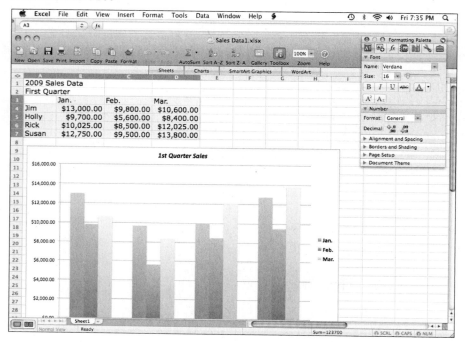

## PowerPoint 2008

Microsoft PowerPoint 2008 is a presentation program. You can use it to present information to an audience, whether it's a live audience, an online audience, or a single viewer. You can use PowerPoint to present a marketing campaign, a school book report, a training course, a class lecture—pretty much anything you need to present to an audience on a screen. The screen can be a computer screen, a projection screen, or even a screen in a kiosk. Much like the electronic version of a slide show, you can use PowerPoint to present your audience with text, graphics, and digital media elements (such as video and audio clips) to explain concepts, strategies, content, and more. As a visual medium, PowerPoint is a very powerful way to get a message across and grab the attention of the targeted viewer. Figure 1.3 shows an example of the PowerPoint program window. Learn more about using PowerPoint in Part IV, "Presenting with PowerPoint."

**FIGURE 1.3**

Microsoft PowerPoint 2008

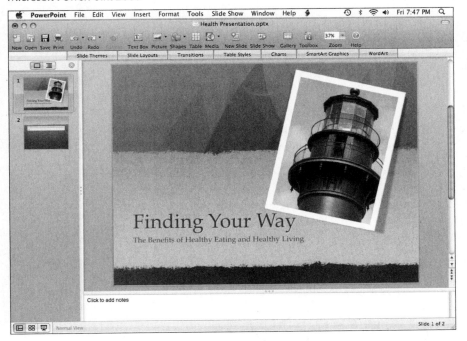

## Entourage 2008

Microsoft Entourage 2008 is a personal information manager program, combining both an e-mail client and a project manager application. In layman's terms, it's like an electronic personal organizer that helps you keep track of e-mail, appointments, to-do lists, notes, projects, and your address book, all in one convenient location. You can quickly jump from sending e-mail to a colleague to setting an appointment on your daily calendar to jotting down a note about an upcoming task, all in the same program window. Like an electronic personal assistant, Entourage can help you keep your busy life ordered and on track. Figure 1.4 shows an example of the Entourage program window. Learn more about using Entourage in Part V, "Working with Entourage."

**FIGURE 1.4**

Microsoft Entourage 2008

# Learning a Little Office History

How about a little back story on Microsoft Office? Sometimes it's interesting to see where computer programs have come from in order to appreciate where they are today in terms of technology and advancements. As it turns out, Microsoft Office has a very rich history. Because Microsoft is so synonymous with Windows, you might think the original Office programs were created for Windows PCs, yes? No. The very first Office suite was created for the Apple Macintosh back in 1989. It was later introduced to Windows users in 1990. The Office suite started out as an interrelated set of desktop applications, called a productivity suite. The very first versions bundled Word, Excel, and PowerPoint together, or Windows users could buy a professional version that included Access and Schedule Plus (neither of which were available for Mac users).

Prior to the bundling of the programs, users previously had to purchase the applications separately. Each program has its own rich history, but at the first "suite" bundle, Word was already up to version 4.0, Excel was version 2.20, and PowerPoint was 2.01. Since that time, each program and bundling suite has made massive progress in features, tools, appearance, and integration. As time progressed, the Office suite evolved to include the Internet Explorer browser, Outlook Express (an e-mail application), and finally Entourage (the Mac version of the popular Windows Outlook program). In addition to the evolving core programs, the software evolved along with the ever-changing computer technologies, changing in appearance and behind-the-scenes functionality.

Incredibly enough, Microsoft Office for Mac has undergone a total of ten manifestations over the course of its history. The last big release of the Office suite for Mac was back in 2004, following the Windows version for Office XP. Microsoft Office 2008 for Mac is the latest big release, nearly coinciding with Office 2007 for

Windows, another monumental release date in Office history. The Windows version features a completely new interface and a new Office Open XML-based file format, which results in the new .docx, .xlsx, and .pptx file extensions for saved document, workbook, and presentation files.

Just in case you ever find yourself on TV's *Jeopardy* game show, here are some little known facts about the individual programs that make up Office 2008 for Mac:

- Word began life in the early 80s as a simple word processor called Multi-Tool Word for Xenix systems and then crossed over to the DOS and Macintosh platforms using the name Word. At first, Word lagged behind its nearest competitor, WordPerfect, but when it switched to a WYSIWYG (What You See Is What You Get) interface, it soon began leading the pack in the software arena.

- Excel was first initiated as a Microsoft-authored program called Multiplan back in 1982 and was later called Excel. In the beginning, it fought for popularity against Lotus 1-2-3, but when Lotus was slow to release a Windows version of its program, Excel gained the lead in popularity and hasn't stopped yet.

- PowerPoint started out as Presenter in 1987, a black-and-white presentation program for creating overhead transparencies, and then became a full-color program. Presenter was later purchased by Microsoft and dubbed PowerPoint.

- Entourage, the newest member of the Office suite for Mac, came along in 2000 and was added to the suite of Office programs in 2001.

As you can guess, marketing, timing, and ever fickle computer users play an important part of the software popularity race. Who knows what the future will bring in the next versions of these programs and bundles? In the meantime, as the latest and greatest version of this widely used set of programs, Office 2008 for Mac has garnered lots of interest and excitement, and it continues to dominate the marketplace today. Are you ready to find out what all the fuss is about? The next section explains what's new and improved in Office 2008 for Mac.

# Discovering What's New and Improved in Office

As all good consumers, we're forever wowed by the latest gadgets and technology, and when it comes to our software, we expect new bells and whistles with each new release. The new Office 2008 for Mac is no exception to this commercial rule of thumb, and as you'll soon see, it combines the best of your favorite Office features with the new Mac OS X-style for a very pleasant overhaul of what was already a best-selling suite of programs. So what's new? You're about to find out.

Overall, you'll see a fresh, new appearance in the user interface for all the programs and much less untidiness than in previous versions. The floating toolbars of previous versions that tended to obscure and clutter your view have been replaced with a single toolbox of task-related palettes that you summon with a click. (In case you're worried, all your old familiar toolbars are still available, if you want them.) Basically, the developers have merged the old Toolbox with the Formatting Palette to create a very useful new Toolbox panel that holds more than just formatting tools.

Speaking of the new Toolbox, you'll find improvements to the features within. For example, the Formatting Palette, shown in Figure 1.5, now features a Document Theme pane with easy access to professional-looking color schemes and styles. The Object Palette now offers easier browsing for shapes, clip art, photos from the iPhoto Library, and larger, easier-to-read symbols. The Reference Tools Palette has added an integrated

Encarta Encyclopedia lookup and bilingual dictionaries. The new Citations Palette available in the Word Toolbox helps you make quick work of managing citations and bibliographies in your documents. There are more changes than listed, but many are simply subtle tweaks in appearance and how much real estate is consumed by the box.

---

**FIGURE 1.5**

Check out Word's new Toolbox.

Another new feature available throughout Office (with the exception of Entourage) is the new Elements Gallery, shown in Figure 1.6. It places a unique variety of drop-in elements you can quickly put to use in your files, ranging from charts and tables to WordArt objects, all within easy access below the default toolbar. These preset elements can really help speed up the time you spend creating documents, spreadsheets, and presentations. Some of the elements are program-specific. For example, Word's Elements Gallery offers drop-in elements commonly found in word-processing documents, while Excel's Gallery features elements for budgets, checkbooks, and invoices. Be sure to spend some time checking out the many elements available. Between these and the new templates found in the Office Project Gallery, you may never have to build another document, workbook, or presentation from scratch again.

## What's Gone from Office 2008?

Sadly, VBA (Visual Basics for Applications), the scripting system used by many businesses to automate workflow, is no longer available. However, Automator, which was introduced with Mac OS X 10.4 "Tiger," lets you easily build workflows by placing commonly used AppleScript tasks in a graphical user interface, which you can learn more about at www.microsoft.com/mac.

**FIGURE 1.6**

The new Elements Gallery is found in Excel.

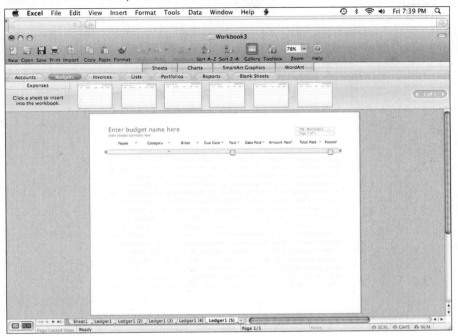

The Office SmartArt graphics feature, shown in Figure 1.7, lets you create spiffy info-based diagrams, charts, and other graphic elements to help you show the relationship between items. You can quickly insert a graphic to show a cycle, process flow, or hierarchy. Pick a diagram style, and fill in the placeholder text with your own text to create a tailored info graphic.

Microsoft has made radical improvements to the Office Help system. You can now connect to the online Help files for the latest information, or toggle between online and offline help with a click of a button. You'll find the Help system easy to navigate and exceedingly fast. Learn more about using the Office Help system in Chapter 4.

You can also now save your work in PDF format, making it even easier to share your files across platforms and across the Internet. While we're on the subject of saving files, another big improvement in Office 2008 is that it supports the new Office Open XML format, a free and open international standard document format for word processing, spreadsheet, and presentation documents. Essentially, this means the specs behind document creation make it easier for all programs to extract information about the document, or to put it more plainly—it is file compatible with Microsoft Office 2007 for Windows. This is very good news, indeed. The XML format is based on the eXtensible Markup Language, which Web pages use. For the end user, this means you'll see new file extensions for the files you save in Word, Excel, and PowerPoint, and you'll be able to swap files with Windows Office users without effort.

You'll find plenty of more new features to get excited about, so let's keep going and look at the major ones for each program.

**FIGURE 1.7**

The SmartArt graphics feature is found in PowerPoint.

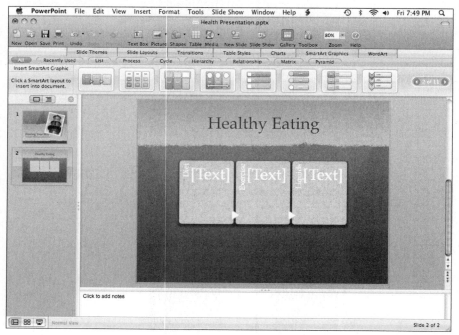

## Word

One of the biggest changes to Microsoft Word is the new Publishing Layout tool. Comparable to Microsoft Publisher for Windows, this new view mode in Word actually switches you over to a built-in desktop publishing application. Here you can choose from a library of publication templates and create professional-looking newsletters, brochures, flyers, invitations, programs, business cards, postcards, catalogs, awards, and menus. With a few quick clicks, you're on your way to filling in the template's placeholder text with your own and producing a polished document on par with anything produced by a professional agency or printing company. You can learn more about this new feature in Chapter 6.

As mentioned previously, another new feature is the drop-in document elements you can add to your Word documents. You can quickly insert a cover page, a table of contents page, a snazzy header or footer, or a bibliography. In previous versions of Word, you had to labor over inserting these elements and getting them to appear just right in your document. Now, they're preset and ready to go through the Elements Gallery. Learn more about using document elements in Chapter 6.

Among the Office Project Gallery's tabs, you can find dozens of professionally designed templates to create all kinds of business and home-use documents. As with any template, you can customize it to suit your needs.

## Excel

You can now insert preformatted ledger sheets, found in the new Elements Gallery, to handle common Excel tasks. For example, you can find sheets for inventory lists, checkbook registers, budgets, stock tracking reports, and more. In the past, users painstakingly built such documents on their own; now they're available with a quick click. No doubt, you'll find them a big time-saver.

Excel also sports a new Formula Builder tool to help you whip up formulas without needing to memorize functions and proper syntax. It's now easier than ever before to find the function you want to apply using a combination help system/wizard.

Related to the new Formula Builder, Excel also now offers a function-based AutoComplete tip box when typing formulas. As you start typing, Excel displays a list of possible matching functions. The Formula AutoComplete feature is a much-needed element to the Excel feature list.

## PowerPoint

Like the other two programs, PowerPoint's new Elements Gallery offers lots of slide themes and custom slide layouts that you can apply, giving you greater versatility and design choice than ever before. PowerPoint also embraces improvements to the Toolbox and the slide show Presenter tools. You can utilize the new Custom Animation tool in the Toolbox to quickly animate slide elements. You can use the Presenter tools for dual-screen setups now, plus the navigation arrows are side by side to save you mouse movements onscreen. If your computer has an Apple Remote, you can use it to navigate a slide show without having to click the mouse.

You also can now send slides to iPhoto using the Save as Pictures command. From iPhoto, you can easily move the pictures to a video iPod for presenting on a video projector or television.

## Entourage

Microsoft has tweaked Entourage to include a much-improved search feature, better junk e-mail filters, an improved Calendar interface, enhanced To Do list, and customizable toolbars. A real bright spot in Entourage is the new My Day feature. It gives you an at-a-glance reference to your appointments and tasks for the day, even if the Entourage program is closed.

# Summary

In this chapter, you learned about the individual components that make up the Microsoft Office 2008 for Mac suite. You also learned a little history about the Office suite and the major changes that occurred prior to the current version covered by this book. Finally, you took a quick look at the various new and improved features and tools available across the Office suite as well as in individual programs. The whole Office world now awaits you, so you'd better get started.

# Chapter 2

# Installing Office 2008

Installing any software may seem like a straightforward task. Just pop in a software CD-ROM, and tell it to go. Sometimes the installation process contains nuances or things you need to know before you ever get started. This chapter describes what system requirements are needed, walks you through the installation process, and shows you how to uninstall a program. You also find a few troubleshooting tips and learn how to check for program updates.

## System Requirements

If you haven't yet installed your copy of Microsoft Office 2008 for Mac, this section explains what system requirements are needed. What is a system requirement, you might ask? It's the minimum necessary elements like a computer processor, type of operating system, amount of memory, and hard disk space your computer needs in order to run the software sufficiently. Some items go without saying, like needing a mouse, a modem or other Internet connection, and a CD-ROM or DVD-ROM in which to insert and install the software. Here's a list of minimum requirements:

- A Mac with an Intel, PowerPC G5, or PowerPC G4 (500 MHz or faster) processor
- Mac OS X version 10.4.9 or later
- 512MB of RAM or more
- 1.5GB of available hard disk space
- HFS+ hard disk format (also known as Mac OS Extended or HFS Plus)
- 1024 x 768 or higher screen resolution monitor

How do you know if you meet these requirements? You need to do a little homework about your computer. Choose ᯤ ⇨ About this Mac to open the About This Mac window, shown in Figure 2.1. Here you find information listed about your

### IN THIS CHAPTER

**Looking at system requirements**

**Installing the Office suite**

**Uninstalling Office**

**Updating your software**

**Troubleshooting problems**

computer's processor and memory. You can click the More Info button for a complete rundown of your computer's inner components, including hardware, networking elements, software, and so on using the Apple System Profiler window.

**FIGURE 2.1**

To find out more about your Mac, display the About This Mac window.

To find out how much space is available on your hard drive, double-click the hard drive icon on the desktop, and then look at the top of the window that appears.

**TIP** Not enough room on your hard drive for all of Office? You can choose to do a custom installation and install only the programs and proofing tools you know you'll use the most. See the next section, "Using the Installer," to learn more.

# Using the Installer

When you install Office 2008 for Mac, the Microsoft Office Installer utility walks you through the necessary steps. The Installer is really just a series of windows, each with a specific part of the installation that requires some interaction on your part. Mainly, you're just clicking the Continue button repeatedly. But some of the windows warrant a bit more input than that, such as choosing a drive in which to store the software, or choosing whether you want a standard or custom installation.

A standard installation installs all four of the Office suite programs, Microsoft Messenger, and all the proofing tools (such as foreign language dictionaries); basically, a standard installation installs everything. A standard installation takes up about 1.1GB of space on your Mac. If you don't plan on using all the programs, you can pick and choose which to install with a custom installation. For example, if you need to save space, you might consider opting out of installing all of the foreign language dictionaries especially if you're not going to use them. Doing so can save you up to a megabyte of hard drive space. If you opt out of a program or feature, you can always pop the CD-ROM or DVD-ROM back in and add an item later.

It typically takes about 3–5 minutes to install the Office 2008 for Mac suite, but your own installation time may vary based on the speed of your computer. Before you begin, you need the user name and password for an administrator's account for permission to install software. Also, you should disable any virus protection applications and close any open program windows.

## Running the Installer

Follow these steps to install Microsoft Office 2008 for Mac:

1. **Insert the software CD-ROM or DVD-ROM.**

2. **Double-click the Microsoft Office 2008 icon on the Mac desktop.**

   The Microsoft Office 2008 window opens, as shown in Figure 2.2.

**FIGURE 2.2**

To start installing, you must first activate the icon on the desktop.

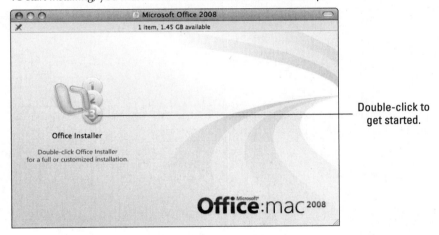

Double-click to get started.

3. **Double-click the Office Installer icon.**

4. **A prompt box appears warning you to make sure your software source is trustworthy; click Continue.** That is, unless you've purchased your software from a seedy underground Internet alley, in which case, you might want to reconsider exactly what you're installing to begin with.

5. **The Welcome screen appears, as shown in Figure 2.3; click Continue.**

6. **The Software License Agreement screen appears with the standard lengthy legalese agreement as shown in Figure 2.4; click Continue.**

> **NOTE** Does anyone ever read a software license agreement? If you prefer to keep installing and read later, you can always click the Print button and print a copy of the agreement.

**FIGURE 2.3**

The real fun starts here when you double-click the Installer utility.

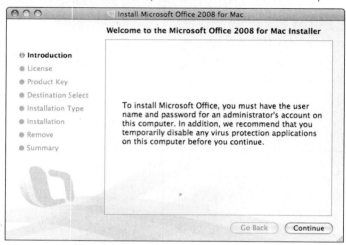

**FIGURE 2.4**

Read all about the legal ins and outs of the software in the license agreement window.

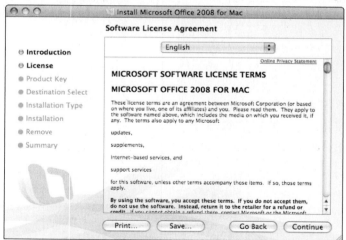

7. The next screen lets you actually agree or disagree to the agreement, as shown in Figure 2.5, so click Agree if you want to continue installing the software.

**FIGURE 2.5**

Specify whether you agree or disagree with the software agreement.

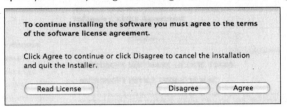

To continue installing the software you must agree to the terms of the software license agreement.

Click Agree to continue or click Disagree to cancel the installation and quit the Installer.

Read License          Disagree     Agree

8. Use the next screen that appears to enter your Product ID and then click Continue.

**TIP**    The product identification number is typically on the CD-ROM or DVD-ROM sleeve that the software came in. This number is pretty important, so it's a good idea to write it down somewhere for safekeeping.

9. If you are prompted to quit any programs you have running, as shown in Figure 2.6, stop and close any open programs, and then click Continue Installation.

**FIGURE 2.6**

Installer asks you to exit any open programs before continuing with the installation.

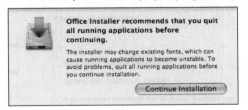

Office Installer recommends that you quit all running applications before continuing.

The installer may change existing fonts, which can cause running applications to become unstable. To avoid problems, quit all running applications before you continue installation.

Continue Installation

10. The Destination Select window, shown in Figure 2.7, asks you to select where you want to install the software; click the volume or drive you want to use, and click Continue.

**FIGURE 2.7**

The Destination window asks you to choose a destination volume or drive.

Click to select
the volume.

11.  When the Installation Type window finally appears, as shown in Figure 2.8, click Install to perform a standard installation.

   ■ To change installation locations, you can click the Change Install Location button and choose another drive.

**FIGURE 2.8**

The Installation Type window prepares you for the nitty-gritty installation procedure.

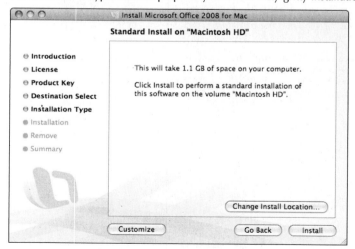

■ Click the Customize button if you want to customize which programs you want to install. This opens another window, shown in Figure 2.9, where you can check or uncheck which program(s) to install or not install.

**FIGURE 2.9**

The Custom Install window lets you control which programs and features are installed on your computer.

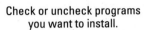

Check or uncheck programs
you want to install.

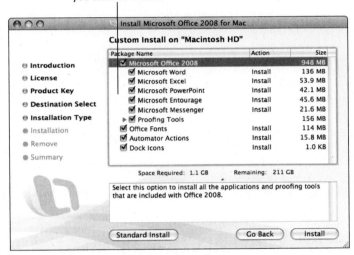

12. **The Installer asks you to type in your administrator password; type it, and click OK.**

   Suddenly, it looks as if the installation is about to begin in earnest, and the Installer begins copying the Office 2008 files to your computer, as shown in Figure 2.10.

13. **Next, the Installer attempts to search for and remove prior copies of any Office programs, as shown in Figure 2.11.** The Remove Office utility searches your computer for previous versions of Office and lets you know what it finds; click Continue at the prompts.

**FIGURE 2.10**

You can watch the installation progress in this window; lots of things installing and counting down. It's very exciting.

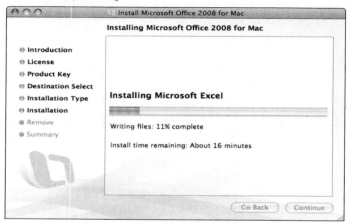

**FIGURE 2.11**

The Installer removes any previous versions of the software.

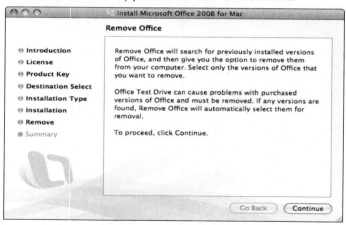

**14.** A final window, shown in Figure 2.12, lets you know the installation is complete; click Close.

**FIGURE 2.12**

Finally, your installation is seemingly at a close . . . almost.

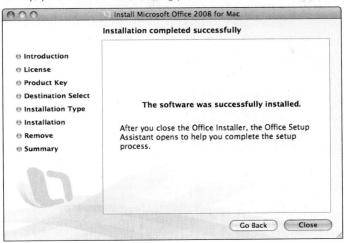

That probably didn't take very long, but it might have seemed like it did with all the starts and stops with input required along the way. Lest you think you're finished, you're not. The Setup Assistant kicks in to ascertain your input a bit longer, as explained in the next section.

## Using the Microsoft Office Setup Assistant

Immediately after you finish installing the Office suite, the Microsoft Office Setup Assistant appears to help you finalize the setup. The first bit of business is to choose whether to participate in the Customer Experience Improvement Program. This is just Microsoft's way of saying it wants to collect information about your program and computer use. You can opt in or out of this "program."

The second bit of business is to read more about the programs, register your software, and check for updates—all of which requires an online connection to complete. You can always revisit the registration option at a later time, but you definitely want to check for updates. This process, once started, may take awhile to complete, but it's worth it to have all the software files up to date and in place.

## How to Register Later

If you chose not to pursue online registration using the Office Setup Assistant, you can always register your software later. You need an Internet connection to finish registering your product. To register, click the program's first menu (Word, Excel, PowerPoint, or Entourage) and click the Online Registration. For example, if you're using Word, choose Word ➪ Online Registration. This opens your default browser window, and you can register your software online.

Follow these steps to finish the installation:

1. **The first screen in the Microsoft Office Setup Assistant window, shown in Figure 2.13, is a Feedback participation invitation; click No or Yes to participate.**

### FIGURE 2.13

The Microsoft Office Setup Assistant lures you in for a little more input before finishing the installation process.

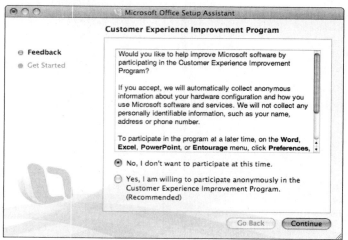

2. **Click Continue.**
3. **The Get Started window, shown in Figure 2.14, offers three options: Learn More, Register, and Check for Updates.**
   - Click the Learn More icon to open your Web browser to the Microsoft Web site and learn more about the product.
   - Click the Register icon to go online and fill out the software registration forms.
   - Click the Check for Updates icon to go online and download the latest software updates.

## What about Microsoft Expression Media?

If you bought the Office 2008 for Mac Special Media Edition, you still have one more program to install. Expression Media, Microsoft's digital asset management program for cataloging and organizing digital media, comes on a separate CD-ROM. You need to follow a separate set of installation steps, which as it turns out, work almost the same as the Office suite installation steps. You need to type in the product key and follow all the Installer screens to complete the installation. After it's installed, it needs updating as well. After you finish checking for updates, you're ready to use the program.

**FIGURE 2.14**

You can visit the Office Web site or register your software now or later, but you really should choose to do an update.

4. **After jumping through all the hoops you want, click Finish or Close based on what final Setup Assistant screen presents itself and eject the CD-ROM or DVD-ROM.**

Now that you've installed the software completely, you're ready to start using the individual programs.

## Uninstalling Office

You can uninstall all or, if you performed a custom install, parts of the Office suite. To uninstall, follow these steps:

1. **Open the Applications folder.**
2. **Double-click the Microsoft Office 2008 folder icon.**
3. **Double-click the Additional Tools folder icon, shown in Figure 2.15.**

**FIGURE 2.15**

Open the Additional Tools folder within the Microsoft Office 2008 folder to find the uninstaller utility.

Additional Tools
icon

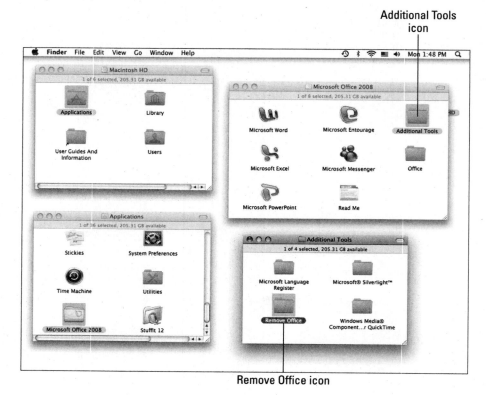

Remove Office icon

4. **Double-click the Remove Office folder icon, as shown in Figure 2.16.**

**FIGURE 2.16**

Activate the Remove Office icon to start removing the software.

5. **Double-click the Remove Office icon.**

   The Remove Office utility (the *uninstaller*) opens and searches your computer to see what programs you've installed, as shown in Figure 2.17.

**FIGURE 2.17**

The Remove Office utility removes Office programs from your computer.

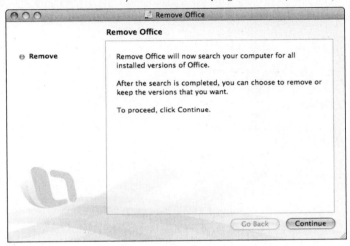

   If you chose a custom install, you can choose which programs to remove.

6. **When the removal is complete, the Removal Utility lets you know it has moved all the necessary files to the Trash; click Finish.**

Your work is almost done. To completely remove the files, you must empty the Trash; choose Finder ➪ Empty Trash.

# Checking for Updates

From time to time, you should check the Microsoft Office Web site for updates of the Office suite. Periodically, Microsoft releases updates you need to keep your software safe to use and up to date, and it releases critical bug fixes to make the programs work better. You can use the Microsoft AutoUpdate feature to check for updates manually or automatically on a schedule. You can schedule updates daily, weekly, or monthly. You also need an Internet connection to perform an update. Be forewarned: Some of the updates are very large, so be prepared for some lengthy download times.

You can check for updates from any Office program following these steps:

1. **Choose Help ⇨ Check for Updates.**

   The Microsoft AutoUpdate window appears, as shown in Figure 2.18.

**FIGURE 2.18**

Use the Microsoft AutoUpdate box to update manually or on a schedule.

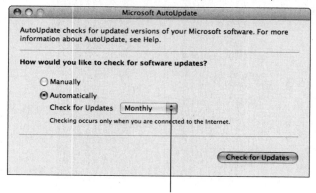

Click to schedule updates.

2. **Choose an update option from these choices:**
   - Click the Manually option to check for updates right now.
   - Click the Automatically option, and click the pop-up menu to set the feature to Daily, Weekly, or Monthly.

3. **Click the Check for Updates button.**

   AutoUpdate begins checking for any updates. If it finds any, it displays a list box, as shown in Figure 2.19.

 If no updates are available, a prompt box appears telling you so. Click OK to exit, and then close the Microsoft AutoUpdate window.

4. **Click the update you want to install.**

5. **Click Install.**

   AutoUpdate begins the downloading process, as shown in Figure 2.20.

   After downloading the update, you need to jump through the installation hoops again, similar to the installation steps you covered earlier, to install the updates on your computer.

**FIGURE 2.19**

AutoUpdate displays the updates.

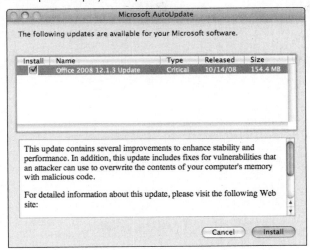

**FIGURE 2.20**

You check on your download progress in the Microsoft AutoUpdate bar.

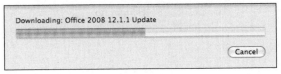

6. When the update is successfully installed, click Finish.
7. Close the AutoUpdate window.

# Troubleshooting

When you install the Microsoft Office 2008 suite, it installs gazillions of pieces of itself in your computer system. Office then keeps track of all your settings and preferences that customize how you use the programs. In the course of use or over the course of time, you may accidentally move a file or delete it, or it just becomes corrupted. You can perform a little test to see if a corrupted file or preference setting is causing problems. Exit all the Office programs, and using Finder open the following folder path: Home ➪ Library ➪ Preferences ➪ Microsoft ➪ Office 2008. In the Office 2008 folder, drag the Microsoft Office 2008

Settings.plist or any other reference or setting files related to the Office programs onto the desktop. The next time you open Word, Excel, PowerPoint, or Entourage, you're starting with new preferences files. If the program operates as expected, you can return to the files on the desktop and send them to the Trash for deletion.

If removing preference files and settings doesn't help clear up a problem, you may need to seek help online. You can find plenty of Mac and Microsoft Office help sources on the Web, but you might start with the Mactopia Help Center (`www.microsoft.com/mac/help.mspx`) or Microsoft's Office forum (`www.officeformac.com`).

Lastly, if you are still experiencing trouble with Office, you can always try uninstalling the programs and reinstalling them again. Keep in mind that in doing so you'll lose all your program preferences. Follow the steps in the section "Uninstalling Office" earlier in this chapter to learn how.

## Summary

Whew! Aren't you glad you're finished with this chapter? Installation and troubleshooting are often nail-biting situations, but with the tools that come with the suite of programs, you've got everything you need to successfully use the software. In this chapter, you learned how to install the Office 2008 for Mac software and check for product updates. You also learned how to uninstall the software, just in case you decided you didn't want to use it anymore, or if you needed to do a reinstall. You also learned how to troubleshoot any problematic files. Now you can relax and start using the programs to get your work done.

# Chapter 3

# Office 2008 Program Basics

After you install Microsoft Office 2008 for Mac and start poking around in all the programs, you'll probably notice something right away. As a suite of integrated programs, the Office 2008 for Mac applications share a similar appearance and many of the same basic features and commands. The title bar, menu bar, and Standard toolbar look very similar from one program to the next, the scroll bars always appear in relatively the same place, and the menu bars display some of the same commands in the exact same way. The beauty of such integration and similarity is that when you learn to use a basic feature or command in one program, the same steps apply for using the feature in the next program. The same is almost true when learning completely new program-specific features—they, too, all seem to work in a similar fashion. All of this integration and similarity make learning to navigate and use the programs much easier and faster.

This chapter is for users who are new to the Microsoft Office suite and need to know how to do very basic tasks. This chapter covers how to start and exit the programs, work with program windows, open files, and use multiple windows. Basic tasks also include how to use menus, toolbars, and scrollbars. If you're a seasoned veteran of the Office programs, you can skip this chapter and move on to building documents, spreadsheets, presentations, calendar schedules, and other Office projects. If you're new to the Office scene, however, this chapter can help you build basic skills and give you the confidence you need to plunge into each Office program.

## IN THIS CHAPTER

Starting and exiting Office programs

Moving, resizing, and hiding windows

Opening Office files

Viewing multiple program windows and files

Using basic program window features

## Starting and Exiting Programs

Let's start with the very, very basic techniques for starting and exiting the Office programs. When you installed Office 2008 for Mac, program icons were put on the Dock. The Mac Dock is a hangout for all your computer's shortcuts. If you move your mouse over the Dock area, as shown in Figure 3.1, you see shortcut icons for Word, Excel, PowerPoint, Entourage, and Microsoft Messenger. To open any of these programs, click the icon. If you're not sure which icon represents which program, simply pause the mouse pointer over the icon to reveal the icon's name.

**NOTE** The first time you open Entourage after installing it, the Setup Assistant utility appears to help you go through the steps of setting up your e-mail account or importing an address book or calendar information.

You also can use Finder to open Office programs. You can find Finder on the Dock as a bluish smiling face on the far left end, as shown in Figure 3.1, or you can find Finder at the top of the Mac window next to the Apple menu. With the Finder window open, navigate to the Microsoft Office 2008 folder. You can find the folder in the Applications folder, as shown in Figure 3.2. Double-click the Microsoft Office 2008 folder, and then double-click the program you want to open.

## FIGURE 3.1

The fastest way to start an Office program is to click its shortcut icon on the Dock.

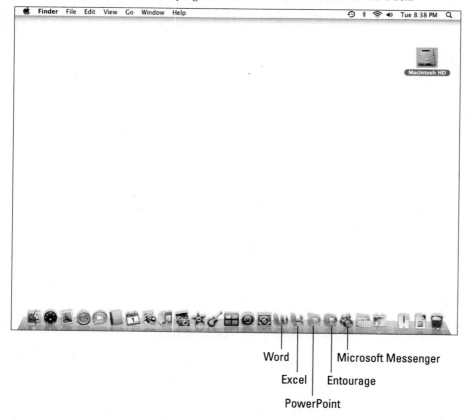

Word

Excel

PowerPoint

Entourage

Microsoft Messenger

**FIGURE 3.2**

You can use the Finder window to open an Office program.

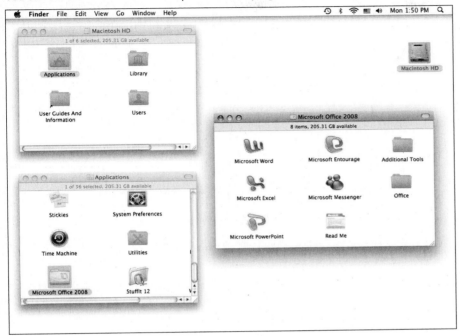

You also can click the program and choose File ⇨ Open on the Finder menu bar, or you can Control+click and choose Open from the contextual pop-up menu that appears.

Exiting an Office program is just as simple as opening it. To close an application, use the program's name menu, such as Word ⇨ Quit Word or Excel ⇨ Quit Excel. This closes the program entirely. Figure 3.3 shows the Quit PowerPoint command for closing the PowerPoint program.

**FIGURE 3.3**

Use the Quit command to exit any program window.

# Working with Program Windows

Every Office program you start opens into its own window. Windows can be moved, resized, minimized, and closed. With the exception of Entourage, when you open a program window, a blank document, workbook, or presentation opens, too. These are essentially windows within windows, which mean you can close or minimize a document, workbook, or presentation window and still keep the main program window open.

## Closing, minimizing, and zooming windows

For controlling windows, the most common tools you use are the program window controls. You can easily spot these buttons because they usually hang out in a cluster in the upper-left corner of windows and dialog boxes. You can use these buttons to minimize, zoom, or close the window. Table 3.1 explains how to use each button.

**TABLE 3.1**

### Program Window Controls

| Button | Description |
|---|---|
| ● | The Close button, the tiny red circle, closes the window to which it's attached. In the case of program windows, the main program remains open. |
| ○ | The Minimize button, the tiny yellow circle, minimizes or reduces the associated window to the Dock. |
| ○ | The Zoom button, the tiny green circle, makes the window as large as possible on the screen. A second click reduces the window to its original size. |

 **TIP** You can find the Minimize and Zoom window controls on the Office program's Window menu. For example, to minimize the window to the Dock, choose Window ⇨ Minimize Window.

When you move your mouse pointer over any of the buttons in the program window controls cluster, tiny icons appear inside each button. The Close button suddenly has a tiny X in the middle, the Minimize button has a dash icon, and the Zoom button has a plus icon. These icons are also clues as to what each button does when clicked.

**NOTE** If a program window button appears dimmed, it means you cannot use it for that particular window. For example, the Toolbox feature operates as a floating window; however, you cannot minimize it, so the Minimize button is dimmed.

If you minimize a window to the Dock, you can maximize it again simply by finding its icon on the dock and clicking the icon. For example, if you save a Word file as Draft01 and minimize it, it waits on the Dock ready for action again, as shown in Figure 3.4. To display it again in the Word window, display the Dock, find an icon for the Draft01 file, and then click the icon. The document is maximized again in the Word program window.

**FIGURE 3.4**

When you minimize a window, it appears on the Dock ready for action when you're ready to summon it back again.

Minimized window

**NOTE** The Zoom button in the program window controls is different from the zoom feature in the Office programs that allows you to change the magnification setting. The Zoom command in Word, for example, lets you magnify a document to see it better or zoom out to get a bird's eye view.

## Moving and resizing windows

To move a window, you can click and drag it by its title bar. If the window is full size, you must reduce the size in order to move it around; click the Zoom button to reduce a window to its original size. To resize a window, click and drag the bottom-right corner of the window, called the Resize control. The corner displays three little lines to let you know it's the Resize control. See Figure 3.5 to see an example of a Resize control.

**FIGURE 3.5**

You can resize a window by clicking and dragging its Resize control, or corner.

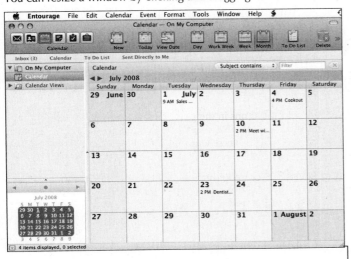

Resize control

## Scrolling around windows

Scroll bars are another important part of the Office windows. Depending on your view magnification setting, the contents of your documents, spreadsheets, and presentations may not always fit entirely onscreen. For example, a long document may exceed the depth of the window, so you must scroll to view the remainder of the document. Office windows can use both horizontal and vertical scroll bars, as shown in Figure 3.6. The horizontal scroll bar lets you move left and right to view a document, while the vertical scroll bar lets you move up and down a page. You can click and drag the scroll box, also called the *scroller,* to quickly move your view, or you can click the scroll arrows found at the end of each scroll bar to move the document view.

## Hiding windows

You can quickly hide a program from view. This can help you reduce onscreen clutter or keep someone walking by from viewing what you're working on. When you activate an Office program's Hide command, the program window is completely hidden from view. To activate the Hide command, choose Word ➪ Hide Word or Excel ➪ Hide Excel. Figure 3.7 shows the Hide command as it appears in PowerPoint. For a quicker hiding action, use the shortcut key: Control+H. To view the window again, you must click the program icon on the Dock.

---

**FIGURE 3.6**

You can use scroll bars to navigate documents.

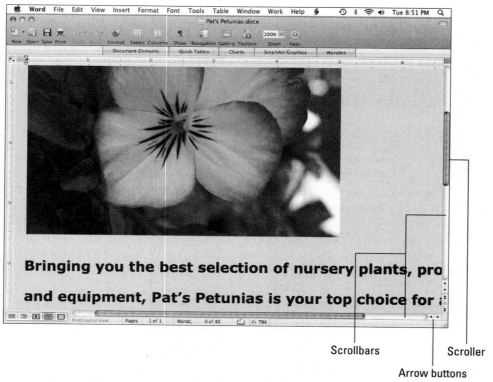

Scrollbars

Scroller

Arrow buttons

**FIGURE 3.7**

You can use the Hide command to hide a window.

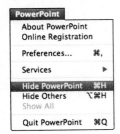

You also can choose to hide all the other open windows and keep only the program window open. To do so, choose Word ⇨ Hide Others or Excel ⇨ Hide Others. When activated, this command hides all other open windows on the Mac desktop. You can use the Show All command to bring them back into view again. Choose Word ⇨ Show All or Excel ⇨ Show All.

# Opening Files

As you work with the various Office programs, you can create files to add content, save the content, and reopen it again to make changes and amendments, add formatting, and more. The term *documents* is sometimes used to describe all the Office files to which you add content and text. However, each program creates a specific kind of file. In Excel, files are called workbooks or spreadsheets. In PowerPoint, they're called presentations. In Word, files are called documents. Entourage doesn't create a specific kind of file.

As you learn about how to use each Office program in this book, you find out how to work with program-specific files. For example, when you read more about using Word, you learn how to save, open, and create new Word documents. For the time being, this section explains some general ways to open Office files.

**TIP** Each Office program, excluding Entourage, keeps a list of recently opened files and displays them in the Open Recent submenu found on the File menu. You can quickly open a recently viewed file by choosing File ⇨ Open Recent and then choosing the file you want to open.

The Office programs offer you several ways to open files, such as using the Open button on the Standard toolbar, or using the File menu and activating the Open command. This inevitably opens the Open dialog box, shown in Figure 3.8. From there, you can navigate to the file you want to open.

You also can open Office files from outside the Office program windows. You can navigate to the file you want to open in the Finder window and double-click the filename. This action opens the program window associated with the file and displays the document. You also can Control+click the filename and choose Open from the contextual pop-up menu that appears. Figure 3.9 shows the Finder window and a list of Office files.

The Open dialog box is an important tool in Word, Excel, and PowerPoint for opening files.

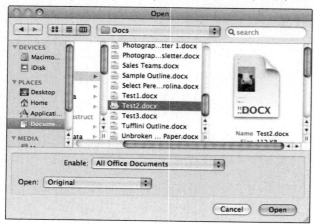

You can use the Finder window to open Office files.

Double-click to open.

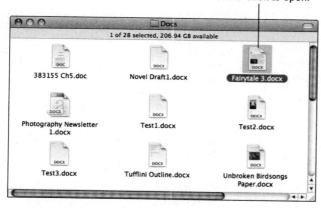

**TIP** You can view a file in the Finder window before choosing to open it in its native application. To view a file, Control+click the filename and choose Quick Look from the contextual pop-up menu. A window opens showing you the file.

# Using Multiple Windows

You can open more than one Office program at a time and switch between them as needed. Called *multi-tasking* in the computer vernacular, this technique allows you to move content from one window to the next. You can use the Cut or Copy commands to cut or copy content in one program, and then activate the Paste command to paste it into the other program. If both program windows are visible at the same time, you also can drag data from one window and drop it into the other to copy it. This technique is called drag-and-drop. You also can use the drag-and-drop technique to move content around within a document. Figure 3.10 shows two Office programs open and viewable at the same time. In most cases, you need to resize two open program windows in order to view them both.

When working with two windows onscreen at once, only one window can be active or current. The active window's tools all appear in full color. An inactive window's tools appear faded or diminished. If the two windows overlap, the window that appears on top of the other is the active window. In Figure 3.10, the calendar is the active window. Click a window to make it active.

You also can open multiple windows in the same program to view and move content. For example, you can open two Excel or Word files and view them both at the same time. Figure 3.11 shows two Word documents open. Again, you can use the drag-and-drop technique or Cut, Copy, and Paste content between the two files. Like the scenario with two open program windows, with two open files, only one can be active or current at a time. The active window's tools appear in full color. Click a file window to make it active.

**FIGURE 3.10**

If you need to multitask between two programs, you can open them both onscreen and view them at the same time.

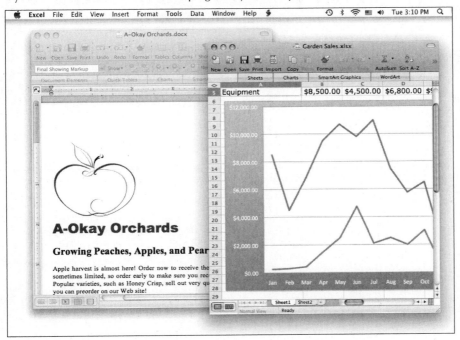

**FIGURE 3.11**

**FIGURE 3.11**

You can also open more than one file at a time in any Office program.

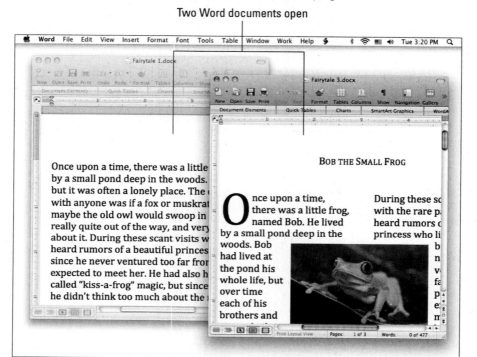

If the two open file windows are maximized to full screen size and only one appears onscreen, you can use the program's Window menu to switch between open files. Shown in Figure 3.12, the Window menu lists all the open files in an Office program.

**FIGURE 3.12**

You can use the Window menu to switch between open files.

The Window menu also has valuable tools for arranging how two or more open files appear onscreen. For example, you can activate the Arrange All command, shown in Figure 3.12, to tile the open files so all appear onscreen at once, as shown in Figure 3.13. To return to a full-screen window, zoom a window with the Zoom program window control button.

You can activate the Split command (refer to Figure 3.12) to split the current window into two scrollable panes, which allows you to view the top of the document in one of the split windows while you use the other split area to view the bottom of the document. Figure 3.14 shows an example of a split Word document. To return to a single window, choose Window➪Remove Split. You can use the New Window command to open a new window with the existing file displayed.

**FIGURE 3.13**

Use the Arrange All command to view multiple files onscreen at the same time in the same program window.

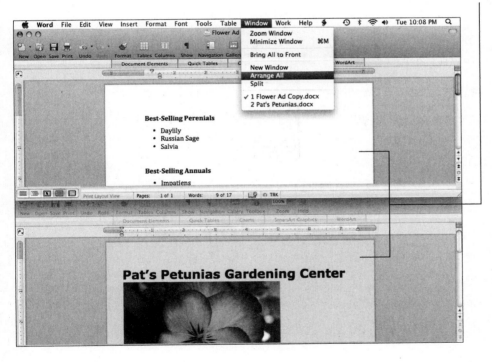

**FIGURE 3.14**

You can use the Window menu to split a single document into two scrollable panes.

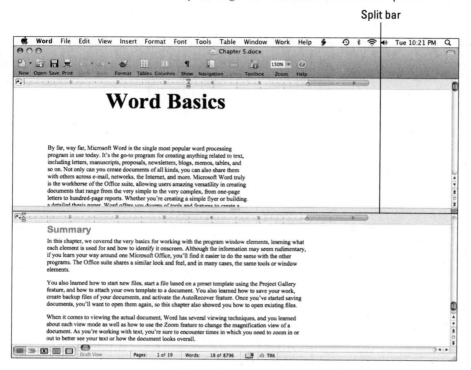

## Using Menus, Toolbars, and the Toolbox

Menus and toolbars are an essential part of every Office 2008 for Mac program. Thankfully, they always work the same, regardless of the program. Office menus and toolbars hold the keys to using a program successfully. They list all the tools and features you use to create, build, format, and generate files and projects. If you learn your way around one menu or toolbar, you pretty much know your way around all. If you're new to Office, this section of the chapter shows you the basic principles behind menus and toolbars.

The Office Toolbox is a revamped feature from Office 2004 for Mac. The new and improved Toolbox is a floating palette that actually combines all the other useful palettes into one location. This section also covers how to use this new feature.

### Using menus

The menu bar, which always appears at the very top of the program window, contains all the commands for activating features, tools, and processes. Figure 3.15 shows the menu bar and the Insert menu displayed from the PowerPoint program window. Commands are organized into related groups headed by a single menu name. So you can expect to find all the commands related to formatting under the Format menu, all the commands related to working with files under the File menu, and so on. To view a group of menu commands, click the main menu group name on the menu bar.

**FIGURE 3.15**

Click a menu name to view commands.

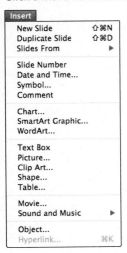

As you can see in Figure 3.15, commands are not alphabetized, but rather they appear in related subgroups. Commands with an ellipsis following the command name open a dialog box where you can give further input about the command. For example, if you activate the Table command shown in Figure 3.15, the Insert Table dialog box appears, as shown in Figure 3.16. You can specify more details about what you want and then click OK to apply the feature, tool, or command. If you decide not to activate it, you can click the Cancel button to exit the dialog box without applying any changes.

**FIGURE 3.16**

The Insert Table dialog box from PowerPoint lets you enter more input about how you want to use the command before carrying it out.

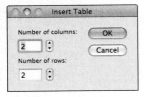

If you click a menu command that has an arrow icon next to it, a submenu appears with more commands. In Figure 3.17, the Slides From command displays three more choices regarding where to get slides from.

**FIGURE 3.17**

Submenus house even more commands in Office.

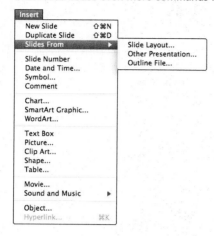

If you prefer using the keyboard to activate commands instead of the mouse, notice that the Office program menus also list keyboard shortcuts you can type. These are listed in the menus to help you learn and memorize the shortcut keys for your favorite tasks.

For many of the actions you perform in the Office programs, you can activate contextual pop-up menus that list commands related to the task at hand. For example, if you Control+click selected text in the Word program, a pop-up menu displays commands you can activate that affect the selected text, such as cutting, copying, or pasting the text or formatting the text. Figure 3.18 shows you an example of a contextual menu. To activate a command on the pop-up menu, click the command. To hide the menu again, click anywhere outside the menu area.

**FIGURE 3.18**

You can use contextual pop-up menus to assign commands related to the current activity.

Ctrl+click to display a contexual menu.

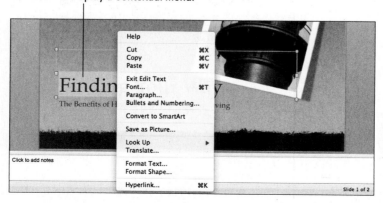

## Using toolbars

All the Office programs display a Standard toolbar by default. This toolbar contains commonly used tools, such as Undo, Redo, and Print. Using these quick-access toolbar tools can save you time ordinarily spent looking through the menus: With the toolbar, the commands are just a quick click away. Figure 3.19 shows the toolbar from the Word program. Notice that some of the tools have tiny arrow icons next to them. You can click the arrow to display a pop-up menu for additional options. For example, if you click the New button's arrow, a pop-up menu appears allowing you to choose what type of new document to create.

You can minimize the Standard toolbar by clicking the tiny oval button located in the far right-upper corner of the toolbar (refer to Figure 3.19). Once minimized, you can click the button again to display the toolbar. You also can turn the Standard toolbar display on and off through the View menu. Choose View⇨ Toolbars⇨Standard, as shown in Figure 3.20. As you can see in the figure, other toolbars are available. In fact, some of the toolbars appear automatically when you are using the toolbar-specific feature. For example, the Reviewing toolbar appears when you activate the Track Changes feature. You can turn toolbars on or off using the View menu (see Figure 3.20). A check mark next to the toolbar name indicates the toolbar is already on display; no check mark means the toolbar is not displayed.

**FIGURE 3.19**

The Standard toolbar offers you quick access to commonly used commands.

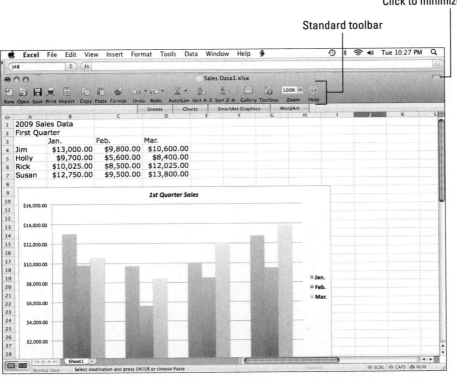

Click to minimize the toolbar.

Standard toolbar

**FIGURE 3.20**

You can use the View menu to toggle the toolbar display on or off.

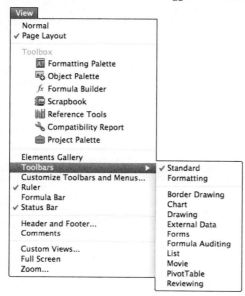

**TIP**    You can customize the Standard toolbar to show only the tools you use the most. See Chapter 34 to learn more.

## Using the Toolbox

New to Office 2008 for Mac, the Toolbox appears by default when you open an Office program for the first time. The Toolbox, shown in Figure 3.21, consolidates what were formerly separate tool palettes in previous versions of the Office programs into one convenient spot for easy access to your favorite tools and features. The palettes change based on the program you're using. For example, in Word the Toolbox includes the Formatting, Object, Citations, Scrapbook, Reference Tools, Compatibility Report, and Projects Gallery palettes. In Excel, the Formula Builder palette is added to the group replacing the Citations palette.

**NOTE**    The Toolbox does not appear by default in the Entourage program window. You can turn it on, however, by choosing Tools ➪ Toolbox ➪ [*palette name*]. You can choose Object Palette, Reference Tools, or Scrapbook. The other three palettes are not available in Entourage.

The Toolbox merges the most commonly used palettes into one spot for easy access. To view any particular palette, just click the associated palette button at the top of the Toolbox. For example, if you click the Formatting Palette button, the Toolbox displays formatting tools in sections or *panes* that you can expand or collapse based on your formatting needs. The name of the current palette always appears at the top of the Toolbox (refer to Figure 3.21).

**FIGURE 3.21**

The Toolbox combines seven palettes into one floating window.

Palette buttons

Toolbox settings button

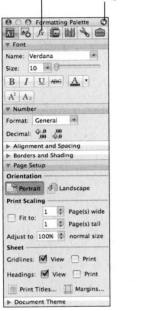

Use either of these methods to open or hide the Toolbox in Word, Excel, or PowerPoint:

■ Click the Toolbox button on the Standard toolbar.

■ Choose View and select the name of the palette you want to display.

**TIP** If the Toolbox button does not appear by default on your toolbar, you can add it using the Customize Toolbars and Menus dialog box. To learn more about customizing which icons appear on the toolbar, see Chapter 34.

Because the Toolbox is a floating window, you can move, minimize, and zoom it using the window's control buttons. You learned about window control buttons earlier in this chapter (see "Closing, minimizing, and zooming windows"). For example, you can zoom the Toolbox so it shows only the palette buttons by clicking the Zoom button. Clicking the same button again restores the full palette. You also can move the Toolbox by clicking and dragging its title bar. To close the Toolbox entirely, click the Close button.

You can customize which panes you want to include in the Toolbox or customize its appearance using the Toolbox Settings dialog box, shown in Figure 3.22. Click the Toolbox Settings button in the upper-right corner of the Toolbox (refer to Figure 3.20) to access this panel. Using the Toolbox Settings options, you can make the Toolbox automatically close or change appearance when not in use, as well as specify which tool panes appear in the palettes. Click OK to save your changes, or click Cancel to exit without saving.

**FIGURE 3.22**

You can customize the Toolbox using the Toolbox Settings.

# Summary

In this chapter, you learned the very basic procedures for starting and exiting the Office program windows. We covered how to open a program window from the Dock or from the Finder window. We also explained the basics for working with the windows themselves, such as moving and resizing windows, and using the program window control buttons. You also learned how to hide windows to reduce desktop clutter.

Although the business of opening program files is covered in the individual chapters dedicated to each Office program, you learned the basic principles for opening files from the Finder window or from the Dock. You can have more than one file or program window open at a time, and this chapter explained how to view and switch between open applications and documents.

Finally, we covered how to use the basic Office program elements: the menu bar, toolbar, and Toolbox. Armed with this knowledge, you no longer have newbie status and can now move forward with gusto in mastering Microsoft Office 2008 for Mac.

# Chapter 4

# Finding Help with Office 2008

Have you ever bought a new gadget that came with an instruction sheet? Did you stop and read the instructions, or did you just plow right in and start using the new gadget? What about those assembly-required gadgets? Did you read the instructions then? Truth is, nobody likes reading the instructions, yet they're often very important in learning how to assemble and use the gadget. Most of the time, we only turn to the instructions when we get into trouble.

Microsoft Office 2008 for Mac also comes with some instructions, called the Help system, and like an instruction sheet, they're relatively brief, not much fun to read, and often lack detail. However, they can help you learn to use the programs, especially when you find yourself in a jam. Granted, they'll never be as good as a handy book like this one, but they'll do in a pinch.

In this chapter, you learn a few things about finding help with Office 2008. Whether you want to look up a feature or learn how to apply a command or you need some assistance with a current task you're trying to perform, you can tap into the Help features for some able assistance. This chapter shows you how. You also might find yourself needing help with words or research from time to time. There's a special type of help you can employ for such instances—the Office Reference tools. This chapter shows you how to look up words using the Dictionary or Thesaurus features, translate text, or look up info in the Encarta Encyclopedia.

### IN THIS CHAPTER

**Making use of the Office Help system**

**Searching for help on Office commands, tools, and features**

**Using the Office Reference tools to find help with words and research tasks**

## Accessing Help

Long, long ago, software manufacturers used to include bulky Help manuals along with the software you purchased for the computer. Those days didn't last too long, especially since it's so much easier to include a manual electronically now and the manuals were quickly outdated anyway. Today, almost every software program you buy comes with electronic Help files. You can use the Office

Help files to find all kinds of information about tools, features, tips, and techniques. Each Office program has program-specific Help files. You won't be able to find information about an Excel function in the PowerPoint Help files. Office Help also works in the background. For example, the Office Help system kicks in when tooltip boxes pop up to reveal the name of a command button or a description of a feature, as shown in Figure 4.1. Prompt boxes that appear the first time you use a complex feature are also an example of the program's attempts to help guide you. Some dialog boxes and windows you encounter offer links to the Help system as well. The point is help is always at hand. To make the most of it, you need to know a few things about how to access it when you need it and how to navigate around the Help window when it's onscreen.

**FIGURE 4.1**

If you're paying attention, Office is always trying to lend a helping hand with tooltips that appear as you pause the mouse over icons and features.

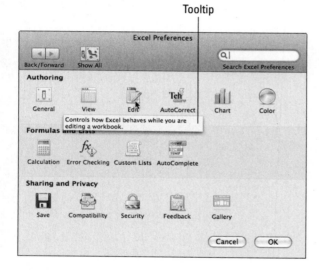

## Opening the Help files

You can find your way to the Office Help system using several different methods. The method you use depends on your preferred work style, whether you like to use menus or toolbar buttons or never let your fingers leave the keyboard. You can employ any of the methods below to access the Help files in any Office program:

- Click the Help button on the Standard toolbar.
- Choose Help ⇨ [*program name*] Help. Depending on the program you're using, the command may say Word Help, Excel Help, PowerPoint Help, or Entourage Help.
- Press ⌘+?.

After you activate the Help command, the Help window appears, as shown in Figure 4.2. This figure shows an example of a Help window from Word 2008.

**FIGURE 4.2**

The Help window first opens to a default Home page, showing links to popular topics and online help.

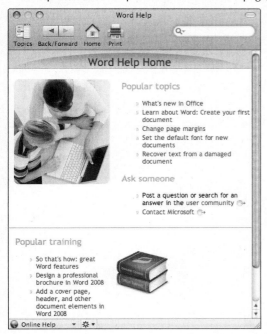

The very first thing you see when you open the Help window is a main page and a title like "Word Help Home" or "Excel Help Home." This title page has a few links you can follow to popular topics. It also has a few links for going online and finding help on the Microsoft Office Mac support Web site. When viewing the Help files, keep your eye out for links that can help you learn more about a topic or take you to information about a related topic. These are often good ways to learn new stuff about a program.

The next section explains how to navigate your way around the window and find the help you need.

## Getting around the Help window

The Help window operates like a mini-window, complete with window control buttons for closing, minimizing, and zooming the window, a toolbar, a viewing pane, and a bottom bar with a couple more tools. When you first open the window, the main Help page appears in the viewing pane, with links to popular topics or the Microsoft Web site. This page is called the Home page.

You have two major options for using the Help window. You can access Online Help or Offline Help. If your computer has a constant Internet connection, you can utilize the Online Help files from the Microsoft Web site. This option is the best because you can always be assured you're accessing the latest information. When you set the window to Offline Help, the help topics are more limited. You can toggle between Online Help and Offline Help using the pop-up option in the bottom-left corner of the window, as shown in Figure 4.3.

## FIGURE 4.3

You can toggle between Online Help and Offline Help.

 To see a list of Help topics, click the Topics button on the Help window's toolbar. This immediately displays the Help Contents as a drawer that slides out from the left side of the window, as shown in Figure 4.4. (If the window is too close to the left side of the computer screen, the Topics drawer slides out on the right side of the Help window.) The Topics drawer has two tabs: Contents and Search. You can use the Contents tab to view the table of contents for the Help files. You can use the Search tab to look up a topic or keyword.

## FIGURE 4.4

The Topics drawer has tabs for viewing the Help topics and searching through the topics.

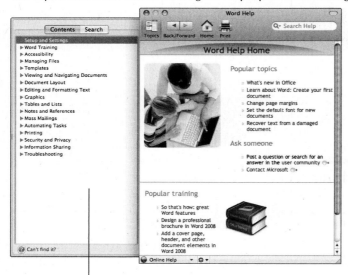

Topics drawer

The Help topics listed in the Contents tab are arranged under headings, and related topics are grouped together. For example, you'll find printing information under the Printing heading or information about templates under the Templates topic. To look through the topics in the Contents tab, click the topic you want to view. The list expands, and you can keep drilling down to find the information you want to read more about. When you find a topic you want to view, click it, and the information appears in the main viewing pane, as shown in Figure 4.5. In some cases, the help information contains links to other topics. Be sure to scroll to the bottom of the Help page to look for other useful information links.

**FIGURE 4.5**

Help topics range from descriptions and explanations to detailed steps, such as the ones shown in this figure.

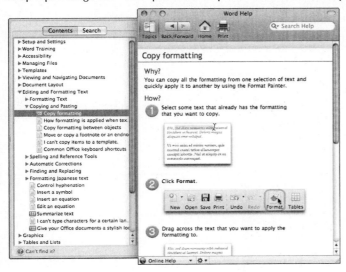

The toolbar at the top of the Help window has buttons you can use to make your way around the Help topics. Table 4.1 explains how you can use each button.

**TABLE 4.1**

# Help Window Toolbar Buttons

| Button | Description |
| --- | --- |
|  | Click the Topics button to open the Topics drawer for viewing Help topics. Click the button again to hide the drawer. |
|  | Click the Back button to return to the previous topic. |
|  | Click the Forward button to move forward a topic. |
|  | Click the Home button to return to the opening Help page. |
|  | Click the Print button to print the current Help topic. |

# Searching for Help

Clicking topics in the Contents tab of the Help window doesn't always produce the immediate results you're looking for. If you know what you want to find, you can use the search tools to look up a specific topic, command, or feature in the Help window. The Spotlight field, located in the top-right corner of the Help window, lets you type a keyword or phrase. As soon as you press Return, the Search tab in the Topics drawer displays any matches, as shown in Figure 4.6. Click a topic to view more about it.

---

**FIGURE 4.6**

You can use the Spotlight search tool to look up topics in the Help window.

Spotlight field

You also can use the Mac OS X 10.5 (Leopard) search field located on the drop-down Help menu on the main menu bar, as shown in Figure 4.7, to look for help. Unlike the Office program search, however, this search tool looks through all the Apple programs. It also does a little something extra. If you're looking for a specific command or feature in the current program, type the word for it in the field, and the menu immediately displays a list of locations where you can find the command. Simply move the mouse over the location, and it's pointed out to you onscreen—literally. The menu where the command is located drops and highlights the command or points it out with a floating arrow. Very impressive!

In addition, the Help menu displays any related topics found in the Mac Help files. Click a topic to open the Mac Help system and view more about the topic.

**FIGURE 4.7**

The Mac OS X search field can point out a command or tool you're looking for.

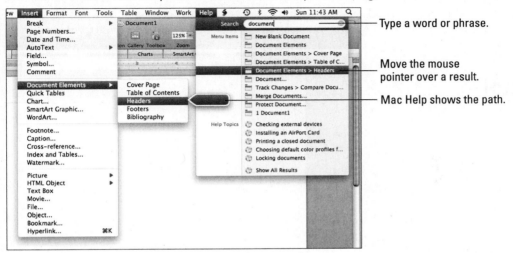

By their very name, you'd think the Help files would be exhaustive in terms of explaining every nuance of a program. Alas, they are not. In fact, it seems that many software manufacturers are being very skimpy in what sort of information is included in the Help system these days. Perhaps they think everyone knows instinctively how to do everything on a computer these days? More likely, they want you to visit their Web sites for the info, and it's often buried where you can't find it easily. Don't give up, though, you can always do a general Web search and perhaps find the information you want elsewhere.

If you still can't find what you're looking for, try some of these Web sites:

- **Microsoft's Online Forum for Mac users:** www.officeformac.com
- **Microsoft's Knowledge Base:** http://support.microsoft.com
- **Mactopia Help Center:** www.microsoft.com/mac/help.mspx

Or better yet, buy a good book (like this one!) so you don't have to waste time on the Internet or looking through the Help system!

# Using the Office Reference Tools

If you ever run into any trouble pertaining to words or language or you need some help researching a topic, the Office Reference tools can really be of great assistance. The Reference tools include a dictionary, thesaurus, text-translation feature, bilingual dictionary, and the Encarta Encyclopedia. You can find all the tools available in one spot—the Reference Tools palette, a part of the new Toolbox overhaul. To view the tools, follow these steps:

1. Click the Toolbox icon in the Standard toolbar if the Toolbox is not already open.

 2. Click the Reference Tools button.

The Reference tools appear, as shown in Figure 4.8.

**FIGURE 4.8**

Use the Reference tools to look up information, find and translate words, look up meanings and synonyms, and search the Web.

> **TIP** You won't find a Toolbox icon on a toolbar in Entourage. Instead, you can access the Reference tools through the Tools menu directly (choose Tools ⇨ Dictionary or Tools ⇨ Thesaurus), or you can activate the Toolbox feature (choose Tools ⇨ Toolbox ⇨ Reference Tools). Both methods open the Reference Tools palette. You can use the same technique in the other Office programs to open the palette.

Each pane listed in the Reference Tools palette can be expanded or collapsed when you click the pane name. Obviously, the screen doesn't have enough room to view all the panes at once, but you can easily display the one you want to use at the moment. The following sections explain how to use each of the tools.

## Using the Thesaurus

Do you ever find yourself in the middle of a document trying to think of another way of saying the same word you used earlier? Don't sweat it; help is here in the form of the Thesaurus tool. You can look up synonyms—words that have the same meaning as another—while you work and quickly insert them into your document, spreadsheet, presentation, or e-mail message.

Follow these steps to look up and insert a synonym:

1. **Display the Toolbox, and click the Reference Tools button.** See the previous steps to learn how to display the Toolbox.

   The Reference tools appear.

2. **Click the Thesaurus section heading.**

3. **Type the word you want to look up, and press Return.**

   The Meanings box lists any meanings for the word, and the Synonyms box lists any synonyms, as shown in Figure 4.9.

**FIGURE 4.9**

You can use the Thesaurus pane to look up and insert synonyms.

4. **Click the synonym you want to use.**

5. **Click the Insert button.**

   The new synonym appears in the document.

You can use these same steps to replace a selected word in a document with a synonym.

You don't always have to open the Reference Tools palette to look up a synonym. If you're working in a document and need to look up a word, you can use the handy pop-up menu to utilize the Thesaurus tool. Simply Ctrl+click a word to display a pop-up menu, as shown in Figure 4.10, and then click the Synonyms command to see a list of synonyms. You can click a synonym from the list to replace the word in the document.

**FIGURE 4.10**

You can use the pop-up menu to look up and insert synonyms when applicable.

Ctrl+click the word to look up.

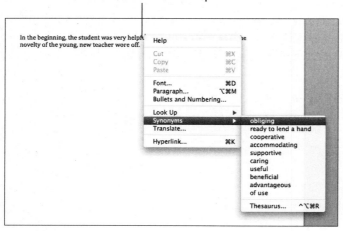

## Using the Dictionary

Do you ever need to look up a word to find its meaning? The Dictionary tool, another valuable part of the Office Reference tools, is ready to assist you. The feature taps into the Encarta World English Dictionary, which contains definitions, pronunciations, word histories, and usage notes. You need an Internet connection to use this feature. Follow these steps to look up a word:

1. **Display the Toolbox, and click the Reference Tools button.**

   The Reference tools appear.

2. **Click the Dictionary pane.**

3. **Type the word you want to look up and press Return.**

   The list box displays any meanings for the word, as shown in Figure 4.11.

You also can Ctrl+click a word to display a pop-up menu and then choose Look Up⇨Definition to open the Reference Tools palette and see the word defined in the Dictionary pane.

**TIP**   Need more room in a Reference Tool pane? You can resize the panes, if needed, to view more information in the list box area. To do so, move the mouse pointer over the three dots at the bottom of the pane until the pointer changes to a double-sided arrow icon; then drag the pane border to the desired height in the palette.

## Using the Encarta Encyclopedia

If any of your Office projects involves researching a topic, you'll be happy to know you can do your research from within the Office program window. For this reference tool, you utilize the knowledge base of the Encarta Encyclopedia. You must have an Internet connection up and running to utilize this feature. Follow these steps to look up a topic:

1. **Display the Toolbox, and click the Reference Tools.**

   The Reference tools appear.

2. **Click the Encarta Encyclopedia pane.**

3. **Type the word you want to research, and press Return.**

   The list box shows the results, as shown in Figure 4.12, including any online links you can follow to view Web pages about the topic.

   If you click a link, your default browser window opens and displays the page.

**FIGURE 4.11**

You can use the Dictionary pane to look up words.

**FIGURE 4.12**

You can use the Encarta Encyclopedia pane to research data.

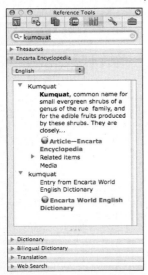

## Translating text

If any of your Office projects or work requires using foreign languages, you may find the Translation feature quite helpful. For example, if you're working on or viewing a letter containing a word you need to translate, you can activate the Translation tool, one of the many helpful tools among the Reference Tools palette. Follow these steps to translate a word:

1. **Display the Toolbox, and click the Reference Tools.**

   The Reference tools appear.

2. **Click the Translation pane.**

3. **Click the From: pop-up menu to choose a language to translate from.**

4. **Click the To: pop-up menu to choose a language to translate to.**

5. **Type the word you want to translate, and press Return.**

   The list box shows the results, including any online links you can follow for additional translation help, as shown in Figure 4.13.

---

**FIGURE 4.13**

You can use the Translation pane to translate words.

Like the Thesaurus and Dictionary tools, you can use a shortcut to translate a word in a document. You can Ctrl+click a word to display a pop-up menu and then click Translate to open the Reference Tools palette and see the word defined in the Translation pane.

**You also can translate an entire document using the online link in the Translation pane and use a Web-based translation service.**

## Using the Bilingual Dictionary

Along with the regular dictionary found in the Reference tools, you also can access a Bilingual Dictionary. The Bilingual Dictionary tool uses local and online bilingual dictionaries and machine translation on the Web. You can translate a single word or a phrase. You need an Internet connection to utilize this tool. Follow these steps to look up a word using the Bilingual Dictionary:

1. **Display the Toolbox, and click the Reference Tools.**

   The Reference tools appear.

2. **Click the Bilingual Dictionary section.**

3. **Click the From: pop-up menu to choose a language to translate from.**

4. **Click the To: pop-up menu to choose a language to translate to.**

5. **Type the word you want to translate, and press Return.**

   The list box shows the results, as shown in Figure 4.14.

**FIGURE 4.14**

You can use the Bilingual Dictionary pane to look up words in other languages.

## Performing a Web search

The last Reference tool to discuss is the Web Search pane located at the bottom of the Reference Tools palette. You can use this feature to research data and find links to Web sites on the Internet. Follow these steps to use the Web Search tool:

1. **Display the Toolbox, and click the Reference Tools button.**

   The Reference Tools appear.

2. **Display the Web Search pane.**

3. **Type the word or phrase you want to look up, and press Return.**

   The list box displays the results, as shown in Figure 4.15.

   You can click any links to open the default Web browser and view the page.

---

**FIGURE 4.15**

You can use the Web Search pane to research the Web for more information.

# Summary

In this chapter, you learned what you can expect to find among the Office Help system files. You learned how to open and navigate the Help window, how to view topics, and how to switch between Online Help and Offline Help. The chapter also covered how to search for a specific command or feature from among the many Help topics. What's more, this chapter showed you how to find help with words and research using the Office Reference tools. The next time you need to look up a synonym or translate a word, you'll know exactly what to do.

# Part II

# Working with Word

# Chapter 5

# Word Basics

B y far, way far, Microsoft Word is the single most popular word-processing program in use today. It's the go-to program for creating anything related to text, including letters, manuscripts, proposals, newsletters, blogs, memos, tables, and so on. Not only can you create documents of all kinds, you also can share them with others across e-mail, networks, the Internet, and more. Microsoft Word truly is the workhorse of the Office suite, allowing users amazing versatility in creating documents that range from the very simple to the very complex, from one-page letters to hundred-page reports. Whether you're creating a simple flyer or building a detailed thesis paper, Word offers you dozens of tools and features to create a professional-looking document in no time flat.

Microsoft Word 2008 for Mac is the latest version of the Office productivity suite, on par with Office 2007 for the PC. Before this, the last big version of Word was Office 2004 for Mac. If you're new to Word, or just trying to get up and running fast with this latest version, this chapter is the place to start. Here, you'll find detailed information about the new and improved interface; learn how to open, close, and save document files; see how to change the way you view text onscreen; and learn about the various ways to add data behind the scenes to a document or protect it from unauthorized use.

### IN THIS CHAPTER

**Exploring the Word window**

**Working with document files**

**Changing views**

**Assigning document properties**

**Protecting documents**

## Navigating the Word Window

Microsoft Word 2008 for Mac sports a much updated look compared to previous versions of the program. With a fashionably tweaked user interface, Word 2008 for Mac now blends in with all the other Office and Mac programs, displaying modern-looking windows, toolbars, and icons. Figure 5.1 shows the new and improved Word window with a blank document displayed. Pretty spiffy, eh? Before you take yours out for a spin, take a few minutes and review the various parts of the program window, as explained in this section.

## FIGURE 5.1

Behold, the new and improved Word 2008 program window. In this figure, the blank document window appears in Print Layout view. Depending on what view mode is selected, your screen may vary in appearance.

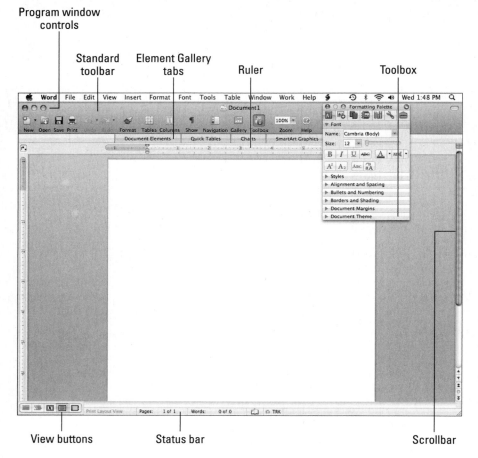

## Viewing window parts

Every Office program window, including Word, has a similar look and feel. This helps the programs seem, well, seamless. After you master the basics in one program, you can count on finding the same tools and icons in the same places in the other programs. So after you figure out your way around Word, for example, you can use those same skills to navigate Excel or PowerPoint. The following descriptions give you a look at the basic window elements.

### Title bar and menu bar

At the top of the Word window, or the top of any program window for that matter, you'll always find a title bar and menu bar. This bar area lists the name of the program, such as Word, and the main menu categories.

# What about Keyboard Shortcuts?

**W**hen assigning commands from Word's menus, you may prefer to keep your fingers flying on the keyboard to save time and effort. There are plenty of keyboard shortcuts for all the Word commands and for all the other programs in the Office suite. Word even helps you learn the shortcuts by listing them next to menu commands. Almost all keyboard shortcuts involve pressing ⌘ while clicking another key, such as ⌘+N to start a new, blank document or ⌘+C to copy selected text. To print out a complete list of Word's entire shortcut keys, follow these steps:

1. **Choose Tools ⇨ Macros.**

   The Macros dialog box opens.

2. **Scroll down the list, and click ListCommands.**

3. **Click Run.**

   The List Commands dialog box appears.

4. **Click Current menu and keyboard settings.**

5. **Click OK.**

   Word creates a table in the document with all the commands and shortcut keys.

6. **Click Print or press ⌘+P to begin printing the list.**

Depending on your document settings, the printed list is probably about 20 pages long and includes shortcuts for commands you may never use. However, having the list is handy while you're trying to learn shortcut keys for your favorite tasks.

To reveal a menu, simply click the menu name and a list of associated or related commands appears. To activate a command, click the command name. Depending on the command, submenus or a dialog box may appear for further input. For example, if a menu command has an arrow icon next to it, a submenu appears when the menu command is selected. If a menu command has ellipses (dots) next to it, a dialog box appears allowing you to give more input before assigning the feature.

Just below the menu bar, you'll find program window controls and the document name. The program window controls, which are the three colored circle icons located at the far left side, allow you to close, minimize, and zoom the document window, as outlined below:

- Click the round red button with an X in the center to close the document window, but leave the program window open.

- Click the round yellow button with a minus in the center to minimize the document window, which transports the window down into the Dock.

- Click the round green button with a plus in the center to maximize or zoom the document window, making the window as large as possible.

The document name at the top of the program window simply lists any assigned name you gave to the saved file. If the document name has not been saved yet, the default name appears, such as Document1, Document2, and so on. You can click and drag the document name icon just like you drag other Mac icons in the Finder. Called the *document proxy icon*, it works just like the folder proxy icons you use in the Finder.

For example, you might drag the current document to another folder or drag it over to the Trash to delete it. You also can ⌘-click the document name to find out the document's location on the hard drive. This works only if the document has been saved.

### Standard toolbar

Directly below the title bar and menu bar is the Standard toolbar. This toolbar displays a row of tool icons for common Word tasks, such as opening or printing documents. To activate a feature or command, just click the associated icon. By default, the Standard toolbar appears every time you create a new document. Depending on the Word task you are performing, other toolbars may appear when needed. Word offers 12 different toolbars, or you can create your own custom toolbar. (See Chapter 34 to learn more about customizing toolbars. To learn more about using toolbars in Office, see Chapter 3.)

> **TIP** You can Control-click an empty area of a toolbar to display a shortcut menu of related commands. For example, if you Control-click the Standard toolbar, you can view commands for changing how icons are displayed on the toolbar, accessing other toolbars, and resetting or customizing the toolbar. For example, if you want to view icons only, click the Icon Only command.

### Elements Gallery

 Located directly below the Standard toolbar, you can use the new Elements Gallery to quickly insert preset design items such as title pages, headers, and tables. The Elements Gallery appears only when using Print Layout, Publishing Layout, or Web Layout views. By default, the Gallery is hidden, showing only a row of tabs. You can display the Gallery by clicking a tab on the bar or by clicking the Gallery button on the Standard toolbar.

If you click a tab, you can view group tabs for specific categories of elements. Figure 5.2 shows the Document Elements tab selected with the Cover Pages group displayed. You can scroll through the list of items and click the one you want to apply.

---

### FIGURE 5.2

The Elements Gallery offers a library of preset design and formatting features you can apply to documents, such as cover pages, headers and footers, and tables.

Click a category to view items.   Click a tab to view categories.

You also can click the Gallery button on the Standard toolbar to view the Elements Gallery, or you can choose View ➪ Elements Gallery. When you finish choosing an element, you can click the Gallery button again to hide the Gallery.

### Ruler

Word's Ruler feature is actually two rulers you can use to help position text and objects and set margins, indents, and tabs. The horizontal ruler at the top of the document shows the horizontal positioning of the page, while the vertical ruler on the left side of the document window shows vertical positioning. You can turn the Ruler feature on or off by choosing View ⇨ Ruler. Learn more about setting tabs, indents, and margins in Chapters 6 and 7.

### Toolbox

The Word Toolbox is packed full of useful tools for completing common tasks. Tools are grouped into palettes that appear as heading bars in the Toolbox. Simply click the palette name to display the palette and view the associated tools and features. You can use this same technique to collapse the palette view again and hide the tools. You learn more about using the Toolbox later in this chapter.

### Scroll bars

As you add more and more text to your document, you can use the scroll bars to move your view of the document. For example, you can drag the vertical scroll box up or down to move around in the document, or you can drag the horizontal scroll box to move left or right. You also can click the scroll arrows to move around the document. In addition, you can use the Navigation buttons to move up or down a page.

### Status bar

The Status bar, located at the very bottom of the screen, offers lots of useful information. For starters, it contains your document's page count, word count, spelling and grammar status, and the Track Changes feature. The far-left side of the bar displays the various view buttons you can apply. To learn more about Word's views, see "Changing Views" later in this chapter. To learn more about the spelling and grammar features, see Chapter 11. To learn about the Word Count tool, see Chapter 9. To learn about the Track Changes feature, see Chapter 10.

## Using the Navigation Pane

 If you're working with particularly long documents, you can use the Navigation Pane to help you view various pages. Shown in Figure 5.3, this pane displays every page in the document. You can scroll through the list and click a page in the Navigation Pane to display the page in the main document window pane. To open the Navigation pane at any time, click the Navigation button on the Standard toolbar or choose View ⇨ Navigation Pane. You can use this same technique to close the pane again. The Navigation Pane has two view modes for listing how pages appear in the pane: Thumbnail or Document Map. Thumbnail view, the default setting, shows each page as an actual picture of the document page, while Document Map view displays the pages in outline format.

**FIGURE 5.3**

You can use the Navigation Pane to make your way through long documents.

Use the scrollbar or
scroll through the pages.

Click to change how
pages are listed
in the pane.

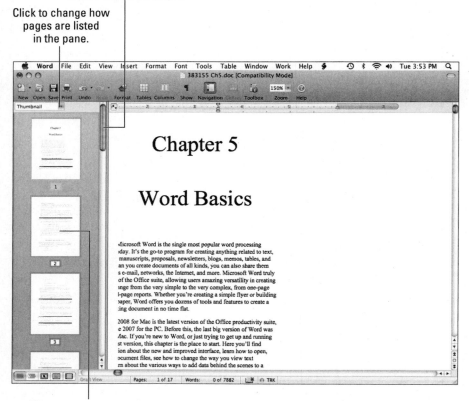

Click a page to view it in
the document window.

## Using the Toolbox

The Word Toolbox consolidates what were formerly separate tool palettes in previous versions of Word into one convenient palette in Word 2008 for Mac. By placing all the common palettes into one easy interface, Word makes accessing commonly used tools and features effortless. Figure 5.4 shows the Toolbox with the Formatting Palette, with the Font and the Alignment and Spacing tools displayed.

**FIGURE 5.4**

The Toolbox consolidates seven palettes into one easy interface.

Palette buttons

Toolbox Settings icon

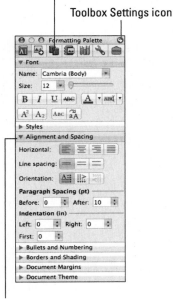

Panes

To open or hide the Toolbox, use any of these methods:

- Click the Toolbox button on the Standard toolbar.
- Choose View ➪ Formatting Palette (or select the name of the palette you want to display).

The Word Toolbox includes the following palettes: Formatting, Object, Citations, Scrapbook, Reference Tools, Compatibility Report, and Projects Gallery. To view any particular palette, click the associated palette button at the top of the palette box. For example, if you click the Formatting Palette button, the Toolbox displays formatting tools in sections or *panes* that you can expand or collapse based on your formatting needs. The name of the active palette appears at the top of the Toolbox. The Formatting Palette (refer to Figure 5.11) has panes for controlling fonts, styles, alignment and spacing, bulleted and numbered lists, borders and shading, margins, and themes. You can click a section or pane name to view its associated tools.

As a floating window, you can move, minimize, zoom, and close the Toolbox. All windows have window control buttons, tiny round colored icons you can use to control the window. To move the Toolbox, drag it by the window's title bar. To zoom the Toolbox so it shows only the palette buttons, click the Zoom button, the tiny round green icon. Clicking the same icon again restores the full palette.

To close the palette window entirely, click the Close button, the tiny round red icon.

Lastly, you can click the Toolbox Settings button, the small gray icon located in the top-right corner of the palette window, to access Toolbox Settings, shown in Figure 5.5. Use the options in this panel to make the Toolbox automatically close or change appearance when not in use or to select which tool panes you want to appear in the palettes. For example, you can instruct the Toolbox to collapse after a set amount of time or close completely. If you make any changes to the settings, click OK, and Word returns you to the Toolbox.

**FIGURE 5.5**

The Toolbox Settings panel allows you to control the appearance of the Toolbox.

# Creating, Opening, and Saving Documents

Files you create in Word are called *documents*. Every time you open Word, a new, blank document is waiting for you to begin using. As you create files in Word, you'll want to open and reuse them again, so mastering the techniques of creating, opening, and saving files is essential to using Word and the rest of the Microsoft Office 2008 for Mac suite.

## Creating new files

Starting new documents is incredibly easy in Word, and you can utilize any of these methods to do so:

- Click the New button on the Standard toolbar.
- You also can click the arrow icon next to the New button to display a menu to specify what kind of new document you want to open: New Blank Document, New Blank Notebook Layout Document, or New Blank Publishing Layout Document.
- Choose File ➪ New Blank Document.
- Press ⌘+N.

Any of the above methods opens a blank document. If you want to create a specific kind of document, you can use Word's Project Gallery. The Project Gallery, shown in Figure 5.6, is your one-stop shop for projects you create in the Office suite. For example, you can create newsletters, business cards, flyers, ledger sheets, resumes, and much more. This feature, also available in Excel, PowerPoint, and Entourage, includes all kinds of ready-made templates for creating documents. The Project Gallery also keeps track of recent project files.

To create a project with the Project Gallery, follow these steps:

1. **Click File.**
2. **Click Project Gallery.**

   The Project Gallery window opens.
3. **Click the New tab.**
4. **Click a document category.**
5. **Click the type of document you want to create.**
6. **Click Open.**

   Word creates and opens the new file.

**FIGURE 5.6**

The Project Gallery offers a variety of templates you can use to create new Word documents.

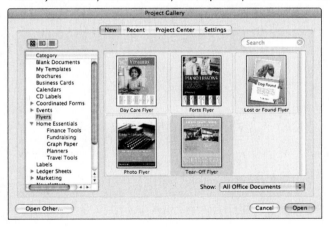

When you create a new project, Word displays the document with placeholder, or dummy, text. You can replace the text with your own text. When you finish creating the document, you can save it with a unique filename and reuse it again later.

## Saving files

After you put lots of work into creating a document, you can save it and revisit it again later to make changes or print it. In fact, if you try exiting the document without saving, Word prompts you to save your data. You can use the Save As dialog box, shown in Figure 5.7, to assign a unique filename to a document, as well as specify a location in which to save the file, choose a file format, or check compatibility.

# Elements Gallery versus Projects Gallery

You may be wondering "what's the difference between the Elements Gallery and the Projects Gallery?" The Elements Gallery focuses on inserting specific types of items into a document, such as preset headers and footers, cover pages, table of contents pages, and more. The Projects Gallery, on the other hand, offers a library of preset templates for creating entire documents. The Elements Gallery, which is only a quick click away using the Gallery button on the Standard toolbar, offers five distinct categories of elements you can add, including charts, tables, and graphics. In many instances, when you add an item from the Elements Gallery, it ends up adding a new page to the document length. So if you're looking for a quick and easy element to insert, check out the Elements Gallery.

 To use the Gallery, click the Gallery button on the Standard toolbar to display the Elements Gallery, or if the category tabs already appear below the Standard toolbar, simply click a category and click the item you want to add. Word immediately adds the item to the document. How easy is that?

---

**FIGURE 5.7**

When saving a file, you specify a unique name for the document and choose a destination where you want to store the file.

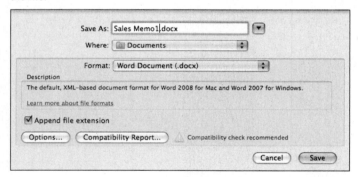

By default, Word documents are saved in the **.docx** file type. This format is an XML-based format for Word for Mac 2008 and Word 2007 for Windows. You can choose another file type, as needed. For example, if you're sharing the file with someone who uses an older version of Word, you can choose an older file format compatible with the program they're using. Word offers a list of common file formats you can choose from, including plain text (.txt), Web page (.htm), and PDF (.pdf). You can also choose from specialty formats, such as Word macro-enabled document (.docm) or Word 2003 XML document (.xml). Word automatically tacks on the file extension for the format you select, such as .docx. You do not necessarily need the file extension letters, but they do help computers identify the type of file it is, so leaving the Append file extension check box selected in the Save As dialog box is a good idea. Table 5.1 defines the available file formats.

**TABLE 5.1**

## Word File Formats

| File Format | Description |
|---|---|
| Word Document (.docx) | Saves the document in XML format for Word 2008 for Mac and Word 2007 for Windows. |
| Word 97-2004 Document (.doc) | Saves the document in a format compatible with Word 98-Word 2004 for Mac and Word 97-Word 2003 for Windows. |
| Word Template (.dotx) | Saves the document in XML template format, compatible with Word 2008 for Mac and Word 2007 for Windows. |
| Word 97-2004 Template (.dot) | Exports a template compatible with Word 98-Word 2004 for Mac and Word 97-Word 2003 for Windows. |
| Rich Text Format (.rtf) | Exports a cross-platform file and preserves the content and formatting for viewing in other programs, such as WordPerfect. |
| Plain Text (.txt) | Exports the document content without formatting, useful for sharing the document if the destination program cannot read any of the other available formats. |
| Web Page (.htm) | Saves the document content for display on the Web, compatible with Mac and Windows Web browsers. |
| PDF (.pdf) | Exports the document as a PDF file. |
| Word Macro-Enabled Document (.docm) | Saves the document with XML-based document format preserving VBA macro coding. Note: VBA macros do not work in Word 2008. |
| Word Macro-Enabled Template (.dotm) | Exports the XML-based template along with VBA macro coding. Note: VBA macros do not work in Word 2008. |
| Word XML Document (.xml) | Saves the document content as an XML file, compatible with Word 2007 for Windows. |
| Word 2003 XML Document (.xml) | Exports the content as an XML file, compatible with Word 2003 for Windows. |
| Single File Web Page (.mht) | Formats the document as a single Web page, including all page elements. |
| Word Document Stationery (.doc) | Exports the document with a Stationery Pad Finder flag, so when it is opened, a new document is created. |
| Speller Customary Dictionary (.dic) | Saves the document as a dictionary file, allowing for stored words and terms not part of the original, main dictionary feature. |
| Speller Exclude Dictionary (.dic) | Saves the document as a dictionary file along with all of your preferred spelling of words. |
| Word 4.0-6.0/95 Compatible (.rtf) | Saves the document as an RTF format compatible with Word 3.0 through Word 6.0 for Mac, and Word 6.0 through Word 95 for Windows. |

When saving files, you also can choose exactly where to store a document. By default, Word is set up to save documents to the Documents folder. If you want to save the file to another folder or drive, you must specify a location.

Before you start saving files, you should know about the Compatibility Report tool. As soon as you open the Save As dialog box, you'll notice a red warning blurb recommending a compatibility check. This feature is helpful if you're sharing documents with people who are using different versions of Word. If you activate the Compatibility Report feature, Word runs a compatibility test and notifies you if it encounters any issues that might cause a problem or not print properly in another version of Word. This same feature is available on the Compatibility tab of the Toolbox. If you're not sharing files, you do not need to run the tool.

Now that you've had a brief overview of the file-saving process, you're ready to save your files. You can utilize any of the following methods to save a document.

### Saving for the first time

The first time you save a file, follow these steps:

1. **Click the Save button on the Standard toolbar, or choose File ⇨ Save or Save As.**
   The Save As dialog box opens, as shown in Figure 5.14.
2. **Type a name for the file.**
3. **Choose a destination folder or drive on which to store the file.**
   - By default, Word saves the file to the Documents folder.
   - Optionally, to save the document in another file format, click the Format arrows and choose a format, as shown in Figure 5.8.
   - Optionally, to check for compatibility issues, click the Compatibility Report button.

### FIGURE 5.8

You can choose from a variety of file formats when saving a file.

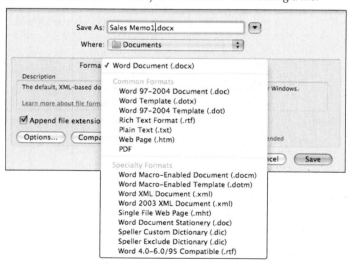

4. **Click Save.** Word saves the document, and the new filename appears at the top of the document window.

If you run the Compatibility Report tool, Word checks the file for compatibility issues and displays a prompt if it finds any. You can view the issues using the Compatibility Report Palette in the Toolbox. You also can access the Compatibility Report feature through the Compatibility Palette on the Toolbox. To learn more about this feature, see "Using the Compatibility Report feature" later in this section.

### Making subsequent saves

After you've saved the file the first time, you don't have to revisit the Save As dialog box again. Instead, employ any of these methods to save your changes:

- Click the Save button on the Standard toolbar.
- Choose File ⇨ Save.
- Press ⌘+S.

### Saving an existing file under a new filename

When you want to save a document with a different name, follow these steps:

1. **Choose File ⇨ Save As.**

   The Save As dialog box opens.

2. **Type a new name for the file.**

3. **Choose a destination folder or drive on which to store the file.**

4. **Click Save.**

   Word saves the document, and the new filename appears at the top of the document window.

### Creating a backup file

In addition to saving your document the regular way, you also can set up Word to create a backup copy of the file when saving. When you activate this option, Word creates two files during the Save process; one is the original and one is a backup file with the name "Backup of" in front of the filename. Both copies are saved in the designated folder or dive. When opting to use the backup feature, consider placing the backup file on a USB drive, an external hard drive, or an iDisk for extra safety. To create automatic backups, follow these steps:

1. **Choose File ⇨ Save As.**

   The Save As dialog box opens.

2. **Type a name for the file.**

3. **Choose a destination folder or drive on which to store the file.**

4. **Click the Options button.**

   The Save options dialog box opens, as shown in Figure 5.9.

5. **Click the Always create backup copy check box.**

6. **Click OK.**

7. **Click Save.**

   Word saves the document and the backup copy to the same folder or drive.

**FIGURE 5.9**

Turn on the backup feature to instruct Word to always make backup copies of a document.

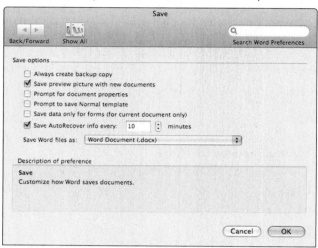

## Using AutoRecover

You can use Word's AutoRecover feature to create automatic saves of your document. In case a power glitch of some sort or a computer failure strikes, you'll have a recently saved copy of your work to reopen. AutoRecover saves the current file as a separate AutoRecover file you can open and save under a new name and keep working on the document. You can set AutoRecover to automatically save every 10 minutes, every 15 minutes, or a time specification based on your needs. You don't want to save too often, like every minute, because the AutoRecover feature slows down your computer for a second or two when it kicks into gear.

To create automatic saves, follow these steps:

1. **Choose Word ➪ Preferences.**

   The Word Preferences dialog box opens.

2. **Under the Output and Sharing group, click the Save icon.**

   The Save preferences appear, as shown in Figure 5.10.

3. **Specify how often you want to save the document in the Save AutoRecover info every box.**

   You can type in a number or click the arrow buttons to arrive at the number you want.

4. **Click OK.**

   Word is now set up to automatically save your file.

 **You also can access the Save preferences through the Save As dialog box. Simply click the Options button in the dialog box while saving a file, and the Save preferences appear.**

**FIGURE 5.10**

Turn on the AutoRecover feature to create automatic saves of your documents.

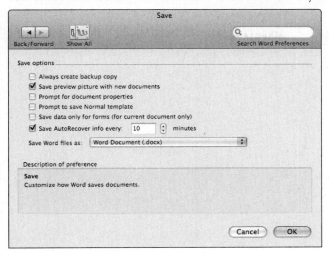

## Using the Compatibility Report feature

The Compatibility Report feature is a helpful tool for users who share their document files with people using older versions of Word. Although you're obviously cooler and more hip for having the latest, greatest version of Word, other users you share files with may be using ancient versions of the program, so sending them a copy of the whiz bang company newsletter you created in Word 2008 may result in lots of frustration on their end if they can't open or view the file properly. That's where the Compatibility Report feature comes in. It checks your document and makes it backward compatible. For example, if your document uses features not available in older versions of Word, the report tool warns you and offers you a way to correct any compatibility issues.

One way to check a document for compatibility is to do so when you first save the file. You can activate a Compatibility Report button in the Save As dialog box. This method is covered in "Saving files," earlier in this chapter. Another way to use the feature is to visit the Compatibility Report Palette in the Toolbox. Here you'll find detailed results of a check, explanations about the issues, and tools for making any fixes or ignoring any problems. Follow these steps to use the Compatibility Report feature:

1. **Display the Toolbox by clicking the Toolbox button on the Standard toolbar or choosing View ⇨ Compatibility Report.**

2. **Click the Compatibility Palette button.**

   Word opens the Compatibility Report Palette in the Toolbox, as shown in Figure 5.18.

3. **Click the Check compatibility with menu, and choose a document type with which you want to compare.**

   Word immediately begins checking the document and displays any issues in the Results box, as shown in Figure 5.11.

**FIGURE 5.11**

You can use the Compatibility Report Palette in the Toolbox to check your document for compatibility issues.

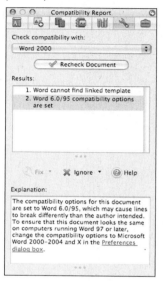

4. **Click a result to view an explanation in the Explanation box.**
   - To fix a problem, click the Fix arrow button and make a selection.
   - To ignore a problem, click the Ignore arrow button and make a selection.
   - You can click the Recheck Document button to check a document again.

## Opening files

After you start creating and saving files, Word makes it easy to open them again. The Open dialog box allows you to open documents stored in various folders and drives on your computer, while the Open Recent submenu on the File menu lists recent files you worked with in Word. You also can use the Project Gallery to open recent Word files.

# Compatibility Preferences

You can control what items are compared in the Compatibility Report using the Preferences dialog box. Choose Word ➪ Preferences to open the dialog box, and then click the Compatibility icon under the Output and Sharing group. This opens the Compatibility options, where you can make your selections. The Options list box contains a wide array of compatibility items you can check or uncheck for testing. You also can reset your document if you chose to ignore the issues. Click OK to exit the dialog box and apply any changes.

## Opening a document with the Open command

The Open command is a quick way to open a file you created; do so by following these steps:

1.  **Click the Open button on the Standard toolbar, or choose File ⇨ Open.**

    The Open dialog box opens, as shown in Figure 5.12.

**FIGURE 5.12**

You can use the Open dialog box to open document files stored on your computer or on other drives or storage devices.

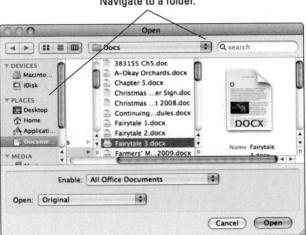

2.  **Click the file you want to open.**
    - You can navigate to a folder or device containing the file you want to open using the Navigation Pane.
    - You also can double-click the document name to quickly open the document.
3.  **Click the Open button.**

    Word opens the document.

**TIP**   If you don't see the file you want in the Open dialog box, you can change what file types are listed. Simply click the Enable menu, and choose a format. For best results, consider changing the setting to All Readable Documents or All Documents so you can view all the document types.

## Opening a document with the Open Recent menu

If you've recently worked with a document, you can quickly access it again using the Recent Files command. Here's how:

# Read-Only and File Copies

The Open dialog box also lets you open a file as a read-only file or as a copy of the original. The Open menu lets you choose from Original, Copy, or Read-Only. The Original setting is selected by default, which simply means whatever document you select to open is the original file. A read-only file does just what the name implies: It opens the document, but does not allow you to make any changes to the content. You can read it, but not edit it. Finally, you can use the Copy feature to open a copy of the original file. If you make changes to the document, you can save them under a new filename and keep the original file intact.

1. **Choose File ⇨ Open Recent.**
2. **Click the file you want to open.**

   If you don't see your file listed, you can click the More button to open the Project Gallery to the Recent documents tab and look for the file.

## Opening a document with the Project Gallery

The Project Gallery is another easy way to access your documents; here's how:

1. **Click File.**
2. **Click Project Gallery.**

   The Project Gallery window opens.

3. **Click the Recent tab.**
4. **Click the document you want to open.**
5. **Click Open.**

   Word opens the file.

## Opening a document based on a template

You can attach a template to any document in Word using the Templates and Add-ins dialog box. Follow these steps:

1. **Choose Tools ⇨ Templates and Add-ins.**

   The Templates and Add-ins dialog box opens, as shown in Figure 5.13.

2. **Click the Attach button.**

   The Choose File dialog box opens.

3. **Navigate to the template file you want to use, and click the filename.**
4. **Click Open.**
5. **Click OK.**

   Word attaches the template to the document.

You also can create a new file based on a preset template found in Word's Project Gallery. See "Creating New Files" earlier in this chapter to learn more.

**FIGURE 5.13**

Use the Templates and Add-ins dialog box to attach a template to the current document.

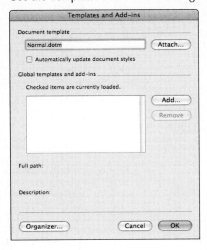

### Searching for a file

You can use the Open dialog box to search for an existing document on your computer. Using the Spotlight text field, which displays the word "search" by default, you can search for a specific filename, a portion of the name, or keywords pertaining to the name. Follow these steps to search for a file:

1. **Display the Open dialog box, as shown in Figure 5.14.** See the previous sections to learn how to open the Open dialog box.

**FIGURE 5.14**

You can use the search feature in the Open dialog box to search for a file to open.

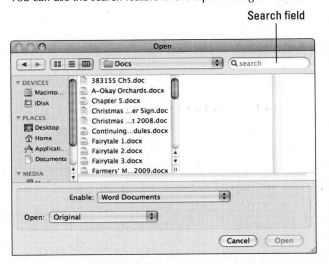

2. **Click inside the Spotlight search field, and type the filename, a portion of the name, or a keyword, as shown in Figure 5.15.**

As you type in the search field, Word lists any possible matches.

You can use the buttons at the top of the search window to target your search.

**FIGURE 5.15**

The dialog box displays any search matches.

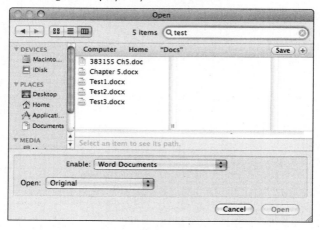

3. **When you find the file you want, double-click the filename to open the document.**

# Changing Views

Word offers a variety of view modes you can apply to help you as you work with your documents, as well as a Zoom feature you can use to magnify your onscreen text. Word's view modes, including the new Publishing Layout view, offer different features for reading and scrolling through a document's text. The Zoom feature, on the other hand, is used to adjust the viewing size of the area you're looking at onscreen. The view you select has no impact on the actual document; rather, it allows you to change how the document appears in the document window. This section examines the various ways you can view documents.

## Using the view modes

You can find five view mode buttons located in the bottom-left corner of the program window on the Status bar. These buttons include Draft, Outline, Publishing Layout, Print Layout, and Notebook Layout views. The View menu offers one more view: Web Layout view. Depending on the view you select, certain onscreen elements, such as toolbars or scrollbars, may or may not appear by default. To change views at any time, simply click the view button you want to use. Word immediately switches views. You also can display the View menu and select a view.

### Draft view

Known as Normal View in previous versions of Word, Draft view displays the document as an unending scrollable window. Basically, the document window looks like a large blank page that fills the screen, as shown in Figure 5.16. Along with the document, Draft view displays the Standard toolbar, the horizontal ruler, and the two scrollbars. In Draft view, blue lines represent page or section breaks, and page layout elements, such as graphic objects or columns, do not appear at all. Draft view is best when you want to focus on writing in your document and not be distracted by other onscreen objects. Draft view allows you to scroll very quickly through the document without waiting for graphic elements to display.

### Outline view

If you prefer building your document in outline format, switch to Outline view, shown in Figure 5.17. Like Draft view, Outline view displays the document as an unending, scrollable window. The Standard toolbar appears, along with the Outlining toolbar featuring tools for editing and adding to the outline hierarchy. As you construct your document, you can use headings to specify an outline hierarchy using the built-in heading styles, such as Heading 1, Heading 2, and so on. After you've defined headings and subheadings, you can enter body text to flesh out your outline and start creating a document. You can rearrange headings and body text as needed, or you can expand or collapse the outline to help you view the topics. You can learn more about using this view in Chapter 6.

---

**FIGURE 5.16**

Draft view displays the document with as few onscreen distractions as possible.

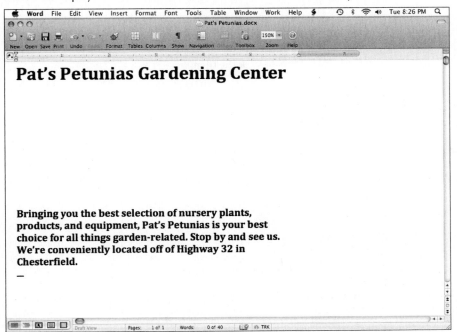

**FIGURE 5.17**

Outline view displays the document in outline format, along with the Outlining toolbar.

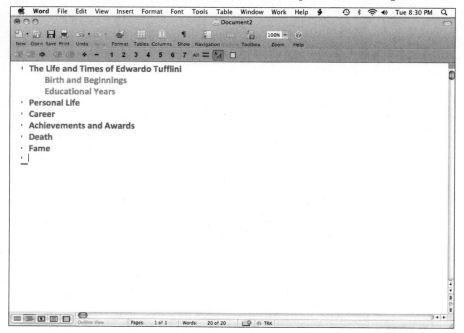

### Publishing Layout view

 New to Word 2008 for Mac, this view offers a full-blown page layout program for creating specialized documents based on templates, such as brochures and flyers. The first time you use this view, a prompt box appears, as shown in Figure 5.18, and asks you to choose how you want to create a document. You can create a new blank document by clicking the Create New button, or you can edit an existing document by clicking the Continue button. You also can click the Don't show this message again check box to discontinue the prompt.

**FIGURE 5.18**

The first time you use Publishing Layout view, a prompt box appears.

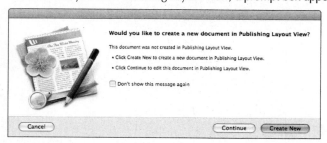

After the document is open in Publishing Layout view, as shown in Figure 5.19, it appears on a drawing table, along with a customized toolbar for the view mode, called the Publishing Layout View Standard toolbar. You can assign a new publication template from the Elements Gallery or create your own custom document from scratch. Like a true page layout program, every element in the document is a moveable box, and you literally lay out your document using these boxes; text appears in a text box, graphics appear in object boxes, shapes appear in boxes, and so on. Learn more about using this feature in Chapter 6.

### Print Layout view

Print Layout view lets you view the document just as it will look when printed. When using this view, the Standard toolbar appears, along with the Elements Gallery, and both the horizontal and vertical rulers. Because you can see all the text and graphical elements in a document using this view, you can quickly manipulate them. For example, you can adjust margins onscreen, edit headers and footers directly, and drag clip art or pictures around and place them where needed.

### Notebook Layout view

Use this view when taking notes or as an organization tool. For example, if you're using a laptop computer in class and taking notes, this view can help you enter notes and draw directly on the document page. The view, as shown in Figure 5.20, looks literally like a school notebook pad, with ruled lines on the page for writing and scribbling and tabs to organize information. You can draw images directly onscreen using the Scribble tool, erase items with an Eraser tool, and type notes and quickly rearrange them by dragging and dropping them in the document. Learn more about using this view in Chapter 6.

---

**FIGURE 5.19**

Publishing Layout view displays the document on a drawing board, along with specialized tools for creating and editing the document.

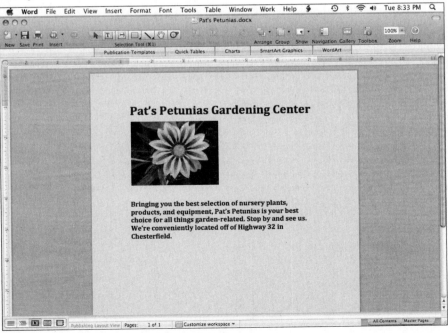

**FIGURE 5.20**

Notebook Layout view displays the document as a collegiate notebook binder.

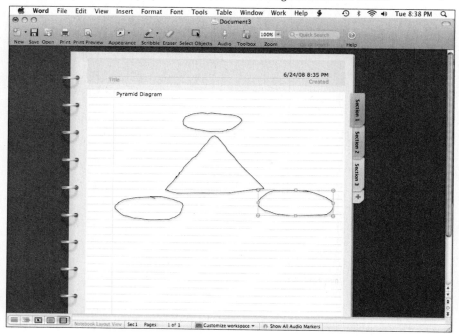

### Web Layout view

If you're planning to convert your document into a Web page, you can use Web Layout view, shown in Figure 5.21, to see what the document looks like in a browser window. In Web Layout view, no page breaks appear, and no ruler is available for setting margins or indents. To learn more about creating Web pages in Microsoft Office, see Chapter 31.

## Using the Zoom feature

You can zoom your document to change its magnification setting. The default setting is 100 percent, but you can choose another percentage to zoom in for a closer look at the document or zoom out for a bird's-eye view. You can use the Zoom button on the Standard toolbar to zoom your view, or you can use the Zoom dialog box. The following sections show you how.

### Using the Zoom tool

To use the Zoom tool on the Standard toolbar, click the Zoom tool's arrow button and click a percentage. Depending on what view you're using, the list of zoom percentages may vary. For example, in Print Layout view, you can choose from 10% to 500%. You also can type a percentage directly into the text field and press Return. You also can choose to view the document in Page Width, Whole Page, and Two Pages views, as needed. Figure 5.22 shows a magnification setting of 200 percent.

**FIGURE 5.21**

Web Layout view displays the document as a Web page.

**FIGURE 5.22**

Using the Zoom tool, you can magnify or zoom out your view of a document.

Zoom tool

### Using the Zoom dialog box

You can use the Zoom dialog box to specify a zoom setting. Follow these steps to open the dialog box:

1. **Choose View ⇨ Zoom.**

   The Zoom dialog box appears, as shown in Figure 5.23.

2. **Click the zoom setting you want to apply.**

   ■ You can type a zoom percentage directly into the Percent field.

   ■ Optionally, you can click the Many pages radio button and choose how many pages you want to view at once with the Page menu.

You can use the Zoom dialog box to set a zoom setting for a document.

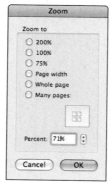

3. **Click OK.**

   Word applies the zoom percentage you specified.

**TIP** If you need to quickly view your document without all the onscreen window elements, choose View ▹ Full Screen. Word displays the document and the menu bar; depending on which view you are using, the Elements Gallery may or may not appear. To return to the regular view again, repeat the step to turn Full Screen view off.

# Setting Document Properties

Whenever you create and save a document, Word saves some data along with the file, called *document properties* or *metadata*. This data includes summary information and statistics about the file, such as when it was created, the last person to save the file, its location, and so on. Quite simply, document properties are a common way to identify and describe any particular document. All Office programs insert some document properties automatically, such as file size and the dates pertaining to file creation.

You can use the Document Properties dialog box to view and set document properties. The dialog box, shown in Figure 5.24, includes five tabs: General, Summary, Statistics, Contents, and Custom. The General tab displays basic information about the file, such as the file type, location, size, creation date, last modified date, and any read-only or hidden attributes settings. The information on this tab is automatically created by Word when you save the file. The Summary tab has a variety of blank text fields you can use to add more information about the file, including title, subject, author, manager, company name, category, keywords, comments, hyperlink base, and what template is attached to the file. You can use these fields, as needed, to add more info. The Statistics tab lists the created and modified dates (again), when it was last printed, who saved the file last, the number of revisions, editing time, and a bunch of statistics on number of characters, words, lines, paragraphs, and pages. The Contents tab displays the contents of the document. Lastly, the Custom tab lets you add your own custom properties to the file, such as client name, destination, and language, and you can set values for each of the properties you add.

**FIGURE 5.24**

You can view properties pertaining to a document using the Document Properties dialog box.

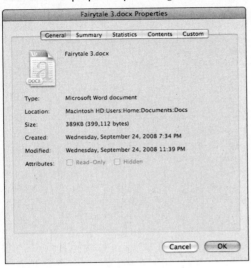

To display the Document Properties dialog box, choose File ➪ Properties. Click the Summary tab, shown in Figure 5.25, to enter your own details about a document. To add custom properties, click the Custom tab and add which new properties you want to include with the document.

**FIGURE 5.25**

The Summary tab has fields for entering your own document properties.

---

## Removing Personal Information

If you'd rather not allow Word to save personal information with your document, you can opt out. To do so, choose Word ⇨ Preferences. The Word Preferences dialog box opens. Click the Security icon, and under the Privacy options, click the Remove personal information from this file on save check box. Click OK, and Word no longer saves your personal information with the document properties.

# Protecting Documents

Word allows you to open and view documents easily. In some cases, perhaps it's too easy, especially when you're trying to keep prying eyes out of important documents. If you're worried about someone viewing personal documents or accessing documents containing private company information, you can utilize Word's document protection features. For example, you can protect your Word files from unauthorized use or changes. Word offers three levels of document protection: read-only, password to open, and password to modify. You can set any of the three security levels using the Preferences dialog box. The following sections discuss how to utilize each of the three security levels.

## Assigning read-only status

To allow others to open and view a document, but not make any changes to the original text or formatting, you can set the document to read-only status. If a user makes changes, Word does not allow them to save the changes. They can, however, save the changes as an entirely new document. This leaves your original document intact. To assign read-only status to a document, follow these steps:

1.  **Choose Word ⇨ Preferences.**

    The Word Preferences dialog box opens, as shown in Figure 5.26.

---

**FIGURE 5.26**

You can access Word's security features through the Word Preferences dialog box.

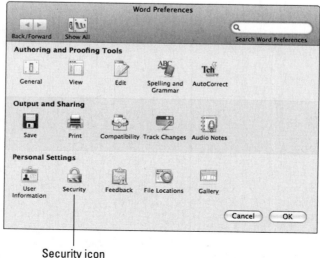

Security icon

**NOTE** You also can access Word's security options through the Save As dialog box. Click the Options button, and then click the Show All icon. This takes you to the same dialog box shown in Figure 5.27, and you can follow the steps in this section to assign read-only status.

2. **Click the Security icon.**

The Security options appear, as shown in Figure 5.27.

**FIGURE 5.27**

Activate the read-only option to allow the document to be opened, but no changes are permitted.

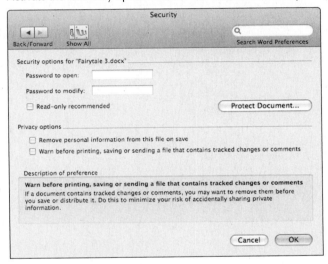

3. **Click the Read-only recommended check box.**

4. **Click OK.**

The document is now protected and can be read but not altered.

After you assign read-only status, you can no longer change the file yourself until you make the security option inactive again. To do so, simply repeat the steps above and deselect the check box.

## Assigning passwords

The other two security levels Word offers have to do with passwords. You can assign a password to a file so that no one can open it except with a password; this is called the Password to Open option. This is the highest level of security you can assign. You also can assign a password to a document that you can share with others to allow edits to the file, but the file remains read-only to anyone without the password.

Passwords you assign in Word are case-sensitive, which means you can use uppercase and lowercase letters, but remember that you must re-enter the letters in the same fashion. Passwords can contain up to 15 characters, and you can use letters, numbers, and symbols. As with any password situation you come across, though, be sure to write the password down and keep it in a safe place. If you lose it, you lose access to your file, too, and no one, not even Microsoft, can help you gain access to the document again.

To assign a password to a document, follow these steps:

1. **Choose Word ⇨ Preferences.**

   The Word Preferences dialog box opens (refer to Figure 5.26).

2. **Click the Security icon.**

   The Security options appear, as shown in Figure 5.28.

**FIGURE 5.28**

You can use the password fields to specify a password for opening the document or a password for making any changes to the document.

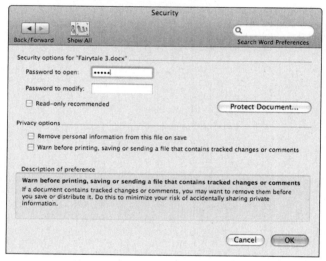

**NOTE** You also can access security options through the Save As dialog box; click the Options button, and then click the Show All icon. This opens the Word Preferences dialog box. You can follow the steps in this section to assign a password.

3. **Click the password field you want to assign, and type a password.**

4. **Click OK.**

   The Confirm Password box prompt appears, as shown in Figure 5.29.

5. **Retype the password exactly as you did the first time.**

6. **Click OK.**

   The document is now protected. The next time you open it, you'll be prompted for a password.

Use the Confirm Password box to confirm your password.

To remove a password, repeat the steps, except delete the text you entered in the password field. When you exit the dialog box, Word saves the changes and removes the associated password.

When sharing a document with others for the purposes of editing and tracking changes, you can activate the Protect Document feature and specify which changes are allowed during the process. To do so, click the Protect Document button in the Security options window (refer to Figure 5.28) and choose whether you want to protect tracked changes, comments, or forms. You can then assign a password to the file.

# Summary

In this chapter, we covered the very basics for working with the program window elements, learning what each element is used for and how to identify it onscreen. Although the information may seem rudimentary, if you learn your way around one Microsoft Office, you'll find it easier to do the same with the other programs. The Office suite shares a similar look and feel, and in many cases, the same tools or window elements.

You also learned how to start new files, start a file based on a preset template using the Project Gallery feature, and how to attach your own template to a document. You also learned how to save your work, create backup files of your documents, and activate the AutoRecover feature. After you've started saving documents, you'll want to open them again, so this chapter also showed you how to open existing files.

When it comes to viewing the actual document, Word has several viewing techniques, and you learned about each view mode, as well as how to use the Zoom feature to change the magnification view of a document. As you're working with text, you're sure to encounter times when you need to zoom in or out to better see your text or how the document looks overall.

Lastly, you learned how to set document properties and how to utilize Word's document protection features to keep your files safe from unauthorized use. Armed with the basics, you're now ready to start building your own Word documents.

# Chapter 6

# Building Word Documents

Building a document may seem like a simple task—just start typing. Alas, there's a bit more to it than that. First, you need to decide what kind of document you're creating. Is it a letter, a report, a blog? Figuring out what type of document you're creating can help you utilize the proper tools and features to get the job done. This chapter teaches you what you need to know to enter basic text or build a complex page layout document.

We go over the rudimentary steps for entering and working with text onscreen, as well as how to move it around, copy it, search through it, and automate it to make document building easier. You also learn how to create tabular columns and regular columns and how to insert specialized character and text features, like drop caps. Finally, you find out that creating complex documents isn't so complex when using Word's outlining, page layout, and notebook features.

## Typing Text

You're probably ready to jump in and just start typing, right? That's the nice thing about Microsoft Word, you can do just that—jump in and start tapping into the keyboard. Click where you want to type in the document window, and let those fingers fly across the keys. As you tap the keyboard, characters, numbers, and symbols magically appear onscreen. That sounds easy enough, eh? Just to help you along, this section covers a few basics about entering text into a document.

When you open a new document, Word places the cursor, also called the *insertion point,* at the top-left area of the document page ready to go. The cursor is the blinking horizontal line marking your current location in the document. If that's where you want to start your document, you can begin typing. However, you may want to start your text in another area of the document. For example, you may want to start your document out with a title page and a title centered smack dab in the middle of the document. In much earlier versions of Word, you couldn't do such a thing, but rather you had to add lots of empty lines to physically move the title down the page to the right location. With newer versions of Word, you can now click and type anywhere and start typing. Well, actually it's a double-click, but you get the general idea. Word calls this feature "click and type." Figure 6.1 shows the feature in action, with the cursor smack dab in the middle of the document ready to go. This works in Print Layout view; see Chapter 5 to learn more about Word's view modes. Print Layout view is a good view mode to use for ordinary document creation. It shows any graphic objects you add, as well as headers and footers.

### FIGURE 6.1

It's incredibly easy to start entering text into a document. Simply double-click where you want to start, and begin typing.

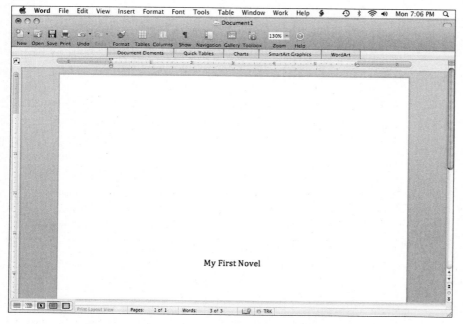

**TIP**     Don't forget—you can magnify your view of a document, including the text you're typing, using the Zoom button on the Standard toolbar. Just click the arrow icon, and choose another magnification setting.

As you move your mouse pointer around the document, the pointer takes on different icons or shapes based on where you're pointing. If you're moving the mouse pointer over the left side of the main document, the pointer looks like a cursor with a bunch of little lines next to it resembling a paragraph of text.

This little paragraph of text icon shows all the lines aligning to the left. This indicates left-alignment, and if you start typing, all of your text aligns to the left. If you move the pointer to the center of the document, as shown in Figure 6.1, the pointer takes on a similar shape, but this time the lines are centered in the tiny paragraph icon. This indicates center alignment, and any text you type from this spot in the document will be centered. If you move the pointer over the right side of the document, the pointer's lines appear lined up on the right, indicating right-alignment, and text you type takes on the same appearance. If you move the pointer over the header area—the space at the very top of the page where you can insert extra text about the document, such as page numbers, titles, author or company name, and so on—the pointer looks like a tiny document page. If you move the pointer over the left margin area, the pointer becomes an arrow icon. You can use this pointer icon later to select lines of text in the document.

Here's the important thing to remember about the mouse pointer/cursor shapes we just discussed: You can double-click in these areas of the document and start typing from that point onward, with the exception of the arrow icon pointer shape that appears in the left margin. You can type header text if you double-click in the header area (which does not appear in Draft view).

**NOTE** You can turn off the Click and Type feature if you don't find a need for it. To turn it off, choose Word ➪ Preferences to open the Word Preferences dialog box. Click the Edit icon to display editing options, and deselect the Enable click and type check box. Click OK to save your changes.

Here are some more tips for typing text:

- You do not need to press the Return key when you reach the right margin. Word starts a new line automatically for you when you reach the margin.

- At the end of a sentence, just press the spacebar once to create a space. In ages past, typists had to insert two spaces with the spacebar key on typewriters to make the text look nice. With today's word processors and printers, such a practice is no longer needed.

- When you're ready to start a new paragraph in your document, you can press Return.

- You do not need to type hyphens for word breaks at the end of a line; Word's hyphenation feature can help you hyphenate later.

- If you notice red or green wavy lines under your text as you type, don't worry. That's just Word's spelling and grammar checking feature pointing out any issues. You can ignore it, turn the feature off, or just turn off spelling or grammar, and leave the other checking feature on. You can learn more about this feature in Chapter 11.

The remainder of this section covers some additional typing features Word offers.

**TIP** If you need to free up some onscreen space for typing, you can close the Toolbox. Just click the Toolbox button on the Standard toolbar to hide the feature. Click the icon again to bring it back.

## Typing with AutoCorrect

Word's AutoCorrect feature is turned on by default. It automatically corrects common spelling problems as you type. You may see it in action as you mistype a word, such as inverting two characters or misspelling a word, and it magically fixes itself. Try it and see for yourself. Type something like *teh* to see AutoCorrect in action. As soon as you type a space after the mistake, AutoCorrect jumps into action and fixes the error. In fact, it happens so fast that you might not even notice it. Autocorrect works behind the scenes to fix mistakes, basing its work on an exhaustive list of commonly misspelled words and special characters. AutoCorrect fixes everything from misspellings to common typos, such as typing two initial capital letters instead of one, or forgetting to capitalize the first letter of a sentence or the names of days.

If you move your mouse pointer over a word that AutoCorrect just fixed, you can display the AutoCorrect smart button, shown in Figure 6.2. Click the button to reveal a pop-up menu pertaining to the word or action. The menu may list an option for changing the word back to the way you originally typed it, an option for stopping any AutoCorrect actions on future uses of the same word, and an option for opening the AutoCorrect dialog box. Of course, you can click any option on the menu to activate the option. There's more you can do with AutoCorrect, including adding to and deleting from its list of misspelled words, or turning the feature off entirely.

### FIGURE 6.2

Click the AutoCorrect smart button to view a pop-up menu of related commands.

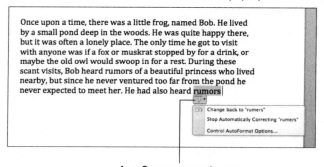

AutoCorrect smart button

You can use the AutoCorrect dialog box to control and change options for the AutoCorrect feature. The dialog box, shown in Figure 6.3, offers various settings for controlling what types of things AutoCorrect checks for as you type and keeps a list of special characters and commonly misspelled words. In addition, you can use the dialog box to access settings for Word's AutoFormat and AutoText tools, covered later in this chapter.

The top of the AutoCorrect list is filled with special characters you can type and replace with emoticons. These are handy if you're typing a blog. As you scroll through the library, you'll quickly see that it's filled with a variety of common words and various ways in which they're mangled during typing.

**FIGURE 6.3**

You can find AutoCorrect's list of commonly misspelled words in the AutoCorrect dialog box, along with options for controlling how the feature checks your text.

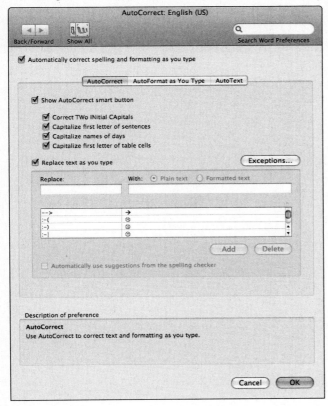

### Adding a word to AutoCorrect

If you find yourself making a mistake on a word not covered in the list, such as the spelling of a corporate name or a person's name, you can add it to the list. Follow these steps:

1. **Choose Tools ⇨ AutoCorrect.**

   The AutoCorrect dialog box opens (refer to Figure 6.3).

2. **In the Replace: field, type the word you commonly misspell, as shown in Figure 6.4.**

3. **In the With: field, type the correct spelling of the word.**

**FIGURE 6.4**

You can use the AutoCorrect dialog box to add and delete words from the list of misspellings.

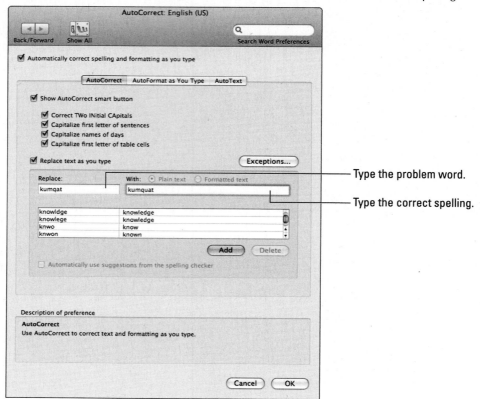

Type the problem word.

Type the correct spelling.

4. **Click the Add button.**

   AutoCorrect adds the word to the list.

5. **Click OK to exit the dialog box.**

The next time you misspell the word, AutoCorrect goes into action and corrects it without any hesitation.

**TIP**   You also can access the AutoCorrect dialog box through the Word Preferences dialog box. Choose Word ⇨ Preferences, and click the AutoCorrect icon. This opens the AutoCorrect dialog box.

### Removing a word from AutoCorrect

If AutoCorrect keeps fixing a spelling or special symbol that you do not want fixed, you can remove the word or symbol from the list. To remove a word, follow these steps:

1. **Reopen the AutoCorrect dialog box, as shown in the preceding steps.**

2. **Scroll through the list of words and special symbols, and click the one you want to remove.**

3. Click the Delete button.

4. Click OK to exit the dialog box.

### Turning off AutoCorrect

Sometimes, you do not want AutoCorrect to fix anything. To undo a correction while typing, press ⌘+Z. This activates the Undo command, and AutoCorrect restores your original typing. (You learn more about the Undo command later in this chapter.) You also can press the F1 key to undo an AutoCorrect action right after you type the word. If you find the feature especially annoying, you can turn it off completely. Use these steps to turn off AutoCorrect:

1. **Reopen the AutoCorrect dialog box, as shown in the first set of steps.**

2. **Deselect the Automatically correct spelling and formatting as you type check box at the top of the dialog box (refer to Figure 6.4).**

3. **Click OK to exit the dialog box.**

   Word turns off the feature.

## Using AutoText

Another Word feature you'll encounter while typing text is AutoText. This feature automatically fills in common words and phrases so you don't have to type the whole thing. For example, if you're typing the name of a day in the week, such as Sunday, AutoText attempts to complete the word for you when you first start typing it. A yellow AutoComplete box appears listing the word in its entirety. You simply press Return, and AutoText fills it in for you. If you ignore the box and keep typing, the AutoText box disappears.

AutoText is part of the whole AutoCorrect group, which includes AutoFormat (you learn about that in Chapter 7). AutoText is turned on by default. Like AutoCorrect, AutoText keeps track of some common words and phrases in its library of entries. For example, if you type *Attention:* or *Dear Sir or Madam:* AutoText offers to help. You may want to add some words or phrases of your own to the library. If you type the name of your company over and over again, for instance, add it to AutoText and make typing easier on yourself. You can add and delete entries using the AutoCorrect dialog box. With the AutoText options displayed, you also can control how the feature works and what items are included in its realm of help.

### Adding a word to AutoText

If you find yourself typing the same word or phrase repeatedly, such as a company name or lengthy motto, you can add it to the AutoText entries list. Follow these steps:

1. **Choose Tools ➪ AutoCorrect.**

   The AutoCorrect dialog box opens (refer to Figure 6.3).

2. **Click the AutoText options, as shown in Figure 6.5.**

3. **In the Enter AutoText entries here: field, type the word or phrase you want to store as an entry.**

4. **Click the Add button.**

   AutoText adds the word to the list.

5. **Click OK to exit the dialog box.**

**FIGURE 6.5**

You can use the AutoCorrect dialog box to add AutoText entries.

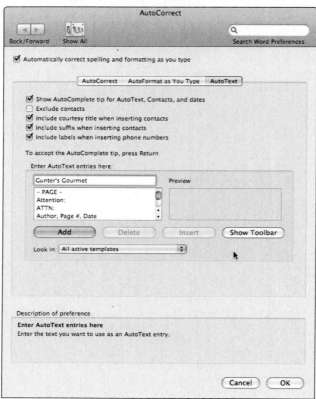

The next time you start typing the word or phrase, AutoText jumps in with an AutoComplete tip box, and you just press Return to complete the entry.

**TIP** You also can access the AutoCorrect dialog box through the Word Preferences dialog box. Choose Word ⌐ Preferences, and click the AutoCorrect icon. This opens the AutoCorrect dialog box.

# Editing Text

After you've started adding text to a document, chances are good that you'll want to change it in some way by making edits. For example, you may want to change a word, retype a sentence, or rearrange a paragraph, and so on. You can easily edit your text in Word, and you can use a variety of techniques to do so. If you've used previous versions of Word or other word-processing programs, the same editing techniques will work in Word 2008 for Mac.

You can edit as you type by using the Backspace key. This technique simply backs up a space to the left of the cursor, erasing what you just typed. You also can use the arrow keys to move to the place you want to edit and press the Del key to erase any characters sitting to the right of the blinking cursor. Pressing the arrow keys ($\uparrow$, $\downarrow$, $\leftarrow$, $\rightarrow$) moves the cursor around the document. To make all kinds of edits to an existing document, you can use selection techniques.

## Selecting text

Learning to select text in Word is a crucial skill necessary for making edits to a document. You can easily select a single character, a word, a sentence, a paragraph, or the entire document. When you select text, it appears highlighted with a bluish-gray block of color. In Word for Windows, you may be used to seeing highlighted text with a black block behind it. Mac users get the cooler bluish block. After you've selected text, you can make changes, such as retyping, changing the formatting, moving or copying the selection, and so on. Figure 6.6 shows an example of selected text.

**FIGURE 6.6**

Selected text appears with a bluish block of color behind it.

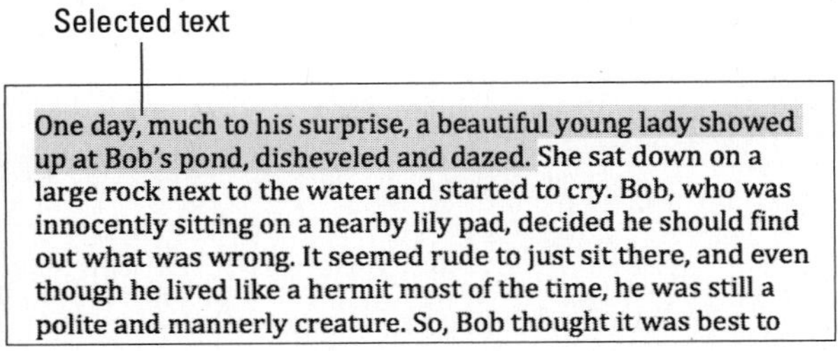

Selected text

> One day, much to his surprise, a beautiful young lady showed up at Bob's pond, disheveled and dazed. She sat down on a large rock next to the water and started to cry. Bob, who was innocently sitting on a nearby lily pad, decided he should find out what was wrong. It seemed rude to just sit there, and even though he lived like a hermit most of the time, he was still a polite and mannerly creature. So, Bob thought it was best to

When it comes to mouse selection methods or keyboard selection methods, it really depends on which you prefer. Some people like the mouse best for editing text, so zooming around the screen with a hand movement seems second nature to them. Other people prefer to keep their hands on the keyboard at all times, fingers flying over the keys. These folks prefer using keyboard techniques for selecting and editing text. A third group of people utilize both the mouse and the keyboard at different times and whims.

### Selecting text with the mouse

Selecting text with the mouse is a pretty straightforward task. You're either clicking and dragging or using some fancy double-clicking and triple-clicking methods. Word offers an invisible selection strip over in the left margin area that you can use to quickly select text. When you move your mouse pointer over the selection strip area, the regular arrow pointer icon points to the right instead of the left, indicating that you're hovering over the selection strip. Table 6.1 explains the various mouse selection techniques.

### Selecting text with the keyboard

As discussed earlier, the arrow keys—$\uparrow$, $\downarrow$, $\leftarrow$, $\rightarrow$—are perfect for navigating around the document from the keyboard and changing the location of the cursor. Like the mouse selection techniques, keyboard selection methods are fairly universal, which means the same methods are common among most word-processing programs and other programs as well. Table 6.2 lists the keyboard shortcut keys for selecting text.

**TABLE 6.1**

## Mouse Selection Techniques

| Selection | Technique |
|---|---|
| A single character | Click in front of the character, and drag across the character to select it. |
| A single word | Double-click the word. You also can click in front of the word and drag across it to select it. |
| A sentence | Click in front of the first word in the sentence, and click and drag across to the end of the sentence. You also can press the ⌘ key and click anywhere in the sentence. |
| A paragraph | Triple-click anywhere in the paragraph, or double-click in the left margin's selection strip in front of the paragraph. |
| A line of text | Move the mouse pointer in front of the line of text and click in the selection strip. |
| The entire document | Triple-click anywhere in the selection strip. |
| Sections of text | Click in the selection strip in front of the line of text you want to start with, and drag down the margin to add more lines to the selection. |

**TABLE 6.2**

## Keyboard Selection Techniques

| Keys and Combinations | Selection |
|---|---|
| Shift+→ | Selects one character to the right of the cursor. |
| Shift+← | Selects one character to the left of the cursor. |
| Option+Shift+→ | Selects from the current cursor location to the end of the word. |
| Option+Shift+← | Selects from the current cursor location to the beginning of the word. |
| ⌘+Shift+→ | Selects from the current cursor location to the end of the line of text. |
| ⌘+Shift+← | Selects from the current cursor location to the beginning of the line of text. |
| Shift+Home | Selects from the current cursor location to the beginning of the line of text. |
| Shift+End | Selects from the current cursor location to the end of a line of text. |
| ⌘+Shift+Home | Selects everything from the current cursor to the beginning of the document. |
| ⌘+Shift+End | Selects everything from the current cursor to the end of the document. |
| Shift+↓ | Selects from the current cursor location to one line down. |
| Shift+↑ | Selects from the current cursor location to one line up. |
| ⌘+Shift+↓ | Selects from the current cursor location to the end of the paragraph. |
| ⌘+Shift+↑ | Selects from the current cursor location to the beginning of the paragraph. |
| Shift+Page Up | Selects a screenful or half page of text from the current cursor upward. |
| Shift+Page Down | Selects a screenful or half page of text from the current cursor downward. |
| ⌘+A | Select everything in the document. |

### Selecting text with the mouse and the keyboard combined

You can use the mouse and keyboard together to make even more quick selections in your document:

- To select words or characters not next to each other, select the first word and then press and hold the ⌘ key while right-clicking the additional words.

- If you want to edit only a portion of a word, such as the first syllable, press the Option key as you drag over the portion you want to select.

- To extend a selection you dragged over with the mouse, just press Shift and click at the end of the additional text you want to select. This works great when extending the section of words, sentences, paragraphs, and other blocks of text.

- To select a sentence, ⌘+click anywhere within the sentence. Word selects the sentence and the period at the end.

- Move the cursor where you want to start selecting text, and press F8. This turns on Extend mode. Now you can use the arrow keys and the Page Up and Page Down keys to select text. To cancel Extend mode, press ⌘+. (period).

## Using Undo and Redo

Ah, the popular Undo/Redo command combo, an essential part of any computer program. The Undo command undoes whatever you just did. This is extremely handy for back-tracking your computer activities, such as undoing a deletion, undoing a typing edit you just made, or undoing the placement of text in a document. If you just click the Undo button on the Standard toolbar, Word undoes your last action. You also can choose Edit ⇨ Undo. Not only does it undo your last action, it also keeps a running list of your actions, a history if you please. If you click the tiny arrow icon next to the Undo button, as shown in Figure 6.7, you can display a menu of– recent actions and choose how many actions to undo. Depending on which action you select, all subsequent actions are undone as well. For example, if you click the tenth action on the list, all the actions from that point to the top of the list are undone as well.

**FIGURE 6.7**

You can use the Undo menu to undo several actions at once.

The Redo command works in the same manner, except it redoes an action. So if you deleted a word, decided to put it back with the Undo command, then decided to delete it again, you can apply the Redo command. Or if you undid a sequence of actions, you can redo them all again using Redo. To activate the Redo command, click the Redo button on the Standard toolbar or Choose Edit ⇨ Redo. Like the Undo command, the Redo command keeps a list or history of actions. If you click the arrow icon next to the Redo button, you can view the history list and choose to redo the actions. You can then choose how far back you want to redo in the list of actions. Anything between the selected action and the top of the list will be redone.

## Moving and copying text

Another very important part of editing text is the ability to move it or copy it around the document or to other files and programs. You can use several methods to move and copy text. The method you choose is entirely up to you and depends on how you like to work onscreen. You can use the drag-and-drop technique, you can use the Edit menu, you can use the context pop-up menu, or you can use the old keyboard shortcut keys.

### Moving text via drag-and-drop

Follow these steps to move text from one location in the document to another or to copy text from one place to another using the drag-and-drop method:

1. **Select the text you want to move or copy.**

2. **Click and drag the text to the location where you want to insert it, as shown in Figure 6.8.** If you want to copy the text instead of just move it, press and hold the Option key while dragging.

   When you release the mouse button, the text is moved or copied.

**FIGURE 6.8**

You can drag and drop text to move it in a document.

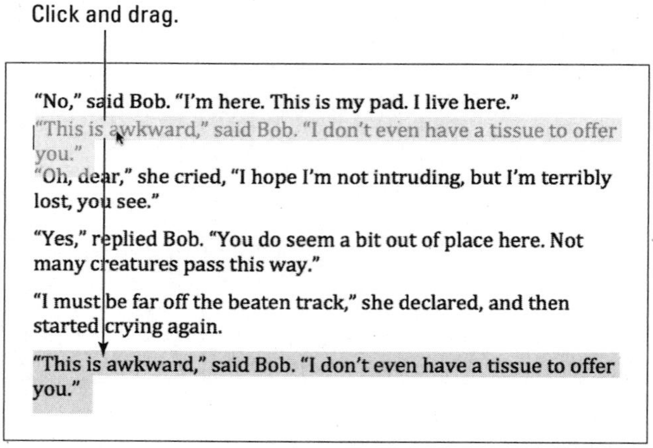

Click and drag.

"No," said Bob. "I'm here. This is my pad. I live here."

"This is awkward," said Bob. "I don't even have a tissue to offer you."

"Oh, dear," she cried, "I hope I'm not intruding, but I'm terribly lost, you see."

"Yes," replied Bob. "You do seem a bit out of place here. Not many creatures pass this way."

"I must be far off the beaten track," she declared, and then started crying again.

"This is awkward," said Bob. "I don't even have a tissue to offer you."

**TIP** You can use the drag-and-drop method to move text to other open programs or out onto the desktop. When you drag text onto the desktop, Word creates a clipping file. These are just text clippings waiting for use later when you drag them back into another document or program. The clipping file remains on your desktop to be reused again. You might use clipping files for text you include in every document you create. The clippings are named Picture Clipping in Finder, even though they only contain text.

## Moving and copying with the Edit menu

Follow these steps to move text from one location in the document to another or to copy text from one place to another using the Edit menu:

1. **Select the text you want to move or copy.**
2. **Choose Edit ⇨ Cut to move the text, or choose Edit ⇨ Copy to copy the text, as shown in Figure 6.9.**
3. **Click where you want to insert the text.**
4. **Choose Edit ⇨ Paste.**

   The text is moved or copied.

**FIGURE 6.9**

You can use the Edit menu's Cut and Copy commands to move or copy text in a document.

## Moving and copying with the context menu

Follow these steps to move or copy text using the context pop-up menu:

1. **Select the text you want to move or copy.**
2. **Right-click the selected text.**

   The context menu appears, as shown in Figure 6.10.
3. **Click Cut to move the text or Copy to copy the text.**
4. **Right-click where you want to insert the text.**
5. **Click Paste.**

   The text is moved or copied.

You can use the context menu's Cut and Copy commands to move or copy text in a document.

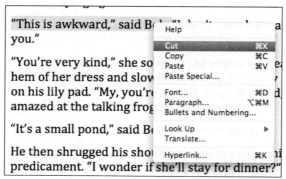

## Moving and copying with shortcut keys

If you're an avid keyboard user, or even if you're not, you're sure to appreciate the keyboard shortcut keys for moving, copying, and pasting text. After you memorize the commands for Word, you'll also find they apply almost globally to every other program. Follow these steps to move or copy text using shortcut keys:

1. **Select the text you want to move or copy.**
2. **Press ⌘+X to cut the text or ⌘+C to copy the text.**
3. **Click where you want to insert the text.**
4. **Press ⌘+V.**

   The text is moved or copied.

## Using the Paste Special command

In addition to a regular paste action, which simply pastes the cut or copied text, you also can activate the Paste from Scrapbook, Paste Special, and Paste as Hyperlink commands, all found on the Edit menu. The Paste from Scrapbook command lets you paste any items you've collected and stored in the Office Scrapbook feature. Learn more about this element in Chapter 33. The Paste as Hyperlink command lets you paste the cut or copied text as a hyperlink in the document. You can use this feature to create links to the original source from which it was copied in the document, becoming a bookmark to the area in the document. Learn more about this element in Chapter 9. The Paste Special command allows you to control how an item is pasted. When you activate this command, the Paste Special dialog box appears, as shown in Figure 6.11. Here you can specify how you want the pasted text treated in the document, as listed below:

- **Microsoft Word Document Object:** Word treats the text as an embedded object, which you can move and resize like any other object.
- **Formatted Text (RTF):** Also known as rich text format, Word retains the font and table formatting of the original source text.
- **Unformatted Text:** Word pastes the text without any of the original formatting.
- **Picture:** Word treats the text as a picture object.
- **Styled Text:** Word copies all the original formatting and styles originally applied to the text.

- **HTML Format:** Word treats the text as Hypertext Markup Language formatting for Web page display.
- **PDF:** Word treats the text as Adobe Portable Document Format.

You also have the option of treating the pasted text as a link, which means the text retains a link back to the original document, and any changes made to the original text are reflected in the pasted text as well. This is very useful when copying and pasting text between two documents. You can activate the Display as icon check box in the Paste Special dialog box to include an icon representing the program in which the pasted text was created. This works only if you paste the text as a link.

---

**FIGURE 6.11**

You can use the Paste Special dialog box to control how you want the copied text to appear.

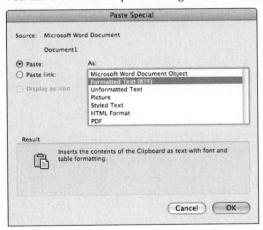

Follow these steps to move or copy text using the Paste Special command:

1. **Select the text you want to move or copy.**
2. **Cut or copy the text as needed.**
3. **Click where you want to insert the text.**
4. **Choose Edit ⇨ Paste Special.**
   The Paste Special dialog box appears.
5. **Click Paste, and choose how you want the text treated.**
   If you choose to paste the text as a link, Word inserts the text as a link to the source file.
6. **Click OK.**
   Word inserts the text.

### Using the Paste Options button

Regardless of which method you use to cut, copy, or paste text, the Paste Options button almost always appears next to the newly pasted text. The Paste Options button is a small, square button that has a clipboard icon on it, as shown in Figure 6.12. When you click the button, a context menu appears with several paste options you can choose from:

- **Keep Source Formatting:** Select this option if you want to keep the text looking exactly like it did from where you moved or copied it. This is the default option.
- **Match Destination Formatting:** Select this option if you want the newly pasted text to match the formatting surrounding it rather than retain its original formatting.
- **Keep Text Only:** Select this option if you don't want to copy any original formatting, just the text.

---

**FIGURE 6.12**

You can use the Paste Options button to control what formatting is pasted along with the text.

You don't have to select any of these options. Word automatically copies all the original formatting along with the text unless you choose otherwise. You can just ignore the Paste Options button and keep right on working. The button disappears as soon as you start typing or choosing other commands. However, if you do want to stop and address how the formatting is handled, the button is handy.

## Removing text

Removing text is an inevitable part of editing. You may need to remove a single character or word, remove text to type new text, or delete entire sentences, paragraphs, or pages of text. Several key tools are in your editing arsenal for removing text. First, you have the Backspace key on the keyboard. Use it as you're typing to quickly delete characters and retype them again. If it's the big guns you need, however, break out the Del key. It's good for all kinds of removal tasks in Word. You can click in a sentence or word and press Del to remove characters to the right of the cursor. You can select any text you want to remove and press Del to quickly delete it from the document. You also can use the Del key to delete selected objects, paragraphs, tables, drawn objects, and more.

If you're looking for a tool for removing formatting and not the text, use the Clear command. Select the text, and choose Edit ➪ Clear ➪ Clear Formatting. You also can remove the contents instead and keep the formatting intact for the replacement text; choose Edit ➪ Clear ➪ Contents. You also can use the Cut command to remove text; choose Edit ➪ Cut.

## Finding and replacing text

As your document grows in length and complexity, you'll encounter times in which you need to find a particular word or phrase in the document. Or perhaps you need to replace a word with another word entirely throughout the document. You can use Word's Find and Replace commands to help you locate text as well as replace it with something else. The Find and Replace dialog box is the nerve center for searching through your document. It includes three tabs: Find, Replace, and Go To. This section discusses how you can use each tab and how to utilize the Advance Find options.

### Finding text

You can use the Find command to locate a specific term or phrase in a document. For example, you might want to check to see if you referenced the full name of a company or find out if you mentioned a particular product name in an article. You can use the Find feature to quickly scroll to the term and check it out. To activate the feature, follow these steps:

1. **Choose Edit ➪ Find, or press ⌘+F.**

   The Find and Replace dialog box opens with the Find tab displayed, as shown in Figure 6.13.

2. **Type the word or phrase you want to look for in the Find what: text box.**

3. **Click Find Next.**

---

**FIGURE 6.13**

Use the Find tab in the Find and Replace dialog box to search for words or phrases in a document.

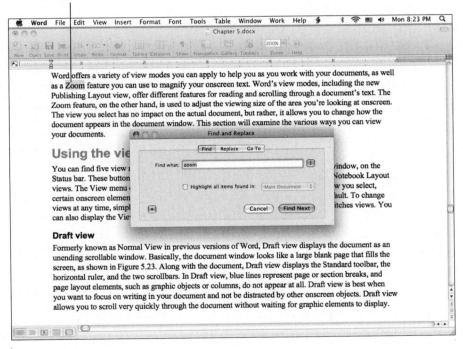

Starting from the current insertion point, Word searches the document and scrolls to the first occurrence, highlighting it onscreen, as shown in Figure 6.13.

If Word cannot find the word or phrase, a prompt box appears telling you so.

If you activate the Highlight all items found in Main Document check box, Word selects every occurrence, and you can apply global formatting changes all in one fell swoop.

Optionally, you can continue searching for additional occurrences by clicking the Find Next button.

4. **When the search is complete, click OK, or exit the dialog box by clicking Cancel.**

## Replacing text

You can use the Replace feature to search through a document for a word and replace it with something else. For example, perhaps you've misspelled a name throughout your document and need to fix each occasion. Instead of endlessly scrolling and reading, you can instruct Word to look for every instance and determine how each one is replaced. You also can search and replace formatting and special characters, such as spaces or hyphens. Follow these steps to find and replace text:

1. **Choose Edit ⇨ Replace, or press Shift+⌘+H.**

   The Find and Replace dialog box opens with the Replace tab displayed, as shown in Figure 6.14.

2. **Type the word or phrase you want to look for in the Find what: text box.**

3. **Type the word or phrase you want to use as replacement text in the Replace with: text box.**

4. **Click Find Next.**

---

**FIGURE 6.14**

Use the Replace tab in the Find and Replace dialog box to find and replace text in a document.

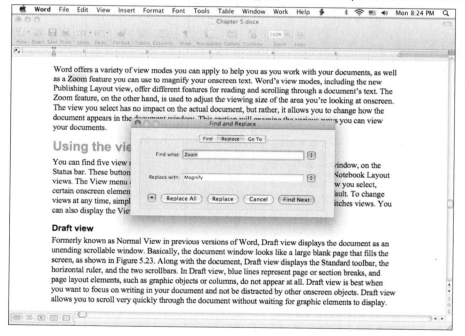

Starting from the current insertion point, Word searches the document and scrolls to the first occurrence, highlighting it onscreen, as shown in Figure 6.14.

If Word cannot find the word or phrase, a prompt box appears telling you so.

5. **Click the Replace button to replace the occurrence.**

   To replace every occurrence in the document, click the Replace All button.

   Optionally, you can continue searching for additional occurrences by clicking the Find Next button.

6. **When the search is complete, click OK, or exit the dialog box by clicking Cancel.**

## Using Advanced Find options

The Find and Replace dialog box can expand to show additional Advanced Find search options you can apply, as shown in Figure 6.15. Click the Expand arrow button to reveal the hidden options. You can click the button again to hide the extra options.

---

**FIGURE 6.15**

You can expand the dialog box to view Advanced Find search options.

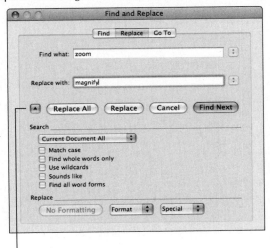

Click to expand or collapse
the Advanced Find options.

You can use the additional search options to narrow down exactly what Word locates in the document. The Advanced Search options are organized into two categories: Search and Find. Here's what you can do with the settings under the Search category:

- **Search pop-up menu:** Click the Search pop-up menu to specify how you want to search the main document: from the current insertion point down or up, from the very beginning of the document, or all open documents one at a time.

- **Match case:** Select this check box to find words that match the specified capitalization you entered.

- **Find whole words only:** This tells Word to search only whole words, not just instances of the string of characters, such as searching for "we" only and not finding "went," "between," and so on.

- **Use wildcards:** Activate this feature to use special characters standing in for actual letters, such as substituting "th*" to find words like "the," "that," "theirs," and so on.

- **Sounds like:** To look for a phonetic spelling of the word, check this option. This is useful if you commonly misspell "their" and "there."

- **Find all word forms:** Check this option to find irregularly spelled nouns and verbs.

You can use the pop-up menus under the Find category to search for specific formatting attributes throughout the document. For example, the Format pop-up menu lets you open specific formatting dialog boxes, such as the Paragraph dialog box, and choose what attributes you want to search for. After making your selections, you'll see what attributes you selected listed under the Find what field at the top of the Find tab, as shown in Figure 6.15.

Here's what you can do with the Find options:

- **No Formatting:** Click this option to stop searching for formatting attributes.
- **Format:** Use this pop-up menu to select which type of formatting attributes you want to include in your search.
- **Special:** Use this pop-up menu to search for special characters in a document.

Just what sort of formatting can you find with the Find and Replace dialog box? Just about any kind of formatting you can think of. You can search your text for a particular font, font size, indents, tab stops, styles, and more. When used in conjunction with the Replace command, you can find formatting throughout a document and replace it with new formatting. Among the list of Format options offered in the Format pop-up menu, you can search for the following attributes:

- **Font:** Finds specific fonts and font characteristics, such as bold, italic, or color.
- **Paragraph:** Finds paragraphs based on indentation, line spacing, alignment, outline level, and page breaks.
- **Tabs:** Finds tab stops by position or type.
- **Language:** Finds text based on a certain language.
- **Frame:** Finds frames and their attributes. (Most people use text boxes instead of frames these days as containers for text that you can freely position and resize on a page.)
- **Style:** Finds styles and style attributes.
- **Highlight:** Finds highlighted text in a document.

You can use the Special pop-up menu in the Find and Replace dialog box to search for special characters and non-alphanumeric characters throughout a document, such as hyphens, en dashes, or em dashes. You also can search for document elements that are not text, such as page breaks, column breaks, or even white space. When you click the Special pop-up menu, the following special character choices appear:

- Paragraph Mark
- Tab Character
- Comment Mark
- Any Character
- Any Digit
- Any Letter
- Caret Character
- Column Break
- Em Dash
- En Dash
- Endnote Mark
- Field

- Footnote Mark
- Graphic
- Manual Line Break
- Manual Page Break
- Nonbreaking Hyphen
- Nonbreaking Space
- Optional Hyphen
- Section Break
- White Space

Simply choose what you want to search for from the list. As soon as you choose a character, it appears in the Find what: text box at the top of the dialog box.

As with any dialog box, you can exit without applying any changes, or in this case without conducting a search, by clicking the Cancel button at any time.

## Using the Go To tab

The Find and Replace dialog box has one more tab you need to know about—the Go To tab. You can use this feature to navigate to a particular location in a document. If your document is very long, the Go To command can help you find your way to a particular spot with greater precision than the scroll bars. Follow these steps to use the Go To feature:

1. **Choose Edit ⇨ Go To. You also can press F5 or press ⌘+G on the keyboard.**

   The Find and Replace dialog box opens with the Go To tab displayed, as shown in Figure 6.16.

 **With some laptop Macs, you must press function+F5 to activate the Go To feature.**

**FIGURE 6.16**

Use the Go To tab in the Find and Replace dialog box to quickly navigate to a particular area of a document.

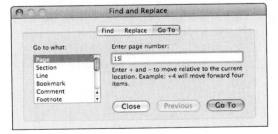

2. **Type the page number you want to go to in the Enter page number text box field.**

   You also can choose to go to another element, such as a bookmark or comment. Simply select the element and enter any name.

3. **Click Next.**

   Word automatically displays the page in the document window.

4. **Click Close to exit the dialog box.**

# Adding Text in Columnar Layouts

As you're building your document and entering text, you may find yourself needing to create columns of some sort. Word offers two ways to create columnar text: tabs and columns. Both allow you to create two or more columns of text on a page. You can use tabs to create lists in columns. You can use the Columns command to create columns in which text flows from one to another, just like a newspaper or magazine layout. You might consider tables as a third way of creating columns, but that topic isn't covered until Chapter 8, where we discuss it in great detail. In the meantime, the following sections walk you through the process of creating tabs and straight-up columns.

## Tabbing text

In the history of typography and the golden age of the typewriter, tabs were an important tool for indenting text for paragraphs and tables. Today's word-processing indentation tools offer much more flexibility, but because people commonly use tabs, they're still around. Tabs are essentially preset indentations across the width of the page. You can use the ruler to view tab stops in a document, as shown in Figure 6.17. By default, every new document you start in Word has invisible, preset left-aligned tabs every half inch across the page. When you press the Tab key on the keyboard, the cursor (or the *insertion point*) moves over approximately one-half inch. Any text you type lines up at this tab stop. If you set your own tab stops, the default tab stops disappear.

**FIGURE 6.17**

You can view tab stops on the horizontal ruler.

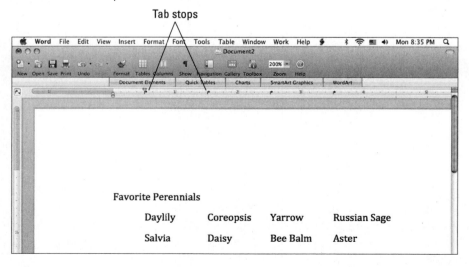

To utilize the default tab stops, just press Tab as you're typing. Many people use the Tab key to create a quick indent at the start of a paragraph. But you can do much more than just create indents: You can create decimal-aligned columns, add leader dashes between columns, and control the alignment of text in a tab column. You can align Tab stops come in five different alignment modes:

- **Left:** Aligns text to the left of the tab column.
- **Center:** Centers text in the tab column.
- **Right:** Aligns text to the right of the tab column.
- **Decimal:** Aligns decimals in the column.
- **Bar:** Aligns text to the left of a vertical bar.

You can set your own tab stops using the ruler or using the Tabs dialog box. You can set tab stops for an entire page before you even start typing. You also can set tab stops for the current paragraph or for selected paragraphs in a document. Be sure to select all the paragraphs you want to include with the new tab stops before you set the tabs.

### Setting tab stops using the ruler

The fastest way to create your own tab stops is to do so directly on the horizontal ruler at the top of the document window. The Tab button, also called the *tab well,* at the far left end of the ruler lets you control what type of tab stop you create. When the button is clicked, as shown in Figure 6.18, you can view the five alignment options. Notice that the pop-up menu has an option for opening the Tabs dialog box. After you select a tab alignment, you're ready to start adding tab stops to the ruler. For example, if you want a tab stop at 2", just click on the 2" mark on the ruler. The little icon that Word adds to the ruler to represent the tab stop also shows the alignment of the tab, as shown in Figure 6.18.

---

**FIGURE 6.18**

The Tab pop-up menu lets you choose a tab type.

Click to display the
pop-up menu.

To set tab stops using the ruler, follow these steps:

1. **Click the Tab button.**
2. **Click a tab alignment.**
3. **Click on the ruler where you want to insert the tab.**

   Word adds the tab stop.

You can easily edit tab stops on the ruler, too. Simply drag them where you want them placed. If you no longer want the tab stop, drag it off the ruler, and it's deleted.

**119**

### Setting tab stops using the Tabs dialog box

The Tabs dialog box lets you set tab stops a bit more precisely than the ruler. You can also use the dialog box to add leader dashes between tabular columns. Leader dashes are dashes or dots that appear after the text and extend to the beginning of the next tab column. Leader dashes can help readers follow a line of text across the tabbed columns.

Follow these steps to set up tabs using the dialog box:

1. **Choose Format ⇨ Tabs, or double-click any tab stop on the ruler.**

   The Tabs dialog box appears, as shown in Figure 6.19.

2. **Type the position you want to assign for the tab stop in the Tab stop position field.**

---

**FIGURE 6.19**

The Tabs dialog box is the place to go to set precise tabs in a document.

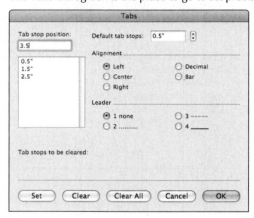

3. **Choose an alignment option from the Alignment radio buttons.**

   Choose a leader character if you want to add leader dashes to the tabbed columns.

4. **Click the Set button.**

   Word adds the tab stop to the list box.

   You can continue adding more tab stops as needed by following Steps 2 through 4.

5. **Click OK to exit the dialog box.**

You can now use your new tabs stops. If for any reason you no longer want a tab stop, reopen the Tabs dialog box, select the tab stop from the list box, and click the Clear button. To remove every tab stop listed, click the Clear All button.

You also can use the Tabs dialog box to set a new default tab stop setting. Just type a new position in the Default tabs text box, or use the arrow buttons to set a new position. When you click OK and exit the dialog box, the new default setting is applied.

**NOTE** If you're serious about placing text neatly across a page, tables are the best way to control the layout of text, even in columnar fashion. To learn more about using tables, see Chapter 8.

# Creating columns

You can use Word's Columns feature to create newspaper or magazine-style columns in a document. When using these types of columns, text flows from one column before proceeding to the next column. You can create columns using the Columns button on the Standard toolbar or by opening the Columns dialog box. You can apply columns to selected text or to a document you just opened. This section shows you how, along with tips on editing columns after you've added them to a document.

## Creating easy columns

The quickest way to create columns is to use the Columns button on the Standard toolbar. You can choose to create as many as six columns in a document. Although the initial pop-up menu shows only four, you can drag past the right edge of the menu to extend the number. Follow these steps to add columns:

1. **Click the Columns button on the Standard toolbar, as shown in Figure 6.20.**
2. **Drag across the number of columns you want to insert.**

   Word creates the columns in the document.

**FIGURE 6.20**

Create quick columns using the Columns button.

You can return a document to single column again by selecting the column text and choosing 1 column from the Columns pop-up menu.

## Creating columns with the Columns dialog box

For more precise columns, use the Columns dialog box shown in Figure 6.21. Here you can choose from preset columns or set your own custom columns. You also can use the options in the dialog box to add a vertical line between columns, adjust the column width and spacing, and specify how columns are applied to the document. Follow these steps to set columns using the dialog box:

1. **Choose Format ⇨ Columns.**

   The Columns dialog box opens, as shown in Figure 6.21.

2. **Type the number of columns you want in the Number of columns field, or select from the Preset column styles.**

   Optionally, to add a vertical line between columns, click the Line between check box.

3. **To set custom columns, click the column you want to adjust and set a new width or spacing.** You can type directly in the fields or use the arrow buttons to adjust the settings.

   To keep the columns equal in width, leave the Equal column width check box selected.

**FIGURE 6.21**

Use the Columns dialog box to set custom columns and features.

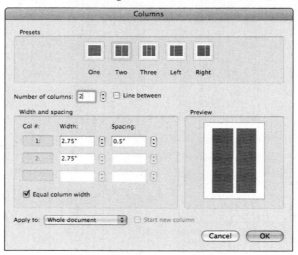

4. **Click the Apply to pop-up menu, and choose how you want to apply the columns.** You can apply them to the selected text, from this point forward in the document, or to the whole document.

The Preview area shows a sample of your column settings.

5. **Click OK to apply the new settings and create your columns.**

## Editing columns

After you've added columns, you can control the column width and how the text flows from one column to the next. You can use the ruler to quickly adjust the width of any column. However, in order to do this, you must use Print Layout view. The column markers appear at either end of the blue "gutter" that signifies the distance between the columns, as shown in Figure 6.22. Simply drag the column markers to change the width.

For more precise controls, revisit the Column dialog box, shown in Figure 6.21, and set your own measurements for column widths in the Width fields for each column. If you leave the column width check box selected, Word makes sure all the columns are always the same width.

To control how text flows from one column to another, you can insert a column break. Column breaks tell Word exactly where you want the text to flow into another column. To insert a column break, click where you want it to start and choose Insert ➪ Break ➪ Column Break. You also can press Shift+⌘+↑. To undo a column break, click in front of the text where the break occurs and press Backspace.

By default, column text is left-aligned, and the right margin is uneven. For some documents, you may prefer both margins to look neat and aligned. You can justify column text for a professional look. To do so, select the text, click the Alignment and Spacing pane on the Formatting Palette, and then click the Justify button.

**FIGURE 6.22**

You can adjust the width of your columns using the ruler.

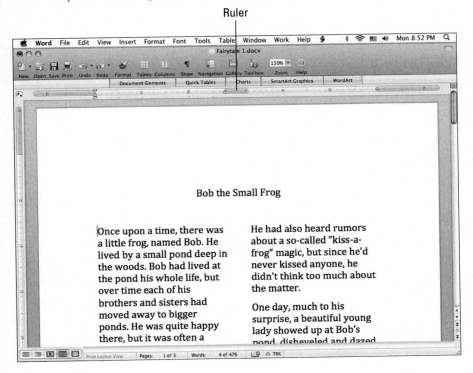

When you apply columns, you may want to turn on automatic hyphenation to automatically break longer words at the right margin. This can help create a straighter, more even right margin for your columns. To turn on the feature, choose Tools ⇨ Hyphenation and click the Automatically hyphenate document check box. Click OK to apply the hyphenation feature to the column text. To learn more about hyphenating in Word, see Chapter 9.

If you're having trouble making your columns come out evenly at the bottom of the columns, try adjusting the paragraph spacing. In the Formatting Palette, click the Alignment and Spacing pane and use the Before and After fields to set space before and after the paragraphs.

# Adding Special Text

Sometimes you may have a need for other kinds of characters in your documents, such as special symbols or drop caps, or you may need to quickly change the case of your text. Word has plenty of tools to help you set specialized text in your documents. This section shows you several ways to insert fancy text elements.

## Adding drop caps

Drop caps are a feature commonly used in publishing in which the first character of a word in the first paragraph is super large compared to all the other text. These extra large capitals are common in books at the beginning of the book or a chapter. You might think you can create the same effect just by making the first character a large font size. Alas, you cannot. The effect also involves dropping the capital letter well below the other characters on the line, and the only way to do that is with the built-in drop cap feature.

To create a drop cap, follow these steps:

1. **Select the character you want to turn into a drop cap.**

2. **Choose Format ⇨ Drop Cap.**

   The Drop Cap dialog box opens, as shown in Figure 6.23.

**FIGURE 6.23**

Set drop caps with the Drop Cap dialog box.

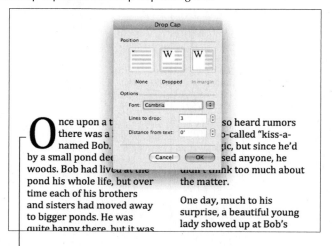

Drop cap

3. **Under the Position setting, choose Dropped.**

   If you prefer to have the drop cap sit by itself in the left margin, click the In margin setting.

4. **To change the font, click the Font pop-up menu and choose another.**

   By default, drop caps drop by 3 lines of text. To change the setting to more or less lines, click the Lines field and set a new number.

   Optionally, Word also sets no distance between the drop cap and the second character. To set some space, click the Distance from text field and set a new measurement.

5. **Click OK.**

   Word applies the drop cap.

Figure 6.23 shows an example of a drop cap applied to text. If you need to edit the drop cap in any way, simply reopen the Drop Cap dialog box and make your adjustments to the settings.

# Adding symbols and special characters

As you're typing along creating a document, you may find yourself needing to insert some characters not found on the keyboard. For example, you may want to insert a copyright symbol, a registered trademark, or an em dash (a very long dash). You can easily add symbols and other special characters using the Symbol dialog box, shown in Figure 6.25. Most fonts include symbols you can insert, but a few are geared just for symbols. The fonts Symbol and Wingdings, for example, offer a huge selection of symbols. If you're looking for a symbol from another language, the font list offers other language selections as well.

Follow these steps to insert symbols:

1. **Click in the document where you want to insert a symbol.**
2. **Choose Insert ➪ Symbol.**

   The Symbol dialog box opens, as shown in Figure 6.24.

**FIGURE 6.24**

Add symbols to your text using the Symbols tab in the Symbols dialog box.

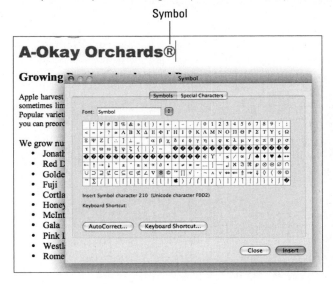

3. **Click the Symbols tab if it's not already selected.**
4. **Click the Font pop-up menu, and choose a symbol font.**
5. **Click the symbol you want to insert.**
6. **Click Insert.**

   Word adds the symbol to the document. The dialog box remains open in case you want to insert more symbols.

7. **Click Cancel to exit the dialog box.**

Follow these steps to insert special characters:

1. **Click in the document where you want to insert a special character.**
2. **Choose Insert ⇨ Symbol.**

   The Symbol dialog box opens.
3. **Click the Special Characters tab, as shown in Figure 6.25.**

---

**FIGURE 6.25**

Use the Special Characters tab to insert em dashes, paragraph marks, or special quote marks.

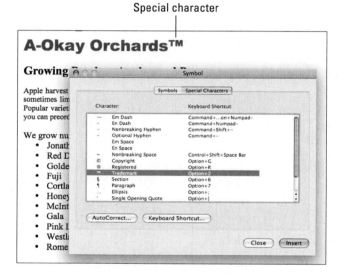

4. **Click the character you want to insert.**
5. **Click Insert.**

   Word adds the special character to the document. The dialog box remains open in case you want to insert more characters.
6. **Click Cancel to exit the dialog box.**

## Changing text case

As you're typing text, you may have occasion to change the text case. Normally, unless you've left the Cap Lock key on, you type using both uppercase and lowercase letters. To quickly change the text case, you can activate the Change Case dialog box, as shown in Figure 6.28. You can choose from five different case options. Follow these steps to change text case:

1. **Select the text you want to change.**
2. **Choose Format ⇨ Change Case.**

   The Change Case dialog box opens, as shown in Figure 6.26.

**FIGURE 6.26**

Use the Change Case dialog box to change the uppercase or lowercase lettering of your text.

3. **Choose an option:**

   ■ Sentence case capitalizes the first word of each sentence.

   ■ Lowercase sets all the text to lowercase text.

   ■ Uppercase creates all uppercase letters.

   ■ Title Case sets capitals for the first letter of every word.

   ■ Toggle Case does the opposite of whatever is typed currently.

4. **Click OK.**

   Word applies the new case.

 You also can activate the Small Caps or All Caps buttons on the Formatting Palette's Font pane to change the text case in a document. The Small Caps button, when clicked, creates formal-looking capital letters, but the characters that were lowercase letters now appear in smaller caps than the capital letters starting each word. Figure 6.27 shows an example of the Small Caps style applied to text.

**FIGURE 6.27**

The Formatting Palette's Font pane also has a couple of text case options you can apply.

BOB THE SMALL FROG

On the other hand, the All Caps button, when clicked, just turns the selected letters to all capital letters. Strangely enough, if you toggle the All Caps button off again, the text reverts to the way you typed it. You can't do this if you typed everything with the Cap Lock key engaged. Word treats the Small Caps and All Caps buttons like formatting you apply, the same as applying bold or italics.

## Adding text boxes

From time to time, you may need to insert a block of text that sits separately from the rest of the document. For example, you may want to set a quote aside in the middle of the document and format it differently to stand out. You can create text boxes to create text that is independent from the rest of the document. Word treats the text box as a graphic object, which means you can move and resize the box as needed, and apply special formatting commands to the object. A text box can have a border or no border at all, and you can even apply a fill color to the box to really set it apart from the rest of the document.

Follow these steps to create a text box:

1. **Choose Insert ➪ Text Box.**
2. **Click and drag across the page to create a box the size you want.**
3. **Type your text, as shown in Figure 6.28.**

**FIGURE 6.28**

Use text boxes to create text that's separate from the rest of your document.

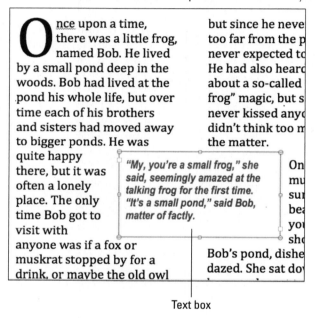

Text box

You can now treat the box like any other graphical element. You can select the box and drag it around to a new location. Simply click the box to select. To assign a line or fill color, select the box and use the settings on the Formatting Palette in the Colors, Weights, and Fills pane. To change the text box formatting, such as setting a new margin or text wrap, click the Text Box pane in the Formatting Palette. You also can double-click the text box to open the Format Text Box dialog box and set line and fill colors, inner margins, change wrapping style, and more. To learn more about formatting objects, including text boxes, see Chapter 30.

# Building Documents Using Outlines

In the preceding chapter, you learned how to use Word's view modes to view your documents in different ways. Outline view is one of those modes, and it truly comes in handy when you're trying to build a document based on an outline. In this section, I'll show you how to use Outline view and start creating a well-planned document. Outlines are all about categorizing and prioritizing your thoughts to help you create a well-constructed document, whether it's an essay, white paper, or report.

As you may remember from your school years, outlines are built on a hierarchical structure with the main points of your idea appearing as Heading 1 level headings, and lesser points trickling down to lower heading levels. Figure 6.29 shows an example of a typical outline created in Outline view. To start your own outline, click the Outline view button, located in the lower-left corner of the program window or choose View ⇨ Outline.

**FIGURE 6.29**

Here's an example of an outline created in Outline view.

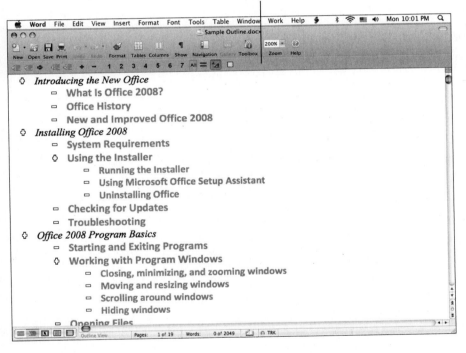

A special toolbar, called the Outlining toolbar, appears with all the tools you need for building an outline, point by point. Table 6.3 explains each of the toolbar buttons.

If you have an existing document you want to view as an outline, you can still use Outline view. When you switch to Outline view, Word uses the headings, line breaks, and indents you typed to display the document in outline form.

**TABLE 6.3**

## Outlining Toolbar Tools

| Button | Name | Description |
|---|---|---|
|  | Promote | Promotes the text one heading level. |
|  | Demote | Demotes the text one heading level. |
|  | Demote to Body Text | Demotes the text to body text. |
|  | Move Up | Moves the text up. |
|  | Move Down | Moves the text down. |
|  | Expand | Expands the selected text. |
|  | Collapse | Collapses the selected text. |
|  | Show Heading 1 | Shows heading 1 only. |
|  | Show Heading 2 | Shows heading 2 only. |
|  | Show Heading 3 | Shows heading 3 only. |
|  | Show Heading 4 | Shows heading 4 only. |
|  | Show Heading 5 | Shows heading 5 only. |
|  | Show Heading 6 | Shows heading 6 only. |
|  | Show Heading 7 | Shows heading 7 only. |
|  | Show All Headings | Shows all headings. |
|  | Show First Line Only | Shows the first line of each heading or paragraph. |
|  | Show Formatting | Toggles outlining formatting on or off. |
|  | Master Document View | Switches to Master Document view (learn more about this coming up later in the chapter). |

## Assigning headings

Outline headings you assign are based on Word's built-in heading styles. Headings can help you arrange your thoughts in an orderly fashion. Heading 1 is the topmost outline heading you can apply, followed by Heading 2, Heading 3, and so on to Heading 7. When you finally get to the point of adding some regular text, you can assign the Body Text style.

To begin any outline, start by typing all the main points as Heading 1 level text in the document. Press Return at the end of each heading and start another heading. You can choose to enter all the level 1 headings first and fill in subheadings afterward, or you can enter in all the text at once and change levels later. It's easy to promote or demote a line to another heading level. To change the heading levels, use any of the following methods:

- To demote a heading, click the Demote button or press Tab.

- To promote a heading, click the Promote button or press Shift+Tab.

- To demote a heading to body text, click the Demote to Body Text button. When you demote to body text, Word applies the Normal style.

As you're building your outline, you'll probably need to move parts of it around. You can rearrange your headings in your outline using several methods:

- You can drag a heading and drop it where you want it to go. Just click and drag the + or − icons in front of the heading to move the heading.

- You can use the Move Up and Move Down buttons on the Outlining toolbar to rearrange headings. Click the heading, and then click a button as many times as you need to move it up or down the outline.

- You can use keyboard shortcuts to rearrange headings; press Control+Shift+↑ or Control+Shift+↓.

## Changing the outline view

By default, Outline view shows all the headings and text you type into your outline. As you work with the material, you may want to view only headings with level 1 assigned, or just view heading levels 1 and 2. You can control which headings appear in the outline using the buttons on the Outlining toolbar. Use these methods to change your view of the headings:

- To expand or collapse a single heading, first click the heading and then click the Expand or Collapse button.

- To view only certain heading levels, click the corresponding level number button on the toolbar. For example, to view only heading level 2 text, click the 2 button. Word shows only the heading level you selected and hides the rest.

- To view the entire outline again, click the All button.

- To view only the fist line of every paragraph, regardless of whether it's a heading or body text, click the Show First Line Only button.

- To collapse a single heading and subheadings, double-click the + icon in front of the heading. Once collapsed, click the − icon in front of the heading to expand it again.

As you've noticed, Word applies some default formatting to your outline text as you assign headings. If you find the formatting distracting, you can turn it off and view just plain text. Click the Show Formatting button on the Outlining toolbar to turn formatting on or off. When you switch to another view, Word keeps the heading style formatting. You can format the document differently as needed.

After completing your outline, you can switch to Print Layout view or Draft view and finish writing the text, fleshing out each heading in the outline.

## Adding outline numbers

For many of us, outlines are associated with all the funny numbering techniques they taught you back when you were learning to write research papers and reports, such as Roman numerals or sequences of tiny iii's. You can find these same numbering sequences in Word today. Word offers seven outline numbering formats you can apply, or you can create your own numbering system. To add numbering, follow these steps:

1.  **Select the entire outline, and choose Edit ⇨ Select All or press ⌘+A.**
2.  **Choose Format ⇨ Bullets and Numbering.**

    This opens the Bullets and Numbering dialog box, shown in Figure 6.30.

**FIGURE 6.30**

The Bullets and Numbering dialog box has a tab devoted to outline numbering systems.

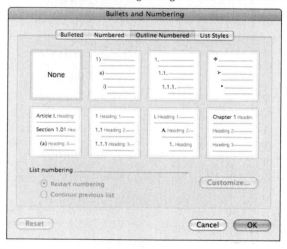

3.  **Click the Outline Number tab.**
4.  **Choose a numbering style.**

    If you don't see a style you like, you can click the Customize button and make your own.
5.  **Click OK.**

    Word applies the numbers to the outline.

# Building Documents Using Notebook Layout View

You can whip up notes for any document you plan to create using Notebook Layout view. One of Word's view modes, Notebook Layout view, looks and acts a bit differently than the other views. Looking just like . . . well, a notebook, this view lets you record notes and random thoughts and rearrange them to start creating a cohesive document. By default, Notebook Layout view appears as a binder with notebook rings. When you first open the view, a clean sheet of ruled "notebook" paper appears onscreen. The pasteboard background behind the notebook is supposed to resemble a desk. Figure 6.31 shows an empty page in Notebook Layout view. It suddenly brings back memories of classes and lectures, doesn't it?

You can use Notebook Layout view to record and organize notes and build a document.

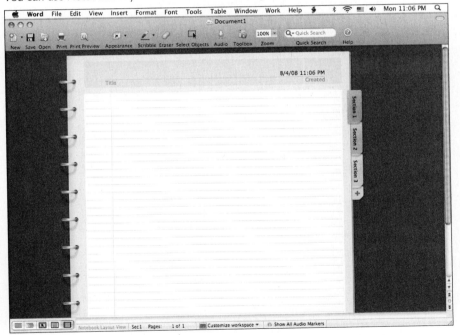

Billing itself as an electronic notebook, Notebook Layout view is ideal for taking notes on a laptop computer, designing an outline, or just gathering materials for a future project. You can even record audio notes using your computer's built-in microphone. You can add tabs to the electronic notebook and organize material into categories, flipping back and forth between your notebook pages. You can even scribble in freehand on the page using a mouse or pen tool. You can add graphics objects, such as AutoShapes, photos, or just about any other type of object you want to place on a page.

To switch to Notebook Layout view, click the Notebook Layout view button or choose View ⇨ Notebook Layout.

As a specialized view mode, Notebook Layout view doesn't play well with the other views in Word, so it's not a good idea to start a document in Print Layout view, and then switch over the Notebook Layout view to finish the document. Rather, this specialized layout view is best for capturing thoughts and ideas. If you do try to convert an existing document into Notebook Layout view, be prepared to lose some formatting, such as headers and footers or caption text. The prompt box shown in Figure 6.32 appears to warn you if you convert an existing document. To create a new document, click the Create New button instead. If you want to convert an existing document, click the Convert button.

**FIGURE 6.32**

If you switch to Notebook Layout view with an existing document open, Word displays this prompt box.

To change your notebook's appearance, click the Appearance button on the Standard toolbar and choose another look. To turn the ruled lines on or off, display the Rule Lines pane in the Formatting Palette and click the Style menu. Choose None to turn the lines off. You also can specify a distance between lines using the Distance setting. To change the pasteboard background, click the Customize workspace button located on the Status bar and choose another design from the pop-up menu.

## Adding note text

To enter note text in Notebook Layout view, just click where you want to insert it and start typing. When you press Return, you start a new paragraph or outline heading. As you enter each line, a tiny gray circle bullet appears over in the left margin. You can see the bullet when you move your mouse pointer over the note text, as shown in Figure 6.33. This bullet works much like the icons that appear in front of headings in Outline view. You can click and drag the bullet icon to move the text around on the page. To create sub-headings under a main heading point in your outline, press Tab. If your text includes subheadings, as in Figure 6.33, you can expand and collapse the headings by clicking the Expand or Collapse arrow icon in the left margin.

The Notebook Layout view offers several special toolbar buttons on the Standard toolbar. Table 6.4 explains each of the buttons you see on the toolbar, including the ones you're already familiar with. The Formatting Palette in the Toolbox also displays some special panes just for working with notebook text and items.

**FIGURE 6.33**

You can enter text and drag it around to rearrange its order on the page.

Draggable bullets

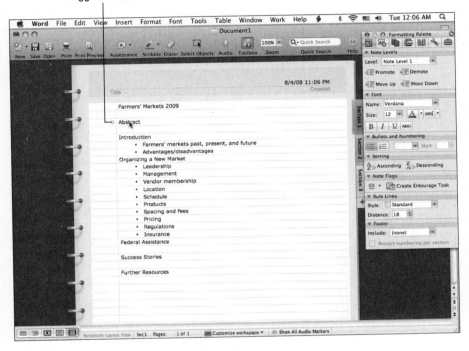

**TABLE 6.4**

## Notebook Layout Tools

| Button | Name | Description |
|---|---|---|
| | New | Creates a new notebook document. |
| | Save | Saves the document. |
| | Open | Opens a new document. |
| | Print | Prints the document. |

*continued*

| | **TABLE 6.4** | (continued) | |
|---|---|---|---|
| **Button** | | **Name** | **Description** |
| | | Print Preview | Opens the document in Print Preview mode. |
| | | Appearance | Changes the appearance of the Notebook and pasteboard background. |
| | | Scribble | Allows you to freehand scribble on the notebook page, turning your mouse into a pen or pencil. |
| | | Eraser | Erases lines you scribble on the page. |
| | | Select Objects | Lets you drag over objects to select them on the page. |
| | | Audio | Displays the Audio Notes toolbar for recording and playing back audio notes. |
| | | Toolbox | Opens the Office Toolbox palettes. The Formatting Palette displays panes geared to Notebook Layout formatting tasks. |
| | 100% | Zoom | Magnifies your view of the notebook page. |
| | Quick Search | Quick Search | Lets you search the notebook for a keyword or phrase. |
| | | Help | Opens the Word Help files. |

**NOTE**   You can use the Formatting Palette's formatting controls in Notebook Layout view just like you do in the other view modes. You can format your text by changing fonts, sizes, and text color, or adding bullets, numbers, borders, or shading. You cannot, however, control alignment or other paragraph formatting options.

To add text on another section tab in your notebook, click the tab heading. Notebook Layout view starts you out with three sections or pages. You can add more if you need them; click the + tab, or Control+click the section heading tab and choose New Section from the context menu. To assign the tabs unique names, double-click the name and type another. Press Return, and the new name is assigned. You also can rearrange sections by dragging and dropping them where you want them to appear in the lineup.

## Organizing notes with text levels

Like Outline view, you can set text levels to promote or demote notes in your notebook outline. Note Level 1 is the highest level, and Note Level 9 is the lowest. You can use the buttons in the Formatting Palette's Note Levels pane to assign text levels, you can drag and drop text to change levels, or you can use keyboard shortcuts. Figure 6.34 shows the Level menu from the Note Levels pane.

---

**FIGURE 6.34**

You can assign levels to your notes using the Note Level headings.

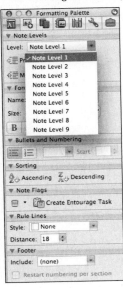

When you first start typing in Notebook Layout view, Note Level 1 is assigned by default. To change the text level, click the line of text and then apply any of these methods:

■ To demote text, click the Demote button in the Note Levels pane in the Formatting Palette or press Control+Shift+→.

■ To promote text, click the Promote button in the Note Levels pane or press Control+Shift+←.

■ To move a line of text up in the outline, click the Move Up button in the Notes Levels pane or press Control+Shift+↑.

■ To move a line of text down in the outline, click the Move Down button or press Control+Shift+↓.

■ Press Control+Tab to indent text without changing text levels.

■ Press Control+Shift+A to expand all levels.

■ To assign a different note level, click the Level menu on the Note Levels pane and choose a level.

To add actual bullets or numbers to your text levels, display the Bullets and Numbering pane in the Formatting Palette and click the Bullets or Numbering button.

## Sorting and flagging notes

You can sort your notes using the sorting commands in the Formatting Palette. Display the Sorting pane in the Formatting Palette, as shown in Figure 6.35, and click either Ascending or Descending. Ascending sorts your notes in ascending order based on the first letter of the text level, while descending sorts the notes in descending order.

**FIGURE 6.35**

The Sorting pane has options for sorting your notes, while the Note Flags pane has options for flagging your notes.

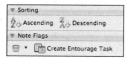

You also can assign a flag to your notes. For example, you can insert a colored check box in front of a text level or assign a priority level. Display the Note Flags pane, click the Note Flag arrow icon, and choose a flag. To turn a note into an Entourage task, click the note and then click the Create Entourage Task button. The Create Task in Entourage dialog box opens, as shown in Figure 6.36. Set a reminder date and time, and click OK to create the task.

**FIGURE 6.36**

You can easily turn a note into an Entourage task.

## Using the Scribble tool

You can create freehand drawings on your notes pages using the Scribble tool. If you have a pen tablet, you can use a stylus to scribble on the page. If you don't, you can use your mouse. Your scribbles may be a bit rough, but with a little practice, you can create some basic shapes. Word treats the drawings as picture objects, which means you can move, resize, and format them like other graphic objects. To learn more about how to work with graphics in Word, see Chapter 30.

 To choose a pen style, click the Scribble button's arrow icon and make your selection. You can draw with a fine point, a very fine point, or a medium point. Basically, the settings control the thickness of your drawn lines. You can choose a color for your drawn lines. To draw on the page, click and drag the mouse or stylus. Figure 6.37 shows an example of drawings on a notebook page.

 Click the Scribble tool again to turn the tool off. You can click the Eraser button and click and drag over the drawing to erase your freehand lines. You can group several drawn shapes into one unit using the Select Objects button. Click the button and drag across all the objects you want to group. Once grouped, you can move them all as one unit. When you select the Scribble tool, the Formatting Palette displays formatting options geared specifically for shapes and lines you draw. Learn more about formatting graphics in Chapter 30.

**FIGURE 6.37**

Use the Scribble tool to create freehand drawings on your notes pages.

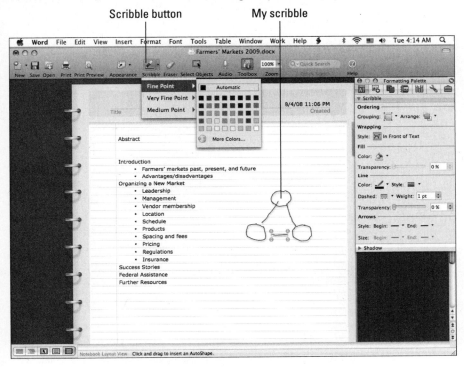

## Using audio notes

If you're using Notebook Layout view in a classroom or lecture environment, you can turn on the audio features and record notes. You can focus on typing the main points and let the audio recording take care of the details. As you type your notes, the audio tool inserts speaker icons for the snippets of audio that match what you typed at the time, synching the audio as you type. You can play back the recording later to refresh your memory about the material covered. Figure 6.38 shows an example of the audio tools.

To turn on the audio tools, click the Audio button on the Standard toolbar or choose View ⇨ Audio Notes. Word displays the Audio Notes toolbar (refer to Figure 6.38). The Audio Notes toolbar displays tools that act just like other recording buttons on other recording devices. For example, clicking the Record button starts recording audio. Clicking the Stop button stops the recording. Table 6.5 explains the Audio Notes tools in greater detail.

Use the Audio Notes toolbar to record audio notes in Notebook Layout view.

Audio speaker icon

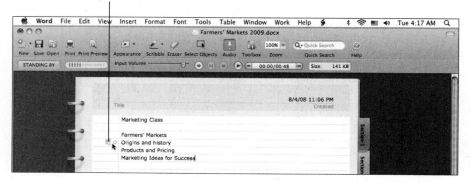

## Audio Notes Tools

| Button | Name | Description |
| --- | --- | --- |
| STANDING BY | Record Status | Displays the recording status as Standing By or Recording. |
| | Input Level Indicator | Displays the microphone volume level. |
| | Input Volume | Lets you drag the slider to increase or decrease the microphone's volume input. |
| | Record | Starts recording audio. |
| | Pause | Pauses audio playback. |
| | Stop | Stops recording or audio playback. |
| 00:00/00:48 | Timeline Slider | Displays the audio recording length. |
| Size: 141 KB | Audio File Size | Displays the audio file size. |

When you're ready to record, click the Record button and begin typing your notes. As you type, Word creates new audio notes for each line you create in the notebook. Click the Stop button to stop recording. To play back the recording, click the Play button or click the audio icon in front of the note text. If you need to pause the recording, click the Pause button.

Any audio notes you record are saved along with the Word document file. If you no longer need the audio recording, you can delete it; choose Tools ⇨ Audio Notes ⇨ Delete Audio from Document.

**NOTE** You can export any audio files you record in Notebook Layout view. Choose Tools ⇨ Audio Notes ⇨ Export Audio. This opens a Save dialog box where you can assign a filename and save it to a specific folder.

# Building Documents Using Publishing Layout View

Hold onto your hats, because this next feature is extremely cool and easy to use, and it can manufacture amazing documents in a flash. New to Office 2008 for Mac, the Publishing Layout view is a built-in desktop publishing program that you can use to create all kinds of professional-looking documents from newsletters and brochures to posters and flyers. You can choose from dozens of well-crafted templates, plop in your own text, and create a snazzy document that's sure to impress and communicate your ideas efficiently.

If you've ever worked with a desktop publishing or page-design program before, you'll find that Word's Publishing Layout application works in much the same way. Publication documents are based on layouts that govern the positioning of text, graphics, and photos on a page. Each object can be moved and edited separately. Depending on what type of publication template you choose, the layout may include more than one page or section. Every publication starts with placeholder text that gives you some idea about the appearance of the text.

In addition to a variety of templates, Word's Publishing Layout view also offers quick access to tools to help you edit and change the text and objects in a layout. You can customize any template to create a publication that suits your needs.

 Click the Publishing Layout View button or choose View ⇨ Publishing Layout to open the feature. Click the Create New button to start a brand new publication, or click the Continue button if you want to edit the existing document in Publishing Layout view.

If you attempt to open an existing document in Publishing Layout view, a Welcome box appears, as shown in Figure 6.39. Click the Create New button to start a brand new publication, or click the Continue button if you want to edit the existing document in Publishing Layout view.

Word opens a new, blank document in Publishing Layout view. To get started, click the Publication Templates tab from the Elements Gallery, and then click the type of template category you want to browse. When you find a template you like, click it, and Word creates it onscreen. Simply insert your own text and photos. It really is as simple as that—and if you're in a hurry, you couldn't ask for a better way to fast-track a document that looks as good as any of the templates available for this feature.

**FIGURE 6.39**

If you attempt to switch views with an existing document, this box appears.

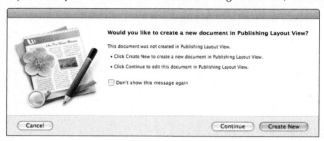

**NOTE** You also can create a new Word publication using the Office Project Gallery. See Chapter 33 to learn more about this feature.

Here's a run-down of the templates you can expect to find in Word's Elements Gallery:

- **Newsletters:** This category lists all kinds of newsletters you can create in Word.
- **Brochures:** This category lists a variety of brochures you can whip up in Word.
- **Flyers:** Choose from several flyer templates available in Word.
- **Invitations:** Choose from informal and formal invitations.
- **Programs:** Create a picture or school program for your next event.
- **Business Cards:** Choose from several professional-looking business card documents you can make in Word.
- **Postcards:** Create a marketing or announcement postcard.
- **Catalogs:** Create a photo catalog or booklet catalog.
- **Awards:** Whip up a nice award document to print out.
- **Menus:** Create a bistro or takeout menu.
- **Posters:** Choose from several poster styles.
- **Signs:** This category lists several signs you can create to announce sales or other events.
- **CD Labels:** You can create your own DVD or CD labels using these Word templates and make use of Avery brand stickers to print them.

As soon as you choose a template from the Gallery, Word creates the document, and it's ready to go. Most templates include placeholder text, as shown in Figure 6.40. You can replace the placeholder text with your own text. The placeholder text is there to show you what the layout and formatting looks like for the template. Of course, you can change the formatting to suit your own needs. To replace the placeholder text, click the text box and start typing. To replace a photo or graphic, drag a photo into the box. You also can Control+click the object and select Change Picture from the context menu. You can then navigate to the image you want to use and insert it instead of the default image.

**FIGURE 6.40**

To start building your publication, replace the placeholder text with your own text.

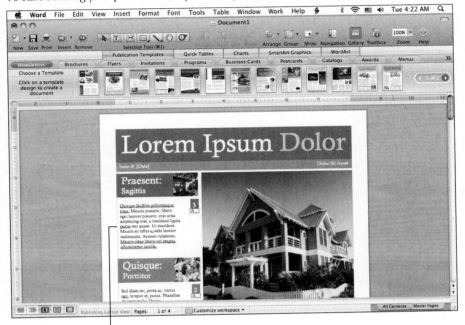

Placeholder text

When you finish creating the publication, you can save the file. To learn more about saving documents, see Chapter 5. To learn more about using graphic objects in Word, see Chapter 30.

For most users, whipping up a quick publication is all that's needed, and filling in placeholder text and photos is pretty straightforward and intuitive. Because all the formatting and design is done for you, the hard part is coming up with your own words. However, as you can see by all the tools available on the Standard toolbar, you can certainly start tweaking a publication's design and formatting if the need arises. You can create your own publication templates, altering the Master Pages to create new designs and layouts, adding your own page elements, and even including movies and sound. You can find tutorials online to help you navigate the techniques and procedures for creating more complex layouts in Word. Of course, if it's real page layout tasks you want to perform, a desktop publishing or page-design program is your best bet. Word's Publishing Layout tools can certainly put you one step closer to a full-blown design program, but even then, it's limited. Regardless of any limitations, including such an innovative feature in Word is a fantastic idea and you're bound to have fun seeing what sorts of publications you can generate using it.

## Summary

This chapter showed you how to start creating documents in Word. First, you learned how to enter and edit text. This chapter taught you how to use AutoCorrect and AutoText to speed up your typing tasks. You also learned how to select and edit text, use the Undo and Redo commands, copy and move text, and find and replace text. You found out how easy it is to give your document structure using columnar layouts using tabs and columns. You also learned how to insert special text elements, like drop caps, symbols, and special characters.

To finish up your education on document building, this chapter instructed you on how to create documents based on outlines and templates using Word's Outline, Notebook Layout, and Publishing Layout views.

# Chapter 7

# Formatting Word Text

Word processing is more than simply typing words on a page. In the past, your only formatting options when creating a document were the margin settings and indenting. Word processing now affords desktop publishing options and control to even the simplest of documents. Your choice of font and color, application of bold and underscoring, and use of spacing often contribute as much to the message conveyed by your document as the text itself. Bulleted and numbered lists can be used to further highlight key points, and they automatically renumber and reformat themselves as you modify the document. Finally, borders and shading columns can provide a final, professional touch to your work.

In this chapter, you learn to use the Formatting Palette for quick changes to your fonts and paragraphs and various dialog boxes that provide even greater control over these options. You learn to control the alignment and spacing of your lines and paragraphs down to the very pixel. You also learn how to format your text with lists, borders, and shading to create the look you want.

## Understanding Formatting

In order to consistently format a document, it's important to know the difference between various elements of your document. Each Word document has three major elements, and different types of formatting can be applied to each:

- **Characters:** A character is the smallest unit in a document. Character formatting includes font name and size, bold or italics, text color and highlighting, and superscripts or subscripts. Character formatting can be applied to a single character or a selection of characters.

- **Paragraphs:** A paragraph in Word does not always have the same definition you learned in English 101. For Word's purposes, a paragraph is a group of text followed by a paragraph break (usually made with the Return key). In some cases, you want a soft return to apply a carriage return without starting a new paragraph in order to preserve formatting. Paragraph formatting includes styles, alignment, spacing, borders and shading, and bullets or numbering.

- **Sections:** A section is used to single out portions of a document for special formatting. A section can be a single paragraph or several pages long. Section formatting includes columns, page numbering, headers and footers, margins, and gutters. Margins and gutters are covered later in this chapter, while columns were covered in Chapter 6 and page numbers and headers/footers are covered in Chapter 9.

In addition to these elements, you can apply formatting to the entire document. Margins and layouts are applied to the document as a whole, although they can be modified within each section. Borders and line numbers also can be applied to the entire document and modified or excluded within particular sections as needed.

# Using the Formatting Palette

 Office makes it easy to see and modify most of the formatting settings in one palette of the Toolbox without having to open multiple menus or obscure your view of your content. If the Toolbox is not already open, you can access the Formatting Palette, shown in Figure 7.1, by clicking the Toolbox icon in the Standard toolbar or selecting View ➪ Formatting Palette. If you've been looking around at the other palettes in the Toolbox, you can switch to the Formatting Palette by clicking the first icon on the left at the top of the Toolbox.

**FIGURE 7.1**

The Formatting Palette contains the most commonly used formatting options.

Depending on which View you're using and the template that's attached to your document, the Formatting Palette contains up to nine panes. When editing text, the following panes are generally available:

- **Font:** This pane contains the most commonly used options for adjusting the appearance of characters.

- **Styles:** This pane allows you to create and apply styles based on the template upon which your document is based. Styles and templates are covered in Chapter 9.

- **Alignment and Spacing:** If you want to center a paragraph or double-space your document (or a portion thereof), this is the pane to change those settings. You also can set the indentation for an entire paragraph or just the first line of same.
- **Bullets and Numbering:** Think of this pane as a list organizer. You can add bullets or numbers to a series of items and format the indentation for those entries.
- **Borders and Shading:** This grouping enables you to set borders of different styles and colors to distinguish tables and text boxes. You also can add shading to a selection.
- **Document Margins:** This pane allows you to set margins for the entire document. You also can determine how much margin space is allocated for headers and footers.
- **Document Theme:** Word comes with several preset combinations of fonts and colors that work well together. You can choose one of these themes from this pane or even create your own.

There are exceptions to this list. Some templates limit access to certain panes, particularly the Document Theme pane. Your options also may be limited when opening a document created in a different word processor or earlier version of Word.

**NOTE** When you add a picture or text box, the panes available on the Formatting Palette change to include options to manipulate those objects. You can learn how to add pictures, clip art, and text boxes in Chapter 30.

You can toggle opening and closing the panes within the Formatting Palette by clicking the pane title. Although you can certainly open all the panes and jump between them at your leisure, this can take up lots of screen real estate. More likely, you'll want to open one or more panes that are specific to your current formatting intent. For example, if you've just created a new document, you may want to use the Alignment and Spacing pane along with the Document Margins pane to set up the overall structure of the document. After those are set, you can close those panes and open the Font and Style panes, where you can apply more specific character and paragraph formatting as you type.

# Changing Fonts and Sizes

One of the most common tasks in Word is controlling the appearance of text. Font changes include everything from the font itself to its size, color, background, and position within a line of text relative to the rest of the text (by way of superscripts and subscripts).

The simplest font change is simply adding bold, italics, and underlining to selected text. Even if you prefer to primarily use the palettes and toolbars for everything else, memorizing the keyboard shortcuts for these three font styles will save you considerable time:

- **Bold:** ⌘+B converts the selection to **bold** type.
- **Italics:** ⌘+I converts the selection to *italic* type.
- **Underline:** ⌘+U converts the selection to <u>underlined</u> type.

You also can use keyboard shortcuts to increase or decrease the font size, change the case of letters, and apply double-underlines and superscripts/subscripts. If you use these elements often, you will want to memorize those shortcuts, as well; you can find a list of them in the Help files by searching on Word keyboard shortcuts. If you don't frequently need these options, you can access them just as readily from the menu or Formatting Palette.

# Different Fonts for Different Purposes

The study of typography can fill volumes. When choosing fonts, you need to consider both aesthetics and practicality. The best way to start is by considering where your document is going to be viewed and its purpose.

If your document's final destination is the Internet, you want to be sure to use a font that can be easily read across multiple computer platforms and browsers. Although Bauhaus 93 looks interesting, if your audience doesn't have that font installed on their systems, it comes up as a much less interesting Arial or Helvetica on their screens. It's better to save the fancy fonts for graphic headers and banners, which can be saved as images, and stick to the basics for your text. The Font Collections option in the font list provides a group of Web-safe fonts for both Macs and PCs.

If your document is going to end up in print, the sky's the limit in terms of font options, but caution is still warranted. Too many fonts on a page can distract the reader from your message. This is doubly true if the fonts don't flow well together. Again, let purpose be your guide. If you're going for a quirky, playful look, you just might get Snell Roundhand and Comic Sans to work together for you. If your purpose is more business-like or attempting to soothe the reader, you'll never want to see those two fonts on the same page. Also keep in mind that if you're ever tempted to use more than three or four fonts in one document, you're probably heading down a dangerous path.

If the process of choosing fonts makes you queasy, you can cure all your ills by applying a Document Theme. This will guide you in font and color selection, ensuring a good result. Document Themes are covered later in this chapter.

## Changing fonts with the Formatting Palette

If you're in the habit of keeping the Toolbox open as you work, the Formatting Palette is the easiest place to make font changes. The Font pane, shown in Figure 7.2, contains all the basic commands to modify the font type, size, and formatting of your text. As you'll see later in this section, the tools here are just a subset of all your font formatting options, but nine times out of ten, these will do the job.

There are two approaches to setting fonts. If you've already typed a block of text, select the text and then click the Name: drop-down in the Fonts pane to select the font you want. If you haven't yet started typing, simply choose a font from the Name: drop-down; any text you type from that insertion point is in the new font.

By default, the fonts appear in the style of the font itself, as shown in Figure 7.3. This can help you choose an attractive font, particularly if you have hundreds installed (and Office 2008 itself adds 125 fonts when you install the application, plus any fonts already installed on your Mac). If you're on a very slow computer, you can speed up the listing a bit by pressing Shift when opening the font list, but the change is generally negligible and makes it harder to browse the font options. To permanently turn off the WYSIWYG (what you see is what you get) display on the font list, go to Word ⇨ Preferences, click the General panel, deselect WYSIWYG font and style menus, and click OK.

**FIGURE 7.2**

The Font pane enables you to quickly change font settings.

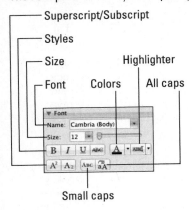

Superscript/Subscript

Styles

Size          Highlighter

Font   Colors   All caps

Small caps

**FIGURE 7.3**

The list of font possibilities is vast, but it also can be overwhelming.

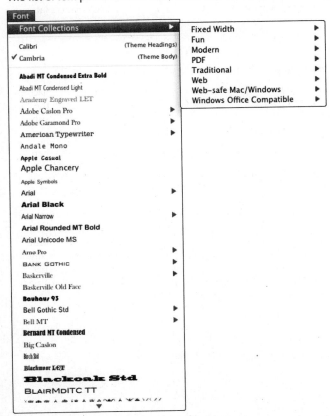

> **TIP** If you know the name of the font you seek, you can type the first couple of letters after you open the font list, and the list scrolls to those letters. This is especially helpful when you don't want to have to scroll through hundreds of fonts to get to Zapf Dingbats, for example.

When you're browsing your font options, be sure to look at the Font Collections option at the top of the list. The Font Collections are groupings of fonts organized by category. These groups are by no means exhaustive, but they can help you get off to a good start.

Below the list of Font Collections are the fonts that are preset for headings and body text in the current Document Theme. If you haven't selected a theme for the document, the defaults are Calibri for Theme Headings and Cambria for Theme Body.

Following the theme fonts is a list of the most recently applied fonts. This is quite convenient when you're creating a multi-font document because after you've applied each of the fonts once, they'll remain at the top of the font list to be readily accessed again, even in a different document.

> **NOTE** If you apply a new font using a Style, the font list does not update its recently used font settings. If you're wondering why a font you've been using throughout a document doesn't appear at the top of the font list, this could be why.

## Changing font sizes

The size of a font determines how much space it takes up on the page or screen. It's important to note that different fonts may appear larger or smaller even if the font size is the same. Also, fonts that appear large onscreen may look smaller in print, and vice versa. For most reports, manuscripts, and letters, the commonly accepted font sizes are 10- or 12-point, with headings being slightly larger. If you're designing a brochure or business card, your size needs may vary much more widely.

You can use several methods for adjusting font size within the Font panel, and any of them can be applied either to a selection or by choosing an insertion point and making a size adjustment to be carried forward to any new text that's added beyond that point:

- Select a point value from the Size drop-down menu.
- Enter a point value into the Size box.
- Use the slider to the right of the Size box. This option works best on a selection because you can see the difference even slight adjustments make to the flow of your text.

> **CAUTION** With monitors capable of handling ever-higher resolutions, it can be difficult to accurately judge font size. Instead of adjusting your font size to make a document more legible onscreen, it's better to adjust your Zoom options.

## Adding color

Unless you've applied a Document Theme or template, the default color for text is black. Adding color to your text can enhance your message considerably, both onscreen and in print. To change the font color, make a selection or set the insertion point, and then click the down arrow to the right of the Font Color swatch. As you can see in Figure 7.4, several color options are immediately available. To select a color, simply click a swatch.

The colors that appear under the Theme Colors heading are variations on the colors for the current Document Theme. If you're using a theme, choosing from these options ensures consistency in your document. If none of these colors appeals to you, click the More Colors button to access the Color Picker. This is the standard Mac OS Color Picker, offering several options to choose additional colors, as shown in Figure 7.5.

**FIGURE 7.4**

The swatches available on the Color Picker vary depending upon the Document Theme.

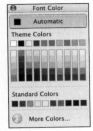

**FIGURE 7.5**

The Mac OS Color Picker extends your color options.

Additionally, you can apply highlighting to the space behind your text. Again, simply make a selection or choose an insertion point, and then click the Highlight button. Unfortunately, you don't have as many color options here as you do when selecting a font color, so it's clearly not intended for extensive design use.

 **TIP** If you want more control over highlighting your text, use the Borders and Shading pane instead of the Highlight tool. Borders and Shading are covered later in this chapter.

# Modifying Fonts with the Font Dialog Box

Although the Font pane provides access to the most common options, if you want full control over your text, you should use the Font dialog box, as shown in Figure 7.6. To access it, choose Format ➪ Font. You also can access the Font dialog box from the context menu when you Ctrl-click in the document. All the options on the Font panel are duplicated in the dialog box, with the addition of other tools, particularly underlining styles, ligatures, and font effects.

**FIGURE 7.6**

The Font dialog box offers additional tools to format characters.

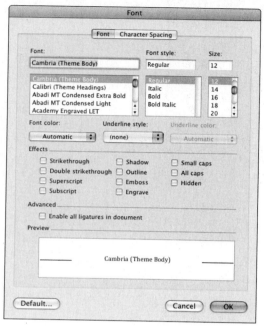

Changing fonts, sizes, and colors work in much the same way in the dialog box as in the palette. To add bold or italic effects, select them from the Font Style list. To add underlining, choose from the Underline Style drop-down list; you'll notice this list has far more options than the simple on/off available from the palette.

**NOTE** The font list in the Font dialog box does not appear in WYSIWYG style. There are better ways to set the font than this, using either the Formatting Palette or the Font menu. The dialog box offers greater control than the Formatting Palette in other areas, however, so it's best to become familiar with both.

## Using font effects

The Font panel contains options for adding superscripts and subscripts, strikethrough text, and changing the case of text. The dialog box contains all these options and more, as shown in Figure 7.7. These options can be used with even greater effect if you apply different font colors and shading to the text. Many of these font effects, particularly Shadow, Outline, Emboss, and Engrave, are used primarily in desktop publishing, so you will generally reserve those for brochures, calendars, and other documents you create in the Publishing Layout.

**FIGURE 7.7**

Font effects can greatly change the appearance of text.

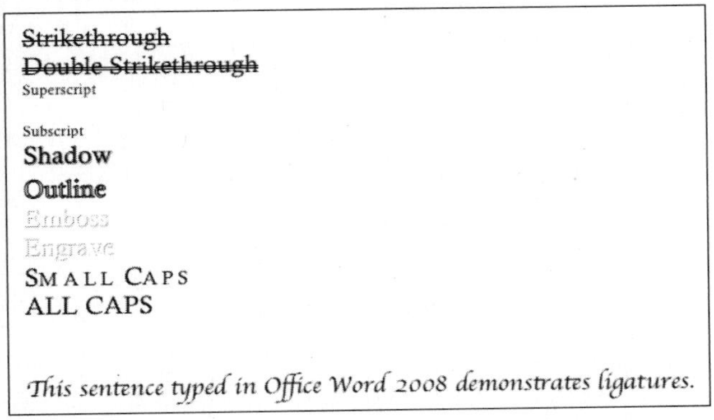

~~Strikethrough~~
~~Double Strikethrough~~
Superscript

Subscript
**Shadow**
Outline
Emboss
Engrave
SMALL CAPS
ALL CAPS

*This sentence typed in Office Word 2008 demonstrates ligatures.*

These are your Font Effect options:

- **Strikethrough and Double Strikethrough:** These give words the appearance of having been crossed out. These effects are sometimes used in contracts when you want to retain the original language for the record while also reflecting the new wording. The single strikethrough effect is available on the Formatting palette, as well as from the dialog box.

- **Superscript and Subscript:** These options shift the selected characters slightly higher or lower on the line. These also are available on the Formatting Palette.

- **Shadow:** This adds a slight shadow below the text. When you're using a small font, this can create a blurred result. For larger font sizes, the effect is more pronounced.

- **Outline:** This effect adds an outline tracing around each character and fills the center with the background color.

- **Emboss:** This makes the letters appear slightly raised from the page. This is used to best effect on a colored background, where it's more noticeable.

- **Engrave:** The opposite of Emboss, this effect makes the letters appear carved into the page. Again, this looks best against a colored background.

- **Small Caps:** This effect converts the lowercase letters in the selection to smaller capital letters, much in the style of block print writing. This is available on the Formatting Palette, as well.

- **All Caps:** This converts all letters in the selection to uppercase. You also can access this option from the Formatting Palette.

- **Hidden Text:** This turns text invisible without deleting it. This feature is helpful to hide your notes or in-house information in a document while retaining them for your own use. Once hidden, you can view this text by choosing Word ➪ Preferences ➪ View, and then turning on Hidden Text. To print hidden text, choose Word ➪ Preferences ➪ Print, and then select Hidden Text from the Include with Document options.

The All Caps effect is deceptively useful. While it may seem that this option is identical to typing with Caps Lock or the Shift key pressed, this is not the case. When you use All Caps, Word recognizes the actual case of the letters. If you later change your mind and want to remove or change the font effect, the word is formatted in the original case in which it was typed.

> **NOTE** The superscript and subscript effects are intended for use in mathematical and scientific equations. If you are creating footnotes in your document, Word automatically formats those correctly without the use of the Font dialog box. See Chapter 9 to learn more about footnotes.

## Using ligatures

Several fonts contain ligatures—characters that appear joined when they're next to each other. These fonts evoke the style of the Middle Ages, when characters were connected to save space on the parchment that scribes used at the time. Apple Chancery is an example of a font that contains ligatures. To turn on ligatures, select the option in the Font dialog box. As shown in Figure 7.7, the first two letters in the example sentence are connected when Ligatures are selected. Note that this change is document-wide—you cannot add ligatures to only one selection of text.

## Character spacing

The Font dialog box also contains less frequently used options to control character spacing, as shown in Figure 7.8. While ligatures are used to connect letters meant to be joined in certain fonts, character spacing allows you to control the scale and spacing, also called *tracking,* of the characters to contract or spread them out to fit the available space, as shown in Figure 7.9. Character spacing is commonly adjusted to minutely contract a verbose heading so it fits on one line. It also can be used in less subtle amounts, with varied results.

**FIGURE 7.8**

The character spacing options are not used often, but they can provide minute control over your text.

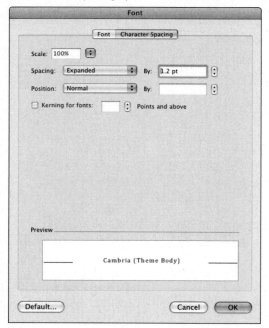

**FIGURE 7.9**

These are some examples of character spacing.

Changing the Scale can **expand** the space a character takes up.

It can also contract the space of characters.

Changing the Spacing controls the space b e t w e e n the characters.

The Position of a character can also be $^ch_an^g_ed$.

Kerning is subtle, best seen on CAPITALS
This line does not have kerning set.

The Scale setting allows you to control the amount of space each character itself takes up. While changing a font's size increases or decreases its vertical height, changing the scale expands or contracts characters horizontally across the line.

The Spacing setting controls the space between characters. Set it to Expanded to increase the white space between characters or Condensed to squeeze the letters together. The By box determines the percentage by which to make the selected spacing change. To see the effect of even small changes, look at the Preview box at the bottom of the dialog box.

The Position options determine the vertical position of characters relative to the baseline. Position can be used to manually set superscripts and subscripts. You also can use this setting to adjust existing superscripts and subscripts if you want them to be higher or lower than the default (which is 3 points in either direction).

Kerning adjusts the spacing between letters in proportional fonts to make them more uniform. Kerning the word MAT, for example would minutely reduce the space between the A and T. Kerning is often used with Japanese characters to control the spacing of the kana or kanji. To use kerning, select the Kerning for fonts check box and set the Points and above box for the text size that should be affected by these adjustments. The final appearance of kerning adjustments can somewhat resemble ligatures, even in fonts that are not designed as such.

# Adding Bullets and Numbers

Lists are used for everything from the mundane, like to-do items and shopping lists, to the professional, such as talking points for a speech or an itemization of features for a book on Office for Mac. In Word, these lists are formatted using Bullets and Numbering.

Bulleted lists are used to present unordered items, such as a team roster. Bullets are markers noting each entry on the list, usually an asterisk, dot, or arrow. Numbered lists are good for ordered, sequential items, such as a plan of action or a step-by-step tutorial on accomplishing a task. The numbers can be the standard 1, 2, 3, or Roman numerals (I, II, III), or even letters (A, B, C). A highly organized list can even combine both bullets and numbers of various formats, such as in a student's formal outline, as shown in Figure 7.10.

**FIGURE 7.10**

Lists can take several forms.

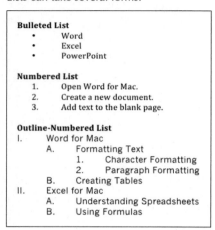

By default, lists are set to automatically format. If you type an asterisk followed by the Tab key followed by some text, Word recognizes this as the start of a bulleted list and formats it appropriately. Word also assumes that the next line is part of the same list, until you hit the Return key twice. Similarly, if you type a number followed by some text, Word assumes this is the beginning of a numbered list. Word is even smart enough to automatically renumber your list if you add items in the middle.

Word does a nice job handling lists, but you may want to modify some of the settings. To access the Bullets and Numbering pane, shown in Figure 7.11, click the Bullets and Numbering title bar in the Formatting Palette. If you want even more control over your lists, select Format ➪ Bullets and Numbering to open the Bullets and Numbering dialog box, shown in Figure 7.12.

**FIGURE 7.11**

The Bullets and Numbering pane allows you to change common list settings.

**TIP** If you do not want Word to make such presumptions, you can deselect Automatic bulleted lists and Automatic numbered lists under Word ➪ Preferences ➪ AutoCorrect ➪ Auto Format as You Type. If you choose to disable this feature, you can still apply formatted bullets and numbering when you need them by using the Bullets and Numbering pane or dialog box (or the Bullets and Numbering buttons on the Formatting toolbar).

---

**FIGURE 7.12**

The Bullets and Numbering dialog box offers even more control over your lists.

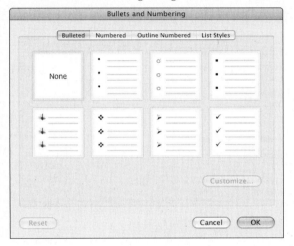

## Changing bullet or number styles

To change a bullet or number style from the Bullets and Numbering pane, click the Style button. For numbered lists, you can choose from Arabic or Roman numerals, letters, or uppercase and lowercase. For bullets, you can choose from filled and hollow circles, arrows, and so on.

In some cases, you'll start a numbered list and then switch to paragraphs that do not require numbers, only to return to the numbered list later on the page. If you type the next number and continue the list, Word picks up the numbering where you left off and continues to format the list. To change the numbering of a list using the Bullets and Numbering pane, follow these steps:

1. **Place the insertion point somewhere in the first item you want to renumber.**
2. **Enter a number in the Start box in the Bullets and Numbering pane.** Word automatically renumbers the rest of the list.
3. **Use the Indent buttons to increase or decrease the indentation of the bullet or item number.**

You also can change the numbering of a list or the bullet style using the Bullets and Numbering dialog box. This not only allows you to renumber the list, but you can change the style and spacing of the bullets or numbering.

To modify a list using the Bullets and Numbering dialog box:

1. **Open the Bullets and Numbering dialog box using one of these methods:**
   - Position the insertion point within the list, and choose Format ➪ Bullets and Numbering.
   - Double-click a list number or bullet.

2. **Choose one of the layouts from the available options (refer to Figure 7.12), or press Customize to access the Customize bulleted list dialog box shown in Figure 7.13 or the Customize numbered list dialog box shown in Figure 7.14.**

3. **To change the number style or bullet character, make your selection in the Bullet Character or Number Format box, depending on the type of list.** In a numbered list, you also can use this area to change the start number.

4. **Set the Bullet or Number Position, which is the indentation point from the left margin.**

5. **Set the Text Position, which is the text indentation from the left margin.** It's usually indented farther than the bullet or number. If the Bullet or Number position is set to indent at 0.25", for example, and the Text Position is set to indent at 0.5", a quarter of an inch appears between the bullet/number and the text. As the text wraps, it automatically indents to the Text Position setting, leaving the bullet or number set apart.

6. **Click OK to return to the Bullets and Numbering dialog box.**

7. **Click OK to apply the new style to the current list.**

**FIGURE 7.13**

The Customize bulleted list dialog box allows you to adjust indenting and bullet styles.

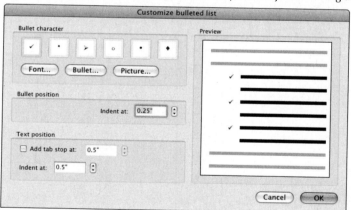

**FIGURE 7.14**

The Customize numbered list dialog box provides options for adjusting numbering and indentation.

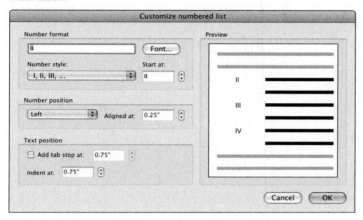

## Customizing bullets

The most common bullets are dots and arrows, but you certainly are not limited to those choices. Some bullets can take on a different appearance just by changing the font. To do this, double-click a bullet in your list to bring up the Bullets and Numbering dialog box. Click Customize, and then click Font from the Bullet character options.

Any symbol can be used as a bullet. In the Customize bulleted list dialog box, click Bullet from the Bullet character options. Choose a symbol from the Symbol dialog box, shown in Figure 7.15. You can view the symbols in other fonts by selecting one from the Fonts drop-down menu. Webdings and the various Wingdings fonts offer interesting choices. After you've clicked a symbol, click OK to return to the Customize bulleted list box, and then click OK to return to the Bullets and Numbering dialog box; a last click of the OK button returns you to your document.

**FIGURE 7.15**

The Symbol dialog box makes any symbol available as a bullet.

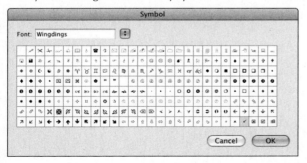

The third bullet customization option is to use a graphic image in place of a bullet. Unfortunately, as of this writing, this feature does not work even with the bullets supplied by Office for Mac, as evidenced in Figure 7.16.

Attempting to customize a bullet with a graphic image results in an error message.

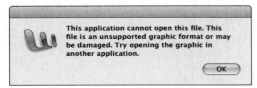

This application cannot open this file. This file is an unsupported graphic format or may be damaged. Try opening the graphic in another application.

OK

## Creating an outline-numbered list

Some lists are so complex that they take on the format of a multi-level outline. There are two ways to create an outline. One is to use Outline view to assign different levels (and related Heading styles) to each level of the outline. As explained in Chapter 6, this is commonly used to lay out the structure of a report with the intent of adding body text at some point. Another method is to use the Bullets and Numbering options to create a multi-level outline, such as a formal outline for a contract or school assignment. You can combine approaches by using the Outline view to format your document and then apply Bullets and Numbering to change the Heading styles. If you use this option frequently, you can save a Template that automatically applies these Heading styles. See Chapter 6 to learn how to create Templates. To learn more about Styles, see Chapter 9.

To create an outline-numbered list, begin with a numbered list: Enter a number, the punctuation you desire, a tab, and the item text, and then press Return. Unless you've turned off this AutoFormatting option, Word automatically begins a numbered list. To indent subheadings, click the Increase Indent button in the Bullets and Numbering pane. To return to a main heading, click the Decrease Indent button.

### Customizing an outline-numbered list

If you want more control over your list, double-click one of the numbers in the list to bring up the Bullets and Numbering dialog box. From here, you can choose a different list format or click the Customize button to gain even greater control. The Customize outline numbered list dialog box, shown in Figure 7.17, allows you to change the format, style, and position of each level of your outline. You can even set some levels as bullets and others as numbers.

### Using list styles

Another approach to using an outline numbered list is to apply a List Style, as shown in Figure 7.18. A List Style is a preformatted series of styles for each level of an outline numbered list. The styles that are installed by Word include options that would apply to contracts or other legal documents. If you've taken the time to carefully customize an outline numbered list, you can preserve your efforts by adding a new List Style based on your outline. When you want to apply the same formatting to another document or list, all the styles will be preset.

**FIGURE 7.17**

The Customize outline numbered list dialog box enables you to design formal outlines.

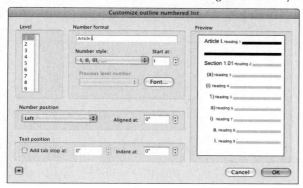

**FIGURE 7.18**

List Styles offer preformatted options for legal documents and contracts, among other uses.

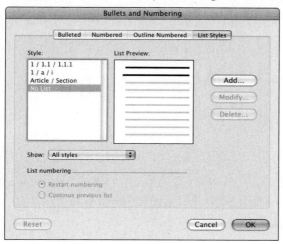

Follow these steps to choose a List Style:

1.  **Double-click a number or bullet within your outline to open the Bullets and Numbering dialog box.**

2.  **Select List Styles to open the List Styles dialog box.**

3. Choose a style.

4. Click OK to return to the Bullets and Numbering dialog box.

5. Click OK to return to your document.

If you want to add your own list style, open the List Styles dialog box and choose Add. You are prompted to create a new style for the list. To learn more about creating and applying styles, see Chapter 9. After you've created a new list style, you can change it by selecting the style from the list and choosing Modify.

> **TIP**
> To quickly remove all list formatting, select the entire list and right-click to access the Bullets and Numbering dialog box from the context menu. Select List Styles, and choose No List. Click OK to save your changes. The style of the list items remains, but any bullets, numbering, and indentation are removed. This tip also can be applied to individual list items.

> **CAUTION**
> Applying List Styles can modify the styles of your entire document. If you apply the Section/Article List Style, for example, all the Headings in your document assume this style, even those not part of the list. User beware!

# Changing Alignment and Spacing

Unlike Font formatting, which applies to characters (or groups of characters), Alignment and Spacing apply to paragraphs. Bullets and Numbering also apply to paragraphs, as you saw in the preceding section, but for a highly specialized purpose. Alignment and Spacing are used to control the general flow of your text across the page.

When modifying Alignment and Spacing formatting, you can either apply it to a selection or choose an insertion point, after which the formatting is applied. As with the other Formatting Palette panes, the Alignment and Spacing pane, shown in Figure 7.19, contains only a subset of a larger set of controls, in this case the Paragraph dialog box, shown in Figure 7.20. To access the Alignment and Spacing pane, click its title heading in the Formatting Palette. To open the Paragraph dialog box, choose Format ⇨ Paragraph.

**FIGURE 7.19**

The Alignment and Spacing pane allows you to modify the flow of text across the page.

**FIGURE 7.20**

The Paragraph dialog box provides a greater degree of control over paragraph formatting.

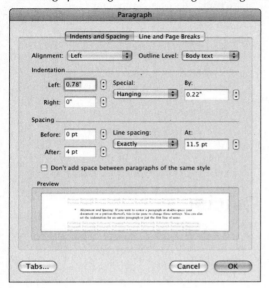

## Setting horizontal spacing

Horizontal alignment controls how your paragraph is aligned relative to the horizontal space of the page.

- **Align Text Left:** Aligns the first character of each line with the left margin. The keyboard shortcut is ⌘+L.

- **Align Center:** Centers the text evenly between the left and right margins. The keyboard shortcut is ⌘+E (remember that ⌘+C is used to copy a selection).

- **Align Text Right:** Aligns the last character of each line with the right margin. The keyboard shortcut is ⌘+R.

- **Justify:** Aligns the first character of each line with the left margin and the last character with the right margin, adjusting the spacing between words and characters as necessary to achieve a balanced appearance. The keyboard shortcut is ⌘+J.

Horizontal spacing can be used in columns, as well. In this case, paragraphs are aligned with the column margins rather than the document margins.

 For best results, turn on hyphenation when using the Justify setting. This allows Word to automatically hyphenate long words to improve the document's appearance.

## Specifying line spacing

Line spacing controls the white space between lines. Letters and other business communications are usually single-spaced. Manuscripts and legal briefs are generally double-spaced, as are most school reports. Brochures and other creative documents can have a wide array of custom spacing options.

The Alignment and Spacing pane offer three line spacing options: single, 1.5, and double. The Paragraph dialog box allows you to control line spacing down to the exact point size (or inch, centimeter, or even millimeter, if you specify in, cm, or mm after entering a number). Three additional options for line spacing are as follows:

- **At least:** If you have text or graphics of different heights within the paragraph, setting this option puts "at least" the specified amount of space between the tallest element on the line and the lines before/after it.

- **Exactly:** If you need to ensure specific line spacing in a document, you can enter it here. Be careful, however, to account for text or graphics that are taller than your specified spacing, as the spacing setting takes precedence over the content, and those tall elements are cut down to size.

- **Multiple:** This option modifies your spacing relative to the standard single-spacing. Setting this for 2.5, for example, gives you results between double- and triple-spacing.

> **TIP**   The Exactly setting can be used to subtly increase the number of lines you can fit on a page. When formatting a manuscript, for example, some editors specify 25 lines per double-spaced page. If you can't quite seem to make it fit, set the line spacing to Exactly 25 pt to provide the appearance of double-spacing, but ensuring everything fits just right.

## Changing text orientation

Text orientation, which is available on the Alignment and Spacing pane as well as the Text Direction dialog box, controls the direction in which the text flows. Generally, English text flows horizontally from left to right. In Word, you can change text to flow vertically, as well, either from top to bottom or bottom to top. This is helpful in Publishing Layout view, where you might have both portrait and landscape elements in the same document or even on the same page, such as a newsletter with an address area that appears on the back cover when the page is folded. These settings also can be used in conjunction with section breaks to change a page to landscape orientation within a document containing other pages in the standard portrait orientation in order to preserve pagination and other formatting. To access the Text Direction dialog box, shown in Figure 7.21, choose Format ⇨ Text Direction.

**FIGURE 7.21**

The Text Direction dialog box allows you to change the orientation of your text.

## Setting paragraph spacing

While line spacing controls the space between lines, many people are still in the old typewriter habit of hitting Return twice at the end of paragraphs to leave additional space between paragraphs. This is "old school." A 21st-century solution is to use Paragraph Spacing to tell Word how much white space to leave between paragraphs. You can set this space to be added before the paragraph, after, or both. Headings and other preformatted styles often make use of paragraph spacing to set those elements apart from body text. You can suppress the addition of paragraph spacing between paragraphs of the same Style by choosing "Don't add space between paragraphs of the same style" in the Paragraph dialog box.

## Setting indents

Another remnant from an earlier time is the use of the Tab key to indent the first line of a new paragraph. The default tab stops in Word are not optimized for this use. Besides, there's no need to go to the extra trouble of using the Tab key when you can set indentation automatically. After you've set the indentation for one paragraph, Word automatically formats subsequent paragraphs with the same settings. Additionally, you can modify the Normal style or any other style to your indentation settings.

Most people think of indentation as something that only applies to the first line of a paragraph, either indenting it inward to specify a new paragraph or moving it negatively to allow the first line to stand out from the lines below (called a hanging indent). In Word, you also can use indentation to adjust an entire paragraph inward from either the left or right margins (or both). This is useful when creating a block quote or formatting poetry.

## Caring for widows and orphans

As paragraphs flow from page to page, they're sometimes broken up in odd places as the text reaches the bottom margin. The first line of a paragraph left alone at the bottom of a page is called an orphan. The last line of a paragraph that flows alone onto a new page is called a widow. To reunite these widows and orphans with the rest of their paragraphs, choose Format ➪ Paragraph to open the Paragraph dialog box and click the Line and Page Breaks tab. Select Widow/Orphan Control to suppress these elements from being left on the page.

The Line and Page Breaks dialog box, shown in Figure 7.22, also allows you to specify paragraphs that should be kept on the page with those that follow it, to keep all the lines of a paragraph together without any page breaks separating them, and to precede some paragraphs by an automatic page break.

**FIGURE 7.22**

The Line and Line Breaks dialog box controls the flow of your paragraphs over multiple pages.

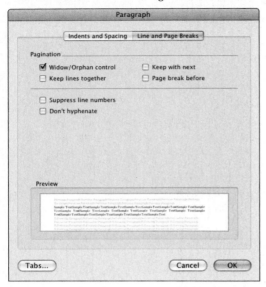

# Adding Borders and Shading

Borders and shading can liven up dull text, emphasize key blocks of text, or provide organization by color-coding information. Even if your final document is going to be printed in black and white, borders and shading can add a professional touch to your piece. If you're working in color, the possibilities are endless.

As with the other formatting options, you can apply borders and shading from within the Formatting Palette, as shown in Figure 7.23, or from the Borders and Shading dialog box, as shown in Figure 7.24. If you're applying shading at various points around your document, you can also use the Tables and Borders toolbar (⌘-click in the toolbar area, and choose Toolbars➪Tables and Borders), as shown in Figure 7.25. The dialog box offers many more options than either the pane or the toolbar, but you may not need more than what those tools provide.

**FIGURE 7.23**

The Borders and Shading pane of the Formatting Palette can add blocks of color to your document.

**FIGURE 7.24**

The Borders and Shading dialog box offers additional customization options.

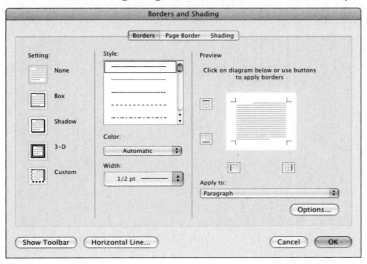

**FIGURE 7.25**

The Tables and Borders toolbar provides formatting options at the top of the window.

## Creating borders

To add a border, first select a block of text. If you want to put a border or shading around an entire paragraph, you can simply click within the paragraph. If you want to put multiple paragraphs into the same block, select all the included paragraphs. If you want to put a border around only certain characters within a paragraph, make that selection. Add the border by choosing a Type from the Borders and Shading pane or a Setting in the Borders and Shading dialog box. If you are adding a border to a table, you can choose to apply the border around the entire table, to the cell divisions within the table, or both.

You can customize borders in several ways:

- **Style:** You can apply a variety of solid and dashed lines to the border, as well as multiple line styles.
- **Color:** You can choose from Word's options or click More Colors to choose from the Mac OS Color Picker. If you have a Document Theme applied, Word's choices reflect different shades of the theme colors, which can help with consistency.
- **Weight:** Border lines can vary in thickness from ¼ point to 6 points.

You also can customize a border by applying different combinations of style, color, and weight, to each side. To control the distance between the border and the text within it, choose Options from within the Borders and Shading dialog box.

 Borders can easily be stylized by opting to apply border lines to only one or two sides rather than boxing in an entire block of text.

Another option in the dialog box is Horizontal Line setting. When you apply this feature, Word adds a graphic horizontal line below the selected paragraph. Horizontal lines used to be important elements in Web design to separate blocks of information, but Web designers more commonly use other formatting options such as Cascading Style Sheets (CSS) these days.

## Adding shading

Shading adds a pattern or color to the white space of a selected area. It can be applied to the area within borders, a text box, or table cells, as well as to any text selection. To add shading, open the Borders and Shading pane in the Formatting Palette and then follow these steps:

1. **Select the area to be shaded.**
2. **Choose a pattern by clicking the arrow next to the Pattern box.** Choosing Solid fills the entire area. Choosing a percentage generates halftones, using the Fill Color for the background and the Pattern Color to modify the fill. Below the percentage options, you can find several patterns, some of which are more subtle than others.
3. **Choose a Fill Color.** This is the color of the background.
4. **Choose a Color (also known as the Pattern Color).** This is the color of the pattern or halftone color. Choosing the Solid pattern is still considered a "pattern" for Word purposes.

**CAUTION** The Pattern and Fill Colors can be tricky. All text has a Clear shading automatically attached to it, transparent by default. When you choose a Pattern and colors, the Fill Color changes this transparent "color." In general, the Pattern Color takes priority, putting down an overlay on top of the fill color. If you change the Fill Color after setting the Pattern Color, however, Word seems to lose track of this precedence and puts a new overlay on top of your Pattern Color, essentially reversing the order of colors in the pattern. It's best to set the Fill Color first and then the Pattern Color. Alternatively, use the Borders and Shading dialog box, where this doesn't seem to be an issue.

If you are using the Borders and Shading dialog box, you can find these options on the Shading tab, as seen in Figure 7.26. The Fill is the color of the background. The Color drop-down below the Shading setting is the color of the pattern. Unlike when you use the Formatting Palette, the dialog box offers a Preview of your changes, allowing you to see how your selection will look before committing to it.

As mentioned earlier in this chapter, Shading can be used in place of the Highlighting Font option to give you more color and formatting choices. Simply select the text to highlight, and choose a Pattern, Color, and Fill Color from the Formatting Palette.

FIGURE 7.26

**FIGURE 7.26**

The Shading options are similar in both the Formatting Palette and the Borders and Shading dialog box.

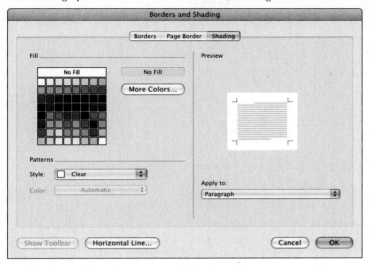

## Applying page borders

Page borders provide exactly what the name implies, a border around the margins of the entire page. Page borders are commonly used to create certificates of achievement and similar items. The options on the Page Borders tab are very similar to those of the Borders tab, with a few extras:

- **Art:** Word offers many graphic borders, many of them around holiday and other themes.
- **Apply To:** This setting determines if the border should be applied to an entire page or just a section.

The Options button at the bottom of the Borders and Page Borders tabs opens the Borders and Shading Options dialog box, shown in Figure 7.27. From here, you can control how far away from the text the selection or page borders are applied.

**TIP** Many people seem to think about word processing from a portrait-only mindset. For documents with little text, you can often get more eye-catching results by taking a different view. Change the orientation of your paper (File ➪ Page Setup ➪ Orientation) to landscape, and you'll have a wider area to add WordArt and otherwise customize your text. Add a page border, and you can create a professional-looking achievement honor for a company employee or even a "diploma" for a kindergarten graduation. You can find many landscape templates for Word on the Internet.

The Borders and Shading Options dialog box controls the margin settings for border frames.

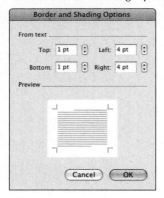

# Changing Document Margins

Although they appear toward the bottom of the Formatting Palette, Document Margins are often one of the first options you modify when creating a new document. Word's default margins are 1 inch at the top and bottom and 1.25 inches on the left and right sides. These settings are fine for business letters, but are far too generous for newsletters, where every bit of space counts.

There are three ways to set margins in a Word document. The Document Margins pane of the Formatting Palette, shown in Figure 7.28, allows you to adjust the four margins as well as the header and footer settings. Headers and footers appear within the top and bottom margin. The setting for headers and footers measures the distance from the edge of the page. Thus, if your top margin is set for 1.25" and your header for 0.5", the header appears 0.5" from the top of the page and 0.75" from the first line of document text.

The Document Margins pane provides quick access to the document and header/footer margin settings.

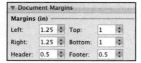

If you're a visual person, you can adjust margins directly within the document window. Switch to Print Layout view (click the Print Layout button at the bottom of the document window, or choose View ➪ Print Layout), and move your cursor to the horizontal ruler at the top of the document. At each end of the ruler, you see a shaded area. This is the margin space. Move your cursor over the area where the margin space ends and the text area begins, and the cursor changes to a double arrow. Click with the double arrow, and you can increase or decrease the margins. Similarly, you can change the margins at the top and bottom of the vertical ruler.

As with all the Formatting Palette panes, the Document Margins pane is a subset of a more powerful dialog box. Choose Format ➪ Document to access the Document dialog box, shown in Figure 7.29. The Preview box gives you an illustration showing how your document will appear when you modify the margins. If you reset the margins to a format you plan to use frequently, click the Default button to make this the default for new documents.

**FIGURE 7.29**

The Document dialog box allows you to set gutters and mirrors and constrain margin changes to sections.

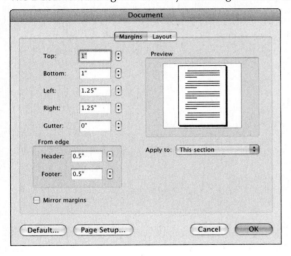

## Setting gutters and mirrors

In addition to the general margin settings, the Document dialog box provides access to gutters. The gutter is the inner margin where the page attaches to the spine of a book when it is bound. If you are planning to bind your finished document, you will want to consider how much gutter space you need to allow for binding, because it varies by type.

If you are using gutters, it is quite likely that you also want to mirror your pages. Bound books are usually printed two-sided. Thus, the odd pages often need a wider left gutter for binding purposes, while their even counterparts need a wider right gutter because they are on the reverse side of the page. To set mirrors, select the Mirror margins box.

## Changing margins and orientation for a section

In Chapter 6, you learned how to use Columns. When you set a portion of a document in column form, Word adds Section Breaks above and below the columnar text. You also can manually insert sections for other purposes, such to format a single page in a different orientation or to customize headers and footers for particular portions of a long document. To add a section break, position the insertion point where you want to place the break and choose Insert ➪ Break ➪ Section Break. You can choose from four types of section breaks:

- **Next Page:** Adds a section break and moves the text following it to a new page. This type of break is useful when changing orientation of a single page (or more).

- **Continuous:** Adds a section break, but keeps the text on the same page. These breaks are commonly used with columns.

- **Odd Page:** Adds a section break and formats the following text as an odd page. This is convenient when using gutters and mirror margins, because you can force new chapters to start on an odd page.

- **Even Page:** Adds a section break and formats the following text as an even page.

If your document contains section breaks, you can set document margins to apply to specific sections. To do this, position the insertion point anywhere within a section. Go to Format ➪ Document to open the Document dialog box. Change the margin settings, and click the Apply To option. You can apply the margin changes to the entire document, just the section surrounding the insertion point, or from the insertion point forward.

# Changing Document Themes

The final pane of the Formatting Palette is Document Theme, as shown in Figure 7.30. Themes are combinations of color schemes and fonts that work well together. These themes are the same as those found in PowerPoint and Excel, making it easy to coordinate your presentations and support documents to present a consistent image. If you choose a theme from the Document Theme pane, Word modifies the styles of your document to automatically apply the colors and fonts of that theme. Word also moves the fonts used for headings and body text to the top of the Font list for easy access.

**FIGURE 7.30**

Word offers a variety of preset color and font themes.

Office provides 50 themes, but you are not limited to these. You can create your own themes by modifying the colors and fonts to suit your needs and clicking Save Theme from the Document Theme pane.

# Copying Formatting

After setting all the formatting options mentioned in this chapter, you're likely to want to use them in other paragraphs and even other documents. The Format Painter can save you time in applying formatting to other paragraphs within the same document. To use the Format Painter, select the characters or paragraph whose formatting you want to copy and click the Format Painter in the Standard toolbar. This "loads" the painter with the formatting for that selection. To apply it, drag the mouse across the paragraph or character(s) to which you want to apply the formatting and release the mouse button. You can apply the Format Painter to multiple paragraphs by double-clicking the Format Painter in the toolbar before loading it. The Format Painter then remains active every time you select a new paragraph or character until you click the paintbrush again to deactivate it. To cancel the Format Painter, press Esc. If you inadvertently applied the paintbrush to the wrong selection, use Undo to remove the formatting.

Another way to copy formatting across selections—and especially across documents—is to create a style. Styles are covered in Chapter 9, but in short, they allow you to group several formatting elements into one customizable command.

> **TIP**    **If you ever feel lost when making font, paragraph, or section changes, you can get your bearings by turning on the formatting codes. Choose View ➪ Reveal Formatting and click a character or within a paragraph to see all the styles and formatting applied to that selection. Choose View ➪ Reveal Formatting again, or simply hit Esc, to exit this mode.**

# Understanding AutoFormatting

Earlier in this chapter, you read about how Word can automatically format lists. Bullets and Numbering are just one (or is that two?) of the options that can be automatically applied using AutoFormatting and AutoCorrect options. AutoFormatting also converts a URL into a hyperlink without your lifting your hands from the keyboard. AutoFormatting can even correct your most common typos, change your quotation marks into "smart quotation marks" (curly quotes), and convert an approximation of a copyright symbol—(c)—into the real thing ©.

To access the AutoCorrect Options, choose Tools ➪ AutoCorrect…. You can get to this dialog box from the Preferences panel (Word ➪ Preferences ➪ AutoCorrect) as well. The AutoCorrect preferences panel is shown in Figure 7.31.

If you are annoyed by Word taking control out of your hands, you can turn off AutoFormatting options. Here's how:

1. **Choose Tools ➪ AutoCorrect….**
2. **Click the tab to switch to the AutoFormat as You Type panel.**
3. **Deselect options you do not need in the panel.**
4. **Click OK.**
5. **Close the AutoCorrect panel.**

## FIGURE 7.31

The AutoCorrect preferences panel allows you to toggle AutoFormatting options on and off.

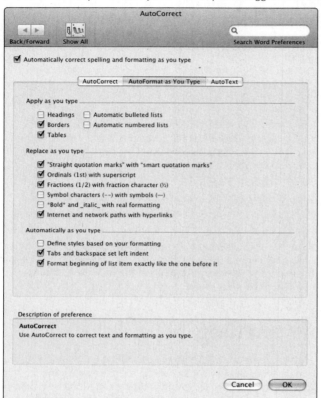

You also can disable AutoFormatting completely by clicking the "Automatically correct spelling and formatting as you type" check box at the top of the AutoFormat as You Type panel. You may be tempted to eliminate the feeling of Big Brother watching over your document, but some of the AutoCorrect features can be helpful if configured correctly. Smart quotation marks do look much more polished than their plain alternatives. Other options may be well-suited for some projects, but not for others. If you're a writer using standard manuscript formatting, you won't want Word to automatically convert your double hyphens (--) into an em dash. You may, however, want to use that em dash conversion on the cover letter that accompanies your submission.

Many options are available in the AutoFormatting panel, as shown in Table 7.1.

**TABLE 7.1**

## AutoFormatting as You Type Options

| Option | Purpose |
|---|---|
| **Apply as you type:** | |
| Headings | When you type a few words and press Return twice, this formats the text as a heading. |
| Borders | If you type three hyphens or underlines in a row and press Return, Word draws a horizontal line across the page. You can change the appearance of this line by using equal signs, tildes, asterisks, or number signs in place of the hyphens or underlines. |
| Tables | This little-known feature automatically creates a table when you type a plus sign (+) followed by a row of hyphens (---), followed by additional plus signs and hyphens across the page, ending with a final plus sign. Each series of plus signs and hyphens indicates the start of a new column. This is most commonly used . by those who create tables in this way on Internet forums and newsgroups. |
| Automatic bulleted lists | As explained earlier in this chapter, typing a common bullet character (*, -, or >) followed by a space or Tab and then some text informs Word that you're starting an unordered (bulleted) list. |
| Automatic numbered lists | Typing a number followed by a Tab (with or without a period or other punctuation following the number) tells Word you're starting an ordered (numbered) list. |
| **Replace as you type:** | |
| "Straight quotation marks" with "smart quotation marks" | Typing quotation marks automatically converts the standard marks to curly quotes. |
| Ordinals (1st) with superscript | When you type an ordinal number, Word automatically raises the letters of the ordinal into a superscript ($1^{st}$ rather than 1st). |
| Fractions (1/2) with fraction character (½) | If you type a common fraction, the type is automatically replaced with the symbol representing the number. |
| Symbol characters (--) with symbols (—) | Typing two hyphens automatically replaces them with an em dash. |
| *Bold* and _italic_ with real formatting | Using asterisks and underlines is a common way of indicating emphasis in newsgroup posts and forums. This option replaces them with actual bold and italic styles. |
| Internet and network paths with hyperlinks | Word automatically converts URLs to active hyperlinks. |
| **Automatically as you type:** | |
| Define styles based on your formatting | If you override the style for a selection once, Word redefines the style based on those new settings. This is usually a good option to disable even if you're using all the others, because it's easy to inadvertently lose your style settings this way. |
| Tabs and backspaces set left indent | If you start a line with the Tab key, Word assumes you want to begin paragraphs to follow with this same indentation. |
| Format beginning of list item exactly like the one before it | If you want to format a list using letters or Roman numerals, Word uses the first item as an example when formatting those that follow. |

In addition to applying AutoFormatting as you create a document, you also can disable these options and instead choose to AutoFormat in one fell swoop on your command:

1. **Follow the instructions above for disabling AutoFormatting as You Type.**
2. **Begin typing your document.**
3. **When you're ready to apply your choice of AutoFormatting options, choose Format ⇨ AutoFormat ⇨ Options.**
4. **Select which options you want Word to automatically format.**
5. **Click OK to accept your settings.**
6. **In the AutoFormat dialog box, choose your method of AutoFormatting:**
   - AutoFormat now: Word applies all AutoFormatting options without any further input from you.
   - AutoFormat and review each change: Word opens a dialog box displaying each change in succession, giving you the option of accepting or rejecting those changes.
7. **Click OK to format your document.**

# Using the Formatting Toolbar

The Formatting toolbar contains a subset of elements from the Formatting Palette. To access the Formatting toolbar, choose View ⇨ Toolbars ⇨ Formatting. The toolbar, as shown in Figure 7.32, appears below the Standard toolbar. If you are transitioning from a PC, toolbars may be a more familiar work environment for you than palettes. The palette and various dialog boxes offer more options, however, so the toolbar is only effective for the most common modifications.

The Formatting toolbar contains elements of several panes from the Formatting Palette.

# Summary

With all the formatting options at your disposal, Word can help you create documents perfect for any objective. You can control the font and its appearance. You can organize lists. Borders and shading highlight key points. The alignment and spacing options, coupled with the margin settings, give you control over how your text flows over the page. Finally, you can use themes to guide you to pleasing color palettes and fonts that work well together.

In the next chapter, you learn how to add tables to organize columns and rows of information.

# Chapter 8

# Adding Tables

Come on over here, pull up a table, and join me in a rousing discussion of Word's table tools. Tables are one of Word's most flexible program features. Tables are widely used to give structure to all kinds of document types, including Web pages, reports, lists, and more. What's the big deal about tables, you may ask? Tables allow you to precisely control the positioning of text and other elements across a page. No other columnar tool does this. Everything you type into a table has its own spot and never encroaches into another cell unless you okay it. Because everything stays in its own cell, you can be sure it's going to look nice, neat, and confined. That's not to say tables are confining. They're anything but confining because of the flexibility they offer. This clearly defined structure, however, is something you can count on when laying out a page design.

In this chapter, you'll learn how to create tables of all types to hold all types of content. You'll find out how to create quick tables using the Elements Gallery, design your own table from scratch, edit tables, make them look extra pretty, and even perform a whiz-bang mathematical formula—that's right, Excel's not the only math wizard in this Office town.

## IN THIS CHAPTER

Creating tables

Navigating tables

Entering table text

Insert and deleting table parts

Formatting tables

## Creating Tables

By their very nature, tables are rectangular in shape and appearance, even if you don't include any set borders to define their edges. Tables are constructed of columns and rows, and the areas in which the columns and rows intersect are called *cells*. Tables are an excellent choice for placing text and other content across and up and down a page. Each cell in a table is like a room in a house, holding the content faithfully. Maybe that's not a very good analogy after all, because you may have some rooms in your house overflowing with content that seems to spill into other rooms. Table cells can expand to fit content as needed, yet still retain the original structure and design. Tables are ideal for making invoices, lists, catalogs, newsletters, reports, calendars, and so on—you name it, a table can help you build it in some form or fashion. For years, Web designers have been using table structures to build Web pages. In this section, I show you all the various methods for creating tables in Word. After you've created a table, you can start inserting text and other types of content.

## Inserting Quick Tables

Word's Elements Gallery comes stocked with a variety of table elements you can use, called Quick Tables. You can find everything from basic tables to more complex table structures. Word's Quick Tables are preset and preformatted, which means all you have to do is plug in your table text and rest assured it's going to look good. When you display the Quick Tables in the Elements Gallery, you can scroll through the list and pick the table element you want to apply. Click the Basic tab to view 12 different tables with various degrees of color and shading applied. Click the Complex tab to view more intricate tables for creating calendars, directions, invoices, or reports.

To assign a table from the Quick Tables library, follow these steps:

1. **Click the Quick Tables tab on the Elements Gallery.**

   Word opens the Quick Tables display, as shown in Figure 8.1.

   **FIGURE 8.1**

   Use the Elements Gallery to insert Quick Tables.

   You can scroll through the tables to find the one you want; move the mouse pointer over a table to view a description.

2. **Click a table.**

   Word inserts it into your document, as shown in Figure 8.2.

Wow. How easy was that? The hard part, as always, is adding your own data to the table cells. When you insert a table, the Formatting Palette adds the Table pane to the list of panes. You can use the tools on the Table pane to edit and work with your rows and columns.

**FIGURE 8.2**

Word inserts the Quick Table into your document.

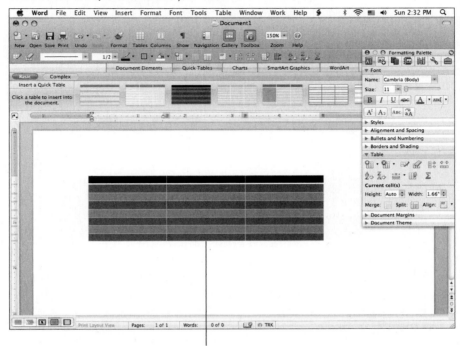

A new Quick Table

## Inserting tables on the fly

 You can use the Tables button on the Standard toolbar to quickly add an instant table. You define how many columns and rows to include, and Word inserts a blank, unformatted table for you. For example, perhaps you're typing along and decide you need a little table to hold some data. Just click and drag, and away you go; click the Tables button and drag across the number of columns and rows you want to insert. Release the mouse button, and the table is inserted. Figure 8.3 shows an example of a table created with the Tables button.

You can use the Tables button to insert a table as you go.

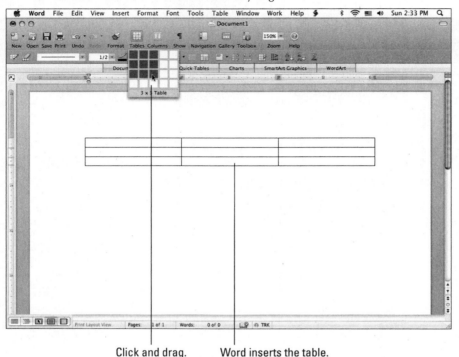

Click and drag.      Word inserts the table.

## Inserting tables with the Insert Table dialog box

If you want to insert a table with a little more planning and thought, use the Insert Table dialog box. Here you can find settings for specifying a table size, controlling how data fits with AutoFit, and applying AutoFormatting. You can learn more about using AutoFormat later in this chapter. The Insert Table dialog box has three AutoFit behavior radio buttons from which you can choose. The Initial column width radio button is set to Auto by default. If you want to set a precise measurement for column width, you can change this setting by typing a measurement. The AutoFit to contents radio button creates narrow columns that expand as you type in your table text. The AutoFit to window radio button spaces the columns evenly across the page.

If you know you're always going to be inserting the same table size, you can make the table settings you specify the default sizes for any new tables you create.

To insert a table, follow these steps:

1. **Choose Table ⇨ Insert ⇨ Table.**

   The Insert Table dialog box opens, as shown in Figure 8.4.

You can use the Insert Table dialog box to set a precise table.

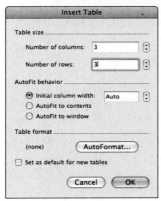

2. **Under the Table size options, specify a number of columns for the table.**

   You can type the number into the field, or you can use the spinner arrows to set a number.

3. **Specify the number of rows you want to create.** Again, you can type the number in directly or use the spinner arrows.

4. **Choose an AutoFit behavior.**

   Optionally, you can AutoFormat your table with the AutoFormat button.

5. **Click OK.**

   Word creates your table, as shown in Figure 8.5.

Look on the Formatting Palette for the Table pane, a collection of tools for working with table elements.

Word inserts a blank table to your specifications.

Tables and Borders toolbar

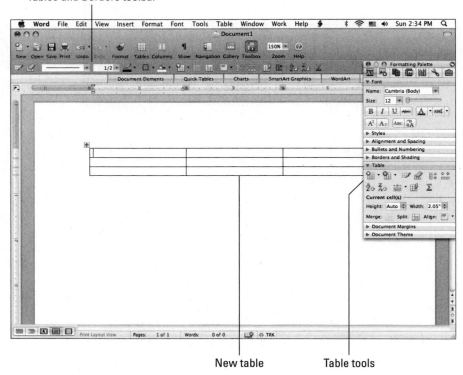

New table          Table tools

## Drawing your own tables

If you're really after a custom table, you can design your own using Word's Draw Table tool. When activated, this tool opens the Tables and Borders toolbar, and you can use the various tools to draw your own table using a pencil tool. By drawing a table, you can control how big it is, how many columns and rows it contains, and the size and spacing of your columns and rows.

To draw a table, follow these steps:

1.   **Choose Table ➪ Draw Table.** You also can click the Draw Table button located in the Table pane on the Formatting Palette.

     The Tables and Borders toolbar opens, and the mouse pointer takes the shape of a pen icon.

2.   **Click and drag the size of the table you want to create in the document, as shown in Figure 8.6.**

3.   **Click and drag each row and column you want to appear inside the table, as shown in Figure 8.7.**

## FIGURE 8.6

Use the pen tool to draw a table on your document.

Click the Draw Table tool.

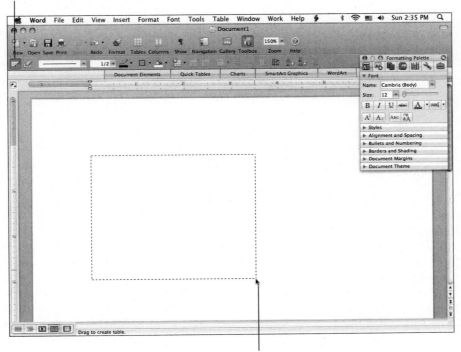

Drag the table size.

## FIGURE 8.7

Drag lines to create column or row borders.

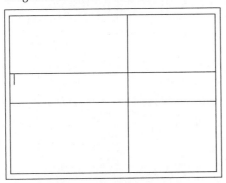

4.   **When the table is complete, click the Draw Table button to turn off the drawing feature.**

You can edit your table at any time by drawing new lines or erasing existing ones. Table 8.1 explains each of the tools available on the Tables and Borders toolbar.

**TABLE 8.1**

# Tables and Borders Toolbar Tools

| Button | Name | Description |
| --- | --- | --- |
| | Draw Table | Turns the drawing feature on or off. |
| | Eraser | Erases table lines you drag over. |
| | Line Style | Changes the line style. |
| 1/2 | Line Weight | Changes the line thickness. |
| | Border Color | Assigns a color to the table borders. |
| | Border | Controls which borders appear on the table. |
| | Shading Color | Assigns a background color. |
| | Insert or Draw a Table | Inserts table elements, such as rows or columns, or open the Insert Table dialog box. |
| | Merge Cells | Merges two or more cells into one large cell. |
| | Split Cells | Splits a large cell into two smaller cells. |
| | Align | Aligns table cell contents. |
| | Distribute Rows Evenly | Evenly spaces your rows throughout the table. |
| | Distribute Columns Evenly | Evenly spaces your columns throughout the table. |
| | Table AutoFormat | Opens the AutoFormat dialog box and applies preset formatting to the table. |
| | Change Text Direction | Changes the direction of text inside a cell. |

| Button | Name | Description |
|---|---|---|
| | Sort Ascending | Sorts the table in ascending order. |
| | Sort Descending | Sorts the table in descending order. |
| | AutoSum | Applies Excel's AutoSum formula to total a row or column. |

These techniques help you utilize the toolbar buttons and tweak your freshly drawn table:

- To erase a line, click the Eraser tool and drag across the line you want to remove.
- To add a new line to create a new column or row, click the Draw Table tool and draw another line on the table.
- To let Word insert a row or column for you, click where you want it to go, click the Insert Table arrow icon, and choose what you want to insert.
- To change the thickness, color, or style of a line, select it and click the appropriate formatting button on the Tables and Borders toolbar.
- To add inner and outer borders to your table cells or whole table, click the Border button and click a border style.
- To merge two cells into one, select both cells and click the Merge Cells tool.
- To split a cell, select it and click the Split Cells tool.
- To control text alignment inside a cell, select the cell, click the Align button, and choose a new alignment.
- To move a row or column border, drag the border.

You can learn more about entering text and selecting table elements later in this chapter.

## Converting text into tables

You can convert existing text within a document into a table. For example, if someone sends you a document with tabbed text, you can convert the text into a table. To make this technique work properly, the text should be in some sort of list format. When converting the text, you can choose to separate the text at the paragraph marks, commas, tabs, or another key. Even then, it might not turn out the way you might expect, so anticipate some editing afterward.

Follow these steps to convert document text into a table:

1. **Select the text, as shown in Figure 8.8.**
2. **Choose Table ➪ Convert ➪ Convert Text to Table.**

   The Convert Text to Table dialog box opens, as shown in Figure 8.9.
3. **Set the number of columns you want to use.**

   Optionally, leave the default Auto as the Initial column width setting to let Word determine the column widths. If you want to set a precise width, type a measurement instead.

**FIGURE 8.8**

To convert text into a table, start by selecting the text.

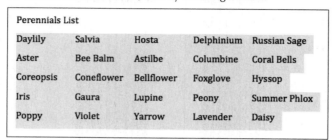

**FIGURE 8.9**

Use the Convert Text to Table dialog box to set up the conversion.

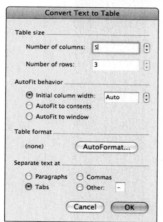

4. Choose how you want the text separated.

5. Click OK.

Word converts the text into a table, as shown in Figure 8.10.

**NOTE** You also can turn table text into regular text. Select the table, and choose Table ⇨ Convert ⇨ Convert Table to Text. In the Convert Table to Text dialog box, choose how you want to separate the table text: paragraph marks, tabs, commas, or another key of your choosing.

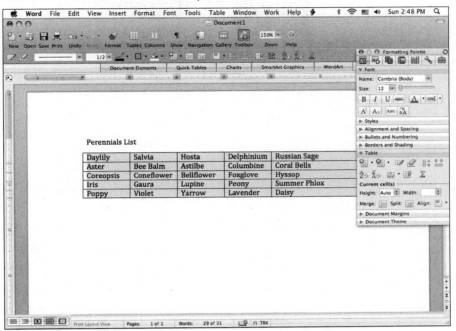

**FIGURE 8.10**

Word turns the selected text into a lovely table.

# Editing Tables

After you have a table inserted into your Word document, you can "set" your table with text and graphics. Insert your forced snicker or guffaw here, because I'm sure that pun has never shown up in a Word chapter before now. With a nicely made table now in place, you can begin entering text into the table cells. You also can start tinkering with the table structure to make it suit your needs. Missing a few rows? Add as many as you like. Need a bigger cell? Merge the cells. Want to dress it all up with a border and shading? Click a few formatting buttons, and you're good to go. Everything about a table is editable, as you're about to find out in this section.

Before we begin, let me also advise you to check out the Tables and Borders toolbar. The Tables and Borders toolbar is extremely handy for performing all kinds of table tasks, so you might want to keep it open while working with tables. Choose View ➪ Toolbars ➪ Tables and Borders.

## Entering table text

Each table cell can contain the content of your choice, such as text, clip art, photographs, drawn shapes and objects, hyperlinks, and so forth. The easiest way to enter text is to click in the first cell and start typing. You can use keyboard shortcut keys to navigate the table as you type so your fingers never have to leave the keyboard. Table 8.2 lists the keyboard navigation keys you can use.

### Table Navigation Keys

| Keys | Navigation Action |
| --- | --- |
| Control+Home | Moves to the first cell in the current row. |
| Control+End | Moves to the last cell in the current row. |
| Control+Page Up | Moves to the top cell in the current column. |
| Control+Page Down | Moves to the bottom cell in the current column. |
| Option+Clear | Selects the entire table. |
| Tab | Moves to the next cell. |
| Shift+Tab | Moves to the previous cell. |

**NOTE** Not all of the shortcut keys listed in Table 8.2 are available on all Mac laptops.

Depending on how you set up your table, the cells may expand to fit the text, or the text may wrap to the next line when it reaches the cell's right margin. If the table is set to AutoFit, the column resizes to fit the text you enter. To turn on the AutoFit feature to resize as you type, choose Table ➪ AutoFit ➪ AutoFit to Contents. In Figure 8.11, the cell holds a long line of text, but the cell originally started out the same size as the other column.

**FIGURE 8.11**

If AutoFit is turned on, Word expands the table cell to fit the text you type.

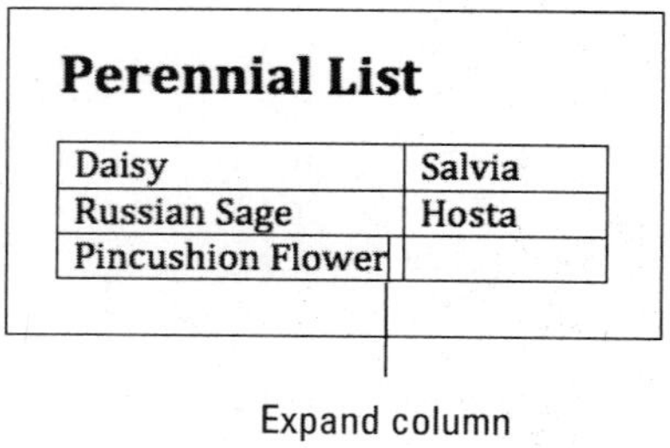

Expand column

If you set up specific measurements for your table columns in the Insert Table dialog box, any text that exceeds the column width is wrapped to the next line in the cell, an action known as *text wrapping*. In Figure 8.12, the same text now wraps to the next line in the cell. If you don't want text to wrap in the table cells, you can turn off the text wrap feature. To do so, you must open the Table Properties dialog box by choosing Table ➪ Table Properties. Next, click the Cell tab, and click the Options button to open the Cell Options dialog box. Deselect the Wrap text check box, and click OK. Click OK again to exit the Table Properties dialog box.

If text wrapping is on, Word wraps the lines of text to fit the cell width.

## Perennial List

| Daisy | Salvia |
|---|---|
| Russian Sage | Hosta |
| Pincushion Flower | |

Wrapped text

If you're typing along and get to the end of the table and need to add another row, just press Tab, and Word inserts it for you so you can keep typing.

Adding text to tables is pretty easy. Adding other types of content is just as easy. Word's tables expand to fit any graphic objects you might add. For example, to add a photo to a cell, click the cell and choose Insert ⇨ Picture ⇨ From File to open the Choose a Picture dialog box. Navigate to the photo you want to insert, and double-click the filename. Word adds it to the table cell, as shown in Figure 8.13. You may have to resize the graphic object to make it fit the way you want.

You can add all sorts of graphical elements into your table cells, such as photos.

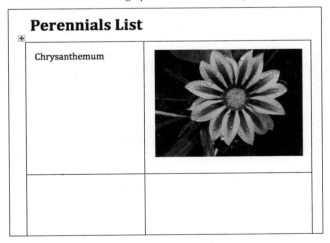

## Perennials List

Chrysanthemum

## Selecting table elements

You need to learn how to select table elements in order to edit them or apply formatting. Selecting parts of a table is sometimes a tricky endeavor. You can select a single cell, groups of cells, columns, rows, or the entire table. You can select text within a cell just like you select any other document text; see Chapter 6 to learn more about basic text selection techniques. Use the following tips and techniques to select table elements:

- To select a cell, click the cell.
- To select multiple cells, drag across the cells.
- To select an entire column, click the top border of the column or Option+click anywhere in the column.
- To select an entire row, click the left border of the row.
- To select an entire table, move the mouse pointer to the upper-left corner of the table and click the table's selection box, or triple-click the beginning of a row. In Figure 8.14, the entire table is selected.
- You also can use the Table menu to select table elements; choose Table ⇨ Select, and then choose the table element.

**FIGURE 8.14**

You can use the table's selection box to select and move the table as a whole.

Selection box

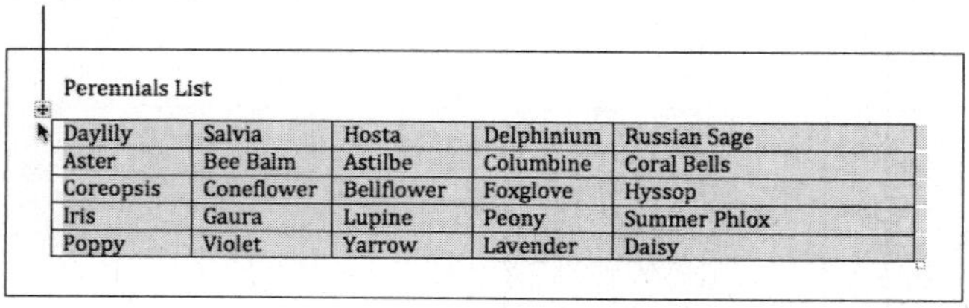

Perennials List

| Daylily | Salvia | Hosta | Delphinium | Russian Sage |
| Aster | Bee Balm | Astilbe | Columbine | Coral Bells |
| Coreopsis | Coneflower | Bellflower | Foxglove | Hyssop |
| Iris | Gaura | Lupine | Peony | Summer Phlox |
| Poppy | Violet | Yarrow | Lavender | Daisy |

## Using the Table pane

When you add a table to a document, the Formatting Palette adds a Table pane to the list of formatting panes, as shown in Figure 8.15. You can find a variety of tools in the pane for working with tables, columns, and rows. If the Formatting Palette is not displayed, click the Toolbox button on the Standard toolbar. Click the Table pane heading to expand the pane and view the tools. To activate a tool, simply click it, or in the case of the Height and Width fields, click the spinner arrows.

Table 8.3 explains the table-oriented tools you can find on the Table pane. Many of these tools can also be found on the Tables and Borders toolbar.

**TABLE 8.3**

# Using the Table Pane

| Button | Name | Description |
|--------|------|-------------|
| | Insert or Draw a Table | Inserts table elements, such as rows or columns, or opens the Insert Table dialog box. |
| | Delete Table | Deletes the selected table. |
| | Draw Table | Turns the drawing feature on or off. |
| | Eraser | Erases table lines you drag over. |
| | Distribute Rows Evenly | Evenly spaces your rows throughout the table. |
| | Distribute Columns Evenly | Evenly spaces your columns throughout the table. |
| | Sort Ascending | Sorts the table in ascending order. |
| | Sort Descending | Sorts the table in descending order. |
| | AutoFit to Contents | Changes the width of the column to accommodate the text. |
| | Table AutoFormat | Opens the AutoFormat dialog box and applies preset formatting to the table. |
| | AutoSum | Applies Excel's AutoSum formula to total a row or column. |
| Auto | Cell Row Height | Increases or decreases cell height. |
| 1" | Cell Column Width | Increases or decreases cell width. |
| | Merge Cells | Merges two or more cells into one large cell. |
| | Split Cells | Splits a large cell into two smaller cells. |
| | Align | Aligns table cell contents. |

FIGURE 8.15

When working with tables, you can quickly access table tools using the Table pane in the Formatting Palette.

## Resizing columns and rows

You can resize the columns and rows in a table, making rows shorter or taller, or making columns thinner or wider. To manually resize columns and rows, move the mouse pointer over the border of any row or column and drag to resize the row or column. Figure 8.16 shows a column resizing by dragging the selected column border.

FIGURE 8.16

To manually resize a row or column, just drag its border.

| Perennials List | | |
|---|---|---|
| Daylily | Salvia | Hosta |
| Aster | Bee Balm | Astilbe |
| Coreopsis | Coneflower | Bellflower |
| Iris | Gaura | Lupine |
| Poppy | Violet | Yarrow |
| Summer Phlox | | |
| Balloon Flower | | |

Drag to resize.

You also can let Word handle all the resizing for you using the AutoFit and Distribute commands. Both of these commands and their subcommands can help you adjust column width and row height to make the table look the way you want. Use any of the following methods to activate the commands:

- To create symmetrically balanced columns and rows, choose Table ⇨ AutoFit and Distribute ⇨ Distribute Rows Evenly or Distribute Columns Evenly. You also can click the Distribute Rows Evenly or Distribute Columns Evenly buttons on the Tables and Borders toolbar.

- To make the table fit the contents of whatever you type into the cells, choose Table ⇨ AutoFit and Distribute ⇨ AutoFit to Contents.

- You also can find the AutoFit to Contents command on the Table pane in the Formatting Palette. Click the AutoFit arrow button, and click AutoFit to Contents.

- Another way to find AutoFit to Contents is to click the Insert or Draw Table arrow button and click AutoFit to Contents.

- Wait, there's one more place to access the AutoFit command: Control-click and choose AutoFit from the context menu and then click the AutoFit command you want to apply.

- To make the table fit the entire width of the page regardless of what you type, choose Table ⇨ AutoFit and Distribute ⇨ AutoFit to Window. You can find the same command available on the AutoFit button on the Table pane or the Insert or Draw Table button on the Tables and Borders toolbar, or you can Control-click and choose AutoFit, AutoFit to Window.

If you prefer to control how big your columns and rows are in a table, you can set your own measurements using the Height and Width fields in the Formatting Palette's Table pane, as shown in Figure 8.17. Simply type a measurement in the appropriate field, or click the spinner arrow buttons to set a measurement.

You also can set the row height, column width, or cell width using the Table Properties dialog box, as shown in Figure 8.18. Choose Table ⇨ Table Properties to open the dialog box. Click the Row tab to set a row height, click the Column tab to set a column width, or click the Cell tab to set a cell size.

---

**FIGURE 8.17**

You can set precise measurements for row height or column width using the Table pane.

**FIGURE 8.18**

You can set precise measurements for a row, column, or cell using the Table Properties dialog box.

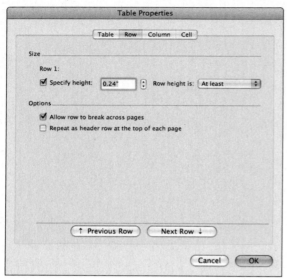

## Inserting and deleting table elements

You can make edits to any of the table elements to modify the table structure. For example, you may find you didn't make your table big enough the first time and you need to add some more rows and columns. Or perhaps you were much too ambitious with the number of cells you created and need to remove some. You find plenty of tools in Word to help you edit the various parts of your tables.

### Inserting columns and rows

If your table needs more columns and rows, you can quickly insert them using the Table menu or the Tables and Borders toolbar. If the Tables and Borders toolbar is not displayed, choose View ➪ Toolbars ➪ Tables and Borders.

Start by clicking where you want to insert a new column or row, and use any of the following techniques:

- To insert a column, choose Table ➪ Insert and choose to insert a column to the right or left of the current cell.

- To insert a row, choose Table ➪ Insert and choose to insert a row above or below the current cell.

- To insert multiple columns or rows, select the number you want of existing columns or rows and apply the Insert Columns or Insert Rows command.

- If the Tables and Borders toolbar is displayed, click the Insert Table arrow icon, as shown in Figure 8.19, and choose what you want to insert. You can insert columns to the left or right or rows above or below.

**FIGURE 8.19**

You can use the pop-up menu to designate how you want columns or rows inserted.

## Deleting columns and rows

You can remove columns and rows you no longer want or need. When you delete columns and rows, any data contained within the cells is deleted as well. Word shifts all the other columns and rows over and up to fill the void. Select the column or row you want to remove, and use any of these techniques:

- To delete a column, choose Table ⇨ Delete ⇨ Columns.
- To delete a row, choose Table ⇨ Delete ⇨ Row.
- You also can Control-click and choose Delete Rows or Delete Columns.

You might think you can simply press the Delete key, but that only deletes the cell contents, not the column or row. Learn how to delete cells entirely coming up next.

## Inserting and deleting cells

You can insert and delete cells in a table. When you insert cells, Word automatically adds a row or column, not just a cell. When you delete cells, Word can literally delete just the cell, leaving a hole where the cell once resided. Whether you're inserting or deleting cells, the steps are the same. The only thing different is the name of the dialog box.

When you add or delete cells, you must tell Word how you want to handle the remaining cells in the column or row. Do you want them to shift left or right, or shift up or down to fill the void? Depending on your location in the table, the option names may vary slightly. Follow these steps to remove cells:

1. **Click where you want to delete a new cell.**
2. **Choose Table ⇨ Delete ⇨ Cells.** You also can click the Eraser arrow button on the Table pane and choose Delete Cells.

   The Delete Cells dialog box opens, as shown in Figure 8.20.
3. **Choose how you want to remove the cells.**
   - To move the existing cells left or up to fill the void, choose a shift option.
   - To remove the entire row or column, click the Delete entire row or Delete entire column radio button.

The Delete Cells dialog box lets you get rid of unwanted cells.

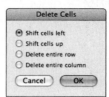

4. **Click OK.**

   Word removes the cells as specified. Figure 8.21 shows an example of a table with one cell removed.

This table is missing one cell.

| We grow numerous Apple Varieties: | |
|---|---|
| Jonathon Gold | Red Delicious |
| Golden Delicious | Fuji |
| Cortland | Honey Crisp |
| McIntosh | Gala |
| Pink Lady | Westland |
| Rome Beauty | |

To insert cells, choose Table ⇨ Insert ⇨ Cells. You also can click the Insert or Draw Table button on the Tables and Borders toolbar, click the arrow button, and choose Insert Cells. The Insert Cells dialog box opens, which looks exactly the same as the Delete Cells dialog box (refer to Figure 8.20). You can choose an insertion option, and click OK to insert the cell.

## Deleting entire tables

You can easily remove tables you no longer want in a document. Select the table (click its table selection box icon in the upper-left corner), and use any of these methods:

- Click the Delete Table button in the Table pane.
- Choose Table ⇨ Delete ⇨ Table.
- Click the Eraser button, and drag across the entire table.

**TIP** You can move a table to another location in your document. The easiest way to move a table is to switch to Print Layout, Web Layout, or Publishing Layout view, select the table selection box, and drag the table to a new location.

### Creating nesting tables

You can insert tables within tables in Word, thus creating *nested tables*. Nested tables are handy when you're using a Word table to create a page layout, or need to present other table information within your main table. To create a nested table, just click inside the cell in which you want to add a table and use any of the table creation methods you learned earlier in this chapter. Figure 8.22 shows a nested table.

**FIGURE 8.22**

You can place a table within a table to create nested tables in Word.

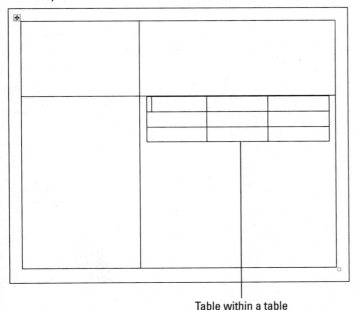

Table within a table

## Merging and splitting cells

Another way you can manipulate a table's structure is by merging or splitting cells. When you merge cells, you take two or more cells and combine them to create one large cell. When you split cells, you're taking a single cell and splitting it into two smaller cells.

To merge cells, follow these steps:

1. **Select the cells you want to merge.**
2. **Click the Merge Cells button on the Tables and Borders toolbar, or choose Table ⇨ Merge Cells.**

   Word merges the cells into one.

To split cells, follow these steps:

1. **Select the cell you want to split.**
2. **Click the Split Cells button on the Tables and Borders toolbar, or choose Table ⇨ Split Cells.**

   Word splits the cell into two.

You also can activate the Draw Table features and simply draw a line to split a cell or erase a line to create a larger cell.

# Formatting Tables

Tables are fairly simple structures, clean and neat in appearance. As such, they look pretty good on their own. You can apply formatting attributes to make them look more interesting. For example, you may want to control how borders are used in a table. You can apply borders to the outside of a table, borders to the inside, borders around every cell, or no borders at all. Borders can help define the structure of your table and make the data within the cells easy to distinguish. Borders are just one example; there are more. Are you ready to see what you can do with formatting? Let's start styling tables.

## Using table formatting attributes

To begin, you'll find options geared just for tables in the Tables and Borders toolbar. You can quickly assign a border; change the line style, thickness, and color; and add shading behind the cell text. To view the toolbar, choose View ⇨ Toolbars ⇨ Tables and Borders. You can play with these attributes as much as you like to create a good-looking table. For example, if you click the Border arrow icon, you can display a pop-up menu of border settings for controlling which lines appear in the table, as shown in Figure 8.23. To apply a border around every cell, choose the All Borders option. To remove any borders, choose the No Border option.

**FIGURE 8.23**

Use the Border control to set different kinds of borders in your table.

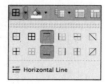

To control the line thickness, click the Line Weight arrow button, as shown in Figure 8.24, and choose a thickness setting from the menu that appears. You can choose from ¼-point thickness to 6-point thickness.

To set a line style, such as dashes, dots, or double-line, click the Line Style button, shown in Figure 8.25, and choose a style.

To change the border color, click the Border Color arrow button and select a color from the color palette, as shown in Figure 8.26.

**FIGURE 8.24**

Use the Line Weight control to set a line thickness for your table borders.

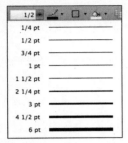

**FIGURE 8.25**

You can assign different styles to borders, including dashes and double-lines.

**FIGURE 8.26**

Use the Border Color control to choose a color for the border lines.

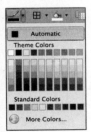

To add a color background, called shading, behind the table cells, click the Shading Color arrow button and choose a color, as shown in Figure 8.27. The palette looks shockingly like the Border Color palette.

Use the Shading Color control to set a background shading in your table cells.

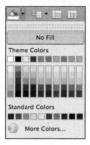

To control the alignment of text within a table cell, you can use the Align button. You also can find table alignment controls on the Table pane in the Formatting Palette. When you click this button, shown in Figure 8.28, you can choose a horizontal or vertical alignment. Your alignment choices are:

- Align Top Left
- Align Top Center
- Align Top Right
- Align Center Left
- Align Center
- Align Center Right
- Align Bottom Left
- Align Bottom Center
- Align Bottom Right

Control alignment in your cells using the Align button.

To create vertical text, click the Change Text Direction button found on the Alignment and Spacing pane. Word rotates the selected cell's text, as shown in Figure 8.29. You can keep clicking the button to arrive at the direction you want to apply.

In addition to these table-specific formatting controls, you also can use the regular formatting tools to change the font, font size, alignment, text color, and so on.

**FIGURE 8.29**

You can create vertical text with the Change Text Direction button.

Change Text Direction

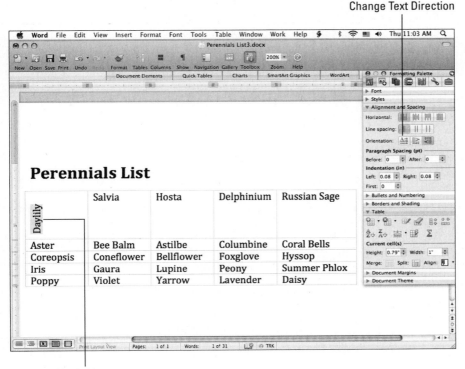

Vertical text

## AutoFormat a table

You can spend lots of time fine-tuning the appearance of your Word tables, tweaking border styles, adding shading, and trying this and that to see how it looks. But if you're short on time and creativity, let Word handle all the formatting for you. How? That's easy—AutoFormatting. The AutoFormat feature taps into a library of preset formatting you can apply to Word tables. The presets include shading for cells, borders, 3-D looks, and more. You can use the Table AutoFormat dialog box to browse through the library of table formatting styles and preview each one. You also can control exactly which formatting attributes to include and which table elements to apply the formatting to—all in one convenient location.

To apply AutoFormat, follow these steps:

1. **Select the table you want to format.**
2. **Click the Table AutoFormat button on the Table pane in the Formatting Palette or on the Tables and Borders toolbar.** You also can choose Table ➪ Table AutoFormat.

   Word opens the Table AutoFormat dialog box, as shown in Figure 8.30.

**FIGURE 8.30**

Scroll through the AutoFormats to find one you want to apply.

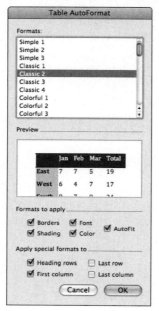

3. **Scroll through the list of formats, and select the one you want.**

   You can preview each format in the Preview area.

   Optionally, you can choose which formats you want to apply by deselecting check boxes.

   You also can choose to apply the formatting to specific parts of your table.

4. **Click OK.**

   Word applies the formatting, as shown in Figure 8.31.

## Adding repeating headings

The first row of a table is typically used as headings in your table structure. For example, your first row might contain labels in each cell for days of the week, financial quarters, category headings, and so on. You may have a table that lists a long inventory of products and prices, for instance. When the table exceeds a document page, you can no longer see the headings for each column. Word has a fix for this, called Heading Rows Repeat. To utilize this command, select the top row of your table and choose Table ➪ Heading Rows Repeat. Word now repeats your top row at the top of each page consumed by your long table.

## Controlling cell margins and spacing

When you create a table, Word assigns default margins inside the cells. You can set your own margins using the Table Properties dialog box. For example, you may want no margins in a cell containing a photo so you can resize it to fit the entire cell, or you may want extra space outside the cells if you're using a table to create a page layout for a Web page. A measurement of .1 or less can make for a very attractive appearance; anything more than this creates a table that resembles a waffle.

**FIGURE 8.31**

For fast table formatting, AutoFormat is the way to go.

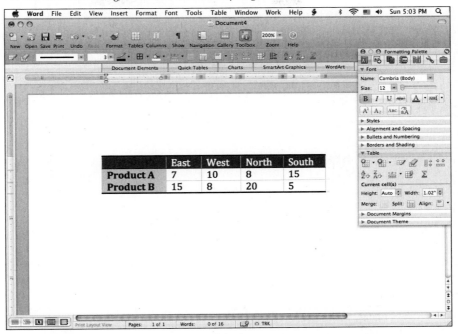

To set cell margins and spacing for the entire table, follow these steps:

1. **Select the table.**
2. **Choose Table ⇨ Table Properties.**

   Word opens the Table Properties dialog box, as shown in Figure 8.32.

3. **Click the Table tab.**
4. **Click the Options button.**

   Word opens the Table Options dialog box, shown in Figure 8.33.

5. **In the Default cell margins fields, set the cell margins you want to use.**

   You can type a measurement or click the spinner arrows to set a measurement.

# Wrapping Text around Tables

You can use Word's text wrapping command to control how document text flows around a table you insert onto a page. By default, the text wrap is set to None, which means text cannot flow around a table. Using the Table Properties dialog box, you can set text wrapping to Around. Choose Table ⇨ Table Properties to open the dialog box. Click the Table tab, and choose the Around text wrapping option at the bottom of the dialog box. When you activate the Around option, you can click the Positioning button to open the Positioning dialog box and set exact positions for the table.

**FIGURE 8.32**

The Table Properties dialog box has settings for controlling the table, rows, columns, and cells.

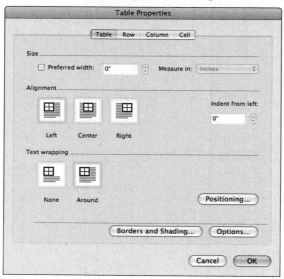

**FIGURE 8.33**

You can control cell margins for the entire table using the Table Options dialog box.

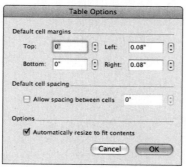

6. To control spacing between cells, set a measurement in the **Allow spacing between cells** field.

   A setting of .1 or less looks great, but a larger setting creates the waffle effect discussed earlier.

7. **Click OK.**

8. **Click OK again to exit the Table Properties dialog box.**

   Word applies the changes to the table.

To set cell margins and spacing for a selected cell or group of cells, follow these steps:

1. **Select the cells you want to edit.**
2. **Choose Table ⇨ Table Properties.**

   Word opens the Table Properties dialog box, as shown in Figure 8.32.
3. **Click the Cell tab.**
4. **Click the Options button.**

   Word opens the Cell Options dialog box, shown in Figure 8.34.

**FIGURE 8.34**

You can control cell margins in the Cell Options dialog box.

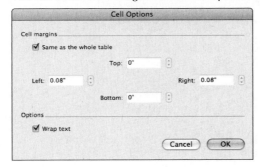

5. **Deselect the Same as whole table check box.**
6. **Set the cell's margins using the Top, Left, Bottom, and Right fields.**

   You can type a measurement or click the spinner arrows to set a measurement.
7. **Click OK.**
8. **Click OK again to exit the Table Properties dialog box.**

   Word applies the changes to the table.

# Performing Table Actions

Lest you think your Word tables are just static containers for text, allow me to introduce you to a couple of unique actions you can perform with your tables. First, you can sort your tables and redisplay their contents based on an alphabetical sort in ascending or descending order. Second, you can use the AutoSum function to quickly produce a sum total for a column or row of numeric data. Sound intriguing? Keep reading.

## Sorting a table

You can sort a table based on a heading. For example, if your table's first row contains headings that describe the rest of the table, you can sort the entire table based on one heading in the table. Perhaps your table lists various types of flowers with headings for Latin plant names, bloom season, and flower color. You can sort the entire list by flower color using the Flower Color table heading.

To perform a sort, follow these steps:

1. **Click the table heading you want to sort by.**
2. **Click the Sort Ascending or Sort Descending button in the Table pane or on the Tables and Borders toolbar.**

   Word sorts the table, as shown in Figure 8.35.

**FIGURE 8.35**

This table is assorted alphabetically based on the listed flower color.

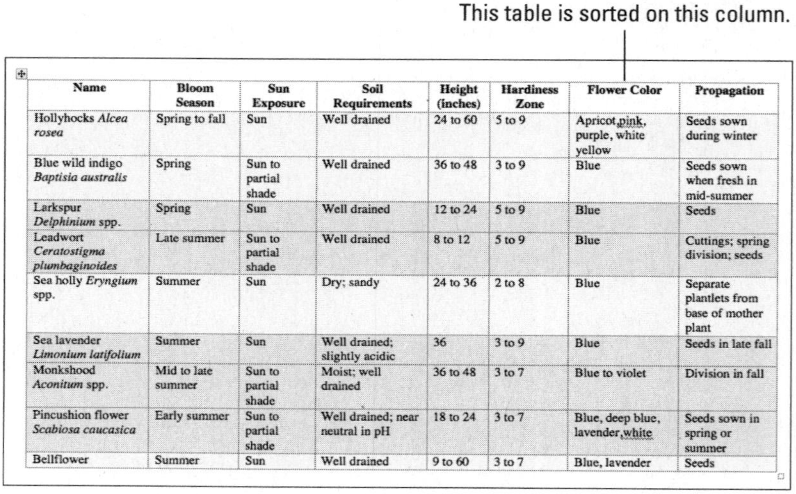

This table is sorted on this column.

| Name | Bloom Season | Sun Exposure | Soil Requirements | Height (inches) | Hardiness Zone | Flower Color | Propagation |
|------|------|------|------|------|------|------|------|
| Hollyhocks *Alcea rosea* | Spring to fall | Sun | Well drained | 24 to 60 | 5 to 9 | Apricot,pink, purple, white yellow | Seeds sown during winter |
| Blue wild indigo *Baptisia australis* | Spring | Sun to partial shade | Well drained | 36 to 48 | 3 to 9 | Blue | Seeds sown when fresh in mid-summer |
| Larkspur *Delphinium* spp. | Spring | Sun | Well drained | 12 to 24 | 5 to 9 | Blue | Seeds |
| Leadwort *Ceratostigma plumbaginoides* | Late summer | Sun to partial shade | Well drained | 8 to 12 | 5 to 9 | Blue | Cuttings; spring division; seeds |
| Sea holly *Eryngium* spp. | Summer | Sun | Dry; sandy | 24 to 36 | 2 to 8 | Blue | Separate plantlets from base of mother plant |
| Sea lavender *Limonium latifolium* | Summer | Sun | Well drained; slightly acidic | 36 | 3 to 9 | Blue | Seeds in late fall |
| Monkshood *Aconitum* spp. | Mid to late summer | Sun to partial shade | Moist; well drained | 36 to 48 | 3 to 7 | Blue to violet | Division in fall |
| Pincushion flower *Scabiosa caucasica* | Early summer | Sun to partial shade | Well drained; near neutral in pH | 18 to 24 | 3 to 7 | Blue, deep blue, lavender,white | Seeds sown in spring or summer |
| Bellflower | Summer | Sun | Well drained | 9 to 60 | 3 to 7 | Blue, lavender | Seeds |

If your table is much more complex, you can perform detailed sorts using the Sort dialog box. Choose Table ⇨ Sort to open the dialog box, shown in Figure 8.36.

## Summing table data

You can use the AutoSum tool to quickly insert a sum of cells in a table. For example, AutoSum automatically sums the row or column based on its location in the table. If you click in the last cell in a row and activate AutoSum, the function totals all the cells in the row to the left of the current cell. If you click in the last cell in a column and activate AutoSum, it totals all the cells above the current cell.

To apply the AutoSum function, follow these steps:

1. **Click the cell where you want to add a sum.**
2. **Click the AutoSum button in the Table pane or on the Tables and Borders toolbar.**

   Word sums the row or column, as shown in Figure 8.37.

You can use other Excel functions in your Word tables as well. Choose Table ⇨ Formulas to open the Formula dialog box, shown in Figure 8.38. By default, the function is set to SUM. To enter another formula, delete the existing field, type an = sign, and enter your formula. To control the format of the numeric results, click the Number format pop-up menu and choose a numeric format. When you click OK, the formula results are applied to the current cell.

**FIGURE 8.36**

Use the Sort dialog box to perform more detailed sorts based on your table headings.

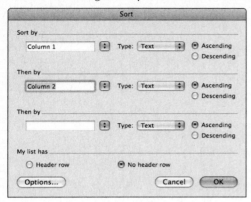

**FIGURE 8.37**

Use the AutoSum tool to add a sum total to a cell.

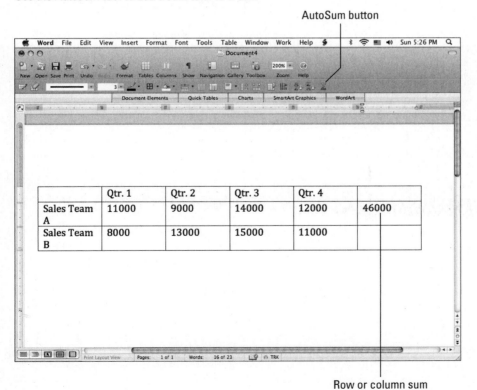

FIGURE 8.38

**FIGURE 8.38**

You can use the Formula dialog box to write formulas for your table.

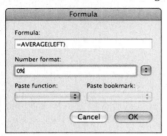

# Summary

In this chapter, you learned a variety of ways to create tables. You learned how to use the Elements Gallery to insert Quick Tables, which are preset table designs that install with Microsoft Word. You also learned how easy it is to build your own tables using the Tables button on the Standard toolbar or the Insert Tables dialog box. If that wasn't enough, you learned how to create custom tables by literally drawing them on the document page. Using the table drawing tools, you can draw the exact size of the table and control where columns and rows appear.

This chapter also showed you what to do after creating a table structure. You learned about the plentiful tools available to help you work with the structure and contents, and make the table look good. You saw how you can choose from a wide variety of preset formatting to apply to your tables through the AutoFormat feature. If you prefer to format manually, the Tables and Borders toolbar offers a variety of tools for editing and working with tables, and you can find the same tools in the Table pane on the Formatting Palette. Both of these areas offer you quick access to table commands, but you also can access table commands through the Table menu.

Regardless of how you create your table, how you format it, or what it holds, you'll quickly see how useful and flexible tables can be in your document building tasks.

# Chapter 9

# Editing Lengthy Documents

Creating a short document can be as easy as opening a new document and typing away. Formatting a long document—one that might require page numbers, footnotes, or an index—is a trickier proposition. Fortunately, Word makes it easy to automatically paginate, customize headers and footers, keep track of footnotes, and even generate a table of contents and an index. This allows you to concentrate primarily on your content rather than its presentation.

If you're someone who works in the world of lengthy documents frequently, styles and templates can be an even greater time-saver. This chapter explains how to use Word features that are helpful in formatting and handling long documents and how to use templates and styles to make the process even easier in the future.

## IN THIS CHAPTER

**Creating and modifying templates**

**Using styles**

**Adding footnotes and indices**

**Formatting headers and footers**

## Using the Navigation Pane

One of the most challenging aspects of working in a long document is navigating the sheer number of pages it can contain. When a document has multiple chapters, a table of contents, footnotes, an index, and so on, wading through these various elements, along with the content itself, can be cumbersome. The Navigation Pane and Document Map can help you quickly locate the page you need.

To access the Navigation Pane, click the Navigation button in the Standard toolbar or choose View➪Navigation Pane. The Navigation Pane, shown in Figure 9.1, opens on the left side of your document. By default, the pane opens in Thumbnail view, providing small images of each page in the document. You can move to a different page by scrolling down the pane to the page you require and clicking the thumbnail.

**FIGURE 9.1**

The Navigation Pane provides a shortcut to access the pages of your document.

NOTE  **The Navigation Pane works regardless of the View you're using. Even if you prefer to work in Draft view, the Navigation Pane displays the pages in Print Layout view for thumbnail purposes. Although too small to read, the Navigation Pane can provide a work-at-a-glance overview of how your pages are flowing, especially if you have headings that stand out as visual landmarks within the text.**

## Switching to the Document Map

A complement to the Navigation Pane, the Document Map provides even more navigational control over your document. To switch from the Navigation Pane to the Document Map, click the down-arrow at the top of the Navigation Pane and switch from Thumbnail to Document Map.

The Document Map, shown in Figure 9.2, displays the headings within the document. The easiest way to create a heading is to apply a Heading style, as explained later in this chapter. You also can create headings in the Outline view by applying an outline level to a text selection, which automatically applies a Heading style, so it's just another means to the same end. Outlines were explained in Chapter 6.

When you open the Document Map, all the sub-headings are fully expanded by default. To close or open a heading to reveal any subheadings, click the triangle to the left of the main heading or Control+click a heading within the Document Map and choose Collapse or Expand. To view only the main headings throughout the document, Control+click within the Document Map and select Show Heading 1. This collapses the entire outline to display only the top level (Level 1 in Outline View or the Heading 1 style) of headings. You can select any level of sub-headings you want to display in the Document Map, using this context menu. Selecting Show Heading 2, for example, collapses the outline to display only Levels 1 and 2.

**FIGURE 9.2**

The Document Map displays all the headings in the document for easy navigation.

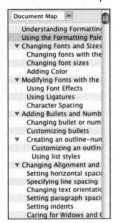

## Customizing the Document Map

Unlike the document window, the Document Map doesn't have a horizontal scrollbar, nor do the headings wrap. If you want to widen the Document Map to see the complete headings, click on the blue Resize bar between the Document Map and the document window. The cursor changes to a double-arrow, allowing you to increase or decrease the size of the Document Map.

By default, the Document Map is formatted in Lucida Grande 12 font. You can change the appearance of the Document Map by modifying its style. To do this:

1. **Click anywhere in the Document Map.**
2. **Choose Format ➪ Style.**
3. **Choose Document Map from the list of Styles.**
4. **Click the Modify button to open the Modify Style dialog box.**
5. **In the Formatting area, choose a new font, size, or any other text effect.**
6. **Click OK to close the Modify Style dialog box, and then click Apply to close the Styles dialog box and apply the new style to the Document Map.**

Other versions of Word also allow you to change the highlight color in the Document Map. In Word 2008, this feature has a glitch. Changing the highlight color also changes the formatting of the actual headings in your document. We hope this bug is fixed in future updates.

**CAUTION**　Although it can be incredibly helpful, Word has a habit of reformatting your document when you use it. Never open a Word file with the Document Map already open. In these conditions, Word often adds extra Level 1 headings to short paragraphs. Also, if you notice that you suddenly have extra Heading 1 entries appearing in your Document Map, check your Undo list to see if Word has used AutoFormat to apply additional headings. An alternative to using the Document Map is to work on long documents in Outline view. This view goes beyond the functionality of the Document Map, allowing you to rearrange your headings, add body text, and quickly format your document. Remember, just because a feature is there doesn't mean you have to use it, nor is it always the best tool for the job.

# Using Styles

Let's say you want to create a heading for a section of your document. You want the heading to appear in a powerful font, stand out from the rest of your text in size and in bold face, with an underline extending across the entire page. If you're creating a short document with only one or two such headings, it may not seem like much to select the text and use the Formatting Palette or dialog boxes to make each of these changes to the selection. If your document is 20 pages long (or even longer), however, with dozens of these headings and subheadings, this task becomes arduous. If the document also contains indented quotations and figures with captions, your focus quickly turns from your content to tedious, repetitive formatting.

A key time-saver in working with long documents is using styles. A style is a collection of formatting instructions that can be applied to a block of text. Rather than changing the font, spacing, and alignment of a paragraph in separate steps, you can create a style containing this group of formatting options and then apply the style in one click. Even more, if you decide to change the formatting for an element of your document, such as the headings, modifying the style automatically updates all the iterations where you applied it.

Some styles are purely for aesthetics, while others have an additional, functional purpose. As you've seen by the description of the Document Map, using the Heading styles can graphically enhance your document and can provide a navigational aid in the Document Map. Heading styles also can be used to generate a Table of Contents, as you see later in this chapter.

## Applying styles

Documents are based on templates, a collection of styles and other settings to format the document. Even when you open a New Blank Document, Word applies the Normal template, containing pre-formatted styles. Other templates, such as the Stationery options in the Projects Gallery, utilize styles to format the document. Templates are explained later in this chapter.

You can make a selection and choose a style to apply, or you can select a style before you begin typing the paragraph. You can apply a style in three ways:

- Choose from the Styles pane of the Formatting Palette, as shown in Figure 9.3.
- Choose Format ⇨ Style to open the Style dialog box, seen in Figure 9.4, and then choose from the Styles list. The dialog box offers the most comprehensive list of available styles and offers a preview of how the style will affect your selection.
- Choose from the Style list in the Formatting toolbar, shown in Figure 9.5. If the Formatting toolbar is not already open, press Shift+⌘+S to open the Formatting toolbar and highlight the Style list.

Some styles are intended to format an entire paragraph, while others can be applied to individual characters or a selection within a paragraph. The four different types of styles are shown in Table 9.1. You can differentiate between the different types by looking at the blue identifier to the right of the style name in any of the three style lists.

**NOTE** If you apply a paragraph style to an individual or selection of characters, Word applies the character formatting of the style to the selection without applying the paragraph formatting of the style. This feature is quirky sometimes, occasionally reformatting the entire paragraph to match the style you apply only to a selection, so stay on your toes and look carefully at the paragraph after making these changes to ensure that you got the expected results.

## FIGURE 9.3

The Styles pane offers a fast way to apply a style.

## FIGURE 9.4

The Style dialog box provides a complete list of styles and options to modify and organize them.

**FIGURE 9.5**

The Style menu in the Formatting toolbar provides easy access to styles and their shortcuts.

**TABLE 9.1**

## Types of Styles

| Identifier | Style Type | Purpose |
|---|---|---|
| ¶ | Paragraph | Can contain a combination of character (font, size, effects, and so on) and paragraph (spacing, alignment, indents, and so on) formatting. Headings are Paragraph styles because they not only determine the appearance of the characters but also their horizontal alignment on the page and the space between the heading and the preceding/following paragraphs. |
| a | Character | Contains character formatting, including font, size, text effects, and color. |
| ⊞ | Table | Contains the formatting for an entire table, including the spacing, borders, shading, and fonts for both the headings and content of the table. Some table styles automatically alternate the shading for alternating rows or columns and adjust themselves as you modify the table. |
| ≡ | List | Contains the numbering and bullet formatting for a list, including all the possible levels within the list. These styles are very limiting, so they are not used very often. The Bullets and Numbering feature provides much more control and is, thus, a better method for formatting lists. |

## Creating styles

You can create a style in several ways. One of the easiest methods is to modify a selection with the formatting options you require and then save the text as a style. Follow these steps:

1. **Type your text, and press Return.**

2. **Select the paragraph, or position the insertion point within the paragraph.**

3. **Use the Formatting Palette, toolbar, or dialog boxes to format the paragraph exactly as you desire.** See Chapter 7 to learn how to format your text.

4. **Create the new style using one of these methods:**
   - Click the New Style… button in the Styles pane of the Formatting Palette.
   - Choose Format ➪ Style, and click the New button.

5. **In the New Style dialog box, shown in Figure 9.6, enter a name for the style in the Name field.**

6. **Click OK.** If you opened the Style dialog box, click Apply to close it.

---

**FIGURE 9.6**

The New Style dialog box allows you to create your own custom styles.

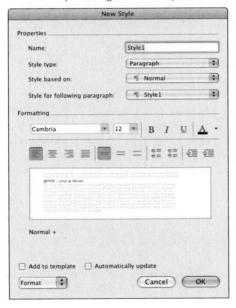

## Naming styles

You also can use a shortcut to create new styles. Follow Steps 1 through 3, click the Style list in the Formatting toolbar, and type a new name. This automatically creates a new style without having to open any dialog boxes. Using the Formatting toolbar to create and apply styles affords another advantage. When you create a new style, you can assign it both a name and a shortcut. If you create a style named Photograph Caption, for example, you can assign it a shortcut named PC. Then, when you want to apply this style, you can press Shift+⌘+S, type PC in the Style box, and press Return.

You can create a shortcut for a style at the same time you create the new style. In either the New Style dialog box or the Style menu of the Formatting toolbar, type the name you want for your new style, followed by a comma and the shortcut. In the example above, you would type "Photograph Caption, PC" when creating the style. The Style menu then recognizes both Photograph Caption and PC as relating to the same style.

Be sure to give your styles meaningful names. You might feel clever when you create a style named Gotcha in the early afternoon, but you will be very frustrated if you can't remember which style you intended for photo captions at midnight when you want to finish a project and get to sleep. In this event, look either at the pop-up tips in the Styles pane of the Formatting palette or the description in the Style dialog box to view the formatting for the styles in your list until you find the one you intended. But it is much simpler to name your styles with care in the first place.

## Using the New Style dialog box

The New Style dialog box, shown previously in Figure 9.6, offers more control over style creation. Instead of creating styles based on examples, you can format them completely within the dialog box using the following options:

- **Name:** This is the name you want to assign to the new style. As mentioned above, you can add a comma and an abbreviation or shortcut for faster access through the Formatting toolbar.

- **Style type:** This refers to the four types of styles—paragraph, character, table, and list. The style type is automatically assigned when you create a style based on an example.

- **Style based on:** A style can inherit properties from existing styles. If you want to make styles to format an envelope, for example, you can create a style for the addressee's name to be in a particular font and alignment, and then create a new style for the address itself based on the addressee style, changing only the size but retaining the font and alignment of the addressee's name. If you later decide to change the font, modify the addressee style, which automatically updates all the styles that are based upon it.

- **Style for following paragraph:** When you press the Return key, the style of the new paragraph is determined by its predecessor. In most cases, the new paragraph inherits the same style as its predecessor. You can, however, instruct the next paragraph to take on a different specified style. The Heading 1 style, for example, automatically formats the paragraph following it with the Normal style. In the envelope example, a paragraph with the addressee style would presumably always be followed by two or more lines utilizing an address style. Thus, the Style for the following paragraph in the Addressee style would be Address (or whatever you named those styles).

- **Formatting:** These are the standard formatting options for both characters and paragraphs. You can access the dialog boxes associated with each formatting option by pressing the Format button at the bottom of the dialog box and choosing the appropriate option. The Preview area displays an example of the formatted text while the exact nature of the style is iterated in words below the preview.

- **Add to template:** Select this box if you want the new style to be added to the current template. Any new documents you create based on this template have this style available. Be careful when adding styles to the Normal template. It's best to keep that uncluttered so you can use it as the basis for new templates.

- **Automatically update:** When selected, this option causes every paragraph formatted with this style to be updated whenever you modify any paragraph with that style. If you want to globally change the style by the new example, this option is very helpful. If you simply want to change one paragraph, however, having this option selected can cause problems.

If you select the Format button, you can choose to open one of several dialog boxes providing complete control over various aspects of your text. You have these options:

- **Font:** This opens the Font dialog box. See Chapter 7 to learn more about font options.

- **Paragraph:** This opens the Paragraph dialog box, also described in Chapter 7.

- **Tabs:** This opens the Tabs dialog box, described in Chapter 6.

- **Border:** This opens the Borders and Shading dialog box, described in Chapter 7.

- **Language:** This opens the Language dialog box. Changing the Language settings for a style opens the dictionary and proofing tools for that language. This is useful when you have a block of text in a foreign language.

- **Frame:** This opens the Frame dialog box. A frame is similar to a text box, but more limited in functionality.

- **Numbering:** This opens the Bullets and Numbering dialog box, described in Chapter 7.

- **Shortcut Key:** This allows you to assign a keyboard shortcut to the style, whereupon you can apply the style using the keyboard instead of using the mouse to access the palette, toolbar, or dialog box. Keyboard shortcuts are covered in Chapter 34.

When you create a new style, it appears in the various style lists after you click OK.

**TIP** Using the New Style dialog box, you can quickly create a complete series of styles. Choose Format ⇨ Style, click the New button, and create the new style. Then press OK to return to the Style dialog box, and press the New button again to repeat the process.

## Modifying and deleting styles

You can modify a style in much the same way as you create one. Select Format ⇨ Style to open the Style dialog box, choose a style from the list, and click the Modify button. Alternatively, hover over one of the styles in the Styles pane of the Formatting palette, click the down-arrow that appears, and choose Modify Style. Either action opens the Modify Style dialog box, shown in Figure 9.7.

**FIGURE 9.7**

The Modify Style dialog box allows you to change the formatting for an existing style.

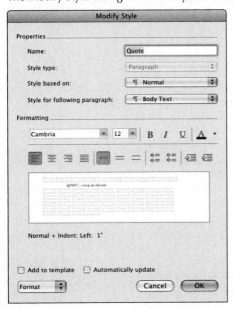

The Modify Style dialog box is almost identical to the New Style dialog box. You can change formatting options in the Formatting area or click the Format button at the bottom to open the various dialog boxes to further modify the font, paragraph, tabs, border, language, frame, numbering, or shortcut key settings.

To delete a style, open the Style dialog box by choosing Format ➪ Style, choose the unwanted style from the list, and click the Delete button. You can delete styles you create, but you cannot delete Word's built-in styles.

## Organizing styles

As you work on a long document or create a series of your own styles, you will want to make them available within other templates. To do this, choose the Organizer button in the Style dialog box. You also can open the Organizer by choosing Tools ➪ Templates and Add-ins and then clicking Organizer. The Organizer, shown in Figure 9.8, helps organize not only styles, but also AutoText entries and custom or modified toolbars.

**FIGURE 9.8**

The Organizer allows you to create a style, AutoText, or toolbar once and copy it to multiple templates.

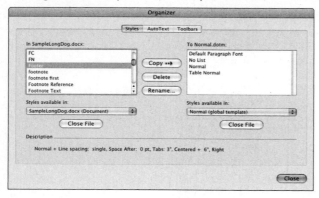

The left box in the Organizer lists the styles in the current document or template. The box on the right lists the styles in the current global template (usually Normal.dotm). If you want to transfer styles between two different templates, click the Close File button under one of the templates and click Open File to choose a new template in that column.

To transfer styles between templates, click a style name in one of the templates and click the Copy button between the two columns. You can transfer styles in both directions; the arrow on the Copy button changes appropriately when you select a style from one of the columns. You also can use the Organizer to delete or rename styles. If the name you gave to a style in one template is not appropriate for the new template, you can copy it and then rename the style. When you are finished, click Close.

**CAUTION**   Be careful when transferring styles, especially to the Normal template. After you click Close, you cannot undo your changes without returning to the Organizer and manually copying or deleting styles.

> **NOTE** You can use the Organizer in the same fashion to transfer AutoText entries and toolbars. Choose the appropriate button at the top of the Organizer dialog box, and the list in each column changes to the related elements.

# Using and Creating Templates

You've already learned lots about templates in this chapter, and we haven't even covered them yet. A template stores your styles, AutoText entries, custom toolbars, document margins, paper type, and all the other myriad settings for your document. You can use a template an infinite number of times without having to rename the document, copy the contents, or save over an existing document. All this is usually handled behind the scenes, and you can get by in Word without ever understanding the details of templates. If you do so, however, you're missing out on one of its most powerful tools.

Templates offer several advantages. If you run a business, edit your child's school newsletter, write papers for school or work, or are writing the great American novel, using a template can ensure a consistent appearance and provide you with shortcuts so you don't have to format each document from scratch. Templates can be transferred to other computers and users, so your co-workers' documents will match yours in appearance, and they'll have access to the same toolbars, macros, and AutoText settings.

Even if you aren't consciously working with templates, they're still working for you. Even blank documents are based on a template (named Normal.dotm), which provides the initial margin and font settings. All the documents in the Projects Gallery are actually templates formatted with the layout and elements you need to create your flyer, calendar, business letter, and so on.

## Attaching a template

A template is a separate file from your actual document. This file is attached to your document, which allows the document to assume all the elements it contains. You can attach a template in Word in three ways.

### Opening a template from the Project Gallery

The Project Gallery contains a wide array of templates for the most common types of documents. These range from simple letterhead for correspondence to elaborate newsletter and flyer layouts in assorted colors. Most of these templates are not specifically intended for lengthy documents, but some can form the basis of such a document. Chapter 5 explained how to use the Project Gallery to create a new document. Now you realize that when you make such a document, you're actually creating a new file and attaching a template.

The Project Gallery also stores any templates you download or create. There are hundreds of templates available for all the Office for Mac applications on the Microsoft Web site (`www.microsoft.com/mac/templates.mspx`). You also may receive templates from co-workers or find them on other Web sites. When you download or receive a template, save it in your User ⇨ Library ⇨ Application Support ⇨ Microsoft ⇨ Office ⇨ User Templates ⇨ My Templates folder. When you revisit the Project Gallery, you will find your templates in the My Templates folder, as shown in Figure 9.9.

> **NOTE** Word templates use a .dot, .dotx, or .dotm extension. Word 2008 can use all three formats. Windows versions of Word, however, do not recognize the .dotm extension. If you plan to share your templates with Windows users, you need to save them with the .dotx extension for Windows 2007 or the .dot extension for any previous versions.

## FIGURE 9.9

Templates you download or create appear in the My Templates folder in the Project Gallery.

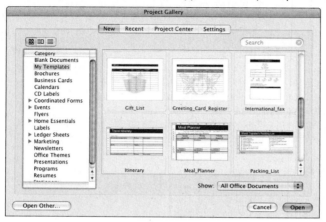

### Attaching a template through the Templates and Add-Ins tool

If you create a new document and later realize you should have attached a particular template, you can do so after the fact. To attach a template to an existing document, follow these steps:

1. **Choose Tools ⇨ Templates and Add-ins.** This opens the Templates and Add-ins dialog box, shown in Figure 9.10.
2. **Press the Attach button.** This opens the Choose a File dialog box, as shown in Figure 9.11.
3. **Select the template you want to attach.** The chooser opens to the User Templates folder (User ⇨ Library ⇨ Application Support ⇨ Microsoft ⇨ Office ⇨ User Templates) by default. If you want to attach one of the built-in templates from the Project Gallery, navigate to Applications ⇨ Microsoft Office 2008 ⇨ Office ⇨ Media ⇨ Templates.
4. **Click Open to select the template and return to the Templates and Add-ins dialog box.**
5. **Click OK to accept your changes and exit the Templates and Add-ins dialog box.**

**NOTE** When you attach the new template, don't expect to see dramatic changes. The styles in the new template don't transfer to the new document unless you check the Automatically update document styles box in the Templates and Add-ins dialog box or copy the styles from the new template to your document using the Organizer. Attaching a template in this manner also does not transfer any graphics or text (called boilerplate) from the template. If those are what you're after, create a new document using the desired template from the Project Gallery and then copy and paste your content there.

### Loading global templates

Some templates are automatically attached to the document without any effort on your part. These are called *global templates,* and they include the Normal.dotm file, which is the default basis of blank documents. Global templates are identical to document templates, but they are automatically available to any document created in Word.

**FIGURE 9.10**

The Templates and Add-ins dialog box enables you to attach and organize templates.

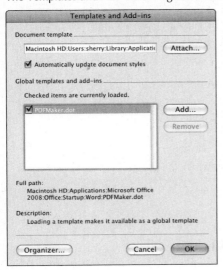

**FIGURE 9.11**

The Choose a File dialog box automatically opens to the User Templates folder.

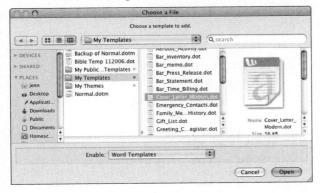

You can create additional global templates and automatically attach them to documents. Unlike document templates, you can attach more than one global template to a single document. Thus, you can create a global template containing toolbars, macros, and AutoText for working with a specific client, and then use that template for any project you're completing for that client. Such a template might contain AutoText that converts the company's initials into the full name of the company, for example. Better still, you can load that template as a global template while still attaching a different template that's specific to the type of document you're creating, such as a meeting agenda.

Global templates are loaded rather than attached. To do this, follow these steps:

1. **Open a new blank document.**
2. **Choose Tools ⇨ Templates and Add-ins.**
3. **Click Add in the Global Templates and Add-ins area.** This opens the Choose a File dialog box.
4. **Select the template you want to load.** This can be any Word template on your computer.
5. **Click Open.**
6. **The new global template appears in the Global Templates list, as shown in Figure 9.12.** The template is checked by default.
7. **Click OK to return to your document.**

**FIGURE 9.12**

You can attach multiple global templates by checking them in the Global Templates list.

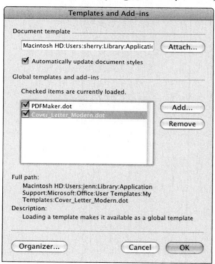

After a global template is loaded, it remains available to any and all documents you create in Word unless you unload or deselect it. In our example from earlier, if all your work for a period of time is for one client, you can leave that client's global template loaded until the completion of the entire project. If you're juggling with multiple clients, you need to load and unload the global template specific to each client as you work.

## Modifying templates

Although the preformatted templates in Word are helpful, they're rarely exactly what you want. Your company might use a different font or color scheme, and it certainly will have its own corporate logo. You might want wider margins on the left so you can punch holes in your document to insert it into a three-ring binder. There's almost always something you'll want to tweak.

To modify a template, edit the template file directly:

1. **Choose File ➪ Open, and navigate to the template you want to modify:**
   - **For templates you've created or installed:** User ➪ Library ➪ Application Support ➪ Microsoft ➪ Office ➪ User Templates.
   - **For built-in templates:** Applications ➪ Microsoft Office 2008 ➪ Office ➪ Media ➪ Templates.
2. **Modify the document as needed using the formatting tools (see Chapter 7 if you need help).**
3. **Save the template:**
   - **To save your changes into the original template:** Choose File ➪ Save.
   - **To create a new template based on the original with your modifications:** Choose File ➪ Save As, and then give the file a new name. Be sure to save the template with the proper template extension (.dotx, .dotm, or .dot) depending on whether the template will be shared with people using Windows.

After you've modified a template, any new documents you create with the template use the new formatting. If you've created previous documents with that template, however, they are not updated. To apply the changes to those documents, open each one and choose Tools ➪ Templates and Add-ins, check the Automatically update document styles box, and then click OK.

## Creating new templates

As you just learned, one of the easiest ways to create a new template is to modify an existing one and then save it under a new name. This allows you to customize your documents without reinventing the wheel. You also can create a template from scratch. Here's how:

1. **Choose File ➪ New Blank Document.**
2. **Set any document formatting options you want: page orientation, margins, tabs, AutoText entries, custom menus and toolbars, and macros.**
3. **Add any boilerplate text and graphics, and set any character, paragraph, and section formatting options.**
4. **Choose File ➪ Save As.**
5. **Click the Format pop-up menu, and choose Word Template.** If your template contains macros, choose Word Macro-Enabled Template from the Specialty options in the Format menu.
6. **Name your template file.**
7. **Click Save.**

After you've created a template, it functions just like any other template. You can open new documents with it using the Project Gallery. You can attach it or load it as a global template. You also can modify it.

# Adding Line and Page Breaks

Styles and templates help you format your document. There's much more to a long document than just the overall appearance, however. As you write the document, many details are sure to crop up. One of these is adding manual breaks in your text.

A break instructs Word to stop the flow of text in some manner. In Chapters 6 and 7, you learned about paragraph, column, and section breaks. Two other types of breaks take on greater importance when preparing lengthy documents.

Line breaks are similar to paragraph breaks. A line break interrupts the flow of text and moves the following text to a new line. Unlike a paragraph break, however, a line break remains part of the preceding paragraph, as does the text that follows. The text after the line break retains the style and formatting of the paragraph, and changes to the paragraph style automatically apply to the entire paragraph. Line breaks also are referred to as *soft returns* and are commonly used when typing an address. To insert a line break, press Shift+Return.

A page break interrupts the flow of text to move the text that follows onto a new page. This is known as a *hard break*. When you insert a hard break, the text that follows forms a new paragraph, even if it's in the middle of a block of text. Hard breaks are often used to position the start of a new heading at the top of a new page. To insert a page break, choose Insert ⇨ Break ⇨ Page Break. For the keyboard shortcut, press Shift+fn+Return.

# Turning On Hyphenation

When you read a newspaper, the columns are both left- and right-justified to create a uniform appearance. In order to preserve this appearance without inserting awkward spaces between words or stretching out letters to fill empty space (as was done in very early versions of word processors), newspapers make heavy use of hyphens to split words between lines. Word does not hyphenate by default, but you can enable the automatic hyphenation feature should you find the need for it.

To enable hyphenation, choose Tools ⇨ Hyphenation. In the Hyphenation dialog box, shown in Figure 9.13, choose Automatically hyphenate document. You also should consider these additional hyphenation settings:

- **Hyphenate words in CAPS:** Most letters typed in all-caps are acronyms, abbreviations, or words that are intended to stand out in your text. This setting is not selected by default because you generally don't want to split this text.

- **Hyphenation zone:** This is the amount of empty space Word allows at the end of a line before automatically breaking up a word with a hyphen. If you set a small hyphenation zone, Word is more diligent about its task, breaking even smaller two-syllable words with hyphens in order to make the margin as even as possible, but at the expense of lots of hyphens. Setting a larger hyphenation zone results in fewer hyphens, which offers more readable text, but sometimes at the expense of a more jagged appearance.

- **Limit consecutive hyphens:** The occasional hyphen doesn't stop your audience from reading your text. Too many hyphens, however, are visually unappealing and lower readability and comprehension. A good general rule is to set this option to 2.

After you enable hyphenation, Word scans the document and inserts hyphens where it thinks they're appropriate, based on its built-in dictionary. Word inserts additional hyphens as you continue to type. If you find this distracting while you work, wait until you've finished entering your content to enable this feature.

---

**FIGURE 9.13**

Word can automatically hyphenate words to preserve the flow of text across columns or pages.

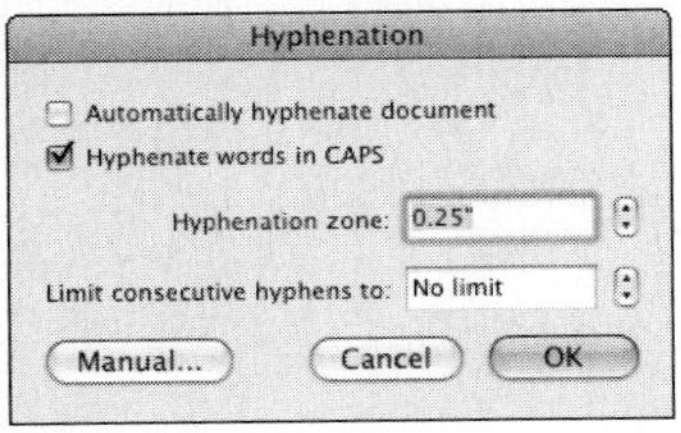

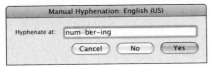

## Manually hyphenating

As its name implies, automatic hyphenation takes place automatically, without consulting you regarding individual changes. If you want more control over your words, use manual hyphenation. This method works similarly to Find and Replace, showing you each proposed instance of hyphenation and allowing you to choose to accept, decline, or reposition the hyphen. You also can select a block of text before enabling manual hyphenation so this process is applied only to a particular section of your document, such as if you have a section with multiple columns within a longer document without columns. To use manual hyphenation, choose Tools ➪ Hyphenation and click the Manual button. Word immediately begins to hyphenate the document or selection, as shown in Figure 9.14.

---

**FIGURE 9.14**

If you choose Manual Hyphenation, Word prompts you to accept, decline, or reposition each hyphen.

> Manual Hyphenation: English (US)
>
> Hyphenate at: | num‑ber‑ing |
>
> Cancel    No    Yes

While automatic hyphenation keeps up with you as you work, manual hyphenation does not update. With this in mind, it's best to apply manual hyphenation only after you've completed any other editing changes to your text.

## Using optional and nonbreaking hyphens

Some words are never meant to be broken, no matter its syllabic breakdown. If you don't want Word to hyphenate a particular word no matter where it falls in your text, click inside the word and press Shift+⌘+ hyphen to encode it with a *nonbreaking hyphen*. Even if you hyphenate automatically or manually later in the editing process, Word leaves this word intact.

Optional hyphens position a hyphen exactly where you want it, but only if the word happens to fall at the end of a line. As you edit your document, an optional hyphen disappears if the word finds itself elsewhere in the text flow, but it reappears if necessary in further edits. These are the types of hyphens used by Word when you enable either the automatic or manual hyphenation options.

## Removing hyphens

If you decide that hyphens are detracting from the visual appearance of your document, you can remove automatic hyphens by returning to Tools ➪ Hyphenation, deselecting the Automatically hyphenate document box, and clicking OK. Word removes any hyphens it automatically placed.

To remove optional or nonbreaking hyphens, use Find and Replace:

1. **Choose Edit ➪ Replace.**

2. **Click the down arrow to open the additional options in the Find and Replace dialog box, if necessary.**

3. **Click Special, and choose either Nonbreaking Hyphen or Optional Hyphen, as shown in Figure 9.15.**

4. **Leave the Replace with box empty.** This removes the hyphen without replacing it with another character.

5. **Click Replace or Replace All.**

**FIGURE 9.15**

Remove nonbreaking and optional hyphens using Find and Replace.

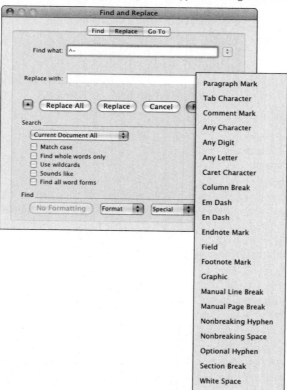

# Adding Headers and Footers

Every page of every document has space at the top and bottom for header and footer information. These areas are positioned within the margins and are used for repetitive information such as page numbering and the document or chapter title. As their names imply, headers appear at the top of the page while footers appear at the bottom.

**TIP** If you just want to add a quick page number to a document, choose Insert ➪ Page Numbers. The Page Numbers dialog box opens, allowing you to set the placement and alignment of the number.

To view the header and footer areas in your document, choose View ➪ Header and Footer. If you are in Draft or Outline view, Word automatically switches to Print Layout view so you can see the areas at the top and bottom of the page, marked in blue. If you are already in Print Layout view, you can double-click in the margin to enter the header or footer area. From here, you can manually enter header and footer details, such as the title of your document, and this information then appears at the top (or bottom) of every page.

When you enter the header or footer area of a document, the Formatting Palette adds a Header and Footer pane, shown in Figure 9.16, to allow you to easily modify the settings. From this pane, you can do the following:

- **Insert Page Number:** This is the most common header or footer content. You can type the word *Page* into the header/footer, add a space, and then insert the page number.

- **Insert Number of Pages:** This field tallies the number of pages in the document and prints that total in the header or footer. You can use this to format a "Page X of Y" type header. To do this, type *Page* and add a space, click the Insert Page Number button, type *of* and a space, and then click the Insert Number of Pages button.

- **Insert Date:** This inserts a date field into the header or footer. This field is updated automatically every time you modify the document, so when you print the document it reflects the date as of printing.

- **Insert Time:** As with the date option, this field automatically updates with the current time when you modify the document.

- **Format Page Number:** This option opens the Page Number Format dialog box. This is explained in detail later.

- **Go To:** These buttons move to the previous or next header or footer and allow you to switch between the header and footer on a page. Because sections of your document can contain different headers, such as a variation on the first page or formatting even and odd pages differently, these buttons are useful when formatting a long document to navigate between each header and footer.

- **Different First Page:** This option allows you to create a unique header or footer on the first page. This is described in more detail later in this section.

- **Different Odd and Even Pages:** This option creates unique headers and footers for odd and even pages, allowing you to alternate the position of the title and page number, for example, between pages for a more professional appearance.

- **Link to Previous:** If your document contains multiple sections, each can have unique headers and footers. When this option is selected, the section inherits the header or footer from the previous section. When deselected, you can create a new header or footer for that section. If your document is divided into chapters, for example, adding section breaks for each chapter and deselecting the Link to Previous option allows you to create a header for each chapter containing the chapter name or number.

- **Hide Body Text:** When you edit a header or footer, the body of your document appears in gray. To focus solely on the header or footer, select this option to completely obscure your body text until you exit the header or footer area.

- **Header/Footer from Top/Bottom:** These are the margin settings for the header and footer. Header and footer margins are measured in distance from the edge of the page, not from your body text. Thus if the header margin is 0.5" and the document margin is 1.25", the header appears 0.5" from the top of the page, and the body text appears 0.75" below the top line of the header.

**FIGURE 9.16**

The Header and Footer pane of the Formatting Palette provides control over these document elements.

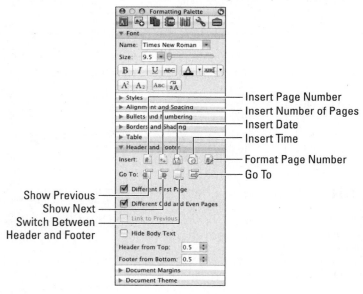

## Formatting page numbers

The Page Numbers dialog box, shown in Figure 9.17, allows for customization of the numbering settings in your document. If your document has introductory material, you can choose to number those pages in lowercase Roman numerals or paginate appendices with letters rather than numbers. Some documents require pagination with the chapter number preceding the page number, as in 1-5 to indicate page 5 in chapter 1. You can do this by choosing the Include chapter number settings. Finally, you can set the starting page number for the entire document or a section.

When creating or modifying a header or footer, you can format it using any of the formatting tools, such as fonts and shading. Headers and footers only have two tab stops set by default—the center and right margin—but you can add or modify them as needed. Widening the margins of headers and footers using negative indents gives the text of your document the appearance of being indented on the page, a nice touch for some applications. For another creative touch, add a graphic to represent the topic of each chapter.

FIGURE 9.17

The Page Numbers dialog box controls starting page numbers and numbering style.

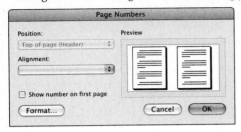

## Creating section-based headers and footers

The first page of a document often requires a different header than the remainder. A first-page header could include contact information, for example. Sometimes the first page doesn't require any header at all, such as if you have a cover page on the document. In that case, you want an empty header for the first page, but the page number, title, and chapter name, for example, on later pages.

To create a different header or footer for the first page, simply select the Different First Page option in the Header and Footer pane. Use the Go To buttons to navigate between the different headers and footers, creating and formatting each. The Format Page Number dialog box allows you to modify the starting page number for the second (and beyond) page heading in order to disregard a cover page from the pagination count.

## Using the Elements Gallery

The Elements Gallery contains several options for headers and footers if you choose not to create your own from scratch. Choose Document Elements from the toolbar, and click either Header or Footer. The Elements Gallery displays several options for the selected element. You can choose to use the same header and/or footer on every page or use different formats for even and odd pages. Click the desired option, and Word inserts the formatting directly into your document. The options in the Elements Gallery offer some interesting ideas, but few of the options are practical for a school paper or manuscript. They do, however, make a good starting point.

The Document Elements Gallery also contains cover pages, bibliographies, and tables of contents. When you create a cover page using the Document Elements, Word automatically inserts a different first-page header and footer. Bibliographies and tables of contents are explained in detail later in this chapter so you'll understand how to create your own, but using these preformatted options can save you considerable time.

The Elements Gallery offers several preformatted header styles.

Alternating headers and footers for even and odd pages is similarly easy. The Different Odd and Even Pages option in the Header and Footer pane creates these additional headers and footers. You also can set this option in the Layout dialog box; access this dialog box by choosing Format ⇨ Document ⇨ Layout. A common use of different odd and even headers would be putting the document title in the header on even pages and the chapter name on the odd pages, with page numbers in the footers for both. Figure 9.18 shows an example of this.

**FIGURE 9.18**

Use headers and footers to full effect by customizing the appearance of odd and even pages.

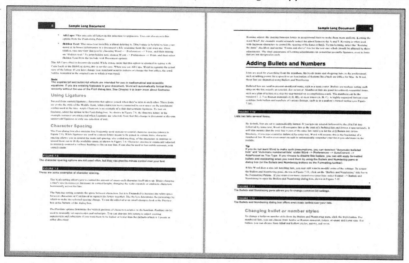

You're on your own a bit, however, if you want to create unique headers and footers for each chapter of a long document. To create a new header for a chapter:

1. **Choose Insert ⇨ Break ⇨ Section Break to insert a section break before the new chapter.** If you want every chapter to start on an odd page, the top of a double-sided page, choose Section Break (Odd Page).

2. **Click View ⇨ Header and Footer, or double-click in the header area on the first page of the new section.**

3. **Deselect the Link to Previous option in the Header and Footer pane of the Formatting Palette.**

4. **Create your new header or footer.**

Repeat these steps for each section of your document. If you change your mind about formatting chapters separately, reselect the Link to Previous option to delete the unique header and footer for that section and reconnect it with the rest of the document.

**TIP**   The Different First Page option applies to each section in your document individually. If you select this option while on the first page of the document, it applies to the first page of the first section. If you select it in a later section, the first page of that section has its own unique header or footer. Use this to your advantage if the first page of each chapter requires unique formatting. For example, because the first page of a chapter usually has a heading (not to be confused with a header) with the chapter number or title, the header on this page doesn't need to duplicate this information.

# Inserting Fields

As you've just seen when adding headers and footers, Word often makes use of fields to mark information that can be automatically updated and is likely to change as the document evolves. When you insert page numbers or a date or time stamp into a header, Word uses a field as a placeholder for this information. Fields can be used in the following ways, as well:

- Generate tables of contents and an index.
- Insert AutoText, such as the filename or author of the document.
- Calculate the number of words in a manuscript or grant submission.
- Create form letters and labels that can be merged with a list of contacts.

At its root, a field is simply a piece of code that processes information within your document. Some fields aid in document navigation rather than presentation. Bookmarks, for example, help you find your place when creating a long document, but they are not intended for print. Instead of manually tracking page numbers, inserting a document's word count, updating the date and time of the current modifications, or finding all the iterations of a particular word or phrase for an index, Word does this for you and makes the data available through fields.

Fields are entered into Word differently than regular text. There are several methods to create a field:

- Choose Insert ➪ Field, and select a category and field type from the Field dialog box, as shown in Figure 9.19. The Description area provides additional information about the selected field.
- Use the Document Elements to insert an element that uses fields, such as a header or table of contents.
- Use a command that inserts a field, such as Insert ➪ Date and Time, Page Number, or AutoText. Some AutoText entries do not insert fields, but most of the Header/Footer entries use fields.
- Use a command that utilizes fields to compile a document element, such as Insert ➪ Index and Tables, Cross-Reference, or Caption.
- Use the Insert ➪ Bookmark command to create a navigational bookmark.
- Press ⌘+F9, and manually type the field code. This is the least-used option because it is far easier to use one of the other methods.

**FIGURE 9.19**

The Field dialog box organizes different types of fields into categories.

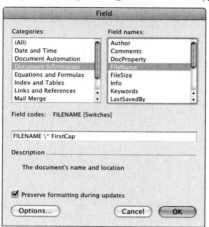

Word does not update fields as you work. As you add more text, for example, the word count field (NumWords) you may have inserted on your cover page continues to display the count as of when you opened the file. The next time you open the file, however, the field displays updated information. You can immediately update a field by Control+clicking within it and choosing Update Field from the context menu (or Option+Shift+⌘+U from the keyboard), or you can update all the fields in the document by pressing ⌘+A to select the entire document and then invoking the Update Field command. To ensure that your fields are always updated before printing, choose Word ➪ Preferences ➪ Print, and select the Update fields option. Keep in mind, however, that this may result in changes to fields you did not want updated before printing, such as the current time rather than the time when you began working on the file.

**NOTE** The Select All command excludes headers and footers. Thus, you cannot update fields within a header or footer using the combination of Select All and Update Fields. To update header and footer fields, you need to enter each header and footer separately. If there are multiple fields within a particular header or footer, however, you can invoke the Select All and Update Field commands to update all of them at once.

## Building and modifying fields

The Field dialog box does more than list the available fields. The Field codes area below the selection boxes show the field code and current options set for that code. These options are known as *switches*. To change a switch, click the Options button. The Field Options dialog box, shown in Figure 9.20, allows you to *build* a field code, customizing its settings to display exactly the information and format you need. In the DATE field, the switch options allow you to display the year in either two-digit or four-digit format, for example.

If you are familiar with field and switch codes, you can edit them directly within the document. Control+click in a field and choose Toggle Field Codes from the context menu. This displays the field code instead of the resulting text, and you can edit this code directly. Whether you display field codes or the field results in Word, the results appear when you print the document.

**FIGURE 9.20**

The Field Options dialog box contains general and field-specific switches.

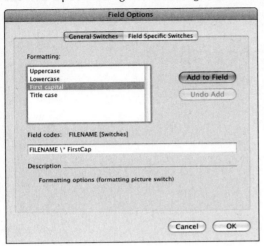

When you select a field, Word displays it with a gray highlight by default. You can turn this off in the Preferences dialog box, but this makes it too easy to confuse it with regular text, which can result in costly errors. To avoid this confusion, change your preferences to always display the gray highlight on fields. Choose Word ⇨ Preferences ⇨ View, and select Always from the Field shading menu. This highlighting shows up only onscreen, not in print. If your document will be read by others onscreen and you want to blend the fields in with your regular text, select Never from the Field shading menu. It is best to wait until you're finished modifying the document before making this selection, however.

Although fields appear with a gray highlight for editing purposes, you can still format them in the same manner as any other text. If you change the highlight or shading color, however, the gray highlight no longer appears on those fields, so use care.

### Locking fields

Locking a field prevents changes to the field code and further updates to the results. After you've put time into creating fields and setting switches, the last thing you want is for a coworker to accidentally change the field code. You also may want to lock a field if you need to change the data from which the field determines its results without changing the information currently in your document. You may want to lock in the results of a formula field that calculates the results of an equation, for example.

To lock a field, press ⌘+F11. If you want to lock all the fields in your document at once, select all the text by choosing ⌘+A. Again, lock fields in headers and footers separately from the body of your document when using the ⌘+A, ⌘+F11 option. If you want to unlock the field to update it at a later time, press Shift+⌘+F11.

### Unlinking fields

Sometimes fields serve a temporary purpose to capture data into a document. To permanently break the link between the results and its field code, press Shift+⌘+F9. This converts the results to regular text and removes the field code entirely.

**CAUTION** Whenever you are working with fields, be sure to save your document often. Word has a tendency to crash when editing fields, and you will lose any unsaved work in the recovery process. This is not a reason to avoid fields, because their benefits outweigh the risks, but you can never save too often!

# Creating Citations and Bibliographies

Scholarly works involve compiling data, opinions, and direct quotes from a variety of sources. This information must be accurately cited to avoid claims of plagiarism. Several styles are accepted for these citations and compilations of source information—known as bibliographies, footnotes, and endnotes. These are the four most common styles and their general uses:

- **Modern Language Association (MLA):** This style is used in literature, the arts, and the humanities.
- **Chicago Manual of Style (Chicago):** This style is used for books, magazines, newspapers, and non-scholarly publications.
- **Turabian:** Intended for general college use, this style closely resembles the Chicago style.
- **American Psychological Association (APA):** This style is used in psychology, education, and the social sciences.

Most scholarly institutions use one of these standards, and they'll clearly express their choice or any unique requirements. Entire books have been written about each of these styles, as each has certain complexities in how various types of source material should be cited. Fortunately, Word makes this process easier through use of the Citation feature.

**NOTE** Although Word's citations features may serve your basic needs, graduate students and academics may find themselves in need of something more robust. Several third-party citation managers integrate well with Word 2008, including Bookends (www.sonnysoftware.com/) and EndNote (www.endnote.com/).

 The Citations Palette, shown in Figure 9.21, is available from the Toolbox, the third tab from the left. The Citations Palette enables you to build a database of all the sources used in your document, which can then be used to create your footnotes, endnotes, and/or bibliography. To add to the database:

1. **Open the Citations Palette.**
2. **Choose the Citation Style you require from the drop-down menu.**
3. **Click the plus sign at the bottom of the palette.** The Create New Source dialog box opens, as shown in Figure 9.22.
4. **Select the Type of Source from the drop-down menu.** Word offers 16 different types of sources, such as book, Web site, or interview. If none of these many types suits your reference, choose Miscellaneous. The form changes to request data pertinent to the source you select.
5. **Click the Edit button to the right of the Author field to open the Edit Name dialog box, as shown in Figure 9.23.**
6. **Enter the Last, First, and Middle names of the author, and press the Add button.** If a source has multiple authors, add each one separately. Use the Up and Down buttons to sort the author names into the proper order for the work.
7. **Click OK to close the Edit Name dialog box.** Word adds the author(s) to the Create New Source dialog box, formatted according to the style you selected.

8. **Fill out the remaining fields.** Required fields are marked with an asterisk; the citation cannot be properly formatted without this information. The Edit button appears next to any fields that might have multiple contributors, allowing you to open the Edit Name dialog box (refer to Step 6) to enter this information.

9. **Click OK to close the Create New Source dialog box and add the source to the Citations List in the Citations Palette.**

---

**FIGURE 9.21**

---

The Citations Palette contains a database of references used in your document.

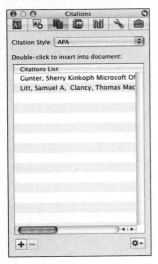

## Editing citation data

You may find that you need to edit a citation after creating it. You may notice a typo or realize you skipped an important field. To edit a citation:

1. **Select the source in the Citations Palette.**

2. **Click the Actions button, and choose Edit Source from the menu.** The Edit Source dialog box opens with the data you entered for that citation.

3. **Edit the source data.**

4. **After you've completed the entry, click OK and return to your document.** Citations that are inserted within the body of your document update automatically.

5. **Citations in footnotes and endnotes are entered as static text and thus do not update.** The easiest way to update these entries is to delete the existing footnote and enter a new one. This is a known issue for this version of Word, and we hope it is resolved in the future.

> **TIP** Creating citations takes time, as you flip through the source material looking for copyright dates, publisher name and location, and so on. If you're creating the citations list as you write, this process can interrupt your workflow. Instead, you can create a brief citation, adding just the barest information to serve as a placeholder and then edit the information later to complete the source data.

**FIGURE 9.22**

Store all the information about your reference in the Create New Source dialog box.

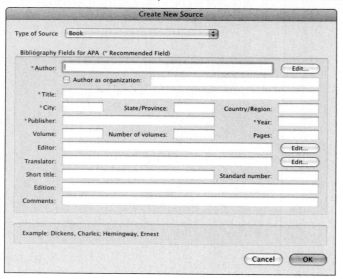

**FIGURE 9.23**

The Edit Name dialog box ensures that multiple author names are sorted and formatted correctly.

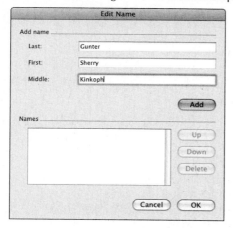

## Managing citations

Most likely, your work or studies are within a particular field, even if only for the duration of a project or semester. As a result, you may often use many of the same reference materials in multiple documents. Word not only stores the citations list for a specific document, it also adds any new citations to a master list. When you create a new document, you can access the master list to add pertinent citations to the current document, saving considerable time re-entering the data. To access the master list, click the Actions button in the Citations Palette and choose Citation Source Manager from the menu. This opens the Source Manager dialog box, as shown in Figure 9.24. Use the Copy button to move sources from the Master list to the Current list. You can create new sources, edit sources, and delete entries from this dialog box as well. Press Close to return to your document.

## FIGURE 9.24

Save time entering reference data by copying previously entered sources in the Citation Source Manager.

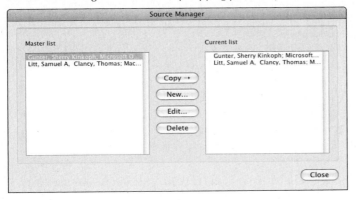

## Using citations

Citations form the basis of footnotes, endnotes, and bibliographies, each of which is explained later in this chapter. You also can use citations within the body of your text. These citations are much-abbreviated, usually containing only the last name of the author and publication date within parentheses next to the quoted text. To add this type of citation, position the insertion point where you want it to appear and double-click the appropriate entry in the Citations list on the Citations Palette. These entries are then supplemented with the full citation in a bibliography or reference section at the end of the document.

### Generating a bibliography

A bibliography alphabetically lists all the reference materials used throughout a paper or report. The bibliography appears at the end of the document. After you have created a complete citations list, you can automatically generate a bibliography using the Document Elements Gallery. To create a bibliography:

1.  **Switch to Print Layout view.**
2.  **Position the insertion point at the end of the document.**
3.  **If you want the bibliography to appear on a separate page, insert a Page Break.** Otherwise, the bibliography appears below your body text, at the insertion point.
4.  **Click Document Elements in the Elements Gallery, and click Bibliographies (or choose Insert ➪ Document Elements ➪ Bibliography), as shown in Figure 9.25.**
5.  **Choose the same Citation Style you selected when creating your Citations list.**
6.  **Select either the Bibliography or Works Cited thumbnail.** Word inserts the appropriate list at the insertion point.

**FIGURE 9.25**

The Bibliography option in the Elements Gallery generates the bibliography seen in the document below.

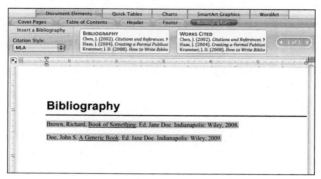

## Formatting bibliographies and works cited

Word inserts bibliographies as one field. If you modify or add entries to the Citations list, you can update this field by choosing Update Citations and Bibliography from the smart menu, the blue arrow that appears to the right of the Bibliography box when you select it.

You also can use the smart menu to convert the entire bibliography to static (regular) text. This makes it easier to edit and format the entries, but you sacrifice the ability to automatically update the bibliography if you later change the Citations list.

## Deleting a citation

Word generates bibliographies using the complete citations list, even if they have not been used within the document. If you have unused citations in your list, you should delete them before creating the bibliography by selecting the citation in the Citations Palette and clicking the minus sign at the bottom of the palette. The minus sign is grayed out if the citation is in use, signaling that the citation cannot be deleted.

Deleting citations within a document varies by how you've used them. To delete a bibliography entry, simply delete the entry as you would any other text. In-text citations, however, function differently than regular text. To delete a citation within the body of a document, select the citation, click the blue area to the left of the field, and cut it from the document (⌘+X).

# Inserting Footnotes and Endnotes

While bibliographies list all your reference materials at the end of the document, footnotes and endnotes are cited within the text numerically, with each number relating to the citation either at the bottom of the page or end of the document. Citations are numbered in order of appearance, unlike the alphabetical listing in a bibliography. To insert a footnote or endnote within Print Layout view:

1. **Position the insertion point next to the material that requires citation.**
2. **Choose Insert ⇨ Footnote.** This opens the Footnote and Endnote dialog box, shown in Figure 9.26.

3. **Set the options for either footnotes or endnotes.** Most footnotes are numbered using the default settings, but you can use an asterisk or other symbol, instead.

4. **If you want to change the numbering style, click the Options button to open the Note Options dialog box, as seen in Figure 9.27.** Click OK after setting your number format options.

5. **Click OK to close the Footnote and Endnote dialog box.** Word positions a superscript-formatted footnote number at the insertion point. It positions a similar number at the bottom of the page and moves the insertion point to the footnote area so you can type the citation.

6. **To insert a reference from the Citations list, open the Citations Palette and double-click a source from the list.** Otherwise, manually type a citation or note.

In Draft view, footnotes and endnotes are entered into a pane that appears at the bottom of the Document Window after Step 5. This pane also provides a shortcut menu that allows you to change the formatting for the separator that divides the document text from the footnotes or endnotes. To jump between the footnote number in the text and the footnote itself, double-click the footnote number. Switch between Draft and Print Layout views to take full advantage of all the footnote and endnote options.

**FIGURE 9.26**

Set footnote and endnote options in the Footnote and Endnote dialog box.

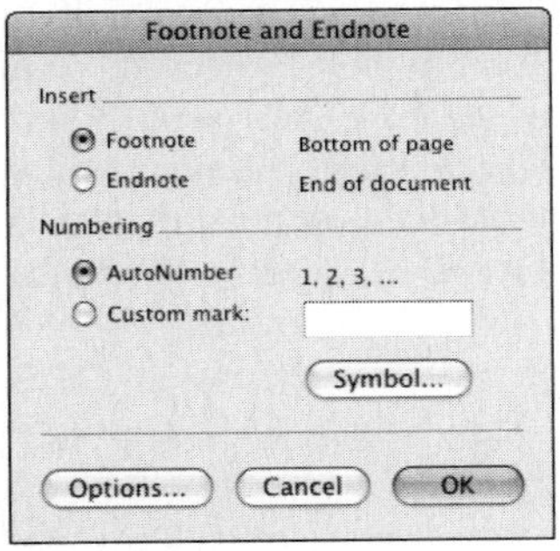

**FIGURE 9.27**

The Note Options dialog box controls the numbering format for footnotes and endnotes.

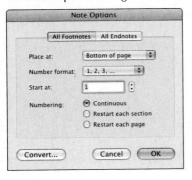

When you want to insert further footnotes, you can simply use a keyboard shortcut to skip Steps 1 through 5. Press ⌘+Option+F to add the next footnote. If you insert a note prior to earlier ones, Word automatically renumbers the list. Figure 9.28 shows an example of a page with footnotes.

**FIGURE 9.28**

Word automatically numbers and formats footnotes and endnotes.

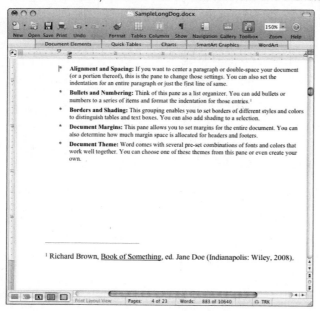

## Converting footnotes to endnotes

If you change your mind between using either footnotes or endnotes, you can convert them. Position the insertion point within the footnote or endnote, and press Control while clicking the mouse button to bring up the context menu. Choose Convert to Footnote or Convert to Endnote, as appropriate. If the Footnote pane is closed in Draft view, choose View➪Footnotes to reopen it and select the notes from the pane.

You also can use footnotes and endnotes concurrently. You may use footnotes as a concordance, adding explanatory comments about the text, and use endnotes for reference citations, or vice versa.

## Deleting footnotes and endnotes

To delete a footnote or endnote, delete the number within the document text. This deletes the number and the related footnote. Word automatically renumbers the remaining notes. Do not delete the notes themselves, because this does not remove the number from the document text.

# Adding Captions

Most long documents make use of visual elements to illustrate the points made in the text. A picture (or table or chart) really can be worth 1,000 words, and if nothing else, they break up long blocks of text to give readers a visual rest. Even these elements, however, need a word or two of note. Captions fill this need, providing a reference number to relate within the text and offering the option of adding an explanation of the object in question.

Word can streamline the captioning process, automatically numbering tables, illustrations, charts, and equations created with Microsoft Equation Editor. To create a caption:

1. **Insert or create the object, and then select it.**
2. **Choose Insert ⇨ Caption to open the Caption dialog box, shown in Figure 9.29.**
3. **Choose a Label type from the pop-up menu.** If you want to create a custom label for your captions, click the New Label button, type your text, and click OK to return to the Caption dialog box.
4. **Choose a position for the caption, either above or below the object.**
5. **If you want to change the numbering format to Roman numerals or letters, click the Numbering button and select your options from the Caption Numbering dialog box, shown in Figure 9.30.**
6. **The Caption box at the top of the Caption dialog box displays the caption formatted according to your selections.** If you want to add any explanatory or identifying information to the caption, add it in this box, being careful not to delete the existing text.
7. **Click OK to close the dialog box and create your caption, as shown in Figure 9.31.**

**FIGURE 9.29**

The Caption dialog box formats a caption for a figure, table, chart, or equation.

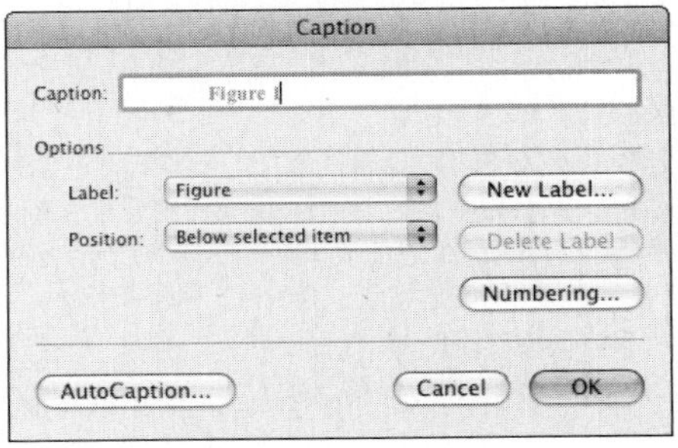

**FIGURE 9.30**

The Caption Numbering dialog box lets you use Roman numerals or chapter numbers.

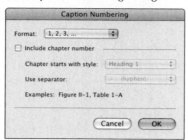

**FIGURE 9.31**

This figure contains both a figure number and supplementary text.

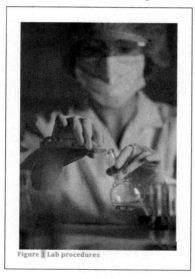

Figure 1 Lab procedures

After you have created captions for your objects, Word automatically keeps them in the proper order. If you move a figure or other captioned object, Word renumbers all the captions.

## Editing captions

Captions use fields, and as such, they have some editing quirks. After you have created a caption, you can edit any explanatory text directly within the document. You cannot, however, change the label on a single caption—for example, to change Figure 1 to Illustration 1. If you need to change just one caption's label, you must delete it and create a new caption for the object.

If you want to change all the captions labeled Figure to Illustration, you can select a caption, choose Insert ⇨ Caption, and make your changes in the Caption dialog box. Be sure to select the entire caption before invoking this command; otherwise, you create a second caption for the selected object.

To delete a caption, select it and press Delete. Any remaining captions in the document are renumbered accordingly. If Word ever loses track of these updates—captions are fields, after all—use the same command you invoke for any other field updates, specifically Option+Shift+⌘+U. If you select all the text (by pressing ⌘+A) first, you can quickly update all the fields throughout the document.

## Using the AutoCaption feature

The Caption dialog box has a button to enable the AutoCaption feature. This feature automatically adds captions as you insert equations, charts, and tables to your document. The AutoCaption dialog box, shown in Figure 9.32, provides a series of check boxes that allow you to turn on the AutoCaption feature just for certain objects. You can still add captions for other objects using the regular Caption tools, and Word tracks all the objects regardless.

To turn off the AutoCaption feature, return to the AutoCaption dialog box and deselect all the check boxes.

**NOTE** The AutoCaption features works only with objects inserted into the document after you've enabled this feature. If you already have items you want to caption in the document, you need to use the regular Caption feature for these.

**FIGURE 9.32**

The AutoCaption feature allows you to take a completely hands-off approach to captioning new objects.

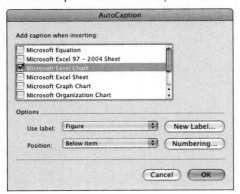

# Navigating with Bookmarks

Although most of the long document features automate processes that contribute to the final presentation of the printed document, Bookmarks are purely navigational in nature. Bookmarks can mark incomplete sections in a work-in-progress, areas of note when passing a document along to a collaborator, or any other place in the work that you want to access easily. You also can use bookmarks as an invisible marker to create a cross-reference to a portion of the document with no other distinguishing features. Whatever the purpose, after you place a bookmark, you can use it to navigate directly to that place in the document.

## Adding and deleting bookmarks

To add a bookmark, select a portion of text or an object, or place the insertion point in the area you want to mark. Choose Insert ➪ Bookmark (or use the keyboard shortcut, Shift+⌘+F5), and provide a name in the Bookmark dialog box, shown in Figure 9.33. Bookmark names must meet the following limitations:

- Must contain 40 or fewer characters.
- No spaces within the name; however, you can use underlines or mixed-case.
- No numbers as the first character in the name, although they can appear elsewhere.

**FIGURE 9.33**

The Bookmark dialog box lists all the bookmarks in the document.

Keep your names descriptive and easy to relate to the text or object. Choosing a clever bookmark name might amuse you at first, but laughter leads to frustration when you can't remember which bookmark leads to which text.

Bookmarks are invisible, because they are not intended to be viewed themselves but simply to mark a location in the document. If you want to view your bookmarks, however, choose Word ➪ Preferences ➪ View, and select the Bookmarks option. Bookmarks appear as a thick I-bar. To return bookmarks to their invisible state, deselect the Bookmarks option in the Preferences panel.

To delete a bookmark, open the Bookmark dialog box (either by choosing Insert ➪ Bookmark or pressing Shift+⌘+F5), click the name of the bookmark, and press the Delete button.

 If you delete the text to which a bookmark is attached, the bookmark disappears as well.

## Using bookmarks

After you've created bookmarks, you can access them in several ways:

- **Go To:** Choose Edit ➪ Go To (or press F5 or ⌘+G) to open the Go To tab in the Find and Replace dialog box. Select Bookmark from the Go to what list, and choose a bookmark from the pop-up menu on the right.

- **Bookmarks dialog box:** Choose Insert ➪ Bookmark (or press Shift+⌘+F5), and double-click the name of the bookmark.
- **Status bar:** Click the Pages area of the Status bar at the bottom of the document window. This opens the Go To tab in the Find and Replace dialog box.

# Using Cross-References

In a long work, such as this book or an academic thesis, if you attempted to explain a point repeatedly each time it relates to something else, the result would be plodding and redundant. Instead, writers use *cross-references,* referring the reader to another chapter or page in the work where they can find related information. You can manually create a cross-reference simply by typing something such as "see Chapter 3" within your text. If you want to call more attention to it, put it on its own line with some sort of cross-reference notation or explanatory text, as in "For more about goose migration patterns, see page 391." These manual cross-references get the job done if your document is completely finished and the page and chapter structure are set in stone. Problems arise, however, if that structure changes. Moving a 5-page section of your work from page 13 to page 210, renders all of your cross-references useless and requires hours of manual labor finding both the cross-references and their new reference points.

To eliminate this problem, Word offers self-updating cross-references. Word's cross-references are similar to hyperlinks in that they are connected to a specific element in your document. Unlike hyperlinks, however, cross-references may refer only to elements within the document.

**NOTE** This is yet another reason why it's more efficient to keep a long document in one file rather than separating the chapters. If you split your work over multiple files, you need to compile them into a master document in order to use cross-references. Master documents are explained later in this chapter.

Cross-references can be linked to the following types of items:

- **Numbered item:** This is an item from a numbered list or a paragraph number when you have enabled line numbers, which are described later in this chapter.
- **Heading:** This is a paragraph formatted with one of the Heading styles.
- **Bookmark:** This is useful when you want to cross-reference a portion of a document that contains none of the other reference types because you can create a bookmark anywhere in the document then use it for cross-reference purposes.
- **Footnote:** This is a citation or explanation positioned on the page below the document text using Word's footnote feature.
- **Endnote:** This is a citation or explanation positioned at the end of the document using Word's footnote (and endnote) feature.
- **Equation:** This is an equation created with Microsoft Equation Editor, a separate application that is included with Office 2008.
- **Figure:** You can use charts, pictures, or other graphic elements with a caption.
- **Table:** This refers to a Word table.

**CAUTION** Cross-references cannot refer to anything within a text box. If you want to cross-reference a text box, create a bookmark before or after the box and then link the cross-reference to the bookmark.

You can choose your own wording for a cross-reference. You probably want to use lead-in text such as *see, refer to,* or *as discussed in.* You also can create a custom Cross-Reference callout, such as the Notes, Tips, and Cautions in this book. Word creates the actual field containing the location of the reference point, but the wording of the call-out is up to you.

To create a cross-reference:

1. **Type your lead-in text.**

2. **Choose Insert ⇨ Cross-reference.** This opens the Cross-reference dialog box, shown in Figure 9.34.

3. **Select the Reference type.**

4. **Choose the Insert reference to option.** The options change depending upon the reference type. Generally, you can choose to refer to the page upon which the element appears or refer to the name (as in a heading) itself. You also can use the more generic "above" or "below."

5. **Choose the reference point in the For which list.** After you've chosen a reference type, Word lists all the elements of that type in the For which heading area of the dialog box.

6. **If you want the cross-reference inserted as a hyperlink, be certain the Insert as hyperlink box is checked.** Hyperlinked cross-references can be useful if your audience will read your work onscreen. If you plan to distribute your work in hard-copy form, using hyperlinks can actually hinder your workflow, however, because they are more difficult to select and edit.

---

**FIGURE 9.34**

Cross-references refer readers to other topics in a document.

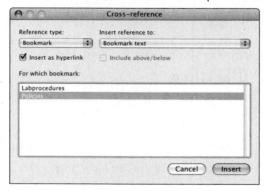

After you insert a cross-reference, Word tracks any changes in location or naming of the referred element. If you change the name of a heading, for example, Word updates any cross-references that refer to that heading by name. Word also updates references as page numbers change when you add to or modify your document.

Cross-references are a type of field. As such, they have all the advantages and disadvantages of other Word fields. Although cross-references should update automatically, Word sometimes loses track of them. To ensure that all your references are up to date, use the Select All (⌘+A) and Update Fields (Option+Shift+⌘+U) commands. To delete a cross-reference, select the shaded field and press Delete.

To modify a cross-reference, select it, choose Insert ⇨ Cross-reference, and then change the settings using the same method you used to create it.

TIP  **You can use cross-references as a navigational tool, just like bookmarks. Press Shift+⌘+F5 to open the Bookmarks dialog box, and click the Hidden bookmarks option. This adds your cross-references to the Bookmarks list.**

# Creating a Table of Contents

Creating a table of contents (commonly known as a TOC) used to be a manual process that took hours to compile and required lots of workarounds in order to prevent it from interfering with the pagination of the rest of the document. As with many of the other tools covered in this chapter, however, Word has automated this task and even updates as pagination changes. As a bonus, you can use a TOC as a navigational element in much the same way as cross-references and bookmarks.

You can create a TOC using either the Document Elements or the Index and Tables dialog box. Each approach has its pros and cons depending on the way you're organizing and formatting your document.

## Using the table of contents document element

The simplest way to create a TOC in Word is to use the built-in heading styles in your document. These are the styles labeled Heading 1, Heading 2, and so forth in the Styles list. Even if you modify the formatting of those styles to meet your needs, applying them to your chapter title (Heading 1) and subsections means your job in creating the TOC is already half-done before you even begin. If you outline your document in Outline view before adding your text, Word applies the appropriate heading styles to each level of your outline.

To create the TOC, first switch to Print Layout view, and then follow these steps:

1.  **Position the insertion point where you want to place the TOC.** You generally want to put this table on the first page of the document or following the cover page and any copyright or title pages.
2.  **Press the Document Elements button in the Elements Gallery.**
3.  **Click the Table of Contents button.** This displays five preformatted options for a TOC, as shown in Figure 9.35.
4.  **Select the Create with Heading Styles radio button.**
5.  **Choose one of the TOC options.** Word inserts the completed table at the insertion point, as shown in Figure 9.36.

**FIGURE 9.35**

The Document Elements Gallery contains several preformatted tables of contents.

**FIGURE 9.36**

The completed table of contents automatically displays the headings and page numbers.

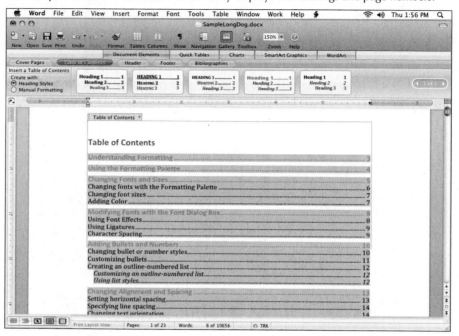

If you prefer to take full control over the text of your TOC but still want to take advantage of Word's formatting options, choose the Manual Formatting radio button in Step 4, and choose one of the TOC options. Word inserts a table of contents with dummy text, which you can then replace. Of course, if you use Manual Formatting, you lose the ability to update the chapter names and page numbers as you modify your document.

**TIP** The more descriptive you make your headings, the more useful they are in a table of contents. If you simply label your chapter titles with the chapter number, they don't provide any insight about their content when the reader scans the TOC. If you give your chapter headings both a number and title, the reader remains oriented in terms of location in the book (number) and content (title). Similarly, subheadings should describe the content within that portion of the chapter.

## Creating a table of contents through the dialog box

As with many Word features, the real secrets of controlling a TOC lie within its dialog box. Using the Index and Tables dialog box, you can set the number of heading levels to appear. More importantly, you can set items formatted with non-heading styles to serve as the entries in the TOC. To do this:

1. **Place your insertion point where you want the TOC to appear.**
2. **Choose Insert ⇨ Index and Tables to open the Index and Tables dialog box.**
3. **Select the Table of Contents tab, shown in Figure 9.37.**

4. **From the Formats list, choose a style for the TOC.**

5. **In the Show levels field, choose how many heading levels should appear in the TOC.** If your document contains only chapter titles, you can display only one level of headings. If your document contains several subheadings, however, determine how many you need to increase the readability and navigation of your document without overwhelming the reader.

6. **Select whether to Show page numbers.** If you are publishing your book in hard copy or PDF format, you most likely want page numbers to appear. If you're publishing the document directly to the Web, page numbers become unnecessary from a navigational stance, so you may deselect this option.

7. **Select whether to right-align the page numbers.** This makes for a more professional appearance.

8. **Select a Tab Leader to separate the chapter title from the page number.** You can choose a dotted, dashed, or solid line. You also can choose (none) if you want white space, instead.

---

**FIGURE 9.37**

The Index and Tables dialog box provides more control over the TOC settings.

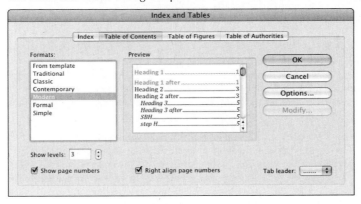

## Using non-heading styles for a table of contents

Although using heading styles makes it easier to format a TOC, all is not lost if you create your own styles. You can tell Word which styles should comprise each level of your TOC, achieving a truly customized result. To assign non-heading styles to a TOC, follow the steps above to set up a TOC in the Index and Tables dialog box, and then click the Options button to open the Table of Contents Options dialog box, shown in Figure 9.38.

Each style that is included in the TOC is assigned a level correlating to its place in the TOC hierarchy. By default, the styles Heading 1, Heading 2, and Heading 3 are assigned to TOC levels 1 through 3, respectively. To assign new styles to the hierarchy, delete these defaults and reassign the numbers to the styles you choose. You can assign more than one style to each level to give those styles equal weight in the TOC hierarchy. If you assign level 1 to every style you want to include, they are all included without any distinction or indenting between them.

Click OK to return to the Index and Tables dialog box, and click OK again to create the TOC.

**FIGURE 9.38**

The Table of Contents Options dialog box allows you to set styles for TOC entries.

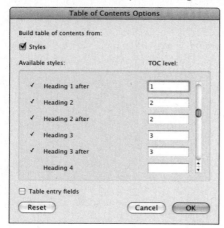

## Changing TOC styles

Word formats your TOC according to the format you select in the Index and Tables dialog box or the Document Element you choose from the Elements Gallery. If you select the From template option in the Format list, click the Modify button to format the styles associated with each level of the TOC hierarchy. This opens the Styles dialog box, as explained earlier in this chapter.

You also can modify TOC styles by choosing Format ⇨ Styles, selecting one of the TOC styles, and clicking Modify. Repeat this for each of the TOC styles to customize the appearance of each level. A trick to retaining consistency between the various TOC styles is to base the lower-level styles (TOC2, TOC3, and so on) on TOC1 using the "Style based on" option, and modifying the style from that foundation, indenting, changing the font size, or adjusting the paragraph spacing for each level.

## Adding other tables

Along with a TOC, Word can generate other lists. A Table of Authorities lists case law citations in legal documents. In terms of the process for creating one, a Table of Authorities is a hybrid of a table of contents and a bibliography. To generate a Table of Authorities:

1. **Select a citation in your document.**
2. **Choose Insert ⇨ Index and Tables, and click the Table of Authorities tab, shown in Figure 9.39.**
3. **Click Mark Citation.**
4. **Choose a citation type from the Category menu.**

5. **If the text should appear differently in the Table of Authorities than it does in the text, modify it in the Selected text box.**

6. **If you have abbreviated further references to this citation in the text, enter the abbreviation in the Short citation field.**

7. **Select Mark to navigate to the next iteration of this citation in your text, or select Mark All to automatically find and mark both the long and short versions of the citation.**

8. **Click Close to return to the Table of Authorities dialog box.**

Repeat these steps for each citation. When you are ready to insert the Table of Authorities, return to the Table of Authorities dialog box. By default, the Table includes All citations. If you want to create a separate list for each type of citation, use the Category menu to select individual types for each table. Select a format for the Table, and click OK.

If you add more citations after generating the Table of Authorities, you can follow the steps above to mark it and then click at the top of the Table and press F9 to update it.

**FIGURE 9.39**

Legal professionals use a Table of Authorities to list legal citations.

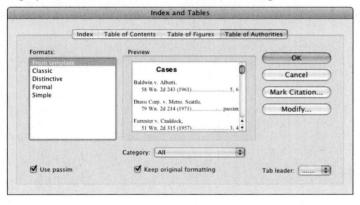

A Table of Figures lists captioned elements in your document. You can create separate lists for equations, figures, and tables. Just as the TOC automatically lists elements formatted with the Heading styles, the Table of Figures locates elements formatted with caption styles. To create a Table of Figures, you must first add captions to the figures throughout your document, as explained earlier in this chapter.

Select Insert ⇨ Index and Tables, and click the Table of Figures tab. The Table of Figures tab, shown in Figure 9.40, is very similar to that of the Table of Contents. The Options button opens the Table of Figures Options dialog box, shown in Figure 9.41, which allows you to identify non-caption styles.

**FIGURE 9.40**

A Table of Figures lists captioned figures, equations, and tables in your document.

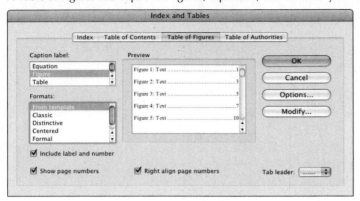

**FIGURE 9.41**

The Table of Figures Options dialog box identifies non-caption styles for use in the Table of Figures.

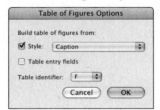

# Creating an Index

Many non-fiction books, such as this one, have an index at the back listing all the pages upon which key terms and concepts appear. Generating a comprehensive index for a book is one of the greatest challenges in the publishing process. In an effort to make this task less onerous, Word provides tools to automate the compilation and formatting of an index.

**NOTE** Although Word does an adequate job of creating an index, any work worth an index probably warrants a professional touch. Entire books have been written about this subject, and the American Society for Indexing provides courses and other resources to train indexers. You, however, most likely would rather focus on the content of your document than studying the ins and outs of indexing. Professional indexers also utilize software applications specific to the task. Although Word does simplify the task of indexing, it is still a very labor-intensive, manual process that involves an understanding of field codes beyond that of the average user. If you decide to proceed with creating your own index in Word, use caution and always save and back up your work often.

Creating an index is a multi-step process. First, you must identify the words and phrases you want to include. Each incidence of those terms must be marked in the document. Then you generate the actual index.

## Creating index entries

Word can't generate an index until it first knows which terms to compile and where they appear in the document. The process for identifying these terms is similar to marking citations in a Table of Authorities. You start by scanning through your document until you come across a word or phrase you want to include in the index. Select the item, choose Insert ⇨ Index and Tables, click the Index tab, and select Mark Entry. Alternatively, you can press Shift+Option+⌘+X to open the Mark Index Entry dialog box, as shown in Figure 9.42.

**FIGURE 9.42**

Each index entry must be marked for inclusion in the index.

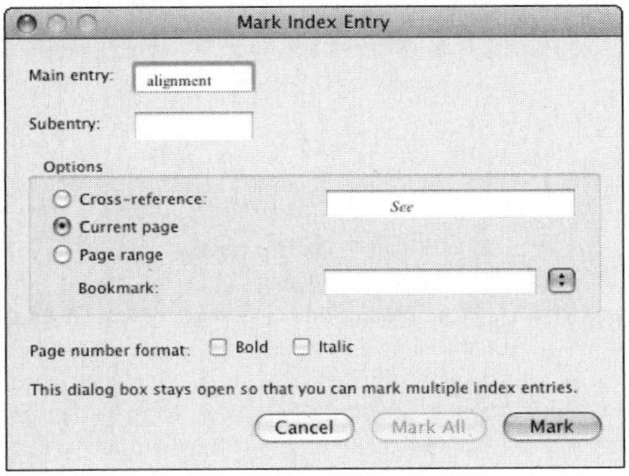

The word or phrase you selected appears in the Main entry field. If you want to capitalize or otherwise modify the entry, you can modify it in this field without changing the text in your document. Your book on literature might refer to William Shakespeare, but you most likely want the index entry to read "Shakespeare, William." You can add a subentry, such as a main entry for Shakespeare, and a subentry for *Romeo and Juliet,* which appears below the Shakespeare entry (usually indented).

Your choice of index references may vary from the words and phrases your readers seek. To aid in navigation, you can create cross-references in the index. Thus, if a reader looked up *Romeo and Juliet* in the index, your book could have an entry reading "Romeo and Juliet, *See Shakespeare, William.*" This would let the reader know to look for the term Shakespeare, where they would then find entries for *Romeo and Juliet.* To add a cross-reference, select the Cross-reference box and type the appropriate text after the word "See"; you can change the word "See" to "See also" if you want to list the entry in both places.

If the topic of the selected word or phrase spans multiple pages, you can specify this in the entry. First, however, you must create a bookmark to reference the range of pages. To do this, return to your document and select the entire range of pages that should be referenced for the entry. Choose Insert ⇨ Bookmark, and create a bookmark as described earlier in this chapter. Then return to the Mark Index Entry dialog box, and select Page range from the Options. Use the pop-up menu to select the bookmark you just created.

After you've set the options for the entry, click Mark. This adds the appropriate field code to your document to mark the selected word or phrase for inclusion in the eventual index. If you want to mark every iteration of this selection, choose Mark All. If a paragraph contains multiple references to the word or phrase, Word marks only the first occurrence, because the index refers only to page numbers or ranges, not to individual iterations on the same page. The Mark All command is case sensitive, so if the original selection is for "dream," Word does not mark the word "Dream," and vice versa.

The Mark commands have a couple quirks you should note. After you press the Mark command, you cannot change your mind and switch to the Mark All button; it becomes grayed out. Also, the Mark command does not navigate through your document searching for the next iteration. If you press the Mark command repeatedly, you simply add more field codes to the same entry rather than locate additional entries. Thus, if you use the Mark command, you need to manually search for additional occurrences of the term. You can, however, keep the Mark Index Entry dialog box open as you scroll through the document.

**NOTE** Although these limitations might make the Mark All option more attractive, this often returns too many entries. Mark All performs a simple search for matching terms; it cannot determine context. If you were to use Mark All on the word *formatting* in this book, for example, only half the references would be germane to using actual Word features. The rest of the entries would be irrelevant for index purposes, such as its occurrence in this paragraph.

When you have finished marking the index entry, press Close. Repeat this process for each word or phrase you want to include in your index. As you can see, this task can take a considerable amount of time, particularly for a very lengthy document.

## Generating an index

 After you complete the process of marking your document, you're almost ready to generate the actual index. First, turn off the display of any field codes in the document (click the Show/Hide icon on the Standard toolbar). These codes do not print, but they do throw off the pagination of your document when generating the index.

Next, position the insertion point where you want to locate it. Most indices appear at the very end of the document, after any bibliography or endnotes. To begin the index on a new page, insert a page break before the insertion point. Choose Insert ➪ Index and Tables. Click the Index tab if the dialog box, shown in Figure 9.43, does not open to it. The Index dialog box functions in much the same way as the Table of Contents. Choose whether to indent subentries by selecting Indented or Run-in Type. Choose a format and the number of columns for the index. Most books use multiple columns, the number of which is based on the dimensions and layout of the printed work.

You can choose to preface the entries for each letter of the alphabet with a heading, if you wish. You also may opt to right-align the page numbers for the entries to the page or column margin. If you are unhappy with any of the formatting in the Preview, press the Modify button to change the Index1, Index2, and Index3 styles.

Click OK to create the index.

## AutoMarking an index

It can take days and innumerable cups of coffee to index an extremely long document. You can streamline this process somewhat by using the AutoMark feature. Rather than individually marking each index entry, you create an *index automark* file (also referred to as a concordance). This file is a separate Word document formatted with a two-column table that contains all the words and phrases you want to include in the index. The column on the left contains the words and phrases you want to mark in your document. The column on the right contains the way in which this selection should appear in the index. To create a subentry, use a colon in the right-hand column, as in Shakespeare:Romeo and Juliet. Figure 9.44 shows an example of an index automark file.

**FIGURE 9.43**

The Index and Tables dialog box formats the index, which is generated from your marked text.

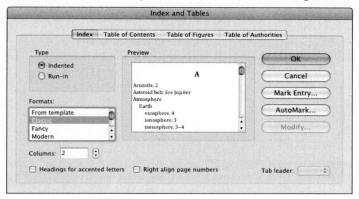

**FIGURE 9.44**

An index automark document lists entries for use in compiling an index in the original document.

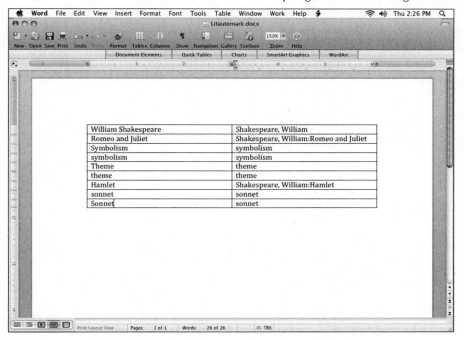

After you have created your list of index entries, save the file and return to your original document. Position the insertion point where you want the index to appear, and choose Insert ➪ Index and Tables. Click the AutoMark button in the Index tab. Navigate to the index automark file, and choose Open. Word searches your document and marks the text according to the concordance. Then you can create the index as normal.

**NOTE** As with the Mark All command, AutoMark cannot separate the wheat from the chaff. Before generating the index, you should scan your document to remove the field codes for any irrelevant entries. Also, AutoMark cannot mark page ranges, resulting in repetitive entries when a topic spans multiple pages.

Although creating the concordance still takes considerable effort, it can save some time. Another advantage of this method is that the same file can be used on multiple documents. Specialists in a particular field can find that this makes the effort pay for itself over the course of several books.

# Adding Line Numbers

If you're a lawyer or screenwriter, your documents are not only lengthy, but they also require precise formatting. One of the necessary formatting elements for these documents is *line numbering*. Line numbers are small numbers that appear in the left margin. They only appear onscreen in Print Layout and Publishing Layout views, but they print from any view.

To add line numbering to your entire document, choose Format ➪ Document and click the Layout tab. Choose where to apply the line numbering, either to a selection (made before opening the Document dialog box), a particular section of the document, or the entire document. Click the Line Numbers button to open the Line Numbers dialog box, shown in Figure 9.45.

In the Line Numbers dialog box, set the start number and interval for the numbering to appear. The From text selection determines the distance the numbers appear from the left margin of the text. The Numbering settings tell Word whether to restart the numbering sequence on every page or section, or to number continuously throughout the document or selection.

**FIGURE 9.45**

Line Numbers can be used to number every line or specific intervals of lines in the document or selection.

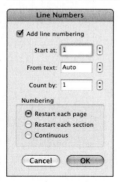

# Using Master Documents

Earlier versions of Word weren't nearly as capable of managing long documents as Word 2008. The file size became cumbersome, resulting in slow scrolling and typing lag. Features using field codes weren't as robust and were extremely buggy, so TOCs and bibliographies were often created manually. The ability to easily share documents and track changes in a collaborative environment was much more restrictive. Microsoft's answer to these issues was Master Documents, a way to link a series of separate documents together into a cohesive whole.

Computers as a whole and Word specifically have evolved over the past several years. Word can now handle documents of several hundred pages quite capably, and the advanced features for long documents make generating TOCs, captions, and indices much easier. Collaborative options are plentiful. As a result, Master Documents no longer serve much purpose. To prove this point, Microsoft has moved Master Documents from the View menu to the Outlining toolbar.

If you have used Master Documents in the past, rest assured that those documents will continue to work in Office for Mac 2008. If you are creating new documents, however, you will find it easier to generate document-wide elements such as TOCs and numbered captions if you keep the entire document in one file rather than a Master Document.

# Summary

By their nature, long documents are content-intensive. Using Word features such as styles and templates, pagination, headers and footers, and fields allows you to keep your focus where it belongs—on your content, rather than getting bogged down in the formatting details. By using the tools presented in this chapter, you can create professional documents that look as good as they read. Understanding these features also allows you to make an educated decision about when they'll save you time or when there is a better alternative for your particular project.

Chapter 10 explains how to use Word in a collaborative environment, sharing comments, and making changes to a document with input from others.

# Chapter 10

# Collaborating on Documents

**M**om always said it was important to share. I'm not sure she meant Word documents, but if she did, Word has some spiffy features to help you share documents and gather everyone's input. Word's collaboration tools can help you collect input from colleagues and merge it all to create one final document. Many job situations require various types of input from a circle of people, each adding their own comments, revisions, and markups to a document. Word's collaboration tools allow you to track all the revisions, whether it's from one person or a whole team of people.

In this chapter, you learn how to use the tracking and revision features to electronically edit a document. You also learn how to add comments to text without changing the original text itself. Then you learn how to use reviewing tools to create a polished, finished document that meets with everyone's approval. If you shared the multiple documents for tracking, you learn how to merge them to make a single document again. If you shared a document with someone who did not use tracked changes, you can still find out what revisions were. This chapter shows you how.

## Adding Comments

First up in the world of collaboration is the topic of comments. What are they, and what can we comment about them? Comments can be used on their own or with the tracking and reviewing tools. A comment is simply a notation another user makes to an existing document without making changes to the text directly. Comments appear in their own "balloons" much like the dialog in cartoons or comics, only more uniform looking. For example, you might get a document back from your boss with comments like "change this," "can we mention this," or "this is all wrong." Before you take it all too personally, the comment feature is a tool

### IN THIS CHAPTER

**Inserting comments**

**Tracking revisions**

**Reviewing changes**

**Merging multiple documents**

**Comparing documents**

for collecting input from others. You also can use comments to leave notes to yourself. For example, you might want to add something later in a particular place in the document. Drop in a comment that reminds you to make the addition.

Figure 10.1 shows what comments look like. Outside the tracking and reviewing feature, comments look like nice round-cornered colored boxes poking out from the edges of a document. You need to use Print Layout or Web Layout view to see the comments. (See Chapter 5 to learn more about using Word's many view modes.) The name of the person who wrote the comment appears at the top of the comment box, along with the date and time the comment was inserted. The area of the document to which the comment addresses appears highlighted in a very light color, and a colored line connects the comment balloon to the area of text on which the person is commenting. I magnified the example in Figure 10.1 by 200 percent so you could clearly read the comment. You may have to do the same on your own screen.

**FIGURE 10.1**

Comments appear as text balloons at the sides of a document.

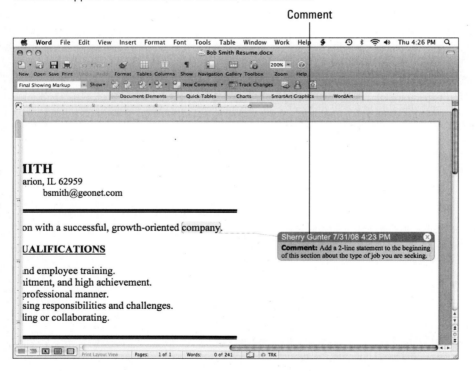

Notice that the comment balloon also features a button with an X in the middle. You might think this is a Close button. It's not. You can click it to delete the comment. If you're looking to turn the comments off, you need to turn off the Markup view; choose View ➪ Markup. This command option toggles markup notations, such as comments, on or off. A check mark next to the command name means the markup notations are on. No check mark means the markup notations are off.

## Adding User Information

**Y**ou may be wondering how Word knows which name to insert along with your comments. Microsoft Office uses the name you specified when you installed the software to mark comments and changes you make using the tracking and reviewing features. If the name is not correct, you can change it; choose Word⇨Preferences to open the Preferences dialog box. Under the Personal Setting options, click the User Information icon. This opens the User Information screen. Type the correct names in the First and Last fields at the top of the screen, along with the initials. Click OK to save your changes. The next time you add a comment, the new name and initials are inserted.

## Adding comments

You can add as many comments as you like to a document. To do so, follow these easy steps:

1. **Select the text to which you want to add a comment.**
2. **Choose Insert ⇨ Comment.**

   Word inserts an empty comment balloon, as shown in Figure 10.2, with your name already filled in, along with the date and time. Word also displays the Reviewing toolbar.

3. **Type your comment text.**
4. **Click anywhere outside the comment when finished.**

---

**FIGURE 10.2**

When you insert a comment, it's a blank box until you fill it in.

To remove a comment, click the comment's X button. This deletes it permanently. You also can Control+click inside the comment and click Delete Comment from the context menu.

If you have Word's Reviewing pane turned on, comments look and work a bit differently, as you see coming up next. For now, though, this is how comment balloons work.

## Adding comments with the Reviewing pane

You can add comments using a pane rather than comment balloons. You may prefer this method if the comment balloons are too hard to read. When activating the Reviewing pane, Word adds a separate pane at the bottom of the window that you can use to add and scroll through comments. Like balloon comments, the Reviewing pane keeps track of who wrote the comment and when it was inserted.

To use the Reviewing pane to enter comments, first turn off the comment balloons. Choose Word⇨ Preferences, click the Track Changes icon, and deselect the Use balloons to display changes check box. Now you're ready to use the pane. Follow these steps:

1. **Choose View ⇨ Toolbars ⇨ Reviewing.**

   This opens the Reviewing toolbar, as shown in Figure 10.3.

**FIGURE 10.3**

Open the Reviewing toolbar to access the Reviewing pane.

Reviewing toolbar

**2.** Click the Reviewing Pane button.

This opens the Reviewing pane, as shown in Figure 10.4.

> **NOTE** You can also open the Reviewing toolbar automatically whenever you add a comment using the Insert menu and choosing Comment.

**3.** Select the text in the document where you want to add a comment.

**4.** Click the New Comment button.

Word inserts a new comment in the Reviewing pane.

**5.** Type your comment.

**6. Continue adding more comments as needed.**

You can press F6 to toggle between the Reviewing pane and the document.

**7. When finished, click the Reviewing Pane button on the Reviewing toolbar again. You can also double-click the dividing bar between the document and Reviewing pane.**

Word closes the Reviewing pane.

You learn more about using the Reviewing toolbar in the next section.

---

**FIGURE 10.4**

You can use the Reviewing pane to insert comments into a document.

Click to reveal the Reviewing pane.

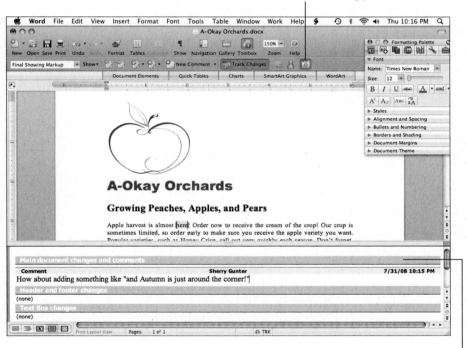

Reviewing pane

# Tracking Changes

You can turn on Word's tracking features and keep track of all the changes users make to a document that's passed around for review. Word's tracking and reviewing features are a big improvement over the old paper and red ink techniques people had to use from ages past. Rather than mark out revisions on paper and scribble in new text between the lines, Word's tracking feature lets everyone add his own input electronically without making a big mess, keeping everything legible and neat.

Just because someone sends you a document file doesn't necessarily mean the tracking and reviewing feature is on. In most cases, you need to turn it on yourself. The easiest way to activate all the tracking tools is using the Reviewing toolbar. Choose View ⇨ Toolbars ⇨ Reviewing. Word adds the toolbar to the top of the program window, as shown in Figure 10.5.

To turn on the Track Changes tool, click the Track Changes button on the Reviewing toolbar. When you do, the TRK icon is activated on the Status bar, and the Track Changes button remains recessed as long as the tool is active. Now you're ready to start editing the document.

## FIGURE 10.5

You can use the Reviewing toolbar to turn on the Track Changes tool.

Another way to turn on the Track Changes feature is to choose Tools ⇨ Track Changes ⇨ Highlight Changes. This opens the Highlight Changes dialog box, as shown in Figure 10.6. Check the Track changes while editing check box, leaving the other two check boxes selected. Leave the Highlight changes on screen check box activated to see the revision marks as you edit. Leave the Highlight changes in printed document check box activated if you want to see the revision marks in the printed document as well. If you want the last two settings turned off, Word still keeps track of all your revisions; you just can't see them onscreen. To exit the dialog box and apply the changes, click OK.

## FIGURE 10.6

You can use the Highlight Changes dialog box to turn on the Track Changes tool.

As you edit the document, Word marks your changes much like the revision marks shown in Figure 10.7. Edits appear marked in color with comment boxes recording each deletion. Each person's contributions are marked in a different color.

**FIGURE 10.7**

When a document is revised, revision marks show up in color, along with any comment boxes.

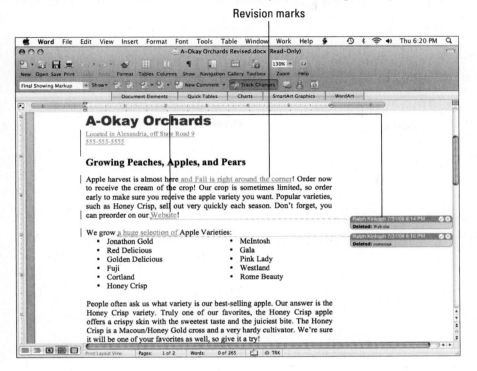

Revision marks

You can control which colors are used with the revision marks using the Track Changes preferences, as shown in Figure 10.8. To open the Preferences dialog box, you can click the Show button on the Reviewing toolbar and click Preferences. You also can choose Word ⇨ Preferences, and click the Track Changes icon. In the Preferences dialog box, you can control how inserted and deleted text appears, how changed formatting and lines appear, what color comments are, and what the comment balloons contain. You can choose which marks to apply as well as which color. The sample area next to each setting shows a sample of what the revision mark looks like. For many users, the default markings work pretty well. After you make any changes, click OK to apply them.

**FIGURE 10.8**

Use the Track Changes preferences to change which markup colors are applied.

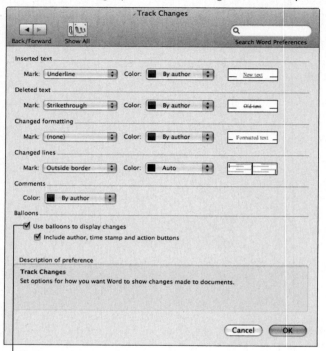

Click to turn off comment balloons.

# Reviewing Changes

When you receive a document with revisions, you can review the changes with some help from the Reviewing toolbar. As explained earlier, you can turn the toolbar on or off by choosing View ➪ Toolbars ➪ Reviewing. The Reviewing toolbar is the easiest way to review changes. Table 10.1 explains what you can do with each button in the toolbar.

**TABLE 10.1**

# Reviewing Toolbar

| Button | Name | Description/Action |
|---|---|---|
| Final Showing Markup ▼ | Display for Review | A pop-up menu lets you choose to view the final document with or without markup, or the original with or without markup. |
| Show ▼ | Show | A pop-up menu lets you change which markups are shown in the document and from which reviewer. |
| | Previous | This highlights the previous revision. |
| | Next | This highlights the next revision. |
| | Accept Change | This accepts the change. |
| | Reject Change/Delete Comment | This rejects the change. |
| | New Comment | This adds a new comment. |
| | Track Changes | This turns the tracking feature on or off. |
| | Mail Recipient as Attachment | This e-mails the document as an attachment. |
| | Send Instant Message | This sends an instant message with Microsoft Messenger. |
| | Reviewing Pane | This turns the Reviewing pane on or off. |

Use the following steps to help you navigate through a document to review the changes:

1. **Click at the beginning of the document, and click the Next button on the Reviewing toolbar to navigate to the first edit.**
2. **To view details about who made the edit, view the comment balloon or click the Reviewing pane button to display the Reviewing pane.**

3. **Click the Accept Change button to accept the revision or Reject Change button to reject the revision.**

   You also can click the arrow icons next to the buttons to reveal additional options for accepting or rejecting, as shown in Figure 10.9.

**FIGURE 10.9**

You can globally accept or reject changes using options in the pop-up menu.

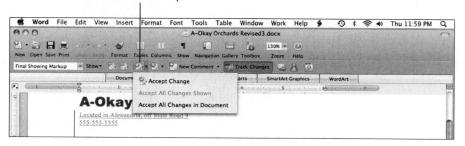

4. **Click the Next button to continue reviewing.**

   If you need to revisit the previous revision, click the Previous button.

   Optionally, to add a response to any comment, click the New Comment button and type your comment text.

5. **When you finish, you can click the Track Changes button to turn the feature off.**

If you trust your reviewers explicitly, you can choose to accept all their revisions. You can do this using the Accept button on the Reviewing toolbar, or you can use the Accept or Reject Changes dialog box. Choose Tools ⇨ Track Changes ⇨ Accept or Reject Changes. This opens the dialog box, as shown in Figure 10.10. You can use the buttons in this dialog box to review changes one by one by clicking the Find buttons to navigate the changes for review. As you click the button, Word highlights the revision in the document for review. You can click the Accept or Reject buttons to determine what to do with each revision, or you can click Accept All or Reject All revisions globally. If you change your mind, click Undo. When you finish, click the Close button.

**FIGURE 10.10**

You can use the Accept or Reject Changes dialog box to globally accept or reject all the revisions in a document.

# Merging and Comparing Documents

The preceding sections discussed tracking changes on a single document that you pass around for review. But what if you send multiple copies of the same document for review and get back multiple changes from multiple people? Relax. Word's gotcha covered. You can merge the edited documents with the original document using the Merge Documents command. On the other hand, what if the people you send the document to fail to utilize any tracking changes tools? What do you do then? Relax again. Word has another feature, called Compare Documents to help you find out what's been changed.

## Merging documents

Let's start with the Merge Documents feature. To create a final document out of numerous documents containing changes using the Track Changes feature, begin by collecting all the documents and locating your original file. Open your file, or any of the others, and follow these steps:

1. **Choose Tools ⇨ Merge Documents.**

   The Choose a File dialog box opens, as shown in Figure 10.11.

**FIGURE 10.11**

Choose a file to merge.

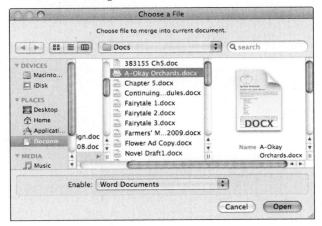

2. **Choose the first file you want to merge with the current file.**
3. **Click Open.**

   Word merges the two files, including all the tracked changes, as shown in Figure 10.12.

   Optionally, if you have more files to merge, repeat Steps 1 through 3.

After merging, you can review the document using the reviewing tools, accepting and rejecting changes as needed.

**FIGURE 10.12**

When you merge two or more documents with tracked changes, Word shows all the revisions from every document.

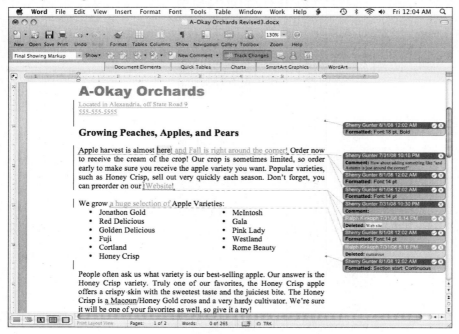

## Comparing documents

If you sent out a document in which the reviewer did not use Track Changes, you can still find out what she changed in the document by comparing it to the original. Here's how:

1. **Open the changed document copy first.**
2. **Choose Tools ➪ Track Changes ➪ Compare Documents.**

   The Choose a File dialog box opens.
3. **Choose the original file you want to compare with the current file.**
4. **Click Open.**

   Word compares the documents and creates a new document based on the original, with the changes marked as tracked changes, as shown in Figure 10.13.
5. **Review the changes using the Reviewing tools.**
6. **Save the document.**

If either document had any revision marks, Word ignores them and examines the unmarked text. If either document has untracked changes, Word prompts you first; click OK to continue, keeping in mind any changes you made to the document while writing it.

**FIGURE 10.13**

When you compare documents, Word creates a brand new document incorporating the other two documents.

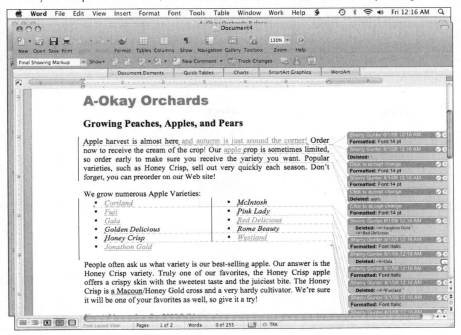

Going forward, if someone sends you a document to revise, tweak its filename to include your initials or a number, and make sure you turn on the Track Changes feature so they'll easily see what changes you make to the text.

## Summary

In this chapter, we covered the various ways other users can add input to a document. You learned how to add comments using comment balloons and the Reviewing pane. You also discovered how to turn on the Track Changes feature to track all the revisions you or anyone editing your document makes. Then you learned how to review revisions made by others to create a final document.

You learned how to merge multiple tracked changes documents into one for reviewing, and you learned how to compare changes between two documents without the Track Changes feature turned on.

# Chapter 11

# Proofing and Printing Documents

While news stories tout the "paperless office," that concept is still more wishful thinking than reality. Most documents created in Word eventually wind up in print form. Before your work is ready for prime time, however, it may require some last-minute touchups. Documents with typos and grammatical errors leave readers with the wrong impression about the capability of the writer. Some documents have specific word or line restrictions, such as magazine and newspaper articles.

One of the advances in our society is the ability to reach masses of people with a single message. This is true in the print world as well as online. Word allows you to type a single document and automatically personalize it for a mass mailing list that gets mailed to hundreds of people.

This chapter is about all those odds and ends you should take care of before hitting the Print button as well as tools that help you make the most of that command.

## IN THIS CHAPTER

**Checking grammar and spelling**

**Assessing compatibility**

**Generating mass mailings**

**Printing documents and envelopes**

## Proofreading a Document

Into every typist's life occasional misspellings must come. Grammatical awkwardness is equally forthcoming, as in the previous sentence. Fortunately, you can correct these problems in Word to avoid embarrassing mistakes on your corporate memo, promotional flyer, or 400-page manuscript.

Chapter 6 explained how to use AutoCorrect. When this feature is enabled, Word catches the most common spelling errors and fixes them without even calling your attention to the change. You can even add your own tricky words to the AutoCorrect list. This feature is not exhaustive, however, so Word offers additional proofreading tools.

## Setting spelling and grammar options

Some people are natural spellers and careful typists who make few errors. Most of us don't come anywhere near this high standard, however, and can use some help. You can customize your spelling and grammar preferences in the Preferences dialog box, shown in Figure 11.1. You reach this dialog box by choosing Word ⇨ Preferences and clicking the Spelling and Grammar button.

**FIGURE 11.1**

Spelling and Grammar preferences enable you to customize Word's proofreading options.

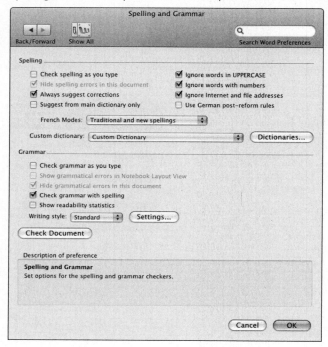

The preference options are extensive:

- **Check spelling as you type:** By default, this option is enabled. Word immediately compares every word you type against its dictionary and marks those that do not match. If you deselect this option, you can still use Word's other spelling tools.

- **Hide spelling errors in this document:** This option disables spell-checking as you type only for the current document. If you are creating a document with lots of non-standard terms, choose this option so Word doesn't fill your text with marks of supposed misspellings.

- **Always suggest corrections:** This option is selected by default. Word takes an educated guess as to possible words you might have intended to type and offers them up in the spelling context menu and Spelling dialog box. If you deselect this option, Word still marks words that don't match any in its dictionary, but doesn't make any alternative suggestions.

- **Suggest from main dictionary only:** Selecting this option turns off any custom dictionaries, forcing Word to use only the main dictionary.

- **Ignore words in UPPERCASE:** Abbreviations and acronyms are usually in uppercase. Selecting this option instructs Word to ignore these words, which might otherwise be flagged as misspellings.

- **Ignore words with numbers:** Word's dictionary contains common number-letter combinations such as 1st and 2nd, but doesn't have a match for CS3 (as in the Adobe Creative Suite) or if you refer to your child as a 3yo (popular shorthand on the Internet for "three-year-old" that's making its way into other casual publications). Select this option to instruct Word to ignore any number-letter combinations.

- **Ignore Internet and file addresses:** This option instructs Word not to check spelling in URLs and file paths, which commonly use non-standard spelling or abbreviations.

- **Use German post-reform rules:** This option is relevant only if you have the German dictionary enabled in Word. The spelling rules for German were reformed in 1996 in an attempt to simplify and standardize the language. Outside of academic and government settings, however, many people still use the pre-reform rules. Thus, Word offers you a choice.

- **French modes:** This option is relevant only if you have the French dictionary enabled in Word. These options determine which set of French spelling rules to honor.

- **Custom dictionary:** You can add new words or terminology specific to your field to a custom dictionary on your computer.

- **Check grammar as you type:** By default, this option is enabled. Word immediately examines every sentence you type against its grammar rules and marks any grammatical errors.

- **Show grammatical errors in Notebook Layout view:** Most documents created in Notebook Layout view deliberately contain disjointed words and incomplete sentences. This option is best left disabled.

- **Hide grammatical errors in this document:** This option disables grammar-checking as you type for the current document only.

- **Check grammar with spelling:** If you want to separate proofreading for grammar from that of spelling, disable this option.

- **Show readability statistics:** This option calculates the approximate reading level of your document based on word usage and complex sentence formation. These statistics are primarily used by teachers, although some fiction authors also use them to get an idea of readability in their work.

- **Writing style:** Your writing style can (and should) vary by the demands of your project. A letter to a friend is less formal than a cover letter for your resume, for example. Fiction writing is much more grammatically relaxed than technical writing. Choose a writing style from the pop-up menu. Choose Custom and then click Settings to pick and choose specific grammatical rules from the Grammar Settings dialog box shown in Figure 11.2.

- **Check/Recheck document:** Click this button to initiate a new review of your document based on any settings you have adjusted.

**FIGURE 11.2**

Customize the grammar rules you want Word to check in the Grammar Settings dialog box.

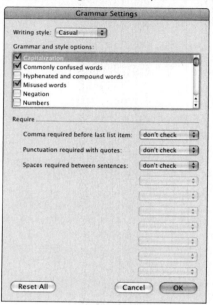

The Grammar Settings dialog box not only lets you customize which rules to follow, but it also provides options to accommodate variations in grammar, such as putting periods and commas before or after the quotation mark at the end of a quote. Also keep in mind that words that can serve as both nouns and verbs often confuse Word's grammar-checking, particularly when they appear in long sentences with subordinate clauses. Many Word users eventually turn off grammar-checking entirely.

If you learned to type in the old days when you always put two spaces after a period, it's a hard habit to break in favor of the new standard of one space. If nothing else, you may want to have Word check for those errors, although you also can do a Find and Replace for that when you complete your document.

**NOTE** Readability statistics offer only a very general approximation of reading level. Word uses the Flesch Reading Ease score and the Kincaid Grade-Level Score to determine readability. Neither score is completely accurate, nor is Word's formula for determining them. It is based on a strict set of grammatical rules with no ability to assess well-crafted passages that break those rules. While the readability statistics may serve as a point of interest and comparison, you should avoid using them as the basis for any choices you make as a writer or for grading someone's work.

### Using Custom and Foreign Dictionaries

Word's main dictionary contains thousands of words, but it is not exhaustive. This is why Word allows you to add words it does not recognize. While it may appear that Word adds these entries to the main dictionary, in fact, it adds them to a custom dictionary. The integration between these dictionaries is so smooth that you may not realize it's even there, but understanding custom dictionaries opens new doors.

You can directly edit the custom dictionary by entering the Spelling and Grammar preferences and clicking the Dictionaries button to open the Custom Dictionaries dialog box, shown in Figure 11.3. Select the Custom Dictionary, and click Edit. All the words you've ever added to the dictionary appear in an editable list. You may add or delete words in this list as well as correct any errors you mistakenly added to the dictionary.

**FIGURE 11.3**

Create additional dictionaries for technical terms.

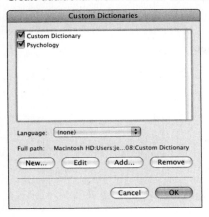

You can create additional custom dictionaries to suit specific purposes. If you are a chemist, for example, create a dictionary for chemical terms. There are two methods for creating a new custom dictionary. Here's the most direct approach:

1. **Open a new blank document.**

2. **Enter each word you want to include on a separate line.**

   The dictionary is case sensitive, so be sure to add both capitalized and lowercase entries as necessary. If you wish, you can sort your entries alphabetically by selecting the list and choosing Table ⇨ Sort. Word automatically realizes you are attempting to sort text paragraphs, so you can just click OK without modifying any of the settings. Sorting your list is optional and doesn't affect its use in Word, but you may find it easier to locate words later if you need to modify or add to the dictionary.

3. **Choose File ⇨ Save (or ⌘+S), and give the dictionary a name.**

4. **In the Format menu, choose Speller Custom Dictionary (.dic) format.**

5. **Navigate to the Library ⇨ Preferences ⇨ Microsoft ⇨ Office 2008 folder.**

6. **Press Save.**

7. **Open the Custom Dictionaries dialog box by choosing Word ⇨ Preferences ⇨ Spelling and Grammar ⇨ Dictionaries, and click Add.**

8. **Navigate to the new dictionary, and click OK.**

Creating a dictionary in this manner makes it easier to use Word's editing and sorting tools and allows you to set the Zoom settings to make the process more comfortable. You also can create custom dictionaries directly in the Custom Dictionaries dialog box:

1. Open the Custom Dictionaries dialog box by choosing Word ⇨ Preferences ⇨ Spelling and Grammar ⇨ Dictionaries.
2. Click New to open the New Dictionary dialog box.
3. Give the dictionary a name, and click Save.
4. Click Edit to open the new dictionary. Word opens a new blank document.
5. Populate the dictionary, typing each word on a separate line.
6. Save the document by choosing File ⇨ Save or pressing ⌘+S.
7. Return to the Custom Dictionaries dialog box to select or deselect the new dictionary.

As you can see, the biggest difference in the two approaches is whether you first add the file to the Custom Dictionary list and then create the entries or you create the dictionary entries first and then add it. Regardless of which method you use to create it, once complete, you can select and deselect it as needed. You can add more words as you encounter them in your document. Note, however, that if you have the default custom dictionary enabled along with those you created, any new words you add as you write automatically go into the default. To add new words to a specific dictionary, you need to go back to Edit mode for that dictionary and manually add to them.

If you work in other languages, Microsoft installs several foreign dictionaries along with the Office applications. To activate one of these dictionaries, you need to tell Word that you're working in another language. Do this by selecting your text and choosing Tools ⇨ Language. Select a language from the Language dialog box and click OK. If you set a different language for only a portion of your document, Word automatically switches to the appropriate foreign dictionary for the selected text and then returns to its native dictionary for the remainder.

### Creating an exclusion dictionary

Word's main dictionary is pre-populated with the most common words, but it does not allow for variations in spelling. The main dictionary contains the word "color," for example, while you may prefer to use "colour." You cannot delete "color" from the main dictionary because it is not editable. Your only alternative, then, is to create an *exclusion dictionary*.

An exclusion dictionary lists words in the main dictionary that you want Word to flag as incorrect. In other words, you're telling Word that its main dictionary is wrong. To create an exclusion dictionary, open a blank document. Enter any standard spellings that you want Word to flag as incorrect. Thus, list the word "color" if you want Word to flag it. As with other custom dictionaries, this list is case sensitive, so you should list both "color" and "Color."

Save your exclusion dictionary in the Library ⇨ Preferences ⇨ Microsoft ⇨ Office 2008 folder. Save in the Speller Exclude Dictionary format. Exit Word and relaunch it for the exclusion dictionary to take effect.

## Checking spelling and grammar as you type

When Word is checking spelling as you type, a red line under a word indicates a spelling error. When you see an error marked in red, you can choose to retype the word correctly or press Control+click on the word to open a context menu with proofing options:

- **Help:** Choose this to open the Help window.
- **Suggestions:** Word makes educated guesses on which word you might have intended and lists them for you to select. When you click a word from this list, Word immediately changes the mis-spelling. If Word cannot determine your intent, this area states "(no spelling suggestions)." If the correct word does not appear on the list, you need to manually correct it.
- **Ignore:** This choice instructs Word to ignore this particular word, regardless of whether it is spelled correctly.
- **Ignore All:** Choose this to instruct Word to ignore this word throughout the document.
- **Add:** This choice instructs Word to add this word to its dictionary.
- **AutoCorrect:** This accesses matching options from the AutoCorrect list. These are usually the same options that appear in the list of suggestions.
- **Spelling:** Selecting this option opens the Spelling dialog box, shown in Figure 11.4.

The Spelling dialog box

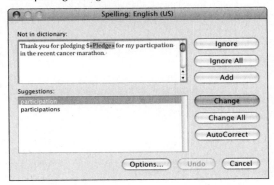

A green line under a word or sentence indicates a grammar error. If you spot the problem right away, you can fix it yourself. Otherwise, press Control+click to open a context menu:

- **Help:** This option opens the Help window.
- **Suggestions:** If the error involves capitalization, contractions, or other minimal adjustments, Word suggests solutions. For other errors, such as passive voice or mistaken noun-verb agreement, Word merely identifies the nature of the problem.
- **Ignore:** Choose this to instruct Word to ignore this particular error.
- **Grammar:** This option opens the Grammar dialog box, shown in Figure 11.5.

**FIGURE 11.5**

The Grammar dialog box

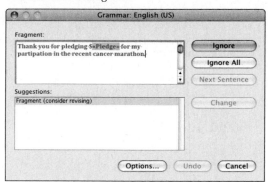

## Checking spelling and grammar on demand

There's much to be said for immediacy, but having Word mark your text as you type can become a distraction. If you find yourself compelled to fix every mistake immediately and then you lose track of what you were typing, you should disable the Check as you type features. Instead, you can check grammar, spelling, or both when you complete your document (or any other time you want to clean up your document). To do this, choose Tools ⇨ Spelling and Grammar (or Option+⌘+L). The Spelling and Grammar dialog box, shown in Figure 11.6, displays each error it encounters in your document, beginning at the insertion point and moving forward. If you want to start at the beginning, position the insertion point at the top of the document before invoking the command.

**FIGURE 11.6**

The Spelling and Grammar dialog box locates each error in the document.

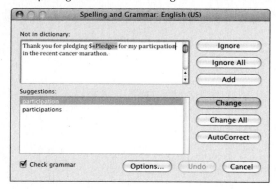

When Word encounters an error, it displays the word or passage in the dialog box. Suggestions on spelling or grammatical matters are listed below the error. To change the word to one of the suggestions, click the correct spelling and press the Change button. To change all occurrences of that misspelling throughout your document, choose Change All. If you want to ignore the error—perhaps it is intentional to illustrate a point or an obscure term or usage—choose either Ignore (for that specific incidence) or Ignore All (to ignore that word throughout the document). If the word is correctly spelled and often-used, click Add to append it to the default custom dictionary. If none of these options solves your problem, you can correct the spelling error directly in the dialog box. Finally, if you commonly make the same typo, click the AutoCorrect button to add the typo and correctly spelled word to the AutoCorrect list.

# Counting Words and Lines

Many writing assignments, from college papers to newspaper and magazine articles, have page, word, or line guidelines. You can see your document's page and word count at the bottom of the document window, as shown in Figure 11.7. If you require more details, such as the number of characters, paragraphs, or lines in the document, click the word count display at the bottom of the window (or choose Tools ➪ Word Count) to open the Word Count dialog box, as shown in Figure 11.8.

Word displays the number of pages and the word count at the bottom of the document window.

The Word Count dialog box provides details about your document's word, line, and character count.

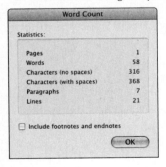

# Inserting a Watermark

A watermark is a faint picture or text that appears behind the text of your document. Watermarks are commonly used to mark documents as a draft or confidential or to add a seal or logo behind the text. This mark appears on every page of the document, which is particularly useful if portions of a draft or confidential document get separated from the cover page, so co-workers or collaborators still know to treat the pages with care.

If you want to add a watermark to your document, choose Insert ⇨ Watermark to open the Insert Watermark dialog box, shown in Figure 11.9.

To use a picture as a watermark, click the Picture radio button and click the Select Picture button. Locate the image you want to use, and click OK. The preview area provides an example of how the document will look with the watermark. The Washout option lightens the picture so it doesn't render your text unreadable. Word automatically scales your image to fill most of the page by default, but you can adjust this setting to make the image smaller.

**TIP** Watermarks interfere less with your text if they're in black and white. Most image-editing applications, including iPhoto, allow you to convert a color image to black and white. You can add a color watermark, but examine your document closely for readability and realize you will use up your color ink cartridges quickly if you apply such a watermark to a long document.

To use text as a watermark, click the Text radio button. The pop-up menu lists several common text options, or you can type your own message. Change the font and size settings as you wish and apply bold or italics. The transparency setting controls how dark the watermark appears on the page. Higher transparency settings fade the watermark so it doesn't detract from the document content. You can apply color to the watermark text, but just as with pictures, this may not be the best choice. Rather than color, the best way to set off a watermark is to orient it at an angle using the Orientation buttons.

Suppose you want to remove a watermark; let's say you edit your draft and are ready to print the final document, so you want to eliminate the Draft watermark. Return to the Insert Watermark dialog box, and select the No watermark radio button.

**FIGURE 11.9**

Watermarks communicate warnings about documents or enhance the visual impression of your work.

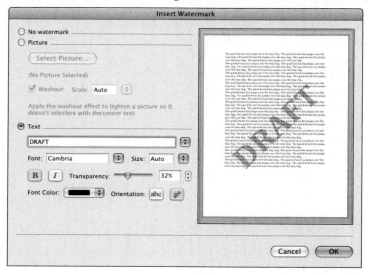

# Printing Documents

You have come up with an idea or assignment, created and formatted a document, added any necessary tables, graphics, bibliographies, and indices, and proofread it. You're now at the moment of truth—time to print.

 The easiest way to print is to click the Print button from the Standard toolbar. This automatically commands your default printer to print one copy of the entire document. Most likely, this is exactly what you need, and you can achieve your final goal with the click of one button. Simple!

You may need two copies of the document, however, or maybe 15 collated copies. In that case, choose File ⇨ Print (or ⌘+P) to open the Print dialog box, shown in Figure 11.10. From here, you can set the number of copies and the collate option, you also can tell Word to print only a particular range of pages. You also can change printers if you have more than one configured.

### FIGURE 11.10

The Print dialog box provides more printing options than the toolbar button.

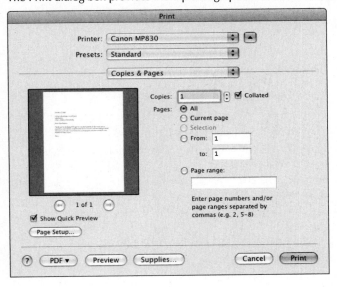

Your print options depend to some extent on your installed printer(s), but most printers offer the following panels in the pop-up menu:

- **Copies and Pages:** This panel includes settings for the number of copies, collation, and the range of pages to print. When setting a page range for printing, you can use commas to separate individual pages, such as 5, 18, 21.
- **Microsoft Word:** This panel allows you to print some of the elements that make up your document, such as the document properties, markup, styles, AutoText, and key assignments. You also can choose to print only odd or even pages, which is useful if you are trying to print on both sides of the page without the advantage of a duplex printer.

- **Layout:** This panel enables you to print multiple pages of your document on one printed page. You can add a border to a page or table without affecting your saved document.

- **Summary:** This panel does not print anything. Instead, it summarizes all the print settings you've chosen on the myriad other panels, giving you an overview of how your document will print.

- **Additional Panels:** Your printer may provide many other panels. The Canon MP830 printer, for example, installs panels for Color Matching, Paper Handling, Cover Pages, Scheduler, Quality and Media, Color Options, Special Effects, Borderless Printing, and Duplex Printing and Margin. Each of these panels provides additional printing options, such as the ability to print on special paper or in duplex (both sides of the page automatically).

After reviewing all the panels and options, you can save your settings for future print jobs. Open the Presets pop-up menu, choose Save As, and name your setting combination. You can save multiple configurations for different uses, saving you time in the future.

The Supplies button in the Print dialog box links to the Apple Store. If Apple sells ink cartridges for your particular printer, you can order them here. Apple does not necessarily have the best prices on printer ink, however, nor does it offer an extensive range of products for all printers.

When you have configured the options to your liking, press Print to send the document to your printer.

## Printing to PDF

The PDF button at the bottom of the Print dialog box provides an additional way to save PDF files. You also can save a document as a PDF using the Save As command, but "printing" to a PDF file provides many more options than simply saving the file in PDF format. The PDF pop-up menu, shown in Figure 11.11, allows you to do the following:

- **Save as PDF:** Use this option to save the document as a standard PDF file.

- **Save as PostScript:** A PostScript file contains embedded printing instructions for professional print shops, which often use PostScript laser printers.

- **Fax PDF:** If your computer is connected by modem to a phone line, you can enter a phone number and fax the document without having to print it first.

- **Mail PDF:** This opens Apple's Mail application and attaches the file to a new message. This feature does not work with Entourage.

- **Save as PDF-X:** A PDF-X file is another standard used by professional print shops.

- **Save PDF to iPhoto:** This saves the file in PDF format and places it in your iPhoto library.

- **Save PDF to Web Receipts Folder:** If your document contains an invoice or receipt, using this option saves the document as a PDF and automatically puts it in your Documents ⇨ Web Receipts folder.

You can do more with PDF files depending upon which applications you have installed in addition to Office. If you use applications such as Journler or Yojimbo, for example, your pop-up menu shows options to Save to Journler and Save to Yojimbo.

**FIGURE 11.11**

Printing to a PDF file offers many advantages.

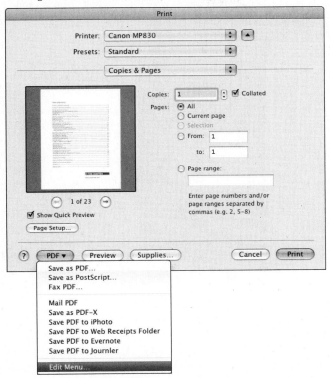

## Previewing documents

As with so many other features, Word offers two methods for previewing your document before printing. Select File ➪ Print Preview to open Word's built-in preview system, shown in Figure 11.12. You can view each page individually or click the Multiple Pages button to view smaller thumbnails of several pages at once. The Zoom menu allows you to increase or decrease the size of the thumbnails for better viewing. You can use the Ruler to change margins, although you should do this in the regular document window instead, for more control.

## FIGURE 11.12

Word's internal Print Preview tool allows you to view your document in its entirety before printing.

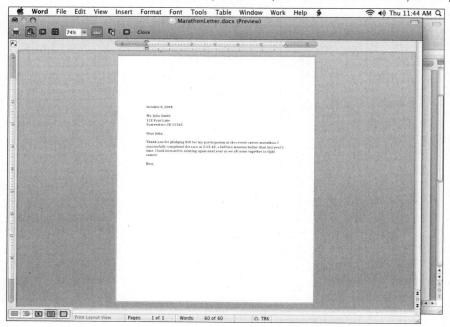

The Preview button in the Print dialog box opens the Mac OS X Preview application, which is considerably more robust than Word's built-in offering. In addition to scrolling through your pages from the Sidebar, you also can annotate your document and scroll in on selected portions for greater magnification. Best of all, Word temporarily converts your file to PDF for the journey to Preview, which provides yet another gateway to PDF conversion if you choose File ➪ Save As in Preview.

## Setting page setup options

Word provides other printer-related options aside from those in the Print dialog box. Choose File ➪ Page Setup to open the Page Setup dialog box, shown in Figure 11.13. From here, select the paper size on which you are printing. If you are working on a tri-fold brochure or envelope, for example, you can switch the orientation of the document from portrait to landscape. You also can scale your document to take up less space on the page, although you can control this better using the margin settings in the document.

Switch the Settings menu to Microsoft Word to apply different printer settings for one portion of a document, as shown in Figure 11.14. For example, you can keep a letter and its envelope in the same document. Set the Page Attributes settings for the letter, and then switch to the Microsoft Word settings and select "This point forward" from the Apply Page Setup settings to pop-up menu. Then return to the Page Attributes settings to set the options for the envelope at the end of the document.

**FIGURE 11.13**

Page Setup provides still more paper and printing options.

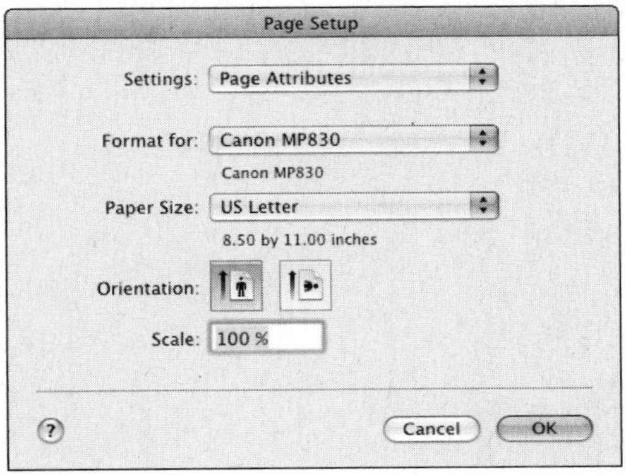

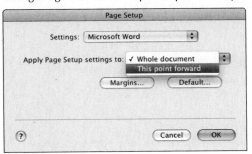

**FIGURE 11.14**

Change Page Attributes for specific portions of your document.

## Printing envelopes and labels

Word makes printing envelopes so easy that it's faster than writing them by hand. A printed envelope lends a much more professional appearance to your correspondence. Word also can print labels for various purposes.

### Creating envelopes

Most printers have slots or tray settings to feed envelopes. To set up Word to print to them, follow these steps:

1. **Choose Tools ⇨ Envelopes to open the Envelope dialog box, as shown in Figure 11.15.**

**FIGURE 11.15**

The Envelope dialog box makes it easy to format the delivery and return addresses.

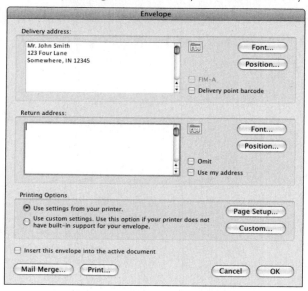

2. **Enter the recipient's address in the Delivery address box.**

   ■ Click the address card icon to select an address from the Office Address Book. Note that this feature does not open the Mac OS X Address Book application, so this feature is helpful only to Entourage users.

   ■ Click the Font button to change the font settings for the address.

   ■ Click the Position button to customize the position of the address on the envelope in the Address Position dialog box, as shown in Figure 11.16.

   ■ The FIM-A option is intended for courtesy reply envelopes, often sent with bills and other forms of mail that have an expected reply. Word formats these envelopes according to the U.S. Postal Service requirements.

   ■ A Delivery point barcode is a scanable code that appears at the bottom of some envelopes. These are not required, but are intended to speed delivery because they enable the USPS to use automated equipment to move your letter along rather than having to hand-sort it.

3. **Enter the Return address.** Business envelopes are often preprinted with a return address, so you may want to deselect this option. You can also choose to omit a return address for anonymity, but the USPS does not guarantee to get such envelopes to their destination if you do not apply proper postage. If you select the "Use my address" option, Word inserts the address you entered in the User Information panel of the Preferences dialog box.

**FIGURE 11.16**

Set the position of the address relative to the edges of the envelope.

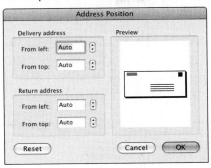

4. **Select either Page Setup or Custom from the Printing Options:**

   ■ **Page Setup:** If your printer has an envelope slot that can accommodate your envelope, choose this option to open the Print dialog box and select the correct paper size for your envelope. This option works best when you are printing on a standard #10 envelope.

   ■ **Custom:** If your printer lacks an envelope feeder or you are printing on a non-standard envelope size, choose this option to specify the size and Feed method from the Custom Page Options dialog box, shown in Figure 11.17.

**FIGURE 11.17**

You can configure any size envelope using the Custom Page Options dialog box.

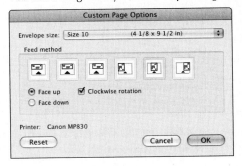

5. **If you want Word to insert the envelope into the document from which you launched the Tools ⇨ Envelope command, select Insert this envelope into the active document.** Otherwise, Word creates a new document for the envelope.

6. **Press Print to print the envelope or OK to create the envelope document or insert it into the active document without printing.**

You also can use the Envelope dialog box to open the Mail Merge Manager for a mass mailing. This is explained later in this chapter.

## Printing labels

Word can create labels of all shapes and sizes. Beyond the traditional return address label, you can use labels for file folders, CDs, and nametags, among other ideas. You can print a single label or an entire sheet of the same label. Follow these steps to create a label:

1. **Choose Tools ⇨ Labels to open the Labels dialog box, shown in Figure 11.18.**

---
**FIGURE 11.18**

Use the Labels tool to create a single label or an entire sheet of them.

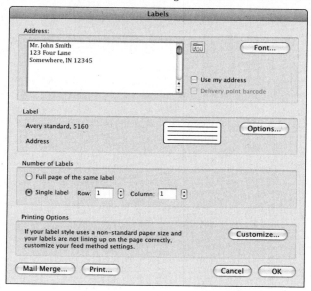

---

2. **Enter the text you want to put on the label.**
3. **Click the Options button to open the Label Options dialog box, shown in Figure 11.19.**
4. **Select your printer type, either dot matrix or laser and ink jet.**
5. **Choose the manufacturer of your labels from the Label products menu.**
6. **Choose a specific Product number, as listed on the box of labels.** The Label information area displays the dimensions of the label, allowing you to verify the specifications for your product.
7. **If you have a generic or unidentified label sheet, choose New Label to enter the dimensions of your labels.**
8. **Press OK to close the Label Options dialog box and return to the Labels dialog box.**

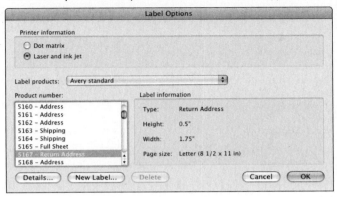

**FIGURE 11.19**

Word offers preset label options for hundreds of label types, including most Avery labels.

9. **Choose to print either a full page of the same label or an individual label.** If you are printing only one label, you can specify the column and row of that label on the page. This allows you to print a single label and save the remaining labels on the sheet for future print jobs.

10. **Press Print to print the labels immediately or OK to create a new document with the labels formatted on the page.**

You can use the Mail Merge button to open the Mail Merge Manager and create a series of labels with different addresses, as explained later in this chapter.

# Creating Mass Mailings

A mass mailing is a form letter sent to multiple recipients. In Word, you can create a letter encoded with fields to customize such information as the recipient address and the salutation. You then merge this letter with a database containing the field data to automate the creation of the individual letters; thus, Microsoft calls this process *Mail Merge*. Don't let this name sell the power of this feature short, however. You can use mail merge to create an address book, product catalog, billing invoices, or even party invitations.

## Creating a form letter

A mail merge brings two types of files together, a data source and the main document (also called the form letter, although that term may not reflect the true nature of the file). The main document contains the body of your project. If you run a marathon for charity, for example, you might create a form letter to thank your donors.

As you prepare your document, think about the unique data you need for each completed copy. For donor thank-you notes, you need the first and last names of the donor, the donor's complete address, and the amount of the donation. By preparing your form letter first, you can ensure that your data source contains all the fields necessary to complete your task.

Save your document in order to preserve your work so far and give the file a name, but leave it open on your screen. Your document is not complete yet, but you need to add a data source before proceeding.

## Using data source files

You can use one of several applications to create your data source. This file contains the unique names and addresses or other custom information you want to include in your merged document. Word can pull this data from an Excel file, FileMaker Pro database, Entourage address book, tab-delimited text file, comma separated value (CSV) file, or a Word table created in a separate document.

No matter the data source, consistency in your data fields is critical to the success of your mail merge. If you do not enter your data consistently—sometimes entering a product's item number into the same field with its name, for example—you create an incomplete and unprofessional catalog. If you want to personalize the salutation in your letter, referring to recipients by their first names, you need separate fields for first and last names so you can select the one you need.

### Creating a new data source

Unless you already have your data compiled in a database or spreadsheet, the fastest way to create a new data source is directly within Word. To do this, follow these steps:

1. **Choose Tools ⇨ Mail Merge Manager to open the Mail Merge Manager Palette, shown in Figure 11.20.**

2. **In the first pane, 1. Select Document Type, click the Create New button and choose the type of mail merge you are creating.** Word automatically assumes your current document forms the main document for the merge.

3. **In the second pane, 2. Select Recipients List, click the Get List button and select New Data Source to open the Create Data Source dialog box, shown in Figure 11.21.**

---

**FIGURE 11.20**

The Mail Merge Manager Palette guides you step by step through the mass mailing process.

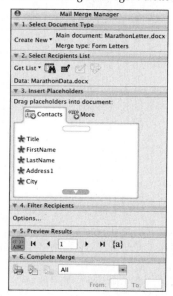

---

**FIGURE 11.21**

Create and remove field names in the Create Data Source dialog box.

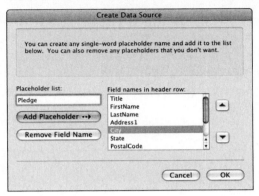

4. In the Field names in header row list, remove any field names you don't require for this project.

5. If you need additional fields, enter a field name in the Placeholder list and click the Add Placeholder button.

6. **Press OK to close the Create Data Source dialog box, and then name and save the Data Source file.** If you will use this data source for future projects, name it something easily remembered. If this compilation of data is unique to this project, you may want to give the file a name related to its associated form letter. If the form letter is named Marathon.docx, for example, the data source file might be named MarathonData.docx.

7. **The Data Form dialog box, shown in Figure 11.22, opens when you save the Data Source file.** Fill in the form for your first record, tabbing between each field. Click Add New to add another record. Use the arrows at the bottom of the dialog box to navigate through records you've already created. Choose Delete to erase the current record. If you delete a record in error, choose Restore to re-populate the form.

8. **When you are finished entering records, click OK.**

If you prefer, you can enter records directly in the data source document instead of through the Data Form dialog box. To do this, press the View Source button to open the data source file. Your data is stored in a regular Word table, and you can add or delete rows (records) or modify any entry. To return to the Data Form dialog box, click the Data Form button on the Database toolbar, which automatically appears when you open the data source file.

## Using existing data sources

If you already have a database in Excel, FileMaker Pro, or Entourage, or a tab-delimited or CSV file, you can merge it with your main document instead of creating a new data source file. With your form letter open, follow these steps:

1. **Choose Tools ⇨ Mail Merge Manager, and click the Create New button to set the document as a form letter, envelope, label, or catalog.**

2. **In the Select Recipients List pane, press the Get List button.**
   - If your file is an Excel spreadsheet or tab-delimited file, choose Open Data Source.
   - If your data resides in FileMaker Pro or your Office Address Book (Entourage), choose the appropriate option from the Get List menu.
3. **Navigate to the file on your Mac, and press Open.**

> **NOTE** Unlike when you create a data source file directly in Word, you cannot edit your records without returning to the original source application.

Whether you create a new data source or use an existing one, you can see the fields listed in the Insert Placeholders pane in the Mail Merge Manager. Now you can add them to your main document.

---

**FIGURE 11.22**

Fill out a Data Form for each record.

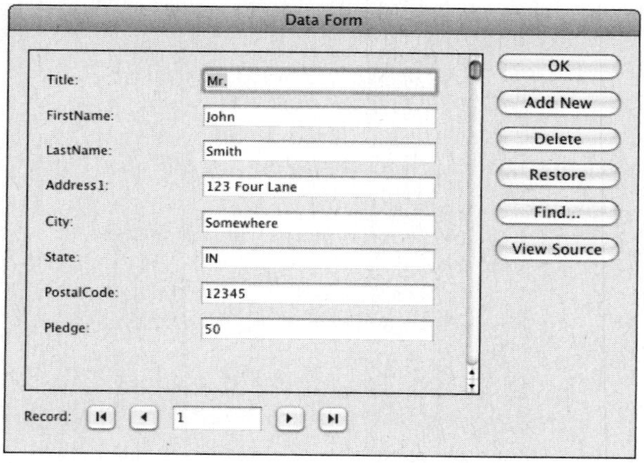

## Adding fields to the form letter

Step 3 in the Mail Merge Manager reads "Insert Placeholders." All the fields for your data source appear in the Contacts list, as shown in Figure 11.23. To add placeholders to your document, simply select one from the list and drag it into your document. Position the placeholder exactly where you want it to appear in the document before releasing the mouse button. You can edit the main document during this process to accommodate the fields. When entering an address, for example, you need to manually insert a comma and a space between the City and State fields.

The More tab in the Insert Placeholders pane provides more advanced options. If you wanted to prepare your letters in advance, for example, but don't yet know your completion time for the marathon you are running the next day, you can insert an Ask query to prompt you for that information before you print the documents. Other options in the More tab allow you to introduce logic into your mail merge, merging only a particular record if certain conditions are met.

When you finish adding placeholders to your document, save the document. Your Mail Merge Manager settings are saved with the document, so if you come back to it later, the data source file is still linked to the main document. You can now use the Filter Recipients pane to group records by specified fields or sort them alphabetically. If you have a large number of letters, for example, you may choose to sort them by state in order to make it easier to comply with the USPS bulk-mailing regulations.

**FIGURE 11.23**

Choose placeholders from the Mail Merge Manager to insert fields into your document.

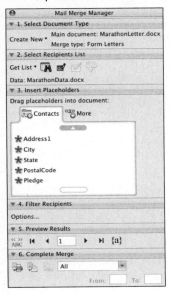

When you are ready to see the merged documents, use the Preview Results pane to browse through them. If only the placeholder fields appear, click the View Merged Data button to display the actual data merged into the document. Review your document carefully for missing spaces and punctuation or the need for other formatting. Remember, you can apply formatting to a field, so you can add bold or italic to the merged data.

If your review meets your requirements, you are ready to complete the merge. The Complete Merge pane, shown in Figure 11.24, provides several options:

- **Merging to the Printer:** If you want to print your merged documents, press this button and then press Print in the Print dialog box. As with any other print job, you can change the number of copies and set other options before printing.

- **Merging to a New Document:** If you want to personalize the merged documents in some way or are simply not yet ready to print, use this option to save the merged letters to a file. Each copy is separated in the new document by a page break and retains all the formatting of the original main document.

- **Merging to Email:** This option is available only if you use Entourage as your default e-mail program. If you meet this criteria, use this option to open the Mail Recipient dialog box, and then use the To menu to specify which field in your data source contains the e-mail addresses to which you want to send the letters. Provide a subject for the e-mails and specify whether the letter should be sent as the body of the e-mail or as an attachment. Click Mail Merge to Outbox to complete the merge and queue up each individual e-mail in your Entourage outbox.

**NOTE**   If you merge into a new document, it no longer has any connection to the original document. If you want to eliminate, filter, or sort records, you need to return to the original mail merge document and create another document (or print at that point). You can, however, manually modify the new document just as you would any other document, such as deleting pages.

**FIGURE 11.24**

The Complete Merge pane gives you some further options for completing your document.

## Creating labels and envelopes in the Mail Merge Manager

As mentioned earlier, you can generate envelopes and labels using the Mail Merge Manager. To create labels, choose Tools ⇨ Mail Merge Manager and then choose Create New ⇨ Labels. Select a product from the Label Options dialog box, and click OK. In the Mail Merge Manager, click Get List from the Select Recipients List pane, use or create a data source, and then continue as you would for a form letter: Choose the placeholders you want to put on the labels, filter and sort the list, preview the resulting label sheets, and then print.

To create envelopes, choose Tools ⇨ Mail Merge Manager and then choose Create New ⇨ Envelopes. In the Envelopes dialog box, leave the delivery field blank, but enter the Return address as you would for a single envelope (explained earlier in this chapter). Click the Position buttons to set the location where the delivery and return addresses should appear, and use the Page Setup or Custom buttons to configure the printer for your envelope size. Proceed to select the data source and follow the other steps for creating a mail merge.

**TIP** If your printer cannot feed multiple envelopes, use the Current Record option from the Merge Data Range pop-up menu in the Complete Merge panel. You can then print one envelope at a time, using the Preview Results to scroll through the records.

# Summary

In this chapter, we covered how to proofread your document as you type and in a final review. Although you can correct most typos and misspellings while you work, it never hurts to give your document a final spelling and grammar check.

You learned how to create watermarks to mark your draft or confidential document in order to remind readers of its status and prevent mass distribution of sensitive material. You learned how to print your document when it's complete and how to print an accompanying envelope or label. If you are sending the same form letter to a long list of people, you discovered that it's easier to create a mass mailing than to manually edit the document and print each letter individually.

You are now armed with the skills to tackle even the most challenging Word documents. It's time to move on to the next application in the Office suite, Excel.

# Part III

# Using Excel

# Chapter 12

# Excel Basics

Ever since spreadsheet applications such as Lotus 1-2-3 took the office world by storm in the early days of the PC, they have been one of the cornerstones of the modern office. Microsoft Excel, to be sure, is far and away the most popular spreadsheet software in existence. Excel is a whiz with numbers, allowing you to build workbooks with many worksheet pages organized in rows and columns. Individual cells in a worksheet can contain numbers, text, or complex formulas to calculate values. Excel goes way beyond number crunching prowess, however, by allowing you to integrate data from databases, generate charts and graphs, collaborate with others, and customize the look and feel of your worksheets to tailor them for specific tasks.

Microsoft Excel started on the Mac and has evolved to keep up with its Windows cousin. If you are new to Excel 2008, this chapter gives you an introduction to the application, including a tour of the various elements that make up the user interface. You learn how to open workbooks, add and delete individual spreadsheets called worksheets to a workbook, apply templates to a workbook, and save them. In addition, you learn how to work with views and create custom views. Finally, you learn how you can protect the data contained in your workbooks.

## Navigating the Excel Window

As with the other Office 2008 programs, Excel 2008 provides an updated look as compared with the previous version released in 2004. The updated toolbars and icons give Excel 2008 a modern, clean look. Figure 12.1 shows the Excel window with a blank worksheet displayed.

Excel features the look and feel common to all Office 2008 programs, the same as you saw with Word in earlier chapters. If you've followed along, you should be able to apply what you learned with Word to make navigating Excel a breeze. Some elements are unique to Excel, however, so look at the following descriptions to learn the basics of the elements that make up the Excel window.

**FIGURE 12.1**

This is the new interface for Excel 2008, with a blank worksheet displayed.

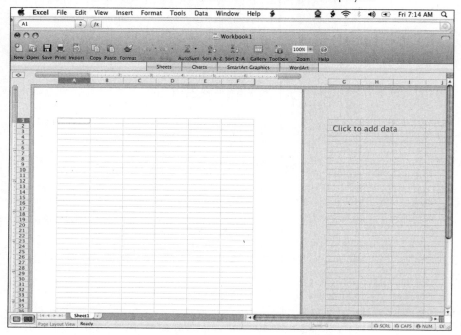

## Title and menu bar

When Excel is active, the top of the screen shows the title and menu bar. This bar shows the name of the program (Excel), along with items that make up the main menu categories. You can click any of the menu items to expand the menu to show related commands and submenus. Submenu items are identifiable by an arrow icon on the right, and selecting these items opens up a new range of items. A menu item with an ellipsis (three dots) at the end opens a dialog box when selected. Figure 12.2 shows the title and menu bar in all its splendor.

**FIGURE 12.2**

The title and menu bar shows the name of the program and the main menu commands.

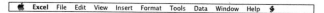

## Formula bar

Below the title and menu bar, but above the main window is an element that's unique to Excel: the formula bar. The formula bar shows the contents—whether data, a formula, or a function call—of the currently selected cell. It can be used edit a formula as well. If the formula bar is not visible, checking the Formula Bar item under the View menu activates it. If it's visible and you would like the screen real estate back, you can hide it by unchecking that menu item or by clicking the small red button on the left side of the bar. The formula bar is shown in Figure 12.3.

**FIGURE 12.3**

The formula bar can be used to create, view, and edit formulas in cells.

By default, the formula bar is docked just under the main menu, but it can be dragged away from that position by clicking and dragging the handle on the left side of the bar. The bar also includes a resize handle in the lower-right corner, which can be used to make the bar wider across the top of the screen if desired. Note that you cannot adjust the size vertically.

Two elements on the formula bar are actually used edit cell contents. On the left side of the bar, the functions drop-down box can be used to choose from commonly used functions, including a More Functions option that opens a dialog box called the Formula Builder. The right side of the bar is an edit control that can be used to view or edit cell contents directly.

See Chapter 15 to learn more about formulas, the formula bar, and the Formula Builder.

Just below the formula bar is the program window, the top of which contains the program window controls and the workbook name. The program window controls—the three colored circle icons located at the far left side—allow you to close, minimize, and zoom the workbook window. (To learn more about how to use the program window controls, see Chapter 3.)

## Rulers

Like Word's rulers, the Excel Ruler feature can be used to help position elements on the screen, set margins, or resize cells to a particular size. The horizontal ruler at the top of the workbook shows the horizontal positioning of items on the page, while the vertical ruler on the left side of the worksheet window shows vertical positioning. You can toggle the ruler feature on or off by choosing View ⇨ Ruler. The rulers are shown in Figure 12.4.

## Scroll box and scroll bars

As you add data that exceeds the viewing space of the window, you can use the vertical and horizontal scroll bars, shown in Figure 12.5, to move around to various parts of your worksheets. For example, you can drag the vertical scroll box up or down to move around in the workbook, or you can drag the horizontal scroll box to move left or right. You also can click the scroll arrows to move around.

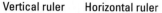

**FIGURE 12.4**

The Ruler feature can be used to set the size of cells, set margins, or position items on a worksheet.

Vertical ruler    Horizontal ruler

## Standard toolbar

Below the program window controls is the Standard toolbar, shown in Figure 12.6. This toolbar displays a row of tool icons for common Excel tasks, including opening or printing workbooks. To activate a feature or command, just click the associated icon. By default, the Standard toolbar appears every time you create a new workbook. Depending on the task you are performing in Excel, other toolbars may appear when needed. Excel offers 12 toolbars, and you can even create your own custom toolbar.

You can control which toolbars appear onscreen using the View menu. Choose View ➪ Toolbars, and click the name of the toolbar you want to display. A check mark next to the toolbar name indicates that the toolbar is displayed; no check mark means the toolbar display is turned off. (See Chapter 34 to learn more about customizing toolbars. To learn more about using toolbars in Office, see Chapter 3.)

**TIP** You can Control+click an empty area of a toolbar to display a shortcut menu of related commands. For example, if you Control+click the Standard toolbar, you can view commands for changing how icons are displayed on the toolbar, accessing other toolbars, and resetting or customizing the toolbar. For example, if you want to view icons only, click the Icon Only command.

**FIGURE 12.5**

Scroll bars let you move around your worksheet.

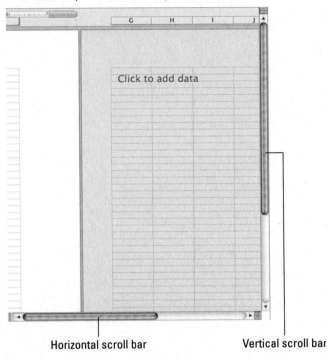

Horizontal scroll bar          Vertical scroll bar

**FIGURE 12.6**

Excel's Standard toolbar gives you quick access to common Excel commands.

## Toolbox

The Excel 2008 Toolbox consolidates what were formerly separate tool palettes in previous versions of Excel into one convenient window. By placing all the common palettes into one easy interface, Excel makes it effortless to access tools and features you use the most. Figure 12.7 shows the Toolbox with the Formatting Palette, with the Font, Number, and Page Setup tools displayed.

The Toolbox combines many tool palettes into one tabbed window.

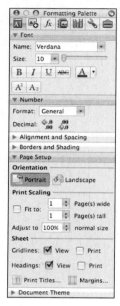

To open or hide the Toolbox, use either of these methods:

- Click the Toolbox button on the Standard toolbar.
- Choose View ➪ Formatting Palette (or select the name of the palette you want to display).

The Excel Toolbox includes tabs for the following palettes: Formatting, Object, Formula Builder, Scrapbook, Reference Tools, Compatibility Report, and Projects. To view any particular palette, click the associated palette tab at the top of the palette box. For example, if you click the Formatting Palette tab, the Toolbox displays formatting tools in sections or *panes* that you can expand or collapse based on your formatting needs. The name of the active palette appears at the top of the Toolbox. The Formatting Palette (refer to Figure 12.7) has panes for controlling fonts, styles, alignment and spacing, bulleted and numbered lists, borders and shading, margins, and themes. You can click a section or pane name to view its associated tools. (To learn more about using the Toolbox, see Chapter 3.)

## Status bar and view buttons

The Status bar, located at the bottom of the program window, shown in Figure 12.8, gives you some useful information on the status of your workbook.

The Status bar shows useful information regarding the current workbook.

The far left side of the Status bar displays the two view buttons you can use to change the way your workbook is displayed. To learn more about Excel's views, see "Changing Views" later in this chapter.

**Ready** The left side of the Status bar shows the current editing mode. The Ready mode is shown when Excel is waiting for you to do something. If you double-click an empty cell to enter new data, it displays Enter. When you double-click on a cell for editing that already has data, it displays Edit. If you are entering a formula and clicking a cell to select it for inclusion with the formula, it displays Point.

Sum=0 The middle of the Status bar includes a menu of handy integrated functions, shown in Figure 12.9. These functions calculates in real time using the numeric values in currently selected cells, whether these values are entered directly or calculated by a formula. The functions available are Average, Count, Count Nums, Max, Min, and Sum. To use one of the functions, click the function area of the Status bar to open the menu and select the function that you want. Then simply select multiple cells with numeric values, and the result of the chosen function with these cells as inputs is displayed right on the Status bar.

If your workbook occupies multiple pages, the middle of the Status bar shows the current page number and the total number of pages in the workbook.

SCRL CAPS NUM The right side of the Status bar has indicators showing the current status of the keyboard. A blue dot is displayed next to the SCRL, CAPS, and NUM indicators when the Scroll Lock, Caps Lock, or Num Lock are active, respectively.

---

**FIGURE 12.9**

Use this handy function menu on the Status bar for instant calculations.

| Help |
| --- |
| None |
| Average<br>Count<br>Count Nums<br>Max<br>Min<br>✓ Sum |

# Creating and Opening Workbooks and Worksheets

Each Office program works with its own file types, and the ones created in Excel are called *workbooks*. To use Excel, you must master the art of opening and working with workbooks, so read this section to learn more.

## Starting a new workbook

As with other Office programs, you can start a new workbook in Excel in several ways:

- Click the New button on the Standard toolbar.
- Choose File ➪ New Workbook.
- Press ⌘+N.

## Adding and deleting sheets

Each workbook contains one or more *worksheets,* with each worksheet implementing the traditional row/column spreadsheet layout. New blank workbooks are created with a single worksheet, but you certainly aren't limited to that. Create a new sheet by doing one of the following:

- Click the Insert Sheet button to the right of the worksheet tabs.
- Choose Insert ➪ Sheet, and choose a sheet type.
- Use the Elements Gallery to select a sheet type. (See more about the Elements Gallery later in this chapter.)

Each worksheet you create is selectable from the tabs at the bottom left, shown in Figure 12.10. Simply click the tab for the worksheet that you want to work with at the time.

### FIGURE 12.10

Worksheet tabs let you choose the individual worksheet that you want to work with.

| Sheet1 | Sheet2 | Sheet3 | + |

## Opening an existing workbook

Of course, after you create workbooks or get them from other people, you will want to open them again. The Open dialog box allows you to open workbooks stored anywhere on your computer. You also can use the Open Recent submenu on the File menu to reopen files that you've worked with recently.

### Opening a workbook with the Open command

Follow these steps to open a workbook via the Open command:

1. **Click the Open button on the Standard toolbar, or choose File ➪ Open.**

   The Open dialog box appears, as shown in Figure 12.11.

2. **Click the file you want to open.**
   - Navigate to a folder or device containing the file you want to open using the navigation pane.
   - Double-click the workbook name to quickly open it.

3. **Click the Open button.**

   Excel opens the document.

> **TIP** If you don't see the file you want in the Open dialog box, you can change what file types are listed. Simply click the Enable menu, and choose a format. For best results, consider changing the setting to All Readable Documents or All Office Documents so you can view all the document types.

### Opening a document with the Open Recent menu

If you've recently worked with a document, you can quickly access it again using the Recent Files command:

1. **Choose File ➪ Open Recent.**
2. **Click the file you want to open.**

   If you don't see your file listed, click the More button to open the Project Gallery to the Recent documents tab and look for the file.

# Read-Only and File Copies

The Open dialog box also lets you open a file as a read-only file or as a copy of the original. The Open menu lets you choose from Original, Copy, or Read-Only. The Original setting is selected by default and simply means that whatever document you select to open is the original file. A read-only file does just what the name implies: It opens the document but does not allow you to make any changes to the content. You can read it, just not edit it. Finally, you can use the Copy feature to open a copy of the original file. If you make changes to the document, you can save them under a new filename and keep the original file intact.

**FIGURE 12.11**

You can use the Open dialog box to open workbook files stored on your computer or on other drives or storage devices.

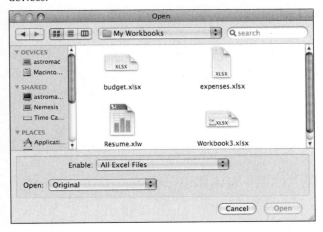

### Opening a document with the Project Gallery

You also can open a document through the Project Gallery:

1. **Choose File ➪ Project Gallery.**

    The Project Gallery window opens.

2. **Click the Recent tab.**

3. **Click the document you want to open.**

4. **Click Open.**

    Excel opens the file.

### Searching for a file

You can use the Open dialog box to search for a workbook on your computer. Using the Spotlight text field, which displays the word "search" by default, you can search for a specific filename, a portion of the name, or keywords pertaining to the name. Follow these steps to search for a file:

1. **Display the Open dialog box.** (See the previous sections to learn how to open the Open dialog box).

2. **Click inside the Spotlight search field, and type the filename, a portion of the name, or a keyword.**

   As you type in the search field, Excel lists any possible matches, as shown in Figure 12.12.

   You can use the buttons at the top of the search window to target your search.

3. **When you find the file you want, double-click the filename to open the document.**

---

**FIGURE 12.12**

The Open dialog box displays any search matches.

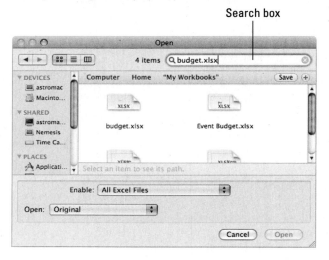

## Using the Project Gallery

Note that when you open Excel directly, a new empty workbook is opened automatically. While the above method opens a blank workbook, you aren't limited to doing it that way. You also can use Excel's Project Gallery, shown in Figure 12.13, to create workbooks that are already tailored for a specific purpose. For example, you can choose from Ledger Sheet templates for your small business or Home Essentials templates for managing household finances and planning.

To create a project with the Project Gallery, follow these steps:

1. **Click File.**
2. **Click Project Gallery.**

   The Project Gallery window opens.

3. **Click the New tab.**
4. **Use the Show drop-down box to select Excel documents.**
5. **Select a category on the left.**
6. **Click the type of document you want to create.**
7. **Click Open.**

   Excel creates and opens the new workbook.

**FIGURE 12.13**

**FIGURE 12.13**

The Project Gallery has a large number of templates that you can use to create new workbooks.

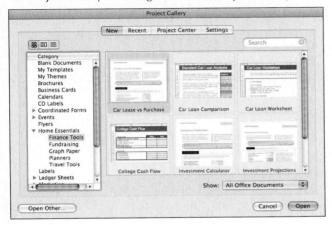

## Elements Gallery

Like Word, Excel has an Elements Gallery, and the differences between it and the Projects Gallery are the same. The Elements Gallery is used to insert specific types of items into a workbook. The Elements Gallery in Excel offers four categories of elements you can add, including sheets, charts, SmartArt Graphics, and WordArt text.

 To use the Elements Gallery, click the Gallery button on the Standard toolbar to expand the category tabs, shown in Figure 12.14. Then choose a category by clicking it, and click the item you want to add. Excel automatically adds the selected item to the workbook or worksheet.

**FIGURE 12.14**

The Elements Gallery can be used to insert pre-built objects into your workbooks.

# Changing Views

Excel 2008 has several ways to alter the way you view your data to make it easier to read or to visualize. To start with, two view modes are selectable from buttons near the Status bar: Normal and Page Layout views. With the Zoom feature, you can either magnify a worksheet to see small text more clearly or zoom out to fit more on the screen at once. This section examines the various ways you can change the view of your worksheets.

## Working with view modes

Two view mode buttons are located on the left side of the Status bar at the bottom of the program window. These buttons allow you to select between Normal and Page Layout views. To change views at any time, simply click the view button you want to use, and Excel immediately switches the view. The views also can be selected from the View menu.

### Normal view

Normal view, shown in Figure 12.15, is the traditional spreadsheet display of a large, unbroken grid of cells that can be panned across using the scroll bars. This mode is optimized for working with data, because it shows the maximum amount of data at once. To activate Normal view, click the Normal view mode button on the Status bar or choose View➪Normal from the menu.

**FIGURE 12.15**

The Normal view makes it easier to work with large amounts of data.

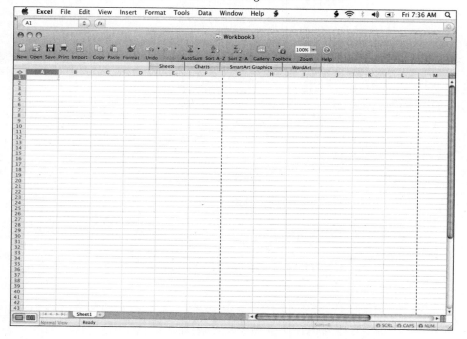

### Page Layout view

An alternative to Normal view is Page Layout view, shown in Figure 12.16. This view—which, oddly enough, is the default view unless you change it in the preferences—is intended to show how your workbook will look when printed. This isn't just a fancy Print Preview feature, however. Worksheets in Page Layout view remain fully editable and functional. To activate Page Layout view, click the Page Layout view mode button on the Status bar or choose View⇨Page Layout from the menu.

### Using the Zoom tool

The Zoom tool on the Standard toolbar can be used to zoom in to or out of the worksheet data. This only affects how the data is displayed on the screen; it doesn't change how it is printed. The selectable zoom range is from between 25% and 200%, in both Normal and Page Layout views. You also can type a percentage directly into the text field and press Return; you can enter a zoom value as high as 400%. You also can zoom in on a selection, and in Page Layout mode, you can zoom to a single page. Figure 12.17 shows a worksheet zoomed to the maximum of 200%.

---

**FIGURE 12.16**

The Page Layout view gives you a feel for how your worksheets will look when printed.

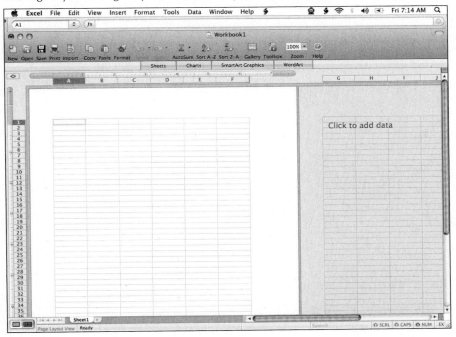

**FIGURE 12.17**

Use the Zoom tool to magnify or shrink your view of a worksheet.

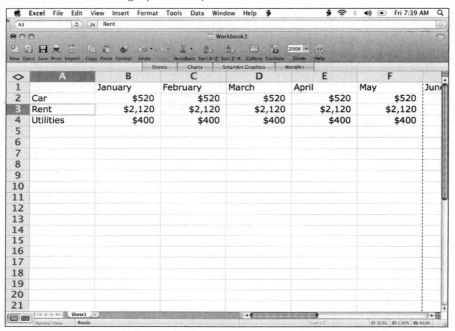

## Using the Zoom dialog box

The Zoom dialog box can be used to specify a zoom setting. Follow these steps to choose a zoom setting using the dialog box:

1. **Choose View➪Zoom.**

   The Zoom dialog box appears, as shown in Figure 12.18.

2. **Click the zoom setting you want to apply.**

   You can select Custom and type a zoom percentage directly into the Percent field.

   You also can choose Fit Selection to have it zoom in on the current selection on the worksheet.

3. **Click OK.**

   Excel applies the zoom percentage you specified.

## Creating custom views

Custom views are a feature new to Excel 2008. With custom views, you can customize the view settings for a worksheet, including hidden rows and columns, zoom settings, print settings, and filter settings, and you can save these settings as a custom view for the workbook. Later, if you've changed the settings again, you can return to your custom view settings.

**FIGURE 12.18**

The Zoom dialog box can be used to choose a zoom setting.

To create a custom view, configure your worksheet the way you want, with hidden rows and columns, print settings, and filter settings. Then follow these steps:

1. **Choose View ⇨ Custom Views.**

   The Custom Views dialog box appears, as shown in Figure 12.19.

**FIGURE 12.19**

The Custom Views dialog box can remember view settings so you can use them again later.

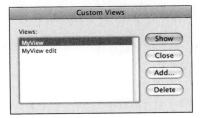

2. **Click Add.**
3. **Enter a unique name for the view, and check the boxes for the settings you want to include in the view.**

   You can choose to include print settings, or hidden rows, columns and filters, or both.

4. **Click OK.**

To restore a view, follow these steps:

1. **Choose View ⇨ Custom Views.**

   The Custom Views dialog box appears, as shown in Figure 12.20.

2. **Select the view to apply by doing one of the following.**

- Click the view, and click the Show button.
- Double-click the name of the view.

3. **Click OK.**

For information on hiding rows and columns and setting up filters, see Chapter 13. For information on print settings, see Chapter 18.

# Saving Excel Workbooks

Obviously, when you create a workbook, you're going to want to save it to your hard drive at some point to make changes, run calculations, or print. Use the Save As dialog box, shown in Figure 12.20, to save a workbook to whatever filename you choose, wherever you want it to be saved on your computer.

**FIGURE 12.20**

Use the Save As dialog box to specify a name and a location where you want to save a workbook.

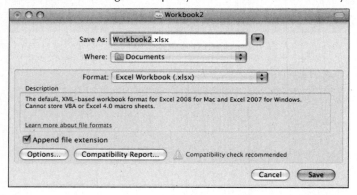

Excel 2008 documents are saved by default as *.xlsx* files. This is a new XML-based format that matches the format used for Excel 2007 for Windows. You also can choose to save files in older Excel version formats or other types including plain text (.txt), PDF (.pdf), CSV (comma separated value, .csv), and more. You also can choose from specialty formats, such as Excel 2004 XML-based spreadsheet (.xlm), Excel macro-enabled workbook (.xlsm), or Excel Add-in (.xla, .xlam). Excel automatically tacks on the file extension for the format you select, so you don't have to add it yourself. You do not necessarily need the file extension letters, but they can be helpful, especially if you plan to share your workbooks with people using Windows. So be sure to leave the Append file extension check box selected in the Save As dialog box. Table 12.1 defines the available file formats.

TABLE 12.1

# Excel File Formats

| File Format | Description |
| --- | --- |
| Excel Workbook (.xlsx) | Saves the file as an XML-based workbook format for Excel 2008 for Mac and Excel 2007 for Windows. |
| Excel 97-2004 Workbook (.xls) | Saves the file in a document format compatible with Excel 98 through Excel 2004 for Mac and Excel 97 through Excel 2003 for Windows. |
| Excel Template (.xltx) | Saves the file as an XML-based template format compatible with Excel 2008 for Mac and Excel 2007 for Windows. |
| Excel 97-2004 Template (.xlt) | Saves the file in a template format compatible with Excel 98 through Excel 2004 for Mac and Excel 97 through Excel 2003 for Windows. |
| Comma Separated Values (.csv) | Save the file as a text file with data from each row saved on a comma-delimited line. |
| Web Page (.htm) | Saves the workbook content as a Web page able to be viewed in popular Web browsers. |
| PDF | Exports the document as an Adobe PDF file. |
| Excel Binary Workbook (.xlsb) | Saves the file as a binary Excel document compatible with Excel 2008 for Mac and Excel 2007 for Windows. |
| Excel Macro-Enabled Workbook (.xlsm) | Saves the document with an XML-based document format preserving VBA macro coding. Note: VBA macros do not work in Excel 2008, but will work with Excel 2007 for Windows. |
| Excel Macro-Enabled Template (.xltm) | Exports the XML-based template along with VBA macro coding. Note: VBA macros do not work in Excel 2008. |
| Excel 2004 XML Spreadsheet (.xml) | Saves the document content as an XML file, compatible with Excel 2004. |
| Excel Add-In (.xlam) | Saves the file as an Excel 2008 for Mac and Excel 2007 for Windows add-in file. |
| Excel 97-2004 Add-In (.xla) | Saves the file as an Excel 97-2004 for Mac and Excel 97-2003 for Windows add-in file. |
| Single File Web Page (.mht) | Formats the workbook as a single Web page, including all page elements. |
| UTF-16 Unicode Text (.txt) | Saves as a Unicode-based, tab-delimited text file. |
| Tab Delimited Text (.txt) | Saves as a standard tab-delimited text file. |
| Windows Formatted Text (.txt) | Saves as a Windows-compatible, tab-delimited text document. |
| MS-DOS Formatted Text (.txt) | Saves as an MS-DOS-compatible, tab-delimited text document. |
| Windows Comma Separated (.csv) | Saves as a Windows-compatible, comma-delimited text document. |
| MS-DOS Comma Separated (.csv) | Saves as an MS-DOS-compatible, comma-delimited text document. |
| Space Delimited Text (.prn) | Saves as a text document padded with spaces for printing. |
| Data Interchange Format (.dif) | Saves as a common spreadsheet format supported by other spreadsheet packages. |
| Symbolic Link (.slk) | Saves data to a text file compatible with Multiplan and other spreadsheet applications. |
| Excel 5.0/95 Workbook .xls | Saves as an Excel 5.0-95 compatible workbook. |

## Saving for the first time

To save a workbook for the first time after creating it, follow these steps:

1. **Click the Save button on the Standard toolbar, or choose File ⇨ Save (or Save As).**

   The Save As dialog box opens, as shown in Figure 12.21.

2. **Enter a filename in the Save As box.**

3. **Choose a destination folder or drive on which to store the file.**

   By default, Excel saves the file to the Documents folder.

   To change the location, click the down arrow next to the filename to expand the Save As dialog and browse to the new location.

   Optionally, to save the document in another file format, click the Format arrow and choose a format.

   Optionally, to check for compatibility issues, click the Compatibility Report button. (See "Checking compatibility" later this chapter for more information.)

4. **Click the Save button.**

   Excel saves the workbook, and the top of the document window shows the new filename.

**FIGURE 12.21**

Expand the Save As dialog box to make it easier to find a location in which to save your file.

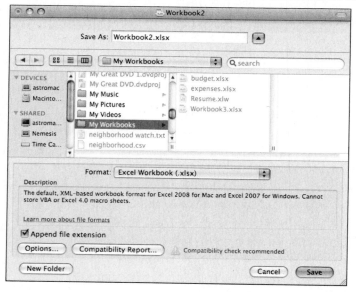

### Subsequent saves

After you've saved a workbook, you can make use of some handy shortcuts to save a workbook again. Use one of these methods to save changes to a file:

- Click the Save button on the Standard toolbar.
- Choose File ⇨ Save.
- Press ⌘+S.

### Saving workspaces

Excel has the ability to save your workspace separately from workbooks. A workspace simply displays information for your workbooks, not the actual information in them. This can be useful if you frequently need to open multiple workbooks at once, for example. If you arrange the workbooks so that information can be viewed side by side (using Window ⇨ Arrange), you can save the workspace so you can compare these same two workbooks later. To save the workspace, do the following:

1. **Choose File ⇨ Save Workspace.**

   The Save Workspace dialog box opens, as shown in Figure 12.22.

2. **Enter a filename in the Save As box.** Workspaces use the .xlw extension.

3. **Choose a destination folder or drive on which to store the file.**

   By default, Excel saves the workspace to the Documents folder.

   To change the location, click the down arrow next to the filename to expand the Save As dialog and browse to the new location.

4. **Click the Save button.**

   Excel saves the workbook, and the top of the document window shows the new filename.

When you open the workspace (using File ⇨ Open), it automatically opens all the workbooks that were open when you saved the workspace and arranges them on the screen in the same way.

---

**FIGURE 12.22**

Save workspaces separately from workbooks so you can restore them later.

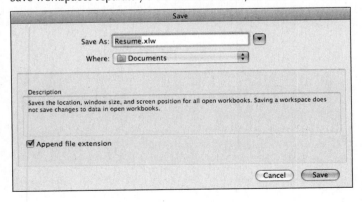

## Checking compatibility

If you need to pass along the workbooks you create to other people, some of them may have older versions of Excel. You can use the Compatibility Report tool to examine the file to find out which features you are using that might not be supported by older versions of Excel for both Windows and Macs. As soon as you open the Save As dialog box, you'll notice a warning recommending that you run a compatibility check. Click the Compatibility Report button to open the Compatibility Report tab of the Toolbox, shown in Figure 12.23. Excel runs a compatibility check on your spreadsheets and lets you know which features won't work in older versions of Excel.

Select the version of Excel you want to test against in the drop-down box. If any problems are reported, you can click them to see a detailed explanation. You can leave the Compatibility Report active while you make any corrections and rerun the check by clicking the Recheck Document button.

**FIGURE 12.23**

Use the Compatibility Report to see how well older versions of Excel will use your workbooks.

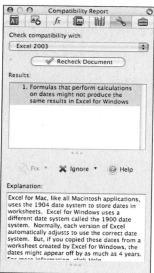

# Setting Workbook Properties

When you save a workbook, Excel saves information along with it called *properties,* or *metadata.* This data includes information about the workbook, including statistics, summary information such as the author or company that created the document, and information regarding the contents of the file, such as the names of the worksheets. This information can be helpful for those who may need to use the workbook later.

Workbook properties can be viewed or set in the Properties dialog box. The dialog box, shown in Figure 12.24, includes five tabs: General, Summary, Statistics, Contents, and Custom. The General tab displays basic information about the file, such as the file type, location, size, creation date, last modified date, and any read-only or hidden attributes settings. Excel automatically creates the information on this tab when you save the file, and it cannot be overridden. The Summary tab has a variety of blank text fields you can use to add more information about the file, including title, subject, author, manager, company name, category, keywords, comments, hyperlink base, and any template that may be attached to the file. Most of these fields are blank by default, and you can choose to enter them as you see fit. The Statistics tab lists the created and modified dates (again), when the workbook was last printed, the person who saved the file last, the number of revisions, and the total editing time. The Contents tab shows the contents of the document, including a list of worksheets. Finally, the Custom tab lets you add your own custom properties to the file. Some are provided by default, including client name, destination, language, phone number, and many more. You can use these or create your own, as well as enter values for any of the properties you create.

**FIGURE 12.24**

Workbook properties can be set in the Properties dialog box.

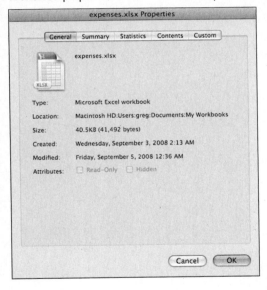

To display the Workbook Properties dialog box, choose File ➪ Properties. Click the Summary tab, shown in Figure 12.25, to enter your own information. Click the Custom tab to add any custom properties.

You can choose whether Excel saves your personal information in the workbook properties. If you are planning to share your workbooks with others, particularly with people you don't know, you may want to keep such information private. To prevent personal information from being saved, choose Excel ➪ Preferences. In the Excel Preferences dialog box, click the Security icon, and under the Privacy options, click the Remove personal information from this file on save check box, as shown in Figure 12.26. Click OK. Personal information is stripped out of the properties of any workbook that you save.

**FIGURE 12.25**

The Summary tab has fields for entering in your own document properties.

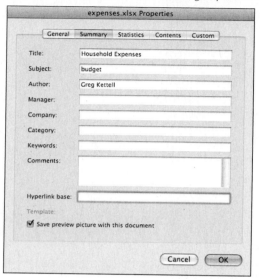

**FIGURE 12.26**

You can keep your personal information out of workbook properties in the Security preferences.

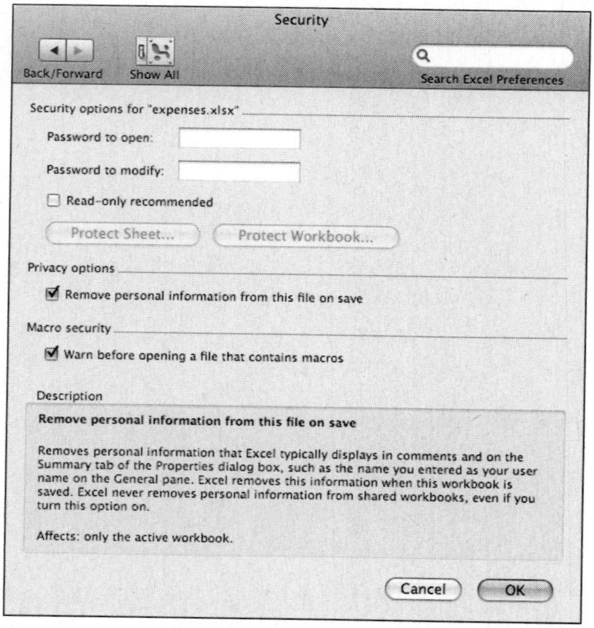

# Protecting Workbooks and Data

Spreadsheets are good with numbers, which makes them a natural tool to use for keeping track of financial information and other important data. Of course, this means that your data is often confidential, and protecting it from snoops (or worse) is crucial. Excel's document protection features provide the means for protecting your important. As with Word, Excel offers three levels of document protection: read-only, password to open, and password to modify. You can set any of the three security levels using the Preferences dialog box. The following sections discuss how to utilize each of the three security levels.

## Assigning read-only status

To allow others to open and view a document, but not make any changes to the original text or formatting, you can set the document to read-only status. If a user makes changes, Excel does not allow him to save the changes. He can, however, save the changes as an entirely new document. This leaves your original document intact. To assign read-only status to a document, follow these steps:

1. **Choose Excel ⇨ Preferences.**

   The Excel Preferences dialog box opens, as shown in Figure 12.27.

**FIGURE 12.27**

Access Excel's Security features through the Preferences dialog box.

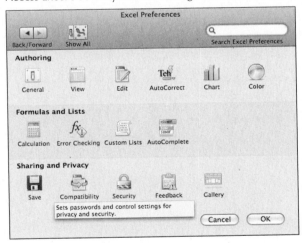

**NOTE** You also can access Excel's Security options through the Save As dialog box. Click the Options button, and then click the Show All icon. Although this dialog box is a little different than the one described in these steps, the options are the same.

2. **Click the Security icon.**

   The Security options appear, as shown in Figure 12.28.

3. **Click the Read-only recommended check box.**

4. **Click OK.**

   The document is now protected and can only be read.

**FIGURE 12.28**

Activate the read-only option to allow the document to be opened, but not changed in any way.

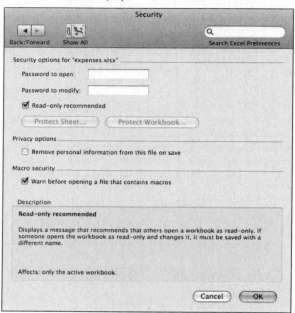

After you assign read-only status, you can no longer change the file yourself until you make the Security option inactive again. To do so, simply repeat the steps above and deselect the check box. As you can see, this is rudimentary security at best, because anyone can uncheck the Read-only recommended box. It's mostly there to protect you from accidentally changing data. To secure the file further, you need to assign a password, as described in the next section.

## Assigning passwords

You can assign a password to protect your workbooks. Excel has two levels of password security: You can assign a password to allow modifications or a password to allow opening of the workbook. The Password to Modify option means that anyone can open the spreadsheet and work with it, but they cannot modify it unless they know the password. The Password to Open option lets you assign a password that must be known to even open the document. You can use both password options at the same time, assigning a different password for those who need full access as opposed to those who need read-only access.

**NOTE**   Passwords you assign in Excel are case-sensitive, which means you can use uppercase and lowercase letters, but you must enter the password in the same way you create it. Passwords can be up to 15 characters long, and you can use letters, numbers, and symbols. As with any password, though, be sure to write it down and keep it in a safe place. If you lose it, you lose access to your file, too, and no one, not even Microsoft, can help you gain access to the document again.

To assign passwords to a workbook, follow these steps:

1. **Choose Excel ⇨ Preferences.**

   The Preferences dialog box opens (refer to Figure 12.27).

2. **Click the Security icon.**

   The Security options appear, as shown in Figure 12.29.

**FIGURE 12.29**

You can use the password fields to specify a password for opening the document or a password for making any changes to the document.

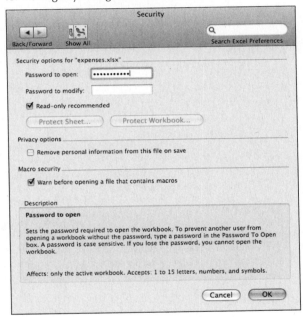

**NOTE** You also can access Security options through the Save As dialog box; click the Options button. This opens the Excel Save Options dialog box, and you can follow the steps in this section to assign a password.

3. **Click the password field you want to assign, and type a password.**

4. **Click OK.**

   The Confirm Password box prompt appears, as shown in Figure 12.30.

5. **Retype the password exactly as you did the first time.**

6. **Click OK.**

   The workbook is now protected. The next time you open it, you'll be prompted for a password.

**FIGURE 12.30**

Use the Confirm Password box to confirm your password.

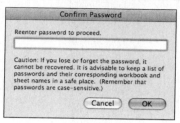

To remove a password, repeat the steps, except delete the text you entered in the password field. When you exit the dialog box, Excel saves the changes and removes the associated password.

When sharing a workbook with others for the purposes of editing and tracking changes, you can activate the Protect Document feature and specify which changes are allowed during the process. To do so, click the Protect Document button in the Security preferences window (see Figure 12.29) and choose whether you want to protect sheets or workbooks. You can then assign a password to the file.

# Summary

In this chapter, we covered the basics for working with the Excel program window, learning what each element of the window is used for and where to find it. The Excel program window is similar to other Office programs such as Word in many ways, but Excel has a number of unique elements that may not be obvious at first glance.

You learned the basics of working with Excel workbooks and worksheets, opening new workbooks, using the Project Gallery to create template-based workbooks, and creating new worksheets and other elements using the Elements Gallery. You also learned how to save workbooks and how to open them again later.

In terms of viewing and editing your workbooks, you learned how to make use of Excel's view modes, as well as how to use the Zoom feature to alter the onscreen magnification of your data. You also learned how to create custom views that enable you to make use of multiple views for each workbook.

Finally, you learned how to set workbook properties and how to make use of protection features to keep your workbooks safe. Now that you have the basics, you are ready to begin exploring Excel further by learning how to enter and edit data.

# Chapter 13

# Entering and Editing Data

Excel worksheets may seem simple at first glance. They are simply tables with rows and columns of numbers, text along with some formulas to calculate values. With this basic organizational structure, Excel can be used to do amazing number crunching feats. However, before you can make Excel jump through hoops with your data, you have to get it into your worksheet in the first place.

The most obvious way to enter data is to type it directly into Excel, and Excel makes it very easy to do this, giving you the ability to easily move around the workbook; enter, edit, and delete data; and efficiently copy and paste. You have automatic completion and automatic fill options for quickly populating cells, and Excel allows you to import data from a variety of data sources.

After data is entered, you can manipulate it to your heart's content, working with ranges or rows and columns by adding, deleting, and sorting them. You can split and freeze sections of a worksheet, and you can hide and show rows and columns, even entire worksheets. In this chapter, you learn how to do all these things and more. By the time you have completed it, you will be able to navigate Excel and confidently work with data.

## Typing Data

You have a mountain of data, and you are ready to begin some serious number crunching. How do you begin? With Excel, it's easy to just jump right in. As you learned in Chapter 12, Excel automatically creates a workbook with an empty worksheet at the ready for you to begin entering data. And the easiest way to enter data, of course, is to simply begin typing it.

When Excel creates a brand-new blank workbook, with no template, the cursor is located in cell A1, which is the upper-leftmost cell in the worksheet. You can simply start typing your data here. Figure 13.1 shows a blank workbook with the default cursor insertion point set on cell A1.

You don't have to start here, of course. Excel makes it easy to move around your worksheet to allow you to begin wherever you like. Read on to learn more.

**NOTE** When we're talking about Excel worksheets, we need a convenient way to refer to the cells, or individual elements, of the worksheet. A cell is referred to by the unique row and column address that identifies it. Columns are referred to by letters, ranging from A to Z, and then continuing with AA, AB, AC, and so on. Rows are numbered starting from 1 and ranging as high as needed. The combination of the column and row is used to refer to an individual cell: A1, B20, AC2048, and so on. This is the convention that we'll use in this and other Excel chapters in this book to refer to cells.

**FIGURE 13.1**

When you create a blank workbook in Excel 2008, the cursor is positioned in cell A1.

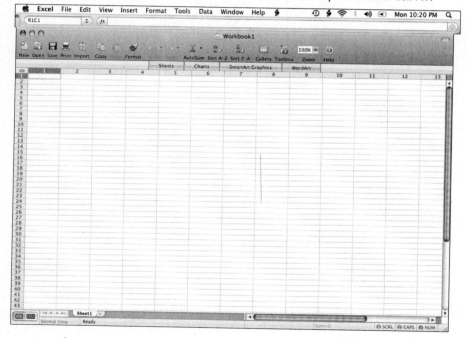

## Moving around

You can use a number of methods to move the cursor to a different cell if you don't want to begin entering data in cell A1. Perhaps the simplest way to select a new cell to insert data into is to click it. That's right—simply click a cell, and begin typing data into it, as shown in Figure 13.2.

This isn't the only way to move around the worksheet, of course. The keyboard offers a number of other ways to do it. Table 13.1 lists the keyboard shortcuts that make it easy to move from cell to cell.

**TABLE 13.1**

## Navigating by Keyboard

| Keypress | Action |
|----------|--------|
| ↑, ↓, ←, → | If the cell is in Ready or Enter mode, you can easily move left, right, up, and down by pressing the corresponding arrow key on the keyboard. |
| Control+↑, Control+↓, Control+←, Control+→ | These key combinations move the cursor to the edge of the current data range. If the current cell has data, using Control plus an arrow key moves to the last cell with data before a blank cell. If the current cell is blank, it moves to the first cell in the direction of the press with data. |
| Tab | This moves to the next editable cell in the current row. |
| Shift+Tab | This moves to the previous editable cell in the current row. |
| Return | This moves down to the next editable cell in the current column. |
| Shift+Return | This moves up to the previous editable cell in the current column. |
| Home | This moves to the beginning of the current row |
| Control+Home | This moves to the beginning of the current worksheet (cell A1). |
| Control+End | This moves to the position of the last cell in use on the worksheet. This cell is the one at the intersection of the rightmost column and the bottommost row that currently have data. |
| Page Down | This moves down one screen. |
| Page Up | This moves up one screen. |
| Option+Page Down | This moves one screen to the right. |
| Option+Page Up | This moves one screen to the left. |
| Control+Page Down | This moves to the next worksheet in the current workbook. |
| Control+Page Up | This moves to the previous worksheet in the current workbook. |
| Control+Tab | This moves to the next open workbook if more than one is open. |
| Control+Shift+Tab | This moves to the previous open workbook. |
| F6 | This moves to the next pane of a worksheet that has been split. See information on splitting a sheet later in this chapter. |
| Shift+F6 | This moves to the previous pane of a split worksheet. |
| Control+Delete | This scrolls the currently selected cell back into the view. |

If you have a large worksheet and you need to move quickly around the sheet, you can use the horizontal and vertical scrollbars. If you know where (or approximately where) in the worksheet you want to go, use the Go To dialog box, shown in Figure 13.3. Follow these steps to use the Go To dialog box:

1. **Choose Edit ⇨ Go To…, press Control+G, or press F5.**

   The Go To dialog box opens, as shown in Figure 13.3.

2. **Type a cell destination in the Reference line, using the row+column nomenclature—for example, A1.**

3. **Click OK to go directly to that cell.**

**FIGURE 13.2**

Click a cell to give it the focus, and you can begin entering data in it.

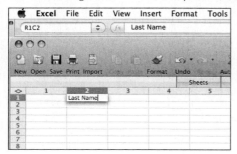

**FIGURE 13.3**

Go directly to a specific cell by using the Go To dialog box.

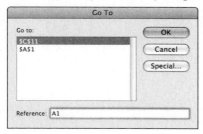

The Go To dialog box has features to make it easier to navigate in your worksheets. As you use it to move from cell to cell, it remembers the last cell you were in and adds it to the Go to: box. You can return to one of those cells simply by clicking it and pressing OK. The Special button allows you to choose criteria for selecting multiple cells (for example, all cells with formulas in them). You will learn more about this feature later in this chapter.

## Entering data

Entering data is as simple as typing it, but as with moving around the worksheet, Excel gives you some options for entering data that make it much easier.

■ When a cell is selected, you can just start typing to begin entering data into it. If the cell already contains data, it is overwritten. When entering data, Excel shows the mode as Enter in the Status bar, as shown in Figure 13.4.

■ If you want to edit a cell with existing data in it, you can double-click in the cell. The cell becomes editable, and the mode shows as Edit in the Status bar.

When you're entering or editing data, some additional keyboard shortcuts make it easier. Table 13.2 shows some keyboard shortcuts for Enter and Edit mode.

**FIGURE 13.4**

When a cell is in Enter mode, you can type new data.

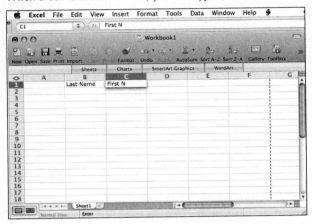

**TABLE 13.2**

## Shortcuts for Entering Data

| Keypress | Action |
|---|---|
| Return | Completes data entry in the current cell and moves to the cell immediately below. |
| Shift+Return | Completes data entry in the current cell and moves to the cell immediately above. |
| Control+Option+Return | Inserts a new line of text in the current cell. |
| Tab | Moves down to the next editable cell in the current column. Completes data entry in the current cell and moves to the next editable cell in the current row. |
| Shift+Tab | Completes data entry in the current cell and moves to the previous editable cell to the left in the current row. |
| Esc | Cancels editing in the current cell. |
| Control+Home | Moves to the beginning of the current worksheet (cell A1). |
| Delete | Deletes the character to the left of the cursor or deletes the current selection. |
| Forward Delete | Deletes the character to the right of the cursor or deletes the current selection. |
| Control+Del | Deletes from the cursor to the end of the current line. |
| ↑, ↓, ←, → | Moves the cursor one character to the left, right, up, or down. |
| Home | Moves the cursor to the beginning of the current line. |
| End | Moves the cursor to the end of the current line. |

## Using AutoComplete

Data entry can involve some drudgery, especially if you find yourself having to type the same data over and over again. Fortunately, Excel comes to the rescue with two features that can make entering cell data easy: AutoComplete and AutoFill.

AutoComplete can help you when you're entering data that you've already entered before. If you are entering data in a cell, and another cell in that column contains data that matches, the AutoComplete feature shows a menu of one or more matching items that you can choose from to complete the cell.

To use AutoComplete, do the following:

1. **Begin typing data in a cell.**

   As you type, the AutoComplete menu shows data from cells that match what you've typed, as shown in Figure 13.5.

   **FIGURE 13.5**

   Use AutoComplete to quickly re-enter values that you've used before.

   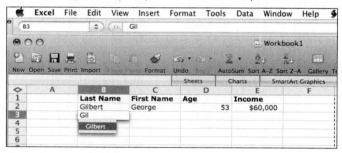

2. **Press the ↓ key to highlight the entry you wish to use, or click it to select it.**
3. **Press Return to have AutoComplete enter that value in the cell.**

**NOTE** Excel automatically completes only those entries that contain text or a combination of text and numbers. Entries that contain only numbers, dates, or times are not completed.

AutoComplete can be a handy option, but it also can be annoying if you find it giving you lots of false matches. Fortunately, you can choose to disable this feature in the Excel Preferences, by doing the following:

1. **Choose Excel ⇨ Preferences, or press ⌘+, (comma).**

   The Excel Preferences dialog box opens.
2. **Click the AutoComplete icon, in the Formulas and Lists section.**

   The AutoComplete Preferences panel is shown in Figure 13.6.
3. **Uncheck the box labeled Enable AutoComplete for cell values.**
4. **Click OK.**

Redo these steps and check the box to enable AutoComplete again if you find that you miss it.

**FIGURE 13.6**

AutoComplete preferences let you control or completely disable AutoComplete functionality.

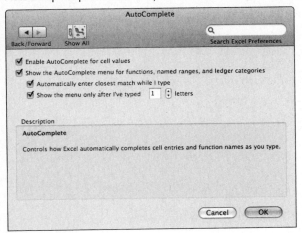

AutoComplete

Back/Forward   Show All                              Search Excel Preferences

☑ Enable AutoComplete for cell values
☑ Show the AutoComplete menu for functions, named ranges, and ledger categories
  ☑ Automatically enter closest match while I type
  ☑ Show the menu only after I've typed  1  ⬍ letters

Description
**AutoComplete**
Controls how Excel automatically completes cell entries and function names as you type.

Cancel    OK

**NOTE** AutoComplete also can be used to complete functions, named ranges, and ledger categories, as you may notice in the Preferences options. These AutoComplete options are described later when those features are covered.

## Using AutoFill

Another handy way to quickly enter cell data is to make use of the AutoFill feature. AutoFill can be used to fill cells automatically with repeating information. This can be useful if you want to set a default value in cells, for example, or if you want to quickly enter a range of numbers or dates. This section shows you how to use the various forms of AutoFill.

### Filling cells with repeating data

If you have data that you would like to duplicate across multiple cells, you can make use of the AutoFill feature to duplicate them as long as the cells are adjacent to one another in either the same row or column. This can be useful for filling a range of values with a default value, for example.

Follow these steps to AutoFill cells:

1. **Select one or more cells that contain the data you would like to duplicate.**
   - Select a cell by clicking it.
   - Click and drag the selection box over a range of cells to select multiple cells.
2. **Click the fill handle, shown as a dot in the bottom-right corner of the selection.**
3. **Drag the selection box to encompass the rows or columns that you want to fill, as shown in Figure 13.7.**
   You can fill only rows or columns with data, not both at the same time.

**FIGURE 13.7**

AutoFill can be used to automatically populate cells with repeating data.

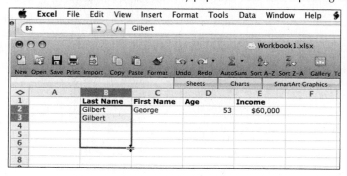

4. **Release the mouse button.**

   Cells are filled with copies of the data in the original cells.

   If the original selection contained multiple rows or columns with different values, all these values are included in the fill.

 When the AutoFill is complete, you will notice the AutoFill Options smart button at the bottom right of the selection range. You can click this button to show a list of fill options, shown in Figure 13.7. Choose one of these options:

- **Copy Cells:** This option copies both data and formatting from the original cells. This is the default option.

- **Fill Formatting Only:** This option copies only formatting for cells, not the cell data. This can be very useful for applying formatting changes to a range of cells without disturbing the data.

- **Fill Without Formatting:** This option copies only data values, but maintains the existing formatting for the target cells.

AutoFill also can be used to enter information in multiple cells at once. To do this, simply select all the cells you want to fill and type the data value. This data is entered into the first cell in the selection, but when you are finished typing, you can press Control+Return to fill the other cells in the selection with the entered value.

You can choose to disable either the fill handle or the AutoFill Options smart button in the Excel Preferences dialog box by doing the following:

1. **Choose Excel ⇨ Preferences, or press ⌘+, (comma).**

   The Excel Preferences dialog box opens.

2. **Click the Edit icon, in the Authoring section.**

   The Edit Preferences panel is shown in Figure 13.8.

3. **Uncheck the box for the AutoFill option you want to disable.**

   - Uncheck Enable Fill handle and cell drag-and-drop button to disable AutoFill altogether.

   - Uncheck the Show Insert Options Smart Buttons item to disable the AutoFill Options smart button after completing an AutoFill.

4. **Click OK.**

**FIGURE 13.8**

You can turn off the AutoFill Options smart button if you'd prefer not to see it.

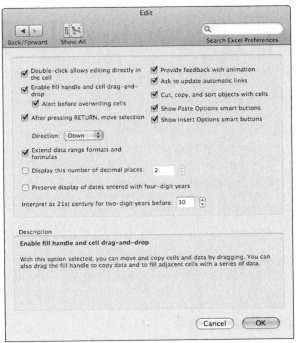

## Continuing a sequence of data values

As exciting as it is to be able to fill cells with the same repeated data, that is just the beginning. AutoFill can be used to continue a series of numbers, text and number combinations, and formulas as well.

For example, if you enter the number 1 in a cell, you can automatically create a numeric sequence by using AutoFill on the value. Subsequent cells have incrementing values: 2, 3, 4, and so on. The same is true for values that start with text and end with a number. You could take a cell with a value of "year 1" and use AutoFill to populate adjacent cells with "year 2," "year 3," and so on. This even works with formulas that reference other cells. As you can see, AutoFill is a valuable time-saving feature indeed.

To use AutoFill to create a sequence of values, do the following:

1.  **Select one or more cells that contain the number or text and number combination that you want to duplicate.**

    ■ Select a cell by clicking it.

    ■ Click and drag the selection box over a range of cells to select multiple cells.

2.  **Click the fill handle, shown as a dot in the bottom-right corner of the selection.**

3.  **Drag the selection box to the right or down to encompass the rows or columns that you want to populate.**

    You can fill only rows or columns with data, not both at the same time.

You can drag up or to the right to populate those cells with a decreasing series of values.

4.  **Release the mouse button.**

5.  **Click the AutoFill Options smart button to choose one of these options:**

    - **Copy Cells:** Copy both data and formatting from the original cells. This functionality works the same as the repeating AutoFill described earlier.

    - **Fill Series:** Fill the cells with incremental values based on the original cell values.

    - **Fill Formatting Only:** Copy only the formatting for cells, not the cell data. This can be very useful for applying formatting changes to a range of cells without disturbing the data.

    - **Fill Without Formatting:** Copy only data values, but maintain the existing formatting for the target cells.

    Cells are filled automatically with a value continuing the sequence of values in the original selection.

    If the original selection contained multiple rows or columns with different values, all these values are included in the fill.

> **TIP** You aren't limited to filling numerical sequences incremented by 1. You can use any arbitrary value by entering data into two cells to begin with and using both as your initial selection. For example, if you'd like to have a series of cells with hundreds values 100, 200, 300, 400, and so on, you can enter 100 in the first cell and 200 in the second cell, and then select both cells and drag to complete the sequence.

## Automatically entering a series of date and time values

You can use AutoFill to quickly populate cells with a series of date and time values, including complete dates, times, weekdays, months, or years. You can use numeric date values or even the names of the months or days of the week, and Excel recognizes them when using AutoFill.

For example, you can enter "January" in a cell and then use AutoFill to populate adjacent cells with "February," "March," and more. Likewise, you can enter "Sunday" and have Excel AutoFill adjacent cells with "Monday," "Tuesday," "Wednesday," and so on.

Follow these steps to fill a series of date values:

1.  **Enter the initial date value in the first cell of the series.** This can be a date, time, weekday, month, or year value.

2.  **Select the cell or range of cells.**

    - Select a cell by clicking it.

    - Click and drag the selection box over a range of cells to select multiple cells.

3.  **Click the fill handle, shown as a dot in the bottom-right corner of the selection.**

4.  **Drag the selection box to the right or down to encompass the rows or columns that you want to populate, as shown in Figure 13.9**

    - You can fill only rows or columns with data, not both at the same time.

    - You can drag up or to the right to populate those cells with a decreasing series of values.

5.  **Release the mouse button.**

6.  **Click the AutoFill Options smart button and choose one of the options, described below.**

    - Cells are filled automatically with a value continuing the sequence of values in the original selection, as shown in Figure 13.10.

    - If the original selection contained multiple rows or columns with different values, all these values are included in the fill.

**FIGURE 13.9**

You can use AutoFill to quickly create an incrementing series of cell values.

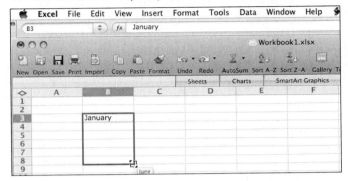

**FIGURE 13.10**

AutoFill is especially useful for creating series of date ranges.

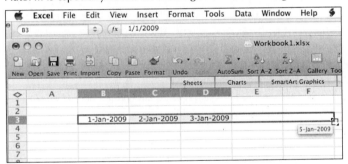

 The AutoFill Options menu has some unique options when entering date ranges. Click this button, and choose one of the options listed below. Some of the options appear only for certain date or time values:

- **Copy Cells:** Copies both data and formatting from the original cells. This functionality works the same as the repeating AutoFill described earlier.

- **Fill Series:** Fills the cells with incremental values based on the original cell values.

- **Fill Formatting Only:** Copies only formatting for cells, not the cell data. This can be very useful for applying formatting changes to a range of cells without disturbing the data.

- **Fill Without Formatting:** Copies only data values, but maintains the existing formatting for the target cells.

- **Fill Days:** Fills the selection with an incrementing sequence of days if the initial selection is a day of the week. If the initial cell contains a date value, it fills the adjacent cells with incrementing date values.

- **Fill Weekdays:** Fills the selection with repeating days of the week, but omits Saturday and Sunday. If a date value is in the initial cell, it fills the adjacent cells with incrementing date values, skipping dates that fall on weekends.

- **Fill Months:** Fills cells with subsequent months of the year if a month name is in the initial cell. If a date value is in the initial cell, it fills adjacent cells with date value incrementing the month.

- **Fill Years:** Uses the date or year in the initial cell to fill adjacent cells with subsequent date or year values, incrementing the year.

## Importing Data

Is all that typing while entering data making your fingers hurt? Fear not, because unless your data is written out on napkins, Excel probably provides a way to import it. One of the most useful features of Excel is the ability to import data from a wide range of file formats.

You can import data from a number of different file formats, including text, CSV and XML. You also can import from databases. In this chapter, you learn how to import data from different file formats. (You learn how to import data from databases in Chapter 17.)

### Importing from text files

Text files are probably the most likely source of imported data that you will want to use with Excel. When importing from text files, the Excel Import utility assumes that data is arranged with one row per line, and each value on a line is separated with a special delimiter character such as a comma, tab, semicolon, or space. Alternatively, values can be organized in fixed-width columns in the text file.

Because text files are naturally organized into rows (individual lines in the file) and columns (values separated by a delimiter, or fixed-width columns), importing the data directly into a worksheet is easy. Follow these steps to import data from a delimited text file:

1. **Click the Import button on the toolbar, or choose File ➪ Import.**

   The Import dialog box opens, as shown in Figure 13.11.

2. **Select the Text File option.**

---

**FIGURE 13.11**

The Import dialog box lets you bring data into a worksheet from external file formats.

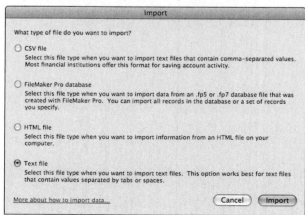

3. **Click the Import button.**

   The Choose a File dialog box opens.

4. **Browse to the file you would like to import.**

5. **Click the Get Data button.**

   The Text Import Wizard dialog box opens, as shown in Figure 13.12.

**FIGURE 13.12**

You can use the Text Import Wizard to tell Excel how data in the file is organized.

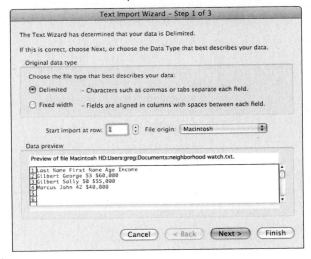

6. **Choose a row to start importing from.** This lets you bypass header rows if there are any.

7. **Choose a File Origin option; your choices are Macintosh, Windows (ANSI), or DOS or OS/2.**

   Files created on different systems may have different character encodings, and this allows Excel to make the best choice in translating.

8. **Click Next.**

   You move on to Step 2 of 3 of the Text Import Wizard, as shown in Figure 13.13.

9. **Choose one or more delimiter characters.** Check boxes are provided for the most common values, or you can enter an arbitrary character to treat as a delimiter.

10. **If the values in your text file are enclosed in quotes, choose double or single quotes in the Text Qualifier list.**

11. **If you would like multiple delimiters to be treated as 1 (useful for spaces), check that option.**

12. **Click Next.**

   You move on to Step 3 of 3 of the Text Import Wizard, as shown in Figure 13.14.

**FIGURE 13.13**

In Step 2 of the Text Import Wizard, you can choose a delimiter character and text qualifier.

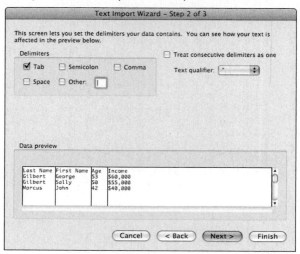

**FIGURE 13.14**

In Step 3 of the Text Import Wizard, you can choose which columns to include as well as set their data types.

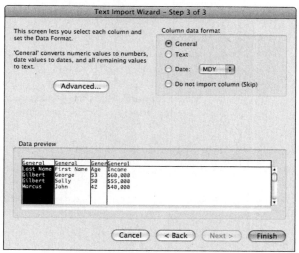

13. **Select each column in turn, and choose a Column Data Type.** You also can choose to not import certain columns.

    You can click the Advanced button, which launches the Advanced Text Import Settings dialog box, which lets you choose characters to use for decimal and thousands separators for numeric data. This can be helpful when importing data from locales that may use different values.

14. **Click Finish to begin the import.**

    The Import Data dialog box is opened, as shown in Figure 13.15.

---

**FIGURE 13.15**
_____

The Import Data dialog box lets you choose a location in the workbook.

15. **Choose a cell to use as a starting point for the data.** By default, the cell that you had selected before you opened the Text Import Wizard is used. You also can choose to have the data imported into a new worksheet.

If the text file that you import data from may change and need to be imported again, you can do so simply by doing the following:

1. **Chose Data ⇨ Refresh Data from the menu.**

    The Choose a File dialog box opens.

2. **Browse to the text file you used for the import.**

3. **Click the Get Data button.**

**NOTE** You can change the properties for refreshing the imported data at any time. Choose Data ⇨ Get External Data ⇨ Data Range Properties, or Choose Data ⇨ Get External Data ⇨ Edit Text Import. If you chose the latter option, browse to the file you imported and make changes to the import properties in the Text Import Wizard again.

## Importing from CSV files

CSV (Comma Separated Value) files are simply text files with a comma used as the delimiter character. Like other text files you can import, data is arranged in rows, and individual values are separated by, you guessed it, commas. Even with the advent of XML, CSV files are still commonly used to transfer data between otherwise non-compatible applications or systems. CSV files may or may not have the text values in quotes.

When you choose the CSV import option, Excel uses the same Text Import Wizard that it does for other text files. The only real difference is that commas are selected by default as a valid delimiter, as you can see in Figure 13.16.

**FIGURE 13.16**

When you import from a CSV file, the Text Import Wizard defaults to a comma for the delimiter.

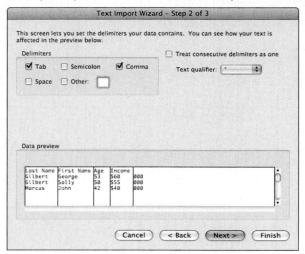

## Importing from HTML files

You can import data from HTML files as well. HTML files are Web pages, and although Excel doesn't give you many options when it comes to importing them, it can still be quite useful.

HTML files can organize data in tables, using the <table>…</table> tag, along with <tr> tags to indicate rows of data and <td> tags to indicate individual cells or columns. When you import an HTML file with a table in it, Excel creates a new workbook with a worksheet containing the table data.

This feature isn't useful as much as for the ability to import Web pages as it is for the fact that other programs including spreadsheet applications can save data as HTML files. This capability not only makes it easier to import the data into Excel, but also creates a nicely formatted HTML file that can be viewed in any Web browser.

## Importing from FileMaker Pro

FileMaker Pro database files can be imported into Excel as well. In order to do this, however, you not only need the database file, but you also need to have FileMaker Pro itself installed on the same computer that you are using to run Excel.

To import data from a FileMaker Pro (.fp5 or .fp7) database, make sure FileMaker Pro is running and then follow these steps:

1. **Click the Import button on the toolbar, or choose File ⇨ Import.**
   The Import dialog box opens.
2. **Choose FileMaker Pro database.**
3. **Click the Import button.**
   The Choose a Database dialog box opens.

4. **Locate the .fp5 or .fp7 FileMaker Pro database file.**

5. **Click Choose.**

   The FileMaker Import Wizard dialog box appears, as shown in Figure 13.17.

**FIGURE 13.17**

You can import data from FileMaker Pro databases using the FileMaker Pro Import Wizard.

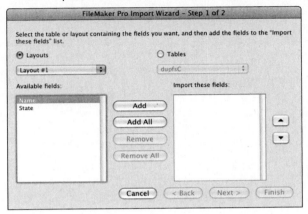

6. **In the Layouts pop-up menu, choose the layout that contains the fields to import.**

7. **If the file is a FileMaker Pro 7 (.fp7) database, you can use the Tables pop-up menu to choose a table with the fields to import.**

8. **Choose the files that you want to include in the import, and click Add to add them to the list. Alternatively, you can choose Add All to automatically add all the fields.**

9. **Click Next.**

10. **On Step 2 of the wizard, you can choose criteria for each field to limit the records to import, much like a database query.** You can choose up to three criteria to use.

11. **Click Finish.**

# Selecting Cells

You've successfully entered some data, either by typing it or by importing it from another source. Now I show you how to work with the data in Excel. For almost any operation you do with cells, you must first select them. Selecting cells can include selecting a single cell, a range of cells, or even multiple individual cells.

To select a single cell, do one of the following:

- Click it.
- Move to the new selection using the arrow keys or the Tab and Return keys.
- Go To a cell using the Go To dialog box, opened by pressing Control+G.

## Selecting a range of cells

To select a range of cells, you can do one of the following actions:

- Click the first cell in the range, and drag the mouse to include the rest, as shown in Figure 13.18.
- Click the first cell in the range, and while holding Shift, click the last cell in the range.
- Click the first cell in the range, and hold down the Shift key while you use the arrow keys to select a range of cells.

### FIGURE 13.18

Select multiple cells by clicking and dragging the selection box over them.

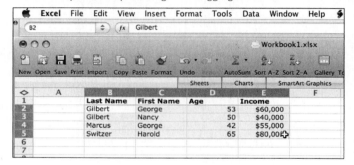

## Selecting multiple cells

You can select multiple arbitrary cells by doing one of the following:

- Click individual cells while holding down the ⌘ key.
- Use the Go To Special dialog box, described below.

The Go To Special dialog box, shown in Figure 13.19, lets you select multiple cells at once that match a specific criteria. You can use it to select all cells that contain formulas, all cells that contain values, or even blank cells. First, open the Go To dialog box by pressing Control+G, and then click the Special button to open the Go To Special dialog box. Table 13.3 lists the criteria available in the dialog box.

### TABLE 13.3

## Go To Special Criteria

| Criteria | Option |
| --- | --- |
| Comments | Select all cells with comments. |
| Constants | Select all cells with constant values. |
| Formulas | Select all cells with formulas. You can limit the selection to formulas that return numbers, text, true/false (logicals), or those with errors. |
| Blanks | Select blank cells. |
| Current region | Expand the current selection to include adjacent cells with data. |

| Criteria | Option |
|---|---|
| Current array | Expand the current selection to include an array if the current selected cell is a member of an array. |
| Objects | Selects all objects in a sheet (including buttons, pictures, and so on). |
| Row differences | Highlights cell differences in selected rows. |
| Column differences | Highlights cell differences in selected columns. |
| Precedents | Highlights cells in the current selection that provide data to formulas. |
| Dependents | Highlights cells in the current selection with formulas that rely on data from other cells. |
| Last cell | Identifies the last cell in a sheet. |
| Visible cells only | Selects cells that aren't hidden. |
| Conditional formats | Highlights cells that have conditional formatting. |
| Data validation | Highlights cells that use data validation. |

**FIGURE 13.19**

The Go To Special dialog box lets you select cells matching specific criteria.

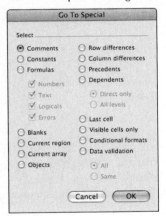

## Adding and Deleting Cells

It is important to have the ability to make changes to your worksheets, and for that reason, Excel makes it easy to add and delete cells. This section shows you how to insert or delete cells in a worksheet and how to delete content in cells.

### Adding cells

The ability to add cells to a worksheet lets you insert data in the middle of existing data in the sheet.

When you insert cells into a worksheet, you need to shift existing cells out of the way. When you insert cells, they are inserted above or to the left of the currently selected cell. Other cells in the same column must be shifted down, or others in the same row must be shifted to the right. You can instead choose to insert a new row above or a new column to the left of the currently selected cell. Follow these steps to insert cells:

**343**

1. Select the cell below or to the right of the place where you want to add cells.

2. Choose Insert ➪ Cells.

   The Insert dialog box opens, as shown in Figure 13.20.

**FIGURE 13.20**

When you insert new cells, use the Insert dialog box to decide how to handle existing cells.

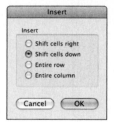

3. Choose one of the options for how to handle existing cells during the insertion:

   ■ **Shift cells right:** Moves cells in the same row to the right.

   ■ **Shift cells down:** Moves cells in the same column down.

   ■ **Entire row:** Inserts an entirely new row above the current selection.

   ■ **Entire column:** Inserts an entirely new column to the left of the current selection.

4. Click OK.

 When you add cells and shift existing cells around, any cell references (such as in formulas) are automatically adjusted to refer to the new locations of those cells.

## Deleting cells

When you delete cells, you run into the same problem with adding them. Existing cells must be shifted to accommodate the empty space in the sheet. You can shift cells in the same column up, shift cells in the same row to the left, or delete an entire row or column. Do the following to delete cells:

1. Select the cell or cells you want to delete.

2. Choose Edit ➪ Delete.

   The Delete dialog box opens, as shown in Figure 13.21.

3. Choose one of the options for how to handle existing cells after deletion:

   ■ **Shift cells left:** Moves cells in the same row to the left.

   ■ **Shift cells up:** Moves cells in the same column up.

   ■ **Entire row:** Deletes the entire row or rows that the selection occupies.

   ■ **Entire column:** Deletes the entire column or columns that the selection occupies.

4. Click OK.

 While Excel updates formulas by adjusting references to cells that have been shifted, formulas that refer to a cell that has been deleted cannot be updated. Instead, they display a #REF!

**FIGURE 13.21**

Deleting cells gives you the opportunity to choose how to handle shifting the remaining cells.

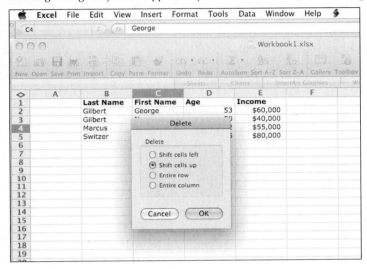

## Deleting content

Sometimes you just want to be able to delete the contents of a cell without having to disturb the other cells in a worksheet. Excel's got you covered here, as well. Do the following to delete the contents of a cell:

1. **Select the cell or cells from which you want to delete the contents.**

2. **Do one of the following:**

   ■ Press the Del key.

   ■ Right-click the selection, and choose Clear.

   ■ Choose Edit ⇨ Clear, and choose one of the options (All, Formats, Contents, or Comments).

**NOTE** If you want to delete any formatting (fonts, colors, and so on) or comments, you must use one of the Edit ⇨ Clear options. The other methods remove content but leave formatting and comments intact.

# Working with Rows and Columns

Now that you have a pretty good handle on working with individual cells, it's time to learn how to work with entire rows and columns at once. You can do so much with rows and columns—add and delete them, resize them, hide them, and split the content of a worksheet into separate panes that can be scrolled independently.

## Adding and deleting rows and columns

Although you saw how to add and delete rows and columns in the process of adding and deleting cells, you can take some specific shortcuts if you specifically want to add or delete rows and columns to a worksheet. To add a row or column, do the following:

1. **Click a cell below or to the right of the point where you'd like to insert the row or column.**
   You also can select a row header or a column header, as shown in Figure 13.22.

2. **To insert a row, choose Insert ⇨ Rows; to insert a column, choose Insert ⇨ Columns.**
   Rows are inserted above the selection, and existing rows are shifted down.
   Columns are inserted to the left of the current selection, and existing columns are shifted to the right.

**FIGURE 13.22**

Select entire rows and columns by clicking the row or column headers.

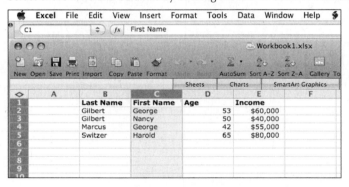

> **NOTE** Don't worry about running out of room for rows and columns. Excel 2008 greatly increases the number of rows and columns allowed in a single worksheet, to match the capabilities of Excel 2007 for Windows. You can have up to 16,384 columns and well over a million rows. You won't be running out of room with Excel 2008!

## Resizing rows and columns

Sometimes rows and columns don't have enough space to show as much information as you'd like. Fortunately, you aren't stuck with the default width and heights. Do the following to resize a row or column.

1. **Position the pointer on the border of the row or column heading that you want to resize.**
   The pointer changes as shown in Figure 13.23.

2. **Drag the row or column border to the size that you want.**

You also can resize rows and columns to more precise values. Right-click a row header and choose Row Height, or right-click a column header and choose Column Width. You can enter a new value to use in the box, as shown in Figure 13.24. The units used are those specified for ruler units. You can change the units used for ruler units in the Excel Preferences, under the General category.

**FIGURE 13.23**

**FIGURE 13.23**

You can resize rows and columns by dragging the borders.

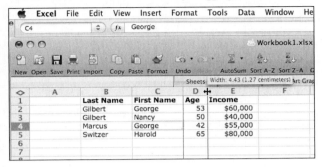

**FIGURE 13.24**

You can specify a precise value for row height or column width.

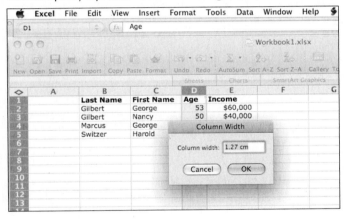

## Hiding rows and columns

Sometimes you may have values or formulas in rows and columns that you'd like to keep, but not make visible to help keep the view uncluttered. Excel gives you the ability to hide rows and/or columns. The data values are still there, and any formulas that make use of them can still do so. An example of when this could be useful is a worksheet to which you add new data in the form of a new row or column every week, and you only need to keep the most recent few months visible.

To hide a row or column, follow these steps:

1. **Right-click the column or row heading that you'd like to hide.**
2. **Choose Hide from the pop-up menu.**

   The row or column you hide is removed from the view, as shown in Figure 13.25.

**FIGURE 13.25**

Hiding rows or columns can help keep your viewable data uncluttered.

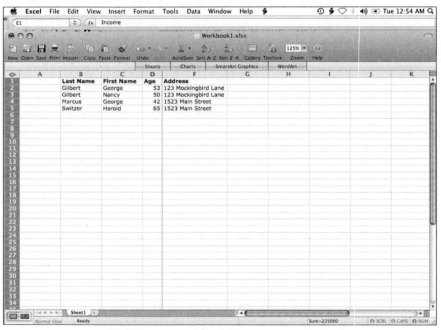

To unhide rows, select the row heading immediately above and below the hidden row. Right-click and choose Unhide, or choose Format ⇨ Row ⇨ Unhide.

To unhide columns, select the column headings on each side of the hidden column. Right-click and choose Unhide, or choose Format ⇨ Column ⇨ Unhide.

**TIP** If the first row or column is hidden, you can't select a row or column above or to the left of it. In this case, you need to use the Go To dialog box to go to cell A1, and then use the Format ⇨ Column ⇨ Unhide to reveal a hidden column A, or Format ⇨ Row ⇨ Unhide to reveal row 1.

## Moving rows and columns

Sometimes you need to reorganize your data, and although cutting and pasting cell contents is not difficult, it can be quite time consuming if you have to do lots of rearranging. Sometimes, you just want to change the order of rows or columns.

It's easy to do this with Excel, because you can easily move rows and columns to new positions simply by dragging and dropping. Follow these steps to move a row or column to a new spot.

1. **Click the Normal View button on the left of the Status bar, or choose View ⇨ Normal.** The worksheet must be in Normal view to move rows and columns.

2. **Select the row or column you'd like to move by clicking the row or column heading.**

3. **Move the pointer below the heading (for columns) or to the right of the heading (for rows), until the pointer changes into a hand, as shown in Figure 13.26.**

**FIGURE 13.26**

Moving row or column data to a new location is as simple as dragging and dropping.

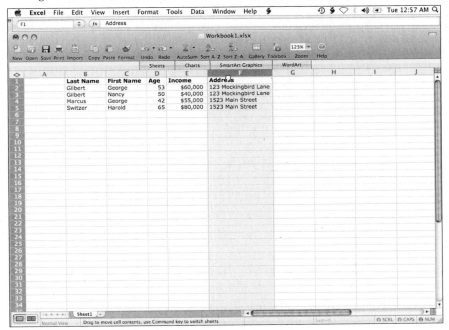

4. **Drag the row or column to a position in between the place you'd like it to be.**

5. **Release the mouse button, and the row or column is moved.**

## Freezing and splitting panes

When you have a large worksheet, you frequently have to scroll from one end to the other to see all your data of interest. Sometimes it'd be nice to be able to freeze part of the worksheet in place so that it is always visible no matter where you scroll. Excel's pane-freezing feature lets you do just that. For example, if the upper portion of your worksheet has column headers, you can freeze them in place so that they are always visible no matter how much you have to scroll in your worksheet.

## Freezing panes

To freeze a portion of a worksheet, do the following.

1. **Click the Normal View button on the left of the Status bar, or choose View ⇨ Normal.** The worksheet must be in Normal view to freeze rows and columns.

2. **Select a cell below and to the right of the row and column you'd like to freeze.**
   - If you only want to freeze rows, make sure the cell you select is in column A.
   - If you only want to freeze columns, make sure the cell you select is in row 1.

3. **Choose Window ⇨ Freeze.**

   You can now scroll the rest of your data sheet without disturbing the frozen portion, as shown in Figure 13.27.

---

**FIGURE 13.27**

---

Freezing a section of the worksheet lets you scroll through your data, but leaves important header rows visible.

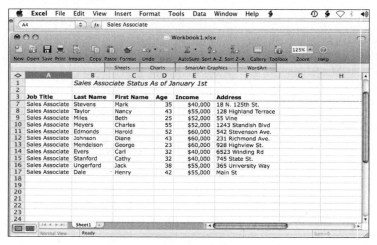

To unfreeze your frozen pane, choose Window ⇨ Unfreeze Panes. You can have only one frozen row and column section of your worksheet at a time.

 **Your frozen pane stays frozen only while you are in Normal view. If you switch to Page view, the panes are unfrozen.**

## Splitting panes

Splitting panes is similar to freezing them. The difference is that Excel lets you scroll each section independently. Follow these steps to split frames.

1. **Click the Normal View button on the left of the Status bar, or choose View ⇨ Normal.** The worksheet must be in Normal view to split rows and columns.

2. **Select a cell below and to the right of the row and column you'd like to split.**
   - ■ If you only want to split rows, make sure the cell you select is in column A.
   - ■ If you only want to split columns, make sure the cell you select is in row 1.
3. **Choose Window ⇨ Split.**

   You can now scroll each split pane independently, as Figure 13.28 shows.

**FIGURE 13.28**

Splitting your worksheet allows you to have multiple independently scrollable sections.

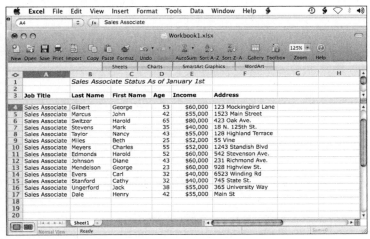

To remove the split panes, choose Window ⇨ Remove Split.

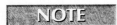 **You can have split or frozen panes, not both at the same time. If you choose to split panes when you already have one frozen, the frozen pane changes to a split pane.**

# Working with Sheets

One of the best innovations in spreadsheets in recent years is the concept of the "3-D" spreadsheet. Three dimensions allow you to have not only rows and columns, but depth as well. Excel's implementation of the 3-D spreadsheet is in the form of *worksheets*. Simply put, worksheets are separate, individual row-column spreadsheet pages. A workbook has a single worksheet in it when it is created, but you can add more. You can give worksheets descriptive names, move them around, and even hide individual sheets. Formulas on one worksheet can reference data on another one, which allows you to build complicated workbooks with data, perhaps imported from a database, hidden away on one worksheet. Meanwhile, users can work with sheets that have cells that are intended for the user to modify or that contain formulas referencing data on the hidden sheets. Individual worksheets are added using the worksheet tabs at the bottom of the program window, as shown in Figure 13.29. In Chapter 12, you learned how to create new worksheets. Now you learn some other tricks for working with them.

**FIGURE 13.29**

You can add multiple worksheets to a workbook.

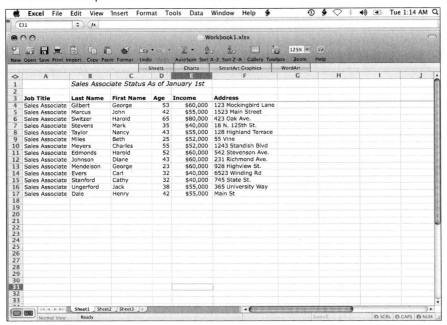

## Renaming sheets

By default, Excel names sheets with the very non-descriptive names Sheet1, Sheet2, Sheet3, and so on. This may be fine if your workbook has a small number of sheets in it, but it can be a bit hard to remember what each sheet is for if you have many of them or if you go a long time before using a workbook again.

Fortunately, Excel makes it easy to rename worksheets to anything that you like. This invaluable feature lets you easily remember what a particular sheet is for simply by glancing at the names on the tabs. To rename a worksheet, do the following:

1. **Select the sheet that you want to rename by clicking its tab.**
2. **Right-click a worksheet tab and choose Rename, or choose Format ⇨ Sheet ⇨ Rename.**
3. **Type the new name directly on the tab, as Figure 13.30 shows.**
    - You are limited to 31 characters for a sheet name.
    - You can use spaces in a sheet name, but you cannot leave it blank or use any of the following special characters: : (colon), \ (backslash), / (forward slash), * (asterisk), [ (left square bracket), or ] (right square bracket).

**FIGURE 13.30**

You can give worksheets more descriptive names.

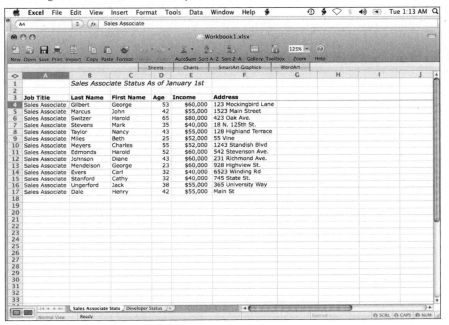

## Moving and copying sheets

When working with large workbooks, you may decide that you'd like to have your worksheet tabs in a different order. You also may want to create a new sheet based on an existing one. Excel lets you do both of these things using the Move or Copy dialog box. You can even move or copy a sheet to an entirely different workbook. Follow these steps to move or copy a worksheet:

1. **Select the sheet that you want to move or copy by clicking its tab.**

2. **Choose Edit ⇨ Move or Copy Sheet from the main menu.**

    The Move or Copy dialog box opens, as shown in Figure 13.31.

3. **If you want to move or copy to a different workbook, choose the open workbook in the To Book drop-down list.**

4. **Choose the sheet that you would like to insert the moved or copied sheet in front of in the Before Sheet list.** Use the (move to end) option to make it the last sheet in the workbook.

5. **If you want to make a copy of the sheet rather than move it, check the Create a copy check box.**

6. **Click OK.**

   If you are copying a sheet within the same workbook, it is created with a numeric indicator at the end of the name in parenthesis.

---

**FIGURE 13.31**

Use the Move or Copy dialog box to move a sheet or create a new sheet based on an existing one.

TIP     **Moving a sheet also can be accomplished in a simpler manner. Click the tab for the worksheet that you would like to move, and drag it to the location where you want it. Excel displays a handy arrow pointing to the location in the sheet tab list where the sheet will go. Release the mouse button to complete moving the sheet.**

## Hiding sheets

At first glance, it may seem odd to want the ability to hide sheets. After all, if you can't see them, what good are they? Hidden sheets let you use them to store data that the user does not need to interact with directly, such as tables imported from a database. Instead, you can use formulas to reference cells on these hidden sheets from elsewhere in your workbook.

To hide a sheet, do the following:

1. **Select the sheet that you want to hide by clicking its tab.**
2. **Choose Format ⇨ Sheet ⇨ Hide from the main menu.**

   The worksheet is hidden from view along with its tab.

To make a sheet visible again, do this:

1. **Choose Format ⇨ Sheet ⇨ Unhide from the main menu.**

   The Unhide dialog box opens, as shown in Figure 13.32. The worksheet is hidden from view along with its tab.

2. **Select the worksheet to unhide from the list.**

3. **Click OK.**

   The worksheet reappears in its original position in the tab order.

---

**FIGURE 13.32**
_____

You can use the Unhide dialog box to make hidden worksheets visible again.

## Changing sheet backgrounds

Let's face it: Spreadsheets aren't always pretty to look at. You can jazz up your Excel worksheets a bit by setting a custom background image. This could be a corporate logo, a picture of money, a picture of your kids—whatever! The sky is the limit.

 Background images are used only for display purposes; they are not included when you print your worksheets. For this reason, you cannot use a background image as a watermark.

To add a background image to a worksheet, follow these steps:

1. **Select the sheet that you want to add a background image to by clicking its tab.**

2. **Choose Format ⇨ Sheet ⇨ Background from the main menu.**

   If the only menu item is Delete Background, then the sheet already has a background. It must be deleted before you can add another one.

3. **In the Choose a Picture dialog box, locate the image file that you would like to use for the background.**

   Just about any image file type that can be opened by QuickTime can be used.

4. **Click Insert.**

   The background image is inserted into the worksheet, as shown in Figure 13.33.

**FIGURE 13.33**

A background image can make your worksheets look nicer.

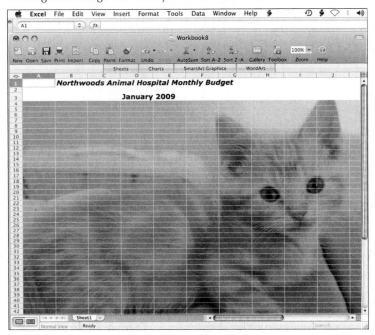

# Working with Named Ranges

You've learned that you can name worksheets to help you keep track of your data, but what about on a finer level? It would be nice to be able to take a smaller chunk of data (such as a cell or group of cells) and give it a name so that you don't have to remember the row and column addresses of every bit of important data in a worksheet.

Excel's Named Ranges feature is intended to do just that. With Named Ranges, you can assign a name to a cell or group of cells and use that name as an input to a formula. This can help keep your formulas easy to read and understand. For example, you could assign name of "SalesTaxRate" to a cell containing the rate and "PreTaxTotal" to a cell containing the total. Your formula to calculate the sales tax would then be something like =PreTaxTotal*SalesTaxRate, instead of something like =E5*E6.

**NOTE** Range names can contain letters, numbers, periods, and underscores. The first character must be a letter or an underscore. Spaces and any other punctuation characters are not allowed, because they could be confused with other uses of these characters in formulas. You also cannot use the name of a valid cell reference, such as A1 or AB120.

## Naming ranges

It's easy to create a Named Range. To do so, follow these steps:

1. **Select the cell (or range of cells) to which you want to assign a name.**
2. **In the Formula bar, type a name in the name box, as shown in Figure 13.34.**
3. **Press Return.**

   The name you enter is applied to the selected cells.

**FIGURE 13.34**

Use the Formula bar to enter a name for a range of cells.

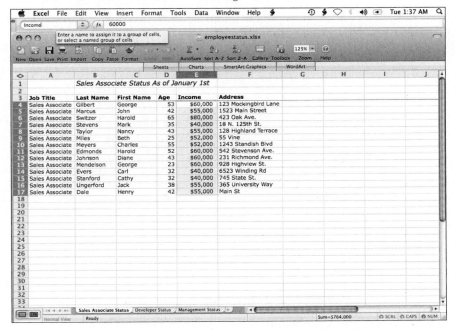

## Reviewing named ranges

After you've created named ranges, you can manage them by choosing Insert ⇨ Name ⇨ Define. This opens the Define Name dialog box, as shown in Figure 13.35.

The Define Name dialog box works at the workbook level, showing you named ranges that are defined on all of its sheets.

**FIGURE 13.35**

Use the Define Name dialog box to manage your named ranges.

Two buttons on the Define Name dialog box help you manage names:

- **Add:** Type a new name into the box at the top, select a cell or group of cells in a worksheet, and click this button to create the new range.
- **Delete:** Select a name from the list, and click Delete to remove it.

At some point, you might need to review your named ranges. You can use the Paste Name feature to paste a list of the names you've created into cells on a worksheet. The list is pasted into two columns—the first with the name and the second with a reference to the cells that the name refers to. Follow these steps to use the Paste Name feature:

1. **Select the cell that will serve as the upper-left corner of the list.**
2. **Choose Insert ➪ Name ➪ Paste from the main menu.**

   The Paste Name dialog box opens, as shown in Figure 13.36.

**FIGURE 13.36**

The Paste Name dialog box lets you paste a single name or the entire list into a worksheet.

3. **Click a name in the list to select it and click OK, or click Paste List to paste them all.**
   - If you choose a single name, a reference to it is pasted into the cell you have selected, and the range of cells that it refers to is highlighted with a blue border.

- If you choose Paste List, your named ranges are pasted into two columns. The leftmost contains the name, and the rightmost contains the cell references. An example of this can be seen in Figure 13.37.

**FIGURE 13.37**

After using the Paste Name feature, you have a complete list of names and the cells they refer to handy.

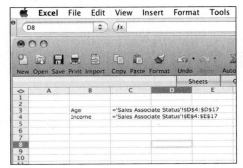

 Named Ranges are primarily used in conjunction with formulas. You learn more about working with named ranges and formulas in Chapter 15.

# Moving and Copying Cells

Face it: When you're designing a worksheet, you might not always place data in the best spot initially. Sometimes you need to move it to a new location on the sheet or even copy it to another sheet or workbook. Fortunately, Excel makes it simple to move or copy data to a new location. Follow these steps to move or copy data to a new location:

1. **Select the cell or cells you want to move or copy.**
2. **Move the mouse pointer to the border of the cell or group of cells.**

    The pointer turns into a hand icon, as shown in Figure 13.38.
3. **Click the mouse button, and drag the cells to the new location.**

    You can make a copy of the cells by holding down Option as you drag the cells. The data in the original cells is left intact.

NOTE When you move or copy cells, any references in the cells or in cells that point to them are not automatically adjusted. If this happens, a cell might display a reference error value #REF!, and you must make manual adjustments to the references. For more information on how to fix references, see Chapter 15.

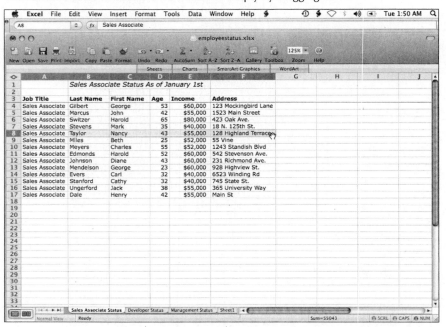

**FIGURE 13.38**

You can move data in cells to a new location simply by dragging it.

# Creating Lists

Excel is a great number cruncher, but that's not the only thing it's good at. It is an exceptionally good data organizer as well, and the designers of Excel for the Mac have taken it a step farther by introducing a Lists feature that gives you even more flexibility.

Lists, like worksheets, are organized into columns and rows. In this respect, they are similar to worksheets, except that they are objects that are themselves embedded into a worksheet. In a sense they are analogous to a database table, and indeed when Excel imports data from a database, it is stored in a list. Figure 13.39 shows a typical list in action.

Excel provides two tools for working with lists: the List Wizard and the List Manager. The List Wizard is a tool that, like other Wizards, can help you step through the process of creating and modifying lists. In the List Wizard, you can choose how many columns should be in a list and the types of data each one should contain. You also can choose formatting options for each list.

When it comes time to edit your list data, you can use the List Wizard to step through everything again; however, the List Manager also helps you work with lists. The List Manager is essentially what makes a list a list, and not just a region in a worksheet. It provides the ability to change sorting and filtering options for each list column and to quickly add columns or rows to lists.

**FIGURE 13.39**

Lists provide a convenient way for working with data.

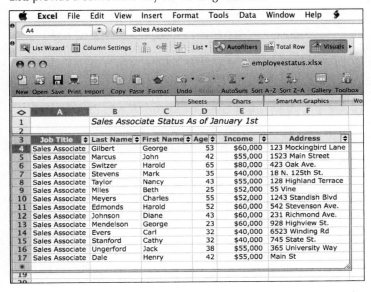

**NOTE** Lists are similar to but not exactly the same as tables in Excel 2007 for Windows; however, the features are not compatible. Workbooks with lists created in Excel for the Mac have any list data preserved when opened with Excel in Windows, but List Manager functionality is not available.

## Exploring the List Wizard

The List Wizard is the tool of choice to use to get the most out of Excel's List feature. While you could create a list without it, the Wizard helps guide new users through the process and shows you options that you might not have been aware of to start with. In this section, you walk through the process and learn about the options available when you create a list.

You can create a list from existing data or create an empty one that you will fill in later. The defining characteristics of a list include columns that are formatted to contain a single type of data each and rows with data in each of those columns that relate to each other.

### Getting started with the List Wizard

The List Wizard is the best way to get started in creating lists. Choose Insert ➪ List to start the Wizard, as shown in Figure 13.40.

The List Wizard consists of three steps. The first step is where you define the data that is to be used for the list. This data can come from an existing group of cells on a worksheet or from an external data source, such as a database. You also can choose to create an empty list in this step, and later steps give you the option to define columns for the list.

**FIGURE 13.40**

The List Wizard makes creating lists easy.

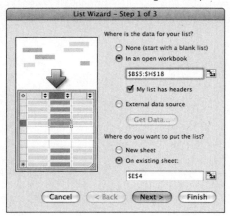

To choose a range of cells, you can either select the range before you start the Wizard or select the range after the Wizard dialog box is already open. If the dialog box is overlaying the area that you want to select, simply drag it out of the way.

**TIP**    If you need to be able to see more of the worksheet under the List Wizard dialog box, click the Collapse button next to each of the range selection boxes to move it out of the way. Click again to expand the dialog box back to its normal size.

The following steps help you in your initial use of the List Wizard:

1. **Choose Insert ⇨ List.**

   The List Wizard dialog box opens, as shown in Figure 13.40.

2. **Choose a source for the data for the list.** Options include:

   - **None (start with a blank list):** This creates an empty list with no data.

   - **In an open workbook:** This lets you select a range of cells to use for the list. If you have a range of cells selected when you start the wizard, they will be referenced here.

   - **External data source:** You can choose to import data from an external source, such as a database. This option is discussed in more detail in Chapter 17.

3. **If your list is in an existing worksheet, check the "My list has headers" box if the first row of the list contains descriptive names instead of data.**

4. **Choose a destination for the list.** You can choose to place it in a new worksheet or on an existing sheet.

   If you choose the "On existing sheet" option, you can optionally specify a new cell location for the upper-left corner of the list.

## Defining columns

The second, and arguably, most important step of the List Wizard, shown in Figure 13.41, lets you define columns for a list. If you are creating a list from existing data, these columns are automatically represented in this step. However, you can use this step to add additional columns to a list (or to an empty list), choose a data type for each column, and choose a formatting option for each column.

The second step of the List Wizard lets you define columns.

Follow these steps to define a column using Step 2 of the List Wizard:

1. **From Step 1 in the Wizard, Click Next.**

   Step 2 is displayed in the List Wizard dialog box, shown in Figure 13.41.

2. **Enter a name for a new column in the Column name box.**

3. **Choose a data type for the column from the Data type drop-down list.** These are described in Table 13.4.

4. **Click Add to add the new column.**

   The new column is added after any selected columns in the list.

You also can use this step to modify existing columns:

1. **Select the column that you wish to modify.**

2. **Enter a new name for the column, if desired.**

3. **Choose a new data type for the column from the Data type drop-down list, if desired.**

4. **Click the Modify button to change the existing column.**

You might be able to figure out how to delete columns from here as well. Simply do the following:

1. **Select the column that you wish to modify.**

2. **Click Delete to remove it from the list.**

**TABLE 13.4**

## List Column Data Types

| Data Type | Description |
| --- | --- |
| Any value | The default setting, this value indicates that cells have no predefined data type. |
| Whole number | The value must be a whole number (no decimal points). |
| Decimal | The value can be any number, including those with decimals. |
| Currency | The value is an amount of currency. |
| Counter | This data type automatically generates a sequential numeric value for each row in the list. |
| Text | The value can be any text. |
| List | Cells can contain one of the values from a list, chosen from a selection of cells. |
| Date | The value must be a date. |
| Time | The value must be a time. |
| Calculated Column | This data type references a formula in another cell, which contains the formula to generate the values for each row. |

You can use the Column Settings dialog box to give you additional options for defining a column, by doing the following:

1. **From Step 2 in the Wizard, select the column you want to change.**
2. **Click the Settings button.**

   The Column Settings dialog box opens, as shown in Figure 13.42.
3. **Enter a new name for the column, if desired.**

**FIGURE 13.42**

The Column Settings dialog box lets you choose advanced column formatting options.

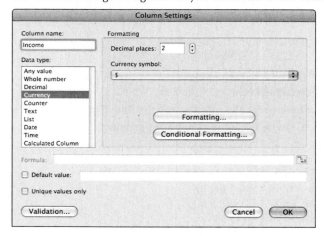

4. **Choose a new data type for the column, if desired.**

5. **Choose formatting options for the column.** Available formats are dependent on the data type you select:

   ■ Choose one of the formatting options provided directly in the Column Settings dialog box, or click the Formatting button to show more advanced formatting options.

   ■ The Conditional button allows you to make formatting dependent on the value in the cell; for example, you can use this to make negative values red.

**NOTE** Formatting is an important subject. Excel's ability to display data in a variety of ways is one of the keys of its power. That's why this book has an entire chapter devoted to the subject of formatting data in Excel. See Chapter 14 to learn how to format text, numbers, currency, and more.

6. **If the data type allows a default value, you can check the Default value box and enter the value in the space provided.**

7. **Check the Unique values only box if you would like the list to ensure rows in this column contain unique values. This option invalidates the default value setting.**

8. **If your data type is List, you can use the Source field to specify a range of cells that contain values for the list.** You can use the Collapse button to hide most of the dialog box and select cells from the underlying worksheet.

9. **If your data type is Calculated Column, use the Formula field to choose a cell that contains the formula to put in the list.**

10. **You can add validation to the column by clicking the Validation button.** Validation is covered in detail in Chapter 14.

11. **Click OK to apply the changes, or click Cancel to leave the column the way it is.**

## Setting list options

Step 3 of the List Wizard is shown in Figure 13.43. This step is used to set options that apply the list as a whole rather than to individual columns. Follow these steps:

1. **From Step 2 in the Wizard, click Next.**

   The List Wizard moves to Step 3, as shown in Figure 13.43.

2. **Enter a name for the list.**

**FIGURE 13.43**

Use Step 3 of the List Wizard to set general list options.

3. **Check the box for Autoformat list after editing if you want to be able to use one of the 16 predefined list formatting styles.** Click the AutoFormat button to open the AutoFormat dialog box, shown in Figure 13.44.

The AutoFormat box lets you choose a predefined style for your list.

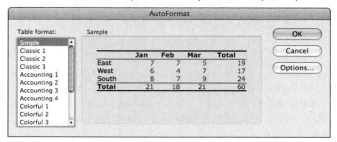

4. **Check the box for Repeat column headers on each printed page if you would like column headings to be printed at the top of every page when you print your workbooks.** The additional column headers are not visible in Excel.

5. **You can add a totals row to the end of your list by checking the box for Show totals row.**

   The Total row is an interesting List feature that lets you apply a formula to the cells in the row. This formula can use any one of the following functions: Average, Count, Count Nums, Max, Min, or Sum. You also can choose to use an arbitrary formula.

6. **Choose one of the Show list visuals options: Auto, On, or Off.** These options control how the List Manager visuals that allow for manipulation of the column data are visible.

7. **Click Finish to complete the Wizard and create the list.**

## Working with lists

After a list has been created, you have many options for changing list properties and working with data. You can use the List Wizard to change list options. You can use the List Manager (the controls visible in a list when you have list visuals enabled), and you can use the List toolbar.

### Using the List toolbar

The List toolbar gives you a convenient way to find all the options available to you for lists, without needing to go through the List Wizard. This toolbar can be activated by choosing View ⇨ Toolbars and then choosing the List option. The List toolbar is shown in Figure 13.45. List toolbar options are described in Table 13.5.

**FIGURE 13.45**

The List toolbar provides you with handy shortcuts for working with lists.

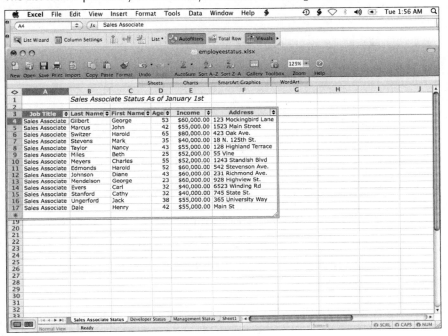

**TABLE 13.5**

## List Toolbar Options

| Button | Menu Item | Description |
|---|---|---|
| | List Wizard | Reactivates the List Wizard. |
| | Column Settings | Opens the Column Settings dialog box for the current selected column. |
| | Insert Column | Inserts a new column into the list, and shifts existing columns to the right. |
| | Insert Row | Inserts a new row above the currently selected cells in the list. |
| | AutoFormat | Opens the AutoFormat dialog box. |

*continued*

| Button | Menu Item | Description |
|---|---|---|
| **List** | List menu | Provides these options for working with lists: List Wizard, Insert Row/Column, Delete Row/Column, Clear Contents, Sort, Filter, Form, AutoFormat, Chart, PivotTable Report, Remove List Manager, and Refresh Data. |
| | AutoFilters | Toggles the AutoFilters controls on the column headers on or off. |
| | Total Row | Toggles the totals row on or off. |
| | Visuals | Toggles the visuals for the List Manager on or off. |
| | More Buttons | Activates a menu with buttons that help in navigating through a list. This menu is shown in Figure 13.46. |

**TABLE 13.5** *(continued)*

**FIGURE 13.46**

These controls activated from the List toolbar make navigating through a list easy.

## Using the List Manager

The List Manager is the collection of visible controls surrounding a list that enable you to work with the data in the list. With the List Manager, you can enter data, add or remove columns or rows, reorganize columns or rows, and choose sorting and filtering options for columns.

### Entering data

Entering data into a list using the List Manager is similar to entering data into a worksheet, but there are some differences. You can click a cell to select it and immediately begin entering data. You can use the Tab key to advance to the next column or Return to move to the next row down. When you tab past the last column in a list, however, the List Manager automatically moves you back to the first column, and down one row.

The List Manager always leaves an empty row at the end of the list. You can use this row to begin entering data for a new row, as shown in Figure 13.47. When you begin entering data, a new empty row is created right below it.

The List Manager automatically adds new rows when you reach the bottom of the list.

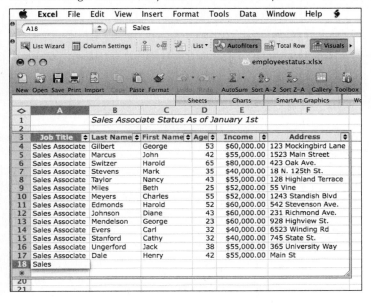

## Using AutoFilter

When you enable the AutoFilter option in the List toolbar, the AutoFilter button on each column heading can be used to activate the AutoFilter menu. This menu, shown in Figure 13.48, allows you to set sorting and filter options for each column.

These options are available in the AutoFilter menu:

- **Sort Ascending:** Sorts the list using this column's values, from lowest to highest.
- **Sort Descending:** Sorts the list using this column's values, from highest to lowest.
- **(Show All):** Makes all rows visible.
- **(Show Top 10):** Activates the Top 10 AutoFilter dialog box, shown in Figure 13.49. This dialog box allows you filter out all except for the top or bottom range of rows. You also can choose the number of rows to include and whether this number refers to a percentage rather than a fixed number of rows.

■ **(Custom Filter):** Activates the Custom AutoFilter dialog box, shown in Figure 13.50. This dialog box allows you filter rows based on two conditions. You can choose an operator for each condition and a value to which to compare the data. You also can choose to require that both conditions apply or specify that either applies using the And and Or radio button selections.

■ **Individual values:** The remainder of the menu shows individual data values in this column. You can select one of these values, and the list is filtered to display only rows that match this value.

---

### FIGURE 13.48

Use the AutoFilter menu to change the sorting and filtering buttons for a column.

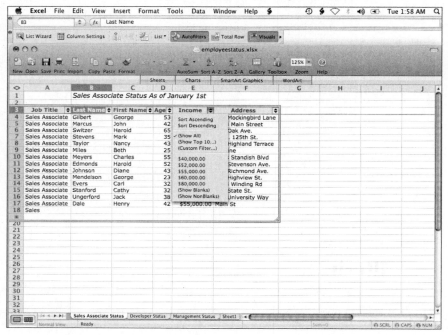

---

### FIGURE 13.49

The Top 10 AutoFilter dialog box lets you choose to show only the highest or lowest ranked rows.

The Custom AutoFilter dialog box lets you perform advanced filtering.

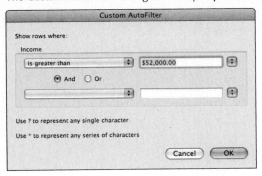

### Reactivating the List Wizard

Although you can do just about anything with a list using the List Manager or the toolbar, you also have the option of invoking the List Wizard again if you so desire. Reactivate the List Wizard using one of the following methods:

- Click in the list to select it, and choose Insert ⇨ List.
- Click in the list, and choose List Wizard from the List toolbar.
- Right-click in the list, and choose List Wizard from the pop-up menu.

Once in the List Wizard, you can change any of the options that you set the first time through the Wizard: add or remove columns, change column data types, and adjust formatting.

# Sorting and Filtering Data

You've read about the sorting and filtering options available in the List Manager, but what if you want to do the same sorts of things with ordinary worksheet data? Excel's got you covered, with advanced sorting and filter options that you can apply to any data in a worksheet.

## Sorting data

When working with large amounts of data, you may need to organize it in such a way that you can easily find data and how it relates to other data. Excel's Sort dialog box, shown in Figure 13.51, lets you choose three columns by which to sort data.

**FIGURE 13.51**

You can use the Sort dialog box to choose which columns to use to sort data in a worksheet.

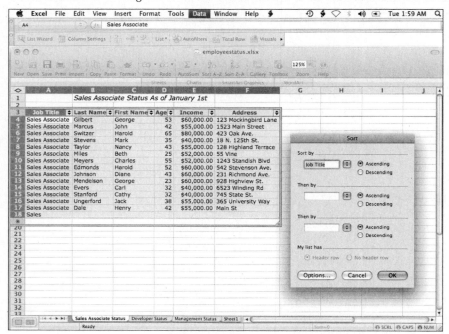

Follow these steps to use the Sort dialog box:

1. **Choose Data ⇨ Sort.**

   The Sort dialog box opens, as shown in Figure 13.51.

2. **Choose a column to sort by from the drop-down menu at the top.**

3. **Choose whether to sort this data in an Ascending (lowest values at the top) or Descending (highest values at the top) manner.**

4. **If you would like to further sort data using other columns, choose sort options for them in the two Then by sections.**

5. **If your data has a row with column header names at the top, choose the Header row option. Choose No header row if you don't have one.**

6. **Click the Options button for additional sorting options, as shown in Figure 13.52.**

7. **In the Sort Options dialog box, choose a First key sort order, which lets you sort by such items as days of the week or calendar month names rather than alphabetically.**

8. **Check the Case sensitive box if you would like sorting to take uppercase and lowercase into account.**

9. **Choose an orientation option if you'd prefer to sort by rows rather than by columns.**

10. **Click OK to close the Sort Options dialog box.**

**FIGURE 13.52**

The Sort Options dialog box gives you additional options for sorting data.

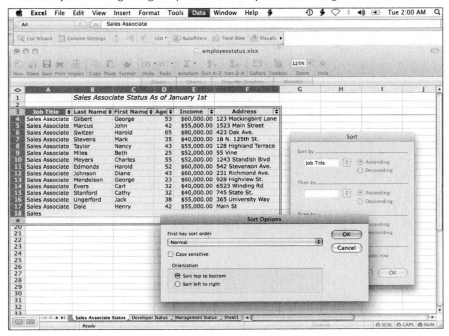

11. **Click OK to close the Sort dialog box and apply the sort options.**

Another way to sort data is to use the AutoFilter menu, just as you did with the List Manager. Read the next section on Filtering to learn more.

# Filtering

Another handy thing to do when you are working with large amounts of data is to filter it so that only the rows that you are interested in are visible, hiding other data out of the way. Excel gives you two ways to filter data in your worksheets: AutoFilter and the advanced filtering options.

## Using AutoFilter

AutoFilter works much like the one in the List Manger. You can use it to sort data by columns in ascending or descending order, or you can filter based on the top or bottom range of values or by conditions. To use AutoFilter, you must first enable it:

1. **Select a cell in the data that you want to sort by clicking it.**
2. **Choose Data ➪ Filter, and check the AutoFilter option to add AutoFilter buttons to each column header, as shown in Figure 13.53.**
3. **Click the AutoFilter buttons for each column heading to set filtering and sorting options for the data.** AutoFiltering works the same way it is described in the List Manager section.

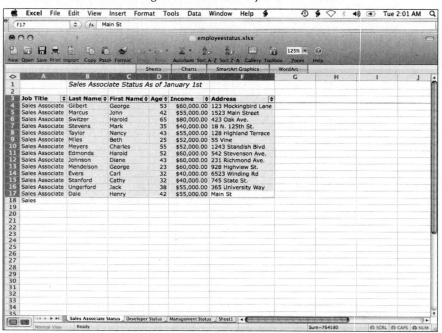

**FIGURE 13.53**

You can use AutoFilter with regular worksheet data just as with Lists.

## Using advanced filtering

As useful as AutoFilter is, it is still limited to a maximum of two filter criteria. If you want to filter by more than that, the Advanced Filter must be used. The Advanced Filter can filter by an arbitrary number of criteria and allows you to filter out duplicate data. You can even use formulas for the filtering criteria.

To use the Advanced Filter, you must set up a range of cells to describe the criteria to use for filtering. The columns for the filtering must match the columns of the data that you want to sort. This data can even be in a different worksheet than the one that contains the data, so you could have data being imported into one sheet while you use the Advanced Filter on another sheet to display the criteria and the data.

Follow these steps to use the Advanced Filter:

1. **Enter a criteria table to match the columns of your data table.** Figure 13.54 shows an example. Choose one of these options:

   ■ Enter a single entry under a column to filter based on that value.

   ■ Enter more than one criteria items in a single row to apply an AND rule.

   ■ Enter more than one criteria on different rows to apply an OR rule.

Also be aware of these restrictions:

■ You can use wildcard characters (the asterisk [*] and the question mark [?]) to substitute for a range of characters or a single character in the filter, respectively.

■ You can use greater than (>) or less than (<) operators with criteria values to allow filtering on a range of data.

■ The criteria values can be generated by a formula. For example, you could build filter criteria to show only data from the current month by using one of the date functions to put the current month in a criteria table.

2. **Click in or select the range of cells that you want to filter.**

3. **Choose Data ⇨ Filter ⇨ Advanced Filter to open the Advanced Filter dialog box, shown in Figure 13.55.**

4. **Click the Criteria range box, and select the cells that make up the criteria table you built in Step 1.**

5. **Click the Copy to box, and choose a cell to use for the destination data.**

6. **If you want to filter out duplicates, check the Unique records only box.**

7. **Click OK to perform the filter.** The filtered data is copied to the new location, as shown in Figure 13.56.

**FIGURE 13.54**

Set up a criteria table with data indicating filtering criteria.

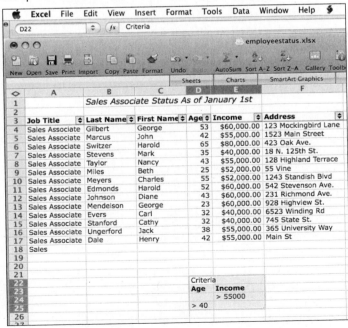

### FIGURE 13.55

The Advanced Filter dialog box lets you choose the range and criteria to filter with.

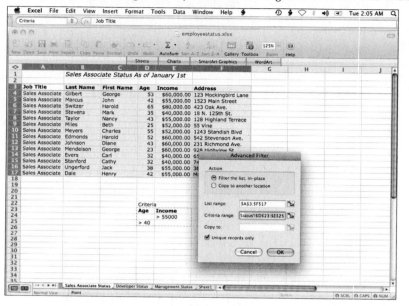

### FIGURE 13.56

Filtered data is copied to a new table.

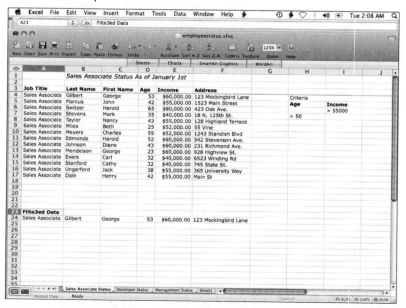

# Finding and Replacing Data

One of the features just about any modern office application needs is the ability to find and replace data throughout a document, and Excel is no exception to this. Find and Replace are stalwart features that can make your life much easier when you have a worksheet with 10,000 rows and you need to locate Fred Robbins, or when you have extraneous data in imported data that you need to remove.

## Using the Find dialog box

To locate data throughout a worksheet or book, you can choose Edit ⇨ Find or press ⌘+F to open the Find dialog box, shown in Figure 13.57. Follow these steps to use this dialog box:

1. **Enter the value you want to search for in the Find what box.**
2. **Choose whether to search within a single sheet or the entire workbook using the Within drop-down list.**
3. **Choose to search by rows or by columns.** This affects the order in which Find locates data.
4. **Choose whether to search in Formulas, Values, or Comments.** You can only choose one of these options.
5. **If you want to do a case-sensitive search, check the Match case box.**
6. **If you want to match entire cell contents, check the Find entire cells only box. Leave this unchecked if you want to match partial cell contents as well.**
7. **Click Find Next to locate the next matching value.** You find values from top to bottom and left to right in your worksheets.
8. **Continue clicking Find Next to locate additional values that match the criteria, if you desire.**
9. **Click Close when you are finished.**

---

**FIGURE 13.57**

You can use the Find dialog box to locate data throughout a worksheet or book.

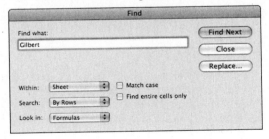

## Using the Replace dialog box

You may notice the button labeled Replace in the Find dialog box. Clicking this button turns the dialog box into the Replace box, shown in Figure 13.58. The Replace dialog box not only lets you locate data in a worksheet, it lets you replace it with a new value. You also can open the Replace dialog box directly by choosing Edit ⇨ Replace.

**FIGURE 13.58**

Use the Replace dialog box to change data.

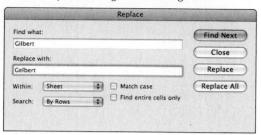

The Replace box offers the same options for locating data as the Find box; however, you have the additional options of entering a new value to replace the old one. As you locate data using the Find Next button, you can choose to replace it with the new value by clicking the Replace button. You also have the option of automatically replacing all the matching data at once by clicking the Replace All button.

**WARNING**    Replace All can be dangerous, because you don't necessarily see all the data that will be changed, and sometimes data that you don't intend to change will be changed inadvertently. It is often better to use the Find Next and Replace buttons to locate and change each item individually.

# Using Undo and Redo

You've seen lots of ways to manipulate data in this chapter, from moving it around, to sorting, filtering, copying, and pasting. You may be thinking that so much could go wrong with all this data manipulation, and you're right. Fortunately, you have a safety net. Excel provides the Undo and Redo functions to allow you to step backward in your editing to undo any change that you have second thoughts about.

As you are making changes to a worksheet, Excel keeps track of all the information you change along the way.

The Undo command (choose Edit ➪ Undo, click the Undo toolbar button, or press ⌘+Z) can be used to step backward through the changes you've made to a worksheet, reverting the sheet to the way it was before. You can perform multiple undos by using this command repeatedly.

The Redo command (choose Edit ➪ Redo, click the Redo toolbar button, or press ⌘+Y) is the counterpoint to Undo. If you decide that you want to undo an Undo command, you can use Redo to reapply it to the worksheet. This can be handy if you are undoing several steps, but accidentally step too far back. Redo can step forward again to reapply those actions.

Although very useful (and sometimes life-saving) commands, Undo and Redo are not without limitations.

- Undo can be applied only to actions in the exact reverse order to when they were first applied. You can't skip a preceding step to undo an even earlier one.
- The Undo history is wiped out every time you save a workbook.

If you need to undo or redo multiple items at once, Excel provides a shortcut using the Undo and Redo buttons on the Standard toolbar. Click the arrow next to the button to bring up a list of undo or redo actions that can be performed. Not only is this a quick and easy way to see the undo history to see the changes that you have made, but you also can use it as a shortcut—simply drag the mouse pointer over multiple actions in the list, and click when you've selected all that you want to undo. This is demonstrated in Figure 13.59.

**FIGURE 13.59**

Multiple undo/redo steps can be performed at once through the Undo button on the Standard toolbar.

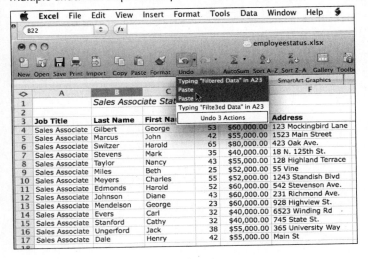

## Summary

Excel is a complex program with many features, and this chapter has covered lots of ground. You learned the basics of entering data into Excel, as well as how to import it from other types of files such as text, csv, or html files. You also learned a number of keyboard shortcuts that can make navigating your worksheets and entering data easier. Basic skills, such as selecting a cell or a range of cells will prove to be invaluable later as you learn to work with formulas, charts, and other advanced Excel functions. In addition, you learned how to work with rows and columns and how to add, delete, and move them around.

You also learned about more advanced features such as named ranges, lists, and sorting and filtering options that give you the ultimate in flexibility when it comes to working with data. In Chapter 14, we cover more ground and show you how to apply formatting to data, including numeric, text, and date formats, as well as visual elements such as fonts and colors.

# Chapter 14

# Formatting Data and Worksheets

You've probably heard it said that quality is more important than quantity. In a way, this can apply to Excel worksheets. How your data is presented can be as important is what it says. In business, you can present reams of data to support your point of view, but if it's hard to read or poorly laid out, your audience is likely to tune out or get frustrated. Properly formatting your data not only helps make your worksheets easier for others to understand, it makes them easier to work with.

The designers of Excel have provided you with an array of formatting options for data and text. You can choose from a huge number of data formats, depending on the data and how you want it presented. Excel lets you format numbers in a variety of ways—as date and time values, currency, percentages, fractions, and more.

In addition to data formats, you can apply style formats to cells and worksheets. You can make changes to character and text formatting, altering fonts, sizes, and colors. You can format cell backgrounds as well, by changing colors, shading, and borders. You can even apply conditional formatting that automatically changes the way numbers are displayed depending on the values; for example, you can highlight negative values in red. You can even create and use styles and themes so you can reapply the same formatting options to other workbooks you create. In this chapter, you learn how you can apply formatting to cells and to your data in order to present your work in the best way possible.

## Formatting Cells

The Format Cell dialog box, shown in Figure 14.1, is your one-stop-shopping place to set most cell formatting options, including number formats, text alignment, fonts, and borders and shading. You can activate it for a single cell at a time to customize its format, or more commonly, for a collection of cells, a row or column, or an entire worksheet or workbook. To activate the Format Cells dialog box, follow these steps:

1. **Select the cell or cells that you want to format by doing one of the following:**
   - Click an individual cell to select it.
   - Select multiple cells by pressing ⌘ and clicking them.
   - Select an entire row or column by clicking the row or column header.
   - Select the entire worksheet using Control+A.
2. **Choose Format ⇨ Cells, or press ⌘+1, or right-click the selection and choose Format Cells.**
   The Format Cells dialog box opens.

**NOTE** Don't activate the Format Cells dialog box while in Edit mode. If you do so, you see only font formatting options. Make sure you are in Ready mode (as shown in the Status bar) in order to get all the formatting options available.

**FIGURE 14.1**

The Format Cells dialog box is where you can find most formatting options.

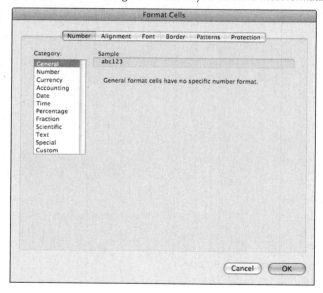

## Choosing a number format

Excel's main purpose is to work with numbers, so it's no surprise that Excel is most flexible when giving you options for formatting them. Numbers are used to represent currency, dates and times, percentages, fractions, and more. If the provided formats aren't enough for you, you can define a custom format that should give you exactly what you need.

The first tab of the Format Cells dialog box is used to choose a data format for numbers in cells (or to set it to use no data formatting whatsoever). Click the Number tab to select number formatting, and choose a data format from the list. Most data types have additional formatting options, which you learn about in this section.

> **TIP** Note that setting a format for a cell doesn't change the underlying data; it only affects how it is presented. You can always see the actual data contained in a cell by double-clicking it (if the cell and worksheet are not protected), or by clicking it and viewing the data on the Formula bar.

## Formatting general

The default format for cells is the first one on the list—the General format. When cells are formatted as General, Excel makes its best guess to display numbers and text. Numbers are generally displayed as they are typed, with a few exceptions. Figure 14.2 shows some examples of General formatting, and the following rules apply to General formatted numbers:

- Numbers are aligned to the left, and text is aligned to the right.
- Trailing zeros entered to the right of a decimal point are truncated.
- Decimals entered without a number to the left of the decimal point are displayed with a single zero.
- Leading zeros on numbers are removed.
- Numbers are displayed using scientific notation if they contain ten or more digits.

**FIGURE 14.2**

With General formatting, Excel attempts to guess how to display numbers and text.

| Cell contents | General format |
|---|---|
| .1234 | 0.1234 |
| 1.0000 | 1 |
| 000052 | 52 |
| 100000000000 | 1E+11 |

## Formatting numbers

You can go beyond Excel's automatic number formatting by choosing the Number data type. This data type lets you choose a consistent format to use to display numbers no matter how they are entered. Figure 14.3 shows the options available when using the Number format. You can set the following options:

- **Decimal places:** Choose the number of digits to display after the decimal point. This can range from 0 to 30.
- **Use thousands separator:** Checking this option causes Excel to display a separator character for every thousands value.
- **Negative numbers:** Choose a conditional formatting option for negative numbers. Typical options are display with a negative sign, display in another color such as red, or display of the number inside parentheses.

> **NOTE** The decimal point, thousands separator character, and formatting options for negative numbers that Excel offers depend on the locale that you've chosen for your computer. Open the System Preferences dialog box, click the International icon, and click the Formats tab to choose a region if you want to change these.

**FIGURE 14.3**

You can choose a variety of display options for number data using Number formatting.

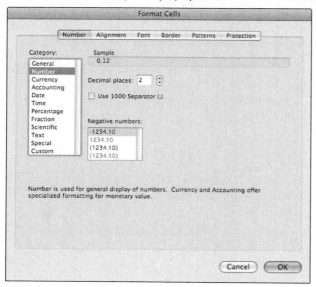

### Formatting currency

Excel is particularly adept at displaying currency values. Symbols for all major currency types are available, and you can adjust decimals and display of negative numbers just as with the General number type, as shown in Figure 14.4. These are your choices:

- **Decimal places:** Choose the number of digits to display after the decimal point. This can range from 0 to 30. Typically, this value is set to accommodate the lowest fractional currency amount, such as cents.

- **Currency symbol:** Select a currency value to use as a prefix to the value. All the common currency symbols are available, or you can choose a three-character abbreviation if the symbol would be ambiguous (MXN for Mexican Pesos, for example). Choose "none" to display no symbol.

- **Negative numbers:** Choose a conditional formatting option for negative numbers. Typical options are display with a negative sign, display in another color such as red, or display of the number inside parentheses.

 If you prefix currency values with the currency symbol such as $ or € as you are entering them, the Currency data type automatically is applied to match.

**FIGURE 14.4**

Currency formatting gives you choices for a currency symbol along with the other number formatting options.

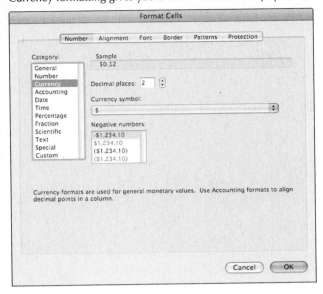

## Formatting for accounting

Accountants need to display currency values for tabulation in columns; as such, the data is easier to read if numbers and currency symbols line up. With the Accounting format option, the currency symbol is aligned to the left of the cell and the value to the right, as shown in Figure 14.5.

With the Accounting data type, negative numbers are displayed in parentheses instead of with a negative sign. The following other options are available:

- **Decimal places:** Choose the number of digits to display after the decimal point. This can range from 0 to 30. Typically, this value is set to accommodate the lowest fractional currency amount, such as cents.

- **Currency symbol:** Select a currency value to use as a prefix to the value. All the common currency symbols are available, or you can choose a three-character abbreviation if the symbol would be ambiguous (MXN for Mexican Pesos, for example). Choose "none" to display no symbol.

**FIGURE 14.5**

Use the Accounting data type to neatly align currency values in columns.

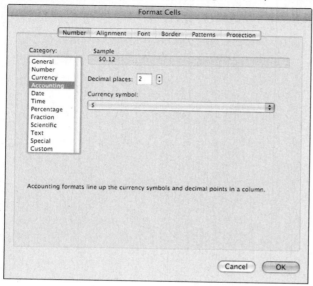

### Formatting dates and time

One of the areas where Excel shines is in the options it allows for formatting date and time values. Several numeric and textual date and time variations are possible. Select the Date item to choose date formats, as shown in Figure 14.6; select Time to display only the time portion. Some options that display both date and time are available for both types.

Unfortunately, unlike its Windows cousin, Excel 2008 is not very adept at displaying date formats for locales that use the Day/Month/Year arrangement rather than the Month/Day/Year format prevalent in the United States. You can get around this by using a Custom format. See "Creating a custom format" in this chapter for more information.

### Formatting percentages

It is often convenient to display fractional values as a percentage. The Percentage data type makes this extremely easy to do. Simply select the Percentage type, as shown in Figure 14.7. The only other option available is the number of decimal places to use.

The Percentage data type takes the value entered in the cell and multiplies it by 100 for display, along with a percent sign (%). For example, the value 0.50 is displayed as 50%, and 2.0 is displayed as 200%.

# Understanding Date Systems

**E**xcel dates and times are represented internally as numeric decimal values, with the whole number portion to the left of the decimal representing the date and the decimal portion representing the time. Unfortunately, a long-standing incompatibility between Mac and Windows versions of Excel has caused some problems over the years. Excel on the Mac traditionally uses January 2, 1904, as the basis for its date values. The date portion simply counts the number of days since then. For example, January 1, 2009, is represented internally by the value 38352. Excel for Windows, however, uses January 1, 1900, as the basis for its dates.

This used to cause major headaches when sharing workbooks between Windows and Macs. Fortunately, this distinction is now largely academic, because Excel allows you to set the base date system to use for a workbook. Although Excel 2007 for Windows still uses 1900 and Excel 2008 for the Mac still uses 1904, an attribute is now saved with the workbook to indicate which system is in use, and it is recognized by either version. You can change the date system in use by choosing Excel ⇨ Preferences and choosing the Calculation icon. Under Workbook options, uncheck the "Use 1904 date system" option to use the Windows 1900 base system standard instead, as this figure shows. Note that this causes any existing dates in a workbook to be set back four years.

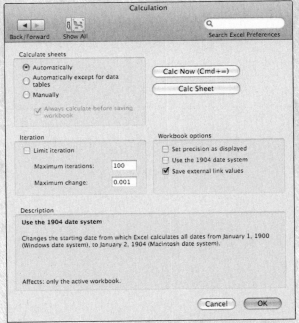

*You can choose a base date system in the Calculation preferences under Workbook options.*

**FIGURE 14.6**

Date and Time formatting options allow you display dates and time values just the way you want them.

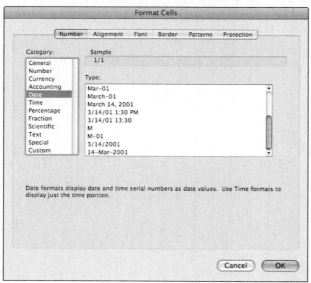

**FIGURE 14.7**

Percentages are a useful way to display fractional data.

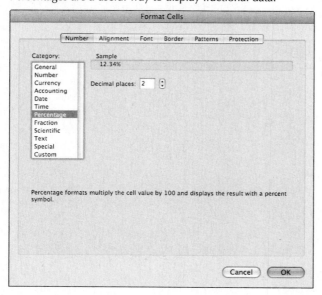

## Formatting fractions

With the Fraction data type, you can choose to display decimal data as the nearest fraction, with a whole number portion and the part after the decimal shown as a numerator/denominator fraction. Select the Fraction data type, and choose one of the fractional values shown in Figure 14.8. If the number cannot be represented entirely by the chosen value, it is rounded for display; the underlying value is never changed.

 **TIP** Some of the fraction types can be most useful for measurements, because portions of an inch are traditionally given in values of half, quarter, eighth, or sixteenth of an inch.

**FIGURE 14.8**

The Fraction formatting type allows yet another way to display decimal data.

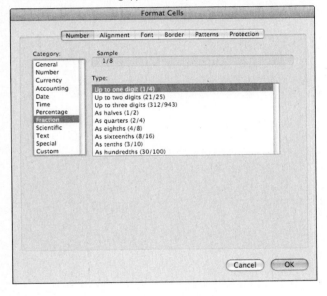

## Formatting scientific values

Scientists and engineers often work with very large or very small numbers, and the number of digits can become unwieldy and hard to see at a glance. With such numbers, the ultimate precision of the value is not as important, so E notation was developed to represent these values in a small amount of space.

With E notation, the decimal point is moved to a more convenient location for display, and the number of places it is moved is displayed after the letter E, along with a sign indicating the direction the decimal point moves. For very large numbers, the decimal point is moved to the left, and the E value is shown with a plus sign. For very small numbers, the decimal point is moved to the right, and the E value is shown with a negative sign. Table 14.1 shows some examples of E notation. Figure 14.9 shows the Scientific formatting options.

**TABLE 14.1**

## Scientific (E) Notation Examples

| Original Value | Shortened Value |
|---|---|
| 30.0 | 0.30E+02 |
| 1,000,000 | 1.00E+06 |
| 0.000056 | 5.6E-05 |

**FIGURE 14.9**

The Scientific data type allows large numbers to be represented in E notation shorthand.

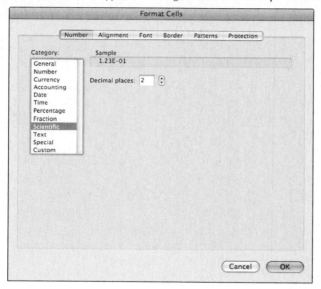

### Formatting text

These number formatting options are nice, but sometimes you just want a cell to display data exactly the way you enter it. The Text formatting option, which is the default for any data that Excel can't determine how to apply another data type to, can be used to force all values to be displayed as entered, with no formatting changes. Figure 14.10 shows the Text formatting option.

### Special formatting

Excel supports some formatting options that just don't fit anywhere else or merit their own category, so they've been tossed into the Special formatting category. These options, shown in Figure 14.11, include Zip code (and Zip +4), phone numbers, and social security numbers. These options are all U.S. formats.

**FIGURE 14.10**

You can choose to display numbers as text, which forces them to be displayed exactly as entered. You have no options for text formatting here.

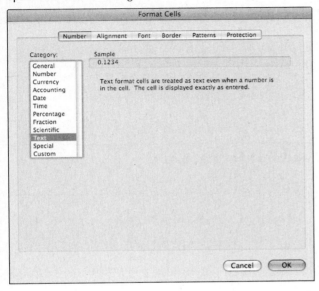

**FIGURE 14.11**

Special formatting is available for Zip codes, phone numbers, and social security numbers.

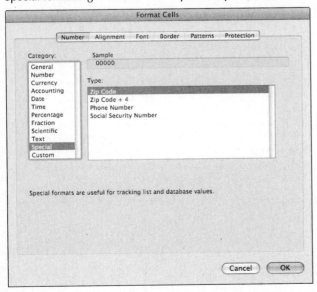

### Creating a custom format

You've looked through all the provided formats and you can't find one that formats numbers (or dates) exactly the way that you like. Fear not, because Excel gives you the Custom formatting option so you can roll your own number formats. With the Custom type, shown in Figure 14.12, you can choose one of the provided basic types as a starting point and modify it to fit exactly the way you want. The Custom options are quite flexible; in fact, they are used to define all the existing formatting types behind the scenes.

 **You can see how the predefined formats are defined by selecting them and then switching to the Custom category.**

The syntax for describing a custom format is a bit arcane, so it's helpful to see a table with the options and examples. Table 14.2 gives a list of codes and what they do. Table 14.3 lists date and time codes.

**TABLE 14.2**

## Custom Number and Text Format Codes

| Number and Text Code | Format |
| --- | --- |
| General | General number. |
| 0 | Single-digit placeholder. Extra zeroes in a format indicate that numbers should be padded with zeros to fit if necessary. |
| # | Single-digit placeholder, but with no zero padding. |
| ? | Single-digit placeholder, which leaves space for zero padding but does not display them. |
| . | Decimal indicator. |
| % | Displays as percentage. |
| , | Thousands separator. |
| E+, E-, e+, or e- | Uses scientific (E) notation. |
| @ | Displays as text. |
| + - $ / ( ) : space | Displays characters directly in the format. |
| \character | Displays the character that follows the backslash. For example, \! displays an exclamation point. |
| "text" | Displays the text inside the quotes. |
| * | Repeats the next character in the format to fill in a custom width. |
| _ (underscore character) | Skips the width of the following character. This can be used to line up one format with another when one displays a character and the other does not. |
| [BLACK], [BLUE], [CYAN], [GREEN], [MAGENTA], [RED], [WHITE], [YELLOW], [COLOR n] | Displays the characters that follow in this color. The n value refers a value from 1 to 56, indicating one of the values of the Excel color palette. |

TABLE 14.3

## Custom Date and Time Format Codes

| Date and Time Codes | Format |
| --- | --- |
| m | Numeric month without leading zero (1-12) |
| mm | Numeric month with leading zero (01-12) |
| mmm | Name of month, abbreviated (Jan-Dec) |
| mmmm | Name of month, unabbreviated (January-December) |
| d | Numeric day of the month, without leading zeros (1-31) |
| dd | Numeric day of the month, with leading zeros (01-31) |
| ddd | Day of the week, abbreviated (Sun-Sat) |
| dddd | Day of the week, unabbreviated (Sunday-Saturday) |
| yy | Two-digit year (for example, 09) |
| yyyy | Four-digit year (2009) |
| h | Hours as a numeric value, without leading zeros (0-23) |
| hh | Hours as a numeric value, with leading zeros (00-23) |
| m | Minutes as a numeric value, without leading zeros (0-59) |
| mm | Minutes as a numeric value, with leading zeros (00-59) |
| s | Seconds as a numeric value, without leading zeros (0-59) |
| ss | Seconds as a numeric value, with leading zeros (00-59) |
| AM/PM am/pm | Use a 12-hour clock |

Each custom format can have up to four sections, separated by a semicolon (;). These sections, from left to right, set formatting for Positive numbers, Negative numbers, Zero values, and Text values. You do not need to use all four sections; if you use one, it is used for all formatting. With two sections, the first is used for positive and zero values, and the second for negative numbers. Formats can be quite complex overall. Table 14.4 shows some examples that you might find useful.

TABLE 14.4

## Custom Format Examples

| Code | Format |
| --- | --- |
| dd/mm/yyyy | Date in day/month/year format, with leading zeros and a four-digit year. Example: 29/03/2009 |
| mmmm d, yyyy h:mm AM/PM | Long format date and time. Example: March 29, 2009 3:29 PM |
| (000) 000-0000 | Displays as phone number. Example: (555) 123-4567 |
| @*. | Text format, but pads the empty space in the cell with a period. Example: John.......... |
| _($* #,##0.00_);_($* (#,##0.00);_($* "-"??_);_(@_) | The standard accounting format: three sections, describing positive, negative, and zero values |

**FIGURE 14.12**

The Custom formatting option allows you to create your own format.

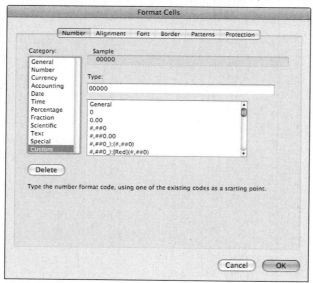

> TIP
>
> Because Excel 2008 provides so many existing formats, you can use them to understand how custom formats work. Select an existing format, and then click the Custom category. The custom format displayed defines the last format you selected.

## Changing alignment and spacing

The second tab on the Format Cells dialog box—Alignment, shown in Figure 14.13—can be used to change the way text is displayed in a cell. You can change the horizontal and vertical alignment and set text wrapping and shrinking, cell merging, and even the orientation of the text. As you can imagine, all these options can lead to some very funky-looking cells.

### Setting text alignment

Setting the horizontal and vertical text alignment can make a difference in how data is displayed in cells with expanded heights or widths, or when a single cell contains lots of data. You can choose from two alignment options: horizontal and vertical.

#### Horizontal alignment

The default horizontal alignment, General, lets Excel try to determine the best way to display data. General alignment displays text aligned to the left and numbers aligned to the right. You can override this setting to have data conform to the alignment of your choice. You have these options:

- **General:** Uses the default alignment that Excel assigns: text aligned to the left, numbers to the right.

- **Left (indent):** Aligns to the left, with an optional indentation value that you can choose in the Indent box to the right of the alignment drop-down list.

- **Center:** Centers data in the cell.
- **Right:** Aligns data to the right of the cell.
- **Fill:** Repeats data to fill up empty space in the cell.
- **Justify:** Spaces text in a paragraph, with the exception of the last line, to fill the cell from left to right.
- **Center across selection:** If multiple cells are selected, this option can be used to center the text based on the width of the selected columns. This is useful for centering titles over multiple columns, for example.

**FIGURE 14.13**

Use the Alignment tab of the Format Cells dialog box to change how text is displayed in a cell.

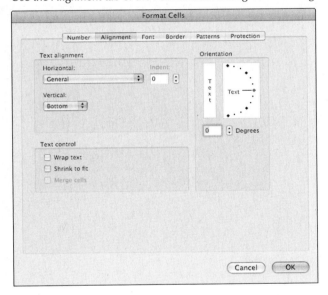

### Vertical alignment

You have these vertical alignment options:

- **Top:** Aligns data with the top of a cell. If the cell grows vertically, data stays in place.
- **Center:** Centers data vertically in the cell.
- **Bottom:** Aligns data to the bottom of the cell.
- **Justify:** Spaces lines of text so they fill the cell from top to bottom.

## Setting text control

When text is too large to fit into a cell, Excel needs to know how to display it. By default with no text control, the data is displayed overlapping the cell next to it. This can be confusing and messy. Figure 14.14 shows some examples of text alignment formatting. These are your options:

- **Wrap text:** Text wraps to additional lines if is too large to fit on a single line.
- **Shrink to fit:** This reduces the size of the text in a cell so it all fits in the size of the cell.
- **Merge cells:** If multiple cells are selected, they are merged together so more space is available for the other formatting options.

### Changing the orientation

The final alignment option for text lets you rotate it through 90 degrees vertical going up, to 90 degrees vertical going down. Simply enter an angle (positive values lead upward, negative values downward), or drag the orientation indicator to where you want.

**FIGURE 14.14**

The various text alignment options give you lots of flexibility.

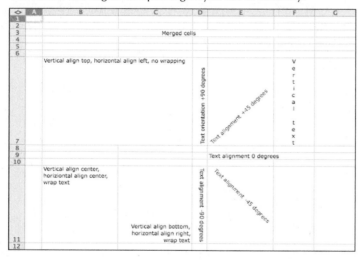

## Changing fonts

On the Font tab of the Format Cells dialog box, shown in Figure 14.15, you can choose from a myriad of text formatting items, including the font style and size, text color, and various effects. Each of these items can apply to an entire cell or to a subset of text in a cell. To apply it to a portion of the text in the cell, you must double-click the cell to get into Edit mode and then select the text you want to change.

As you make changes to the font settings, the Preview window shows you how these settings will make your text look.

### Choosing a font

The most important choice on this tab is the font to use. The right font can make the difference between readable text in a worksheet and a frustrating experience. Choose a font from the Font list. If you know the name of the font you want to use, you can type it into the Font box directly. The list scrolls as you type so you can quickly locate the correct font.

**FIGURE 14.15**

The Font tab of the Format Cells dialog box lets you customize how text is displayed.

After you've chosen a font, you need to choose a style for it. Your options are Regular (no style), Italic, Bold, or Bold Italic.

Finally, choose a size for the font. Most fonts allow from 6 to 72 points in size. If a value you want to use is not listed, you can enter it directly in the Size box.

## Applying character formatting

Choosing a font is simply the first step. You can apply additional formatting attributes to your data as well. These include various text effects as well as underline styles that are unique to Excel.

### Underline options

Excel gives you several underline styles, with two that are useful for worksheets oriented toward accounting:

- **None:** Text is displayed without being underlined.
- **Single:** Text is displayed with a single line under it.
- **Double:** Text is displayed with two underlines. The second line is above the line used for the single underline. The spacing of the lines is not affected by the font size.
- **Single Accounting:** Text is displayed slightly higher with more space between the font and the underline.
- **Double Accounting:** In this double underline setting, the second line is below the one used for single accounting.

### Effect options

With effects, you can add more attributes to your data to present it in a special way. Effects can be applied alone or together, and each can be set individually. (Subscript and Superscript are exceptions; only one of those effects can be applied at a time.) These are your options:

- **Strikethrough:** Text is displayed with a line through it.
- **Superscript:** Text is displayed slightly smaller and above the main text. This is frequently used for exponents.
- **Subscript:** The text is displayed slightly smaller and below the main text.
- **Outline:** Only the outline of the text is displayed.
- **Shadow:** A drop shadow is displayed below and to the right of the text. The color of the shadow is similar to the text color chosen for the cell, only lighter.

### Normal Font

The Normal Font check box can be used to return a cell to its default formatting. This restores any font, effects, and colors that you have chosen for a cell.

## Changing text color

Nothing changes a worksheet from drab to interesting more than adding color. Colors can be used to make certain data stand out. For example, you could make cells in which you intend to have values manually entered appear in one color, cells that are locked appear in another color, and formulas in yet another color.

Excel offers a palette of 56 colors to choose from; simply use the Color drop-down list, shown in Figure 14.16, to make your choice. Keep in mind any background color that you may want to use. If you use a dark background, you should stick with lighter font colors. Darker colors are okay on white or lighter background colors. See "Setting a background pattern" for information on setting background color.

**NOTE**   Of special interest is the Automatic option. This option may seem to always make your text black, so you may wonder why they bother with this option. It is useful when you save a worksheet as an HTML page for viewing in a Web browser, because the browser takes the user's default color preference for both the text color and the fill color. Therefore, if you don't have any other color changes, you should consider leaving the default setting of Automatic in place out of consideration for people who may view your worksheets over the Web.

## Adding and modifying borders

Another option for custom cell formatting is to use the border feature. Borders can be used to accentuate a cell, a range of cells, or a row or column. You can disable borders to give your worksheets a clean look. Most aspects of a cell's border presentation can be set independently of one another. You can turn each border on and off individually and even give each one a unique color if you like. Figure 14.17 shows the Format Cells dialog box's Border tab.

**FIGURE 14.16**

Text color changes can have a dramatic effect on your worksheet's presentation.

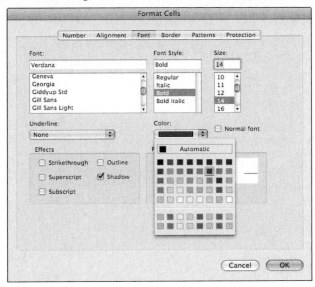

**FIGURE 14.17**

Use border settings to accentuate a cell or a section of cells.

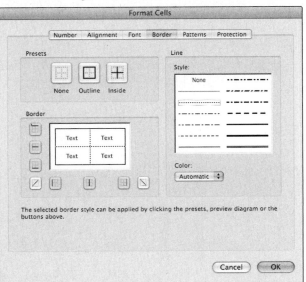

To change cell borders, follow these steps:

1. **Select a cell or range of cells, and open the Format Cells dialog box as described earlier.**

2. **Choose a line style, if desired.** The default is a solid line, but other options are available, including thicker lines, a double line, various broken and dashed lines, as well as no style at all.

3. **Choose a color for the border, if desired.**

4. **Click one of the preset buttons to apply borders:**

   - **None:** This option removes all borders.

   - **Outline:** This option adds borders in the selected style to the outside borders of the selection.

   - **Inside:** This option adds borders in the selected style to the inside borders of the selection. This setting has an effect only when multiple cells are selected.

5. **If you want to enable or disable an individual border, use one of the individual border buttons located in the Border section.** You also can toggle borders on and off by clicking them directly in the preview window.

6. **If you want to give some borders a different style or color, repeat Steps 2 through 5 for those borders.** One popular option is to make outline borders thicker and darker, but leave inside borders lighter or dashed.

7. **Click OK to apply the border change.**

**NOTE** Cells share borders with other cells, and a conflict can occur as to which border setting is used. In general, the last border setting made overrides a previous one. For example, if you make the right border of a cell red and then the left border of the adjacent cell blue, the blue border is used.

## Setting a background pattern

The final step in customizing a cell's format is to set a background color or pattern. This is done on the Patterns tab of the Format Cells dialog box, shown in Figure 14.18.

Even though the tab is labeled Patterns, the most common option to set here is the solid background color of a cell. To do so, simply choose one of the 56 offered colors in the palette. The Sample window shows you a larger filled area of the color. Click OK to apply the new color.

If you like, you can set a pattern for the cell's background instead. The patterns you can choose from include a variety of horizontal, vertical, and diagonal lines, as well as some crosshatch patterns. You can use these patterns to emphasize certain cells. To set a pattern, choose one from the drop-down menu shown in Figure 14.19. Use the same menu again to choose a color to use for the pattern.

**TIP** If you want cell text to be readable against the pattern, use a lighter pattern color to go with darker cell colors.

**FIGURE 14.18**

Use the Patterns tab to select a background color or pattern for your cells.

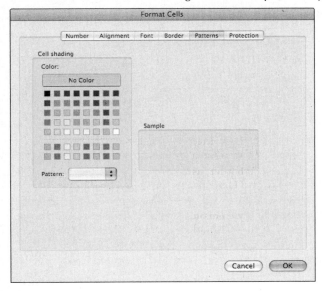

**FIGURE 14.19**

Selecting a background pattern can give cells a unique background look for emphasis.

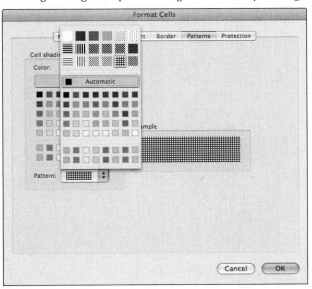

# Using the Format Toolbar

So far, we've been focusing on the Format Cells dialog box, and with good reason: It's the place to go for all the formatting options available to you. You can use other tools to set formatting, one of which is the Formatting toolbar, shown in Figure 14.20. If the Formatting toolbar is not visible, you can enable it by choosing View ⇨ Toolbars and checking the Formatting option.

### FIGURE 14.20

The Formatting toolbar presents a handy way to apply the most commonly used formatting options.

Table 14.5 shows the options available on the Formatting toolbar.

### TABLE 14.5

## Custom Format Examples

| Icon | Function |
|---|---|
|  Verdana ▾ 10 ▾ | Lets you choose a font name from the drop-down menu, along with the font size. |
|  **B** | Sets selected text Bold. |
|  *I* | Sets selected text as Italics. |
|  U | Underlines the selected text. Only the standard single line underline is available here. |
|   | Aligns text to the left. |
|   | Centers text in the cell. |
|   | Aligns text to the right. |
|  ⟨A⟩ | Merges selected cells, and centers text within the combined cell. |
|  $ | Applies the Accounting data format. |
|  % | Applies the Percentage data format. |
|  , | Applies the standard numeric format, with two decimal places and the thousands separator. |

| Icon | Function |
|------|----------|
| | Increases the number of decimal places displayed by one. |
| | Decreases the number of decimal places displayed by one. |
| | Decreases indent. |
| | Increases indent. |
| | Lets you choose a border style from the drop-down menu. |
| | Lets you choose a background fill color. |
| | Lets you choose a text color. |

# Using the Formatting Palette

The Formatting Palette is part of the Toolbox floating palette, as shown in Figure 14.21. The Formatting Palette doesn't give you as many formatting options as the Format Cells dialog box, but it does give you more to work with than the Formatting toolbar. It also puts all the controls within a single click without forcing you to try to remember which tab contains a particular setting. An additional advantage is that changes are applied in real time to your worksheets, so you don't have to make all your formatting choices and click OK to see them; you can decide whether a particular format works as you're making changes. If the Formatting Palette is not visible, you can activate it by choosing View⇨Formatting Palette.

The Formatting Palette offers some unique controls for formatting cells and is organized in categories that can be expanded or closed, depending on which ones you want visible. The following categories are available:

- **Font:** Here you can set all the usual font selection options, including typeface, size, color, and effects. One unique option available here is the slider control that can be used to select a font size.
- **Number:** This category can be used to set basic number formatting. While all the number format data types are available from this list, only one of each type is available. If it's not exactly what you want, you have to use the Format Cells dialog box. You also can increase or decrease the number of decimal points visible using buttons located here.
- **Alignment and Spacing:** You can select the most common text alignment options, as well as orientation, text wrapping, and cell merging in this category.
- **Borders and Shading:** Choose a border style and color, or set the background color of a cell in this category. For added convenience, you can use the Draw by Hand button to change borders directly on the worksheet.
- **Page Setup:** This category can be used to configure your worksheets for printing. These options are discussed in detail in Chapter 18.
- **Document Theme:** This category lets you choose a document theme, which is discussed later in this chapter.

**FIGURE 14.21**

The Formatting Palette provides a convenient place to make the most common formatting changes.

# Copying Formatting

So you've spent hours creating the perfect formatting, and you're very happy with how it looks. The only problem is that you now want to apply the formatting to other worksheets or workbooks. Fortunately, you don't need to redo each individual format setting from scratch: Excel gives you the ability to copy formatting from one cell and paste it directly into another.

The easiest way to copy formatting is to use the Format Painter icon on the Standard toolbar. Follow these steps to copy formatting from a cell or range of cells to another:

1. **Select the cell or range of cells that contain the formatting that you want to copy.**
2. **Click the Format Painter icon on the Standard toolbar.**
3. **Select the cell or range of cells to which you want to copy formatting.**
   The formatting is automatically applied.
4. **Repeat Steps 2 and 3 to apply the formatting to additional cells, as shown in Figure 14.22.**

**FIGURE 14.22**

The Format Painter feature makes it easy to copy formatting from cell to cell.

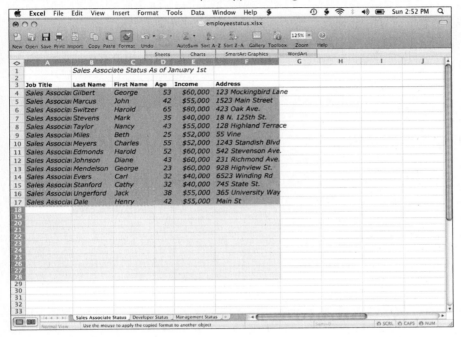

Another way to copy formatting is to use the Paste Special feature. By default, all formatting is copied when you copy and paste a cell, but the Paste Special dialog box lets you be a little more selective. Here's how:

1. Select the cell or range of cells that contain the formatting that you want to copy.
2. Copy them to the clipboard using one of the Copy commands—for example, by choosing Edit ➪ Copy.
3. Select the cells to which you want to copy the formatting.
4. Choose Edit ➪ Paste Special to open the Paste Special dialog box.
5. Select the formatting options that you want to copy. You can choose just to copy formats or just copy number formats and values, along with some other options shown in Figure 14.23.

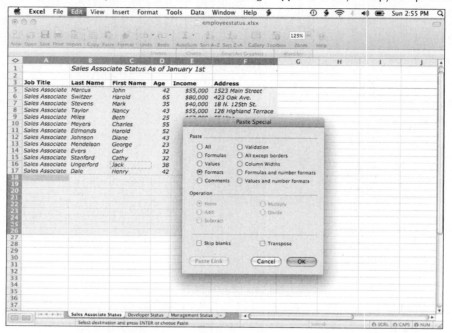

**FIGURE 14.23**

You can use Paste Special to control how formatting is applied when you copy and paste cells.

# Using AutoFormat

Even though you want pretty worksheets and all this formatting stuff makes sense, it still seems too much like work to get a professional-looking result. What you really want is a feature that automatically formats an entire worksheet to save you some time. Excel's AutoFormat feature can do just that. AutoFormat gives you 17 options that immediately make your worksheets look like a pro did them, even if this is your first day using the program.

AutoFormat is really designed around table type data. It applies font, color, number, and border formats to the range of cells you select. Unfortunately, you have to enter the data and text yourself. To use AutoFormat, follow these steps:

1.  **Select the cell range to which you want to apply the formatting.**
2.  **Choose Format ➪ AutoFormat.** The AutoFormat dialog opens, as shown in Figure 14.24.
3.  **Choose a format style that matches your desired look and the purpose of your workbook.**
4.  **Click the Options button to reveal a set of check boxes that let you choose a subset of the format options to apply.** Check and uncheck these as desired.
5.  **Click OK to apply the formatting.**

**FIGURE 14.24**

Use AutoFormat to instantly apply professional-looking formatting to your data.

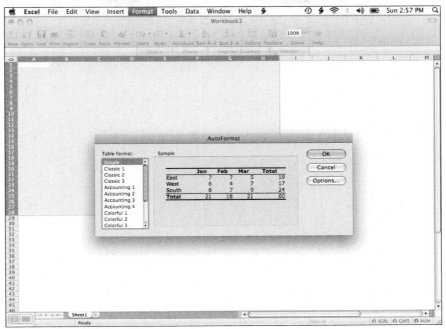

After you have applied AutoFormat formatting, you are free to make further changes using any of the methods described in this chapter, using the Format Cells dialog box, the Formatting toolbar, or the Formatting Palette.

# Applying Conditional Formatting

Conditional formatting is a feature of Excel that lets you set rules for how cell formatting will look. Each cell can have up to three rules; if the conditions of a rule are met, the formatting is applied. You can use conditional formatting to emphasize values that are of interest, such as when a value is outside of a desired range—say, when your budget goes negative. To define conditional formatting for a cell, follow these steps:

1. **Select the cell or range of cells to which you want to apply conditional formatting.**
2. **Choose Format ➪ Conditional Formatting.** This opens the Conditional Formatting dialog box, shown in Figure 14.25.

**FIGURE 14.25**

Conditional formatting alters a cell's formatting depending on rules you create.

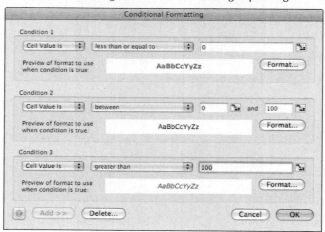

3. **Under Condition 1, choose whether you want the condition to be triggered from a value or from the result of a formula.** The formula option is often more useful, because cells with formulas are more likely to have changed data. However, the value option gives you flexibility in choosing operators. These are your choices:

   - **Cell Value Is:** If you choose this option, select a conditional phrase from the next pop-up menu, and then enter a value to compare it to in the last field.
   - **Formula Is:** Enter a formula that evaluates to either TRUE or FALSE.

4. **Click Format, and choose the formatting options for font, border, and patterns.** Conditional formatting has a limited subset of formatting options available. For example, you can't choose a different font or font size, but you can choose a font style (bold, italics, or underline), underline and strikethrough effects, and text color. Figure 14.26 shows the Font tab of the conditional formatting version of the Format Cells dialog box.

5. **Click OK to add the format.**

6. **To add additional conditions, click the Add button in the Conditional Formatting dialog box.** You can have up to three conditions; if none of them evaluates to TRUE, the normal cell formatting applies. If more than one condition evaluates to TRUE, the first one that does so applies.

**FIGURE 14.26**

Conditional formatting gives you a limited subset of font options.

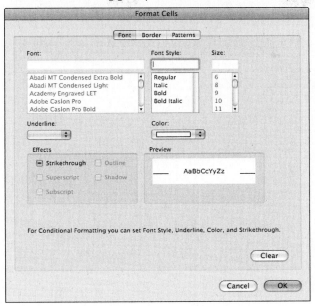

# Using Styles

You may find yourself using the same formatting options over and over again, and it can be painful and time consuming to have to redo them every time. Fortunately, Excel gives you the ability to save formatting options so that they can be reused again later. Your styles are saved along with the workbook, and it's easy to refer to them again in order to apply that style (or a portion of it) to additional cells. You can even copy a style to another open workbook.

**TIP** Excel remembers which styles have been applied to a cell. If you make modifications to the style, the formatting changes are automatically applied to all cells that use the style. This can make it easy to make sweeping formatting changes to a workbook simply by changing a couple styles.

## Creating styles

You can base a style on an existing format, create one from scratch, or do some combination of the two. Follow these steps to create or modify a style:

1. **Select the cell or cells that contain the formatting you want to use as the basis for the style.**

2. **Choose Format ⇨ Style to open the Style dialog box, shown in Figure 14.27.**

**FIGURE 14.27**

Use the Style dialog box to create and manage saved formatting styles.

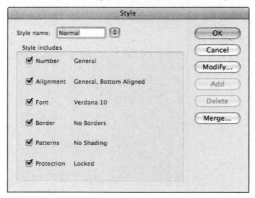

3. **If you want to make changes to the formatting or are creating formatting from scratch, click the Modify button.** Then make formatting changes in the Format Cells dialog box as described earlier in this chapter.

4. **Uncheck any formatting styles that you don't want to include in the style.** You can include or exclude number, alignment, font, border, pattern, and protection styles.

5. **Enter a name for the style in the Style Name box.**

6. **Click Add to create the new style.**

7. **Click OK to apply any changes to the style to the selected cells.**

## Applying styles

After you create a style, you can easily apply it to other cells. You also can choose to apply one of the standard styles that have been provided. Follow these steps to apply a style:

1. **Select the cell or cells to which you want to apply the style.**

2. **Choose Format ⇨ Style to open the Style dialog box.**

3. **Choose a style from the Style Name menu.**

4. **Uncheck the style attributes you don't want to apply, if any.**

5. **Click OK to apply the style.**

## Copy and merge styles

After you are happy with a style, you likely will want to use it all the time, in all your workbooks. Excel makes it easy to merge styles from one workbook into another so you can do just that. Follow these steps to merge styles from one workbook into another:

1. **Open the workbook containing the styles you want to copy.**
2. **Open or create the new workbook.**
3. **In the new workbook, choose Format ⇨ Style to open the Style dialog box.**
4. **Click Merge.**
5. **Choose the source workbook in the Merge Styles dialog box, shown in Figure 14.28.**
6. **Click OK to apply the styles.**

**FIGURE 14.28**

The style merge feature makes it easy to copy styles from one workbook to another.

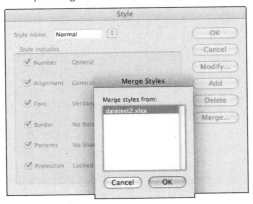

**NOTE** When you merge styles from another workbook, there is a chance that the names of those styles will conflict with styles in the destination workbook. If this occurs, Excel gives you a warning and asks if you still want to merge the styles. If you say yes, the existing styles using those names are replaced by the new ones and any cells that make use of those styles have formatting changed to match.

# Applying Document Themes

While you were learning about the Formatting Palette, you may have noticed that we skipped over the Document Theme pane. Document themes are combinations of color schemes and fonts that work well together. Excel can use the same themes as Word and PowerPoint, which makes it very easy to coordinate your presentations and supporting documents so they present a consistent image. However, themes have a significant limitation in Excel; they don't apply to worksheets directly, only to charts, SmartArt graphics, shapes, and pictures. If you make use of any of those features, however, use themes to provide consistency with Word and PowerPoint documents.

To apply a theme to your workbook, do the following:

1.  **Open the Formatting Palette, and expand the Document Themes section if it's collapsed.** This pane is shown in Figure 14.29.

2.  **Choose a theme from the list, or browse for a custom one that you created in PowerPoint.**
    If you prefer, you can choose a color combination and font individually.

---

**FIGURE 14.29**

---

Document themes can be applied to SmartArt, charts, shapes, and pictures to provide a consistent look with Word and PowerPoint documents.

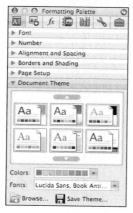

Office provides 50 themes, but you are not limited to these. You can create your own themes by modifying the colors and fonts to suit your needs and then clicking Save Theme from the Document Theme pane.

# Summary

Formatting can make a plain, mundane worksheet special—if not exciting, at least a little more pleasant to look at and work with. Excel 2008 provides an array of formatting options. You learned how to apply number formatting to cell values to allow them to contain general formatting, numbers, currency, accounting, date and time values, percentages, fractions, and scientific values. If that's not enough, you learned how to create custom formats as well.

You also learned how to apply formatting to the text in your worksheets, giving you the ability to change fonts, alignments, line wrap functionality, and even text orientation. You learned how to set borders and color information for cells.

This chapter showed you how to apply formatting using the Format Cells dialog box, the Formatting toolbar, and the Formatting Palette. You learned how to use AutoFormat and Conditional Formatting and how to create and apply styles and document themes.

In the next chapter, you learn how to work with formulas and functions to perform a wide variety of computational tasks.

# Chapter 15

# Using Formulas and Functions

Ychor can use spreadsheet software for a variety of uses, from simple jobs like making lists and organizing tables, all the way up to database-like duties. With such extreme versatility, it's no wonder that a spreadsheet program, along with a word processor, has become one of the must-have programs in any office suite.

However, the heart of a spreadsheet program is the ability to make complex calculations quickly and easily using formulas and functions. Excel 2008 is definitely no slouch in this area. With more than 300 built-in functions and an extensive formula building capability, Excel 2008 should be able to satisfy the most power-hungry data cruncher.

A downside to all of this power is that creating formulas is often an arcane art, with many options and difficult-to-understand syntax. With Excel 2008, Microsoft's designers sought to improve things in this regard with a new feature called the Formula Builder. This new tool can help reduce the amount of time and effort it takes to create formulas.

In this chapter, you learn how formulas work, from the basics on up. And yes, you get a tour of the Formula Builder to see just how easy building formulas can be. In addition, you learn about Excel's built-in functions and the services they provide. You also learn how to troubleshoot any problems you might encounter with your formulas and function calls.

## Working with Formulas

Formulas are a complex subject, but an important one to understand before you can begin to get the most out of Excel. Before you dig into how to create and use formulas, it's a good idea to take a look at this subject from the top and explore just what formulas actually are and what they can do.

Workbooks and worksheets contain various data elements that do nothing by themselves. In order to make use of Excel's computational abilities, you must use formulas to establish relationships between the various data entities. These relationships can be simple, as in the case of working with data in one or two cells, or quite complex, covering many cells and even spanning multiple worksheets.

## Understanding formulas

A formula in Excel is created in a cell and is usually hidden from view, unless you are editing the cell or looking at the Formula Bar, of course. The purpose of a formula is to calculate some value to display to the user. All formulas have the same basic structure: They start with an equals sign (=), which is followed by one or more operands (values to act on, which can be static values, cell references, or functions) and operators, which are mathematical symbols used to calculate a result, including subtraction (-), addition (+), multiplication (*), division (/), and exponentiation (^). Together, these items form an expression that evaluates to the value that users see when they look at the cell.

Figure 15.1 shows a formula that's about as simple as you can get. Two cells, A1 and A2, contain values. Cell A3 contains a formula that adds together the values in these two cells. While the cell shows the calculated value, you can see the formula used to calculate this simple example in the Formula Bar.

### FIGURE 15.1

A formula is simply an expression that computes a value to be displayed in a cell.

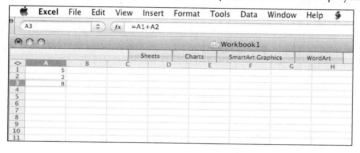

The formula, =A1+A2, consists of two operands, which in this case are references to values contained in other cells. The expression's operator, the plus sign, is adding the values in these two cells in real time. If you change the value in A1, for example, the formula recalculates the value and immediately displays the new value in cell A3. Now let's go into more detail on how you can create formulas in your own worksheets.

### Understanding operands

You can think of operands as the bits of data that Excel works with when calculating a result. In the simple addition formula =A1 + A2, A1 and A2 are cell reference operands.

Formulas operands can be any one of the following things:

- **Value:** A numeric or text value entered directly into the formula.
- **Cell reference:** The contents of a worksheet cell—for example, A1.

- **Cell range:** A rectangular region of cells—for example, A1:C10.
- **Range name:** A name you've assigned to a range of cells.
- **Function name:** Function calls return a value, which is then used in the formula calculation.

These operands can be used directly in the formula, or they can be passed to a function as a parameter where even more complex calculations can be done. The end result is a pretty limitless calculation engine.

## Understanding formula operators

Excel has four types of operators that can be used for different types of formulas: arithmetic, comparison, text, and cell reference operators. Some simple formulas may make use of only one of these operators. Others may make use of multiple operators of different types. It all depends on what you are trying to accomplish.

### Arithmetic operators

Arithmetic operators are used to calculate a numeric value. The operands for arithmetic operators can be number values, cell references to cells containing number values, or functions that return a number value. Table 15.1 provides a list of the arithmetic operators that Excel recognizes.

**TABLE 15.1**

# Arithmetic (Computational) Operators

| Symbol | Meaning | Example |
|--------|---------|---------|
| + | Addition | 5 + 5 |
| - | Subtraction or | 10 - 6 |
| | Negation | -15 |
| * | Multiplication | 10 * 10 |
| / | Division | 10 / 2 |
| ^ | Exponentiation | 10 ^ 2 |
| % | Percentage | 35% |

### Comparison operators

Another type of operator is the comparison operator. These operators are used to compare one value with another, and they return either a logical value of TRUE or FALSE value depending on whether the comparison is valid. Comparisons can be done between any two of the same type of data: numeric or text strings. Table 15.2 shows the available comparison operators.

 **NOTE** The logical value TRUE is equivalent to a numeric value of 1, and FALSE is equivalent to a numeric value of 0.

**TABLE 15.2**

## Comparison Operators

| Symbol | Meaning | Example |
|--------|---------|---------|
| = | Equality | A1 = B1 |
| > | Greater than | A1 > B1 |
| >= | Greater than or equal to | A1 >= B1 |
| < | Less than | A1 < B1 |
| <= | Less than or equal to | A1 <= B1 |
| <> | Not equal to | A1 <> B1 |

Comparison formulas can be quite useful in conjunction with Conditional Formatting, as discussed in Chapter 14. You can use it to display a different message in the cell depending on whether the result is TRUE or FALSE. You also can use the logical function "IF" to display different values depending on the result of a comparison, like this:

```
=IF(A1 > A2, A1, A2)
```

This formula compares the value in cell A1 with the value in A2. If A1 is larger, its value is displayed in the cell. If not, the value in A2 is displayed.

### Text operators

Only one text operator exists: the ampersand (&), as shown in Table 15.3. The operator joins two text strings together, resulting in one combined long string. You also can use it to append text to numeric or other data types, such as numeric. When you do this, the entire result is made into a string.

**TABLE 15.3**

**Text Operators**

| Symbol | Meaning | Example |
|--------|---------|---------|
| & | Text concatenation | A1 & "degrees" |

### Cell reference operators

Some function calls can take many cell references as parameters, and cell reference operators are used to combine cells and cell references so that they can be passed without having to identify each cell individually. Table 15.4 shows a list of operators that can be used on cell references.

**TABLE 15.4**

## Cell Reference Operators

| Symbol | Meaning | Example |
|--------|---------|---------|
| : | Range operator, to indicate a range of cells from upper-left to lower-right corner. | A1:D10 |
| (space) | Intersection: Only cells that are in both of the intersecting ranges are included. | SUM(A1:A10 A1:C5) = SUM(A1:A5) |
| , | Union: All cells are included in the calculation. | SUM(A1, B1, C1:C10 ) |

### Explaining precedence

When you are building a complex formula, with many operands and operators, it is not always immediately obvious how the operands and operators should be arranged to produce the desired result. Take the following formula:

    =5 + 4 * 3

Do you want to add 5 + 4, and then multiply by 3, for a result of 27? Or do you want to add 5 to the product of 4 * 3, which would be 17? This ambiguity can get even worse for more complex examples; to resolve it, the concept of precedence was created. *Precedence* holds that some operations should be evaluated before others, to remove any such confusion. Operations that are evaluated first are said to be of a higher order. Excel's order of operator precedence follows that of other computer languages. Table 15.5 shows the operators from top to bottom in order of precedence.

**TABLE 15.5**

## Operator Precedence

| Operator | Description |
|----------|-------------|
| : | Range operations |
| (space) | |
| , | |
| - | Negation |
| % | Percent |
| ∧ | Exponentiation |
| * and / | Multiplication and division |
| + and - | Addition and subtraction |
| & | Concatenation |
| =, <>, <=, >=, <, > | Comparison operators |

In the previous example, it is clear that the multiplication operation occurs first, so the result of the formula =5 + 4 * 3 is, in fact, 17.

So what if you wanted to ensure that the addition portion occurs first? You can put a portion of a formula you want evaluated first in parentheses like this:

```
=(5 + 4) * 3
```

Operations in parentheses take precedence over any other operator precedence order. In this case, the formula evaluates to 27. Enter each of these two formulas in an Excel cell to see for yourself.

Through operator precedence and the use of parentheses—and even nested parentheses—you can create very complex formulas indeed.

## Writing formulas

Excel makes it easy to enter formulas, especially those with cell references. You can just type them into the cell where you want them. The following steps are pretty basic:

1. **Select the cell that you want to contain the formula.**
2. **Type an equals sign (=). This puts Excel into Enter mode.**
3. **Enter the operands and operators that make up the formula.** If you want to use cell references as operands, you can use one of the following ways to enter them:

   - You can simply type the name of the cell you want to reference, using row-column nomenclature (for example, A1). You can enter a range of cells by specifying the upper-left and lower-right corners of the range separated by a colon (for example, A1:D10).

   - You can click the cell or select a range of cells that you want to add references to. This puts Excel into *Point* mode, which is indicated on the Status bar. As you click cells, you see them surrounded by colored boxes with drag marks at the corners; these can be used to expand the cell reference to include a range.

   - You can use the arrow keys to move to other cells, and press the spacebar to add a reference to the formula. When you press the spacebar, the focus returns to the formula to allow you to enter an operator or another operand.

   - You can select entire rows or columns as ranges by clicking the row or column headings.
4. **After you have completed the formula, press Enter to add the formula to the cell.**

   The cell now displays the value (if any) that the formula calculates.

Even though the cell is now displaying the value that the formula, you can still get back to the formula and edit it if necessary. Simply double-click the cell to put it back into Edit mode, and make any changes that you like. Another option is to use the Formula Bar, which is explained in the next section.

### Using the Formula Bar

Excel's Formula Bar, shown in Figure 15.2, can be used to enter and edit formulas as well as other cell values. Using the Formula Bar has several advantages over editing formulas directly in a cell.

When you select a cell, its name is shown in the name box on the left side of the bar. The name box also is where you can enter names for named ranges. If you have named ranges in your workbook, you can select the cells that make up the range using the selection menu for the name box.

The formula edit box gives you more room to work with than a typical cell, which makes it easier to see and work with long formulas. When you select a cell that contains a formula, it is displayed in the Formula Bar while the calculated value is still shown in the cell. You can edit your changes directly in the Formula Bar, and when you are finished, press Return to apply the changes to the cell.

**FIGURE 15.2**

The Formula Bar can be used to enter and edit formulas.

Two other buttons on the Formula Bar may be of use:

 The Cancel button on the right side of the bar is used to cancel any editing changes you may have made since you started editing the cell. This can be very helpful, especially if you accidentally click a few too many cells in Point mode.

 You can use the Formula Builder button, to the left of the bar, to tell Excel that you want to enter a formula the box. Clicking it opens the Formula Builder dialog box, either ready to add a new formula or to edit an existing one. You learn about the Formula Builder next.

### Using the Formula Builder

The newest addition to the world of Excel formula editing is the new Formula Builder, which is an enhancement of the old Excel Insert Function dialog box. The Formula Builder not only makes it easy to find and use functions, but it also helps you build the entire formula expression one step at a time, providing input boxes for each element in the formula.

To open the Formula Builder, shown in its empty cell state in Figure 15.3, do one of these three things:

- Choose View ⇨ Formula Builder to open the Toolbox directly on the Formula Builder tab.
- Click the Insert Formula button on the Formula Bar.
- Click the Toolbox icon on the Standard toolbar, and then choose the Formula Builder tab.

**FIGURE 15.3**

The Formula Builder is a new feature in Excel 2008 that can help both novice and experienced Excel users quickly create useful formulas.

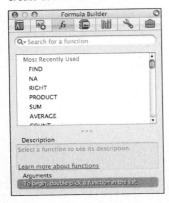

The Formula Builder is really geared toward creating formulas that use functions, and we get to that use later in this chapter. However, it is more versatile than that. It can be used as a simple mathematical formula builder, as well. Follow these steps to add a formula using the Formula Builder:

1. **Select the cell in which you want to enter a formula.**

2. **Open the Formula Builder using View ⇨ Formula, or one of the other methods discussed previously.**

3. **Scroll down the list of functions to the one that says Add, Subtract, Multiple, or Divide, and double-click it.**

   You can make it easier to find by typing the first part of the name, "Add", into the search box, as shown in Figure 15.4.

### FIGURE 15.4

Searching for a partial name can narrow down the long list of functions, or in this case, the Add, Subtract, Multiply, or Divide option.

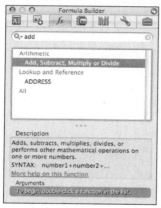

4. **Select the box labeled "number1" by clicking in it.**

5. **Enter the first value for the calculation.** You can either enter a value directly or click a cell to add a reference.

6. **Choose an operation to perform using the pop-up menu in the operation box.** The default is addition.

   Note that unary operators such as negation and percent are not available in this menu. If you want to use one of these operators, enter it in the same box as the value.

7. **Enter the second value for the calculation in the box labeled "number2."**

8. **If you want to add more arguments to the formula, click the Add an Argument button.**

   You can use this button to insert arguments in the middle of the formula by using the buttons next to existing arguments or at the end by using the one on the last argument.

9. **Repeat Steps 6 through 8 for any additional arguments.** Figure 15.5 shows a longer formula created in the Formula Bar.

**NOTE** The Formula Builder can make creating long formulas easy, but it is fairly limited when it comes to precedence, and especially with arguments in parentheses. In order to have arguments in parentheses evaluated, the entire section in parentheses must be entered as a single value in one of the argument boxes.

---

**FIGURE 15.5**

With the Formula Builder, you can easily create formulas with several operators and operands.

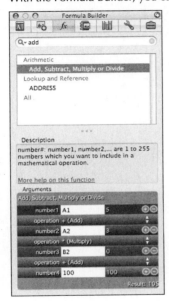

**TIP** As you enter values into the Formula Builder, the boxes are color-coded to match any selected cell references in the worksheet. This can allow you to easily see at a glance exactly where a formula is getting its data and can help with troubleshooting problems.

# Exploring Absolute and Relative Cell References

Up until now, the cell references that you have seen are known as *relative* references. Relative references are actually stored behind the scenes as offsets from the cell containing the formula, to the referenced cell. Relative references are the default kind of reference used by Excel, and for the most part, they work fine. Problems come into play when you copy a formula to another cell. The offsets are copied exactly, so the formula no longer references the original cells, but rather new cells determined by the same offsets.

This can actually be quite useful if you have columns of data and you are using a formula to calculate a total or average; you can copy and paste the formula to a cell in an adjacent column, and the references are updated to use the new cell. Figure 15.6 shows an example of how this can be useful.

## FIGURE 15.6

Relative cell references let you easily copy a formula to another cell and have it work with new data. In this case, the average function was copied from column D to column E, where it now refers to the cells in column E, thanks to relative references.

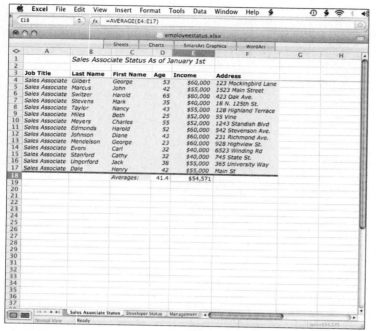

## Using absolute references

Sometimes, however, you want a formula to refer to the same cell at all times, even if you copy and paste the formula to a new location. To handle this situation, Excel offers the concept of *absolute* references. Absolute references use dollar signs ($) in the cell address to indicate whether the row, the column, or both portions of the reference should remain fixed. Table 15.6 shows the four references that are possible.

## TABLE 15.6

### Relative and Absolute Cell References

| Symbol | Example |
|--------|---------|
| A1 | Relative reference for both row and column (default). |
| $A1 | Absolute reference for the column, relative reference for the row. |
| A$1 | Relative reference for the column, absolute for the row. |
| $A$1 | Absolute reference for both row and column. |

**TIP** You may be wondering how you can make cell references absolute without having to type the addresses manually. After all, Excel offers Point mode, which makes adding relative addresses easy. Point mode always initially adds a cell reference as a relative one, but you can use the keyboard shortcut ⌘+T to quickly toggle a reference through all four referencing options.

## Using named ranges

If you are planning to use lots of absolute references to cells and cell ranges, you might consider using a named range instead. Named ranges allow you to assign a name to a collection of cells, which you can refer to in formulas in place of the cell addresses. Creating named ranges is covered in Chapter 13.

When building a formula, you can make use of your existing named ranges by substituting the name of the range wherever you might use a cell reference. You can even use named ranges with the cell reference operators such as union (comma) and intersect (space). Figure 15.7 shows a formula that calculates an average using a named range.

---

**FIGURE 15.7**

Named ranges can be used in place of cell references in formulas.

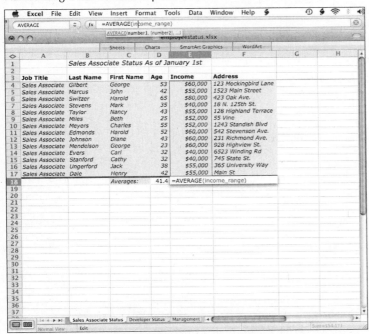

**NOTE** Named ranges are always treated as absolute references when copying cells.

If you aren't sure about the name of the range and you are in the middle of typing a formula, Excel provides a way to paste a range name into the formula without missing a beat. Try these steps:

1. **Begin typing the formula, in a worksheet that has named ranges defined.**
2. **When you reach the location in the formula where you want the reference, choose Insert ⇨ Name ⇨ Paste.** The Paste Name dialog box opens, as shown in Figure 15.8.
3. **Click the name of the range from the list.**
4. **Click OK to paste the name into the formula.**

You can use the Paste Name feature to quickly add a range name into a formula.

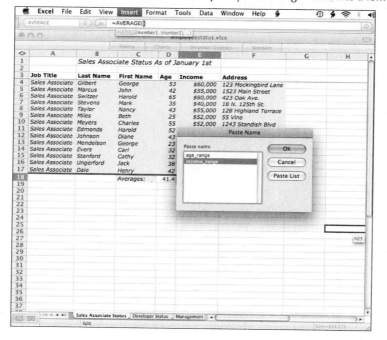

## Naming formulas

You learned how to assign names to cell ranges in Chapter 13, but that isn't the only use for names. You can assign names to frequently used formulas that you create so that they can be reused without your having to retype them (or copy and paste them). This can help make your worksheets tidier and easier to understand. Follow these steps to name a formula:

1. **Choose Insert ⇨ Name ⇨ Define to open the Define Name dialog box.**
2. **Enter the name that you want to use for the formula in the Names in Workbook box.**

3. **Enter the formula into the Refers To box, exactly the way it would be entered into a cell.** Be sure to copy a good, working version of the formula from the cell and paste it into this box. Figure 15.9 shows an example of this.

4. **Click OK.**

The formula you've named can now be used anywhere in your worksheet simply by entering it in a cell as follows, substituting the name of the formula you created in place of *MyFormulaName*:

    = MyFormulaName

---

**FIGURE 15.9**

Defining a formula in the Define Name dialog box makes it easy to reuse later.

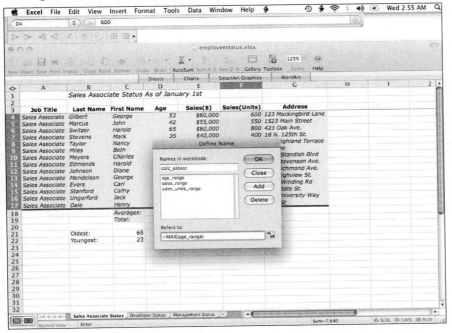

# Working with Functions

While formulas that make use of simple arithmetic operators are pretty handy to have, the real power of formulas comes into play when you couple them with functions. Functions are built-in formulas that you can use to do more complex calculations or other things not possible with just using arithmetic formulas. Earlier in this chapter, you saw a hint of what functions can do in the form of the IF and SUM functions. They often can be used to perform calculations on entire cell ranges.

# Understanding functions

As you've seen in this chapter, you can create formulas in cells that can perform calculations on data in other cells using cell and range references. Functions greatly expand what you can do in formulas. With more than 300 functions available, you're almost sure to find a function that can do what you need. Excel formulas are grouped into categories including database, date and time, engineering, financial, information, logical, lookup and reference, math and trigonometry, statistical, and text.

Many functions are adept at working with cell ranges. These functions can be used to calculate statistical information on a large block of data with very little work; you just need to provide a cell range or a named range. The following example shows a common function used to calculate an average:

```
=AVERAGE(C1:C50)
```

This formula calls the AVERAGE function with a range of cells encompassing C1 through C50. This next function call shows how you can reference an entire column in a formula. The SUM function adds all the values in the referenced range. You can see that, for a large number of values, the function is easier to use than adding each cell together individually.

```
=SUM(C:C)
```

You can even use the results of functions as operands in formulas or as arguments for other functions, or you can use formula operators to combine them. Three more common functions typically used with ranges include MIN, MAX, and COUNT:

```
=MIN(D5:D100)
=MAX(A9:X9)
=COUNT(E:E)
```

As you may have guessed, MIN returns the lowest value in the cell range, MAX returns the highest value, and COUNT returns a count of all the cells with values.

# Exploring function categories

Excel has far too many functions available to go into detail on each one for this book; however, you need to understand the types of functions that are available and some examples of each type. A full listing of functions and information on each one can be found in the Excel 2008 Help files. The following is by no means an exhaustive reference, but we hope it gives you an idea about the types of functions available in each category.

## Using database functions

Database functions are similar to the math functions you've already seen, except they are intended to work with data imported from database tables. Use of databases is discussed in Chapter 17. Database functions include:

- **DAVERAGE:** Returns an average of selected database entries.
- **DCOUNT:** Returns a count of cells that contain numbers.
- **DCOUNTA:** Returns a count of cells that contain numbers or text.
- **DGET:** Returns a single record that matches specific criteria.
- **DPRODUCT:** Returns the product of selected database entries.
- **DSUM:** Returns the sum of selected database entries.
- **DSTDV:** Computes a standard deviation based on a sample of database entries.

## Using date and time functions

Date and time functions are used to return current date and time values or to calculate date or time values. Many date and time functions are geared around accounting uses. Some of the more common functions include:

- **DATE:** Calculates the serial date value (days since 1/1/1904) given a year, month, and day.
- **DATEDIF:** Calculates the number of days, months, or years from one date to another.
- **NOW:** Returns the serial date and time value of the current date and time.
- **TODAY:** Returns the serial date value for the current day.

## Using engineering functions

The engineering functions include number base conversion functions (from decimal to hexadecimal, decimal, binary, or octal) and functions for advanced math for working with complex (imaginary) numbers. Some of these functions include:

- **DEC2HEX:** Converts a decimal number (base 10) to hexadecimal (base 16).
- **HEX2DEC:** Converts a hexadecimal number to decimal.
- **IMSUM:** Returns the sum of imaginary numbers.
- **IMLOG10:** Returns the base-10 logarithm of a complex number.

## Using financial functions

Financial calculations are one of the mainstay uses for Excel. Therefore, many functions are geared toward financial calculations. The following list is a sampling:

- **ACCRINT:** Returns the accrued interest for a security that pays periodic interest.
- **EFFECT:** Returns the effective annual interest rate, given the nominal rate and the number of compounding periods.
- **PMT:** Calculates the periodic payment for an annuity, given the term, rate, and present value.
- **RATE:** Returns the interest rate per period of an annuity, given a payment period, payment, and present value.
- **SLN:** Returns the straight-line depreciation of an asset from a starting to ending value, over a period of time.
- **YIELD:** Returns the yield on a security that pays periodic interest.

## Using information functions

Information functions return...well...information regarding the status of the workbook, cells, and data values:

- **CELL:** Returns information regarding formatting, location, or contents of a cell. For example, =CELL("row", D10) returns the row number for cell D10, which is, of course, 10.
- **INFO:** Returns information regarding the current operating environment. For example, =INFO("release") returns the current version of Excel.
- **ISNONTEXT:** Returns TRUE if the value of the argument is not text.
- **ISNUMBER:** Returns TRUE if the value of the argument is a number.
- **ISTEXT:** Returns TRUE if the value of the argument is text.
- **N:** Returns the value converted to a number.

## Using logical functions

Logical functions expand the capabilities of the logical operators and include the following:

- **AND:** Returns TRUE if all of its arguments are TRUE (non-zero).
- **FALSE:** Returns the logical value FALSE.
- **IF:** Performs a logical test, and returns one of two different actions depending on the result of TRUE or FALSE.
- **IFERROR:** Returns TRUE if the argument evaluates to an error value.
- **NOT:** Reverses the logic of its argument; IF(TRUE) would return FALSE.
- **OR:** Returns TRUE if any of its arguments are TRUE.
- **TRUE:** Returns the logical value TRUE.

## Using lookup and reference functions

Lookup and reference functions can be used to access information in an array or reference. Arrays are multidimensional collections of values of arbitrary data types. An example of an array with two rows and four columns might be { "A", "B", "C", "D"; 1, 2, 3, 4 }.

- **COLUMNS:** Returns the number of columns in a reference.
- **INDEX:** Uses an index to choose a value from an array or reference.
- **LOOKUP:** Searches an array or vector (row or column) to return a value.
- **ROWS:** Returns the number of rows in a reference.

## Using math and trigonometry functions

Math and trigonometry functions can be used to perform advanced mathematical calculations. Some examples are:

- **ABS:** Returns the absolute value of an argument.
- **CEILING:** Rounds a number to the nearest integer or multiple of significance.
- **COS:** Returns the cosine of an angle, specified in radians.
- **DEGREES:** Converts radians to degrees.
- **FACT:** Returns the factorial of a number.
- **FLOOR:** Rounds a number down toward the nearest integer.
- **LOG10:** Returns the base-10 logarithm of a number.
- **MMULT:** Multiplies to matrices, specified as arrays.
- **PI:** Returns the value of pi.
- **PRODUCT:** Multiplies the arguments, and returns their product.
- **RADIANS:** Converts degrees to radians.

## Using statistical functions

Statistical functions operate on ranges and can be used for analysis of their data:

- **AVERAGE:** Returns the average of all the arguments.
- **FORECAST:** Returns a value along a linear trend.
- **GROWTH:** Returns values along an exponential trend.
- **MEDIAN:** Returns the median of the given arguments.
- **MODE:** Returns the highest value in all the arguments.
- **POISSON:** Returns the Poisson distribution.
- **STANDARDIZE:** Returns a normalized value.
- **STDEV:** Returns the estimated standard deviation of a sample.

## Using text functions

Excel isn't only about numbers; sometimes you need to work with text values as well. The following functions can be used to manipulate text:

- **FIND:** Locates a string inside another string, and returns its location. This is case-sensitive.
- **LEFT:** Returns the leftmost characters in a string, given a string and a count.
- **LEN:** Returns the length of a string.
- **RIGHT:** Returns the rightmost characters in a string, given a string and a count.
- **SEARCH:** Finds one text value inside of another, and returns its location. This is not case-sensitive.
- **SUBSTITUTE:** Replaces a portion of a string.
- **TRIM:** Removes spaces from the beginning and end of text.
- **UPPER:** Converts the text argument to uppercase.

# Using AutoComplete

You've been exposed to the AutoComplete feature that can be used to quickly fill cells with data values that Excel already has entered. AutoComplete can be used to assist in entering formulas, too. As you are typing a formula name into a cell, Excel provides a pop-up window with matching function names that you can choose from. You can use the arrow keys or the mouse to select a function from the list to enter it in the cell. After the formula has been added, you see a tooltip that lets you know which arguments the function is expecting. Figure 15.10 shows an example of AutoComplete in progress.

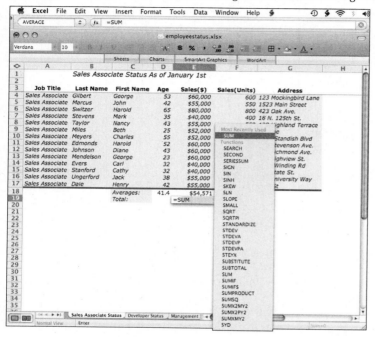

**FIGURE 15.10**

**FIGURE 15.10**

AutoComplete can be used to assist in entering function names and arguments.

## Using AutoSum functions

Some functions are so useful and universally used, that Excel's designers felt that they deserved a way to add them quickly from the Standard toolbar. The AutoSum button can be used with a selected range of cells in a row or column to add a formula that works with them. The following steps explain how to use the AutoSum functions:

1. **Select a range of values in either a row or column.**

2. **Click the AutoSum button on the toolbar to add a SUM function formula.**

   You also can click the arrow to the right of the AutoSum button to add other common functions instead, including Average, Count Numbers, Max, and Min.

   You can even choose to launch the Formula Builder from this menu, but this is not recommended because it won't reference the selected cells correctly.

3. **A formula with a function using the selected cell range reference is added below the selected cells (or to the right, if a row range was selected).** Figure 15.11 shows the AutoSum function in use.

## FIGURE 15.11

The AutoSum feature can be used to quickly add common functions that work on row or column data.

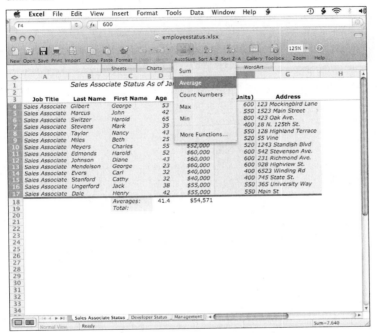

You can actually use the AutoSum functions if you have more than one column or row selected. Excel simply adds a formula after each row or column that references cells from that row or column. Excel uses the direction with the most entries—horizontal or vertical—to determine whether the formula should go after a row or below the column.

# Fixing Formula Errors

Just as with computer programming, it is easy to introduce errors when working with formulas and functions. Fortunately, Excel provides several ways to help locate and resolve errors.

## Checking for errors

When a formula in Excel encounters an error, the result typically is displayed as an error message in the cell. For the most part, Excel error messages start with a pound (#) sign, which should alert you right away that there is a problem. Figure 15.12 shows some common error message on display in a cell.

## FIGURE 15.12

Errors displayed in formula cells can be the first sign that there's a problem with a formula.

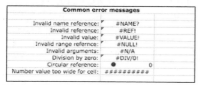

| Common error messages | |
|---|---|
| Invalid name reference: | #NAME? |
| Invalid reference: | #REF! |
| Invalid value: | #VALUE! |
| Invalid range refernce: | #NULL! |
| Invalid arguments: | #N/A |
| Division by zero: | #DIV/0! |
| Circular reference: | ● 0 |
| Number value too wide for cell: | ######### |

The errors on display are as follows:

- **#NAME?:** The cell contains an invalid name reference. This can happen if you enter a name incorrectly when building a formula or delete a name that is still used in formulas.

- **#REF!:** The cell contains an invalid reference. You can get this if the cell that your formula was referring to is deleted (by deleting the row or column containing the cell) or the formula with relative references is moved so that the referenced cell is a row or column before A1.

- **#VALUE!:** The formula contains a reference to a cell with invalid data for the formula's calculations.

- **#NULL!:** The formula contains no valid cell references. One way that this can occur is if you use the intersection (space) operator with two ranges that don't intersect.

- **#N/A!:** The formula contains invalid arguments. This can happen if required arguments are missing.

- **#DIV/0!:** A calculation being performed by the function results in a division by zero error.

- **#########:** A numeric or formula generated value is too wide to fit in the current column width. Expand the column size to accommodate it. This error also can occur if you use a negative numeric value as a serial date. Only positive values can be used as dates.

 When an error is encountered, cells also typically contain a green triangle in the upper-left corner. Clicking the cell to select it also shows the Error menu button floating off to the left side of the cell. Click it to open the error menu, shown in Figure 15.13.

## FIGURE 15.13

A drop-down error menu can be used to assist you in tracking down errors.

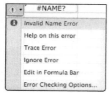

The following items are displayed on the menu:

- **Help on this error:** Choose this option to open Excel Help for more information on the error.

- **Trace error:** You can use this menu item to draw an error from the cell to any references that are invalid.

- **Ignore error:** This item removes the error menu, but any error message resulting from the formula is still shown in the cell.
- **Edit in Formula Bar:** This item opens the Formula Bar at the current cell so that you can edit the formula.
- **Error checking options:** This item opens the Error Checking pane in the Excel Preferences, where you can set various options for error handling of formulas and other potential problems. This pane is shown in Figure 15.14.

**FIGURE 15.14**

You can configure error handling preferences in the Error Checking pane.

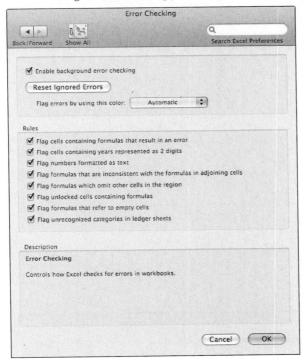

## Showing formulas in the worksheet

By default, Excel displays formula results in the cells that contain formulas. In order to see the actual formula, you have to select the cell and look at the formula in the Formula Bar. However, it can be useful at times to see all the formulas in a worksheet at once, to help solve problems or even just to see at a glance which cells contain formulas and which contain data. You can tell Excel to display all the worksheet's formulas by following these steps:

1. **Choose Excel ⇨ Preferences to open the Preferences dialog box.**
2. **Click the View icon to open the View pane.**

3. Check the Show Formulas box in the Window Options section, as shown in Figure 15.15.

**FIGURE 15.15**

Use the Show Formulas option to make Excel display formulas in your worksheet rather than the calculated results.

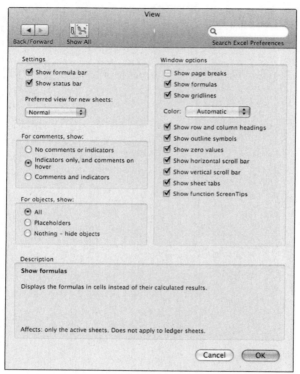

4. **Click OK.** Figure 15.16 shows what a worksheet looks like with formulas displayed.

 **You can quickly toggle between values and formulas by pressing Control+`.**

## FIGURE 15.16

Displaying formulas can be helpful when troubleshooting worksheets.

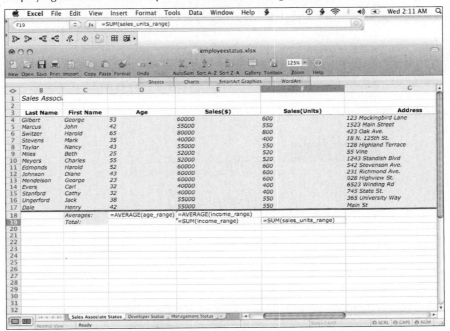

## Using the Formula Auditing toolbar

Another tool that can be invaluable in working with formulas and functions is the Formula Auditing toolbar. This toolbar can help you to easily see the relationship between formulas and referenced cells by drawing arrows between formulas and referenced cells, tracing errors, adding comments, and highlighting cells that contain invalid data. You can activate the Formula Auditing toolbar by choosing View ➪ Toolbars and checking the Formula Auditing item. Figure 15.17 shows the Formula Auditing toolbar.

## FIGURE 15.17

The Formula Auditing toolbar can help you trace problems with your formulas.

The following section provides you with some information regarding the use of the Formula Auditing toolbar buttons.

## Tracing precedents

You can use the Formula Auditing toolbar to trace the precedents in a formula. As the name implies, precedents are cells that are used as a source for the current cell's formula—essentially, the cell references that the formula uses. Follow these steps to display precedents:

1. **Select a cell containing the cell references you want to trace. You can select only a single cell at a time.**

2. **Click Trace Precedents on the Formula Auditing toolbar.**

   Arrows are drawn from the cell references to the selected cell, as shown in Figure 15.18. Cell ranges have only a single arrow drawn, but the range is surrounded by a box of the same color as the arrows.

---

### FIGURE 15.18

Tracing precedents can help you see at a glance which cells a formula references.

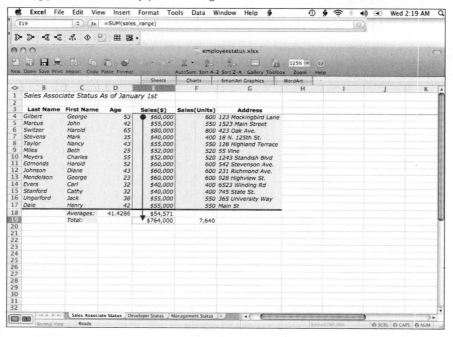

To remove the arrows, make sure the target cell is selected and click the Remove Precedent Arrows button.

Use the Remove All Arrows button to remove all arrows, whether precedent or dependent.

## Tracing dependents

Tracing dependents works the opposite of the precedent tracing. When you trace dependents, Excel draws arrows from cells to formulas that reference them. This lets you see at a glance all the formulas that make use of a particular value. Follow these steps to display dependents:

1. **Select a cell containing the value that you want to trace. You can select only a single cell at a time.**

2. **Click Trace Dependents on the Formula Auditing toolbar.**

   Arrows are drawn from the cell to any cells that reference it, as shown in Figure 15.19.

### FIGURE 15.19

You can trace dependents to see which formulas make use a particular cell.

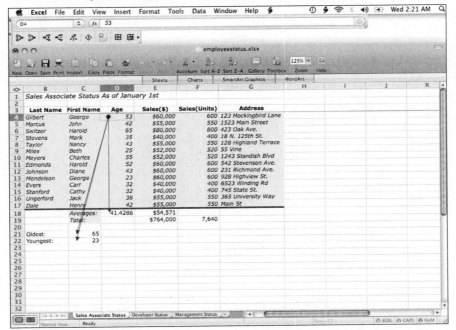

 To remove the arrows, make sure the target cell is selected and click the Remove Dependents Arrows button.

## Tracing errors

 If a cell contains an error, the Trace Errors button can be used to draw errors to the offending cells. You can clear the errors by clicking the Remove All Arrows button.

## Adding comments

 The Comment button provides a way to easily add comments to a cell. Comments can be used to provide some explanation for the data in a cell or for a formula that you create. Figure 15.20 shows the comment editor.

**FIGURE 15.20**

You can help make your worksheets easy to understand by attaching comments to cells.

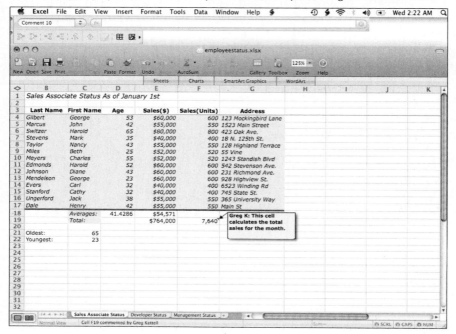

Cells with comments have a small visible triangle in the upper-right corner. You can hover the mouse over it to make the comment visible.

To remove a comment, right-click the cell and choose Delete Comment.

### Highlighting invalid data

 If any of your cells have data validation rules in place, and data values exceed those rules, you can use the Circle Invalid Data button to highlight them. Data validation rules normally prevent you from entering an invalid value in a cell, but such cells can contain formulas that return results outside the validation range. The validation rules also can be changed, causing previously acceptable data to fail the check. Figure 15.21 shows a worksheet with circles around invalid data.

## FIGURE 15.21

Validation circles can help you find cells that fail data validation checks.

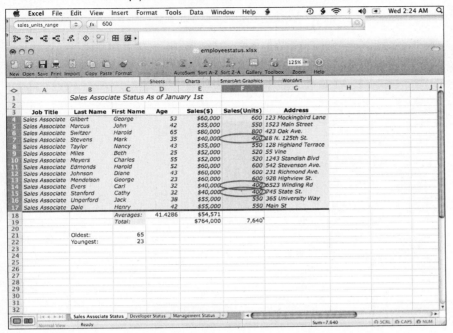

NOTE    You can add validation rules to cells or a range of cells by choosing Data ⇨ Validation and configuring rules in the Data Validation dialog box.

 Click the Clear Validation Circles button to remove validation.

# Controlling Automatic Recalculation

When you enter a formula or change a data value in a cell that is referenced by a formula, Excel automatically recalculates the cell. In most circumstances this is desirable, because you don't have to worry about recalculating the worksheet yourself. However, with large worksheets with many complex calculations, it can take anywhere from a few seconds to a minute or more to recalculate. Fortunately, Excel gives you the ability to turn off automatic recalculation if it takes too long each time. Follow these steps to set the automatic recalculation options:

1. **Choose Excel ⇨ Preferences to open the Preferences dialog box.**
2. **Click the Calculation button to open the Calculation pane, which is shown in Figure 15.22.**

**FIGURE 15.22**

You can disable automatic calculations in Excel Preferences to speed up working with complex worksheets.

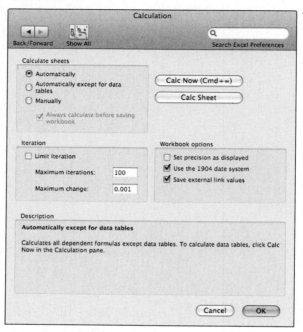

3. **Choose one of these options for recalculation:**

   ■ **Automatically:** Excel recalculates the worksheet every time a change is made to a formula or referenced data.

   ■ **Automatically except for data tables:** All calculations are performed automatically except for those that reference data tables.

   ■ **Manually:** All recalculations must be done manually. If you select this option, you can optionally uncheck the Always calculate before saving workbook box if it is taking a long time to save.

4. **Click OK.**

If you choose to do calculations manually, you see the Calculate message appear in the Status bar whenever an update is needed. To recalculate, you can go back to the Calculation pane of the Preferences dialog box and click Calc Now to recalculate every open worksheet or click Calc Sheet to recalculate only the currently active worksheet.

**TIP**  It can be a pain having to go back to the Calculation pane every time you want to recalculate the worksheet. However, you can use ⌘+@= keyboard shortcut to force a recalculation at any time.

# Summary

To begin to unlock the power of Excel's calculation engine, you need to use formulas, because without them, Excel is nothing more than a fancy list-maker. A formula is used to calculate a result that will be displayed in a worksheet cell. Formulas utilize operands including values, functions, and cell references, along with operators for arithmetic and comparison operations. You learned how you can enter formulas in several different ways—directly into a cell, in the Formula Bar, or in the new Formula Builder Palette of the Toolbox. Much of the power of formulas comes from the ability to deal with cell references and ranges. You learned how to use both relative and absolute references, as well as how to use named ranges in formulas.

To really get the most out of formulas, Excel provides more than 300 built-in functions that can do many different sorts of calculations with all Excel's data types. You learned that there are several categories of functions that cover a wide range of capabilities. Some of these include database, mathematics and trigonometry, date and time, financial, and text functions. Finally, you learned about some of the errors that can occur with formulas, the error messages that are displayed, and how to find more information in order to correct the problem.

# Chapter 16

# Creating Charts

Nothing gives your Excel numbers more impact than a chart. Charts can provide your audience with a visual understanding of what your numbers really mean and where your information is going. As it turns out, an overwhelming number of the human population is visually oriented anyway, so turning your numerical data into a visual format makes perfect sense and is sure to reach the widest audience. Think about it—staring at a column of numbers in a worksheet does not really have much impact, but when you present that same column of numbers as a pie chart or bar chart, then you begin to really see what each number represents. Suddenly, the ordinary number speaks volumes as it relates to the other data. The visual impact is quick and to the point.

Whether you're using a simple pie chart or a detailed scatter chart, Excel charts give your numbers a professional polish and the visual oomph needed to quickly convey the importance of your spreadsheet information. This chapter explores the various ways you can build and format charts. You learn how to use the new Elements Gallery to quickly choose a chart type, how to format various elements of a chart, and how to edit the chart data to suit your needs. You also learn all the necessary chart terminology and the details about each chart type.

## IN THIS CHAPTER

**Inserting charts**

**Adding formatting attributes to charts**

**Editing chart parts and data**

**Using advanced charting techniques**

## Adding Charts

In the Excel family, charts are the buttoned-up spreadsheet's funky, artistic cousin. Charts can take ordinary numerical data and make it look expressive and interesting, sort of like having an interior decorator over to rethink the display of your drab columns and rows. Adding charts in Office 2008 is easier than ever. In previous versions of Excel, the tried and true Chart Wizard walked you through all the necessary steps for building a chart. The process took several dialog boxes and lots of decisions. Today, the Chart Wizard is gone, and the new Elements Gallery is the go-to feature for charting and assigning other graphical objects. It offers a special category just for charts. All you have to do is open the Gallery to the Charts tab and pick a chart. It really is that easy. The Gallery lists a dizzying array of chart types to choose from, ranging from area charts to line charts, to surface charts, and every chart in between. So before you begin trying them out, look at what goes into basic chart anatomy and determine what chart type works best for your data.

## Understanding chart parts

Charts are generally comprised of several key features or parts. Granted, not all charts look the same, but the general elements are usually consistent throughout the charting vernacular, with a few exceptions. For example, you can expect to find a legend, and maybe some axes and data points on a typical chart, and every chart includes a plot area and a chart area regardless of what kind of chart it is. To truly utilize your charts, you need to know basic chart terminology and how these chart parts work together. Start by looking at Figure 16.1. It shows a simple marked line chart that tracks monthly sales totals for four salespeople over the course of three months. When plotting this data in a worksheet, your sheet would contain a row for each salesperson and a column for each month. The intersecting cells where the rows and columns meet hold the sales totals for each month. You also could arrange the data another way, and show rows for each month and columns for each salesperson. No matter the arrangement, the result is a chart that emphasizes each person's contributions and compares them to the group.

### FIGURE 16.1

This worksheet example tracks sales figures over the course of three months. The resulting line chart shows lines for each month and data markers on each line pinpointing each employee's sales totals.

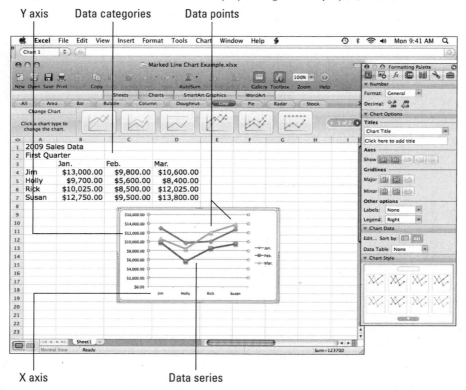

## Data points

*Data points* are the individual values you plot in a chart. In Figure 16.1, for example, the monthly sales total for each salesperson becomes a data point in the chart. In other words, the individual cell data is plotted as data points in the chart. *Data markers* are the graphical elements that represent data points in a chart, such as bullet points or shapes.

## Data series

The *data series* is a group of related values in a chart. In Figure 16.1, the data series is the group of values over three month's time for each salesperson. Most charts use more than one data series, as is the case when tracking sales figures for four different salespeople. Each person's sales figures across three months become a data series. In many instances, the data series is the row of data or column of data in a worksheet.

## Data categories

*Data categories* are the categories you assign in a worksheet to organize data. In Figure 16.1, the data categories are the month names at the top of the data that organize the sales totals.

## Axes

The *axes* in a chart display the horizontal and vertical scale upon which the data is plotted. The X axis, also called the *category axis,* is the horizontal scale, while the Y axis, also called the *value axis,* is the vertical scale. Depending on the chart style, one of the axes corresponds to the row or column headings in your worksheet. For example, in Figure 16.1, the marked line chart shows monetary values on the Y axis and salespeople names on the X axis. The plot area shows how much money each salesperson generated each month.

In Figure 16.2, the same data is plotted as a clustered cylinder column chart. Instead of lines, cylindrical columns indicate the changes in values, yet the X and Y axes stay the same.

---

**FIGURE 16.2**

In a clustered cylindrical column chart, the data points appear as cylindrical columns. The X axis shows the individual salespeople, while the Y axis shows monetary values, and the columns show how much in sales each person contributed to the whole.

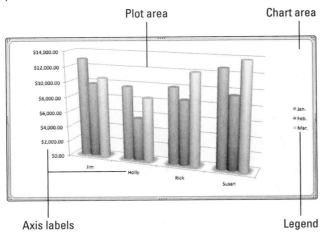

### Axis labels

*Axis labels* help identify what data is being plotted out in the chart. Labels in the worksheet can include data titles, names, categories, time intervals, months, years, and so on. In Figure 16.2, the Y axis labels indicate amounts for the monetary scale for the chart data, while the X axis labels represent each salesperson. Other charts you create might use labels like "Income in Millions" or "Projected Sales Growth."

### Plot area

The *plot area* is the middle of the chart where all the data appears. The plot area includes data points, data markers, data series, data labels, gridlines, and so on. For many charts, the plot area appears as a rectangle. In other charts, like pie charts and doughnut charts, the plot area is circular in shape.

### Legend

The *legend* is a summary or map of what the chart is plotting, much like a map key. Depending on the type of chart, the legend identifies the data series and differentiates between the series. For example, in Figure 16.2, the legend shows each month's color and name as it appears in the plot area. Most legends appear to the side or top of the plot area.

### Chart area

The *chart area* is, quite simply, the entire chart. The chart area includes the plot area, axes, legend, and any chart title text. It also includes any borders you assign to the chart. You'll notice when you insert a chart into your worksheet, it appears as its own object as a box, which means you can move it, resize it, copy it, and delete it.

### Gridlines

*Gridlines,* also called tick marks, appear in the plot area to help your audience line up chart data with the scale it is illustrating. In other words, gridlines or tick marks can help with readability of your chart. You can use major gridlines to show units or minor gridlines to further break up the scale between units. Figure 16.3 shows a chart with minor gridlines turned on.

### FIGURE 16.3

This chart shows gridlines, a chart title, and a legend. You can use the chart options on the Format Palette to add features to your charts.

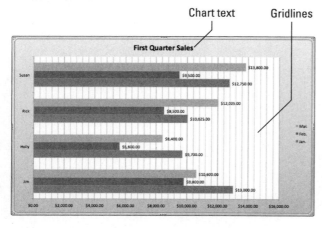

# Using Data Series in Excel

**O**f all the charting terminology you encounter in Excel, the concept of data series is often the most confusing. A data series is a group of numbers that appear as a single column or row of cells in your worksheet. If your worksheet is tracking company revenue, for example, you might have a column of number data for expenses and another column of number data tracking income. Both of these columns of numbers are considered data series in Excel. When you turn the numeric data into a chart, such as a bar chart or column chart, Excel creates a set of bars or columns for each data series. The data series tracking expenses appears in a different color in the chart than the data series tracking income. If the worksheet tracks expenses and income across several months, the corresponding chart will show the same color for each data series, so the bar or column showing expenses in January is the same color as the bar or column showing expenses in June. Like-colored bars or columns always depict the same data series, making it easy to see what goes with what in a chart.

Most charts you create will track more than one data series. However, you don't want to include too many data series in a chart, or the chart becomes too difficult to follow. Instead of charting a year's worth of monthly sales figures, for example, consider consolidating them into quarters.

Something else to note about data series: If the selected chart data in the worksheet has more rows than columns, Excel plots the data by column. If the chart data has more columns than rows, Excel plots the data by row. If there are an equal number of both, Excel plots by rows. You can always change the plotting arrangement later to reverse its appearance in a chart.

### Chart text

In addition to labels that appear on your axes, you also can add chart titles, subtitles, and other text information. By default, Excel does not create a chart title for you, but you can easily add one later. You also can format the text to help improve the appearance of your chart data.

## Choosing a chart type

Excel offers a dizzying array of chart types and variations of each kind. Before you begin turning your spreadsheet information into a chart, it is a good idea to determine what sort of chart is best suited for your data. At its heart, Excel's charting feature can compare data in five fundamental ways, as outlined in Table 16.1. Choosing the type of comparison you want to make can help you narrow down what type of chart to use. For example, a pie chart is perfect for comparing expenditures in a household budget, while a bar chart works well for comparing individual data, such as sales totals from a group of stores. Finding the right chart type can save you time and effort at the start of your charting tasks.

**TABLE 16.1**

## Chart Comparisons

| Comparison | Description |
| --- | --- |
| Time Series | Compares values from different time periods to show changes over time. For example, comparing sales figures for every month of the year is a time series comparison. |
| Correlation | Compares data series to form correlations. For example, comparing TV viewing ratings nationwide to viewing ratings in a particular age group is an example of correlation comparison. |

*continued*

| **TABLE 16.1** | *(continued)* |
|---|---|
| **Comparison** | **Description** |
| Part-to-Whole | Compares individual values to the sum of a data series. For example, comparing sales for a particular model number for a gadget to overall gadget sales is a part-to-whole comparison. |
| Whole-to-Whole | Compares individual values to each other, or a data series to another data series. For example, comparing sales for gadgets from one manufacturer to the sales of the same gadgets from another manufacturer is a whole-to-whole comparison. |
| Geographic | Compares values using a geographic basis. For example, comparing sales from each state or sales by country is an example of geographic comparison. |

Although you can preview any chart type using the Elements Gallery, the following descriptions might give you greater detail about the particular chart type and how it is used. In addition to the standard chart types, Excel's charting feature includes several subtypes for each. Subtypes include stacked, 100% stacked, and 3-D versions of the standard chart types. For example, you can assign a standard column chart, or you can use a stacked, 100% stacked, or 3-D subtype. The stacked subtype means the data series is displayed in one column or, in the case of the bar or line charts, whatever the chart's data point style dictates. The measurement of the chart element, such as the height of a column in a column chart, is the sum of the values for that particular data series category, yet each portion appears as a segment in the column. The 100% stacked subtype displays the percentages of the data series total, essentially showing how each value contributes in percentage to the whole.

Lastly, the 3-D subtype artistically renders the chart so that it appears three dimensional in perspective. Surface charts are the only Excel chart type that offers true three-dimensional aspects in plotting data. The other 3-D subtypes use three-dimensional graphics to create a 3-D appearance only. I'm anxiously looking forward to the day they start integrating 3-D glasses with viewing charts in Excel. That should really make the data pop!

### Area chart

Area charts are most appropriate for showing trends or amounts of change over a period of time or across categories. Because area charts display the sum of the values, this chart type is useful for showing how the various parts contribute to the whole. Each line in an area chart represents a single data series. Area charts come in three versions: area, stacked, and 100% stacked. Plus, each version has 3-D renderings, making for a total of six different area charts. The stacked area chart shows trends in contributions over time or categories, while the 100% stacked area chart shows the percentage each value contributes over time or categories. Figure 16.4 shows an example of a stacked area chart.

### Bar chart

Bar charts show comparisons between data using rectangular horizontal bars. Bar charts are great for emphasizing differences in data series. Bar charts come in several versions, the main differences being the graphical presentation of the bars themselves. You can assign a clustered bar, stacked bar, or 100% stacked bar, or 3-D versions of all three. If you are not fond of rectangular bars, you can use cones, cylinders, or pyramids instead. Each of the other graphical styles also has 3-D perspectives. In total, you have 15 different bar charts to choose from. Figure 16.5 shows a clustered bar chart.

**FIGURE 16.4**

Area chart

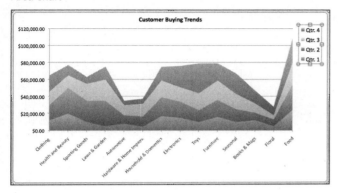

**FIGURE 16.5**

Bar chart

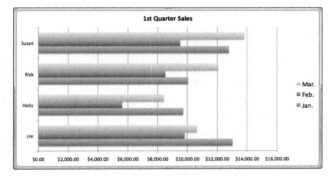

### Bubble chart

Bubble charts are similar to XY (scatter) charts. They compare sets of three values: X, Y, and a third variable. Data markers appear as circular bubbles on the actual chart, with the largest bubble expressing the third variable in the set. For example, you might use a bubble chart to compare the number of products, sales totals, and the percentage of market share. In order to use a bubble chart, you need to place all the X values in one row or column, all the corresponding Y values in adjacent rows or columns, and the bubble values in the next adjacent row or column. Unlike some of the other chart types, bubble charts offer only two flavors: bubble or 3-D bubble. To view a bubble chart, see Figure 16.6.

Bubble chart

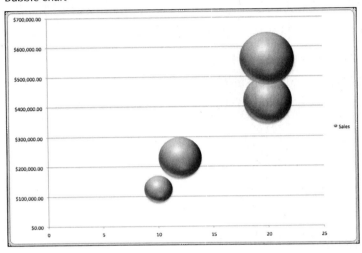

## Column chart

Column charts show changes in data over a period of time or compares data. This chart type is good for displaying two or more values side by side. Column charts, like bar charts, use rectangular shapes to illustrate the extent of comparison, but the shapes run vertically instead of horizontally. Also like bar charts, column charts can be clustered or stacked using columns, cylinders, cones, or pyramids. You also can assign 3-D versions of each kind. In total, you can choose from 19 column charts. With sheer numbers alone, column charts win the popularity contest among chart types. Figure 16.7 shows an example of a clustered column chart.

Column chart

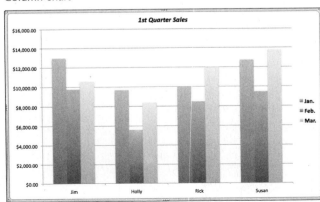

## Doughnut chart

Doughnut charts, like the one shown in Figure 16.8, are circular and display data series in rings with a big, empty whole in the middle. Much like pie charts, doughnut charts allow readers to see the relationship of parts to the whole. Unlike pie charts, however, which show only one data series, doughnut charts can illustrate more than one data series. Each ring in the doughnut represents a different data series. You can assign a regular doughnut chart or an exploded doughnut chart. Don't worry, no real explosives are involved. Instead, it's simply an effect that makes the data appear to emanate from the center of the doughnut. It's a strange name, really.

**FIGURE 16.8**

Doughnut chart

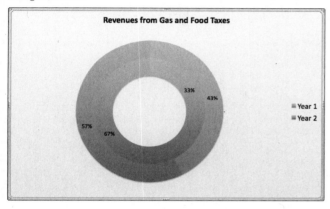

## Line chart

Line charts are useful for showing trends in intervals, like time. You can use this chart type to track data points over time or categories with data markers or data points at the crucial intervals of change. For example, you might use a line chart to show the rate of change over time, using one or more data series. Each series has its own line on the chart. Line charts include regular line, stacked line, 100% stacked line, marked line, stacked marked line, 100% stacked marked line, and 3-D line. The marked versions of this chart type use small graphical shapes as data points along the line being charted. Figure 16.9 shows an example of a line chart.

## Pie chart

Using a single data series, a pie chart shows how the individual values are proportional to the sum of the values. Turning a household budget into a pie chart is a good example of this chart type. Each item in the budget appears as a wedge or piece of the pie, and the wedge size is proportional to the whole budget. The pie chart subtypes include 3-D pie, pie of pie, and exploded pie. Like the exploded doughnut chart, nothing is really exploding, rather the illusion of pie parts breaking off and emanating from the center. For an example of a pie chart, see Figure 16.10.

**FIGURE 16.9**

Line chart

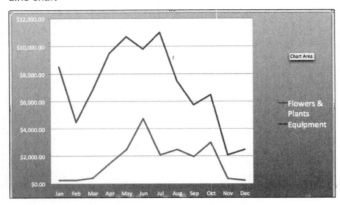

**FIGURE 16.10**

Pie chart

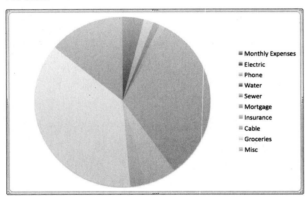

### Radar chart

You can use radar charts, as shown in Figure 16.11, to display changes in values relative to a center point. As such, Radar charts look much like spider webs. Data points closest to the center represent low values, while data points further from the center represent higher values. You might use a radar chart to look at several factors all related to one item, such as comparing NFL quarterbacks' statistics or average monthly temperatures in the three most populated countries. Radar charts come in three flavors: radar, marked radar, and filled radar. The marked radar style shows values as data markers on the chart, while a filled radar style fills in a color for the data series area covered.

**FIGURE 16.11**

Radar chart

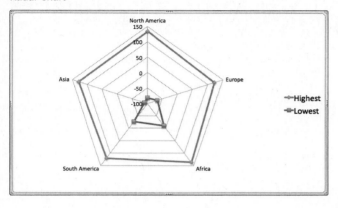

## Stock chart

You can use Excel's stock charts to illustrate the fluctuation in stock prices. Stock charts come in four varieties: high-low-close, open-high-low-close, volume-high-low-close, and volume-open-high-low. You can also use them to chart scientific data, such as daily temperature values. When preparing data for a stock chart, you must organize the data in the right order on the worksheet. For example, to use a high-low-close stock chart, you must list three series of values, listing the high values first in one column, then the low values in the next column, and then the closing values in the final column. If you do not enter the values in the correct order, your chart will not be accurate. See Figure 16.12 to view a sample of a high-low-close stock chart.

**FIGURE 16.12**

Stock chart

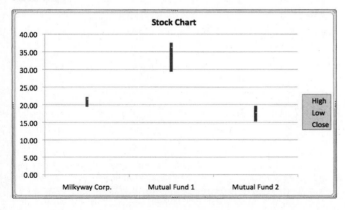

## Surface chart

Surface charts, also called contour maps, look like topographical maps, as shown in Figure 16.13. They allow you to illustrate combinations between data values. Surface charts work by comparing how a variable (Z) changes according to two other variables (X and Y). This is the same as an actual topographical chart that shows how altitude (Z) changes with longitude and latitude (X and Y) on the earth's surface. Surface charts use colors and patterns to show where data values are the same. You can choose from 3-D surface, wireframe 3-D surface, contour, or wireframe contour charts. The wireframe perspective displays the chart data with a grid that flows with the rise and fall of values, while the contour perspective looks more like a folded map.

**FIGURE 16.13**

Surface chart

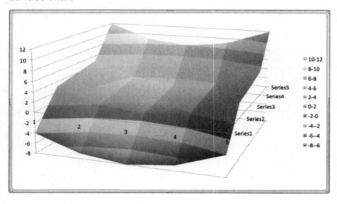

## XY (Scatter) chart

XY, or *scatter,* charts are used to illustrate relationships between numerical values or compare trends across uneven time periods using two or more data series. Scatter charts plot paired variables on a grid to view the relationship between them. Scatter charts come in the following styles: marked scatter, smooth marked scatter, smooth lined scatter, straight marked scatter, and straight lined scatter. Figure 16.14 shows an example of a straight marked scatter chart.

Even though Excel offers a variety of chart types, most people find themselves using the same few over and over again. The most commonly used chart types are column, pie, scatter, area, and line charts. All in all, choosing a chart type really comes down to deciding the best way to present your data, making it easy to understand at a glance. Let your guiding philosophy be this: Always choose a chart type that conveys your message in the simplest possible way.

# Inserting a chart

Inserting a chart is easier than ever in Office 2008. Before you apply Excel's charting feature, you must first figure out which data to include in the chart. This may seem rather obvious, but it is often easy to miss something in your selection. Think about what data you want to emphasize as you're making your selection. When selecting data, keep the following points in mind:

■ Be sure to select any text labels appearing in the columns or rows to include with the chart data. For example, if your worksheet has text headings at the top of each column for your data series, be sure to include those cells, or if your rows include text labels for items, be sure to include those.

**FIGURE 16.14**

Scatter chart

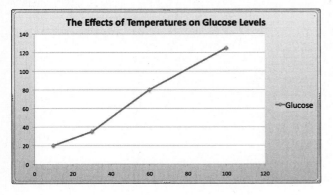

- Unless the numbers are a part of your chart data, it is not necessary to include cells containing totals, such as a total at the bottom of a column.

- You may find it easier to place a data series in a column rather than a row. This tends to keep your numeric data adjacent to each other and most resembles a list, which is how most people are used to seeing number data.

- Do not include blank rows or columns in your selection, or your chart will end up with gaps, and your audience won't understand where they came from.

- You can, in fact, also choose data to chart from non-adjacent cells. To do so, press and hold the ⌘ key while clicking the cells you want to include in the selection.

Now that you know which data to include in your chart, you are ready to insert a chart. Use the following steps to create a chart in Excel:

1. **In your worksheet, select the data that you want to turn into a chart.**

2. **Click the Charts tab on Elements Gallery.** You also can use the Insert menu; choose Insert ➪ Chart to display the Charts tab. Figure 16.15 shows the Elements Gallery with the Charts tab displayed. Notice the chart types arranged as tabs at the top of the Gallery.

3. **You can now cycle through the various chart types in the Gallery, clicking each tab to view its subtypes.** Not all the subtypes fit onscreen, so you must use the scroll arrows at the far right end of the Gallery to view additional subtypes.

4. **To apply any chart to your data, just click the chart you want on the Charts tab.** Excel immediately creates a chart and places it on the worksheet as a floating object, much like a graphic or picture.

The chart object is treated as an embedded object in Excel. Figure 16.16 shows a newly inserted chart. Excel isn't always very careful about where it places a chart. Notice in this figure, the chart partially obscures the underlying data. I have not touched the chart yet in any way, honestly! Excel just thought that would be a good place for it, I guess. The good news is that because it's an object, the chart is moveable and resizable, and you can delete it when you no longer want it on the sheet. If you continue clicking other chart types in the Gallery, and as long as the chart is still selected on the worksheet, Excel continues to update the chart object to a new type. The chart is linked to your worksheet data, so if you make any changes to the cells associated with the chart, Excel updates the chart to reflect your changes.

**FIGURE 16.15**

The Charts tab on the Elements Gallery gives you fast access to every kind of chart you can create in Excel.

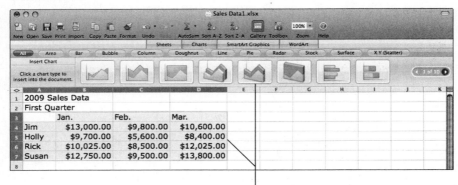

Select the worksheet data, then choose a chart type.

 Something else happens onscreen regarding charts: Whenever you select a chart, the Formatting Palette displays options specifically geared to charts. Unless, of course, you've turned off the palette, in which case, just click the Toolbox icon on the toolbar or click View ➪ Formatting Palette. Figure 16.16 shows the Formatting Palette along with all the charting tools displayed. The Chart Options, Chart Data, and Chart Style sections appear, along with other tool groups needed for working with graphic objects. You can display or hide the various groups as needed. Just click the group name to display or hide the tools. You can learn more about the charting tools in "Formatting Charts" later in this chapter.

Now that you have a chart inserted onto your worksheet, make sure it's in the right location and the right size. To move a chart at any time, follow these steps:

1. **Move the mouse pointer over the border edge of the chart object.** The mouse pointer takes on the shape of a four-sided arrow pointer.

2. **Click and drag the chart to a new location on the worksheet, and drop it in place.**

**TIP**   Want to move the chart to another sheet? You can use the Chart menu; choose Chart ➪ Move Chart. This opens the Chart Location dialog box. Click the As new sheet option, and click OK. Excel automatically creates a new sheet and inserts the chart. By default, Excel names the sheet "Chart1," unless you typed a new name in the text field.

To resize a chart, follow these steps:

1. **Hover the mouse pointer over a corner of the selected chart object until the pointer takes the shape of a double-sided arrow pointer.**

2. **Click and drag to resize the chart.**

   ■ Drag toward the middle of the chart to make the chart smaller.

   ■ Drag away from the middle to make the chart larger.

   ■ If you press and hold the Shift key while dragging, Excel resizes the chart proportionately, which means all four sides are resized simultaneously and equally.

You also can remove a chart entirely from the worksheet by selecting the chart and pressing Delete. That's all there is to it. You can use the same technique to delete individual chart elements. If you ever accidentally delete the wrong chart or item, you can always activate the Undo command. Press ⌘+Z, or choose Edit ➪ Undo.

---

**FIGURE 16.16**

After you create a chart, the chart appears selected onscreen, and the Formatting Palette displays charting tools.

Chart tools appear in the Formatting Palette

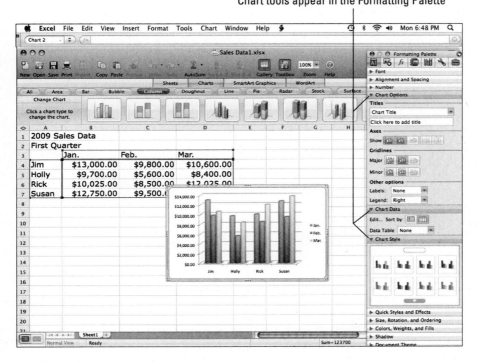

## What About a Copy?

You can cut, copy, and paste chart objects. For example, you may want to copy a chart onto another work-sheet, into another workbook, or to another document altogether. You can use the standard Cut, Copy, and Paste commands to cut and copy charts. With the chart selected, click the Copy button on the toolbar. You also can use the Edit menu; choose Edit ➪ Copy. Switch over to the receiving sheet, workbook, or document, and click the Paste button or use the Edit menu again; choose Edit ➪ Paste. For quicker copying and pasting, press ⌘+C on the keyboard to copy and then press ⌘+V to paste, or use the shortcut menu; press Control, click the chart to view the menu, and then click Copy or Paste.

# Editing Chart Data

After inserting a chart, make sure you've referenced the correct data. If something looks amiss, you can make adjustments to the data using the Select Source Data dialog box or window. You can access this feature in several ways. If the chart is selected and the Formatting Palette is displayed, you can click the Edit button in the Chart Data pane of tools. You also can use two other methods to open the dialog box. You can use the Chart menu by choosing Chart ⇨ Source Data, or use the shortcut menu by pressing Control, clicking anywhere on the chart, and then clicking Select Data. The Select Data Source dialog box, shown in Figure 16.17, displays the selected data range in the Chart data range field. Notice that the starting cell and ending cells in the range are absolute references.

**FIGURE 16.17**

The Select Data Source dialog box lets you redo your data range for a chart.

Click to collapse the dialog box.

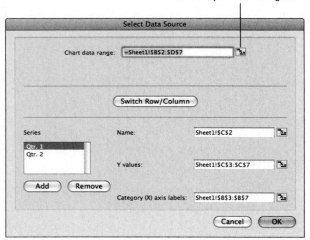

If the Chart data range box does not show the correct range, click the collapse button at the far-right side of the text box to minimize the dialog box. After it's minimized, you can select the correct range in the sheet and then click the expand button to view the entire dialog box again. Figure 16.18 shows a collapsed dialog box with the expand button. You also can type a range directly into the Chart data range field.

**FIGURE 16.18**

Collapse the dialog box to get it out of the way for selecting a new range, and then click the expand button to bring the dialog box back into full view.

Click to restore the dialog box.

If you prefer to see the horizontal (X) axis and vertical (Y) axis switched in your chart, you can click the Switch Row/Column button. This same command is accessible in the Formatting Palette under the Chart Data options. You can click the Sort by Row button or the Column button to swap axis orientation. When activated, this command causes Excel to reverse the two axes on the chart.

You can make changes to the individual data series in a chart using the Name and Values fields in the Select Data Source dialog box. In the Series box, select the series you want to edit. You can change the name of the selected series as it appears in the Legend by typing a new name in the Name field. You can change which cells are associated with the range using the Y values or X values field. Like the Chart data range field, you can click the collapse button to minimize the dialog box and select cells in the worksheet, and then click the expand button to maximize the dialog box again. Alternatively, you can type a range directly into the field. To remove a series from the chart, select the series and click the Remove button or press Delete. Any changes you make in the dialog box are immediately reflected in the chart. However, the changes are not permanent until you apply them using the OK button. After you finish editing the data, click OK to close the dialog box and apply any changes. If you decide not to apply any changes, click the Cancel button instead.

 **Don't forget that if you make changes to the data on the worksheet, Excel also updates the data in your chart automatically.**

# Formatting Charts

Excel's charting tools include numerous ways to change and improve the appearance of your charts. You may want to change fonts, make the chart text larger and easier to read, add a title, add labels to the data points, rearrange items, and much more. Granted, Excel's charts look pretty darn good from the get-go, but you can always make them look even better. This section shows you how to tap in to the many tools available for making your charts look great. As with any formatting tools you use, be careful not to go overboard with all the bells and whistles. If you make your chart too busy with fonts, colors, and chart elements, your audience will be distracted by the chaos and miss the message your chart is trying to convey. Simplicity is the best approach for formatting.

## Formatting with the chart tools

When you select a chart, which you can do simply by clicking the chart object, the Formatting Palette automatically displays groups of tools related to charting, such as options for adding titles or displaying axes, gridlines, or labels. These groups, also called sections or panes, organize the options into logical sections. In addition, other graphic-related groups appear on the palette. We examine the main charting group first.

The Chart Options tools, which appear in Figure 16.19, include features for formatting the axes, gridlines, labels, and legend, and adding a title. You can use the Titles options to add a title to your chart. By default, titles appear at the very top of the chart, unless you move them to another location. To add a title, click the Titles field and click Chart Title. Depending on your chart type, you also can add titles to various axes on the chart. Next, click inside the field below the Titles field, where it says "Click here to add title," and type your title text. Anything you type appears automatically at the top of the chart. The title is actually contained in a text box on the chart, which means you can move or resize the box as needed.

**FIGURE 16.19**

The Chart Options tools help you to fine-tune a chart's title, axes display, gridlines, data point labels, and legend.

You can use the Axes Show buttons, shown in Figure 16.19, to change how axes appear in a chart. The buttons act as toggles that turn an axis on or off. Click the Primary Vertical Axis or Primary Horizontal Axis buttons to toggle the X or Y axis on or off. In the case of stock or surface charts, you can toggle the Depth Axis on or off with the button. If your chart utilizes a second vertical or horizontal axis, you can toggle it on or off using the Secondary Vertical Axis or Secondary Horizontal Axis buttons. (The secondary axes are useful only if you're charting two different measurement scales on the same chart.)

The Gridlines buttons, shown in Figure 16.19, toggle gridlines on or off in the plot area. The Major buttons allow you to display the Vertical, Horizontal, or Depth gridlines for the major units of measurement in your chart. Use the Minor buttons to control the same gridlines for minor units.

Under the Other options section, shown in Figure 16.19, you can find controls for data point labels and the chart legend. Click the Labels field to view which data point labels you can turn on or off. Click the Legend field, and choose a position for the legend.

The Chart Data group of tools, shown in Figure 16.20, has only three options: the Edit button, Sort by toggles, and the Data Table field. You can use the Edit button to quickly open the Select Data Source dialog box and make changes to the data referenced by the chart. See the preceding section, "Editing Chart Data," to learn more about making changes to the source data upon which the chart was built.

**FIGURE 16.20**

The Chart Data tools can help you edit your referenced data, switch columns and rows, and include original worksheet data along with the chart.

You can click the Sort by buttons to swap the horizontal (X) axis and the vertical (Y) axis in a chart. For example, perhaps your quarterly sales worksheet originally showed all the sales staff names in a column and all the month names in a row, but now that you see it in a chart, it might look better reversed. You can click the Row or Column button to switch the display.

If you plan on copying your chart to another document or program, you can use the Data Table feature to include the original worksheet cell data along with the chart. Click the Data Table field, and select an option. Choose Data Table to include the cell range from the worksheet that you originally used to create the chart. Excel inserts the cells at the bottom of the chart, looking much like they do in your original sheet. In essence, you've added a little bit of your worksheet to your chart, cells and contents combined. This little chunk of your worksheet is called a *data table*. If you want to add a legend key to the data table, choose the Data Table with Legend Keys option. Excel then adds the legend key information to the front of the data table. Figure 16.21 shows an example of a data table added to a chart. To remove the data table later, choose the None option instead.

The Chart Style group on the Formatting Palette shows a variety of color schemes you can apply to your chart. You can peruse from a long list of color selections, clicking the arrow buttons at the top and bottom of the group to view more. When you find a color scheme you like, click it and Excel applies it to the chart. The color schemes mainly involve changing the appearance of the graphics in a chart, such as the bars or columns in the plot area. Several of the schemes also include backgrounds for the entire chart area. Figure 16.22 shows the Chart Style group.

If you don't quite find the color scheme you wanted for a chart, you can look elsewhere in the Formatting Palette. The Document Theme section, shown in Figure 16.23, lists a myriad of preset, professional color schemes you can apply to your charts. Themes can help give all your Office documents, including work-sheets and charts, a cohesive and similar feel. If you find a theme you like, click it to apply it to the selected chart. The Quick Styles and Effects group, shown in Figure 16.23, displays options for adding fill colors to your chart backgrounds and individual chart elements, along with tools for adding shadows, glows, reflections, 3-D effects, and text transformations. Not all the options are available for every chart, but you still can find plenty of styles and effects to play with and create just the right look for your data.

You can add cells from your worksheet to the chart, allowing other users to see the original data upon which the chart is based.

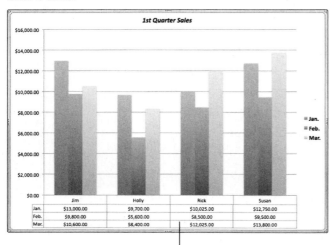

Data table

Change your chart's color scheme by selecting a new scheme from the Chart Style group.

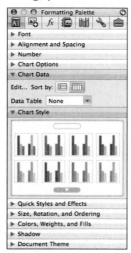

**FIGURE 16.23**

The Formatting Palette also offers general groups of tools for formatting graphic objects, whether a chart or clip art.

You can use the tools in the Colors, Weights, and Fills section, also shown in Figure 16.23, to assign individual fill colors, line colors, and thicknesses to various parts of a chart. The Shadow section offers tools for creating and editing shadow effects. To learn more about using the formatting tools for graphic objects, see Chapter 30.

**NOTE**    Many of the formatting tools on the Formatting Palette also are available through dialog boxes. Like many commands among the Office suite, the tools show up in two or more places. Don't be alarmed by the duplication. Just use the method that best suits your work needs. The next section shows you how to use the dialog boxes to edit individual chart items.

## Formatting individual chart elements

What about formatting individual parts of a chart? Can you do that in Excel? Of course you can. Every element or item in a chart can be formatted. Plus, you can add additional elements if you need them. You can open a detailed formatting dialog box for every element in a chart and make changes to the attributes assigned to the element. For example, you can make all kinds of formatting changes to a data series in a bar chart. You can change the fill color of the bar, change the line color and thickness, add shadow and 3-D effects, change the way an axis is plotted, add labels, change the series order, and more. Best of all, you can make all these changes in one convenient location—the Format Data Series dialog box, as shown in Figure 16.24.

For quick and easy formatting, you can always use the Formatting Palette. It offers lots of tools you can use to change fonts, alignment, fill colors, shadows, and more. It also includes groups of tools tailored just for charts: Chart Options, Chart Data, and Chart Style. See the preceding section to learn how to use the chart-specific tools in the palette.

### FIGURE 16.24

You can open the Format Data Series dialog box to make changes to a selected data series in your chart.

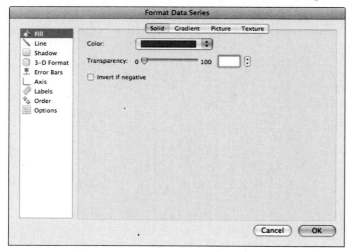

Depending on the chart element, different formatting categories are available, and the name of the formatting dialog box changes as well. If you edit the plot area, for example, the dialog box is called the Format Plot Area box. If you edit an axis, the Format Axis dialog box appears. It's the same dialog box in principle, but it shows element-specific commands and tools each time. The formatting options for a data series in a pie chart differ from the options available for a Line chart. To summon any formatting dialog box, simply double-click the chart element you want to edit. You also can use the Format menu; choose Format ⇨ and then choose the name of the selected chart item, such as Chart Area. In Figure 16.25, the legend is selected in the chart, and the Format Legend dialog box is displayed. The formatting dialog boxes are multi-tabbed based on what formatting option you select in the category list box.

To help you understand the various formatting options you can apply to your charts, let's go through the basic chart elements and how to format each using the appropriate Format dialog box.

### Format the chart area

You can change the appearance of the chart area using the Format Chart Area dialog box. The chart area includes the background upon which the chart plot, legend, and title sit, and the fonts assigned to the chart. It also includes chart properties for controlling the embedded positioning of the chart. To open the dialog box, hover your mouse pointer over an empty area of the chart until the name of the element appears next to the pointer in a ScreenTip. If it says "Chart Area," double-click to open the dialog box. You also can use the Format menu to open the dialog box; click inside the chart area and choose Format ⇨ Chart Area.

**FIGURE 16.25**

The Format Legend dialog box offers categories of settings for changing the legend's fill color and line style, applying a shadow effect, changing the font, and controlling the positioning of the legend on the chart.

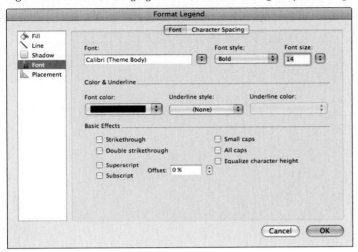

> **NOTE** The Format Chart Area dialog box for a surface chart includes an extra formatting category—3-D Rotation. The settings in this category let you control the rotation properties for the surface chart's three axes and the scaling depth and height for the unique appearance of this chart type.

# Formatting for Objects

Many of the formatting categories and options available in the Format dialog box for chart elements also are applicable to other graphic objects you might insert into a worksheet. For example, if you insert clip art, an AutoShape, or an image file, Excel treats them all as objects in the worksheet. This means you can move, resize, and format them as needed. After you learn how to apply formatting to one object, you can use the same techniques and settings to format another kind of object. In other words, if you master creating gradient effects for charts, you can use the same tools to create gradient effects for other graphics, such as shapes or clip art. In some cases, the formatting categories and options you come across while working with chart elements are available only for other types of graphic objects. In such instances, the tools or settings appear grayed out in the Format dialog box, and you cannot activate them at all. Also, the formatting tools contain lots of repetitiveness. The same formatting categories and options are available to many of the same chart parts. For example, you can set a gradient effect for the chart area and use the same tools to create gradients for a data series. To learn more about formatting other graphic objects in Excel and all the other Office programs, see Chapter 30.

### Formatting with Fill options

The Format Chart Area dialog box, shown in Figure 16.26, starts out with the Fill category at the top of the list, which offers options for controlling the fill color. By default, the color is set to white for any new chart you create. You can change the color to another solid color, change it to a gradient effect, insert a picture as a background, or apply a texture effect. With the Fill option selected, you see four tabs at the top of the dialog box: Solid, Gradient, Picture, and Texture. To change the background color, click the Solid tab, click the Color field, and choose a new color from the pop-up palette. To make the background transparent, choose the No Fill option. If the Theme Colors and Standard Colors don't offer enough selections, you can click More Colors to open the Colors dialog box for more color options.

**FIGURE 16.26**

The Format Chart Area dialog box lets you change the chart background fill.

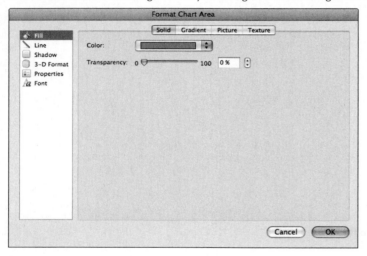

To apply a gradient effect, which is simply a blend of colors or intensities, click the Gradient tab, as shown in Figure 16.27. You can use this tab to add a gradient based on one or more colors. The Gradient tab has two main areas of controls: Styles and direction, and Color and transparency. Start by selecting a color (or colors) with the Color field under the Color and transparency settings. The Gradient box immediately shows a sample of the selected color, along with some funny-looking markers. The color white is assigned by default, allowing you to create a blended effect between the color you chose and white. You can select and drag the markers to make adjustments to the color intensity. To add another color to the mix, click the Add Color button to add another marker to the sample, and use the Color field to change the color. You can then drag the new marker to adjust the intensities of the blend. To remove a color marker, select it and click the Delete Color button.

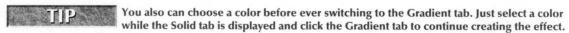 **TIP** You also can choose a color before ever switching to the Gradient tab. Just select a color while the Solid tab is displayed and click the Gradient tab to continue creating the effect.

Next, click the Style field and choose a gradient style. None is selected by default. You can pick from Linear, Radial, Rectangle, and Path. If you choose a Linear effect, the gradient shows a color changing in intensity from one side to the other. You can make adjustments to the angle of the effect, either by turning the Angle dial or setting a degree in the degree field. If you select a Radial or Rectangular gradient, you can specify a direction for the color graduation.

For a more subtle effect, make adjustments to the Transparency setting. You can drag the Transparency marker to make changes or set a percentage level in the number field. After you've set up your gradient just the way you like it, you can click OK to exit the dialog box and apply your new formatting to the chart.

Use the Gradient tab to create a gradient effect for the chart background.

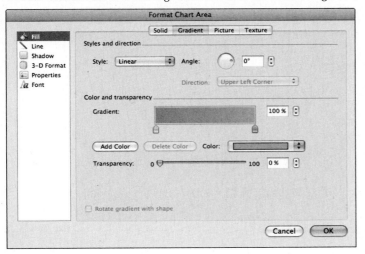

If you'd rather use a picture as a chart background, click the Picture tab in the Format Chart Area dialog box and click the Choose a Picture button. This opens the Choose a Picture dialog box, and you can navigate to the picture file you want to use. After you locate the image file, double-click it to add it to the Picture tab. You can then make adjustments to the transparency level, tiling (how an image repeats itself to fill the space), or rotation. Figure 16.28 shows the Picture tab with a picture ready to apply.

To use a texture as a background in your chart, click the Texture tab in the Format Chart Area dialog box and select from the list of preset textures. Figure 16.29 shows the Texture options. You can adjust the transparency setting of the texture by dragging the marker or setting a specific percentage of transparency.

**NOTE** The Gradient, Picture, and Texture tabs all include a check box for rotating the item with the shape. If you enable this option, Excel allows the formatted background to be rotated along with the chart object.

### Formatting with Line options

The Line category of formatting options offers three tabs you can use to control the border line of a chart: Solid, Gradient, and Weights & Arrows. By default, Excel applies a light gray border, but you can choose another color and control the thickness of the border line. To change the line color, click the Solid tab, click the Color field, and pick another color. To adjust the transparency setting, drag the Transparency marker or set a specific percentage. To turn the line color into a gradient blend, click the Gradient tab and choose a gradient Style and color. (Refer to the preceding section to learn how to apply a gradient effect, as shown in Figure 16.27.) To Change the line thickness and style, click the Weights & Arrows tab, as shown in Figure 16.30. Here you can use the Line style settings to change the line thickness, apply a dotted or dashed line border, and set the end cap type or corner shape. You also can directly type a line thickness into the Weight field. The Arrows settings are activated only when you format gridlines or axes in a chart.

**FIGURE 16.28**

Use the Picture tab to add an image file to the chart background.

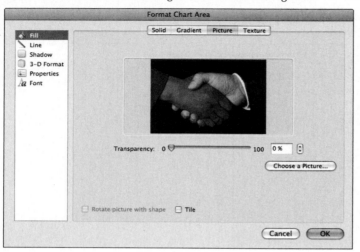

**FIGURE 16.29**

Use the Texture tab to add a preset texture to the chart background.

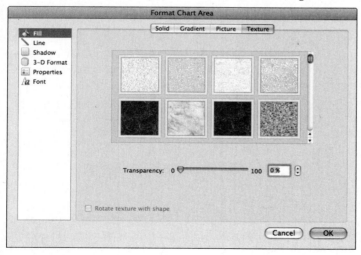

### Formatting with Shadow options

Click the Shadow category to view shadow effects you can assign to the chart area. The shadow options make the chart seem to cast a shadow behind it onto the worksheet. You might use this feature to give your chart the illusion of dimension. Click the Shadow check box, shown in Figure 16.31, to activate the settings. You can then change the shadow style, angle, color, size, blur effect, distance from the chart object, or transparency level.

**FIGURE 16.30**

You can add a border to the chart and use the Line settings to format the border line.

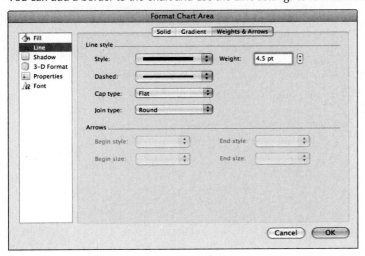

**FIGURE 16.31**

You can add a shadow effect to the chart and use the Shadow settings to format the effect.

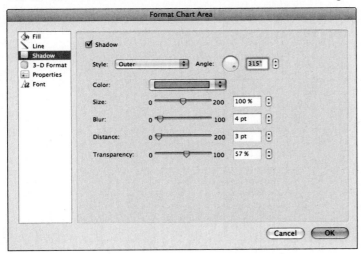

### Formatting with 3-D options

Click the 3-D Format category to view 3-D settings you can assign to the chart area. You can choose from setting bevel effects, which add a dimensional bevel to the chart's edges, or setting depth and surface effects, which also lend a three-dimensional appearance to your chart. You can learn more about these settings in Chapter 30.

### Formatting chart properties

Click the Properties category in the Format Chart Area dialog box to view properties pertaining to object positioning. Figure 16.32 shows the Properties settings. At first glance, you might think the object positioning refers to controlling the exact position of a chart in a worksheet. It actually allows you to control how an embedded chart is positioned with cells in the worksheet. You can allow the chart to move and size with cells, move but don't size with cells, or don't move or size with cells at all. You also can deselect the Print object check box to prevent the chart from printing along with the worksheet. The Locked check box locks the chart only if the worksheet itself is protected. Learn more about protecting sheets and workbooks in Chapter 12.

### Formatting with Font options

When you insert a chart into your worksheet, one of the first things that may bother you is the extremely small type for the chart text, whether axes labels or the legend. Thankfully, you can set a larger (or smaller) font size for the text. For quick font controls, you don't have to look any farther than the Formatting Palette. Click the Font pane to view tools for changing the font, size, and color, and applying basic formatting, such as bold, italic, or underlining. However, because we're talking about the Format Chart Area dialog box in this section, you'll be happy to know you can find font and character spacing tools among the Font category of formatting options. With the Font tab selected, as shown in Figure 16.33, you can view Font, Color & Underline, and Basic Effects settings. To change the font, click the Font field and select another font. To change the style, such as regular, bold, italic, or bold italic, click the Font style field and pick the formatting you want to apply. To change the text size, click the Font size field and click a new size. As you make your selections, Excel immediately previews the formatting on the chart itself.

The Color & Underline settings allow you to change the font color and apply an underlining style and color. Click the appropriate field, and make your selection. The Basic Effects settings offer check boxes for turning on strikethrough, superscript, subscript, or capitalization options.

Click the Character Spacing tab to view settings for controlling the spacing between lines of text when two or more lines appear together in a chart and the spacing between characters.

---

**FIGURE 16.32**

The Properties settings help control how charts are embedded, printed, or protected.

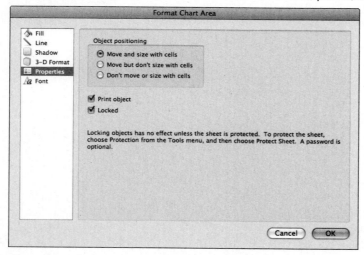

**FIGURE 16.33**

The Font settings allow you to set fonts, sizes, color, and character spacing for your chart text.

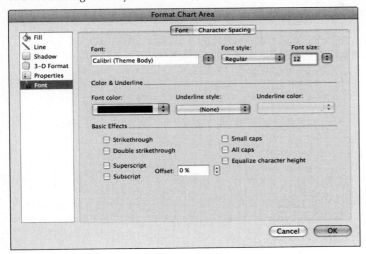

After you finish making changes to the chart area formatting, click OK to apply them to the chart.

### Format the plot area

You can change the appearance of the plot area using the Format Plot Area dialog box. The plot area includes the actual chart layout upon which the data series and axes sits. To open the dialog box, hover your mouse pointer over the middle area of the chart until the name of the element appears next the pointer in a ScreenTip. If it says "Plot Area," double-click to open the dialog box. You also can use the Format menu to open the dialog box; click inside the plot area, and choose Format ⇨ Plot Area.

The Format Plot Area dialog box features four of the same categories found in the Format Chart Area dialog box: Fill, Line, Shadow, and 3-D Format. Instead of formatting the chart background, however, the settings control how the plot area appears. To review how these formatting controls work, revisit the preceding section, "Format the chart area."

### Format a data series

To change the appearance of a single data series, you can open the Format Data Series dialog box. For example, you may want to assign another color to the data series columns of a column chart or the bubbles of a bubble chart. Or perhaps you'd like to use a texture or gradient effect instead of a solid color. To open the dialog box, hover your mouse pointer over a data series in the chart until the name of the element appears next the pointer in a ScreenTip. If it says "Series," double-click to open the dialog box. You also can use the Format menu to open the dialog box; click inside the chart area, and choose Format ⇨ Data Series.

The Format Data Series dialog box lists nine categories of formatting options, as shown in Figure 16.34. You've already learned about the Fill, Line, Shadow, and 3-D Format categories in the previous sections. Depending on the chart type, the Error Bars, Axis, Labels, and Options categories may appear in the list. As an advanced charting technique, the Error Bars category is covered in the "Advanced Charting," up next in this chapter.

## What Happened to the Chart Toolbar?

The good ole' Chart toolbar is still available in Excel 2008. You can still use it as a handy toolbar for editing charts. To open the toolbar, choose View ⇨ Toolbars ⇨ Chart. Excel displays the toolbar at the top of the program window. You can use the toolbar to edit individual chart elements, access the Format dialog box, toggle the legend or data table on or off, swap rows and columns, or change text direction. The toolbar may really come in handy when you're having trouble selecting individual items in a chart, such as an axis or data series. Simply click the Chart Objects field, and click the item you want to select in the chart. After you have the item selected in the chart, you can click the Format Selected Object button in the toolbar to summon the Format dialog box for that particular element.

### FIGURE 16.34

The Format Data Series dialog box has options for changing the appearance of a data series.

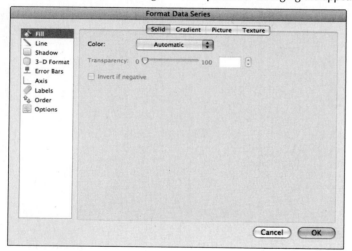

> **NOTE**   If two or more series appear in a chart, the order category may appear in the Format Data Series dialog box, allowing you the option of changing the order in which the series appears in the chart.

### Formatting the axis

The Axis category is pretty simple. You can choose to plot the series on the primary axis or a secondary axis. For example, in some charts, you want to plot two different measurement scales, such as charting the mean soil temperature in both Fahrenheit and Celsius scale. To show both scales in the chart, turn on the Secondary axis in the Axis category, as shown in Figure 16.35. To return to just one scale again, click the Primary axis option.

### Formatting labels

By default, Excel does not add labels to a data series on the plotted chart. Instead the X or Y axis shows any labels associated with the charted data. To make the information easier to read, however, you may want to turn on certain labels. We've already covered how to turn on simple data series labels using the Chart

Options pane on the Formatting Palette. Now look at the Labels category in the Format Data Series dialog box, shown in Figure 16.36. Depending on the chart type and data series, you can choose from six data labels: None, Show value, Show percent, Show category name, Show category name and percent, or Show bubble sizes. In a pie chart, you may want to show percentages in each pie wedge, for example. If you click the Show percent option, Excel displays a percentage label in each pie segment. If you're charting lots of data, you may want to go a step further and add a legend key next to each label, sort of like a color tag to help match up the selected series with the legend.

**FIGURE 16.35**

Some charts require two measurement scales, such as a scale for both Fahrenheit and Celsius. You can create a secondary axis using the Axis category.

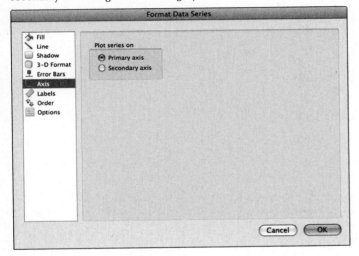

### Formatting options

For all those little extra features, like adding drop lines to a data series or changing pie slice color variation, you can look in the Options category. This category's features vary from chart type to chart type. Some types, like the line chart, offer settings to add drop lines, high-low lines, and up-down bars to the data series in the chart. Others, like the radar chart, use this category to vary colors by point or add category labels.

 **If you're using a line chart, the Format Data Series dialog box includes categories for formatting markers, such as changing the marker fill color, line thickness, and style.**

### Format a single axis

You can change the appearance of an axis using the Format Axis dialog box. The axis is the vertical (Y) or horizontal (X) scale on the chart. You can edit each individually. To open the dialog box, move your mouse pointer over the axis of the chart until the name of the element appears next the pointer in a ScreenTip, and then double-click to open the dialog box. You also can use the Format menu to open the dialog box; click inside the chart area, and choose Format ➪ Axis.

**FIGURE 16.36**

You can use the Labels category to turn labels on or off on the plotted area of the chart.

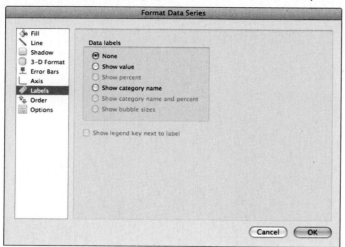

The Format Axis dialog box displays the same categories you've already learned about in the previous sections: Fill, Line, Shadow, 3-D Format, or Font. As always, the categories vary based on the chart type. In addition to those already covered, you may see these categories: Text Box, Number, and Scale.

The Text Box category, shown in Figure 16.37, displays settings for controlling text layout, AutoFit, and internal margins. You might notice when you select an axis to edit, it appears to be in a text box. As such, you can control how the text appears within the framework of the box. Click the Vertical alignment field to change the vertical positioning of text within the text box. By default, Excel places text horizontally in the text box for most chart types; however, you can rotate the text to make more room for your axis labels as they span the length of the scale. Click the Text direction field and select a text direction. Some chart types also let you change the order of lines and apply the AutoFit options to fit text. Lastly, you can use the Internal Margin settings to set margins around the inside of the text box.

To view number formats for your axis number data, click the Number category. The settings in this category are the same as those available through the Number pane on the Formatting Palette or in the number formats found in the Format Cells dialog box. The settings are not available for all chart types or axes.

Finally, the Scale category, shown in Figure 16.38, features settings for controlling the axis scale. You can set minimum and maximum amounts, display major or minor units, or change the display units entirely. For example, you may want to display hundreds instead of thousands or add labels to the units to help describe them for the user. The Scale options also include settings for reversing values, using a logarithmic scale, or displaying horizontal axis crosses.

## Format a legend

To change the appearance of a chart's legend, you can open the Format Legend dialog box. To open the dialog box, hover your mouse pointer over the legend until the name of the element appears next the pointer in a ScreenTip. If it says "Legend," double-click to open the dialog box. You also can use the Format menu to open the dialog box; click inside the chart area, and choose Format ⇨ Legend. The Format Legend dialog box displays the following categories: Fill, Line, Shadow, Font, and Placement. You've already learned how to use the first four, now let's look at the Placement category. The choices in this category control how a legend is positioned in the chart: bottom, top right, top, right, or left. The same options are available on the Chart Options pane in the Formatting Palette. Simply choose a position that best suits your chart.

**FIGURE 16.37**

You can use the Text Box category in the Format Axis dialog box to control axis text.

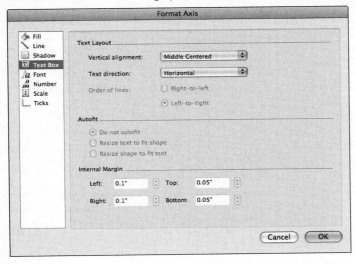

**FIGURE 16.38**

The Scale category, found in the Format Axis dialog box, has settings for controlling the appearance of the axis scale.

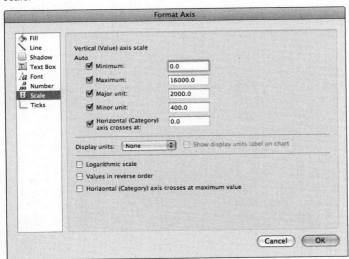

### Format a chart title

You can use the Format Title dialog box to make changes to a chart title, with the exception of actually editing the chart text. (To edit text, use the Chart Options pane in the Formatting Palette.) The dialog box offers six formatting categories: Fill, Line, Shadow, 3-D Format, Text Box, and Font. You can use the categories to change the fill color background of the legend, add a border or shadow, change the font or size, or control the positioning of text within the title text box. All these formatting categories are covered in previous sections.

### Format gridlines

The Format Gridlines dialog box is handy for making changes to the gridlines in the plot area. The dialog box offers three formatting categories: Line, Shadow, and Scale. You can use the categories to change the line color, thickness, add shadow effects, or turn major and minor tick marks on or off. All these formatting categories have been covered in previous sections, so flip back to review the options. You also can use the Formatting Palette to edit gridlines; you'll find the gridline tools in the Chart Options pane.

### Moving and deleting chart elements

One last thing you can do to individual chart elements: You can move them around the chart or delete them entirely. For example, if you don't like where the legend is positioned, you can click it and move it to another area of the chart. Or if you decide you don't like the chart title, you can delete it. Select the title text box, and press Delete.

> **TIP**   You can use the Drawing toolbar to add other elements to your charts, such as shapes or text boxes. For example, you may want to add another text box to insert a paragraph about the chart data. To learn more about using the Office 2008 graphics tools, see Chapter 30.

# Using Advanced Charting Techniques

Excel has several advanced charting features you can utilize if your charting needs require them. You can add versatility to your charts using error bars or trend lines. For most charting tasks, the wide selection of chart types offered by the Elements Gallery suffices. However, you may encounter instances where additional features are needed. This section goes over a few advanced charting techniques you can try.

## Adding error bars

Some chart types, such as column charts, let you add error bars to the chart. Error bars allow you to show variability in the measures plotted in the chart. For example, if your chart tracks a stock or plots data from an opinion poll, you can use error bars to set the margin of error or range of movement that surrounds the data. Error bars let you specify a range around each data point. The range appears as an actual bar on the data series. Most charts place error bars along the horizontal (Y) axis. Scatter charts are the only charts that allow vertical (X) axis error bars. You can add error bars to area, bar, bubble, column, line, and scatter charts. Figure 16.39 shows the Error Bars category in the Format Data Series dialog box.

To add error bars, double-click the data series you want to edit. This opens the Format Data Series dialog box. You also can click the data series and choose Format ⇨ Data Series to open the dialog box. Next, click the Error Bars category from the list box. Among the Display options, click the type of error bar you want to add. This activates the Error amount settings. Now choose which error amount you want to utilize in the chart. As soon as you click OK to close the dialog box, Excel applies the range bars to the chart.

If you decide later to remove the bars, revisit the Format Data Series dialog box and select the None option.

**FIGURE 16.39**

The Error Bars category offers settings for adding error bars to a chart.

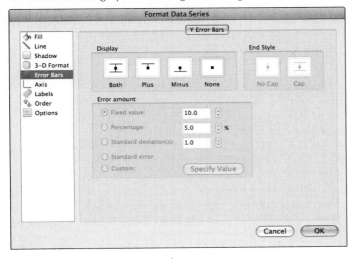

## Adding trend lines

One of the biggest attractions of using charts in Excel is their ability to show trends over time or categories. To further assist you in visually displaying such trends over the course of time, you can add trend lines to your chart. How does this feature work, you might ask? It works by using a mathematical model to accentuate patterns in the data and project future patterns. Trend lines are available only in unstacked area charts, bar charts, bubble charts, column charts, line charts, scatter charts, and stock charts. Because trend lines are helpful in making predictions regarding patterns in your charts, you might expect to find the feature lurking in a Format Data Series dialog box, but alas, it is not there. Instead, you must use the Chart menu to assign trend lines. Start by selecting the data series to which you want to apply a trend line. Next, choose Chart ➪ Add Trendline. This opens the Format Trendline dialog box.

Hauntingly similar to the Format Data Series dialog box, the Format Trendline dialog box offers four formatting categories: Line, Shadow, Type, and Options. We covered the Line and Shadow categories back in "Formatting individual chart elements," so we skip the coverage here. However, click the Type category to view the elusive trend line options. Figure 16.40 shows the Type category displayed in the Format Trendline dialog box.

Click the Trend/Regression type you want to apply. Depending on which type you select, additional parameters can be set. Excel adds a preview of the line in the chart and adds a description in the legend. Look at the descriptions for each type of trend line:

- **Linear:** If your chart already looks like a line, this type of trend line works well. It closely follows rising or falling data as a line.

- **Logarithmic:** If your chart data climbs and falls rapidly and then levels out, a logarithmic trend line works best. It exhibits a sharp curve at one end and gradually evens out.

- **Polynomial:** If the chart data has numerous highs and lows in a rhythmic manner, a polynomial trend line may be the answer for your chart. Polynomial trend lines have large curves or humps.

**FIGURE 16.40**

You can add a trend line to a data series using the Format Trendlines dialog box. This feature is accessible through the Chart menu.

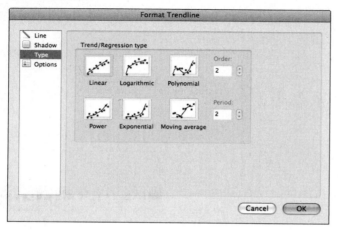

- **Power:** If your chart data shows steadily increasing or decreasing rates, power trend lines can easily show the acceleration with a smoothly curving upward line.

- **Exponential:** If the chart data changes at an ever-increasing or decreasing rate, an exponential line is better for showing a curving line.

- **Moving Average:** If your chart data shows cycles happening, a moving average trend line makes a good choice. It tries to smooth out fluctuations in the data.

After establishing a trend line, click the Options category to find settings for naming the trend line, forecasting it forward or backward, or adding an R-squared value (this statistical value calculates how accurate the trend line fits the data). After you finish setting any additional options, click OK to apply the trend line to your chart.

## Summary

In this chapter, you learned how to add, edit, and format charts. You learned about each type of chart available in Excel, how to insert a chart, and how to change the various aspects of a chart to improve the overall appearance of the data. We started out by exploring the chart types and finding out which ones were best suited for certain types of data. Next, you learned about the various elements that go into charts, such as the plot area, axes, and legend. You saw how easy it is to add charts using the new Elements Gallery. We went on to cover how to use the formatting tools available on the Formatting Palette to make your charts look good, as well accessing formatting settings for all the individual chart elements through the Format dialog boxes. Finally, you learned how to utilize some of the more advanced charting techniques in Excel, such as adding error bars and trend lines. As you can now see, charting your spreadsheet data has never been easier than it is in Office 2008.

# Chapter 17

# Using the Excel Database Tools

Today's Information Technology-driven offices have one thing in common: They all tend to have lots of different types of data that need to be processed. Whether it's bookkeeping, trend analysis, sales information, or basically anything, it seems that every bit of data is stored in a database for use and archival purposes.

Although Excel itself isn't really a database (at times it can almost pass for one), its variety of functions and features for working with tabular data makes it a natural complement to one. If you find yourself having to crunch numbers often, you'll find Excel's ability to pull data right from a database to be invaluable. Excel takes advantage of the power of Structured Query Language (SQL), the standard language of relational databases, to build queries that can encompass data spread over multiple relational database tables, join the data, and bring it into an Excel workbook for your use.

In this chapter, you learn how to configure Excel 2008 to use Open Database Connectivity (ODBC) to make a connection to a remote database. You also see how to use Microsoft Query to build the database request and retrieve data into a worksheet. Once there, you see how to make the best use of the data by using PivotTables, Goal Seek, and Scenarios to analyze it.

Finally, this chapter shows you some other Excel 2008 data analysis tools that can help make your number-crunching tasks faster and easier. You learn how to use Goal Seek to work backward to find data values and how to use the Scenario Manager to let Excel run various test cases into your formulas and summarize the results.

## Retrieving External Data

Databases come in all shapes and sizes. There are huge enterprise-class databases with many gigabytes of storage, two of the most popular being Oracle and Microsoft SQL Server. There are medium-sized open source databases such as MySQL and PostgresSQL that drive cost-conscious businesses and legions of Web applications. And there are smaller, desktop-class databases such as Microsoft Access and FileMaker Pro, which are used for smaller data storage and analysis tasks.

# The ODBC Connection

The Mac is usually praised as a system that is easy to use and understand, but unfortunately that doesn't always extend to the sometimes arcane science of ODBC. With several versions of OS X available just in the past few years, and with both PowerPC and Intel CPU native application support needed, not to mention the popularity of numerous database products, companies that create ODBC drivers have a hard time keeping up.

The major databases such as SQL Server and Oracle don't offer ODBC drivers for OS X, so people must turn to a third-party driver to get connected to those databases. Some open source databases such as MySQL do offer Mac ODBC drivers, but getting these running can sometimes require you to become more of a guru than you might like.

Fortunately, two major third-party vendors offer ODBC drivers for a variety of database platforms, and both offer good products for a small fee. They offer ease of installation and configuration, and you can turn to them for help with any issues that you may encounter. The two companies are OpenLink Software (`www.open-linksw.com`) and Actual Technologies (`www.actualtechnologies.com`). Both offer ODBC drivers that connect to SQL Server, Oracle, MySQL, and more. They even provide trial versions of their products so you can see which you like best.

No matter the size, and how differently they are designed, most databases have some things in common. For example, some standards have evolved over the years for database connectivity. Many databases offer a "native" interface that allows clients to gain efficiency by connecting to them directly, but the disadvantage of this is that each application must know how to make the native connection. This puts the burden on database makers and application developers to create drivers so the products can talk to one another.

To solve this, a standard for database connectivity was created to provide a middle ground. Open Database Connectivity (ODBC) was designed by the SQL Access Group in 1992 to give database makers a standard interface to their products that any application can use. From the application point of view, adding ODBC support means they can automatically take advantage of any database that provides such an interface.

## Connecting to your database

Excel 2008 can use its ODBC connectivity to retrieve data from any number of databases, so long as the database provider (or a third-party) provides an ODBC driver that works with the Macintosh's operating system. Fortunately, drivers for all of the most popular databases are available, and in many cases you have more than one option.

While drivers can come from a variety of vendors and third-party providers, after they are installed, you can create Data Source Name (DSN) entries to control access to a particular database in the ODBC Administrator utility, which can be found in your Applications/Utilities folder. Although a thorough explanation of this utility is outside the scope of this book, any driver that you purchase or download should have instructions for installing and configuring connections and likely makes use of this or a similar ODBC administration tool. Figure 17.1 shows the ODBC Administrator at work.

The two main types of DSNs that you can use with Excel are System and User. A User DSN can be used only by the user who sets it, which in most cases will be you. A System DSN, on the other hand, can be used by any user account that is set up on your computer. If you are the only user on your computer, the distinction may not seem important, but if others use your system and also need to be able to access the database, then you are better off creating a System DSN unless there is a specific reason to deny other users access. The following steps are typical in defining a database connection, in this case using the OpenLink driver to talk to a MySQL database:

## FIGURE 17.1

You can use the ODBC Administrator to configure Data Source Names that point to your database.

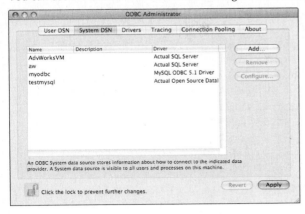

1. Locate and install an ODBC driver for your database.
2. Open the ODBC Administrator (in Applications/Utilities).
3. If necessary, unlock it by clicking the lock icon in the lower-left corner and entering your administrative password.
4. Click the System DSN tab.
5. Click Add.
6. Choose the appropriate ODBC driver from the provided list, shown in Figure 17.2.

## FIGURE 17.2

Choose an ODBC driver that is appropriate for the type of database to which you are connecting.

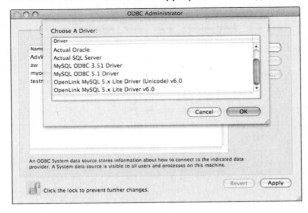

7. **Enter the connection information for your database.** Every database type and driver has its own setup wizard, but most ask you to enter a DSN name, connection information including a hostname or IP address, ports, and a username. Figure 17.3 shows a typical one.

You also may be asked to provide a password, but this is typically used only in the setup to obtain information from the database and then to test the connection.

Some drivers have many connection options, some are simpler. In general, you should leave settings at the default values unless you know what you are doing or have specific instructions from a database administrator.

8. **Most driver setup wizards have a way of testing the connection at the end of the process, so verify that everything works before clicking the Finish button.**

### FIGURE 17.3

Most DSN configurations involve entering information in a setup wizard.

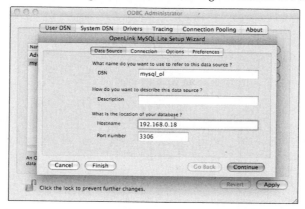

> **NOTE** File DSNs also are supported by some ODBC administration tools, most notably the iODBC Data Source Administrator provided with OpenLink and some other drivers. As the name implies, file DSNs store connection information for a database in a text file that the application can then read.

## Importing data using ODBC

Excel is capable of importing data from a variety of sources, including database and various file formats. In Chapter 13, you learned about the basics of importing some types of external data, including from text files, CSV files, and FileMaker Pro databases. Now you learn how to import directly from an ODBC connected database into Excel. After you have a database driver installed and a DSN configured, you're ready to begin.

To retrieve data from a relational database, you have to first be able to define the tables and query parameters to retrieve it. Relational databases consist of one or more tables, each of which may have data that relates to another table. For example, you could have a table containing Orders, with fields (called *columns* in database parlance) that contain an order date, product number, quantity, and other relevant information, including a customer ID. The customer ID would relate to another table called Customers, which could contain information such as addresses and phone numbers. The Structured Query Language (SQL) was designed to be able to work with relational data, and it has numerous options for building queries.

Explaining how to make queries using SQL syntax is beyond the scope of this book; in fact, entire books have been written just on this subject. Fortunately, you don't need to learn SQL in order to import data into Excel, because Microsoft thoughtfully included a tool called Microsoft Query, which lets you easily create queries and test them visually. (If you happen to know SQL, you are, of course, free to use it.)

## Opening the connection

Learning how to work with Microsoft Query is the key to mastering Excel's data importing power. But first, you need to tell it which data source you want to use. Follow these steps to get started:

1. **In Excel, choose Data ⇨ Get External Data ⇨ New Database Query.**

   This launches the iODBC Data Source Chooser dialog box, which is a bit like a stripped-down version of the ODBC Administrator tool you used to create the data source. In fact, if you somehow skipped that step, you can do it from here, as well. (Add, Remove, Configure, and Test buttons are available here that you can use to manage your DSNs.) Figure 17.4 shows the Data Source Chooser dialog box.

2. **Click the tab of the DSN type you created: User, System, or File.**

3. **Click the data source name.**

4. **Click OK.**

   At this point, you likely will be asked for authentication information in the form of a username and password to access your database. Figure 17.5 shows an example, but yours may look different depending on the ODBC driver you are using. See the documentation that came with your ODBC driver if you have questions about what to enter here.

5. **Enter your username and password, and click OK (or Connect, depending on your driver).**

If all went well, you should now be in Microsoft Query with a floating palette of tables, similar to that shown in Figure 17.6. (Of course, the tables in your database will be different!)

---

**FIGURE 17.4**

The first step in creating a query is to choose your data source.

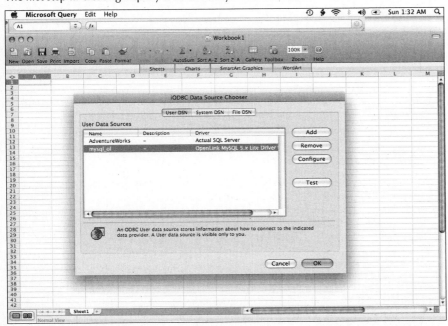

**FIGURE 17.5**

In most cases, you are prompted to provide authentication information.

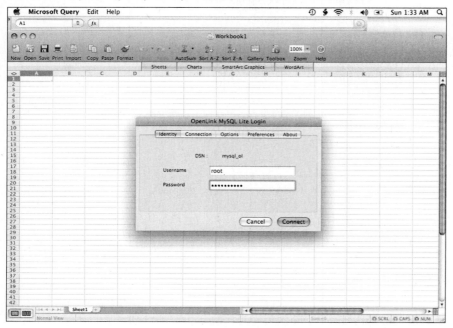

At the top of the Microsoft Query menu, you see four buttons, which are the main controls for working with queries:

- **Query View:** Use this view when you want to construct a query visually, using boxes and lines to show tables and references.

- **SQL View:** Use this button to toggle the view to SQL view, where you can see the SQL statement that your query is using. You can edit the SQL statement directly if you prefer.

- **Show Tables:** This can be used to open the Tables Palette again if you happen to close it.

- **Test!:** Run the query as it currently exists. If successful, you see the data you import displayed in the lower portion of the screen.

Below the buttons, a portion of the screen is reserved for displaying either the selected tables or the SQL code depending on the view you select. Under that are controls for working with data that you retrieve (the Fields pane). The lower portion of the screen is reserved to show data retrieved using the Test! button (the Data pane).

Now, let's begin building a query.

**NOTE** For this chapter, you will see data presented from the 'Sakila' sample database created for MySQL. This sample represents a video rental store customer and inventory database. **More information about the Sakila database can be found at:** dev.mysql.com/doc/sakila/en/ sakila.html.

**FIGURE 17.6**

Use Microsoft Query to begin building a database query.

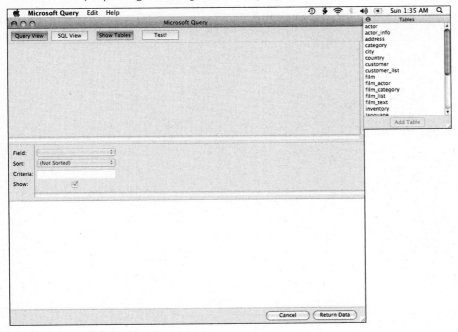

## Creating the query

The easiest way to create a query is to use the Query view. Click that button, and open the Tables Palette if it's closed. Then follow these steps:

1. **Click a table name in the Tables Palette to select it.**
2. **Click Add Table.**

   A box with the fields (or columns) in the table is displayed in the Tables pane. You can drag this box around within the window if you like.
3. **Select fields to retrieve in the query by double-clicking them.**

   Fields appear in the Fields pane as you double-click them.

   The first field listed in every table is the * wildcard. This can be used to include all fields in the query.
4. **Repeat Steps 1 through 3 for any additional tables or fields you want to include in the query.**
5. **Click Test! to run your transaction.** The data matching your query should be retrieved and displayed in the Data pane, similar to that shown in Figure 17.7.

**FIGURE 17.7**

Construct a query by choosing tables and fields, and use the Test! button to retrieve the data.

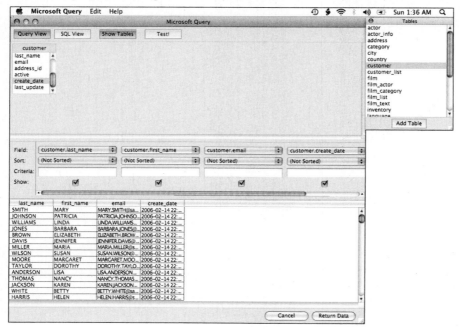

### Removing tables and fields

If after adding tables and fields to a query you decide you don't want them included any more, it's easy to remove them.

To remove a field from the Fields pane, right-click or Control+click in the field box, outside of any of the controls. Then choose Delete.

Tables can be removed from the Tables pane in the same way. Right-click or Control+click on a table, and then choose Delete.

### Refining queries

Although it's possible that you want to retrieve all the data in the tables that you've chosen, it is more likely that you'd like to refine the query and restrict it to only retrieving the values that you like. You can accomplish this in two ways. One is by specifying criteria for chosen fields to limit the values that can be retrieved. The other way is to create joins between tables.

#### Specifying criteria

In the Fields pane, you may have noticed the Criteria field. This field can be used to limit the records returned by a query by specifying criteria that a particular field must match. Every potential record retrieved is evaluated against all the criteria. If it doesn't match any of them, the record is excluded from the results.

Figure 17.8 shows a sampling of data from the Sakila database's film_list view, which is used as an example for the various criteria options.

**FIGURE 17.8**

Retrieved results can be limited by specifying criteria for key fields.

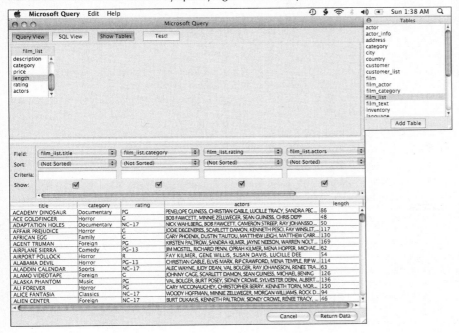

The following are some examples of criteria you can specify to restrict data from the film_list table:

- You can use the LIKE operator to restrict data to that which matches a partial string. For example, you can restrict the film_list query to only include movies that being with the letter A by using **LIKE 'A%'**. Criteria text must be enclosed in single quotes. The % character is a wildcard character meaning that the results can include titles that start with 'A' followed by any other text. Likewise, **LIKE '%KIRSTEN PALTROW%'** applied to the actors field would limit the query to movies with that actress in the cast.

- You can use mathematical operators such as equals (=), greater than (>), greater than or equal (>=), less than (<), less than or equal (<=), and does not equal (<>). These operators can be used on numeric, date, and text fields. **> 120** applied to the length field would retrieve movies longer than two hours. Likewise, you can retrieve movies in the Horror category by applying **= 'Horror'** to that field.

- You can use the IN operator to match a field to values in a list. For example, you can limit results to PG-13 rated movies or higher using this criteria applied to the rating field: **IN ('PG-13', 'R', 'NC-17')**.

- You can find records that are missing data. Use the IS NULL operator in the criteria box for a field to retrieve records with null values in the field.

- You can use the NOT operator in front of most of these criteria to negate the results. For example, NOT LIKE '%KIRSTEN PALTROW%' applied to the actors field returns all movies that don't include her in the cast.

### Choosing a sort order

If you add individual fields rather than the * wildcard, you can specify a sort order for your fields. Sort orders are applied from left to right. Options include no sorting (in which case data is retrieved in the order that it exists in the database table), Ascending (from lowest to highest, numerically or alphabetically), or Descending.

### Joining tables

If your query includes data from multiple tables, you can refine the query in another way: You can create *joins* between tables. Joins are key to the power of a relational database, because they are used to define the relationship between one table and another. You can create several types of joins, and the type you choose is important to ensure that your query returns the correct results. To create a join, do the following:

1. **Click a field in a table in the Tables pane.**
2. **Drag the field name to another table.**

   The Join dialog box appears, as shown in Figure 17.9.

3. **If the fields you are joining have the same name, Excel automatically adds it to the Second Field box; if not, choose a field to use for the join comparison from the list.**
4. **Choose a join operator.** In most cases, you can leave this as the default value of Equals (=), but you can use other operators to join based on unequal relationships between the fields as well.

---

**FIGURE 17.9**

Use the Join dialog box to define a relationship between fields in different tables.

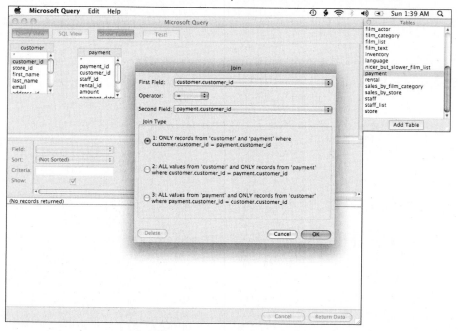

5. **Choose the join type.** The default choice, item 1, specifies an inner join where both tables must have matching fields. Options 2 and 3 are used to specify outer joins. Inner and outer joins are explained in more detail below.

6. **Click OK.** The Tables pane now shows a line between the joined fields indicating the relationship, as shown in Figure 17.10.

You can edit or delete a join by right-clicking (or Control+clicking) the join line in the query view. The two types of joins are described here:

- **Inner join:** The default type of join, an inner join selects records where the joined fields in both tables match. If one record doesn't have a matching record in the other table based on this field, neither record is included in the results. Figure 17.10 shows an inner join between the inventory. film_id field and the film_list.FID field. A result set using an inner join can include multiple entries for each record, because you can have many records in each table matching.

- **Outer join:** An outer join selects all the records from one table regardless and includes records from the second table when a match exists. When a record from the table that's contributing all its records can't be matched with a record from the other table, the record still appears in the result set. Empty cells are used in place of data when no matching record is found in the other table.

**FIGURE 17.10**

Joins are indicated in Query view by lines drawn between the fields.

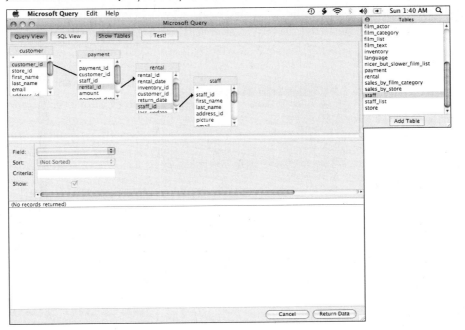

Although most of the commands for refreshing data can be done with the Excel main menu, you might find it more convenient to work with the External Data toolbar, shown in Figure 17.13. This toolbar is activated automatically when you import data, but you also can activate it manually by choosing View ➪ Toolbars and checking the External Data item.

## Refreshing data

After you've defined the query and imported data into a worksheet, it's simple to keep it up to date; just refresh the data. The refresh command causes the query to be executed again without having to go back through Microsoft Query. Instead, it's all done behind the scenes. You have these two options for refreshing the data:

- **Refresh Data:** This command executes a query for the currently selected data range.

- **Refresh All:** If your workbook has multiple queries defined, this command causes them all to be refreshed. This button also is useful if you have only one query, because it's active no matter what you have selected.

## Editing a query

It's not a problem to make a change to a query that you've saved. Simply click the Edit Query button on the External Data toolbar, or choose Data ➪ Get External Data ➪ Edit Query to return to the Microsoft Query application. Make your changes, and click the Return Data button to refresh the data on your worksheet.

---

**FIGURE 17.13**

The External Data toolbar puts database commands at your fingertips.

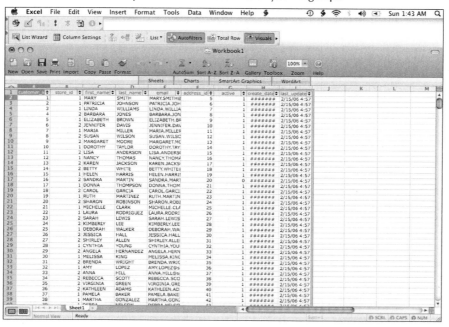

You can change data range properties, too. Click the Data Range Properties button on the External Data toolbar, or choose Data ⇨ Get External Data ⇨ Data Range Properties to reopen the External Data Range Properties dialog box described earlier in the chapter.

## Using parameters

You may think it's silly to have to edit a saved query if you want to search for a particular name or other field value. Well, you're right, and Excel provides a way to not have to do this by allowing you to define parameters for queries. After you've defined parameters, you can edit your queries to prompt for the values you want to search for.

Remember when I said you didn't need to know SQL syntax to build queries? Well, parameters are an exception to this. Although Excel itself is fully versed in parameters, the Mac version of Microsoft Query lags behind its Windows cousin in this regard. You can define query parameters in Microsoft Query, but it's not versed in the syntax for parameters while using the Query View, so you are forced to enter parameters using the SQL View.

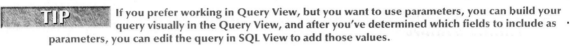 **TIP** If you prefer working in Query View, but you want to use parameters, you can build your query visually in the Query View, and after you've determined which fields to include as parameters, you can edit the query in SQL View to add those values.

### Defining parameters

The following steps illustrate how to add parameters to a database query:

1. **Click in the data range that you want to modify.**

 2. **Edit the query by choosing Edit Query on the toolbar or by choosing Data ⇨ Get External Data ⇨ Edit Query.**

3. **Click the SQL View button to switch to that view.**

4. **Add to the query's WHERE clause if it has one (you can create one if it doesn't have one).** Instead of a value to compare a field to, use a question mark (?). The following example shows a query from the customer table. We added a WHERE clause that uses the LIKE operator for string comparisons:

   `SELECT customer.* FROM customer WHERE customer.last_name LIKE ?`

   Figure 17.14 shows SQL View with the sample query.

5. **Click Return Data to return to Excel.** You can't switch back to Query View after making this change, because Microsoft Query doesn't recognize the parameter syntax and gives you an error. Likewise, you can't run a test because Microsoft Query doesn't know how to prompt you for parameters.

**FIGURE 17.14**

Parameter fields must be specified using SQL View.

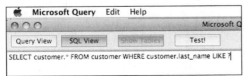

### Setting parameter options

After you have parameters defined for the query, Excel recognizes this and allows you to set parameter options such as a prompt, default value, or cell to use for the source. You should notice that the Query Parameter button on the toolbar and Parameters menu item is made active as well. Follow these steps:

1. **Click in the data range to select it.**

2. **Click the Query Parameter button on the toolbar, or choose Data ⇨ Get External Data ⇨ Parameters.** This open the Parameters dialog box, shown in Figure 17.15.

**FIGURE 17.15**

Choose settings for defined parameters.

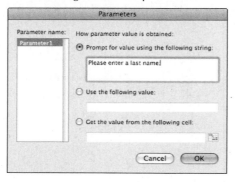

3. **Choose one of the parameter options:**
    - **Prompt for value:** You can enter text that will be used as a prompt so you don't have to remember which parameter is which.
    - **Use the following value:** You can predefine a value to pass to the query. Use this setting if you don't expect to change a value often, but still want the options.
    - **Get the value from a cell:** This option lets you use a cell reference as the input to a parameter. This can be useful if you want to use the results of a formula as the parameter value.

4. **Click OK.**

5. **Refresh the data by pressing the Refresh Data button or by choosing Data ⇨ Refresh Data.**

6. **You should now be prompted for a parameter.** For our example, we entered J%, as shown in Figure 17.16.

**FIGURE 17.16**

When you refresh data, you have the opportunity to enter a parameter value to pass to the query.

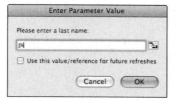

If all goes correctly, your list is refreshed with the data that matches the query. Figure 17.17 shows the results of our sample query. Now, every time you run the query, it plugs in the value of the parameter—from the cell, from the value you entered, or from a prompt.

# Analyzing Data with PivotTables

Now that you've successfully imported data into a worksheet, it's time to remember why you wanted to do this in the first place: You want to take advantage of the power of Excel to work its number-crunching magic on it. One of the best ways this can be accomplished is through the use of PivotTables. A PivotTable is a special type of report that can help you analyze a set of data with contiguous values by letting you arrange it in a variety of ways. This section explains how you can build a PivotTable and illustrates with some examples. Figure 17.18 shows the data that we use for the examples.

**FIGURE 17.17**

The query is executed with the parameter you entered as one of the search criteria.

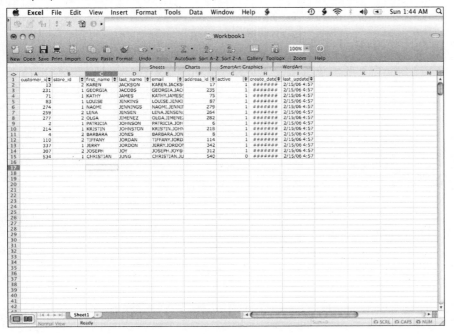

**FIGURE 17.18**

Here is the data that we have returned from a query to use as the basis for the PivotTable report. It includes customer, payment date, amount, movie title, and store manager information.

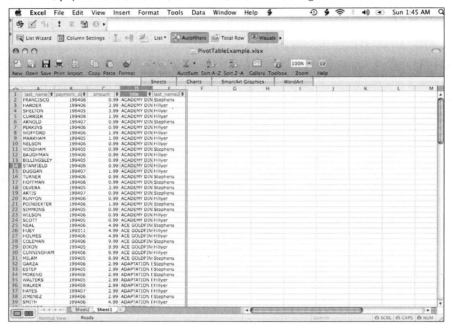

## Creating PivotTables

It's easy to build a PivotTable using the PivotTable Wizard. Perhaps the easiest way is to just get started. Suppose you want to create a table from a data range that you have imported into a worksheet. Follow these steps:

1. **Select a cell in the data range that you want to use as the source of data for the PivotTable.**

2. **Choose Data ⇨ PivotTable Report.**

   The PivotTable Wizard is launched, as shown in Figure 17.19.

3. **In Step 1, select the first option for a data source: Microsoft Excel list or database.**

   You also can retrieve data directly from an external data source using Microsoft Query or choose multiple ranges to consolidate for the report. You can even use another PivotTable as a data source.

4. **Click Next.**

5. **In Step 2 of the Wizard, shown in Figure 17.20, verify that Excel chose the correct data range that encompasses your selected cell.** Make adjustments if necessary.

6. **Click Next.**

7. **In Step 3, shown in Figure 17.21, you can choose to place the table in a new worksheet or an existing sheet.** For this example, choose an existing sheet.

8. **You can click the Options button to open the PivotTable Options dialog box, shown in Figure 17.22.** In this dialog box, you can set various formatting and data options for the PivotTable.

**FIGURE 17.19**

The PivotTable Wizard makes it easy to create a PivotTable from your data.

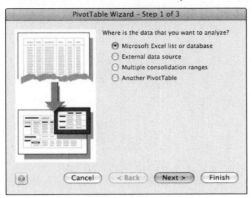

**FIGURE 17.20**

Verify the range to use for the table.

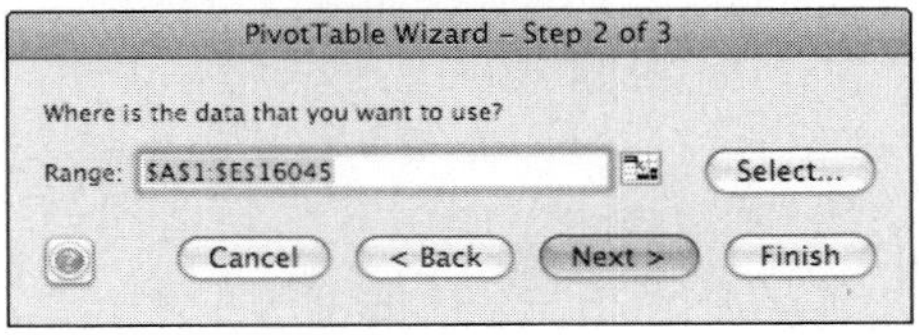

**FIGURE 17.21**

Choose which worksheet you want to use for the PivotTable.

9. **You can click the Layout button to choose the cells to use for a preliminary layout.** This layout can be changed later as you work with the table.

10. **Click Finish to create the table.** Figure 17.23 shows the blank PivotTable ready to have fields assigned to it.

**FIGURE 17.22**

Choose formatting and data options for the table, or accept the defaults.

**FIGURE 17.23**

An empty PivotTable created by the Wizard is ready to receive data. The PivotTable toolbar has been opened to assist in adding data.

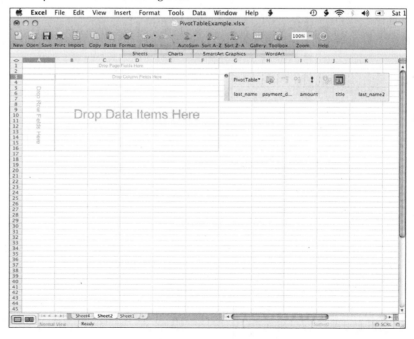

## Analyzing PivotTable data

In essence, a PivotTable is a multi-dimensional report that can be used to analyze multi-column data in various ways. To do that, you need to assign fields from the source data to the row, column, and data portions of the table, and let Excel do all the work to calculate totals based on the data.

When displaying a PivotTable, you first need to know which field you are ultimately interested in. In the case of our sample data, we want to get a sum of the payment totals for each movie title, so we drag the amount field to the data section. Because we want to tabulate payments per title, we can drag the title field to the rows section. Finally, we can drag the payment_date field to the columns section. By default, Excel automatically calculates a grand total for each title by summing the values for each month. It also calculates a grand total for each payment month, shown at the bottom of each column. This is shown in Figure 17.24.

### FIGURE 17.24

By dragging and dropping different fields to the rows and columns, you can create PivotTable reports that show many different details from the same data. Here, we are generating a grand total for rental payments on each title.

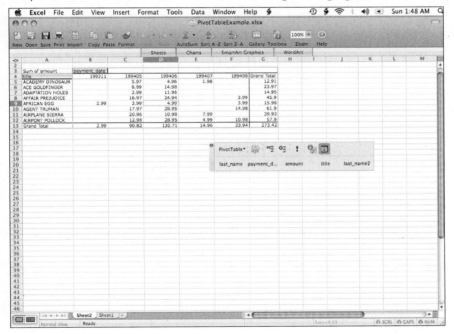

Now, suppose we want to look at it differently and see how much each customer may have spent. We can replace the field used for the PivotTable rows with the last_name field, which is the last name of the customer. Figure 17.25 shows the new PivotTable.

**FIGURE 17.25**

By changing the field used for the PivotTable rows, we can generate a completely different table using the same data values.

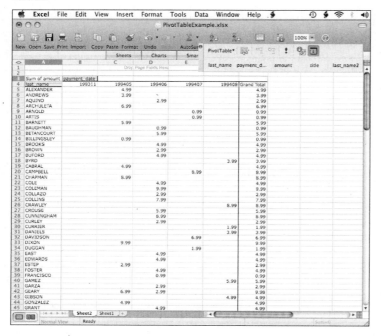

Just to make it clear, let's try one more example. We'll keep the title in the rows spot and add last_name2, which is the name of the store manager. As Figure 17.26 shows, we can now see at a glance how much was spent on each title for each manager.

As you can see, PivotTable reports offer lots of options when it comes to viewing data.

**FIGURE 17.26**

In this example, we can see a PivotTable report showing payments per manager per title, along with grand totals.

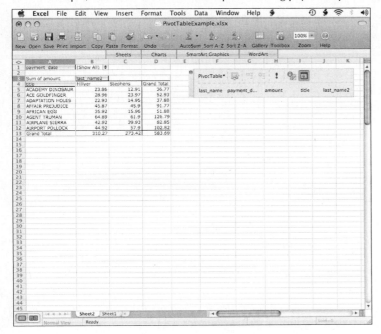

## Using advanced PivotTable settings

So far you've seen much of what PivotTables can do, but we've barely scratched the surface. If you have looked closely, you have seen another section of the PivotTable report labeled "Drop Page Fields Here." This can be used to add yet another dimension to the PivotTable Report. If you drag one of your fields to this portion, you can filter your report to show items matching only a single value of that field. Figure 17.27 shows title versus payment date, but only for one manager.

 You can do a number of things to customize your reports using the PivotTable toolbar. First, you can reactivate the PivotTable Wizard by clicking the Wizard button.

 You can use the Field Settings button to set various parameters for the fields. Simply select a cell containing a value from the field you want to modify, and click the button. This activates the Field Settings dialog box, shown in Figure 17.28.

## FIGURE 17.27

Using the Page field area, we can filter the data by a single value of that field. In this case, the table now shows sales for a single manager, Stephens.

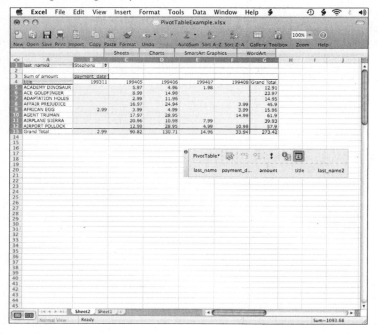

## FIGURE 17.28

Use the Field Settings dialog box to configure advanced settings for field display.

You can change these items:

- **Name:** If you don't like the chosen name for a field, you can rename it to make your reports a little more readable. For example, we could change "last_name2" to "manager" to make it more clear what that field represents.

- **Subtotals:** If the field is created from a calculation, you can change the function used to create it. The standard Excel functions of Sum, Count, Average, Max, Min, Product, and Count Nums can be used.

- **Hide Items:** You can choose to hide certain fields, if you want to exclude them from the report.

- **Number:** You can change the number format for fields that contain number values.

- **Hide:** You can completely hide this field in the report.

- **Advanced:** This launches the PivotTable Field Advanced Options dialog box, shown in Figure 17.29. In the Advanced dialog box, you can set AutoSort, AutoShow, and Page field data retrieval options.

**FIGURE 17.29**

The PivotTable Field Advanced Options dialog box can be used to set sorting and AutoShow options.

# Using Goal Seek

When you're doing calculations, sometimes you know the result you are looking for, but you need to know what you have to do to achieve it. You can think of this as a reverse calculation, which can be handy for calculating loan terms and other financial calculations.

Excel's Goal Seek feature is designed to let you do that. Goal Seek works best when you already have data and formulas for your calculation in place and working correctly. Simply tell Excel which cell contains the formula, what the goal value is, and which cell contains the data value that you would like to change in order to meet your goal. Figure 17.30 contains an example of a worksheet with a formula in place to calculate an automobile loan.

## FIGURE 17.30

Goal Seek is used with a working formula in place. It can vary one of the input values until the formula's result matches a goal value.

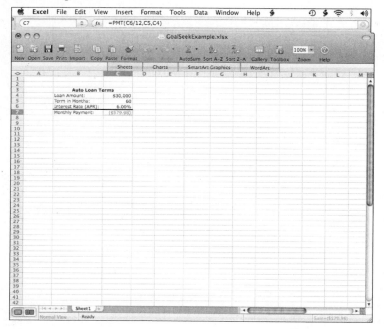

You can see in this example that cell C7 contains a formula for a loan payment:

    =FMT(C6/12, C5, C4)

C6 contains the annual percentage rate (FMT requires a percentage rate based on the payment cycle, so it needs to be divided by 12 to get the monthly interest rate). C5 contains the term of the loan in months, and C4 contains the original amount of the loan. In this example, the monthly payment for a $30,000 loan for 60 months at an APR of 6.00% results in a monthly payment of $579.98.

Suppose we can only afford to pay $500 a month. In this case, we'd either need to lower the interest rate, increase the term, or decrease the loan amount. Goal Seek allows us to test any of these options.

To use Goal Seek for this example, follow these steps:

1.  **Select the cell that contains the formula.** In this example, it's C7.
2.  **Choose Tools ➪ Goal Seek.** This opens the Goal Seek dialog box, shown in Figure 17.31. The Set cell should already reference the selected cell.

 **The Set cell always contains a formula or function.**

3.  **Enter a value in the To value box.** This is the desired result of the calculation.
4.  **Select one of the loan parameter cells as the Changing cell.** The changing cell must always refer to a cell containing a value, not a formula or function.

**FIGURE 17.31**

Use the Goal Seek dialog box to choose the Set cell, the target value, and the cell to change.

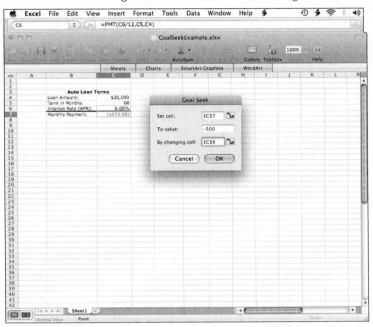

5. **Click OK.** Excel attempts to calculate a proper value for the selected variable in order to have the formula result be the target value.

While it is calculating a goal, Excel displays the Goal Seek Status dialog box, shown in Figure 17.32. The Goal Seek Status dialog box shows you the calculations in progress. While Goal Seek runs, it iteratively substitutes new values into the Changing cell until it has run the calculation 100 times or has found an answer that is within .001 of the target value. (The maximum iterations and maximum change settings can be altered in the Calculations pane of the Excel Preferences dialog box.) If Goal Seek is unable to come up with a solution, the Step and Pause buttons become active, and you can use them to perform further iterations to try to reach your goal.

# What Happened to Solver?

If you are an Excel for the Mac veteran, you may remember the Solver tool, which was a more heavy-duty, "what-if" analysis tool compared to Goal Seek. Unfortunately, the original version of Solver made heavy use of Visual Basic for Applications (VBA), and when support for VBA was removed in Office 2008, features like Solver went with it, to the great consternation of Mac Excel power users everywhere.

Fortunately, the company that created Solver in the first place, Frontline Systems, has taken on the task of rewriting Solver using AppleScript, and it's available today as a free download. Visit www.solver.com/mac to learn more about Solver for Excel 2008 as well as other Solver products.

**FIGURE 17.32**

After running Goal Seek, the target value has reached the desired value, and the interest rate has been changed in order to meet the goal.

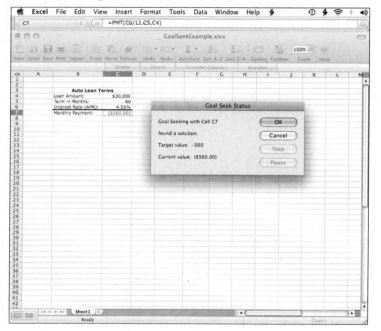

# Using Scenarios

Excel can be a great tool for analyzing "what if" types of questions. You can use formulas and functions to create complex calculations, and then plug different data values into referenced cells to see how it changes the results. One problem with this is that you need to keep track of all the changes you make, and you may even need to save multiple versions of your workbook with different values in order to be able to go back to a particular calculation.

Excel 2008 offers a tool called the Scenario Manager to help you deal with these sorts of questions. You can use this tool to make changes to data values in a number of cells and save them under a unique scenario name, which can later be used to revisit or demonstrate how changes in values affect the calculations.

## Adding scenarios

A scenario is simply the set of values that Excel can automatically plug into specified cells in your worksheets. This capability can be especially handy if you have a formula that calculates a result based on multiple input values. The following steps show how to use the Scenario Manager to create different scenarios:

1. **Open the worksheet that you would like to run scenarios against.**
2. **Choose Tools ⇨ Scenarios to open the Scenario Manager dialog box, shown in Figure 17.33.**

**FIGURE 17.33**

You can use the Scenario Manager dialog box to manage different "what-if" cases for a worksheet.

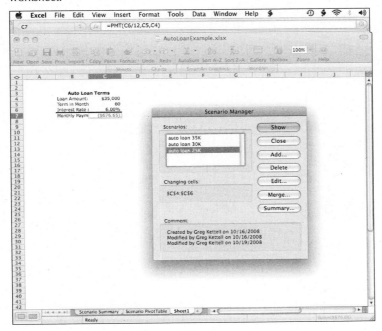

3. **Click Add to open the Add Scenario dialog box, which is shown in Figure 17.34.**

4. **Type a unique name for the scenario in the Scenario name box.** Ideally, the name should provide some indication as to what conditions the scenario is testing.

5. **Enter cell references for the cells to change in the Changing cells box.** You can collapse down to the worksheet and select cells or to a range of cells. Use the ⌘ key when selecting non-adjacent cells to add them.

6. **Choose protection options for the sheet.** These take effect if you enable protection on the worksheet. Protection is explained in Chapter 12.

   ■ **Prevent changes:** This prevent users from making changes to the scenario if the worksheet is protected.

   ■ **Hide:** This hides the scenario from view if the worksheet is protected.

7. **Click OK to open the Scenario Values dialog box, shown in Figure 17.35.**

8. **Enter the values that you want to use for this scenario for each selected cell.**

9. **If you want to create more scenarios, click Add and repeat Steps 4 through 8.**

10. **Click OK.** All scenarios that you've created are now visible in the Scenario Manager.

**FIGURE 17.34**

Define a scenario by specifying the cells that can be changed.

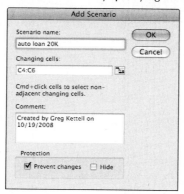

**FIGURE 17.35**

Enter new values for the changing cells in the Scenario Values dialog box.

After you've created scenarios, you can test them using the Scenario Manager. Simply select the scenario you want to run, and click the Show button. The worksheet is updated with the saved values and the results recalculated. If you reach a scenario that you'd like to stick with, you can click the Close button to return to the worksheet. Alternatively, you can build a summary of all the scenarios, as explained later in this chapter.

**TIP** To make your scenarios easier to understand at a glance, name your cells and use those names when entering changing cells. You can find more information about naming cells and ranges in Chapter 13.

## Merging scenarios

Suppose you have workbooks with similar layouts (say, monthly or yearly reports), and you want to run the same scenarios in each of them. The Scenario Manager offers a merge capability that allows you to use scenarios created in one workbook in another. Note that this works only if the input cells are exactly the same between the two worksheets; otherwise, you must edit the imported scenarios. Follow these steps to merge scenarios from another workbook:

1. Open the workbook containing the original scenarios and the new one to which you want to add them.
2. In the new workbook, choose Tools ➪ Scenarios to open the Scenario Manager.
3. Click Merge to open the Merge Scenarios dialog box, shown in Figure 17.36.

**FIGURE 17.36**

You can merge scenarios from one workbook to another if the changing cells will be the same.

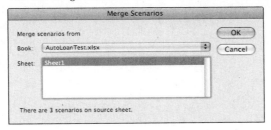

4. Choose the workbook to import scenarios from the Book list.
5. If the workbook has multiple sheets, choose the sheet with the scenarios.
6. Click OK. The scenarios are added to the worksheet.

## Generating a scenario summary

After you've created a few scenarios, it's nice to be able to see the effects of different data values all in one location. The Summary feature can be used to generate a new worksheet with either formatted data values or a PivotTable with the scenario values for further work. Follow these steps to create a scenario summary:

1. Open the Scenario Manager.
2. Click Summary.
3. Choose the option you want: Scenario Summary or Scenario PivotTable.
4. Enter the cell reference for the cell that contains the result of the calculation if it isn't correct.
5. Click OK. A new worksheet with either the Summary (shown in Figure 17.37) or PivotTable is created in the workbook.

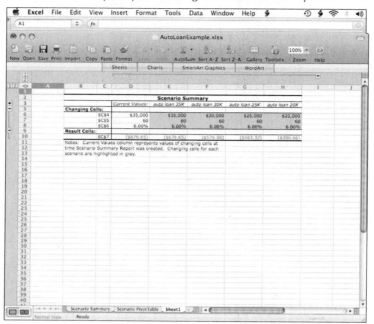

**FIGURE 17.37**

A Scenario Summary lets you see at a glance the result of all your scenarios.

## Flagging for follow-up

Sometimes when you are working with data, you may see something that catches your attention that you want to revisit at some point. You can flag your data for follow-up and get a notification to take a look. This can be helpful if you are working with data that you expect to be refreshed regularly. For example, you can set a follow-up notification for a time that is some point after the data has been modified so you'll be reminded to run a report. Another case where this could be useful is when you notice something amiss that you don't have time to deal with right away. Simply flag for follow-up, and you won't have to worry about it. To use this feature, choose Tools ➪ Flag for follow-up, and select a data and time in the Flag for Follow Up dialog box, shown in Figure 17.38.

**FIGURE 17.38**

You can use the Flag for follow-up feature to notify you to follow up on this document.

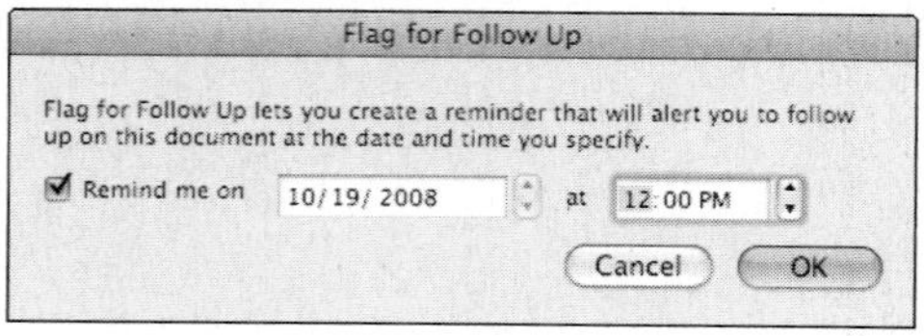

# Using Data Forms

The data form feature of Excel is intended to provide a quick and easy way to both manage and search for records in a list. If you have a row-column list with column headers, whether or not it uses the List Manager, do the following to use it in a data form:

1. **Click any field in the list.**
2. **Choose Data ⇨ Form.**

   The Data Form dialog box opens, as shown in Figure 17.39.

   The dialog box is given a title that is the same as the worksheet from which it's launched.

3. **To add new records to the list, click the New button or scroll to the end of the list, fill in the values in the fields, and click the New button again.**
4. **To search the list, click the Criteria button.** Enter a value to search for in one of the data fields, and click the Find Next or Find Prev buttons.

**FIGURE 17.39**

Data Forms can provide a simple interface for manually plugging in or searching for data values.

# Summary

Databases are ubiquitous in the corporate world, and being able to access and work efficiently with that data is a must. Excel's database connectivity capabilities using ODBC give it great flexibility in terms of the number and types of databases and data it can work with. All you need to get started is an ODBC driver for your particular database, and several third-party companies make drivers for the most popular database systems.

You learned how to create queries using the Microsoft Query tool and how to import that data into a worksheet. From there, it's a simple matter of utilizing the data, and one of the most powerful number-crunching tools Excel offers is the PivotTable report. This report can take data and present it in a myriad of ways, offering you tremendous flexibility in terms of finding out exactly what you want your data to tell you.

Finally, some additional Excel tools including Goal Seek and Scenarios were introduced, and you learned how to use them for "what-if" calculations. Finally, you saw yet another way to enter and search for data in your worksheets using the Data Form tool.

# Chapter 18

# Proofing, Printing, and Collaborating in Excel

Your presentation is in two days, and you've got PowerPoint slides ready to go. Now all you need to do is to be able to present the numbers that you've crunched in Excel, and you're all set. What you need to do is print your worksheets so the content is both clear and visually appealing. While the slides are what people see at the presentation, the Excel printouts are what they take back with them to study.

Or maybe you're a project manager tracking team progress over the course of a development cycle. You've been tracking everybody's assigned tasks and estimates in an Excel spreadsheet, and you need to print them so everyone can discuss them at the weekly meeting.

What these examples show is that no matter how productive we've become in the modern computer-enabled office, we still need to print stuff. Sometimes, it's just easier to sit with a printout and a highlighter, making notes.

This chapter explores Excel's print capabilities and shows you how to get the most from hard copies of your worksheets. However, if you're striving for electronic sharing, we show you how your team can work together using Excel's collaboration features, too.

## Proofreading Workbooks

At first glance, it might not seem that Excel workbooks would need extensive proofreading, but if you think about it, Excel workbooks contain text information almost as often as they have numbers. Field names, headings, instructions, and lists are just as deserving of proofreading as a newsletter that you are creating in Word. Fortunately, Microsoft agrees, so it provides many of the same proofreading capabilities in Excel that it does throughout the Office suite.

Although Excel doesn't include some of the more advanced features that Word offers in this area, such as automatically correcting spelling as you type or a grammar checker, it does include some other autocorrect options, a spell-checker that uses the same dictionary that other Office applications use, and the ability to access the dictionary and thesaurus references.

## Checking spelling

While Excel doesn't include Word's ability to autocorrect spelling mistakes as you type, it does include the same manual spell-checking capabilities. Before you print or share a workbook, run it through the spell-checker to clean up any problems. To do this, choose Tools ⇨ Spelling. The Spelling dialog box, shown in Figure 18.1, displays each error it encounters in your workbook. The spell-checker begins at currently selected cell, and continues to the end of the sheet before asking if you want to start over at the top.

When Excel encounters an error, it displays the word in the dialog box, with suggested spellings listed below the error. To change the word to one of the suggestions, click the correct spelling and press Change. To change all occurrences of that misspelling throughout your document, choose Change All. If it isn't an error at all, such as with technical terms, names, or other uncommon words, you can choose either Ignore (for that specific incidence) or Ignore All (to ignore that word throughout the workbook). If it's a word that you expect to use often, click Add to append it to the default custom dictionary.

If none of these options solves your problem, you can correct the spelling error directly in the dialog box. Finally, if you commonly make the same typo, click the AutoCorrect button to add the typo and correctly spelled word to the AutoCorrect list.

### FIGURE 18.1

The Spelling dialog box locates each error in the document.

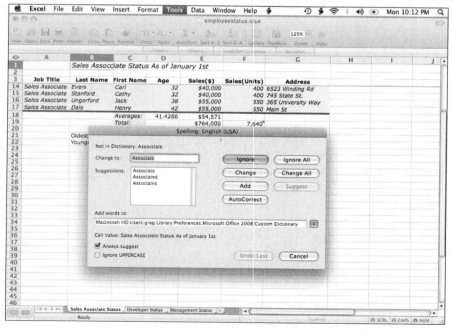

## Looking up words

A handy feature that Excel includes in its Toolbox is the ability to look up words in a variety of reference works, including a dictionary, a thesaurus, the Encarta online encyclopedia, or even on the Web. You can even do translations or look up foreign language words. Choose View ⟿ Reference Tools to activate the Toolbox on the Reference palette, shown in Figure 18.2. You can go directly to the dictionary (which is online, so it requires you to have an active Internet connection) by choosing Tools ⟿ Dictionary. You can reach the Thesaurus directly by choosing Tools ⟿ Thesaurus.

## Enabling AutoCorrect

In Chapter 6, you learned about using the AutoCorrect feature in Word. Well, Excel has AutoCorrect capabilities of its own, even if they are a bit more limited. Choose Excel ⟿ Preferences, and click the AutoCorrect tab to open the AutoCorrect Preferences panel, shown in Figure 18.3.

---

**FIGURE 18.2**

Use the Reference Tools Palette to look up words in various reference works.

**FIGURE 18.3**

Enable AutoCorrect options in the Excel Preferences to help correct errors as they are typed.

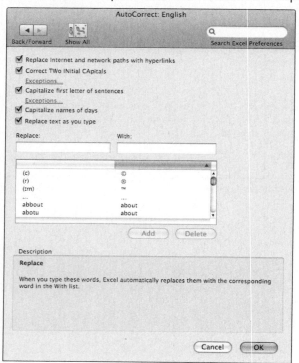

With AutoCorrect, you can have Excel automatically catch some common mistakes as you are typing, such as extra or missed capitalization and capitalization of the names of days of the week. It also provides a list of words and phrase that it automatically corrects as you type. This list includes some words with commonly transposed letters and misspellings, as well as some automatic translation of such things as copyright or trademark symbols. You can add or remove items from this list as you see fit or add them from the spell-checker.

# Printing Worksheets and Workbooks

Your workbook is completed, and you've proofread it and corrected spelling errors, so now it's time to print. You might want to print the entire workbook or just a single sheet or a portion of a sheet. Some options for formatting workbooks only apply when printing or in Page Layout mode, such as headings and footers. In this section, you learn how to define print areas, preview your workbooks before you print them, and configure the various print options for Excel.

## Defining a print area

Sometimes you don't want to print an entire workbook or worksheet, but only a portion of it. For example, you might have a section of a sheet that includes lots of data, and another section with formulas and formatting for display, for example. You can define a print area to include only the formatted part, but leave the raw data alone. To define a print area, select the range of cells that you want to include and choose File ⇨ Print Area ⇨ Set Print Area. A dashed line is displayed around the selected area to remind you that a print area is defined, as shown in Figure 18.4.

If you want to print multiple areas of the worksheet, you can choose File ⇨ Print Area ⇨ Add to Print Area. When you print, each print area is printed on a separate page. Choose File ⇨ Print Area ⇨ Clear Print Area to remove all defined print areas.

## Changing page setup

Before you print, you can configure quite a few options for your workbook to display in the best way possible. These options include page orientation, scaling, margins, headers and footers, and more. Choose File ⇨ Page Setup to open the Page Setup dialog box, shown in Figure 18.5.

---

**FIGURE 18.4**

When you define a print area, it is marked with a dashed line around it, and printing is restricted to print area content.

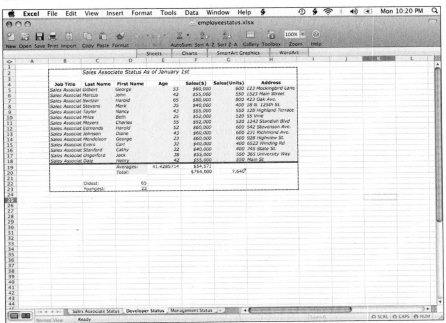

### Setting page orientation and scaling

Click the Page tab to set options that for printing the page as a whole. They include the following:

- **Orientation:** You can choose between Portrait and Landscape orientation. Worksheets often have a layout that is wider than it is tall, so the Landscape option can come in quite handy.

- **Scaling:** You can scale the worksheet to a percentage of its normal size, or you can have it automatically scaled to fit into a certain number of pages or even a single page. Scaling can be useful when your worksheets are just too large to fit on a single page. Rather than have a few columns print on another page, scale the whole printout to fit. Use the Print Preview feature to verify that your scaling settings are just the way you like them.

- **First page number:** You can leave this set to Auto to have Excel automatically determine a page number to start with when printing page numbers. You can specify 1 or some other number to customize the page numbering.

- **Print Quality:** Choose High or one of the specific print quality settings.

---

**FIGURE 18.5**

The Page tab of the Page Setup dialog box is used to configure scaling and orientation options.

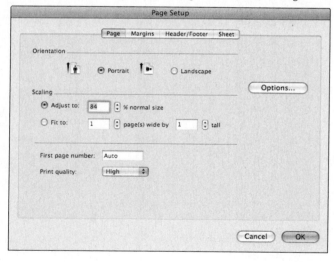

### Setting margins

Click the Margins tab, shown in Figure 18.6, to make changes to the margins of your printouts. You can set the width of the left, right, top, and bottom margins, as well as the margins for the header and footer. Units are inches, centimeters, or millimeters, depending on the units you have defined in the General panel of the Preferences dialog box.

You can configure centering options on this tab as well. Check the Horizontally or Vertically boxes to control centering. This is particularly useful when printing a small worksheet or data range.

**FIGURE 18.6**

The Margin tab is used to set page margins and centering options.

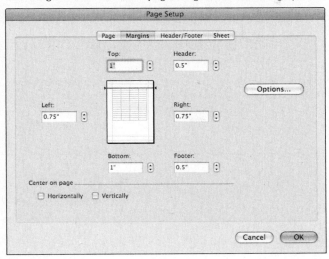

## Setting headers and footers

Click the Header/Footers tab, shown in Figure 18.7, to add or edit headers and footers. You can use headers and footers to customize the information to the top and bottom of every printed page, including page numbering, company information, or workbook filename. As their names imply, headers appear at the top of the page, while footers appear at the bottom.

**FIGURE 18.7**

The Header/Footer tab lets you customize the information printed at the top and bottom of each page.

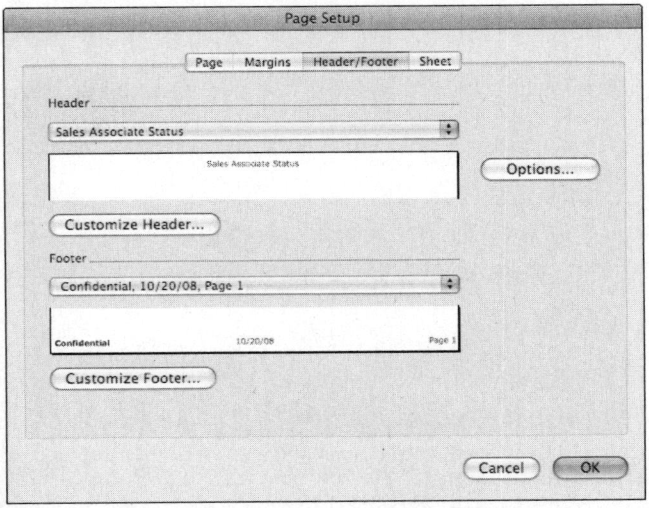

From this tab, you can manually enter header and footer details, such as the title of your workbook, and this information then appears at the top (or bottom) of every page. Headers and footers have three sections each: left, center, and right. Each section can be customized individually to give you exactly the information you want.

The easiest way to add a header or footer is to choose one from the list of headers and footers that Excel already knows about. These are a mix of previously used headers and footers, filename information, and some standard ones. Choose one from the pop-up menu for both the header and footer.

If one of the provided headers or footers isn't quite what you want, you can click the Customize Header (or Customize Footer) button to create your own. These buttons open the Header and Footer dialog boxes, shown in Figure 18.8. Note that these dialog boxes are identical in terms of features.

**FIGURE 18.8**

The Header dialog box can be used to create custom headers.

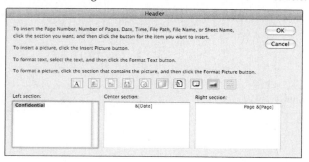

In the Header (or Footer) dialog box, you can enter information for the left, center, and right sections. Several buttons allow you to enter some pre-formed bits of text and auto-generated text:

- **Format Text:** This lets you customize the font and effects used for the text. You can set it for the entire box or just for a selected portion of the text.

- **Insert Page Number:** This is the most common header or footer content. You also can type the word "Page" into the header/footer, add a space, and insert the page number.

- **Insert Number of Pages:** This field tallies the number of pages in the document and prints that total in the header or footer. You can use this to format a "Page X of Y" type header. To do this, type "Page" and add a space, click the Insert Page Number button, type "of" and a space, and then click the Insert Number of Pages button.

- **Insert Date:** This inserts a date field into the header or footer. This field is automatically updated every time you modify the document, so when you print the document it reflects the date of printing.

- **Insert Time:** As with the date option, this field automatically updates with the current time when you modify the document.

- **Insert File Path:** This inserts the path to the workbook into the header or footer. If you organize your documents in hierarchical folders or on a network share, this can help you remember where the original workbook lives.

- **Insert File Name:** This inserts the filename of the current workbook.

- **Insert Sheet Name:** This can be used to insert the name of the worksheet. This can be useful if you use custom worksheet names, and why wouldn't you?

- **Insert Picture:** This can be used to insert a picture such a company logo. The picture can be in any of the supported Office picture file formats.

- **Format Picture:** This button becomes active when you've added a picture. It opens the Format Picture dialog box, where you can scale the picture and enter cropping settings. You can make some color settings including black and white, grayscale, watermark, or automatic. You also can adjust brightness and contrast.

To view the header and footer areas in your document, change to Page Layout view by choosing View ➪ Page Layout. This view shows your documents as they will be printed (with some exceptions, such as the fact that print area settings are ignored), including headers and footers. If you are already in Page Layout view, you can double-click directly in the header or footer areas to edit them directly in the document.

You can go directly to the Headers/Footers tab of the Page Setup dialog box by choosing View ➪ Header and Footer.

### Setting sheet options

The final tab of the Page Setup dialog box is the Sheet tab, shown in Figure 18.9. Click the Sheet tab to configure information relevant to printing worksheets, including titles, page order, and other formatting settings.

**FIGURE 18.9**

The Sheet tab of the Page Setup dialog box is used to control how worksheets are printed.

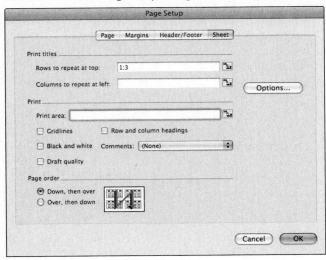

The following settings are available:

- **Print titles:** You can set aside some number of rows and columns to use as titles on each page. This option is useful if you are printing columns of data that have title and header information in the first rows or wide rows with headers on the left. Note that you can't enter a number here, but rather you can enter a row reference such as 1:3 to repeat the first three rows or A:A to use the leftmost column. You can choose a range of cells by clicking the collapse button and selecting them directly from the sheet.

- **Print area:** You can enter or select a range of cells to use as a print area. This has the same effect of defining a print area as the File ⇨ Print Area commands do.

- **Gridlines:** Checking this option causes gridlines to be included in the printout. They are not included by default.

- **Black and white:** Check this option to force the printout to be in black and white even on a color printer. With some printers, you can save color ink with this setting.

- **Draft quality:** Check this to force the printout to be in the lower-quality draft mode to speed up printing.

- **Row and column headings:** Check this box to have Excel's row and column identifiers added to printouts.

- **Comments:** Choose a setting for printing comments. Choices are None, at the end of the sheet, or as displayed on the sheet.

- **Page order:** Choose to print down, then over or Over, then down. These options control the order in which pages are printed when your workbooks are more than one sheet wide and more than one sheet long.

### Setting more page setup options

Each tab of the Page Setup dialog box has an Options button. Click this button to open another Page Setup dialog box similar to the one available in Word and shown in Figure 18.10. In this dialog box, you can set some additional page settings. You can choose paper size, a printer to format for, and orientation and scaling settings (which are identical to settings described earlier). You also can choose to save these settings as the default using the Settings selection.

**FIGURE 18.10**

Use the Options button to open additional page setup options.

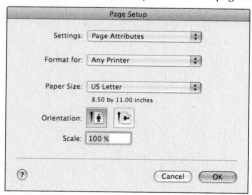

## Printing data

 The easiest way to print is to click the Print button from the Standard toolbar. This automatically prints one copy of the current sheet to the default printer. If this is what you want, then great! If not, you can use the Print dialog box to choose some additional options. Choose File ⇨ Print (or ⌘+P) to open the Print dialog box, shown in Figure 18.11. (If the Print dialog box isn't fully expanded, you can click the down arrow button next to the Printer selection box to expand it.) From here, you can set the number of copies and the collate option, and you can tell Excel to print only a particular range of pages or worksheets. You also can change printers if you have more than one configured.

**FIGURE 18.11**

The Print dialog box can be used to customize print output.

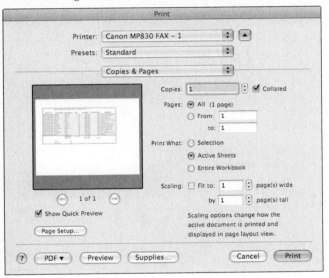

Many options are available in the Print dialog box, including these more common ones:

- **Printer:** If you have multiple printers on your system, you can select one here. You also can use this as a jumping off point to configure a new printer.

- **Presets:** You can save settings that you commonly use by choosing Save As from this pop-up menu and entering a name. When you wish to reuse those settings, you can choose it by name from this menu.

- **Print Options:** This pop-up menu lets you change the view of the Print dialog box to allow for advanced settings. The views available in this menu may vary depending on your printer and driver, but may include some of the following: Copies & Pages (the default), Layout, Color Matching, Paper Handling, Paper Feed, Cover Page, Scheduler, Quality & Media, Color Options, Special Effects, and Duplex Printing and Margin. That's lots of options and more than we have room to cover in this book, but information on these settings is available in the Excel Help file. The Summary view is the last option on the menu and allows you to review all of the settings.

- **Copies:** Choose the number of copies to print. Check the Collated box to ensure that an entire copy of the document prints before the next one is started. Uncheck this box to cause each copy of an individual page to be printed before the next page.

- **Pages:** Choose the pages to include in the printout—either All or a range. You can use the Quick Preview view to get an idea about what each page would include.

- **Print What:** You can choose to print the selected region of the active sheet, the entire active sheet, or the entire workbook.

- **Scaling:** You can choose a scaling option here to force the document to fit within a certain number of pages wide and tall.

- **Show Quick Preview:** Check this box to enable the small quick preview window. You can use the arrow keys to move from page to page.

- **Page Setup:** This opens the Page Setup dialog box.

- **Preview:** This lets you preview the document in the OS X Preview application.

- **PDF:** This menu includes options for saving the formatted document as a PDF or PostScript file, mailing it, or faxing it.

- **Supplies:** This launches a Web browser to navigate to a site where you can purchase printer supplies such as toner or ink cartridges.

- **Print:** This prints the document using the entered settings.

## Previewing your work

With Excel 2008, Microsoft decided to drop Excel's built-in preview functionality in favor of the OS X Preview application, shown in Figure 18.12. And no wonder: Preview gives you a great deal of flexibility in working with the formatted document. In Preview, you can choose individual pages from the sidebar on the right or use the scrollbar to scroll through your pages. You also can perform all the other functions that Preview can do—save the printout in PDF or as an image, delete individual pages that you don't want to include, and even mark up text and add annotations. You also can print directly from Preview application. To preview, click the Preview button from the Print dialog box.

### FIGURE 18.12

Excel uses the OS X Preview application to perform print preview duties.

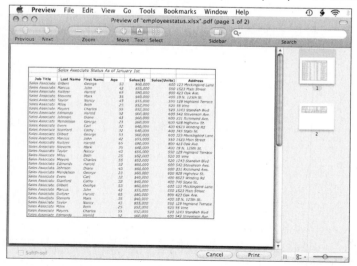

# Using Collaboration Features

When you work in a team environment, several people often need to work with the same documents. This can be true especially for workbooks, which are often used as continually updating "working documents." Excel sees lots of use because of its ability to make lists, track schedules and estimates, and work with oft-updated financial and other numeric data. Because Excel is included in every version of the Microsoft Office suite on both the Mac and Windows, a huge number of people can make use of it.

## Sharing workbooks

One of Excel's unique features in the Office suite is its ability to share workbooks. At first glance, this may not seem particularly useful; after all, any document can be "shared" if it sits on a network file server and multiple people have access to it. Excel, however, goes beyond this by including features that allow users to make changes to worksheets *at the same time*. That is to say, when you enable workbook sharing, Excel keeps track of who has the worksheet open, and who has saved it most recently. When you attempt to save over somebody else's changes, Excel merges their changes into your workbook first. Best of all, this feature is compatible with other versions of Excel such as Excel 2003 and Excel 2007 on Windows, so for once you don't have to forgo a feature if you are the lone Mac user in the office. Sound useful? Read on.

### Enabling worksheet sharing

You can use workbook sharing automatically with any workbook; you just have to enable it first. This couldn't be simpler though; simply choose Tools ⇨ Share Workbook to open the Share Workbook dialog box, shown in Figure 18.13.

**FIGURE 18.13**

The Share Workbook dialog box is used to control how and who can access a shared book.

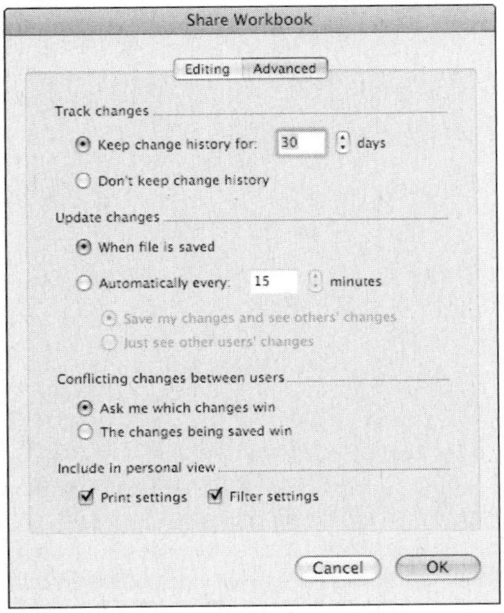

On the Editing tab, check the Allow changes by more than one user at the same time option to enable sharing. That's it! Your workbook can now be shared, after you click the OK button, that is.

On this tab, you also can see a list of people who have the worksheet open. You can also remove them from this list if necessary. This is sometimes necessary if the person who opened the workbook doesn't close it before disconnecting from a network share or powering off his computer. When this happens, Excel doesn't get a chance to remove them from the list before closing.

You can set some additional options on the Advanced tab, shown in Figure 18.14. These are as follows:

- **Track changes:** You can keep track of the change history for a period of time. The default is 30 days. The change history can be viewed either directly in the document or on a history worksheet. We cover more on this feature later.

- **Update changes:** Choose how to apply updates that other people may have saved. The default is to update them whenever the file is saved, but you can choose a time interval to perform updates, and choose whether this interval should update the saved document with your changes or just merge any saved changes into your open document.

- **Conflicting changes between users:** If another user changes information in a workbook—such as a cell data value or formula—and you also change the same value, you will have a conflict when the changes are updated. This setting controls how conflicts are handled. You can choose to have the user prompted to choose which change to use (highly recommended) or just have the most recent version of the changes take precedence.

- **Include in personal view:** These settings allow individual users' print and filter settings to be saved with the workbook. This can be useful if users make use of different printers.

**FIGURE 18.14**

The Advanced tab of the Share Workbook dialog box lets you control how changes are tracked and updated.

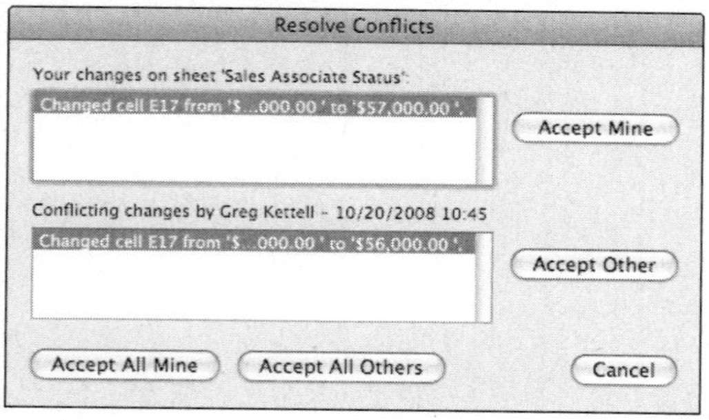

**Saving and resolving conflicts**

When two users are editing the same workbook frequently, conflicts can occur if they update the same data in the document at the same time. When this occurs, and you configured the Workbook Share settings to prompt the user to resolve conflicting changes, the Resolve Conflicts dialog box, shown in Figure 18.15, is launched. In this dialog box, you can see how each user changed the workbook, with your changes on the top and the saved changes on the bottom. You can select individual items and click the Accept Mine button to have your changes take effect or Accept Other to keep the saved version. If there are many changes, you can use the Accept All Mine or the Accept All Others buttons to choose either all your changes or all the saved changes. You can click Cancel here if you don't want to risk making any changes, in which case your changes are not saved.

**FIGURE 18.15**

When you save a shared workbook with conflicting changes, Excel asks you how to resolve it.

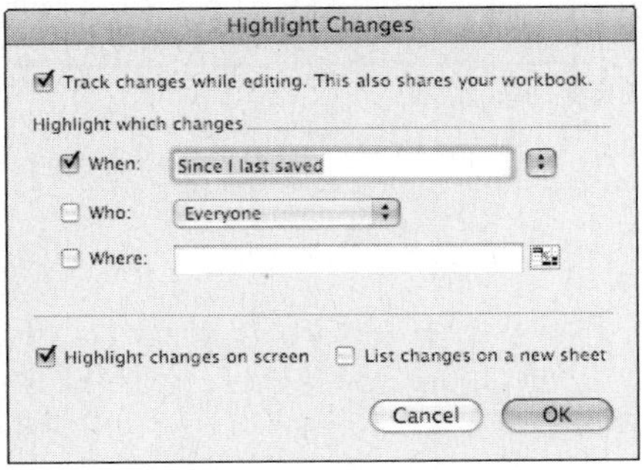

**NOTE** Excel is smart enough to handle conflicts with comments on its own. If you have added a comment in the same cell that the saved copy has, Excel automatically merges the comments together.

### Merging documents later

Although Excel can automatically merge changes when you save on top of a changed document, sometimes you don't have the luxury of working that way. Sometimes you or your teammates need to take work home or otherwise work remotely with files, and you may not be connected to the network. Sometimes you mail a copy of a document for review to many people, and you want the ability to merge all their changes into your original workbook. This is easy to do with the Merge feature. To manually merge changes from another workbook, simply save it to a location on your hard drive or on a network share, and choose Tools ➪ Merge Workbooks. As with the automatic merge, any differences are automatically incorporated into the open workbook, and any conflicts are handled according to the sharing settings.

## Tracking changes

When multiple users are making changes to a workbook, it can be nice to track the changes so you can decide to accept or reject them, or at least to see what those changes were. The Track Changes feature in Excel can be used in both ways.

### Highlighting changes

If you would like to see the changes that other users (and you) have made, choose Tools ➪ Track Changes ➪ Highlight Changes. The Highlight Changes dialog box is launched, as shown in Figure 18.16.

You have these options in this dialog box:

- **Track Changes while editing:** Check this option to enable change tracking while editing. This option is automatically enabled when workbook sharing is turned on, and vice versa.

- **Highlight which changes:** You can choose to highlight changes made during a specific time period, for specific users, or in a portion of the workbook. The options are When, Who, and Where. Uncheck all the options to track all changes in the history:

  - **When:** Highlight changes made over a time period. Sub-options are Since you last saved, All, Not yet reviewed, and Since Date.

  - **Who:** Highlight changes made by Everyone, Everyone but you, or just you.

■ **Where:** If you are interested only in changes made in a specific region of the worksheet, choose a region to put in this box.

**FIGURE 18.16**

Use the Highlight Changes dialog box to control how Excel indicates changes in progress.

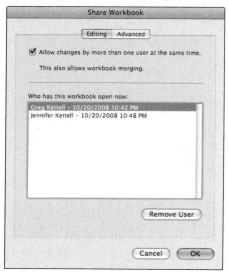

■ **Highlight changes on screen:** Check this option to have changes highlighted on the screen, shown in Figure 18.17. You can move the mouse pointer over a highlighted cell to see exactly what has changed in a pop-up window.

■ **List changes on a new sheet:** If checked, a special worksheet named History is created with a list of changes. This worksheet cannot be deleted or modified directly. The History worksheet is shown in Figure 18.18.

**FIGURE 18.17**

Highlighting changes on the screen lets you see at a glance when changes have been made.

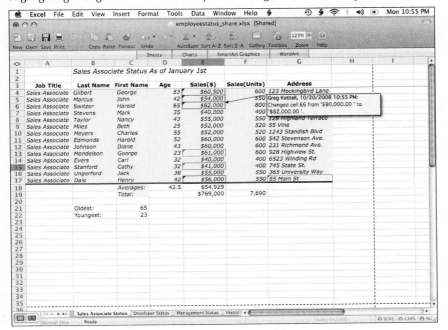

## Accepting and rejecting changes

When tracking is enabled, you have the opportunity to accept or reject changes if you like. Choose Tools ➪ Track Changes ➪ Accept or Reject Changes. Before the command is executed, Excel must save the workbook and merge any changes that are pending. After all changes are merged and any detected conflicts resolved, Excel opens the Select Changes to Accept or Reject dialog box, shown in Figure 18.19.

## FIGURE 18.18

If you prefer to get a listing of changes made, you can have them appear on a separate worksheet.

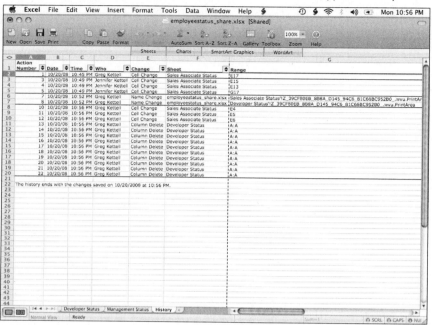

In this dialog box, you can make the same three choices (When, Who, and Where) that are described earlier for the Highlight Changes dialog box. The choices act a little differently, however:

■ **When:** Highlight changes made over a time period. You can accept or reject changes Not yet reviewed and Since Date. Use the Not yet reviewed option if you want to get a chance to accept or reject all changes and keep up with it. If your document has lots of changes and you want to decide only on the most recent ones, choose Since date and adjust the date as appropriate.

■ **Who:** Accept or reject changes made by Everyone, Everyone but you, or just you. If you are the main reviewer of other people's changes, you might find the Everyone but you option preferable.

■ **Where:** If you are only interested in changes made in a specific region of the worksheet, choose a region to put in this box.

Leave all boxes unchecked if you want the opportunity to accept or reject all changes. After you've selected which changes to review, click OK. Excel then iterates over all the changes in the workbook. If it finds changes that haven't been accepted or rejected yet, the Accept or Reject Changes dialog box, shown in Figure 18.20, is opened.

**FIGURE 18.19**

Use the Select Changes to Accept or Reject dialog box to decide which changes you want to approve.

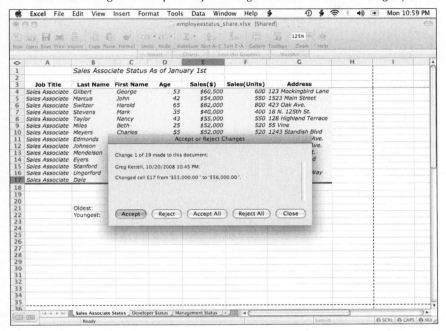

**FIGURE 18.20**

The Accept or Reject Changes dialog box iterates over unreviewed changes and gives you an opportunity to keep them or revert to the original setting.

In the Accept or Reject changes dialog box, you can choose to accept or reject an individual change, or accept or reject all remaining changes. When you accept them, the changes are applied to the worksheet. If you reject changes, they revert to the way they were before the change. You can stop at any time by clicking the Close button, and any remaining unreviewed changes are still available the next time you run the command.

If a particular item has been changed multiple times since the last time you reviewed changes, you have the opportunity to choose any of the change values, as shown in Figure 18.21. Click one of the changed values to select it, and click Accept. When you have finished reviewing all the changes, save the workbook to ensure that the next time you review it, you only need to see new changes.

---

**FIGURE 18.21**

If multiple changes have been made to an item, you have the opportunity to accept any of them.

## Using the Reviewing toolbar

Sometimes when you are reviewing a worksheet for somebody, all you really want to do is add comments to ask questions or point something out. Then, when you send it back to them or merge changes, they can use the Track Changes feature to scan through the comments and accept or reject them as they see fit. The Reviewing toolbar can make things easier for both the reviewer and the workbook author by letting you easily add comments, navigate from comment to comment, and show or hide comments. Choose View ➪ Toolbars, and check the Reviewing item to make it visible, as shown in Figure 18.22.

The Reviewing toolbar has the following options:

 ■ **Add Comment:** Use this button to add a comment to cell that doesn't have one. Enter the text for the new comment, and press Return.

 ■ **Edit Comment:** If a cell you have selected already has a comment associated with it, this button appears in the toolbar instead of the Add Comment button. You can add new text to a comment, but you can't change any existing comment text. You also can control how big the comment pop-up box is by resizing it using the mouse.

 ■ **Previous Comment:** Find the previous comment in the workbook from the current selection.

 ■ **Next Comment:** Find the next comment in the workbook from the current selection.

 ■ **Show Comment:** Use this button to make a comment in the current cell visible, even if the mouse pointer is not hovering over the cell.

 ■ **Show All Comments:** This button forces all comments to be visible onscreen. Click it again to hide them all.

 ■ **Delete Comment:** Use this button to remove the currently selected comment.

 ■ **Update File:** This button merges any saved changes from other users into the current document. This button does not cause changes made by you to be saved, however.

 ■ **Mail Recipient (As attachment):** To facilitate the review process, this button can be used to send the workbook to an e-mail address as an attachment. The workbook is sent with the Reviewing toolbar active so that the recipient can add/review changes.

**FIGURE 18.22**

The Reviewing toolbar can be used to cycle through workbook comments.

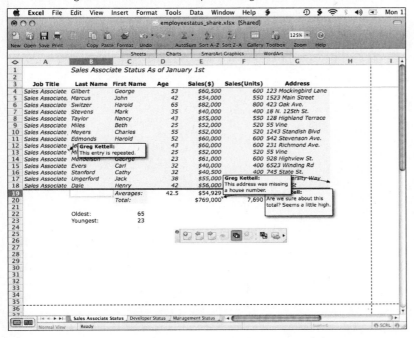

# Summary

Excel is a great tool to use in a team environment, whether you prefer to work with hard copy printouts or electronically. You can take advantage of Excel's advanced printing and previewing features to create printouts that show your work in the best light. You can print workbooks in whole or in part, and adjust, scale, and add headers and footers to identify the content. When you are ready to print, you can preview your work in the OS X Preview application, which lets you add annotations and markup to the document, delete any extraneous pages, or save the formatted output in a variety of formats, including PDF.

If collaborating with coworkers is more your thing, Excel's workbook-sharing feature makes it possible for several people to make changes to a workbook at once. Excel can track changes made by others and automatically merge them into your copy of the workbook when you save or at a specified interval. You can view the change history to see any changes that have been made in a specified amount of time, or even step through changes one by one to accept or reject them. Finally, the Reviewing toolbar can help you if you rely on having people add comments to a workbook as they review it. You can use this toolbar both to add and edit comments, but also to step from one to another, delete comments, or even mail the workbook directly to a reviewer (or from a reviewer back to you).

# Part IV

# Presenting with PowerPoint

# Chapter 19

# PowerPoint Basics

PowerPoint is the most widely used presentation software on the planet. In fact, Microsoft brags that 30 million presentations are created using the software every day. I'm not sure how they're counting all those, unless everyone's e-mailing them to Bill Gates saying "Hey, look what I made!" Regardless, there is no doubt that PowerPoint is the number one choice when it comes to creating an informative visual display that communicates a message and looks good in the process.

As a presentation program, PowerPoint helps you present information to a target audience. Using a graphical approach in the form of slide shows, PowerPoint is widely used in business and classroom environments to explain or present an idea, a process, a series of information, or just images. You can narrate your presentations yourself while giving them or record narration to go along with them. You can give a presentation using a computer, on a projector screen, or on the Web, or you can print your slides for distribution. The best part is that your presentations always turn out looking professional and polished!

A PowerPoint presentation typically consists of text, graphics, movies, or other objects positioned in layouts on pages, which are called *slides*. You can make the elements move in and out of a slide using custom animations, and you can make slides move from one to the next using transitions. In this chapter, you learn about the various parts of the program window; creating, opening, and saving presentations; changing view modes; assigning presentation properties; and protecting your presentations from unwanted changes.

## Navigating the PowerPoint Window

Microsoft has tweaked the appearance of PowerPoint along with improvements to all the other Office programs. If you've used previous versions of the software, you'll quickly notice subtle changes to the user interface: It now displays modern-looking windows, toolbars, and icons. Figure 19.1 shows the new and improved PowerPoint window with a blank slide displayed. If you're new to PowerPoint, or if you've used it before and need a refresher course, this section reviews the various parts of the program window.

**537**

**FIGURE 19.1**

Check out the new and improved PowerPoint 2008 program window. In this figure, the blank slide appears ready for text or graphics.

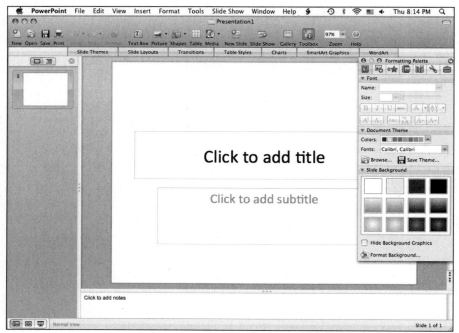

**NOTE**    Depending on how your PowerPoint program is set up, you may be presented with the Project Gallery as soon as you start PowerPoint. This Gallery helps you quickly create an Office file of any kind. If you want to create a PowerPoint presentation based on a template, click the Presentations category and choose a template. To skip the Gallery, click the Cancel button. To stop it from appearing by default, choose PowerPoint ➪ Preferences, click the General tab, and deselect the Show Project Gallery at startup check box.

## Viewing window parts

Like all the other Office programs, PowerPoint features a similar look and feel that gives all the programs a seamless appearance. If you've already mastered the basics in one program, such as Word or Excel, you can count on finding the same tools and icons in the same places in PowerPoint. The following descriptions give you a look at the basic window elements found in PowerPoint.

### Title bar and menu bar

At the top of the PowerPoint window are a title bar and menu bar, as shown in Figure 19.2. This bar area lists the name of the program and the main menu categories. To display a menu, click the menu name and a list of related commands drops down from the menu bar. To activate a command from the menu, click the command name. Depending on the command, submenus or a dialog box may appear for further selections. If you click a menu command that has an arrow icon next to it, a submenu appears. If you click a menu command that has ellipses (dots) next to it, a dialog box opens, and you can specify more input before assigning the feature.

The title bar and menu bar display the name of the program and the main groups of menu commands.

Just below the menu bar are program window controls and the presentation name, if you've assigned one. The program window controls, which are the three colored circle icons located at the far-left side, allow you to close, minimize, and zoom the window, as outlined below:

- Click the round red button with an X in the center to close the slide window but leave the program window open.

- Click the round yellow button with a minus in the center to minimize the slide window, which transports the window down into the Dock.

- Click the round green button with a plus in the center to maximize or zoom the slide window, making the window as large as possible.

 **Remember, the program window controls only show icons in the circles when you move the mouse pointer over a control button.**

The presentation name at the top of the program window simply lists any assigned name you gave to the saved file. If the presentation has not been saved yet, the default name appears, such as Presentation1, Presentation2, and so on. You can click and drag the presentation name icon just like you drag other Mac icons in the Finder. Called the *document proxy icon,* it works just like the folder proxy icons you use in the Finder. You can drag the current presentation to the Trash to delete it or drag it to another folder. You also can ⌘+click the presentation name to find out the presentation's location on the hard drive. This works only if the presentation has been saved.

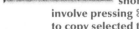 **Keyboard command lovers will be happy to know they can still use oodles of keyboard shortcuts in PowerPoint to activate commands and features. Most keyboard shortcuts involve pressing ⌘ while clicking another key, such as ⌘+N to start a new, blank presentation, or ⌘+C to copy selected text. Keep a lookout for new keyboard shortcuts you can learn scattered about the PowerPoint menus.**

### Standard toolbar

The Standard toolbar appears below the title bar and menu bar, shown in Figure 19.3. This toolbar displays a row of tool icons for common tasks, such as opening or printing presentations, adding slides, and so on. To activate a feature or command from the toolbar, just click the associated icon. The Standard toolbar appears every time you create a new presentation in PowerPoint. You can add or subtract icons from the toolbar to create your own custom toolbar. Chapter 34 teaches you how to customize toolbars. To learn more about using toolbars in Office, see Chapter 3.

The Standard toolbar displays tools for performing common PowerPoint tasks with a click of a button.

## Toolbar Tips

You can use five other toolbars in PowerPoint in addition to the Standard toolbar, and you can control which toolbars appear onscreen using the View menu. Choose View ➪ Toolbars, and click the name of the toolbar you want to display. A check mark next to the toolbar name indicates the toolbar is displayed; no check mark means the toolbar display is turned off. If toolbars are taking up too much real estate onscreen, you can turn them off to free up space.

You also can Control+click an empty area of a toolbar to display a shortcut menu of related commands. For example, if you Control+click the Standard toolbar, you can view commands for changing how icons are displayed on the toolbar, accessing other toolbars, and resetting or customizing the toolbar. For example, if you want to view icons only, click the Icon Only command.

### Elements Gallery

The new Elements Gallery sits directly below the Standard toolbar, and you can use the Gallery to quickly insert preset design items such as slide themes, layouts, transitions, and tables. By default, the Gallery is hidden, showing only a row of tabs. You can display the Gallery in its entirety by clicking a tab on the bar or by clicking the Gallery button on the Standard toolbar. If you click a tab, you can view group tabs for specific categories of elements. Figure 19.4 shows the Slide Themes tab selected with the Built-in Themes group displayed. You can scroll through the list of items and click the one you want to apply.

**FIGURE 19.4**

The Elements Gallery offers a library of preset design items you can apply to your slides.

You also can choose View ➪ Elements Gallery to view the Gallery. When you finish choosing an element, you can click the Gallery button on the toolbar to hide the Gallery.

### Toolbox

The PowerPoint Toolbox, shown in Figure 19.5, is the place to go for quick access to useful tools. Tools are grouped into palettes that appear as heading bars in the Toolbox. Click the palette name to display the palette and view the associated tools and features. You can use this same technique to collapse the palette view again and hide the tools. You learn more about using the Toolbox later in this chapter.

### Slide pane

The large main area of the program window is the slide pane, shown in Figure 19.6, displaying the current slide. Use this area to view and work with your slide and the various slide elements, such as text boxes. As you add slides to the presentation, a vertical scroll bar appears. For example, you can drag the vertical scroll box up or down to move around in the presentation. If you zoom your view, a horizontal scroll bar appears and you can drag the horizontal scroll box to move left or right to move around the slide. In addition, you can use the Navigation buttons to move up or down a slide.

**FIGURE 19.5**

The Toolbox includes a variety of palettes full of tools for common tasks, such as formatting tools.

**FIGURE 19.6**

Use the scroll bars to move around and view different slides in your presentation.

### Slides/Outline view pane

The narrow vertical pane on the left side of the program window, shown in Figure 19.7, displays in Normal view the individual slides that make up your presentation. You can use the pane to navigate between slides by clicking the slide you want to view. The pane also switches to Outline view, shown in Figure 19.8, allowing you to see your entire presentation in an outline form. You can click the buttons at the top of the pane to toggle between Slide view and Outline view.

**FIGURE 19.7**

Click the Slides button to view a navigation pane containing all the slides in your presentation.

Click to toggle between
Slides and Outline views.

**FIGURE 19.8**

Click the Outline button to view an outlining pane containing all the slides in your presentation in outline format.

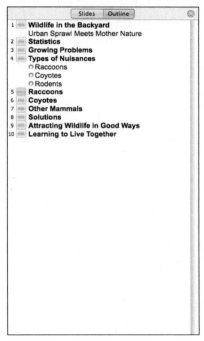

### Notes pane

You can use the Notes pane, shown in Figure 19.9, to add notes about a slide. The notes do not appear in the actual presentation, but rather, you can use them yourself when giving the presentation. They appear only on your computer screen, not on the projected screen. You also might use the Notes pane to add notes to yourself about items you need to add to the slide later or a task you need to accomplish before completing the slide.

**FIGURE 19.9**

Use the Notes pane to add notes about a slide.

Welcome the group and introduce the panel.

Add notes here.

### View buttons

Three important view buttons are located in the Status bar at the very bottom of the screen, as shown in Figure 19.10, for switching between view modes. You can switch among Normal view, Slide Sorter view, and Slide Show view. Learn more about these views later in this chapter.

**FIGURE 19.10**

Use the view buttons to switch among Normal view, Slide Sorter view, and Slide Show view.

# Creating, Opening, and Saving Presentations

Files you create in PowerPoint are called *presentations*. You also may see them referred to as *documents* from time to time. The terms are interchangeable. As a matter of fact, just about every file you create using the Office suite can be referred to as a document file. Whenever you open PowerPoint, there's a new, blank presentation waiting for you to start using. Granted, the presentation is made up of just one blank slide, but you can easily build from there, adding more slides or "pages" in the presentation. Naturally, as you create files in PowerPoint, you'll want to open and reuse them again, so understanding the techniques of creating, opening, and saving files is essential to using PowerPoint. This section of the chapter shows you how to do all three.

# Creating new files

It's very easy to start new presentations in PowerPoint. Use any of these methods:

- Click the New button on the Standard toolbar.
- Choose File ➪ New Presentation.
- Press ⌘+N.

Any of the above techniques opens a blank presentation. If you want to create a specific kind of presentation, you can use PowerPoint's Project Gallery. The Project Gallery (refer to Figure 19.11) is available in PowerPoint, Word, Excel, and Entourage, and includes all kinds of ready-made templates. For example, you can find templates for creating photo albums, pitch books, quiz shows, and widescreen presentations in PowerPoint. The Project Gallery also keeps track of recent project files.

To create a project with the Project Gallery, follow these steps:

1. **Click File.**
2. **Click Project Gallery.**

   The Project Gallery window opens, as shown in Figure 19.11.

**FIGURE 19.11**

The Project Gallery offers a variety of templates you can use to create new PowerPoint presentations.

3. **Click the New tab.**
4. **Click the Presentations category.**
5. **Click the type of presentation you want to create.**
6. **Click Open.**

   PowerPoint creates and opens the new presentation file.

As soon as you create a new project with the Project Gallery, PowerPoint displays the presentation along with placeholder boxes for text and graphics, such as photos or clip art. You can replace the placeholder objects with your own text and photos. When you finish creating the presentation, you can save it with a unique filename and reuse it again later.

## Which Gallery Is Which?

The Office Suite includes more than one thing called the "Gallery." So what's the difference between the Elements Gallery and the Projects Gallery? As you learned earlier in the chapter, the Elements Gallery lets you insert specific types of items into a presentation, such as preset layouts or transitions. The Projects Gallery lets you choose to insert entire presentations from a library of preset templates. So the difference is specific items versus actual presentation templates.

You can click the Gallery button on the Standard toolbar to display the Elements Gallery, which offers seven distinct categories of elements you can add, including slide themes and layouts. If you're looking for a quick and easy element to insert, check out the Elements Gallery. If you're looking to use an entire presentation, use a template from the Project Gallery.

### Saving files

After creating a presentation, you can save it and open it again later to make changes. If you try exiting the presentation without saving, PowerPoint prompts you to save your data. As you've seen in Word and Excel, you can use the Save As dialog box, shown in Figure 19.12, to assign a unique filename to a presentation, as well as specify a location in which to save the file, choose a file format, or check for compatibility.

**FIGURE 19.12**

When saving a file, you specify a unique name and choose a destination where you want to store the file.

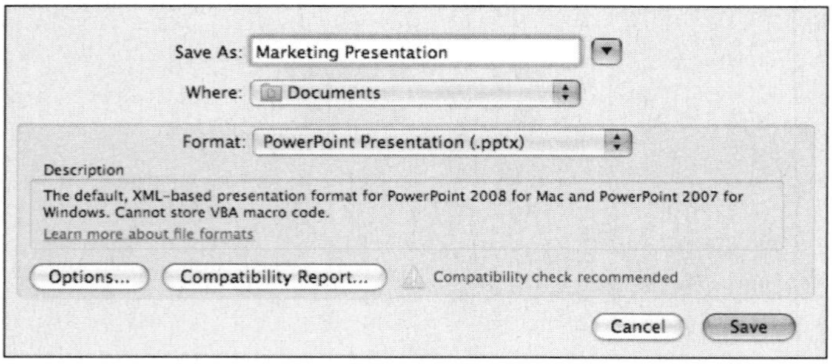

All PowerPoint presentations are saved in the *.pptx* file type by default. This format is an XML-based format for PowerPoint for Mac 2008 and PowerPoint 2007 for Windows. You can choose another file type, as needed. For example, if you're sharing the file with someone who uses an older version of PowerPoint, you can choose an older file format compatible with the program they're using. You also might choose to save every slide as a graphic to be viewed or copied into another application. The following table defines the available file formats:

**TABLE 19.1**

# PowerPoint File Formats

| File Format | Description |
| --- | --- |
| PowerPoint Presentation (.pptx) | Saves the file in an XML-based document format for PowerPoint 2008 for Mac and PowerPoint 2007 for Windows. |
| PowerPoint 97-2004 Presentation (.ppt) | Saves the file in a document format compatible with PowerPoint 98-PowerPoint 2004 for Mac and PowerPoint 97-PowerPoint 2003 for Windows. |
| PowerPoint Template (.potx) | Saves the file in an XML-based template format, compatible with PowerPoint 2008 for Mac and PowerPoint 2007 for Windows. |
| PowerPoint 97-2004 Template (.pot) | Saves the file in a template format compatible with PowerPoint 98-PowerPoint 2004 for Mac and PowerPoint 97-PowerPoint 2003 for Windows. |
| PowerPoint Package | Saves the presentation and any linked files to one folder. |
| Movie (.mov) | Exports the presentation as a movie file that can be played in the QuickTime Player. |
| Web Page (.htm) | Saves the presentation content for display on the Web, compatible with Mac and Windows Web browsers. |
| PDF | Exports the presentation as a PDF file. |
| PowerPoint Show (.ppsx) | Saves the file with XML-based presentation format that always opens in Slide Show view as soon as the file is opened. |
| PowerPoint 97-2004 Show (.pps) | Opens the file in Slide Show view, compatible with PowerPoint 98 through PowerPoint 2004 for Mac, or PowerPoint 97 through PowerPoint 2003 for Windows. |
| PowerPoint Macro-Enabled Presentation (.pptm) | Saves the presentation content as an XML-based format, preserving any VBA macro code. (Note: VBA macros do not work in PowerPoint 2008.) |
| PowerPoint Macro-Enabled Template (.potm) | Saves the presentation as an XML-based template format, preserving any VBA macro code. (Note: VBA macros do not work in PowerPoint 2008.) |
| PowerPoint Macro-Enabled Show (.ppsm) | Saves the presentation as an XML-based presentation format, preserving any VBA macro code. (Note: VBA macros do not work in PowerPoint 2008.) |
| Outline/Rich Text Format (.rtf) | Exports the outline text from your presentation to a file that can be read in other programs, such as Microsoft Word. |
| Office Theme (.thmx) | Saves the presentation font, color scheme, and background to be used as a new theme. |
| JPEG | Exports each slide in the presentation as a JPEG graphic file. |
| PNG | Exports each slide in the presentation as a PNG graphic file. |
| GIF | Exports each slide in the presentation as a GIF graphic file. |
| BMP | Exports each slide in the presentation as a BMP graphic file. |
| TIFF | Exports each slide in the presentation as a TIFF graphic file. |

When saving files, you can choose exactly where to store a presentation. PowerPoint is set up to save presentations to the Documents folder. If you want to save the file to another folder or drive, you must specify a location.

The last thing to mention about saving files is the Compatibility Report tool. When you open the Save As dialog box to save a file, you'll notice a red warning blurb recommending a compatibility check. This feature is helpful if you're sharing documents with people who are using different versions of PowerPoint. If you activate the Compatibility Report feature, PowerPoint runs a compatibility test and notifies you if it encounters any issues that might cause a problem in another version of PowerPoint. This same feature is available on the Compatibility tab of the Toolbox. If you're not sharing files, you do not need to run the tool.

You're probably ready to start saving your own files, so without further adieu, use any of the following methods to save a presentation.

### Saving for the first time

The technique for saving a presentation for the first time probably seems pretty standard by this point in the book since you've already learned how to save Word documents and Excel workbooks, and the process always works the same way; however, I need to tell you these things anyway. It's the law in computer book publishing. Here's the skinny on saving a presentation the first time:

1. **Click the Save button on the Standard toolbar, or choose File ⇨ Save or Save As.**

   The Save As dialog box opens (refer to Figure 19.12).

2. **Type a name for the file.**

3. **Choose a destination folder or drive on which to store the file.**

   By default, PowerPoint saves the file to the Documents folder.

   Optionally, to save the presentation in another file format, click Format arrows and choose a format, as shown in Figure 19.13.

   Optionally, to check for compatibility issues, click the Compatibility Report button.

> **NOTE**    If you run the Compatibility Report tool, PowerPoint checks the file for any compatibility issues and displays a prompt if it finds any. You can view the issues using the Compatibility Report Palette in the Toolbox. See "Using the Compatibility Feature" later in this section to learn more.

4. **Click Save.**

   PowerPoint saves the presentation, and the new filename appears at the top of the window.

You also can access the Compatibility Report feature through the Compatibility Palette on the Toolbox. To learn more about this tool, see "Using the Compatibility Report feature" later in this section.

### Subsequent saves

After you've saved the file the first time, you don't have to keep reopening the Save As dialog box again to save. Instead, you can apply any of these methods to save your changes:

- Click the Save button on the Standard toolbar.
- Choose File ⇨ Save.
- Press ⌘+S.

PowerPoint saves the file using the same filename you established before, updating any changes you made to the file. If you do need to change something, such as a storage location, use the Save As dialog box again.

**FIGURE 19.13**

You can choose from a variety of file formats when saving a presentation.

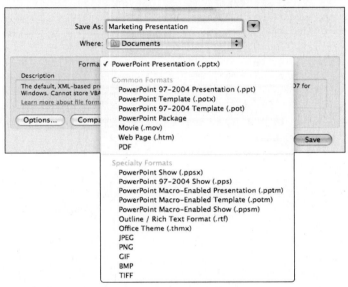

## Saving an existing file under a new filename

What if you want to create a copy of your presentation and make a few changes, but still keep the original intact? No problem. Just save it under a new filename. Follow these steps when you need to save the file again with a new name or to a new location:

1. **Choose File ⇨ Save As.**

   The Save As dialog box opens.

2. **Type a new name for the file.**

3. **Choose a destination folder or drive on which to store the file.**

4. **Click Save.**

   PowerPoint saves the presentation, and the new filename appears at the top of the window.

## Using AutoRecover

PowerPoint's AutoRecover feature is a clever feature for creating automatic saves of your presentation in case there's a power shortage or computer failure. With AutoRecover activated, you'll have a recently saved copy of your work to reopen again just in case of such a disaster. AutoRecover works by saving the current file as a separate AutoRecover file that you can open and save under a new name. You can set the AutoRecover to automatically save every few minutes; however, for best results, consider setting the feature for every 5 to 10 minutes. A shorter setting slows down your computer every few minutes.

To create automatic saves, follow these steps:

1. **Choose PowerPoint ⇨ Preferences.**

   The PowerPoint Preferences dialog box opens.

2. **Click the Save icon.**

   The Save options appear, as shown in Figure 19.14.

You can turn on PowerPoint's AutoRecover feature to create automatic saves of your presentations.

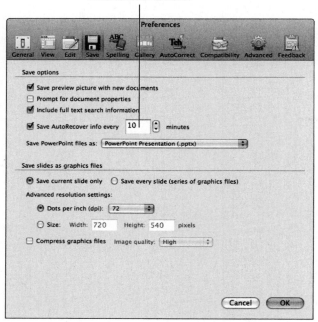

Set the minutes for the
AutoRecover feature.

3. **Specify how often you want to save the document in the Save AutoRecover info every box.**

   You can type in a number or click the arrow buttons to arrive at the number you want.

4. **Click OK.**

   PowerPoint is now set up to automatically save your file.

## Using the Compatibility Report feature

You may remember that this feature was discussed in Chapter 5 with Word. It works the same way in PowerPoint. The Compatibility Report feature is a helpful tool for users who share their presentation files with people using older versions of the software. It checks your file and makes it backward compatible. For example, if your presentation uses features not available in older versions of PowerPoint, the report tool prompts you with a warning box and offers you a way to correct any compatibility issues.

You can activate the Compatibility Report feature through the Save As dialog box or through the Compatibility Report Palette in the Toolbox. The advantage of using the palette method is that you'll find detailed results of a check, explanations about the issues, and tools for making any fixes or ignoring any problems. Follow these steps to use the Compatibility Report feature in the Toolbox:

1. **Display the Toolbox by clicking the Toolbox button on the Standard toolbar or choosing View ⇨ Compatibility Report.**

2. **Click the Compatibility Report Palette button.**

   PowerPoint opens the Compatibility Report Palette in the Toolbox, as shown in Figure 19.15.

**FIGURE 19.15**

You can use the Compatibility Report Palette in the Toolbox to check your presentation over for compatibility issues.

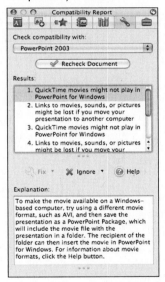

3. **Click the Check compatibility with menu, and choose a document type with which you want to compare.**

   PowerPoint immediately begins checking the presentation and displays any issues in the Results box.

4. **Click a result to view an explanation in the Explanation box.**

   To fix a problem, click the Fix arrow button and make a selection.

   To ignore a problem, click the Ignore arrow button and make a selection.

   You can click the Recheck Document button to recheck a document again.

## Opening files

After you've started creating and saving files in PowerPoint, you'll want to open them again later to view or edit the presentation. You can use the Open dialog box to open presentations stored in various folders and drives on your computer, or you can use the Open Recent submenu on the File menu, which lists recent files you worked with in PowerPoint. A third option is to use the Project Gallery to open recent PowerPoint files.

The following sections explain how to use each method.

### Open a presentation with the Open command

This method is a quick and easy way to access your presentations:

 **1.** **Click the Open button on the Standard toolbar, or choose File ➪ Open.**

The Open dialog box opens, as shown in Figure 19.16.

### FIGURE 19.16

You can use the Open dialog box to open presentation files stored on your computer or on other drives or storage devices.

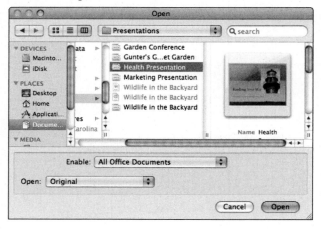

**2.** **Click the file you want to open.**

You can navigate to a folder or device containing the file you want to open using the navigation pane.

You also can double-click the presentation name to quickly open the presentation.

**3.** **Click the Open button.**

PowerPoint opens the presentation.

**TIP** You can click the Enable menu and choose a format if you don't see the file you want in the Open dialog box. For best results, consider changing the setting to All Readable Documents or All Office Documents so you can view all the document types.

### Open a presentation with the Open Recent menu

If you've recently worked with a presentation, you can quickly access it again using the Open Recent command:

1.  **Choose File ➪ Open Recent, as shown in Figure 19.17.**
2.  **Click the file you want to open.**

    If you don't see your file listed, you can click the More button to open the Project Gallery to the Recent documents tab and look for the file.

**FIGURE 19.17**

You can use the Open Recent menu to open recent files.

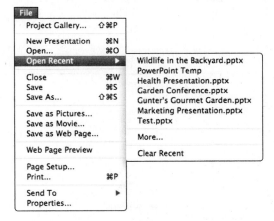

### Open a document with the Project Gallery

Another easy way to find your presentations is to use the Project Gallery; here's how:

1.  **Click File.**
2.  **Click Project Gallery.**

    The Project Gallery window opens, as shown in Figure 19.18.

## Original, Copy, or Read-Only

The Open menu in the Open dialog box lets you open a file as an original, as a read-only file, or as a copy of the original. Click the Open menu arrow buttons to choose from Original, Copy, or Read-Only. The Original setting is selected by default and simply means whatever presentation you select to open is the original file. A read-only file does just what the name implies: It opens the presentation, but does not allow you to make any changes to the content. Finally, you can use the Copy feature to open a copy of the original file. If you make changes to the presentation, you can save them under a new filename and keep the original file intact.

---

FIGURE 19.18

You can use the Project Gallery to open recent files.

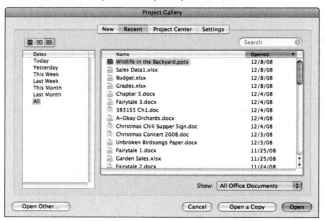

3. **Click the Recent tab.**

4. **Click the presentation you want to open.**

5. **Click Open.**

   PowerPoint opens the file.

### Search for a file

You can use the Open dialog box to search for an existing presentation on your computer. Using the Spotlight text field, which displays the word "search" by default, you can search for a specific filename, a portion of the name, or keywords pertaining to the name. Follow these steps to search for a file:

1. **Display the Open dialog box.**

2. **Click inside the Spotlight search field, and type the filename, a portion of the name, or a keyword.**

   As you type in the search field, PowerPoint lists any possible matches.

   You can use the buttons at the top of the search window to target your search.

3. **When you find the file you want, double-click the filename to open the presentation.**

# Changing Views

PowerPoint offers a variety of view modes you can apply to help you as you work with your presentation, as well as a Zoom feature you can use to magnify a slide. This section examines the various ways you can view your slides and presentations.

## Using the view modes

PowerPoint offers three view modes for working with slides: Normal view, Slide Sorter view, and Slide Show view. Available as icons you can click in the Status bar area, you can switch between views depending on the work you want to accomplish.

 Normal view, the default view shown in Figure 19.19, displays individual slides for you to work on and edit. Within Normal view, you can choose to work with slides or outlines. Notice that the window is divided into three panes in Normal view: the Slides/Outline pane, the main Slide pane, and the Notes pane. You can use the Slides/Outlines pane to switch between navigating slides and viewing the presentation in outline format. You can use the Notes pane to add any notes to a slide for your own viewing. You can resize the borders of panes to increase or decrease their sizes. Just click and drag a pane's border to resize a pane.

**FIGURE 19.19**

Normal view

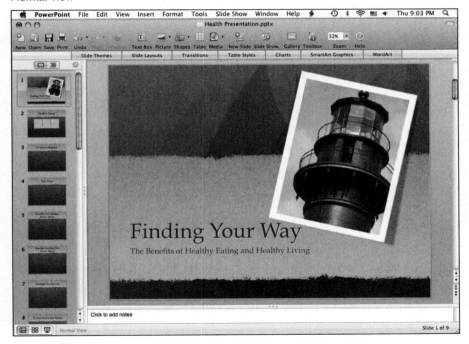

 When you're ready to start assembling your presentation in earnest, you can switch to Slide Sorter view, shown in Figure 19.20. You can use this view to make changes to the slide order, apply transitions and special effects, and rehearse the show.

**FIGURE 19.20**

Slide Sorter view

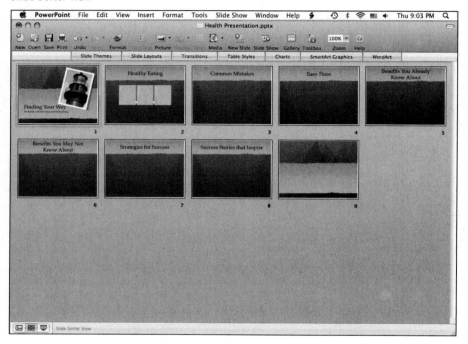

 You can use the Slide Show view, shown in Figure 19.21, to actually see the slide show as your audience sees it. When you switch to this view, the slides are enlarged to encompass the entire screen, obscuring the title bar and menu bar, toolbars, scrollbars, and Status bar. You can navigate between slides by clicking or by using the pop-up menu located in the bottom-left corner of the screen.

## Using the Zoom feature

As with Word and Excel, you can zoom your PowerPoint presentation to change its magnification setting. You can choose a percentage to zoom in for a closer look at the slide or zoom out for a bird's eye view. PowerPoint features two ways to zoom. You can use the Zoom button on the Standard toolbar to zoom your view, or you can use the Zoom dialog box. If you're in Normal view, the Zoom feature lets you zoom your view of a slide. If you're in Slide Sorter view, the Zoom setting controls the size of the slide display in the sorter window. Alas, you cannot use the Zoom feature in Slide Show view.

**FIGURE 19.21**

Slide Show view

The following sections show you how to use the Zoom tool and the Zoom dialog box.

### Using the Zoom tool

To use the Zoom tool on the Standard toolbar to change the zoom setting, click the Zoom tool's arrow button and click a percentage, as shown in Figure 19.22. PowerPoint immediately changes the magnification. That's all there is to it.

### Using the Zoom dialog box

You can use the Zoom dialog box to specify a zoom setting. Follow these steps to open the dialog box:

1.  **Choose View ➪ Zoom.**

    The Zoom dialog box appears, as shown in Figure 19.23.

## FIGURE 19.22

Using the Zoom tool, you can magnify or zoom out your view of a slide in Normal view.

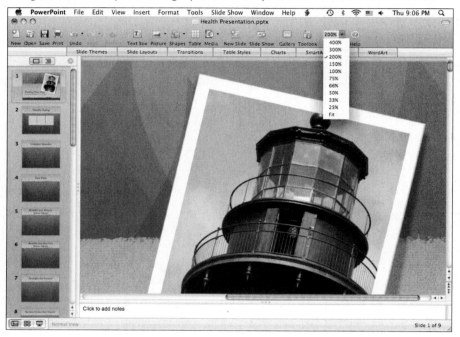

## FIGURE 19.23

You can use the Zoom box to set a zoom setting.

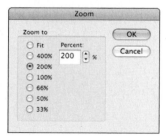

2. **Click the zoom setting you want to apply.**

   You can type a zoom percentage directly into the Percent field or click the arrow buttons to set a percentage.

3. **Click OK.**

   PowerPoint applies the zoom percentage you specified.

> **TIP**  You can use PowerPoint's Rulers and Guides to help you position objects onscreen. To turn on the vertical and horizontal rulers, choose View ⇨ Ruler. To turn on guide lines, choose View ⇨ Guides and choose a guide option. Dynamic Guides, Snap to Grid, and Snap to Shape guides are turned on by default.

# Setting Presentation Properties

PowerPoint saves data along with your file whenever you create and save a presentation. This special data is known as *document properties* or *metadata*. Document properties are a common way to identify and describe any particular file. All Office programs insert some properties automatically, such as file size and the dates pertaining to file creation. Other property data can include summary information and statistics about the file, such as when it was created, the last person to save the file, and its current location. You can use the Document Properties dialog box, shown in Figure 19.24, to view and set properties for a PowerPoint presentation file.

**FIGURE 19.24**

You can view properties pertaining to a presentation using the Document Properties dialog box.

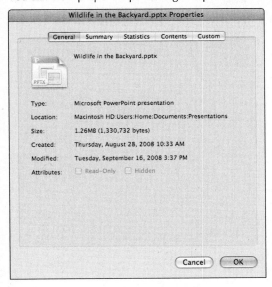

The dialog box features five tabs of properties: General, Summary, Statistics, Contents, and Custom. The General tab displays basic information about the file, such as the file type, location, size, creation date, last modified date, and any read-only or hidden attributes settings. The information on this tab is automatically created by PowerPoint when you save the file, and you cannot make changes to it. On the other hand, the Summary and Custom tabs do allow you to enter your own information. The Summary tab has a variety of blank text fields you can use to add more information about the file. For example, you can include information such as a title, subject, author, manager, or company name. You can type in a category, keywords, comments, or hyperlink base. The tab also lists any templates attached to the file. The Statistics tab lists the created and modified dates again, when the file was last printed, who saved the file last, the number of revisions, editing time, and a bunch of statistics on the number of notes, words, paragraphs, and slides. The Contents tab displays contents of the document. Lastly, the Custom tab lets you add your own custom properties to the file, such as client name, destination, language, and so on, and set values for each of the properties you add.

To display the Document Properties dialog box in PowerPoint, choose File ➪ Properties. Click the Summary tab, shown in Figure 19.25, to enter your own details. To add custom properties, click the Custom tab and add which new properties you want to include with the file.

**FIGURE 19.25**

The Summary tab has fields for entering in your own file properties.

# Summary

In this chapter, you learned your way around the PowerPoint program window. Like the other Office programs, you learned where to find all the common tools and features for using the program. Not so surprisingly, the tools and features are located in pretty much the same places you discovered them in the other programs.

You discovered how to use the three view modes to view your slides and change the magnification setting to zoom your view while you work. You also learned how to create new presentations, save presentations, and open existing presentation files. Lastly, you learned how to control some of the properties that describe your file that are saved with the document. With all this basic information out of the way, you're ready to start building your own presentations.

# Chapter 20

# Building Presentations

What goes into a typical presentation, you might wonder? Blood, sweat, and tears might be the common answer, but with a little help from PowerPoint, the quantities of each are more than manageable. You might even be able to build PowerPoint presentations without breaking a sweat at all. The process is quite painless and, I daresay, can even be easy and enjoyable. Of course, good advance planning can really help speed your work along.

The goal of any presentation is to get your point across, whether you're speaking to one person or thousands. PowerPoint can help you make your point through the use of text, graphics, movies, and sound. Your presentation may require just a few slides, or many slides, but no matter what elements you place in a slide, it still has to communicate your message effectively. The starting point of any presentation is deciding upon the message. After you've figured out what you're trying to convey, you can start building your presentation.

A typical slide's content is controlled by its layout, whether you use a preset layout or design your own. You control what information each slide contains and what format the information takes, such as text, a video clip, a sound clip, or a picture. In this chapter, you learn how to add content, assign layouts and themes, add and delete slides, create presentations using outlines, and control slide masters. In other words, it's time to start making your presentation.

## Planning a Presentation

Have you been asked to give a presentation before? After the initial panic, the first thing you typically need to do is a little preplanning. It might be natural to assume that PowerPoint does all the work for you, but the reality is that PowerPoint can only help you so far. PowerPoint is just a tool, after all, and you're the real star of the presentation. So it's really up to you to make the presentation a success, and the best path to success is planning. With that said, before you ever start typing slide text or picking slide layouts, take time to figure out your goals for the presentation. These tips may help you get started:

- Start by asking yourself what it is you want to convey in your presentation. What is it you want your audience to gain? Do you want to inform them, enlighten them, teach them something new, convince them to do something, inspire them, or make them take some sort of action?

- Once you've figured out the overall goal, determine who your audience is. Who are you presenting to? Is it peers, your boss, a large group of people, students, friends? Determining your audience can help you put yourself in their shoes and think about what might make the presentation interesting to them. It will also help you know what sort of language to use—whether they'll expect any industry jargon, for example.

- Outlining can really help you narrow the focus of your presentation so you make sure to cover each topic with a slide. You can use PowerPoint's outline tool or import an outline from Word. You learn about using PowerPoint's outlining feature later in this chapter.

- After you've determined your message, your audience, and a rough idea of where you're going with the presentation, take time to gather the information you want to present. For example, if your presentation requires charts or graphs, have them ready. If your presentation needs special files, such as movie or sound clips, assemble them in a folder where you can easily find them when you're ready for them. If you want to illustrate the slides with photos, locate them and keep them in one handy spot.

- Where and how are you giving the presentation? Are you using your computer, a laptop, someone else's computer? Are you going to need any special equipment to give the presentation? Do you need a video projector? If you're using a projector, what sort of screen are you projecting on? You may save yourself a headache or two if you figure out in advance what equipment you need in order to make your presentation. If you're using someone else's equipment, take time to learn how it works, or make sure you've scheduled it in advance.

- Practice makes perfect. Practice giving your presentation. Practice your timing, making sure you're covering everything within the allotted time frame, and practice your delivery so you sound polished and knowledgeable. Consider giving the presentation to a colleague or trusted friend for input. Whatever you do, make sure to proofread your slides thoroughly. There's nothing more detracting than misspellings while you're trying to talk about something important.

To learn more tips on delivering a successful presentation, see Chapter 23.

# Using Outlines

PowerPoint's outlining feature is a great way to build a presentation. You can quickly whip up key points you want to make as slide titles and flesh them out further as you go along. For example, you may start by typing all the main points you want to make and see how they flow. Then you might go back to each slide and add more text, such as bullet points or body text, to support the main ideas. If you don't want to be distracted by slide design or layouts, the outlining feature can really help you focus on the message you want to convey. You can easily edit the slides in the outline until you're satisfied with the overall content and then switch back to Slide view to finish adding visual elements to illustrate the slides, add transition effects, and insert animations.

## Creating an outline

To use PowerPoint's outlining tools, switch to Normal view and click the Outline icon in the Slides/Outline view pane. PowerPoint displays the Outline pane along with the main Slide pane, shown in Figure 20.1, but now the Outline pane is wider to accommodate your outline text. To add text, just click in the Outline view pane and start typing. Press Return to create a new slide. As you type text, the main Slide pane shows the text being added to the actual slide.

**FIGURE 20.1**

One way to start building a presentation is to create an outline.

Click the Outline tab icon to view the Outline pane.

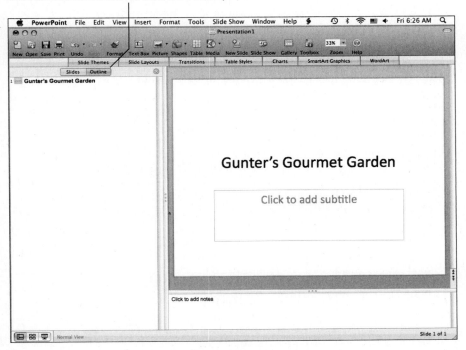

The slides you add in Outline view are numbered, and each heading you type is a title in a slide. You can add subheadings, bulleted text, and other body text by promoting and demoting text levels. You can press Tab to demote a title into a bullet point. If you press Tab again, you can demote the text to a lower level. You also can turn on the Outlining toolbar for quick access to tools for promoting and demoting text, moving the slide order around, expanding and collapsing the outline, and turning formatting on or off. To display the toolbar, choose View⇔Toolbars⇔Outlining. The outlining tools featured here are very similar to those found in Microsoft Word (see Chapter 6). Figure 20.2 shows the Outlining toolbar in place.

### FIGURE 20.2

You can use the Outlining toolbar to work with the outline levels.

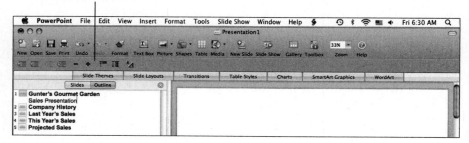

Outline toolbar

If you prefer using the keyboard to work with outline text, see Table 20.1 for an explanation of how to use keyboard keys to control the text level in your outline.

### TABLE 20.1

## Outlining Keyboard Shortcuts

| Keyboard Keys | Description |
| --- | --- |
| Return | Starts a new slide and title text, or if you're typing a bulleted list, starts a new bullet. |
| Tab | Demotes the selected text. |
| Shift+Tab | Promotes the selected text. |
| Shift+⌘+N | Inserts a new slide. |
| ⌘+D | Duplicates the current slide. |
| Delete | Deletes the selected slide. |

You can click a slide icon in the Outline view pane to select the slide. You also can drag the slide to a new location to change the slide order. The text in the Outline view pane can be selected just like any other text. For example, to delete a word, double-click the word to select it first.

 To return to Slide view again at any time, click the Slides tab at the top of the Slide/Outline view pane.

## Importing a Word outline

If you've used Microsoft Word to help plan an outline for a presentation, you can easily import the outline into PowerPoint and create the presentation. To export the file from the Word program window, choose File ➪ Send To ➪ PowerPoint. This opens the PowerPoint application and turns the Word outline into a presentation outline. You also can import the file within the PowerPoint window; however, the file must be saved first in Word as an .rtf file type. Then you can import from PowerPoint; choose Insert ➪ Slides From ➪ Outline File. This opens the Choose a File dialog box. Navigate to the .rtf file you saved in Word, and double-click the filename to insert it into PowerPoint. PowerPoint turns every level 1 heading in the Word outline into a slide in the presentation.

# Adding Slide Content

As I mentioned, slides can contain all kinds of content, including text, clip art, photos, movie clips, sound clips, drawn shapes, and more. A slide is much like a single page in a document, holding whatever content you designate. If you create a presentation based on a template, your slides already have placeholder objects for holding text or graphics. You can fill in the placeholder objects with your own text and graphics as needed. If you build a presentation from scratch, PowerPoint starts you out with a single slide with a default layout. Here again, you fill in the slide with whatever content is needed.

It's actually quite easy to start adding content. Normal view mode works best for adding slide elements. To add text to the current slide, just click the text box object and type your own text. To add your own graphics, click the graphic object and replace it with your own artwork. This section shows you how to start building your presentations by working with layouts and adding new slide content.

## Working with layouts

A layout is like a map of where everything goes on a slide. Layout boxes dictate the area consumed by text or graphics on a slide, and the boxes can be resized and moved around to customize a layout. You also can add or remove layout boxes to customize the appearance of a slide or which elements appear within it. Look at the blank slide shown in Figure 20.3. Notice the two text boxes on the slide, one for a title and another for a subtitle. PowerPoint makes it extremely easy to add a title and subtitle in this layout. Just click in each box, and type your text. This particular layout is great for a title slide at the start of your presentation. In fact, that's the name of this particular layout—Title Slide.

**FIGURE 20.3**

This slide layout includes text boxes for a title and subtitle text.

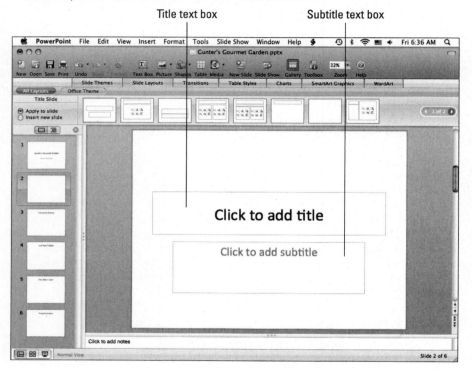

Now look at another layout, shown in Figure 20.4. This layout has a text box for a title and a large box for bulleted text or any other slide element you want to add. The icons in the center allow you to control exactly what appears in the box. You can choose from the following: Insert Table, Insert Chart, Insert SmartArt Graphic, Insert Picture from File, Insert Clip Art, and Insert Movie from File. If you want to add text, just start typing. If you'd rather add another type of slide element, click the appropriate icon. Depending on what you click, a dialog box or Gallery choices appear to help you narrow down what you want to insert. The name of the standard layout in Figure 20.4 is Title and Content.

**FIGURE 20.4**

This slide layout lets you add a title for the slide and a slide element of your choice.

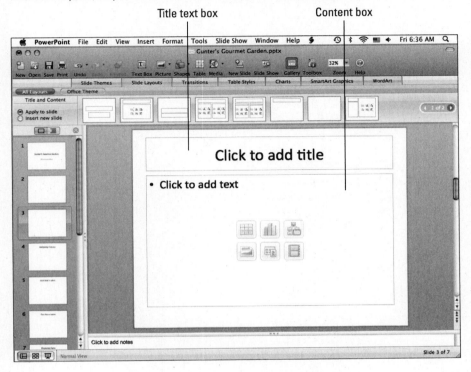

You can change the slide layout at any time. Follow these steps to assign a new layout:

1. **Click the Slide Layouts tab on the Gallery, or choose Format ➪ Slide Layout.**

   PowerPoint displays the Slide Layouts, as shown in Figure 20.5.

   You can scroll through the layouts to find the one you want, or you can hover the mouse pointer over a layout to view its description at the left end of the Gallery.

2. **Click the layout you want to apply.**

   Optionally, you can apply the layout to the current slide or insert it as a new slide. Click the appropriate radio button at the left end of the Gallery.

You can customize any object on a slide by moving or resizing the object. For example, if a text box isn't large enough to contain the text you want to convey, you can resize the box and make it bigger. Or if the box is in the wrong spot, you can move it anywhere else on the slide. This is true for any item you add to a slide, including tables, clip art, or movie clips.

 You can create your own layout using the various slide elements. For example, you can add a text box, picture, clip art, shape, table, or movie. You can find all these elements on the Insert menu, as shown in Figure 20.6. Choose Insert ➪ Text Box to add a text box, for example. When you select any of these options, you can drag across the slide to create the box to hold the element and then fill the box with the content desired.

**FIGURE 20.5**

Use the Slide Layouts tab on the Gallery to change the slide layout.

The highlighted layout's name          Slide Layouts tab          Layout options

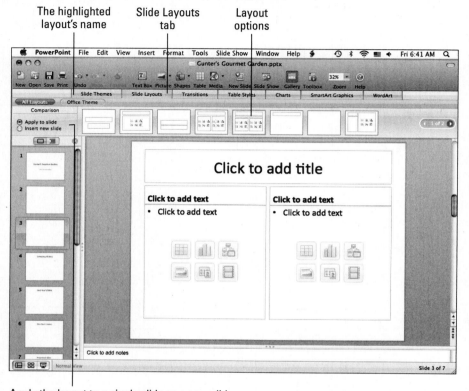

Apply the layout to a single slide or a new slide.

You also can customize a layout by removing slide elements you don't need. For example, you can remove a subtitle text box if your presentation doesn't require one. Click to select the element you want to remove, and then press Delete.

**NOTE** To customize an entire presentation, make your changes to the slide master. Learn more about using slide masters coming up later in this chapter.

## Adding text

To add text to an existing text box, simply click inside the box and start typing, as shown in Figure 20.7. A cursor appears inside the text box, and you can use the same typing techniques you learned about in Word to enter and work with text in PowerPoint. You learn how to format the text in Chapter 21.

**FIGURE 20.6**

You can add new slide elements using the Insert menu.

**FIGURE 20.7**

You can add text to a slide using text boxes. Many of the standard layouts have text boxes ready to use.

Click in a text box and start typing.

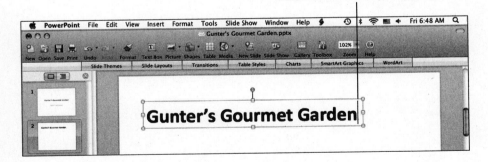

To add a new text box to a slide, follow these steps:

1.  Click the Text Box button on the Standard toolbar, or choose Insert ⇨ Text Box.
2.  Click and drag across the slide where you want to insert the box, as shown in Figure 20.8. You also can just click inside the slide to place the box.
3.  Type your text.

**FIGURE 20.8**

Click and drag the size of the text box you want to create.

Click to add text boxes.

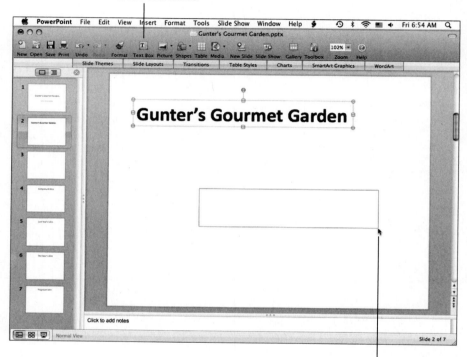

Click and drag to create a new text box.

You can move and resize the text box as needed. Click the text box, move the mouse pointer over the box until it becomes a four-sided arrow pointer, and then click and drag the box to a new location. To resize the box, move the mouse pointer over a corner or middle border area until the pointer becomes a two-sided arrow pointer. You can then click and drag to resize the box.

## Adding clip art

 If your slide layout already has an option for inserting clip art, click the Insert Clip Art icon. This opens the Clip Gallery shown in Figure 20.9. You can use this Gallery to search for a particular type of clip art or browse through the various categories to find something you want to use. To browse, choose a category and look through the artwork displayed in the Clips list box. The Category list displays 31 categories, each holding a collection of clip art related to the category. When you find something you want to use, click it in the Clips pane and click the Insert button, and it's added to your slide. You also can just double-click the clip art to insert it immediately.

You can always preview clip art before inserting it. To do so, select it and click the Preview check box. This opens a larger preview window. Deselect the check box to close the window.

**FIGURE 20.9**

You can use the Clip Gallery to add clip art to your slides.

Choose a category.

Peruse clip art.

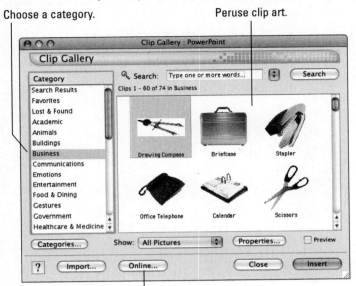

Click to download clip art.

If you don't find what you want by browsing through clip art, you can search for a particular item by typing in a keyword or phrase in the Search field. You also can look for more clip art online and download artwork into the Clip Gallery using the Online button. You learn more about working with clip art in Chapter 30.

To insert a new clip art element onto a slide, follow these steps:

1. **Click the Picture button's arrow on the Standard toolbar and click Insert Clip Art, or choose Insert ➪ Clip Art.**

2. **The Clip Gallery appears (refer to Figure 20.9).**

3. **Choose a category.**

4. **Click a clip to insert.**

5. **Click the Insert button.**

    PowerPoint inserts the artwork, as shown in Figure 20.10.

Like the text boxes you previously learned about, you can move and resize the clip art as needed. Click the clip art to select it, move the mouse pointer over the box until it becomes a four-sided arrow pointer, and then click and drag the box to a new location. To resize the clip art, move the mouse pointer over a corner or middle border area until the pointer becomes a two-sided arrow pointer. You can then click and drag to resize the artwork. To keep the artwork to scale, press and hold the Shift key while dragging the corner. You also can rotate the artwork, format it, and more. To learn how, see Chapter 30.

**FIGURE 20.10**

Every element you add to a slide appears in its own box area.

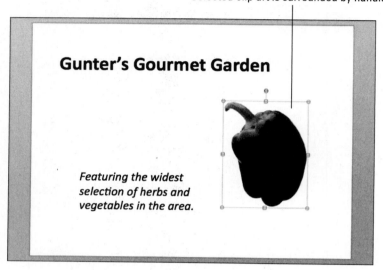

Selected clip art is surrounded by handles.

# Gunter's Gourmet Garden

*Featuring the widest selection of herbs and vegetables in the area.*

## Adding a picture

You can easily insert digital photos or graphic files stored on your computer into your PowerPoint slides. If your slide layout already has an option for inserting a picture, click the Insert Picture from File icon. This opens the Choose a Picture dialog box shown in Figure 20.11. Navigate to the folder or drive containing the photo, click the filename for the photo you want to insert, and click the Insert button. PowerPoint immediately adds it to the slide.

To insert a new picture element onto a slide, follow these steps:

1. **Click the Picture button's arrow on the Standard toolbar and click Insert Picture, or choose Insert ⇨ Picture.**
2. **The Choose a Picture dialog box appears (refer to Figure 20.11).**
3. **Navigate to the file you want to insert.**
4. **Click the Insert button.**

   PowerPoint inserts the picture, as shown in Figure 20.12.

You can move and resize the picture or graphic. Click the picture to select it, move the mouse pointer over the image until it becomes a four-sided arrow pointer, and then click and drag the picture to a new location. To resize the picture, move the mouse pointer over a corner or middle border area until the pointer becomes a two-sided arrow pointer. You can then click and drag to resize the picture. You also can rotate the picture or adjust its formatting. To learn more about using and editing photos and other graphics in Office, see Chapter 30.

**FIGURE 20.11**

You can use the Choose a Picture dialog box to add photos and other graphic files your slides.

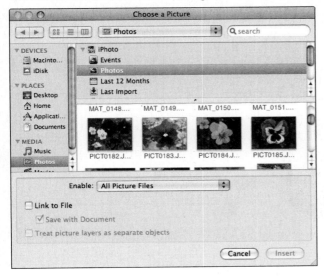

**FIGURE 20.12**

Photos can really help convey a message and make your slide more interesting. Of course, you'll want to choose images that pertain to your content.

## Adding a table

You can add tables to your slides and populate them with data. The quickest way to insert a table is to choose a table from the preset tables available in the Elements Gallery. Click the Table Styles tab, as shown in Figure 20.13, and browse through the tables until you find the one you want. Click it, and the Insert Table dialog box opens, as shown in Figure 20.14. Specify the number of columns and rows you want, and click OK to create the table on the slide.

**FIGURE 20.13**

You can use the Table Styles tab in the Elements Gallery to insert tables.

**FIGURE 20.14**

You can use the Insert Table dialog box to specify how many columns and rows to use in a table.

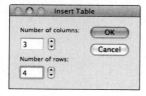

If your slide layout already has an option for inserting a table, click the Insert Table icon. This, too, opens the Insert Table dialog box shown in Figure 20.14. Set the number of columns and rows you want to create and click OK. PowerPoint immediately adds the table to the slide, and you can fill in the cells with your own text. Figure 20.15 shows a simple table added from the Elements Gallery.

To insert a new table element onto a slide, just click the Table button on the Standard toolbar and drag across the number of columns and rows you want to create. You also can choose Insert ⇨ Table to open the Insert Table dialog box (refer to Figure 20.14) and set the number of columns and rows to insert.

PowerPoint's tables work just like tables in Word. You can use the Tab key to move from cell to cell, and you can resize columns and rows by dragging their borders. You also can move and resize the entire table just as you would any other slide element you add. To learn more about using tables, see Chapter 8.

## Adding a chart

You can add charts to your slides and populate them with data with a little help from Excel. The quickest way to insert a chart is to choose a chart type from the preset charts available in the Elements Gallery. Click the Charts tab, as shown in Figure 20.16, and glance through the charts until you find the one you want. Click it, and Excel opens with a worksheet ready to go. Fill in the data, and close Excel to return to PowerPoint.

**FIGURE 20.15**

Any table you insert from the Elements Gallery is already formatted and ready for data.

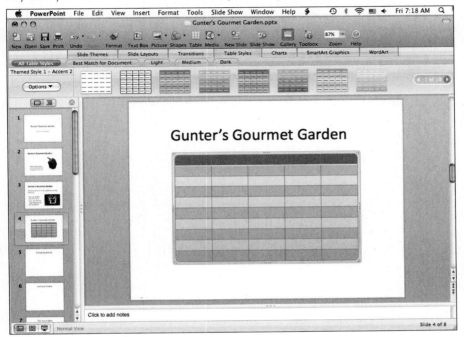

**FIGURE 20.16**

Insert a chart using the Elements Gallery.

 You can click the Insert Chart icon in a layout's content box to display the Charts styles in the Elements Gallery.

After you insert a chart, as shown in Figure 20.17, you can move and resize it. Click the chart to select it, move the mouse pointer over the chart until it becomes a four-sided arrow pointer, and then click and drag the chart to a new location. To resize the chart, move the mouse pointer over a corner or middle border area until the pointer becomes a two-sided arrow pointer. You can then click and drag to resize the chart. To learn more about using charts, see Chapter 16.

## FIGURE 20.17

Charts appear in their own boxes, which you can move and resize as needed.

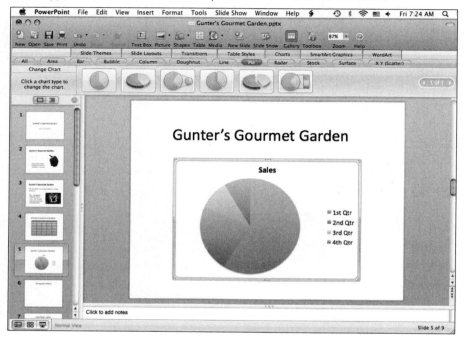

## Adding a SmartArt graphic

The Office SmartArt graphics are handy pre-drawn artwork you can use to diagram processes, cycles, work-flows, hierarchies, relationships, and more. Click the SmartArt Graphics tab on the Elements Gallery to view a list of all kinds of SmartArt, as shown in Figure 20.18. If your slide layout already has an option for inserting SmartArt, click the Insert SmartArt Graphic icon.

## FIGURE 20.18

You can add SmartArt graphics to diagram or explain relationships.

From the Gallery, click the artwork you want to insert, and a Text Pane appears where you can enter the data to make the art, as shown in Figure 20.19. You can type your text in the pane window or directly into the box on the slide.

## FIGURE 20.19

Fill in the boxes with your own content.

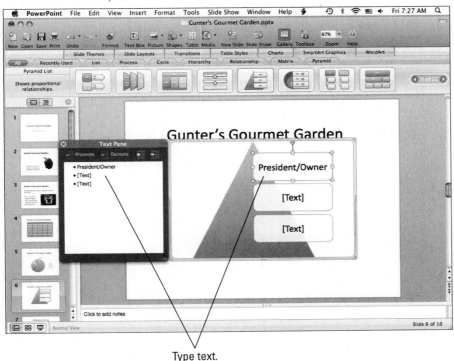

Type text.

 If you want to insert shapes into your slide, you can display the Object Palette in the Toolbox, or choose Insert ⇨ Shape, or click the Shapes button on the Standard toolbar. From the palette, click the shape you want to insert, and click where you want it to appear on the slide.

**CROSS-REF** See Chapter 30 to learn more about using shapes and other graphic objects in the Office programs.

### Adding a movie or sound clip

 You can add a movie clip to your slide by clicking the Media button on the Standard toolbar and clicking Insert Movie. You also can choose Insert ⇨ Movie. If your layout shows a content box, you can click the Insert Movie from File icon. Any of these methods opens the Insert Movie dialog box, shown in Figure 20.20. Locate the movie file you want to insert, select it, and click Choose.

PowerPoint immediately adds it to the slide, but not before asking you how you want the movie to play, as shown in Figure 20.21. You can choose to play the movie automatically or when clicked.

**FIGURE 20.20**

You can use the Insert Movie dialog box to add movie clips to your slides.

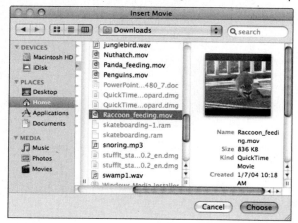

**FIGURE 20.21**

PowerPoint prompts you to choose how you want the movie to play.

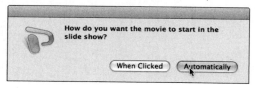

When you insert a movie clip, the Toolbox displays a new pane in the Formatting Palette—the Movie pane, shown in Figure 20.22. When you display this pane, you can find settings for controlling the movie's playback in a slide. You can change how the movie plays, adjust sound volume, hide the movie, play the movie full-screen, loop the playback over and over again, or rewind after playing. You can click the Play button at the top of the Movie pane to view the movie while editing the slide. To include the QuickTime movie controls with the clip, click the Show Controller button. The QuickTime movie controls appear at the bottom of the clip, with buttons for playing and pausing the playback.

Just like all the other slide elements you add in PowerPoint, you can move and resize the movie element as needed.

When you add a movie clip, it's generally embedded as a link, so if you're copying the presentation onto another computer, be sure to copy the movie file as well. If you'd like everything kept together so you don't have to worry about copying individual elements, you can save the presentation as a package instead. Choose the PowerPoint Package file format when saving the presentation.

 You also can add sound clips to a slide. Click the Media button on the Standard toolbar and click Insert Sound and Music, or choose Insert ➪ Sound and Music ➪ From File. Either method opens the Insert Sound dialog box, shown in Figure 20.23. Locate the sound file you want to insert, select it, and click Insert.

**FIGURE 20.22**

Use the Movie pane in the Formatting Palette to set playback controls, volume, or looping.

QuickTime playback controls

**FIGURE 20.23**

You can use the Insert Sound dialog box to add sound clips to your slides.

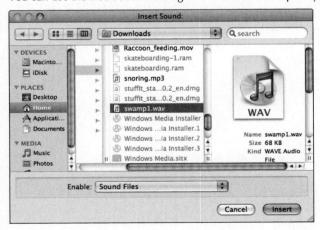

PowerPoint immediately adds it to the slide as a tiny speaker icon, but not before asking you how you want the sound to play, as shown in Figure 20.24. You can choose to play the sound automatically or when clicked.

As soon as you insert a sound clip, the Toolbox displays a new pane in the Formatting Palette—the Sound pane, as shown in Figure 20.25. This pane has settings for controlling the sound's playback in a slide. You can change how the sound plays, adjust the volume, hide the clip, or loop the playback over and over again. You can place the sound icon anywhere you want on a slide or resize it as needed.

**FIGURE 20.24**

When inserting sounds, choose how you want them to play.

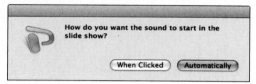

**FIGURE 20.25**

Use the Sound pane in the Formatting Palette to set playback controls for the sound clip.

Sound pane

Sound icon

Like movie clips, sound clips are embedded as links, so if you're copying the presentation onto another computer, be sure to copy the sound file as well. To keep all the slide elements together, such as movie and sound clips, you can save the presentation as a package by choosing the PowerPoint Package file format when saving the file.

# Assigning Themes

You can use themes to give your presentation a coherent look and feel. Themes are premade designs that come in a variety of color schemes, font styles, and background graphics. When you assign a theme, any new slides you add use the theme as well, making it easy to keep your slide formatting looking the same for each slide. Because a theme really sets the tone for a presentation, be choosy and select a theme that suits your audience and your presentation topic. To assign a theme at any time, click the Slide Themes tab in the Elements Gallery and choose a theme, as shown in Figure 20.26. You also can choose Format ⇨ Slide Theme ⇨ From Gallery.

Use the professionally designed Office themes to give your presentation a coherent look and feel for every slide.

You can peruse a variety of themes in the Gallery. Click a theme to view it on a slide. Figure 20.26 shows the Median theme applied to a slide. As you move the mouse pointer over the themes, the theme name appears on the left side of the Gallery. You can continue trying out themes until you find the one you want. Click the Slide Themes tab again to hide the thumbnail icons.

> **TIP** If you have customized themes or other themes stored on your computer, you can assign them to presentations. Choose Format ⇨ Slide Theme ⇨ From File to open a dialog box where you can navigate to the theme you want to apply.

You also can find themes in the Project Gallery. If you want to start a new presentation and a new theme at the same time, choose File ⇨ Project Gallery to open the Project Gallery. Click the New tab, and choose the Office Themes category. You can inspect the choices, and select the one you want to assign with the new presentation file you're creating.

## Inserting Other Objects

You can insert other types of objects onto your PowerPoint slides, including Word documents and Excel sheets. To insert such an object, choose Insert ⇨ Object to open the Insert Object dialog box. Select the type of object you want to insert. You can create a new object or nab an existing file to insert. If you create a new object, you're taken to the source application to create the object. When you're finished creating the object, exit the application window to return to PowerPoint where your new document appears inserted into the slide. If you insert an existing object, you can use the Insert as Object dialog box to navigate to the file and add it to the slide.

# Navigating and Working with Slides

As you start building a presentation, you'll probably need to manipulate the slides from time to time. For example, you may want to delete slides you no longer need or add new slides in the middle of the presentation to cover any points you missed. This section shows you how to man-handle your slides by adding, deleting, moving, and hiding slides.

## Navigating slides

You can move around a presentation and view your slides in several ways. If you're in Normal view, the most obvious way is to use the Slides/Outline view pane, as shown in Figure 20.27. In Slide view, you can click a thumbnail of a slide, and it suddenly appears in the main Slide pane for viewing in detail. You can use the vertical scroll bar to move around from slide to slide, click the arrow buttons to move up or down the presentation one slide at a time, or drag the scrollbar to move to a slide.

The current slide always appears highlighted in the Slides/Outline view pane, and the slide number appears in the bottom-right corner of the Status bar.

Chapters 22 and 23 show you how to navigate slides in Slide Sorter view and Slide Show view, respectively.

**FIGURE 20.27**

You can navigate among your slides using the Slide/Outline view pane; just click a slide to view it.

Click a slide to navigate to that slide.

Use scroll arrows to navigate among slides.

## Adding and deleting slides

The tasks of adding and deleting slides are essential to building a presentation. Unless you're presenting a one-slide show, you're probably going to want to add new slides to your program. Use any of these methods to quickly insert a slide:

- Click the New Slide button on the Standard toolbar.
- Choose Insert ⇨ New Slide.
- Press Shift+⌘+N.
- Control+click the current slide, and choose New Slide.

If your presentation has a theme assigned, PowerPoint adds the theme to the new slide. After you have a new slide in place, you can change its layout and start adding content.

You also can duplicate an existing slide in a presentation. For example, perhaps you want to use the same layout, but change the wording of the text slightly. To duplicate a slide, click the slide and press ⌘+D, or choose Edit ⇨ Duplicate. PowerPoint inserts the duplicate right after the current slide.

To remove a slide you no longer want as part of your presentation, select the slide in the Slide view pane and use any of these techniques:

- Press Delete.
- Choose Edit ⇨ Delete Slide.
- Control+click the slide, and choose Delete Slide.

## Moving slides

You can move slides in Normal view easily. Just click the thumbnail of the slide you want to move in the Slides/Outline view pane, and drag and drop it where you want it to go. If you're viewing your presentation as an outline, you can use the same technique; just click and drag the tiny icon in front of the slide you want to move. You also can use the standard Cut, Copy, and Paste commands to move slides around.

You can use the drag-and-drop method to move slides in Slide Sorter view, too, as you learn in Chapter 22.

## Hiding slides

If you'd like to skip slides rather than delete them entirely, you can hide them in a presentation. PowerPoint keeps the slides where they are, but skips them during a slide show. Select the slide or slides you want to hide and choose Slide Show ⇨ Hide Slide, or ctrl+click the slide and choose Hide Slide. PowerPoint marks the hidden slide in the Slides/Outline view pane with a tiny white box around the slide number.

You can follow the same steps to unhide the slide.

 If you want to display any hidden slides during the actual presentation, you can press H when the preceding slide appears.

## Inserting slides from other presentations

You can bring in slides from other presentations to use in the current presentation. This is a great way to recycle material, build on previous shows, or utilize a well-received program. Choose Insert ⇨ Slides From ⇨ Other Presentation. This opens the Choose a File dialog box shown in Figure 20.28.

**FIGURE 20.28**

PowerPoint lets you insert slides from other presentations.

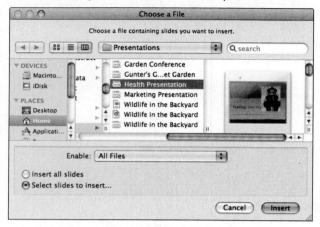

You can navigate to the presentation you want to use and click it. In the area at the bottom of the dialog box, choose whether you want to insert all the slides or select specific slides to insert. If you choose the former, PowerPoint automatically imports all the slides and inserts them after the current slide. If you have a theme applied to the current presentation, PowerPoint adds the theme to the imported slides.

If you choose to import only specific slides, the Slide Finder box opens and you can click which slides to insert. As shown in Figure 20.29, the Slide Finder dialog box shows thumbnails of every slide in the presentation. You can click which slide or slides you want to import, and then click the Insert button. When finished, click the Close button to close the dialog box.

**FIGURE 20.29**

You can pick and choose which slides to import.

# Working with Slide Masters

Have you ever worked with slide masters before? At first mention it sort of sounds like a gang of Samurai PowerPoint users or a *Star Wars* subplot, doesn't it? Perhaps you're picturing a cluster of Ninjas in white robes belting out PowerPoint commands while defensively positioned in a circle? As far as I know, there are no PowerPoint Ninjas, but slide masters are a good thing to know about. Not many people are aware of slide masters and how they can help you tailor-make a presentation.

The slide master is the blueprint of your presentation. It's a special slide that works behind the scenes to determine the look of all the slide elements for the entire slide show. That slide master stores information about how text and objects are placed, what fonts and sizes are used, and which backgrounds, color schemes, and special effects are assigned. This probably doesn't sound very exciting at first, but as it turns out, slide masters can help you create a custom presentation. For example, did you know you can tell PowerPoint to put your company logo on every slide? By placing the logo on the slide master, it's always inserted into every slide in the entire presentation. You don't have to do a thing; the logo is already added for you.

That's not all the customizing you can do. You can change the font, font size, text color, text box size, and anything else you want to modify and affect every slide. For example, you may want the slide title text boxes to appear in a different location than the default layout dictates. You can reposition and resize s tandard layout elements on the slide master to create a custom layout as well as a custom presentation.

In order to edit a slide master, you must first switch over to slide master view. Choose View➪Master➪Slide Master. PowerPoint displays the Master toolbar, and the master slide appears at the top of the Slides/Outline view pane, as shown in Figure 20.30. All the other standard slide layouts are listed below the master slide. This means all the standard layouts are subservient to the master slide. You can make changes to the objects in the master slide that affect all the other layouts. For example, if you want the title text to appear in a different default font, apply the font to the title text box on the master slide.

 You also can create a new standard layout to use in your slide show while in slide master view. Any new layout you create is added to the list of layouts that appear on the Slide Layouts tab in the Elements Gallery. To create a brand new standard layout, click the space between the master slide and the first standard layout listed in the left pane. On the Master toolbar, click the Insert New Layout button. A new layout appears in the Slides/Outline view pane, as shown in Figure 20.31. Using the tools on the Master toolbar, add any placeholders you want to put in the new layout. For example, if you want a generic content box that can hold anything from text to SmartArt graphics to movie clips, click the Content button and draw the box on the slide. The Master toolbar also has buttons for drawing plain old text boxes for content, tables, charts, SmartArt graphics, clip art, pictures, and media clips if you want a specific kind of content box.

**FIGURE 20.30**

Switch to slide master view to create a custom presentation.

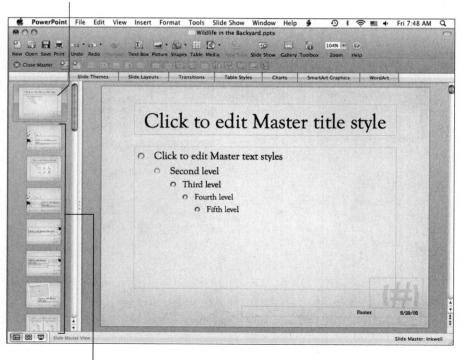

# Other Masters in PowerPoint

Not only does PowerPoint have a slide master, but it also has handout masters and notes masters. Like the slide master, both the handout and notes masters act as blueprints for any handouts and notes you create. Handouts are simply special page designs you can create containing one or more slides to print out and distribute to your audience. Notes are like handouts, displaying both the slide and any note text pertaining to the slide, and also can be used as handouts or just as notes for yourself. You can control the appearance of either feature using the appropriate master. To change the handout feature, choose View ⇨ Master ⇨ Handout Master. To change the notes feature, choose View ⇨ Master ⇨ Notes Master. You can make edits to the elements as needed, such as changing headers and footers, fonts, and so on. When you finish, click the Close Master button to exit and apply the changes.

## FIGURE 20.31

You can create new layouts in the slide master, or you can modify existing layouts.

Master toolbar

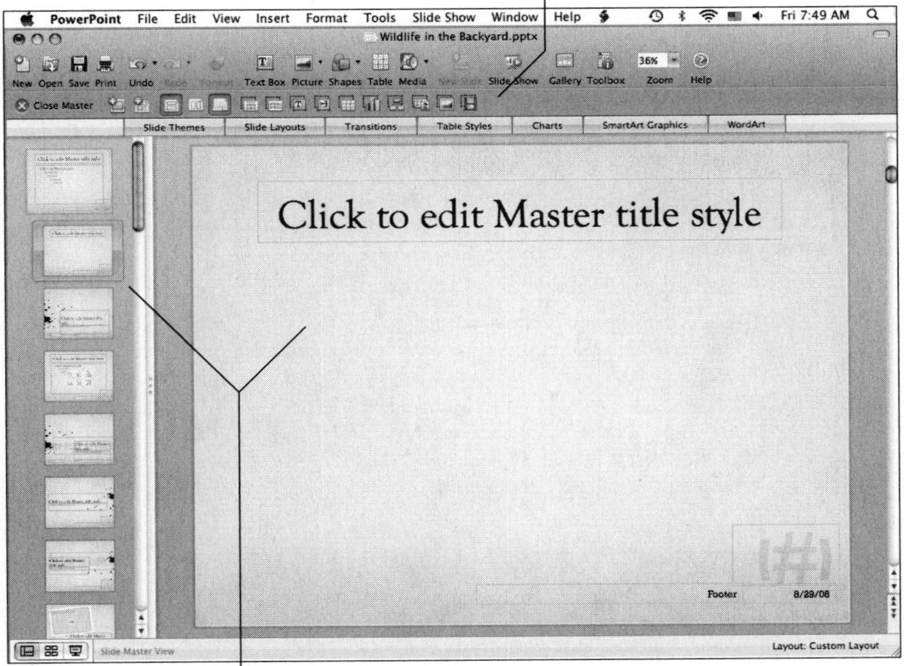

Add your own custom layout.

PowerPoint gives any new layouts you create a default name of Custom Layout. If you create more than one, it starts numbering them. To give the new layout a unique name instead, ctrl+click the thumbnail slide and choose Rename Layout. Type a new name in the Rename Layout dialog box and click OK.

**⊗ Close Master** When you finish editing a master slide, modifying a standard layout, or creating a new layout, you must click the Close Master button on the Master toolbar to exit. If you made a new layout, PowerPoint saves the custom layout and places it at the front of the Slide Layouts list in the Elements Gallery.

As you're editing the slide master, keep in mind that the changes apply only to the current presentation. If you edit a standard layout while in slide master view, any existing slides in the presentation based on the layout are not updated. Only new slides based on the changed layout reflect the modifications you make. For this reason, it's a good idea to modify the slide master to your specifications before building a new presentation.

You can revisit the slide master at any time to make changes. You also can delete any layouts you no longer want.

# Summary

In this chapter, you learned some valuable tips for getting started with planning a presentation. It's worth mentioning again how much of a time-saver it is to plan everything in advance. This can help you assemble and prepare your presentation more quickly, and anticipate problems that may occur. First and foremost, make sure you have a clear idea of what your presentation's message is and who the target audience is. After you've nailed these two items down, you can start plugging away at building a presentation.

PowerPoint's outlining feature can help you build a presentation from the ground up, establishing main presentation points in an outline form and building on them to include meatier content. You learned how to use the Slides/Outline view pane to whip up an outline. You also learned how to import outlines from Word.

When it comes to assembling slides for a slide show, PowerPoint does all the design work for you through themes and layouts. You can create your own layouts, of course, to make custom presentations. PowerPoint merely guides you in laying out the content, however. It's up to you to create the actual content. Placeholder boxes make it easy, though, to position various slide elements and help present your material in the form of text, visuals, and sound. This chapter showed you how to apply layouts and insert individual content elements into your slides. You also learned how to create a custom presentation by tweaking the slide master—your presentation's blueprint for overall appearance and design. Now you're ready to move on to formatting slide elements.

# Chapter 21

# Formatting Slides

As the author and creator of the presentations you make in PowerPoint, you have complete control over how things look. You're in charge of everything from fonts and sizes to backgrounds and color. This may seem a little overwhelming at first, but as you'll soon see, PowerPoint makes it easy to manage all these things through formatting controls found throughout the program. Even if you turn over most of the formatting to PowerPoint's themes or templates, chances are good that your slides will need a little tweaking from time to time. You may need to make the font more legible on a background or make the bulleted text larger to fill up some space. In this chapter, you learn how to utilize all the formatting controls to make your presentations look their very best.

## Formatting Text

Many presentations utilize text boxes to convey a message. As such an important slide element, text boxes are often one of the first things you need to format when you're making changes to the appearance of a slide. For example, sometimes you can improve the legibility of slide text simply by making it bold or bigger. Or maybe you want to add emphasis by italicizing a keyword or phrase in a text box. This section covers all the various formatting techniques you can apply to your presentation text. When it comes to formatting techniques, PowerPoint has a myriad of options to help you quickly change the appearance of text and text boxes in your slides and change the formatting of other slide elements.

When applying formatting to text in PowerPoint, you can select the text box by clicking the box border, or you can select text within the text box. You can use the same text selection techniques you learned in Word to select text in PowerPoint. For example, you can click and drag to select words with the mouse, or you can double-click to select a single word or triple-click to select a sentence. Learning to select a slide element is the key to applying any sort of formatting changes.

## Using the Formatting Palette

Your first stop for any formatting needs is the Formatting Palette. The Formatting Palette is one of several palettes contained within PowerPoint's Toolbox feature. As shown in Figure 21.1, the Formatting Palette is the first palette in the Toolbox bunch. On this palette are settings and options for formatting the text font and size, alignment, bullets and numbering, backgrounds, and so on.

 If the Toolbox is not displayed, click the Toolbox button on the Standard toolbar. Click the Formatting Palette icon at the top of the Toolbox to display the formatting options. Notice that the formatting controls are grouped into panes in the Formatting Palette. PowerPoint changes which panes appear in the palette depending on the task at hand. If you click a text box element on a slide, the palette displays 11 panes you can use to format the element. If you click an empty area of a slide, the palette displays only three panes. You can expand or collapse the panes to view or hide the options.

You can hide or display the Toolbox by toggling it on or off using the Toolbox button on the Standard toolbar. You also can open the Toolbox to a specific palette using the View menu; choose View ⇨ Formatting Palette, for example. In addition to the Formatting Palette, you can find formatting controls through the Format menu.

 If you're unhappy with any formatting you apply to a slide element, you can click the Undo button on the Standard toolbar to quickly undo it. Or you can choose Edit ⇨ Undo.

---

**FIGURE 21.1**

You can use the Formatting Palette in the Toolbox to quickly access common formatting features and settings.

Click to display the Formatting Palette.

## Applying bold, italics, and underline

**B**
**I**
**U**

If it's quick and easy formatting you want, look no further than the Bold, Italics, or Underline commands. These three common formatting commands are found in just about every computer program involving text. With a click of any of these commands, you can make your text appear bold, italicized, or underlined. You can find the Bold, Italic, and Underline commands on the Formatting Palette in the Toolbox or in the Format dialog box. Click the Toolbox icon and click the Formatting Palette button to display the options, or choose Format ⇨ Font to open the Font dialog box. You also can Control+click the text and choose Font to open the dialog box. If you're using the Toolbox to assign the formatting, just click the button for the formatting you want to apply. In Figure 21.2, the first word in the title text box appears in bold, the second word is italicized, and the third word is underlined.

---

**FIGURE 21.2**

Here are examples of bold, italics, and underlining at work in a text box.

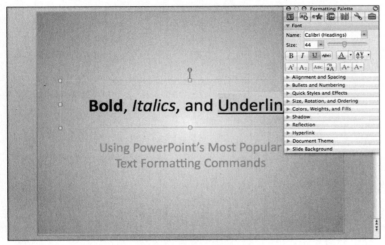

If you're using the Format dialog box to apply simple formatting, as shown in Figure 21.3, click the Font style drop-down menu and choose Italic, Bold, or Bold Italic. To apply underlining, click the Underline Style menu and choose a style. Use the Format dialog box when you want to find a greater selection of underline styles to apply to your text. The Underline button on the Formatting Palette only applies a default underlining style.

## Formatting with fonts and sizes

One of the most common formatting tasks you'll perform in PowerPoint is changing the font and size of your slide text. A font governs the appearance of text characters, and the font size, naturally, determines how big or small the text is. You can use the Font pane in the Formatting Palette to change fonts and sizes, or you can use the Format dialog box.

To change the font using the palette, start by selecting the text and making sure the Font pane is displayed in the Formatting Palette. You can click the Font arrow button to view a drop-down list of fonts, as shown in Figure 21.4. Click the one you want to apply, and PowerPoint immediately changes the selected text. To change the font size, click the Size arrow button and choose another size, or you can click and drag the Size handle to the right of the Size setting.

**FIGURE 21.3**

You can use the Format dialog box to apply bold, italics, or underlining to your slide text.

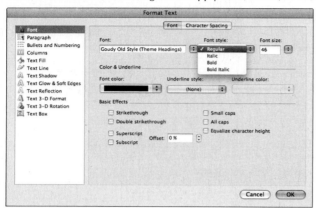

**FIGURE 21.4**

You can change the font and size settings on the Font pane to format your slide text.

You also can use the Format dialog box to set a new font and size. Choose Format ⇨ Font to open the dialog box. Click the Font tab if it's not already displayed. You can click the Font arrow button to display a pop-up menu of fonts to choose from and make your selection, as shown in Figure 21.5. To change the size, click the Font size pop-up menu and choose a size, or type a size directly into the field. Click OK to exit the dialog box and apply any changes.

## FIGURE 21.5

You can use the Format dialog box to set the font and size for text.

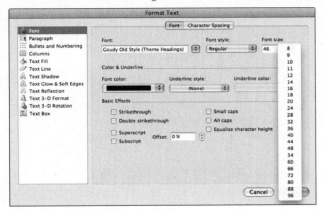

 The Formatting Palette has two handy buttons for quickly resizing selected text: Increase Font Size and Decrease Font Size. A click of either button bumps your text up or down a font size. Keep clicking to continue resizing. You won't find these commands in the Font dialog box. They're available only on the Formatting Palette of the Toolbox, as shown in Figure 21.6.

## FIGURE 21.6

Use the Increase Font Size or Decrease Font Size buttons to quickly increase or decrease your slide text.

Click a size button.

# Keep It Simple

**D**on't use too many different fonts and sizes in a presentation, especially on one slide. Among PowerPoint's themes and templates, you'll notice that only one or two fonts are used on most layouts. This creates a nice flow in appearance, making the text easy to read on each slide. If you use more than one or two fonts, the effect becomes jarring and distracting for the audience. Stick with what the pros know: Pick a font and use it consistently.

The same is true of font sizes. If you use too many on a single slide, you'll end up with a messy-looking slide that's hard to follow. Be careful when trying to fill up space. A little extra space between elements provides a nice cushion, and if you pack too many elements into one slide, it looks crowded. Keep your slides simple, and your audience will pay attention to your message instead of the chaos onscreen.

## Formatting bullets and numbering

Lists can make your slides more readable and visually interesting, and you can use either bulleted or numbered lists in PowerPoint. You can change bulleted and numbering formats for slide text using the Bullets and Numbering pane in the Formatting Palette. For starters, you can toggle bullets or numbers on or off using the Type buttons: Bullets and Numbering. To apply bullets to selected text, click the Bullets button; to apply numbers, click the Numbering button. Figure 21.7 shows an example of a slide with bulleted text. The pane also features controls for setting a color for the bullets or numbers and changing the indentation.

**FIGURE 21.7**

Use bulleted or numbered lists to organize and present information in a slide.

You can change the style of the bullets or numbers using the Style pop-up menu, shown in Figure 21.8. You can choose from several bullet and number styles, such as open bullets or check marks. In the case of numbers, you can choose from several number styles including Roman numerals and letter numbering.

**FIGURE 21.8**

Use the Style pop-up menu to change the bullet or number style for a list.

If the pop-up menu doesn't display the style you're looking for, you can open the Format Text dialog box to the Bullets and Numbering tabs, as shown in Figures 21.9 and 21.10. You can access the dialog box through the Bullets and Numbering command at the bottom of the Style menu, or you can choose Format ➪ Bullets and Numbering. This dialog box features a variety of styles as well as settings to customize your own list style. For example, in the Bullets tab you can change the color and size of the bullets. In the Numbering tab, you can customize a start number for a list, as well as change the color and size of the numbers.

**FIGURE 21.9**

Find more bullet styles in the Bullets tab of the Format Text dialog box.

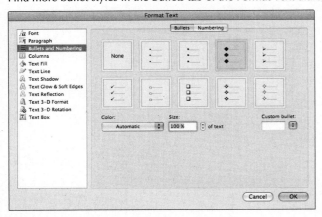

**FIGURE 21.10**

**FIGURE 21.10**

Customize number styles in the Numbering tab.

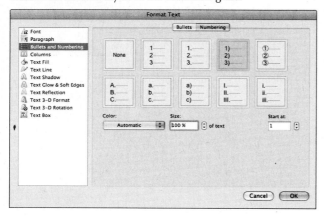

## Formatting with alignment and spacing

You can use the Alignment and Spacing pane in the Formatting Palette to control how text is positioned within a text box. The pane, shown in Figure 21.11, offers controls for horizontal and vertical positioning and controls for changing the orientation of the text within a text box. Here you'll find common alignments such as left, center, right, and justified.

**FIGURE 21.11**

The Alignment and Spacing pane features controls for setting alignment and spacing in your text.

You'll also notice additional alignment and spacing controls in the pane. For example, the Wrap text check box lets you choose to wrap a text box around a graphic object, while the Shrink text to fit check box automatically resizes the text to fit within a box. The buttons under the Paragraph Spacing and Columns area let you control space between paragraphs and turn the selected text into columns.

In addition to the Alignment and Spacing pane, you also find alignment controls in the Format menu; choose Format ⇨ Alignment, and choose an alignment. To view Paragraph formatting options, choose Format ⇨ Paragraph. This opens the Format Text dialog box to the Paragraph controls, shown in Figure 21.12. Here you can choose additional alignment, indentation, and spacing settings.

**FIGURE 21.12**

Find additional spacing options in the Format Text dialog box in the Paragraph category.

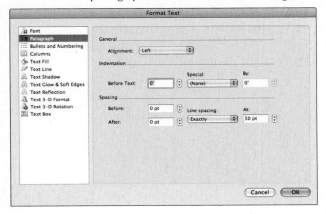

 Character spacing, which is the space between individual characters you type, has a control on the Formatting Palette. Look in the Font pane for the Character Spacing button. You can choose from Very Tight, Tight, Normal, Loose, Very Loose, and More Spacing. If you click the More Spacing option, the Format Text dialog box opens to the Character Spacing tab, where you can set additional spacing and kerning controls.

## Formatting with color

 You can use the Font Color command to assign color to your slide text. Click the Font Color arrow button, shown Figure 21.13, to display a pop-up palette of colors you can choose from, including a set of colors to complement any themes you assign.

You can click the More Colors option on the Font Color menu to open the Colors dialog box and set a custom color for your text. To match an existing color, use the Pick A Color command. To set additional text colors, such as fills and outlines, open the Format Text dialog box by choosing the Text Effects option form the Font Color menu. From the Format Text dialog box, shown in Figure 21.14, you can use any of the text categories to apply formatting. For example, you can click the Text Fill and Text Line categories to reveal settings for creating an inside fill color for the text and an outer border. This works well with a heavy or thick font type. You also find options for creating glowing text, text with shadows, reflecting text, 3-D text, and rotated text.

**FIGURE 21.13**

You can use the Font Color feature to assign a color to your slide text.

**FIGURE 21.14**

Use the Text categories in the Format Text dialog box to create all kinds of specialized formatting attributes.

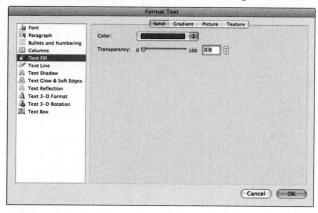

You can find controls for text boxes in the Format Text dialog box, shown in Figure 21.15. Select the Text Box category to find settings for text layout within a text box, settings for controlling margins, and settings for controlling how text fits inside the text box.

 **TIP** You can double-click the border of any text box to quickly access the Format Text dialog box and choose what formatting you want to change.

The Text Box category in the Format Text dialog box offers settings for controlling text box elements in your slides.

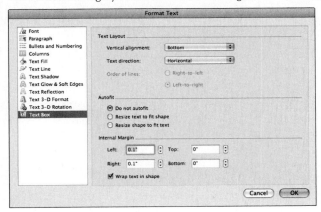

## Applying Quick Styles and Effects for text

You can use PowerPoint's Quick Styles and Effects pane to apply a reusable artistic style to text boxes, pictures, charts, tables, and other slide elements. Depending on which slide element you're working on, different Quick Styles are available to apply. When formatting text boxes, you can choose from Quick Styles, Shadows, Glows, Reflections, 3-D Effects, and Text Transform. Click the Quick Styles and Effects pane to view your options, as shown in Figure 21.16.

Use the Quick Styles and Effects pane to assign specialized text effects.

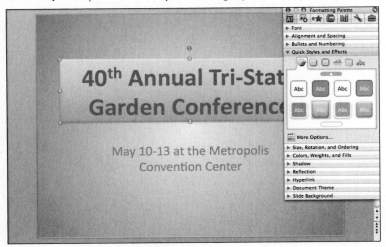

You can click a style button to view a menu of effects. You can choose from the following styles:

- **Quick Styles:** Click this style to display a menu of text box color backgrounds to apply to the text.
- **Shadows:** The Shadows styles include effects that create the illusion of shadows behind your slide text.
- **Glows:** Choose from a menu of effects that create the illusion of glowing text on a slide in this style category.
- **Reflections:** Styles in this menu create a reflective effect for your slide text.
- **3-D Effects:** This category creates various 3-D effects, but is applicable to picture boxes rather than text.
- **Text Transforms:** Create specialized text effects, such as circular text or arched text, in this category.

You can click the More Options button at the bottom of the pane to open the Format Shape dialog box and change the effect's fill, line, shadow colors, and so on.

## Copying formatting

 If you've spent lots of time applying formatting to a slide element, you may be happy to know that PowerPoint has an easy way to redo all the formatting and apply it to another text box in your presentation. You can use the Format button on the Standard toolbar. Simply select the text or text box containing the formatting you want to copy, click the Format button, and drag across the new text or click the text box to which you want to copy the formatting.

# Easy Formatting for Slide Elements

Aside from text boxes, you can apply formatting to other slide elements in your presentation. Although you can learn more about formatting graphic objects in Office in Chapter 30, we touch on some of the easy formatting options available in PowerPoint in this section. For example, you may decide a clip art box needs a new color background or shape, or the photo you inserted may need a frame. You can use several techniques to apply formatting to other slide elements, including clip art, pictures, charts, tables, and SmartArt graphic objects.

Depending on which slide element you're currently working with, the handy Formatting Palette on the Toolbox offers panes specific to the element. For example, if you click a clip art or picture element, the Picture pane appears, as shown in Figure 21.17. If you click a table, the Table pane appears on the palette. You can use the element-specific pane to make formatting changes to the object. In addition to the element-specific pane, the Formatting Palette may display panes for formatting the size, rotation, and ordering of the object, borders and shading, shadows, and reflections.

If the Formatting Palette doesn't offer enough options for you, you also can double-click the border of a slide element or Control+click the element to open its Format dialog box, shown in Figure 21.18. The dialog box offers many of the same settings found on the Formatting Palette, as well as some additional options not found on the palette. For example, if you double-click a picture or clip art element, the Format Picture dialog box opens, and you can choose a category and options for formatting the element.

**FIGURE 21.17**

PowerPoint displays element-specific panes for formatting individual slide elements.

Picture pane

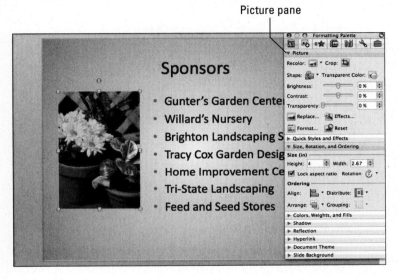

**FIGURE 21.18**

You can find formatting options for slide elements in the element-specific Format dialog box.

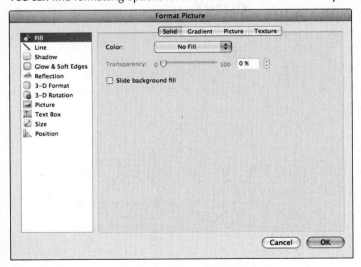

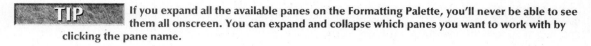
> **TIP** If you expand all the available panes on the Formatting Palette, you'll never be able to see them all onscreen. You can expand and collapse which panes you want to work with by clicking the pane name.

## Applying Quick Styles and Effects

For easy formatting effects, turn to PowerPoint's Quick Styles and Effects pane. You can use the controls in this pane to apply a reusable style to text boxes, pictures, charts, tables, and other slide elements. As you learned in the text formatting section, this pane displays different Quick Styles depending on what kind of slide element you're formatting. When formatting a picture or clip art element, you can choose from Quick Styles, Shadows, Glows, Reflections, and 3-D Effects. Not all styles and effects are available for every slide element. Click the Quick Styles and Effects pane to view the styles and effects, as shown in Figure 21.19.

### FIGURE 21.19

Use the Quick Styles and Effects pane to assign frames, shadows, 3-D effects and more.

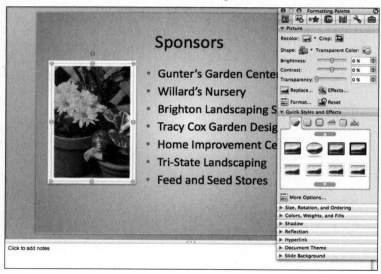

You can choose from the following styles:

- **Quick Styles:** This option displays a menu of frames and other background color effects to apply to the element.
- **Shadows:** This option displays a menu of shadow styles to create the illusion of shadows behind the slide element.
- **Glows:** This option displays a menu of glow effects to create the illusion of glowing object.
- **Reflections:** This option displays a menu of reflection styles to create the illusion of a reflection of the slide element.
- **3-D Effects:** This option displays a menu of various 3-D effects.

If you click the More Options button at the bottom of the pane, the element's Format dialog box appears where you can further customize the effect.

## Formatting with shadows and reflections

You can whip up customized shadow and reflection effects for slide elements using the Shadow and Reflection panes on the Formatting Palette. For example, the Shadow pane, shown in Figure 21.20, lets you control the angle of the effect and the style, color, distance, blur, and transparency of the shadow. You can experiment with the controls to create your own specialized effect.

**FIGURE 21.20**

The Shadow pane offers controls for creating customized shadow effects.

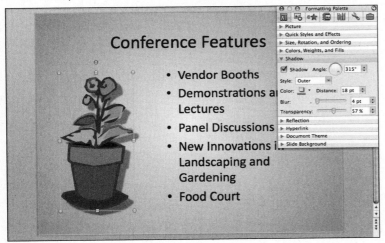

You can find the same controls and more in the element's Format dialog box; double-click the element's border area or Control+click the element and choose the Format command.

Like the Shadow pane, the Reflection pane, shown in Figure 21.21, offers controls for customizing a reflection effect. You can set a transparency level, size, and distance for the reflection.

## Formatting with colors, weights, and fills

The Colors, Weights, and Fills pane on the Formatting Palette contains settings for controlling the fill color and line style for a slide element. The fill color is the interior color of a selected element, while the line style is the outer border of an element. For example, you can select a clip art object and click the Fill Color button to change the clip art's fill color. You can customize the effect further by setting a transparency level. You might add a border to an element and make it thick or change its color to match the slide theme. The Colors, Weights, and Fills pane, shown in Figure 21.22, includes controls for customizing any fill or line styles, and you can experiment with the controls to create your own specialized effect.

**FIGURE 21.21**

The Reflection pane offers controls for creating customized reflection effects for your slide objects.

**FIGURE 21.22**

The Colors, Weights, and Fills pane is the place to go to set fill colors and lines for a slide element.

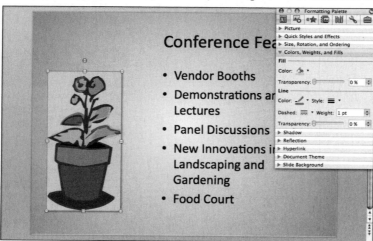

## Formatting for size, rotation, and slide order

The Size, Rotation, and Ordering pane in the Formatting Palette includes options for setting a precise size for a slide element. Do you need to rotate a piece of clip art, change the alignment positions of objects, or change the order of shapes stacked in a slide to create artwork? You can find controls for all these formatting options in this one pane. Shown in Figure 21.23, you can use these options to perform a variety of edits based on size, rotation, and order. For example, if you want to move several slide elements at once, you can group them with the Grouping command, or if you want to distribute the objects equally on the slide, you can use the Distribute command. If you want to tilt a picture slightly, you can rotate it left or right, or flip it horizontally or vertically. This is handy if you need a piece of clip art to face into the slide, for example.

**FIGURE 21.23**

To control the size, rotation, and order position of an object, use the Size, Rotation, and Ordering pane.

The Arrange setting, part of the Ordering option group, helps you control how items are ordered in a stacking scheme on the slide. Your options are Bring to Front, Send to Back, Bring Forward, and Send Backward. For example, if you have several shapes you want to place behind a text box, you can use the Bring Forward or Bring to Front commands to place the text box on top of the stack. This means you can still read the text, yet see the other shapes in the background behind the text box.

## Customizing themes

In Chapter 20, you learned how to assign themes to a presentation using the Slide Themes tab on the Elements Gallery. You can customize any assigned theme using the Document Theme pane in the Formatting Palette. As you already know, themes assign preset color schemes, fonts, sizes, and backgrounds to a presentation. In the Document Themes pane, you can choose a different color scheme for a theme, change the font associated with the assigned theme, and save the settings as a new theme. Figure 21.24 shows the Document Theme pane. With a little tweaking, you can make your presentation look just the way you want, and themes make sure every slide has a similar look and feel.

If you have any previously saved themes, you can assign them using the Browse button. When clicked, this button opens the Choose Themed Document or Slide Template dialog box where you can navigate to the saved theme file you want to apply.

**FIGURE 21.24**

You can customize a slide theme using the Document Theme pane.

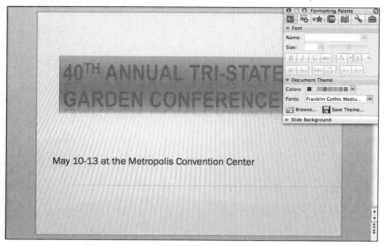

# Working with Backgrounds

Slide backgrounds appear behind the text boxes and other elements you place on a slide. PowerPoint offers a library of preset backgrounds you can assign, or you can choose to use a solid background color. The Slide Background pane, shown in Figure 21.25, lets you choose from several styles.

**FIGURE 21.25**

You can set a different slide background using the preset styles found on the Slide Background pane.

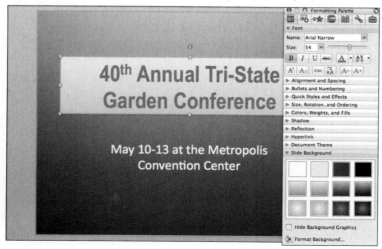

If, for example, a theme's background objects are distracting you while building a slide, you can hide them by activating the Hide Background Graphics check box in the Slide Background pane.

You can customize your own background style using the Format Background dialog box, shown in Figure 21.26. For example, you can set a new solid fill color for a background, control its transparency level, or import a photo to use as a background. You also can find a library of preset textures you can use as slide backgrounds. The Format Background dialog box has two categories: Fill and Picture. Each category has a unique set of tabs with options you can set.

**FIGURE 21.26**

Use the Format Background dialog box to set a solid color, gradient, picture, or texture as a background for your slides.

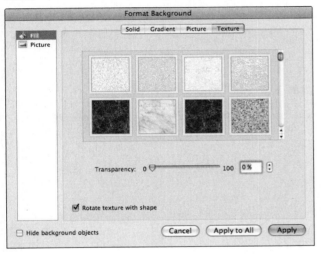

## Customizing with the Slide Master

If you want to incorporate a company logo or other image into every slide background, you can add the graphic or image to the slide master. As explained in Chapter 20, PowerPoint's slide masters are the blueprint of every presentation, working behind the scenes to control the background elements, theme elements, fonts, layout positioning, and headers and footers in a slide. If you place graphics or photos on a slide master's background, PowerPoint is sure to include the images on every slide in the presentation. To learn more about using slide masters, see Chapter 20.

# Summary

In this chapter, you learned how easily you can apply formatting attributes in PowerPoint. You learned how to format text by changing its font and size, color, and alignment. You also learned how to customize bullets and numbers for lists in your slides. Another way to customize a slide is to format individual slide elements, such as clip art, pictures, charts, and tables. You can use the panes and options found on the Formatting Palette to make changes to your slide elements. For example, you can customize a clip art image by adding a border or assigning a shadow effect. There's no end to the combination of formatting attributes you can apply, and PowerPoint makes it easy to experiment with the settings to create just the right look. You can even customize themes to work the way you want.

As you saw in this chapter, the Formatting Palette is the main hangout for all the major formatting attributes you might want to apply. However, if you're looking for even more formatting controls, just open the slide element's Format dialog box.

# Chapter 22

# Fine-tuning a Presentation

You've worked hard assembling a presentation, adding slide content, and formatting your slides. While you certainly can give your presentation as is, you also can do more. You can fine-tune a presentation by adding transition effects, animation effects, and sound or music. Consider these elements the icing on the presentation cake, so to speak. You can polish a presentation by adding special effects, such as making bullet points fly in one at a time, setting time lengths for each slide to appear onscreen, and recording narration to accompany a presentation. Just between us, this is where the real fun begins for assembling a presentation—controlling how slides progress from one to the next and assigning animations to make your slide elements interesting and eye-catching.

In this chapter, you learn how to work with slide transitions, rearrange slides in Slide Sorter view, add animation effects, add sound or narration, and use action buttons. You also learn how to rehearse the timings for the show. The end result of these techniques is a presentation that's professional, enjoyable to watch, and successful in conveying your message to an audience in meaningful ways.

## Rearranging Slides

When you're ready to start organizing your slides and fine-tuning what appears in your presentation, switch over to Slide Sorter view. Click the Slide Sorter View button located in the bottom-left corner of the program window. This view mode gives you a bird's eye vantage point for surveying all of a show's slides, as shown in Figure 22.1.

You can increase or decrease the number of slides shown on a single screen by using the Zoom feature to adjust the magnification setting. To see larger slides, increase the magnification setting. To zoom out and view more slides, decrease the magnification.

Acting rather like a light-table for viewing actual slides, you can use Slide Sorter view to get a general idea about your content and presentation flow, moving slides as needed, or hiding slides you don't want to include with the show. You can double-click any slide in Slide Sorter view to open the slide in Normal view and make edits.

**FIGURE 22.1**

PowerPoint's Slide Sorter view is the place to view all the slides in a show and make adjustments to the arrangement.

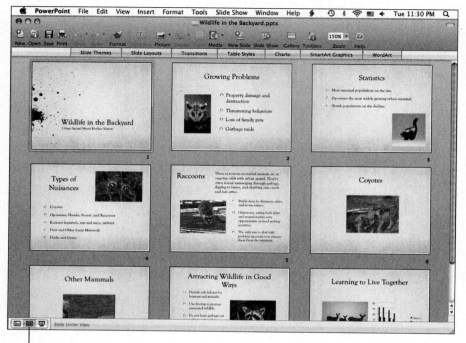

Slide Sorter View button

Use any of these techniques to rearrange and work with your slides:

- To move a slide, click it and drag it where you want it to appear.
- To hide a slide, Control+click the slide and choose Hide Slide, or choose Slide Show ⇨ Hide Slide. PowerPoint marks the slide number with a gray box to indicate it's hidden in the presentation.
- To delete a slide, click it and click Delete, or choose Edit ⇨ Delete Slide. You also can Control+click and choose Delete Slide from the pop-up menu.
- To duplicate a slide, click it and choose Edit ⇨ Duplicate, or Control+click and choose Duplicate Slide.

# Adding Transition Effects

Transitions control how slides move from one to the next in a slide show. Without any transitions assigned, PowerPoint simply changes slides instantly or cuts to the next slide. The effect can be a bit jarring. If you prefer something a little smoother, try assigning one of many preset transitions found in PowerPoint's Transitions library, shown in Figure 22.2. PowerPoint offers more than 60 transition effects, ranging from slow dissolves and fades to wipes and shape transitions.

**FIGURE 22.2**

You can add transitions to slides using the Transitions library found in the Elements Gallery.

Mind you, we can't easily demonstrate what PowerPoint transitions look like in a book. You must see them for yourself to appreciate their artistic accomplishments. Because the transition possibilities are vast, you can get carried away easily and want to assign all kinds of transition effects to a single slide show program. Do yourself and your audience a favor by reining in the urge to use every transition effect in the library. Instead, keep to simple effects and use them sparingly. One or two different types in a single show is a good general rule. The entire idea behind transitions is to provide a way to move from one slide to another, creating segues that moves your audience along with the message you're trying to convey. Sometimes, you'll want a dramatic transition, and other times something less showy will suffice.

The transitions you do end up selecting should mesh nicely with the type of show you're giving. For example, if your presentation is all about launching a new product line, then by all means, try some fancy transition effects. On the other hand, if your presentation is more on the somber tone, simpler transition effects work best with the content.

## Assigning transitions from the Elements Gallery

Transitions appear in between two slides, controlling how the first slide moves to the second slide. The transitions are divided into six unique categories: Fades and Dissolves, Wipes, Push and Cover, Stripes and Bars, 3-D, and Random. The All Transitions category lists all the available transitions. When you click a transition, PowerPoint immediately previews it in the selected slide. The selected transition's name appears on the left end of the Gallery. You also can move the mouse pointer over the transitions and view the name of the transition before assigning it.

Follow these steps to assign a transition from the Elements Gallery:

1. **Click the first slide to which you want to assign a transition.**
2. **Click the Transitions tab in the Elements Gallery, or choose Slide Show ➪ Transitions. You also can Control+click the slide in Slide Sorter view and choose Transitions from the pop-up menu.**

   PowerPoint displays the transitions, as shown in Figure 22.3.
3. **Click the type of transition you want to create from among the Transition tabs.**

   You can use the scroll arrows at the far right end of the Transitions library to browse the category's transitions.
4. **Click a transition to preview the effect on the selected slide and assign the transition.**

   You can continue testing transitions until you find the one you want to keep.

When you assign a transition, PowerPoint displays a tiny transition icon in the bottom-left corner of the slide's thumbnail in Slide Sorter view, as shown in Figure 22.4.

**FIGURE 22.3**

You can view the name of a transition at the left end of the Gallery.

The selected transition's name

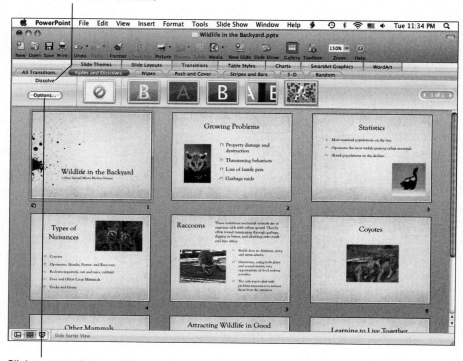

Click to customize a transition.

You also can apply the same transition to every slide by first selecting the slides. Choose Edit ⇨ Select All to select every slide, or press Ctrl+a, and then click a transition from the Gallery.

You can revisit the Transitions library at any time to assign a different transition to a slide. To remove a transition, click the No Transition choice at the far left end of each category.

## Setting transition options

You can customize your transition effects using the Transition Options dialog box, shown in Figure 22.5. You can use this dialog box to set a different transition effect, adjust the speed of the transition, add a sound to the transition, and choose how to advance the slide. To open the dialog box, click the Options button located at the far left end of the Gallery bar.

The dialog box is divided into three areas. You can choose from three transition speeds: Slow, Medium, and Fast. Fast is the default option. You can slow down the effect, if desired. When you select a speed option, PowerPoint previews the speed effect in the preview thumbnail.

**FIGURE 22.4**

Slides with transitions display a tiny transition icon in Slide Sorter view.

Transition icon

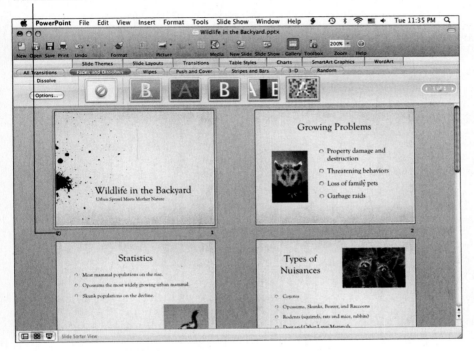

**FIGURE 22.5**

Customize transitions using the Transition Options dialog box.

PowerPoint installs with a library of sound effects from which you can choose. You can assign a sound along with a transition using the Sound pop-up menu. For example, at the beginning of your slide show, you may want to insert the sound of applause or clapping to a transition from the opening slide to the start of the show. You also can choose to loop the sound until the next transition.

The Advance slide options let you control how a transition advances to the next slide, either on mouse click or automatically. You may, for example, want to advance the slide after 10 seconds, or you may prefer to click to move to the next slide.

After you set any transition options, you can click the Apply button to exit the dialog box and add them to the effect. You can apply the same transition to every slide using the Apply to All button.

# Adding Animation Effects

You can use animation effects to animate slide elements. Also called *builds,* animations allow you to add movement to text boxes, bullet points, clip art, pictures, tables, charts, and SmartArt graphics. For example, you might make bullet points fly into the slide as you talk about each point. This can keep the audience from reading ahead so they focus on what you're trying to say.

As with transition effects, you can easily be caught up in the Hollywood special effects that animations offer. However, it's one thing to dazzle your audience, and it's quite another to distract them from your message with a dizzying array of flying bullet points, chart parts that boomerang back and forth, and spinning clip art. Try to keep the animation effects to a minimum, and use effects that suit the tone of your presentation as well as the tone of the audience. With that said, do have some fun seeing what's available in the effects library. It might inspire you to new artistic heights.

PowerPoint divides the animation effects into three main categories: Entrance effects, Emphasis effects, and Exit effects. The Entrance effects are designed to help a slide element make an entrance onto the slide. The Emphasis effects help to emphasize an element. The Exit effects determine how a slide element exits the slide. Within each of the main categories, PowerPoint divides the effects into subcategories, such as Basic and Exciting. You can assign multiple effects to an element for each of the main categories. For example, you might have a bullet point fly into the slide, make it blink to emphasize the point later, and then make the point disappear.

 You can add and manage animation effects using the Custom Animation Palette in PowerPoint's Toolbox. Click the Toolbox button in the Standard toolbar to display the Toolbox, and then click the Custom Animation button to view the palette. The palette keeps a list of all the effects you add, and you can change their order or delete effects you no longer want.

To assign an effect, follow these steps:

1. **Click the slide element you want to animate in Normal view.**
2. **Display the Custom Animation Palette, shown in Figure 22.6.**
3. **Click the type of effect you want to assign: Entrance effect, Emphasis effect, or Exit effect.**

    PowerPoint displays the last few effects you previously assigned. You can choose an effect from the list or open the full library of effects.

4. **To choose from the complete list of effects, click the More Effects command.**

    PowerPoint opens the Animation Effects dialog box, as shown in Figure 22.7.

**FIGURE 22.6**

Use the Custom Animation Palette to add and edit animation effects.

Custom Animation icon

**FIGURE 22.7**

To choose from all the available effects for the category, open the Animation Effects dialog box.

5. **Click the effect you want to add.**

   PowerPoint immediately previews the effect. Each time you test out an effect, PowerPoint previews it on the actual slide in Normal view.

6. **Click OK.**

   PowerPoint adds the effect to the list box in the palette, as shown in Figure 22.8.

**FIGURE 22.8**

PowerPoint keeps track of all the animation effects you assign by listing them in the list box.

Play button

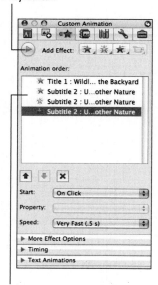

The slide's animation effects

 You can click the Play button at the top of the palette to see the effect in action again on the slide. To remove an effect, select it in the list box and click the Delete button. To move the effect order, select the effect and click the Move Up or Move Down arrow button.

If you switch over to Slide Sorter view, you'll notice a tiny animation icon at the bottom-left corner of any slide with an animation effect assigned, as shown in Figure 22.9.

 **If you assign an animation effect to a bulleted list, PowerPoint animates each bullet point individually.**

**FIGURE 22.9**

You can tell which slides have animation effects assigned by the tiny animation icons.

Animation icon

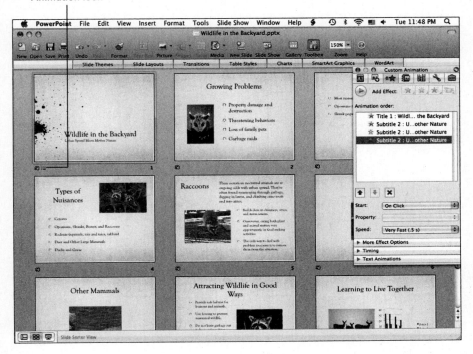

## Customize animation settings

You can customize an effect using the Start, Property, and Speed settings located below the list box in the Custom Animation Palette, as shown in Figure 22.10. Start by selecting the effect you want to modify from the list. You can click the Start pop-up menu to choose when you want the effect to play: On Click, With Previous, or After Previous. The default setting is On Click. When you click the mouse or a keyboard key, PowerPoint plays the animation. If you choose the With Previous setting, the effect begins at the same time as the effect just above it in the list. If you choose the After Previous setting, the effect begins as soon as the previous effect finishes.

**FIGURE 22.10**

Use the Start, Property, and Speed settings to fine-tune an effect.

The Property pop-up menu lets you control from which direction the effect happens, such as flying in from the top of the slide. Not all animation effects have properties you can set.

The Speed pop-up menu lets you choose from five speed settings: Very Slow, Slow, Medium, Fast, and Very Fast. The speeds range from half a second to 5 seconds in length.

After you start adding effects, you may need to reorder them in the palette. You can click an effect in the list and change its order by clicking the Move Up and Move Down arrow buttons. To remove an effect entirely, click the Delete button.

## Assigning more effect options

The More Effect Options pane includes options for adding sounds to an animation effect or options for choosing what you want PowerPoint to do after the animation plays. Click the pane heading to view your options, as shown in Figure 22.11. To add a sound effect to the animation effect, select the effect from the list box, click the Sound pop-up menu, and choose a sound effect, such as applause or a camera click.

Click the After animation pop-up menu to control what you want to happen to the element after the animation plays. You can choose to change the element to another color, hide it, or hide it when the next animation effect plays. Choose the Don't Dim option to leave the element onscreen after the animation plays, which is the default setting.

**FIGURE 22.11**

Use the More Effect Options pane to assign sounds or control the after effect state of the slide element.

## Setting animation timings

Click the Timing pane in the Custom Animation Palette to view several timing settings you can assign to an animation. As shown in Figure 22.12, you can use the Delay box to set a delay for the selected effect. For example, you may want to delay the effect for a few seconds. Use the Repeat pop-up menu to instruct the effect to repeat however many times you choose. Click the Rewind check box to return the appearance of the element to the same state as before the animation played.

**FIGURE 22.12**

You can use the Timing pane to set timing options for a selected animation effect.

## Applying text animation settings

If you're assigning animation effects to a text box, you can use the Text Animations pane to view and set additional options, shown in Figure 22.13. For example, you can choose to animate each letter, each word, or all at once using the Animate Text pop-up menu. You can use the Group Text pop-up menu to treat text lines as a single object, or you can animate them one line at a time according to their outline level. If the text is inside a shape object, you can choose to keep the two grouped together for the animation effect by checking the Animate attached shape check box. Lastly, click the In reverse order check box to make the lines of text appear in reverse order on the screen.

**FIGURE 22.13**

You can use the Text Animations pane to set animation options for text boxes.

## Applying chart animation settings

If you're animating a chart, the Chart Animations pane is available on the Custom Animation Palette, as shown in Figure 22.14. You can click the Group graphic pop-up menu to choose whether the chart element appears all at once or by data series. You also can start the animation effect with a blank chart background and then add the finished chart. Just click the Start animation by drawing the chart background check box.

**FIGURE 22.14**

You can use the Chart Animations pane to set animation options for charts.

# Adding Slide Controls and Action Buttons

You can embed slide controls into your presentation that allow you to jump to other slides or control the pace of the show. For example, if you're designing a training module or self-guided presentation, embedded slide controls allow other users to run the presentation, choosing when to move forward or go back a slide. The slide controls are actually action buttons found in the Object Palette. Action buttons are predesigned buttons for common slide show tasks, such as Forward or Back. You also can find action buttons for playing a sound or a movie clip. PowerPoint includes 12 predesigned buttons, one of which is a custom button. When adding slide control or action buttons, you must specify a particular action to carry out, such as a hyperlink to another slide, an object action, or an action that opens and runs another program.

When embedding slide controls, you can choose to embed them on a particular slide or include them on every slide in the program by placing them on the slide master. (See Chapter 20 to learn more about working with slide masters.) You can find slide controls and action buttons in the Object Palette, or you can add them through the Slide Show menu. If you use the Slide Show menu, PowerPoint automatically opens the Action Settings dialog box, where you can assign an action to the newly drawn button. The dialog box offers two tabs: Mouse Click and Mouse Over. If you want the user to click the button to perform an action, use the Mouse Click tab settings. If you want the action to take place if the user moves the mouse pointer over the button, use the Mouse Over settings.

Follow these steps to add slide control action buttons from the Slide Show menu:

1. **Display the slide on which you want to place an action button.**
2. **Choose Slide Show ⇨ Action Buttons ⇨ click the name of the button you want to create.**
3. **Click and drag on the slide to create the button, as shown in Figure 22.15.**

**FIGURE 22.15**

Drag the button size you want to create.

Click and drag to draw the button.

As soon as you finish dragging, PowerPoint creates the button and automatically opens the Action Settings dialog box, shown in Figure 22.16.

**FIGURE 22.16**

Use the Action Settings dialog box to assign an action to the button.

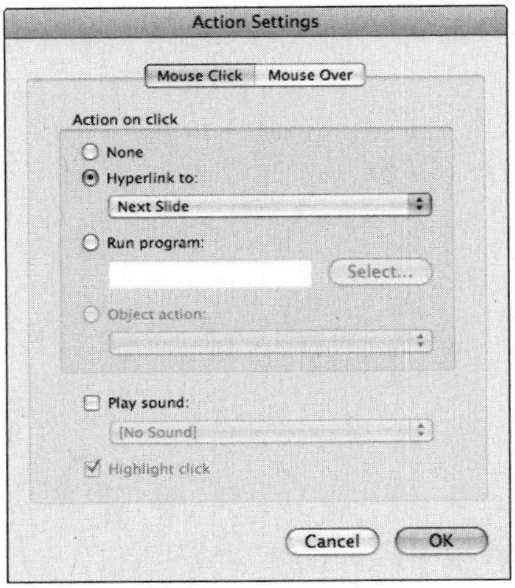

4. **Click the Hyperlink to pop-up menu, and choose where you want to jump to when clicked.**

5. **Click OK to exit the dialog box.**

You can now test your new button in Slide Show view. Click the Slide Show View button to start the presentation. When you reach the slide containing the button, click it to test its action. If you need to change what action the button does, you can reopen the Action Settings dialog box and make the necessary changes; Control+click the button, and choose Action Settings.

Follow these steps to add slide control action buttons to your slide from the Object Palette:

1. **Click the Object Palette button in the Toolbox.**

2. **Click the Shapes button.**

3. **Click the categories pop-up menu, as shown in Figure 22.17, and choose Action Buttons.**

   The list box displays the 12 action buttons for PowerPoint, as shown in Figure 22.18.

4. **Click the button you want to assign, and drag it onto the slide.**

   PowerPoint inserts the slide control, as shown in Figure 22.19.

**FIGURE 22.17**

Switch to the Action Buttons category to find preset slide control buttons.

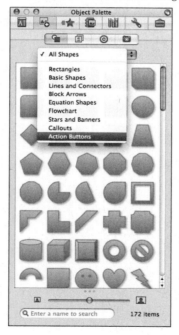

**FIGURE 22.18**

You can choose from 12 different action buttons, including slide controls for running a slide show.

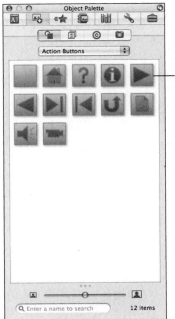

Click and drag a button into the slide.

5. **Control+click the button, and choose Action Settings.**

   The Action Settings dialog box opens (refer to Figure 22.16).

6. **Click the Hyperlink to pop-up menu, and choose where you want to jump to when clicked.**

7. **Click OK to exit the dialog box.**

You can format an action button by changing its color, adding a shadow effect, or adding any other special graphic effect. Double-click the button to open the Format Shape dialog box, as shown in Figure 22.20. To change the button color, click the Fill button and choose another color from the Color pop-up palette. You can use any of the other formatting options to change the appearance of the button.

**FIGURE 22.19**

Slide controls appear as buttons to be clicked by you or another user.

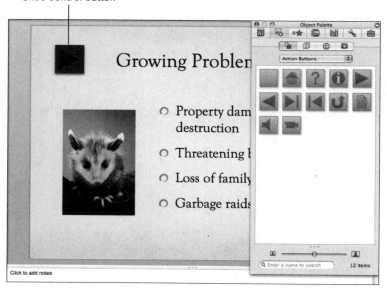

**FIGURE 22.20**

Use the Format Shape dialog box to change the formatting of an action button.

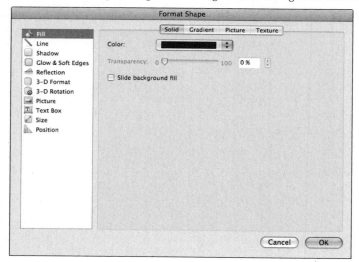

# Adding Sound and Narration

You can add sound to a slide presentation in the form of sound clips, soundtracks, and recorded narration. You've already learned how to add sound effect clips from the PowerPoint library to transitions and animation effects. Chapter 20 explained how to add both movie clips and sound clips to slide content. Now you'll learn how to play a music CD, add a soundtrack, and add narration.

## Play a CD during a presentation

You can play a music CD during a slide show presentation as background music. The nice thing about a music CD is that you don't have to worry about importing a large sound file along with your PowerPoint file. Instead, the computer plays the music directly from the CD.

Follow these steps to add music to a presentation:

1. **Insert the music CD into your computer's CD-ROM drive.**
2. **Click the slide where you want the soundtrack to start playing in Normal view.**
3. **Choose Insert ⇨ Sound and Music ⇨ Play CD Audio Track.**

   PowerPoint opens the Play Options dialog box, as shown in Figure 22.21.

**FIGURE 22.21**

Use the Play Options dialog box to specify tracks to play.

4. **Choose the track you want to start playing under the Start options.**
5. **Choose the track you want to stop playing at under the End options.**

   Optionally, you can loop the sound by clicking the Loop until stopped check box.

6. **Click OK.**

   PowerPoint asks you how you want the sound to start, as shown in Figure 22.22.

7. **Click When Clicked to play the sound when clicked, or click Automatically to have the sound start playing automatically when the slide appears.**

   PowerPoint adds a sound icon to the slide.

To test the sound in Normal view, double-click the sound icon, as shown in Figure 22.23.

**FIGURE 22.22**

A prompt box asks you how you want to start the sound.

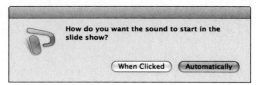

**FIGURE 22.23**

A CD sound icon appears on the slide indicating music.

CD sound icon

## Play a soundtrack throughout a presentation

You can add a soundtrack to play along with your PowerPoint presentation. For example, you may use a soundtrack as background sound that plays throughout the entire presentation.

Follow these steps to add music to a presentation from a CD or your computer's library:

1. **Click the Media button on the Standard toolbar and click Insert Sound and Music, or choose Insert ⇨ Sound and Music ⇨ From File.**

    The Insert Sound dialog box opens, shown in Figure 20.24.

2. **Navigate to the sound file you want to insert, select it, and click Insert.**

    PowerPoint prompts you to choose how you want the sound to start and then adds a sound icon to the slide.

3. **Click the sound icon in the slide as shown in Figure 22.25.**

**FIGURE 22.24**

The Insert Sound dialog box allows you to insert a sound file into your presentation.

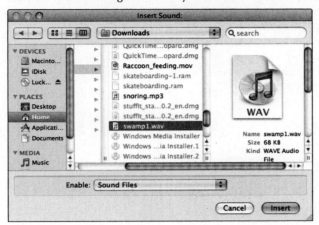

**FIGURE 22.25**

Click the sound icon, and then use the Sound pane on the Formatting Palette to set a play option.

Sound icon

4. **Display the Formatting Palette and the Sound pane.**

5. **Click the Play pop-up menu, and choose Across Slides.**

   If your slide show runs longer than the music file, you can click the Loop Until Stopped check box to keep the music playing.

To test the sound in Normal view, double-click the sound icon. To remove the sound, click the icon and press Delete.

## Recording narration

If you have a microphone attached to your computer or a built-in microphone on your computer, you can record your own narration to add to a presentation. By default, narration files are embedded with the presentation. If you like, you can link the narration file you create to the slide show. Sound files are often very large, so linking can save you space by storing the narration elsewhere.

When you start recording your narration, PowerPoint switches you to Slide Show view and displays the first slide. As you start recording, you can advance to each slide to narrate. If you make any mistakes, you can stop the process and start all over again. At the end of the narration process, PowerPoint prompts you to save the timings to correspond with the narration file.

Follow these steps to add narration:

1. **Open the slide on which you want to start a narration clip.**
2. **Choose Slide Show ⇨ Record Narration.**

   PowerPoint opens the Record Narration dialog box, as shown in Figure 22.26.

**FIGURE 22.26**

Use the Record Narration dialog box to set up and record your presentation narration.

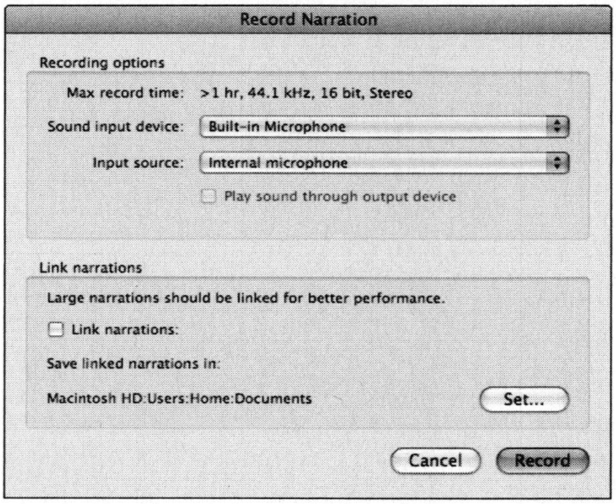

   Optionally, if you need to change the input device or input source listed, click the appropriate pop-up menu and make your selection.
3. **When you're ready to start recording, click the Record button.**

   PowerPoint starts the presentation in Slide Show view.
4. **Begin your narration for the first slide. When you're ready to move on, click the slide to advance to the next slide.**
5. **Continue narrating for each slide.**
6. **When you finish, click the Stop button.**

   PowerPoint saves the recordings, and a prompt box appears, as shown in Figure 22.27, offering to save the slide timings as well.
7. **Click Yes.**

   Another prompt box appears asking if you want to review the timings in Slide Sorter view, as shown in Figure 22.28.
8. **Click Yes.**

   PowerPoint switches to Slide Sorter view, as shown in Figure 22.29.

Notice in Slide Sorter view timings appear under each slide. These indicate the length of time each slide will appear onscreen in the actual slide show. Learn more about slide timings in the next section.

**FIGURE 22.27**

PowerPoint prompts you to save the slide timings.

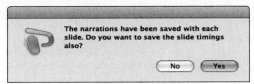

The narrations have been saved with each slide. Do you want to save the slide timings also?

No    Yes

**FIGURE 22.28**

A second prompt box appears to see if you want to switch to Slide Sorter view and see your timings.

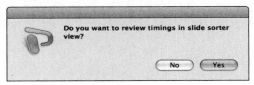

Do you want to review timings in slide sorter view?

No    Yes

**FIGURE 22.29**

PowerPoint switches to Slide Sorter view.

Timings

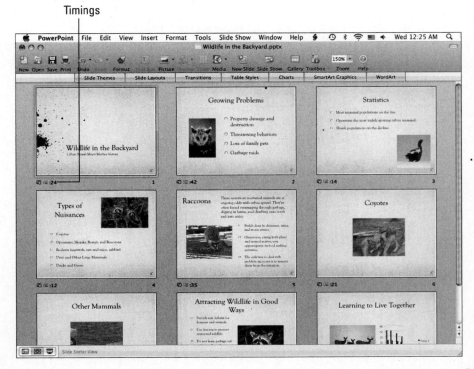

## Recording Individual Sounds

**I**f you'd rather not record a long narration, you can record individual sound clips and save them to each slide to play. To do so, click the slide first and choose Insert ➪ Sound and Music ➪ Record Sound. This opens the Record Sound dialog box, where you can choose your input device, assign a unique name to the clip, and start recording. When you finish, click Stop and then click the Save button. PowerPoint saves the clip and inserts a sound icon onto the slide. See Chapter 20 to learn more about inserting sound clips onto slides.

# Rehearsing Timings

PowerPoint has an extremely useful feature to help you run through your presentation and get an accurate timing for each slide. Called Rehearse Timings, this feature keeps track of how long you want each slide to appear onscreen. It does this by running through the actual slide show, with you determining how long each slide appears. A running clock at the bottom-right corner of the slide shows you the time. When you advance to the next slide, a new clock appears for that particular slide. When you finish, all the recordings appear along with the slides in Slide Sorter view.

To rehearse your slide show and assign timings, follow these steps:

1. **Choose Slide Show ➪ Rehearse Timings.**

   PowerPoint starts Slide Show view and displays the first slide, as shown in Figure 22.30.

2. **After the slide has appeared as long as you require, click the slide to advance to the next slide.**

3. **Repeat Step 2 for each slide in the presentation.**

   When you've rehearsed the whole show, a prompt box appears asking if you want to save the timings.

4. **Click Yes.**

   PowerPoint saves the timings and displays them in Slide Sorter view, as shown in Figure 22.31.

**FIGURE 22.30**

You run through the actual slide show to record your timings with the Rehearse Timings feature.

Recording time clock

**FIGURE 22.31**

Timings appear in Slide Sorter view under each slide.

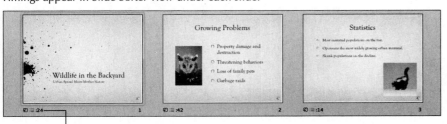

Rehearsed timings

# Summary

In this chapter, you learned your how to reorder your slides using Slide Sorter view. Slide Sorter view is handy for viewing your overall presentation and quickly making changes to slide order and viewing timings, transitions, and more. You also learned how to apply transition effects to move from one slide to the next and how to animate individual slide elements to add visual interest to your presentation. You discovered how to customize the special effects to suit your presentation needs.

This chapter also introduced you to PowerPoint's action buttons for creating slide controls. These buttons allow users to navigate the presentation without you. You also learned how to add CD music and narration to your presentation.

Lastly, you learned how easy it is to rehearse a slide show and make sure the timings are just right to give your presentation.

# Chapter 23

# Preparing and Presenting a Slide Show

A t last, your big moment is here. It's time to actually give the presentation you've been working on so hard, building, tweaking, and rehearsing these past few weeks, days, or hours. Like any performer, you're probably pacing backstage waiting, giving yourself a pep speech, and hoping the audience likes what you've done. Before you know it, the appointed moment is here. The lights dim, the stage is ready, and the crowd roars in expectation. Are you ready to wow them?

Granted, giving a PowerPoint presentation is not like giving a rock concert, and it's doubtful you'll have screaming fans showering you with adoration, but perhaps you'll find some gratification in your presentation. The best reward is an audience that's captivated by your information and attentive to your slides and your accompanying message.

In this chapter, you learn how to set up and run a slide show, paying particular attention to the tools needed to navigate the show while it's running. You also learn the various avenues for presenting, how to create and print notes, and how to create your own custom shows.

### IN THIS CHAPTER

**Setting up your slide show**

**Creating a custom show**

**Understanding presentation scenarios**

**Navigating a slide show**

**Printing presentations**

## Setting Up a Slide Show

Before you give a slide show presentation, you need to do a little setup work. One of the ways you can set up a slide show is by using the Set Up Show dialog box. You can even create your own custom slide show. This section shows you how to utilize the dialog box controls.

### Choosing a show type

Before you present a slide show, you can specify a show type. You can choose from three types of slide shows: a show presented by you using the full screen, a smaller screen show browsed by someone else, or a full-screen self-running show browsed at a kiosk. A kiosk is an enclosed structure with an open window displaying a computer screen running a looped program, or in the case of a slide show, a looped presentation. Kiosks are common in places like malls, trade shows, conference centers, and so on. The first option is the default option in PowerPoint. If you want to choose either of the other two, you must use the Set Up Show dialog box.

You can use the dialog box to set looping to make the show run continuously, turn off any narration or animation effects, advance the slides manually or automatically, or even choose to show only a range of slides. If you choose a manual advance, you can move through the slide show one slide at a time based on mouse clicks. If you used the Rehearse Timings command to record any timings, as you learned about in Chapter 22, the timings option is already selected for you.

To specify a show type, follow these steps:

1. **Choose Slide Show ➪ Set Up Show.**

   PowerPoint displays the Set Up Show dialog box, as shown in Figure 23.1.

   **FIGURE 23.1**

   You can use the Set Up Show dialog box to specify a show type.

   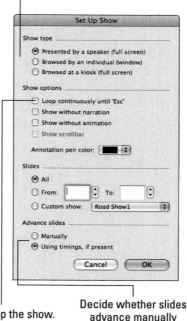

   Choose a show type.

   Click to loop the show.

   Decide whether slides advance manually or automatically.

2. **Under the Show type options, choose the type of show you want to create.**

   Optionally, under the Show options, you can choose to loop the presentation, include narration or animation effects, and display a scrollbar. The last option is available only if you're using a windowed slide show style.

   You also can set the pen color for any onscreen note-taking you plan to do during the show.

Optionally, under the Slides options, you can choose which slides to include in the show. You also can choose whether you want the slides to advance manually or automatically.

**3. Click OK.**

PowerPoint applies your changes to the presentation.

## Creating a custom show

You can create custom shows in PowerPoint to tailor your slides for a particular audience. For example, you may want to recycle a show, but cut a few slides to meet shortened time requirements, or you may want to cut out a few slides you don't want a particular audience to see. You can customize exactly which slides appear in a show and save the custom treatment. PowerPoint saves the custom show as part of the original presentation file. You can create as many custom shows based on one presentation as you need. You cannot, however, add new slides without adding them to the original presentation. You can only customize what's already in the original presentation.

To create a custom show, follow these steps:

**1. Choose Slide Show ⇨ Custom Shows.**

PowerPoint displays the Custom Shows dialog box, as shown in Figure 23.2.

**FIGURE 23.2**

The Custom Shows dialog box lets you set up custom presentations.

**2. Click New.**

The Define Custom Show dialog box opens, as shown in Figure 23.3.

**3. Type a name for the custom show.**

**4. Click which slide you want to include.**

**5. Click the Add button to add it to the list.**

**6. Repeat Steps 4 and 5 to continue adding just the slides you want.**

Optionally, you can use the arrow buttons to rearrange the slide order. Select the slide number, and click an arrow button to move the slide up or down in the list order.

**7. Click OK.**

PowerPoint adds the show to the list box shown in Figure 23.4.

**FIGURE 23.3**

Use the Define Custom Show dialog box to customize a show.

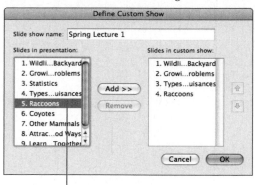

Build a custom show
slide by slide.

**FIGURE 23.4**

PowerPoint keeps track of all the custom shows associated with the presentation.

8. **Click Close.**

    Optionally, you can click the Show button to view the custom show. To view the show in Presenter view mode, leave the Open custom show in Presenter View check box selected and click the Show button.

After you have several custom shows saved with a presentation, you can do the following by reopening the Custom Shows dialog box:

- To remove a show from the list, click it and click the Remove button.

- To edit which slides appear in the custom show, select it and click the Edit button to revisit the Define Custom Show dialog box and make your changes.

- To duplicate a custom show, click the show and click the Copy button.

- To view a custom show at any time, open the Custom Shows dialog box, click the show you want to view, and click the Show button.

# Ways to Present a Slide Show

Years ago, the words "slide show" conjured up nights trapped at Uncle Jack and Aunt Edna's house watching photos projected onto the wall of their latest trip to the Grand Canyon. In today's culture, "slide show" is more synonymous with PowerPoint presentations. Like Uncle Jack and Aunt Edna, you can still project a slide show onto a wall. You also can use a variety of other methods to present the show.

## Presentation scenarios

A standard way to present a slide show is to project it onto a screen or wall. To do this, you need a projector. You hook up your computer to the projector and present the show to a group of people, such as in a classroom or conference room scenario. A projector is ideal for larger groups. A variety of multimedia projectors on the market today are available in a wide range of price points, from $500 at the low end to $20,000 at the high end. Used primarily for business presentations, multimedia projectors are much like a combination overhead projector/DVD player/PowerPoint presenter all rolled into one device. They allow you to project a presentation directly from your PC. Most major electronics manufacturers offer such devices today, and most projectors are both Mac and PC compatible. Just about every multimedia projector includes a remote, which is handy for slide show presenters to advance or pause a program. Of course, another simple option is to give a presentation directly on your computer with a user or small group huddled around the screen.

If you are a frequent traveler and plan on giving presentations on the road, you should consider a slimmer projector, one that doesn't weigh too much. Slim, personal multimedia projectors weigh in at 15 pounds or less, making them about the same size as a laptop. Some are as small as five pounds. Portable projectors cost anywhere from $1,000 to $8,000. If you're giving presentations for a company at corporate headquarters, a larger, more expensive model probably suits your needs more. Most of the larger projectors include extra video ports, laser pointers, and other bells and whistles. If you plan on giving presentations in one spot all the time, consider a fixed installation projector. These are usually mounted in large conference rooms or auditoriums, and they typically weigh up to 100 pounds. At this stature, these projectors provide the highest resolution settings and work well for classrooms and large group training situations.

Multimedia projectors use either LCD or DLP displays. LCDs offer brighter pictures, but DLPs give greater contrast and deeper background imaging. You also can find LCOS projectors (liquid crystal on silicon), which use aspects of both LCD and DLP projectors, but they're very, very expensive.

Brightness and resolution are the specs to look for in the world of multimedia projectors. Lamp types, also known as projector bulbs, are a crucial component when figuring out which projector to buy. Generally speaking, the brighter the room in which you are projecting, the brighter your projector lamp should be; lamp brightness is measured in ANSI lumens. A minimum of 300 lumens or higher is good for relatively dark rooms. If it's a larger room, 500 lumens is the absolute minimum. If the room is a large auditorium, 750 lumens or higher is the way to go. If it's a sunny conference room, you may need up to 2,500 lumens. Because most projectors range from 1,000 to 10,000 lumens, you should be able to find a projector that meets your requirements. Most multimedia projectors today use 1,500 to 2,000 ANSI lumens and higher as the standard. The most common lamp types are UHP, UHE, and halide. Each type differs in lamp life. You can expect anywhere from 1,000 to 4,000 hours from a lamp. As with all things technical, nothing's worse than having a projector lamp blow the day of the big presentation. So make sure you choose a projector with a bulb that you can easily and quickly replace or have on hand as a backup. Bulbs are notoriously expensive, so check the cost of a replacement bulb at the time you're purchasing a projector. The cost can very well influence your decision regarding what device to buy.

Resolution, or the number of pixels on a screen, is another big factor in multimedia projectors. If your presentations require the sharpest images possible, then you need a projector that supports the highest resolution settings. The standard today is SVGA (800×600) and XGA (1024×768).

**639**

You may be tempted to hunt for a bargain projector. This may do if you're on a very tight budget, but if you want a long-term piece of equipment, you need a projector that meets your long-term needs. Be sure to ask about customer support policies before you buy, price the replacement bulbs, and find a reputable seller who's willing to help you.

As far as actual projection goes, it's always better to project your show onto an actual projector screen. These are designed for use in larger classroom or auditorium settings, and they make projected images much more visible. A plain wall will do in a pinch, however.

Another popular way to present a show is to use your laptop computer. You can easily run a presentation on your laptop screen. Because laptops are so portable, you can haul one anywhere to make a presentation. For example, if you're presenting to a new client in his office, you can simply set the laptop down in front of the client and run the show. The laptop scenario is great for one-on-one presentations, or small groups that can easily gather around the screen and view the show.

If you cannot give a presentation in person, you can save the show to a CD-ROM and hand it off for viewing at the other person's convenience. You also can set up a slide show to run on the Internet as a Web page.

If you can't deliver the actual show using any of the methods described, you can print out the slides to give to someone. You also can print them to transparencies and show them on an overhead projector.

## Presentation tips

Is this your first time giving a presentation? Or are you looking for a few tips to make your slide shows more engaging? Here are a few helpful tips if you're giving a presentation before a live audience:

- Always start out by welcoming your audience. Don't just jump in and start showing slides; instead, briefly tell what you're presentation is and give your audience some idea of how long it will be, how you want to handle questions, and whether they need to take notes.

- Open with something that grabs the audience's attention. Depending on the type of presentation, you may try an opening joke to relax the audience. Another option is to solicit audience participation right off the bat. Ask some questions that allow people to respond as a group and find out how the audience relates to your topic.

- Introduce yourself. Take time to explain why you're there to give the presentation, what makes you a specialist on the topic, and what your background is related to the topic or the presentation at hand.

- Do you tend to be a bit nervous when speaking in public? Try to relax. If that's entirely impossible, the next best thing is to fake it. Pretend to be relaxed, and don't let on that you're not!

- Talk directly to the audience as much as possible. Nobody wants to sit through a presentation being read from a script with the speaker looking down at his notes all the time. Glancing at the slides is fine, but don't turn your back on the audience the entire show. The only exception to this is if the room is so completely dark that no one would notice.

- Your presentation's slides shouldn't contain all the text of your lecture, just the highlights. It's up to you to fill in the details with your speech.

- At the end of the show, take time to review your points and presentation goals. If you're opening the lecture up for a question/answer time, be sure to define the timeframe.

- End by thanking your audience for their time, and be sure to offer any contact information or additional steps they need to take.

- Take time to evaluate your performance after the fact. Make notes on where you can improve the presentation, and consider collecting feedback from audience members.

# Running a Slide Show

Are you ready to actually run the show? We hope you've rehearsed, set up all the required equipment, and everything's ready to go. This section shows you how to navigate a show and utilize PowerPoint's presenter tools.

## Starting and navigating a slide show

Starting a show is incredibly easy. From the PowerPoint window, you can use any of these methods to start a show:

- Click the Slide Show button on the Standard toolbar.
- Click the Slide Show View button in the lower-left corner.
- Choose Slide Show ⇨ View Slide Show.
- Press ⌘+Return.

Depending on what hardware you're using, your presentation shows up onscreen with the first slide. For example, if you're showing the presentation on a single monitor, the first slide fills the entire screen. If your situation involves two screens, the slide appears only on the projected screen or secondary monitor, while your laptop's screen becomes the command center of your presentation. In this scenario, the laptop screen utilizes the Presenter Tools view mode. You learn more about this view mode coming up.

If your presentation is set on manual, it's up to you to advance each slide. You can do this by clicking the screen or pressing the spacebar. If a slide has animation effects assigned, such as bullet points that fly in one at a time, each click you make brings another bullet onto the slide. If you've assigned timings to your show, the slides advance according to the timings you set. You can interrupt the timings by clicking the slide.

By default, PowerPoint displays a small pop-up menu button in the lower-left corner of the slide screen, as shown in Figure 23.5. You also can move the mouse pointer to the corner to display the button. You can click this button to display a pop-up menu of navigation commands and tools, as shown in Figure 23.6. You also can Control+click the screen to display the menu.

**FIGURE 23.5**

Look for the pop-up menu button in the lower-left corner of the slide.

Wildlife in the Backyard

Pop-up menu button

**FIGURE 23.6**

You can use the pop-up menu to access slide show commands.

The pop-up menu offers several navigation commands: Next, Previous, Last Viewed, Go to Slide, and End Show. In addition, you can apply the following options using the menu:

- To choose a custom show to run, click the Custom Show command and select the show.
- To go to a black screen, click the Black Screen command.
- To pause the show, choose Screen ⇨ Pause.
- To change the pointer, click the Pointer Options command and choose an option: Automatic, Hidden, Arrow, Pen, or Pen Color.

 **Need help navigating? From the pop-up menu, choose the Help command to open a Slide Show Help window full of navigation hints.**

Although the pop-up menu is handy, for a much more seamless presentation, consider using keyboard shortcuts to navigate your show. Table 23.1 lists the keyboard shortcuts you can use to navigate a slide show. Notice that some of the navigations you can perform can be activated by a variety of keys.

**TABLE 23.1**

## Navigation Controls

| Navigation | Description |
| --- | --- |
| Move to next slide or animation effect | Mouse click, spacebar, Return, N, Enter, →, ↓, Page Down |
| Move to previous slide or previous animation effect | ←, ↑, Page Up, P, Delete |
| Move to a particular slide in the presentation | Type the slide number and press Return |
| Move to the first slide | Home |
| Move to the last slide | End |
| Move to a black slide | B, period |
| Move to a white slide | W, comma |
| Show or hide the arrow pointer | A, = |
| End the slide show | Esc, ⌘+period, hyphen |
| Stop or restart a self-running show | S, + |
| Erase any onscreen drawings | E |
| Change pointer to pen | ⌘+P |
| Change pointer to arrow | ⌘+A |
| Hide the pointer and the pop-up menu button | ctrl+H |
| Automatically show the pop-up menu | ⌘+U |
| Go to the next hidden slide | H |

When you reach the end of the slide show, PowerPoint returns you to the view you were previously using in the program window.

# Controlling Navigation through Preferences

Another way to control how your slide show appears during a presentation is to use PowerPoint's Preferences dialog box. Choose PowerPoint ➪ Preferences to open the dialog box, and click the View tab. Under the Slide Show options, you can click the Slide Show Navigation pop-up menu and choose whether you want the pop-up menu button to appear on slides or to display no slide show controls at all. You also can specify whether you want to activate the pop-up menu by pressing Control+click or whether to end with a black slide.

## Using pointer tools

PowerPoint's pop-up menu that appears in a slide show presentation offers several pointer options you can assign. By default, the mouse pointer does not appear onscreen during the show; it's set to Automatic, which means it does not appear unless you move the pointer. You can turn the pointer on, if desired, or turn it into a pen. To view the pointer at all times, click the pop-up menu button and choose Pointer Options ➪ Arrow, as shown in Figure 23.7. The pointer now appears onscreen.

**FIGURE 23.7**

Control what role the mouse pointer takes using the Pointer Options.

To hide the pointer completely, choose Pointer Options ➪ Hidden. To return the pointer to the default setting, choose Pointer Options ➪ Automatic.

You can write on a slide using your mouse by turning the pointer into a pen. For example, you may want to circle an important fact or figure on a slide, or write a word or phrase, underline a keyword, or draw a simple sketch. To turn on the Pen tool, choose Pointer Options ➪ Pen. PowerPoint displays the pointer as a pen icon, as shown in Figure 23.8. Click and drag the pen to write on the slide.

FIGURE 23.8

**FIGURE 23.8**

You can write on your slides by turning the pointer into a pen.

### Attracting Wildlife in Good Ways

- Provide safe habitat for humans and animals.

- Use fencing to prevent unwanted wildlife.

- Do not leave garbage out in bags or loose bins.

- Use natural sprays and chemicals to discourage animals.

Use the Pen tool to write on-screen.

By default, the pen color you draw with is set to black. You can assign another color to make the pen easier to see on the screen; choose Pointer Options ➪ Pen Color, and choose a color. To erase anything you draw, click the pop-up menu button and choose Screen ➪ Erase Pen.

## Using Presenter Tools

If you're using a multimedia projector to display your slide show, you can use PowerPoint's Presenter Tools to help you run the show from your computer or laptop screen. The Presenter Tools display in a special view mode on your laptop or computer. While the presentation's slides appear projected on the wall or projection screen, the computer screen allows you to see notes, the next slide, a clock, and more, as shown in Figure 23.9. Acting like a command center, the Presenter Tools let you control and survey what's going on in your presentation.

**FIGURE 23.9**

Use the Presenter Tools to control the presentation.

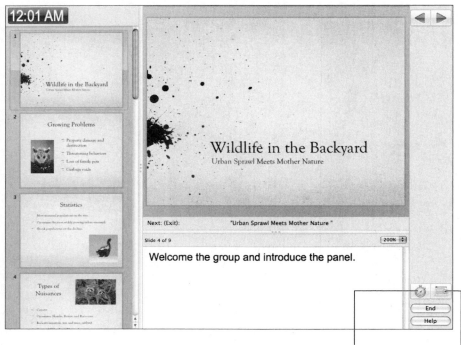

Clock button        Preview window toggle

To view the Presenter Tools, choose Slide Show ⇨ View Presenter Tools. PowerPoint splits the screen into panes. The clock in the upper-left corner shows the current time. When the show starts, it keeps track of the elapsed presentation time. You can toggle the clock display on or off by clicking the Clock button located in the bottom-right corner of the view mode.

The Slides pane works just like does in the PowerPoint program window, listing thumbnails of each slide. To view a slide from the display, click it. The main Slide pane shows the slide currently being projected. The Notes pane displays any notes assigned to the current slide. You can actually edit notes within this pane. For example, you may want to make note of someone's question or make a note of a slide that elicited the best response. Just click in the pane and type. You can use the Zoom button in the top-right corner of the pane to magnify your view of the Notes text.

The Previous and Next arrow buttons in the top-right corner let you move back or forward in your presentation. In addition to these navigation buttons, you can use any of the presentation navigation keys you learned about earlier from within Presenter Tools view.

The Preview window is a tiny window showing you the next slide to appear in the show. Like the clock feature, you can toggle the Preview window on and off. Click the Preview button located next to the Clock button to toggle the feature on and off. Directly below the toggle buttons are buttons for ending the program or for accessing help about keyboard navigation keys.

If your slide show has preset timings assigned, the Presenter Tools view shows the slides advancing auto-matically. You can interact with the show at any time to override the timings. To turn the Presenter Tools off, just click the End button or press Esc.

# Printing Presentations

You can print various aspects of your PowerPoint presentation. For example, you may want to print your slide notes to have them handy while giving a presentation, or you may want to print slides to show someone who could not attend the presentation. This section shows you how to print in PowerPoint.

## Making changes to Page Setup

You can use the Page Setup dialog box to control the size of your printouts, which printer to use, and what paper size to apply. The settings in this dialog box also control the size of slides as they appear on the computer screen. To open the dialog box, choose File ⇨ Page Setup. The dialog box, shown in Figure 23.10, includes slide size and page orientation options, as well as access to headers and footers, notes and handouts, and printer options.

**FIGURE 23.10**

You can use the Page Setup dialog box to set slide sizes and other page and printing options.

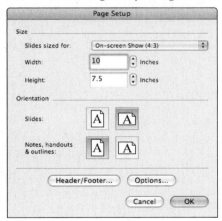

To change the size of the slides for printing purposes, click the Slides sized for pop-up menu and choose a preset size. If you prefer to set a custom size, you can enter your own dimensions in the Width and Height boxes. To change the slide orientation, click the setting you want to apply under the Orientation options.

**NOTE** Among the preset sizes on the Slides sized for pop-up menu, On-screen Show (4:3), Letter Paper (8.5×11 in), and Overhead all use the same slide size—10×7.5 inches.

Click the Options button to open another dialog box for setting paper size and scale options. You also can find these options in the Print dialog box, which you learn about later in this chapter.

### Adding headers and footers

A header is text that appears at the top of every slide, while footer text appears at the bottom of every slide. You might add a footer that lists the company name at the bottom of your presentation or the name of the class you are teaching, or you might add slide numbers to every slide. To add header and footer text to a slide, click the Header/Footer button in the Page Setup dialog box. This opens the Header and Footer dialog box, as shown in Figure 23.11. You also can access header and footer features through the View menu; choose View ⇨ Header and Footer.

**FIGURE 23.11**

You can add header or footer text to a slide by going through the Page Setup dialog box.

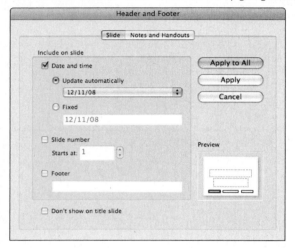

With the Slide tab selected, you can view fields and check boxes in the Header and Footer dialog box for adding footer elements to a slide. You cannot, however, add header text to a slide. For example, you can insert the date and time and update it automatically or insert a fixed date. You can include slide numbers and tell PowerPoint which number to start on. Or you can type your own footer text, such as a company name. If you don't want the footer text shown on the title slide, be sure to click the Don't show on title slide check box. After you've selected which options you want to include, click the Apply button to add to the current slide, or click the Apply All button to add the information to every slide in the presentation.

To add header or footer text to handouts and notes, click the Notes and Handouts tab, as shown in Figure 23.12. Nearly identical to the previous dialog box, you can add the date and time, page number, or footer text. You also can add header text. Simply make your selections, fill in any fields as needed, and click the Apply to All button.

**FIGURE 23.12**

Use the Notes and Handouts tab to set up headers and footers for printed materials.

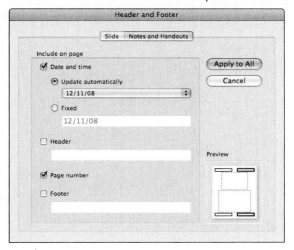

## Printing slides, handouts, and notes

To print your presentation, choose File ➪ Print. This opens the Print dialog box, as shown in Figure 23.13. You can tell PowerPoint exactly what you want to print, whether it's slides, handouts, or notes. The Print dialog box is packed full of options for controlling which printer is used, how many copies are printed, which slides are printed, how the slides fit onto the printed page, options for printing in PDF format, and so on.

To specify what to print, click the Print What pop-up menu and make a selection. You can choose to print slides, handouts, notes, or the presentation in outline form. If you choose to print slides, you can use the Slides options to specify which slide numbers to print. PowerPoint prints a single slide on each printed page.

The Handouts print option, shown in the pop-up menu in Figure 23.14, is great if you want to create handouts of your presentation. When you choose this option, PowerPoint prints thumbnail versions of the slides and fits them onto the printed page in the layout you designate. You can choose to print anywhere from two to nine slides per printed page.

**FIGURE 23.13**

Use the Print dialog box to print out slides, handouts, notes, and outlines.

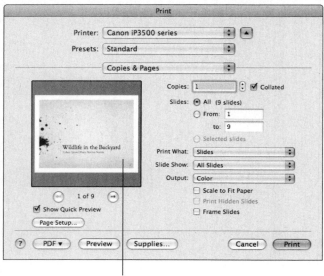

Preview the printed slides.

**FIGURE 23.14**

You can choose from a variety of handout layouts to print.

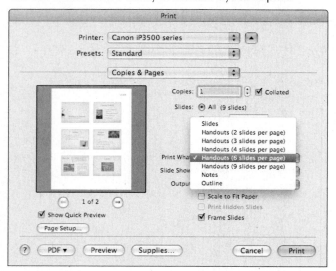

If your presentation includes notes for each slide that you want to distribute, you can choose the Notes option from the Print What pop-up menu, as shown in Figure 23.15. When you select this option, PowerPoint prints a thumbnail of the slide along with any note text assigned to the slide.

**FIGURE 23.15**

If your slides include notes, you can print thumbnails of the slides and note text to use as handouts or to use to help you give the presentation.

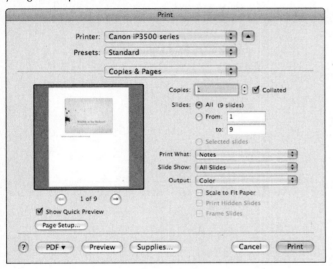

The Preview window shows you what your printouts will look like. When everything's set the way you want it, click the Print button to send the information to your printer.

You also can convert your presentation into a PDF file, which anyone with a PDF viewer can read as a document. To choose a PDF format, click the PDF button at the bottom of the Print dialog box. Here, you can find commands for saving as a PDF, faxing as a PDF, emailing as a PDF, and so on.

## Saving Slides as Other Objects

If your intended audience needs to view a presentation as another format besides a slide show, you can save the presentation as a movie, you can save individual slides as graphics, or you can even send the presentation to your video iPod. For example, you can save a show as a QuickTime movie, which can be viewed if the user has QuickTime installed. You also can save individual slides as graphic files and send them to Mac's iPhoto program for importing into iMovie.

## Saving a presentation as a QuickTime movie

QuickTime is a very popular multimedia framework designed to view digital video, movie clips, sound, text, animation, and more. As a viewer program, QuickTime is available for free, and as a helper app, many people have it installed for viewing multimedia content on their Web browsers. If you know someone who doesn't have PowerPoint, but does have QuickTime, you can save your presentation as a QuickTime movie to be viewed in the QuickTime player. When you create a movie file, PowerPoint saves it in the .MOV file format.

When saving a slide show as a movie, you can designate optimizing features, set movie screen dimensions, set looping, and specify which PowerPoint elements to include, such as transitions, soundtrack, or movie player controls. By default, PowerPoint is set up to save the presentation in a 640×480 movie size. You can set a custom size, if desired. You also can choose to disregard transition effects and turn off the sound. If you want users to control the movie, you can add movie player controls. If you want the move to be self-running, you can apply the Loop Movie command.

To save a slide show as a QuickTime movie, follow these steps:

1.  **Choose File ➪ Save As Movie.**

    The Save As dialog box opens, as shown in Figure 23.16.

---

**FIGURE 23.16**

You can turn any presentation into a QuickTime movie and access movie options for optimizing the process.

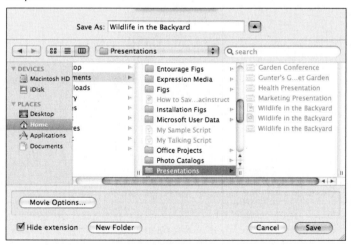

2.  **Type a name for the movie file.**
3.  **Navigate to the folder or drive where you want to save the file.**
4.  **Click the Movie Options button.**

    PowerPoint opens the Movie Options dialog box, as shown in Figure 23.17.

**FIGURE 23.17**

Use the Movie Options dialog box to fine-tune your QuickTime movie settings.

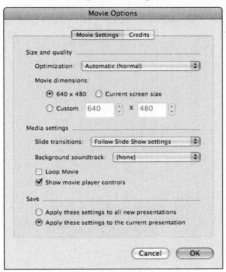

5. **In the Movie Settings tab, you can set size and quality settings, media settings, and save options.** Make your changes, as needed.

   Optionally, you can save your movie settings for use with other presentations you save as QuickTime movies using the Apply these settings to all new presentations radio button.

6. **Click the Credits tab, as shown in Figure 23.18.**

7. **Type any movie credits you want associated with the presentation.**

8. **Click OK.**

9. **Click Save.**

   PowerPoint saves the file as a QuickTime movie.

You can now open the saved file in the QuickTime Player window and view the presentation, as shown in Figure 23.19.

**NOTE** QuickTime doesn't actually support PowerPoint's slide transitions, but it does its best to duplicate them with QuickTime equivalents. If you keep your transitions really simple, like fades, the results are the same.

**FIGURE 23.18**

Use the Credits tab to type any movie credits you want to appear with the movie.

**FIGURE 23.19**

Users can view your presentation as a movie file in the QuickTime Player window.

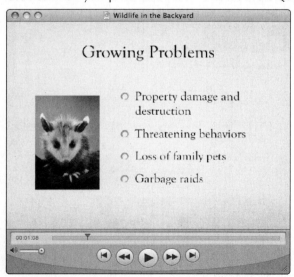

# Saving slides as graphics files

You can turn a slide into a graphic and use it in another program or share it as a photo. You can then easily share the graphic files of all or parts of your presentation with other users regardless of whether they use PowerPoint. Mind you, transitions, animations, and sounds are not part of this process.

## Save as pictures

To save your slide show as a collection of individual picture files, follow these steps:

1. **Choose File ⇨ Save As Pictures.**

   PowerPoint opens the Save As dialog box, as shown in Figure 23.20.

**FIGURE 23.20**

Use the same old Save As dialog box to save slides as graphics files.

2. **Navigate to the folder or drive where you want to store the files.**

3. **Type a name for the files.**

   If you're saving more than one slide as a graphic, PowerPoint sequentially adds numbers to the filename you specify.

4. **Click the Format pop-up menu, and choose a graphic file type.**

   JPEG and TIFF work well for photos, while GIF and PNG formats work well for smaller files and Web images.

5. **Click the Options button.**

   PowerPoint opens the Preferences dialog box, as shown in Figure 23.21.

**FIGURE 23.21**

You can choose to turn a single slide into a graphic file or make the entire presentation into a collection of graphic files.

6. **Under the Save slides as graphics files heading, choose whether you want to save the current slide or all the slides.**

   Optionally, you can adjust the resolution settings and size dimensions or apply compression.

7. **Click OK.**

8. **Click Save.**

   PowerPoint saves the files.

## Send to iPhoto

You can send all the slides in your presentation to the iPhoto program and save them as photo files, use them in an iPhoto slide show, or import to iMovie. To save your slide show as a collection of individual picture files, follow these steps:

1. **Choose File ➪ Send To ➪ iPhoto.**

   You also can specify which slides you want to send by selecting them in the Slides/Outline View pane.

   The Send to iPhoto dialog box opens, as shown in Figure 23.22.

2. **Type a name for the photo album.**

3. **Click the Format pop-up menu, and choose a graphic file type.** You can choose JPEG or PNG.

4. **Click a radio button to send all the slides or just the selected slide.**

5. **Click the Send to iPhoto button.**

   iPhoto opens to finish the procedure and display the slides as photos as a new album, as shown in Figure 23.23.

**FIGURE 23.22**

You can send your slides to iPhoto to save them as high-quality graphics or turn them into an iPhoto slide show.

**FIGURE 23.23**

After you import your slides into iPhoto, you can turn them into a slide show, send them to a Web page, or burn them to a DVD.

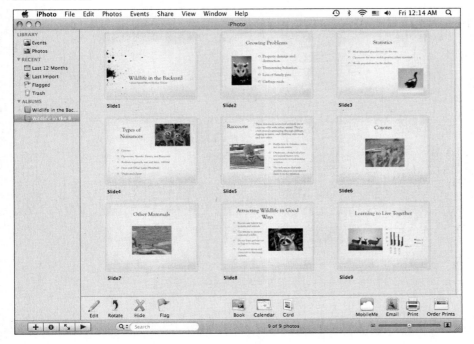

## Saving a presentation as a Web page

Do you want to turn your presentation into a Web-worthy slide show? You can, using PowerPoint's Save as Web Page command. When you turn a presentation into a Web page, PowerPoint handles all the coding and JavaScript programming needed to create the file. As with movies and graphics, you can expect to lose transition and animation effects in the process, and other slide elements may not translate well either. However, if you keep your graphics simple, the transition should prove acceptable.

The first thing you should do is to preview your presentation as a Web page. Choose File ➪ Web Page Preview. PowerPoint creates all the necessary HTML components and displays everything in your default browser window, as shown in Figure 23.24. The page looks very much like the PowerPoint program window, but the slides in the Slides/Outline View pane are links, and navigation buttons at the bottom allow the user to move back and forth between slides.

**FIGURE 23.24**

Preview your presentation first before turning into a Web page.

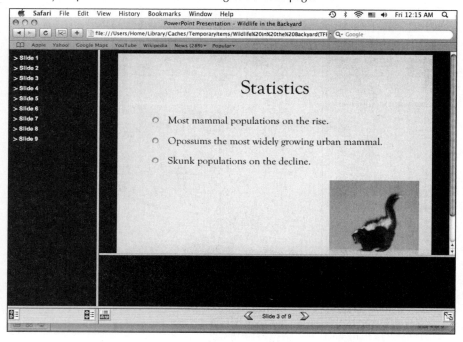

To save the presentation as a Web page, or more appropriately a set of HTML pages, follow these steps:

1. **Choose File ➪ Save As Web Page.**

    PowerPoint opens the Save As dialog box, as shown in Figure 23.25.

2. **Navigate to the folder or drive where you want to store the file.**

3. **Type a name for the file.**

4. **To set additional options, click the Web Options button.**

    PowerPoint opens the Web Options dialog box, as shown in Figure 23.26.

    ■ The General tab lets you add a document description.

    ■ The Files tab offers two save options for updating links and including the original file with the presentation file.

    ■ The Appearance tab, shown in Figure 23.26, lets you set Normal or Full screen view, change presentation colors, and include navigation buttons.

**FIGURE 23.25**

Here's the familiar Save As dialog box to save your presentation as a Web page this time.

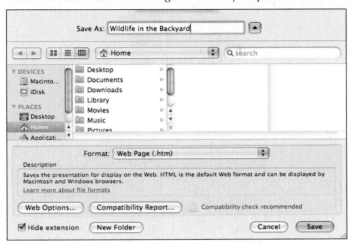

**FIGURE 23.26**

Use the Web Options dialog box to set additional options for your HTML files.

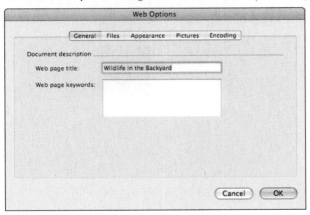

- The Pictures tab enables PNG as an output format and sets a target monitor screen size.
- The Encoding tab lets you save the document in another language format.

5. **Click OK.**

6. **Click Save.**

PowerPoint saves the files.

# Summary

In this chapter, you learned how to set up a slide show and create custom shows based within the main presentation. You also learned about the various ways you can give a show using different hardware scenarios, and we gave you a few presentation tips to help you manage the speaking end of a live presentation.

You also learned how easy it is to actually conduct a presentation using PowerPoint's navigation tools and commands and using the Presenter Tools. You discovered how to turn your slide content into printed materials, including handouts and notes. Finally, this chapter taught you how to turn a slide show into graphics files, a QuickTime movie file, and a Web page.

With the slide show ins and outs behind you now, you're well on your way to the fame and fortune that awaits you on the PowerPoint presentation circuit. Enjoy your time in the limelight!

# Part V

# Working with Entourage

# Chapter 24

# Entourage Basics

If you're like most people today, your life is pretty complicated and often feels like it's going in a million different directions. Wouldn't it be nice to hire a personal assistant, someone who could come in each day and tell you what's on the agenda, where you need to go, what things need to be done, answer important e-mails, and hand you a nice cup of coffee? Entourage can do that, electronically speaking of course—except for the cup of coffee part. It doesn't do coffee. Not yet anyway. I hope to hear about an update soon to synchronize Entourage with a coffee pot. What a programming coup that would be!

Even without the cup of coffee part, Entourage is a great tool for keeping track of your busy life. Acting as both a project manager application and an e-mail client, Entourage can help you organize appointments, plan events, jot down notes, manage addresses and phone numbers, juggle a to-do list, and e-mail colleagues, friends, and family. It's starting to sound like you ought to be paying it to do all those things. At its very heart, Entourage is a tailored organizational tool you can use to help your complicated life seem a bit less complicated and a bit more organized. In this chapter, you learn how to set up Entourage, find your way around the program window and features, and import your favorite electronic address book.

## Using the Setup Assistant

When you first open Entourage, a Setup Assistant politely appears to ask you some pertinent questions before jumping into the program. This feature helps set up your e-mail accounts, import your address book, import any calendar info you have hanging around, and get everything up and running. Like many complex programs, Entourage needs some information from you first before it can get to its job being your personal information manager (PIM).

## Understanding Internet E-mail

There are three types of Internet e-mail accounts: Web-based, POP (Post Office Protocol), and IMAP (Internet Message Access Protocol). Web-based mail, also called Web mail, works by using both Web browsers and the Internet to allow access to e-mail from anywhere in the world. POP e-mail works by allowing access to a shared server, and after you download e-mail to your computer, it's removed from the shared server. IMAP combines features of both Web e-mail and POP e-mail, allowing users to download messages as well as store them online. Of the three, POP accounts are the most common type of e-mail account. Examples of POP servers include Yahoo! Mail and Gmail, while IMAP servers include AOL Mail. Entourage supports all three types, but not all can be accessed through Entourage for free. Some e-mail service providers charge a fee for accessing e-mail through an e-mail client like Entourage. If you encounter trouble setting up an e-mail account in Entourage, you may need to check with your e-mail service provider to find out what type of service you use.

If you've never used Entourage and you're a new Mac user, you can start using Entourage without needing to import anything. If you're a seasoned Mac user and you've been using another e-mail program, chances are good you can import all the info into Entourage, such as your saved e-mail messages and address book. Lastly, if you've been using a previous edition of Entourage, the Setup Assistant can help you easily migrate all your info into the new edition.

When creating a new account, you must input all the necessary information about your e-mail account's incoming and outgoing server, server type, your account ID, and your password. If you're using a popular e-mail provider, such as Yahoo! Mail, EarthLink, Hotmail, or Gmail, the Setup Assistant can automatically fill in the information for you. If you're using a lesser-known service, you need to gather all the details and be prepared to enter them into the required fields.

If you're using Entourage through a corporate network, your e-mail account may run on a Microsoft Exchange server, a centralized system for handling networks in an office environment. If this is the case, you need to let the Setup Assistant know by checking the My account is on an Exchange server check box in the Set Up a Mail Account window, the second part of the Setup Assistant's walkthrough session.

Follow these steps to set up Entourage anew:

1. **From the Setup Assistant's Welcome window (also called a *page* by the Setup Assistant), shown in Figure 24.1, click the Start using Entourage without importing anything radio button.** This tells Entourage to create new e-mail and calendar data from scratch.

   If you're importing or upgrading, you'll choose the appropriate option and view some different windows, as explained at the end of these steps.

**NOTE** You also can set up new e-mail accounts at any time from the Entourage window. Choose Entourage ➪ Account Settings to open the Accounts window, click the New arrow button, and select Mail. This opens the Account Setup Assistant, and you can follow the instructions in each window to set up an account. Many of the steps are the same as those outlined in this section.

2. **Click the right-arrow button to continue.**

   The Set Up a Mail Account window appears, as shown in Figure 24.2.

**FIGURE 24.1**

The Entourage Setup Assistant can help you get started with setting up your e-mail, calendar, and address book.

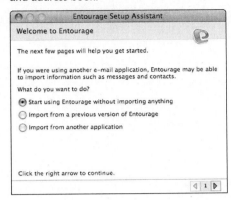

**FIGURE 24.2**

Add your e-mail address in the Set Up a Mail Account window.

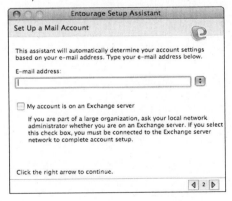

3. **Type in your e-mail address, and click the right-arrow button to continue.**

4. **Setup Assistant tests the configuration settings and shows the results, as shown in Figure 24.3. Click the right-arrow button to continue.**

   If Entourage does not recognize your e-mail server, the Setup Assistant window says "Automatic Configuration Failed." You need to manually insert all the required information in the next window.

5. **The Verify and Complete Settings window, shown in Figure 24.4, offers fields for filling in and verifying your e-mail account information. Fill out the fields as required by your e-mail service.**

**FIGURE 24.3**

The Setup Assistant tests your mail account settings and tells you how it went in the Automatic Configuration Succeeded window.

**FIGURE 24.4**

You can fill in your e-mail account information in the Verify and Complete Settings window, including your account ID, password, and mail server addresses.

Click to save your password in the Mac Keychain.

Set a server type.

NOTE    If you don't know your account info, you need to contact your e-mail service. Check with your e-mail provider to learn more. If you're using another e-mail program, you also might glean this information from the program's account settings.

6.  **Click the right-arrow button to continue.**

The Verify Settings window appears, as shown in Figure 24.5.

**7.** **Click the Verify My Settings button.**

The Setup Assistant checks your information to see if it's all valid and displays the results. If you've missed something, you need to return to the previous window and correct any errors.

**8.** **If everything checks out, click the right-arrow button to continue.**

The Setup Complete window appears, as shown in Figure 24.6, the final Setup Assistant window.

**9.** **Assign a name to your account as it will appear in Entourage.**

- Leave the Add this new e-mail address to your "Me" contact check box activated to add the address to your address book feature in Entourage.

- Leave the Include this account in my Send & Receive All schedule check box activated if you want this account checked automatically when sending and receiving e-mail.

**FIGURE 24.5**

The Setup Assistant verifies all your account settings to make sure everything's in order and working properly.

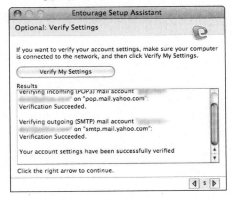

**FIGURE 24.6**

You can assign a unique name for your account, such as Yahoo! Mail or Hotmail Account.

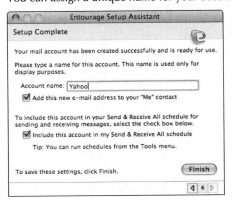

10. **Click Finish to exit the Setup Assistant.**

Entourage prompts you to make the program the default e-mail client, as shown in Figure 24.7.

11. **Click Make Default if you want Entourage to open whenever you click an e-mail link on a Web page; click No if you prefer to use another e-mail client as your default client.**

### FIGURE 24.7

One more thing before you can use your new account: Entourage wants you to make it the default e-mail client.

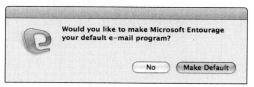

If you are using another e-mail program as your main e-mail client, Entourage can switch you over and import all the saved e-mail messages and address book data. You still work your way through the Setup Assistant steps; however, your windows will vary slightly from the previous set of steps, and depending on how successful the import is, you may have to input more account information, or you may be allowed to skip steps entirely. From the very first Welcome to Entourage window the Setup Assistant presents, you can click the Import from a previous version of Entourage radio button (refer to Figure 24.1). When you make this your selection in the first Setup Assistant window, the next window you see is the Choose an Application window, as shown in Figure 24.8.

### FIGURE 24.8

Choose an e-mail program you want to import in the Choose an Application window.

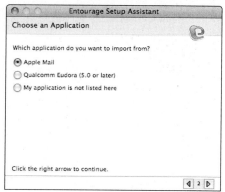

As you can see from the figure, the list of e-mail programs is a bit slim. You can select from two: Apple Mail or Qualcomm Eudora (5.0 or later). If you're using one of these programs, select one and proceed to the next window, shown in Figure 24.9, where you can choose exactly which program elements you want to import.

**FIGURE 24.9**

When importing from Apple Mail or Qualcomm Eudora, you can specify which program elements you want to import.

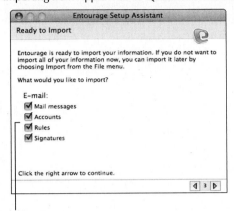

**Select or deselect
items to import.**

If your e-mail program is not one of these two programs listed, you can tell the Setup Assistant that your application is not listed. When you proceed to the next window, the Setup Assistant explains that you can import mail messages in the MBOX format or import address books from the comma-delimited or text file format. After making your selection, you can specify which elements you want to import, such as rules, signatures, messages, and so on. Your list of import elements varies based on the type of import you select. When the import finally starts, it could take quite some time, so be patient.

If you are upgrading from an older version of Entourage, you can select the Import from a previous version of Entourage radio button in the Setup Assistant's Welcome window (refer to Figure 24.1). After making this selection, the next screen you see is the Import window, shown in Figure 24.10. Choose which application you're upgrading from, and then continue through the setup process to import the data.

**FIGURE 24.10**

The Setup Assistant's Import window lets you upgrade from a previous version of Entourage.

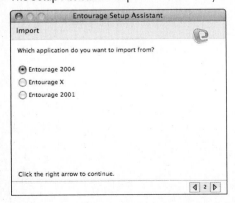

You can use the Account window to edit your e-mail account in Entourage. Choose Entourage ➪ Account Settings. Next, double-click the e-mail account you want to edit to open the Edit Account dialog box. Here, you can change any settings, including Account ID, POP server, or SMTP server, and password, as well as access advanced options for sending and receiving messages. See Chapter 25 to learn more about editing and deleting existing e-mail accounts.

# Navigating the Entourage Window

Entourage looks and acts a bit different than the other Office programs. Rather than dealing with just one work area window holding a document or spreadsheet, Entourage is composed of several key features. You can toggle between them based on what task you want to perform. Unlike the other programs, however, the Entourage window layout is primarily made of panes. You can still use a Standard toolbar at the top of the window to quickly perform common tasks, and the menu bar holds all the commands for using various features and tools. If you're new to Entourage, take a moment and familiarize yourself with the main features and window elements.

## Viewing the main Entourage features

When you open the program, you'll notice six nicely lined-up icons on the left side of the Standard toolbar, shown in Figure 24.11. These icons represent the six key features. You can click an icon to view the feature. The following sections provide a rundown on what each feature does.

**FIGURE 24.11**

You can switch between the main features using these icon buttons found on the Standard toolbar.

### Mail

Mail is the Entourage e-mail client. You can use the Mail feature to send and receive e-mail, sort e-mail, apply rules and filters to messages, and perform all the usual e-mail tasks and activities. Figure 24.12 shows a typical Mail window and layout. The Inbox appears by default and displays any e-mail messages in the two panes. You can learn more about using the Mail feature in Chapter 25.

### Address Book

Use the Address Book to store and manage contact information. Shown in Figure 24.13, the Address Book displays a list of names and e-mail addresses, along with what other pertinent information you prefer to save with each person. Learn more about entering and editing contacts in Chapter 25.

## FIGURE 24.12

You can use Mail to perform e-mail tasks and organize your messages.

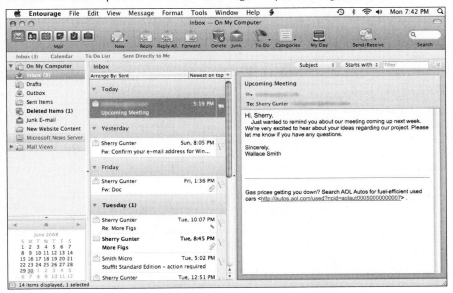

## FIGURE 24.13

You can use the Address Book to manage a contact list.

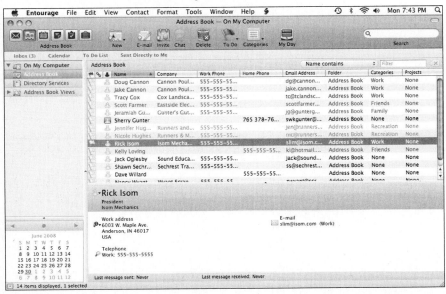

### Calendar

Track your busy schedule using the Calendar. The Calendar lets you view and set appointments, events, recurring meetings, and anything else related to your time management. Figure 24.14 shows the Calendar in Monthly view. Learn more about using the Calendar in Chapter 26.

**FIGURE 24.14**

You can use the Calendar to manage your schedule.

### Notes

Jot down thoughts, reminders, and other items using the Notes feature, shown in Figure 24.15. Much like an electronic pad of paper, you can make notes to yourself and use them with projects and tasks. Learn more about the Notes feature in Chapter 27.

**FIGURE 24.15**

You can use the Notes feature to literally keep notes about whatever you like.

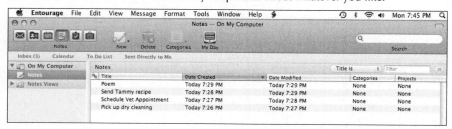

## Tasks

Keep on target with your priorities using the Tasks feature to make to-do lists, as shown in Figure 24.16. Whether you're just making a list of home projects you need to tackle or a detailed list of everything you need to complete a work project, the Tasks feature can help you achieve your goals. Learn more about Tasks in Chapter 27.

**FIGURE 24.16**

You can use Tasks to keep on top of things you need to do.

## Project Center

You can use the Project Center, shown in Figure 24.17, to centrally create and direct projects from all across the Office suite. You can manage notes, documents, e-mail messages, tasks, and schedules. The Project Center brings together documents, files, contacts, tasks, and more. Learn more about using the Project Center in Chapter 27.

**FIGURE 24.17**

You can use the Project Center to manage projects big and small.

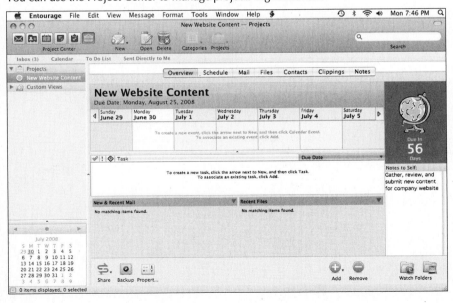

## Viewing window elements

Although very different in appearance from the other Office programs, Entourage still displays several of the same program window features. The following descriptions give you a look at the basic Entourage window elements.

### Title and menu bar

At the top of the Entourage window sits the title and menu bar. This area lists the name of the program and the main menu categories. To reveal a menu, click the menu name; to activate a command, click the command name. Submenus or dialog boxes may appear for further user input. Figure 24.18 shows the Tools menu displayed.

**FIGURE 24.18**

Entourage's title and menu bar display the name of the program and the main groups of menu commands.

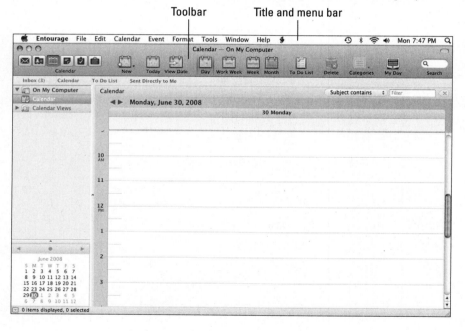

Below the menu bar sit the window controls that allow you to close, minimize, and zoom the document window.

### Toolbar

Directly below the title bar and menu bar is the one and only toolbar found in Entourage. The toolbar displays a row of tool icons for common Entourage tasks. The commands and tools that appear on the toolbar change based on whether you're viewing Mail, the Address Book, the Calendar, Notes, Tasks, or the Project Center. To activate a tool or command, just click the associated icon.

## Panes

The Entourage feature windows utilize panes, shown in Figure 24.19, to list items such as tasks or e-mail messages. You can resize the panes to view more or fewer items onscreen. To resize a pane, move the mouse pointer over a pane border until the pointer icon changes to a double-sided arrow pointer, and then click and drag to adjust the pane size. Any pane border that has a tiny dot in the middle can be dragged to resize the pane.

**FIGURE 24.19**

Areas within an Entourage feature are divided into panes for easy viewing.

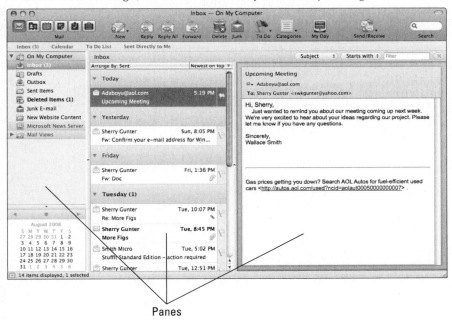

Panes

# Summary

In this chapter, you learned how to use the Setup Assistant to set up Entourage to work with your e-mail service provider. Entourage can help you create a new account, import an existing account, or upgrade from a previous version of the program. Setting up e-mail accounts has many nuances, so if you run into any trouble, be sure to check with your e-mail service provider for more information.

This chapter also introduced you to the six main features Entourage offers: Mail, Address Book, Calendar, Notes, Tasks, and Project Center. You can learn more about using these features in the chapters that follow.

You also learned how to find your way around the program window, viewing familiar and new program window elements. Now you're ready to start e-mailing, scheduling, and organizing your messages, appointments, tasks, and projects.

# Chapter 25

# E-mailing with Entourage

You can use Entourage to communicate electronically with the world at large, whether your world is a group of friends and family, a corporate network of colleagues, underlings, and bosses, or just the Internet as a whole. If you're like most computer users today, e-mailing is an essential, nay, a crucial part of your daily technology experience. For many of us, a day without e-mail is like a day without sunshine, or a day without breathing, or a day without . . . well, you get the picture. For many of us, e-mail is vitally important.

You can use the e-mail feature in Entourage to send and receive e-mail and file attachments, read newsgroups, organize contacts, and more. In this chapter, you learn how to set up an e-mail account, send and receive messages, build your contacts list in the form of an Address Book, filter out junk e-mail, juggle attachments, and view newsgroups. As you can see, lots of components are packed into Entourage, so let's not waste any more time out here in the chapter lobby. Let's start e-mailing!

## Setting Up an E-mail Account

As you discovered in Chapter 24, the very first time you use Entourage, a Setup Assistant appears to help you set up your e-mail accounts. If you have already stepped through the process, you probably already have an e-mail account set up to use. If not, you can start a new one. You also can add other accounts as needed. For example, you may have one e-mail account at work and a free account for personal use. You can configure Entourage to manage all your accounts in one convenient spot.

You can use the same Account Setup Assistant you learned about in Chapter 24 to add new e-mail accounts to Entourage. To set up another e-mail account, follow these steps:

1. **Choose Entourage ➪ Account Settings.**

   Entourage opens the Accounts window, as shown in Figure 25.1.

2. **Click the New button.**

   The Account Setup Assistant appears, as shown in Figure 25.2.

3. **Type the account's e-mail address in the text box.**

   If you're using an account on an Exchange server, you need to check with your network administrator for additional setup information.

---

### FIGURE 25.1

Use the Mail tab in the Accounts window to keep track of your e-mail accounts.

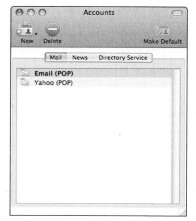

---

### FIGURE 25.2

The Account Setup Assistant walks you through the process of setting up an e-mail account.

4. **Click the right arrow button to continue.**

5. **Setup Assistant tests the configuration settings and shows the results, as shown in Figure 25.3.** Click the right arrow button to continue.

   If Entourage does not recognize your e-mail server, the Setup Assistant window says "Automatic Configuration Failed." You need to manually insert the required information in the next window.

   Next, the Verify and Complete Settings window appears, as shown in Figure 25.4, offering fields for filling in and verifying your e-mail account information.

6. **Fill out the fields as required by your e-mail service.**

7. **Click the right arrow button to continue.**

**FIGURE 25.3**

Setup Assistant tests your mail account settings and tells you how it went in the Automatic Configuration Succeeded window.

**FIGURE 25.4**

Fill in your e-mail account information in the Verify and Complete Settings window, including your account ID, password, and mail server addresses.

**NOTE**    If you don't know your account info, check with your e-mail provider to learn more. If you're using another e-mail program, you might also glean this information from the program's account settings.

The Verify Settings window appears, as shown in Figure 25.5.

**FIGURE 25.5**

Setup Assistant verifies all your account settings to make sure everything's in order and working properly.

8. **Click the Verify My Settings button.**

   Setup Assistant checks your information to see if it's all valid and displays the results. If you've missed something, you'll need to return to the previous window and correct any errors.

9. **If everything checks out, click the right arrow button to continue.**

   The Setup Complete window appears, as shown in Figure 25.6.

10. **Assign a name to your account as it will appear in Entourage.**

    Leave the Include this account in my Send & Receive All schedule check box activated if you want this account checked automatically when sending and receiving e-mail.

11. **Click Finish to exit the Setup Assistant.**

    Entourage adds the new account to the list of existing accounts in the Accounts window, as shown in Figure 25.7. You can return to this window at any time to edit an account or remove it entirely.

**FIGURE 25.6**

You can assign a unique name for your account using this window.

**FIGURE 25.7**

The Accounts window lists the newly added account.

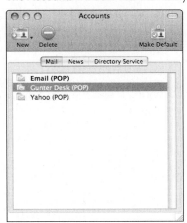

To edit an account, select it in the Accounts window and choose File ➪ Open Account, or Control+click the account name and choose Open Account. This opens the Edit Account dialog box, shown in Figure 25.8, and you can make changes to the account settings.

To remove an account, select it in the Accounts window and click the Delete button.

**FIGURE 25.8**

You can make changes to your account's settings using the Edit Account dialog box.

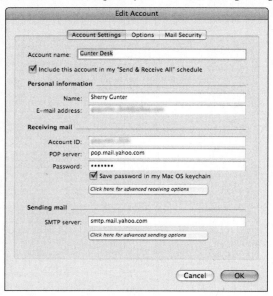

# Working with the Mail Tool

As you learned in Chapter 24, Entourage is comprised of six main tools, one of which is Mail. All the e-mailing you do with Entourage takes place using Mail. As it turns out, Mail is often considered the real workhorse among the Entourage tools. You can use Mail to send and receive messages, file attachments, and newsgroup postings. You can use the various features in Mail to filter your messages, manage messages, set up message rules, schedule e-mailing tasks, and more. In this first section, you learn how to open and view the Mail window.

## Introducing Mail

To use the e-mail feature in Entourage, just click the Mail button on the Standard toolbar. Or you can choose View➪ Go To➪ Mail or press ⌘+1. When you display the Mail tool, the Inbox folder list appears by default, as shown in Figure 25.9. The Standard toolbar also changes to show buttons for working with the e-mail. When you click another Entourage tool, such as Calendar, the Mail tools disappear.

**FIGURE 25.9**

The Inbox appears by default when you use the Mail feature in Entourage.

Mail tool

The main Mail view displays three panes: the Folders List pane, the mini calendar pane, and the main list pane for viewing messages. Messages you receive are shown in the Inbox, a special folder in Entourage (refer to Figure 25.9). The Inbox folder displays by default when you click the Mail button. To view a different folder, such as the Outbox, just click the folder name in the Folders List pane. To return to the default Inbox view again, click the Inbox folder name. You also can change the various ways you view messages using Mail Views, which you learn about coming up shortly.

Here's a rundown of the main Mail folders:

- **Inbox:** Displays your e-mail messages.
- **Drafts:** Lists any e-mail messages you are currently composing.
- **Outbox:** Displays messages waiting to be sent.
- **Sent Items:** Lists all the e-mail messages you have previously sent.
- **Deleted Items:** Lists deleted messages.
- **Junk E-mail:** Lists junk e-mail and spam messages.

## Checking E-mail on Online Accounts

Two common types of e-mail accounts are POP and IMAP. An IMAP account typically keeps e-mail messages on a server rather than downloading them onto your computer like a POP account. Entourage lets you treat a POP account like an IMAP account and keep your messages on the server. This is handy if you're planning a trip and want to check your messages at a glance without wanting to download everything. It does this by downloading only the header information. This Entourage feature is called *online access*. To set up an account in this way, choose Tools ➪ Accounts and double-click the account name. In the Edit Account dialog box, click the Options tab and turn on the Allow online access check box. When you activate this feature, Entourage adds a folder for this to the Folders List pane, which then lets you check for e-mail with just one click on the folder name. You can browse headers for e-mail messages stored on the server without downloading the messages, but if you see a message you need to view in its entirety, you can click it. When you use this Entourage feature, the messages remain on the server and are not downloaded onto your computer.

In addition to folders, the Folders List pane displays any Office project folders you are working on; to learn more about using projects, see Chapter 27. The Folders List pane has main headings you can expand or collapse to view sublists of folders, or views. For example, you can expand or collapse the top heading, My Computer, to view or hide the Mail folders.

## Using Mail Views in the Folders List

You can find the Mail Views in the Folders List pane, located in the far-left pane in the program window. You can expand and collapse various headings in the Folders List pane to view different aspects of the Mail feature. The Mail Views themselves are useful for filtering out messages you don't want to see and concentrating on those you do want to view. You can use the Folders List pane to view filtered lists of e-mails in any of your mail folders, such as viewing all the flagged or high-priority messages. To display the filtered Mail Views in the Folders List, click the Expand arrow next to the Mail Views heading, as shown in Figure 25.10. To see a particular filtered list, click the view name, such as Unread or Received Today. You can choose from the following filtered list views:

- **Due Today:** Displays all the e-mail items associated with a due date.
- **Family Category:** Displays only messages assigned to the Family category.
- **Flagged:** Displays any flagged e-mail messages.
- **High Priority:** Displays all the high-priority messages.
- **Personal Category:** Displays all the messages to which the Personal category is assigned.
- **Received Today:** Displays only the messages you received today.
- **Sent Directly to Me:** Displays messages addressed only to you and no one else.
- **Unread:** Displays all the unread messages.
- **Work Category:** Displays all the messages to which the Work category is assigned.

**FIGURE 25.10**

You can filter your view of message items using the Folders List pane.

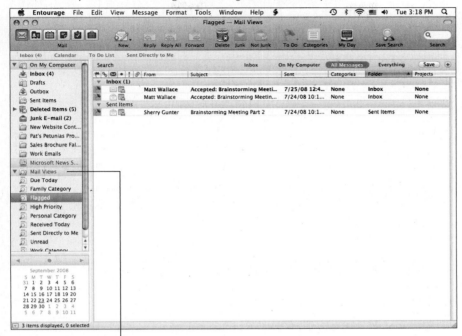

Use Mail Views to
filter your view of
messages.

To return to the regular Inbox view, click the Inbox folder in the Folders List pane.

## Inbox columns and icons

As you start receiving messages, different icons appear in the columns in the list pane, helping you to quickly ascertain pertinent information about the messages. The Inbox folder divides the list pane into columns. The columns display the message sender, the subject line, the date it was sent, and any categories or projects assigned to the message. Table 25.1 explains the columns and what type of icons you can expect to see.

**TABLE 25.1**

## Inbox Columns

| Column | Description |
| --- | --- |
| To Do Flag Status | This column displays messages requiring action. Gray by default, the icon in this column changes to red to indicate that this message requires action, and Entourage adds it to your To Do list. When the item is completed, you can click the icon again to make it green, indicating it's completed. |
| Links | This column indicates whether the message is linked to another message, a calendar event, a task, or a note. |
| Online Status | This column shows the online server status of your IMAP messages. Different icons appear to indicate if a message has been only partially received, deleted from the server, or fully downloaded the next time you contact the server. |
| Status | This column shows the message status. Several different icons may appear in this column to indicate whether the message has been read, answered, redirected, or forwarded. |
| Priority | This column indicates the message priority: Highest, High, Low, Lowest, or Normal. |
| Attachments | An icon in this column indicates that one or more files are attached. |
| Digital Signing | A padlock icon in this column indicates the message is digitally signed, meaning it's tamper-proof. |

# Receiving and Sending E-mail

When you start and setup Entourage, your Inbox shows one e-mail already received. This is actually the welcome message from Microsoft, and it's built into the program. In case you were excited about receiving your first e-mail in Entourage, it didn't come via e-mail. It's preprogrammed to be in the Inbox. Don't let that get you down, however, because your Inbox is sure to be full of messages soon enough.

## Checking for e-mail

To check for new messages, use any of these methods:

- Click the Send/Receive button on the Standard toolbar.
- Choose Tools ➪ Send & Receive ➪ Send & Receive All.
- Press ⌘+K.

If you have more than one account, you can check for messages on a specific account; choose Tools ➪ Send & Receive ➪ and click the name of the account.

Anytime you activate the Send & Receive command, Entourage checks the mail server for any incoming messages and sends any outgoing messages you have waiting in the Outbox. This includes downloading or uploading any file attachments.

**TIP** You can restrict the download size of your e-mail messages, which is handy if you have a slow dial-up connection. Choose Tools ➪ Accounts, double-click the account, and then click the Options tab. Click the Partially receive messages over 20KB check box. You can choose a smaller or larger kilobyte setting, if desired. Once activated, this feature tells Entourage to grab only the first portion of the e-mail message.

## Would You Like Sound with That?

**B**y default, Entourage is set up to play sounds for various mail features. For example, when you receive mail, a chime sounds. You can turn the sounds on or off to suit your own likes or dislikes. Choose Entourage ⇨ Preferences to open the Preferences dialog box. Under the General Preferences category, click Notification. Under the Sounds settings, choose which sounds you want to hear by selecting check boxes, or turn sounds off by deselecting check boxes. Click OK to exit the dialog box and save your changes.

### Reading e-mail messages

There are two ways to read a message you receive in the Inbox. You can open the message in its own message window, or you can use the Preview Pane.

To read an e-mail message in its own window, simply double-click the message in the Inbox. This opens the message, as shown in Figure 25.11. From the message window, you can choose to reply to the sender of the message, reply to everyone on the message list, or forward the message to someone else. The toolbar at the top of the window also includes commands for deleting the message, moving it to the Junk e-mail folder, printing the message, or assigning the message a priority status, category, or project.

**FIGURE 25.11**

You can open the message window to read the message.

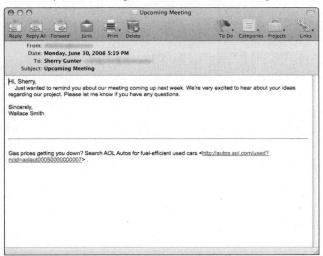

After you've read the message, you can decide what to do with it then and there, or j
window. To close the window, simply click the window's Close button.

You also can set up Entourage to include a Preview Pane, which shows the selected e
main Mail window in its own pane, as shown in Figure 25.12. To turn on the feature
Preview Pane ⇨ Below List or On Right.

**FIGURE 25.12**

You can use the Preview Pane to view messages in the Inbox.

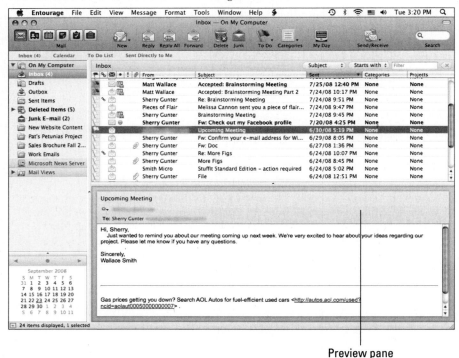

Preview pane

You can move through messages in the Inbox Preview Pane by clicking the ↓ or ↑ key. You also can use the View menu to move to the next or previous message.

## Creating and sending an e-mail

When you're ready to create a new e-mail message, Entourage opens a blank message window and a pop-up window for addressing the message. You can use the Tab key to move from field to field or just click in the field box to fill in the appropriate data. The pop-up window, shown in Figure 25.13, offers four buttons and three text fields for entering e-mail addresses. Each text field has a specific purpose:

■ **To:** This field is the place to enter e-mail addresses of the primary people to whom you want to send a message. If the address you start typing already exists in your Entourage Address Book, Entourage automatically tries to fill in the rest for you. If you enter more than one address, be sure to separate them with commas. Any address you enter in this field appears at the top of the message for anyone to see.

■ **Cc:** Standing for "carbon copy," this field is for addressing secondary recipients. Like the To field, any address you enter in the Cc field appears at the top of the message for anyone to see.

■ **Bcc:** Meaning "blind carbon copy," use this field to send the message to a secondary recipient without the primary recipient knowing about the secondary recipient. This field is very handy for sending a message to lots of people without including everybody's e-mail addresses in the message itself, thus avoiding the potential for spammers to see your e-mail address.

**FIGURE 25.13**

When you open a new message window, the pop-up window for addressing the e-mail appears onscreen.

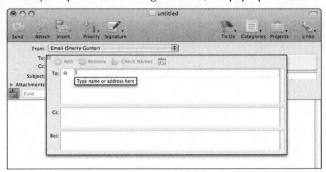

**TIP**   You can access your Address Book contacts using the Address pop-up window. Click the Address Book button to view your list of contacts. To add a name to your current e-mail, double-click a name from the list. Click the Address Book button again to toggle the list display off.

After addressing the e-mail, you can fill out the Subject line with a subject title, as shown in Figure 25.14. This title information lets the recipient know about the nature of your e-mail message. You should always include a brief subject line in your messages. Some e-mail programs filter out unmarked subject messages as spam or junk mail.

**FIGURE 25.14**

You can fill out the rest of the message fields to finish composing your e-mail.

Use the main text box
to compose your message.     Addresses     Subject line

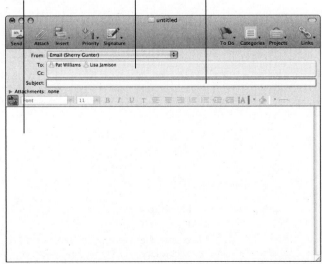

You can use the large text box area in the message window, shown in Figure 25.14, to compose your e-mail. You type your message just as you would type a letter in Word. E-mail formatting typically falls into two categories: plain text and HTML. With plain text, you can't format with special formatting, such as bold or color. With HTML formatting turned on, you can. You can toggle between the two types using the Use HTML button. If you opt for HTML formatting, the toolbar at the top of the text box includes commands for controlling the font, size, style, alignments, and other simply formatting features. Most e-mail client programs can read HTML today, but the process is not always successful. In other words, don't spend lots of time trying to format your message to look pretty. There's no guarantee the recipient will see the message the same way in which you formatted it. For best results, keep the formatting simple or plain.

**NOTE**    The spell-check feature is turned on by default, so you may see Entourage correcting misspellings as you type. To turn the feature off, choose Entourage ➪ Preferences to open the Preferences dialog box. Under the General Preferences category, click Spelling. Deselect the Check spelling as you type check box to turn off automatic spell-checking.

To create a new e-mail, follow these steps:

1. **Click the New button, or choose File ➪ New ➪ Mail Message.**

    An untitled Mail message window opens along with a pop-up window, called the Address pop-up window, for addressing the message.

2. **In the pop-up window, type the e-mail address or addresses in the appropriate fields, as shown in Figure 25.15.**

    Optionally, you can click the Address Book button to view contacts in your Address Book and double-click names to add them to the message. The Address Book button toggles the Address Book on or off in the pop-up window.

3. **Click anywhere outside the pop-up window or just keep pressing Tab until the window closes.**

**FIGURE 25.15**

Use the Address pop-up window to enter e-mail addresses to which you want to send your message.

Address Book button

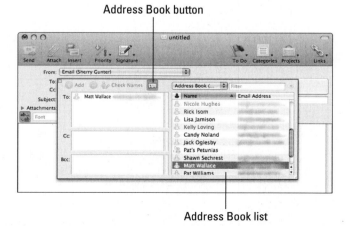

Address Book list

4. **Click in the Subject line, and type a subject header, as shown in Figure 25.16.**
5. **Click in the message text box, and compose your e-mail message.**

6. **Click the Send button, or choose Message ⇨ Send Message Now.**

   If you're connected to the Internet, Entourage sends your message.

**FIGURE 25.16**

Fill out the subject header and compose your e-mail message.

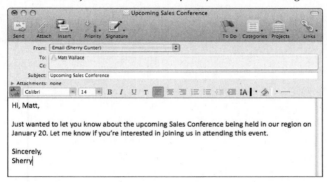

If you prefer to send the message at a later time, choose Message ⇨ Send Message Later. If you want to save your message as a draft and work on it again later, press ⌘+S to save the message in the Drafts folder. You can reopen it again and send it when you're ready.

### Assigning flags, priorities, and categories

The toolbar at the top of the message window includes several buttons for prioritizing, flagging, or categorizing a message. For example, you may want to flag the message as High priority, alerting the recipient that the message requires attention. You also can assign a category to a message, such as Family or Personal, or add the message to the To Do list. These options can help you keep track of your Entourage information. You can flag, prioritize, and categorize any message you send, as well as messages you receive. Figure 25.17 shows the buttons found in a typical message window.

**FIGURE 25.17**

You can use the Priority, To Do, Categories, and Projects buttons to organize and keep track of your e-mail messages.

Here's how you can use the message window's toolbar buttons to flag, prioritize, or categorize:

- **Priority:** Use this button to set a message priority level: Highest, High, Normal, Low, or Lowest. By default, all messages are set to Normal priority unless you specify otherwise.
- **To Do:** You can flag a message with a due date using this button, helping you to keep track of when a message needs to be completed. When you activate a flag, Entourage adds a flag icon to

the Inbox column and adds the message to your To Do list. You can choose from the following denotations: Today, Tomorrow, This Week, Next Week, No Due Date, Choose Date, Add a Reminder, Mark as Complete, or Clear To Do Flag.

- **Categories:** Organize your messages by categories, such as Family or Work. Categories are simply labels to help you keep track of your Inbox information.
- **Projects:** If a message pertains to an Office project you're working on, you can use the Projects button to assign the message to a project. This can help you keep all the related project items grouped together.

In addition to finding these buttons on the message window's toolbar, you also can access the settings through the Message and Edit menus.

### Inserting pictures, backgrounds, sounds, or movie clips

You can insert a picture, background picture, sound, or movie clip into your e-mail message. To do so, click the Insert button and choose the type of media you want to insert. Or you can choose Message ➪ Insert ➪ and pick a media. The appropriate Choose a File dialog box opens, and you can select the specific file to insert. Entourage places the media object directly into your message, as shown in Figure 25.18.

---

**FIGURE 25.18**

You can insert different types of media into your message, such as a photo.

Click to insert media.

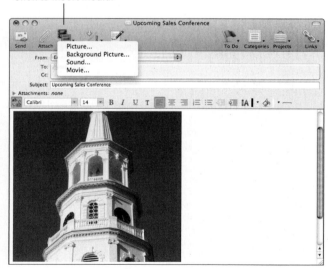

If you change your mind, you can Control+click the photo or clip and choose Cut. This deletes it from the message.

You also can send files as attachments. Learn more about this option coming up later in this chapter. To learn more about working with graphics in Office, such as photos, see Chapter 30.

# Replying to an e-mail

 Replying to any message is easy. From the Inbox, select the message and click the Reply button, or choose Message ➪ Reply. You also can double-click the message and click the Reply button in the message window. Either route opens a new message window, as shown in Figure 25.19. Unlike a blank message window, however, the Reply window has the sender's e-mail address filled in already, and the Subject line filled in with the original e-mail's subject line and the letters "Re:" in front. The "Re:" is commonly thought to mean "reply" or "regarding," but technically it's Latin for "in the matter of." This lets the original sender know it's a reply to the message he sent to you. This pre-addressing can be a real time-saver. You also can add other recipient's names to the address fields; click the field and type the address.

**FIGURE 25.19**

When you reply to a message, Entourage reuses the sender's e-mail address and subject line.

Re appears in the subject line.

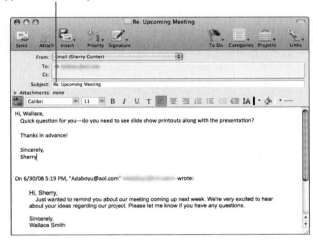

By default, Entourage also includes the original message text in the text box field (refer to Figure 25.18). You can type your response above the original message text or in the original text, or you can remove the original text entirely. When you're ready to send the e-mail, click the Send button or choose Message ➪ Send Message Now.

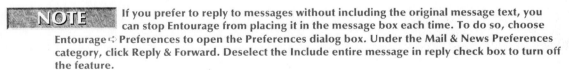 **NOTE** If you prefer to reply to messages without including the original message text, you can stop Entourage from placing it in the message box each time. To do so, choose Entourage ➪ Preferences to open the Preferences dialog box. Under the Mail & News Preferences category, click Reply & Forward. Deselect the Include entire message in reply check box to turn off the feature.

 If the message was originally addressed to two or more people, you can choose to send your reply to everyone on the list. To do so, select the message in the Inbox and click the Reply All button, or open the message window and click Reply All.

## Forwarding an e-mail

You can forward a message to a new recipient. You can forward it just as you received it, or you can forward it as an e-mail attachment. To send along a message as is, select it in the Inbox and click the Forward button on the Standard toolbar, or if you're viewing a message in a message window, click the Forward button on the window's toolbar.

Entourage opens the message in a new message window and the pop-up Address window. Fill in the recipient's e-mail address, and click anywhere outside the Address window. As shown in Figure 25.20, the Subject field is already filled in, this time with the letters "FW:" preceding the header. "FW" stands for "forward." You can add your own message text to the existing message. By default, Entourage also includes the original message text in the text box field (refer to Figure 25.19). When you're ready to send the e-mail, click the Send button or choose Message ➪ Send Message Now.

To forward an e-mail as an attachment rather than a message, click the message in the Inbox and choose Message ➪ Forward as Attachment. Entourage opens a new message window with only the Subject field filled in; address the message as you normally would, and compose the message. Under the Attachments heading, the forwarded e-mail appears as a document attachment, as shown in Figure 25.21. When you're ready to send the e-mail, click the Send button or choose Message ➪ Send Message Now.

You can redirect a message rather than forward it. Redirecting sends the original message without adding any information from you in the message. With a redirected message, the recipient sees only the sender's name as the sender, not your name. This is handy if you don't want to be included in any e-mail exchanges between the two people. To redirect a message, choose Message ➪ Redirect. Unlike forwarded messages, you cannot add a comment to a redirected message. All you can do is add the recipient's e-mail address.

---

**FIGURE 25.20**

When you forward a message, Entourage reuses the subject line.

FW appears in the Subject line.

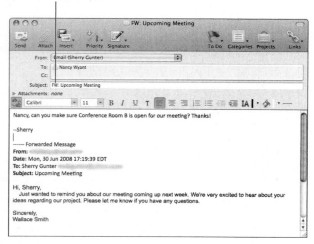

**FIGURE 25.21**

You can forward an e-mail as a file attachment.

File attachment

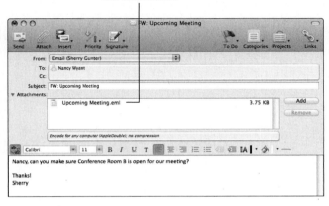

## Adding a signature

Many users often include signatures at the bottom of their messages, typically containing contact information and a company logo, or in the case of personal e-mails, a popular saying, quote, or personal statement. A signature is simply preset text you add to the bottom of an e-mail message saving you the trouble of typing the information each time. You can create as many signatures as you like or edit the default Standard signature. To create your own signatures in Entourage, follow these steps:

1. **Choose Tools ⇨ Signatures.**

   Entourage opens the Signatures window, as shown in Figure 25.22.

**FIGURE 25.22**

You can use the Signatures window to manage your signatures.

2. **Click the New button.**

   An untitled signature form opens, as shown in Figure 25.23.

**FIGURE 25.23**

You can use the signature form window to create a new signature.

Enter a name for the signature.

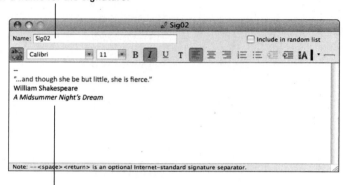

Type the signature.

3. **Type a unique name for the signature, such as My Work Sig or Personal Sig01.**

4. **Type your signature text, and format it the way you want it to appear in your e-mail messages.**

   You can use the toolbar buttons to apply formatting to the signature text.

5. **Press ⌘+S, or choose File ⇨ Save.**

6. **Close the signature form window.**

   Entourage adds the signature to the list box.

7. **Close the Signatures window.**

**TIP**    If you have a library of different signatures, you can instruct Entourage to include a random signature in an e-mail message. Click the Include in random list check box in the signature form window while creating a new signature or editing an existing signature.

To use a signature in a message, simply click the Signature button on the message window's toolbar and select the signature you want to apply. You also can choose Message ⇨ Signature ⇨ and select a signature to use. Entourage adds the signature to the bottom of your e-mail message, as shown in Figure 25.24.

## Cleaning Up Messages

Every time you forward a message, more quoting brackets are added to the original message. After a couple hundred forwards to a message, the brackets can make the original message downright illegible. Entourage features a handy tool you can use to clean up heavily forwarded message text, and you can apply it before sending the e-mail to someone else. Simply choose Edit ⇨ Auto Text Cleanup ⇨ and choose the type of edit you want to perform. For example, to clean up quoting marks, choose the Remove Quoting command. To fix paragraph wrapping, choose Rewrap Paragraphs.

Signatures are a great way to insert contact information or personal statements into your e-mail messages.

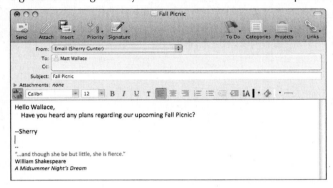

You can return to the Signatures window at any time to create new signatures, delete ones you no longer want, or edit existing signatures.

## Scheduling message checking

By default, Entourage is set up to check for new messages whenever you start the program, every 10 minutes while you're using the program, and when you close the program. You can turn the feature off or set a different schedule. For example, you may only want to check for messages manually or set a longer length of time between checking the server for messages. You can do all this through the Schedules and Edit Schedules feature. The Schedules window, shown in Figure 25.25, keeps track of all the scheduled items you set in Entourage. You can access the window by choosing Tools ➪ Edit Schedules.

Use the Schedules window to schedule when Entourage checks e-mail, deletes mail, and performs other functions.

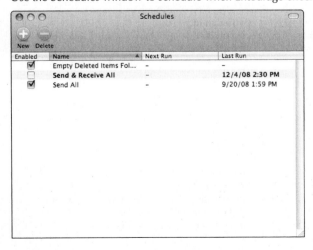

## Automatic Signatures

You can tell Entourage to add the same signature to every e-mail message you send. You can do this through the Accounts window. Choose Tools ⇨ Accounts. Double-click the account you want to edit to open the Edit Account dialog box. Click the Options tab to find the Message options. Click the Default signature pop-up menu, and choose your signature. Click OK to exit the dialog box and apply the change. The next time you send an e-mail, Entourage automatically adds the signature.

Entourage includes three default schedules already set in the Schedules window:

- **Empty Deleted Items Folder:** This item deletes messages from the Deleted Items folder. By default, this scheduled item takes place manually, which means it's up to you to delete messages.

- **Send & Receive All:** This item sends and receives messages as a repeating schedule every 10 minutes while you're using Entourage.

- **Send All:** Set to manual, this action sends all messages waiting in the Outbox without checking for incoming messages.

You can edit these existing schedules, remove them entirely, and add your own schedules to the list. For example, you may want to schedule when Entourage removes messages from the Deleted Mail folder. When setting a scheduled item, you can define its name, when it happens, and what happens. The "when" options let you determine when a schedule runs. When defining a scheduled item, you can choose from the following "when" actions:

- **Manually:** A scheduled item with this designation does not really run until you tell it to by choosing Tools ⇨ Run Schedule.

- **At Startup:** This item runs as soon as Entourage opens.

- **On Quit:** This item runs when Entourage closes.

- **Timed Schedule:** You can specify your own time settings when you want this item to run.

- **Repeating Schedule:** You can set a schedule to run at regular intervals using this designation.

- **Recurring:** You can set a schedule to run in a recurring pattern over the course of time you define.

The "what happens" options, called the Action options in the Edit Schedule window, let you determine what happens when a schedule runs. You can choose from these actions:

- **Receive Mail:** Receives e-mail messages from your server.

- **Receive News:** Receives the latest newsgroup postings.

- **Send All:** Sends all mail waiting in the Outbox.

- **Run AppleScript:** Runs a specified AppleScript.

- **Delete Mail:** Sends any mail in the Deleted Items folder to the Trash.

- **Delete Junk Mail:** Empties the Junk E-mail folder.

- **Launch Alias:** Opens an alias to any document or program on your computer.

- **Excel Auto Web Publish:** Works with Excel's Save As Web Page feature to keep a workbook current on the Web.

When you define the "when" and "what" of a scheduled item, you typically must define a few more parameters to set the scheduled item into play. For example, if you set up a schedule to delete mail at startup, you can specify a folder to delete and an age of the messages within the folder such as removing any messages older than 14 days. You also can add more When and Action items to a schedule using the Add Occurrence and Add Action buttons. You can add up to three items to a scheduled item using the Add Occurrence button under the When options. You can add dozens of actions using the Add Action button under the Action settings. You also can remove occurrences and actions you no longer want to associate with the scheduled item.

To add a scheduled item, follow these steps:

1. **Choose Tools ⇨ Run Schedule ⇨ Edit Schedules.**

   The Schedules window opens, as shown in Figure 25.25.

2. **Click the New button.**

   The Edit Schedule dialog box opens, as shown in Figure 25.26.

**FIGURE 25.26**

Use the Edit Schedule dialog box to create new scheduled e-mailing tasks or edit existing tasks.

3. **Type a name for the scheduled item in the Name text box.**

4. **Under the When options, choose when you want to run the schedule.**

   You can click the When pop-up menu and choose Manually, At Startup, On Quit, Timed Schedule, Repeating Schedule, or Recurring.

   If the item includes parameters, such as setting a time or date, fill in the parameters as needed.

   Optionally, you can check the Only if connected check box to perform the action only when connected to your Internet Service Provider.

5. **Under the Action options, click the pop-up menu and choose an action.**

   If the item includes parameters, such as setting a time or date, fill in the parameters as needed.

6. **Click OK.**

   Entourage adds the item to the schedule.

7. **Click the Schedule window's Close button to exit the window.**

After you've scheduled an item, you can do the following:

- To run a scheduled item, choose Tools ⇨ Run Schedule ⇨ and click the item. If the scheduled item has a specific time set to run, it does so automatically.
- To turn off a scheduled item, just deselect its check box in the list. When you deactivate a scheduled item, Entourage no longer follows its schedule.
- To edit an item, double-click it and make changes to the settings.

**TIP**   Do you want to read your messages offline? You can. Choose Entourage ⇨ Work Offline. Now you can read messages and write replies without having to worry about Entourage trying to go online for scheduled e-mail retrievals.

## Sending an automatic response

You can create an automatic e-mail reply to any messages you receive. This scenario is ideal if you need to be away from the office for awhile or if you're going on vacation. You can create an automatic response that states when you'll be back and who the sender might contact in the meantime. One way to create an automatic response is to set up a message rule. The catch to using this method is that Entourage has to be running while you're away.

When setting up a message rule, you give the rule a unique name and control the "ifs" and "thens" of the scenario. In this case, the "if" is if you receive a message, and the "then" is then Entourage sends a response.

To set up a message rule, use these steps:

1. **Click Tools ⇨ Rules.**

   The Rules window opens, as shown in Figure 25.27.

2. **Click the New button.**

   The Edit Rule dialog box opens, as shown in Figure 25.28.

---

**FIGURE 25.27**

Use the Rules window to create and manage message rules.

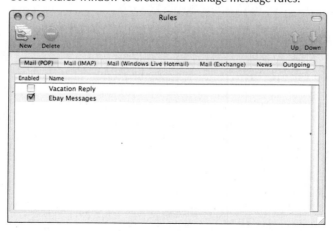

3. **Type a name for the rule in the Rule name field, such as Vacation Response.**

   Optionally, you can change the All message pop-up menu to narrow down which messages to respond to, such as sending an automatic response only to certain people.

4. **Under the Then options, just below the Add Action button, click the pop-up menu and change the Change status to Reply.**

**FIGURE 25.28**

New rules are created in the Edit Rule dialog box, where you complete a form and make your option selections.

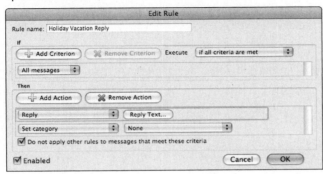

5. **Click the Reply Text button.**

   Entourage opens a Reply Text dialog box, as shown in Figure 25.29.

**FIGURE 25.29**

Type the reply you want to send when Entourage generates an automatic response.

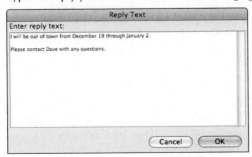

6. **Type the reply you want Entourage to send.**

7. **Click OK.**

   Notice that the Enabled check box is enabled by default. Leave this check box selected.

8. **Click OK again to exit the Edit Rule window.**

Entourage adds the rule to the list box, as shown in Figure 25.30. Leave the Enabled check box selected to turn the automatic response on now, or deselect the check box to turn the rule off until you need it later.

**FIGURE 25.30**

Use the Rules window to control which rules are turned on or off.

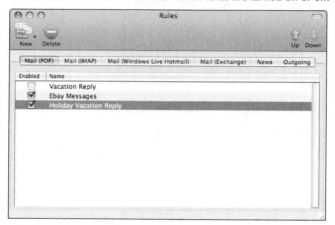

9. **Close the Rule window when finished.**

You learn more about setting other types of message rules in the next section.

If you're using a Microsoft Exchange account, you can use the Out of Office Assistant to generate an automatic response. Unlike a message rule that requires Entourage to be running to create an e-mail response, the Out of Office Assistant works with the mail server running Microsoft Exchange to create your reply. To activate this feature, click the Microsoft Exchange account in the Folders List pane, choose Tools ⇨ Out of Office, and click Send Out of Office messages. Type your reply text, and you're ready to go. If you need to set additional options, such as start and end dates, click More Options.

# Managing Messages

After you start accumulating messages in your Inbox, you'll need to figure out what you want to do with them all. Entourage makes it easy to manage your messages using all kinds of tools and features. For example, you can delete old messages, archive messages, print them, and so on. Like the other Office programs, message files are stored in folders on your computer after you download them. By default, messages are directed into the Inbox folder when you first receive them. You can move them into other folders, create new folders for organizing messages, or delete messages you no longer want to keep. This section shows you the various tools for keeping your messages organized and managing the growing pile of e-mails.

## Deleting messages

You can delete messages you no longer need to see in your Inbox. When you delete a message from the Inbox or other mail folders, Entourage moves the message to the Deleted Items folder. To permanently remove the message, you must then delete it from the Deleted Items folder.

To delete a message, use any of these methods:

- Select the message in the Inbox, and click the Delete button in the Standard toolbar.
- Choose Edit ➪ Delete Message, or press ⌘+Del.
- Select the message in the Inbox, and press Del.
- Control+click a message in the Inbox, and choose Delete Message.
- In the message window, click the Delete button in the toolbar.

To remove more than one message from the Inbox, you can select multiple messages and apply a deletion method. Simply click the first message in the group you want to delete, press and hold the Shift key, and click the last message in the group. Entourage highlights the messages. To select non-contiguous messages, press and hold ⌘ while clicking the messages.

To permanently delete messages from the Deleted Items folder, use any of these methods:

- Control+click the Deleted Items folder name in the Folders List pane, and choose Empty Deleted Items from the pop-up menu.
- Choose Tools ➪ Run Schedule ➪ Empty Deleted Items Folder.
- Open the Deleted Items folder, select the message you want to delete, and click the Delete button. Entourage asks you to confirm the deletion.

## Printing messages

You can quickly print any message you receive. To do so, select the message in the Inbox and choose File ➪ Print. This opens the Print dialog box, shown in Figure 25.31, and you can adjust any printer settings before committing the e-mail to paper. For example, you can choose to include headers or footers with the printout, choose the number of copies and pages, and so on.

If you're viewing a message in its message window you can activate the Print button and print the message directly without opening the Print dialog box. Just click the Print button on the window's toolbar. If you do want to open the Print dialog box, click the Print button's arrow icon and choose Print.

## Filing messages

You can organize your messages by filing them away. You can do this by storing them in unique folders. By default, all incoming messages are stored in the Inbox folder until you do something else with the messages. Also by default, Entourage is set up with two preset folders you can use for messages you don't want to keep or messages you don't want to look at right away: the Deleted Items folder and the Junk E-mail folder. In addition to these folders, you can add other folders and subfolders to help you manage your e-mail. To create a new folder, choose File ➪ New ➪ Folder. Entourage adds a new, empty folder to the list pane and lets you type a unique name. Type a name, and press Return.

**FIGURE 25.31**

The Print dialog box

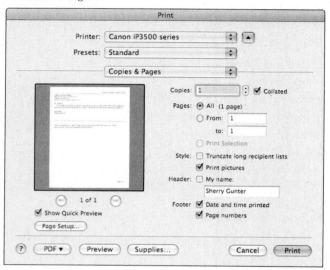

Use any of these methods to file your messages:

- You can quickly drag a message from the Inbox and drop it into any folder in the Folders List pane.
- Select the message in the Inbox, and choose Message ➪ Move To ➪ Choose Folder. This opens the Move To dialog box where you can select the folder in which you want to store the message.
- Control+click a message, choose Move To ➪ Choose Folder, and select the folder from the Move To dialog box.
- To make a copy of the message and place the copy in a folder, press and hold Option while dragging the message. The original message stays where you found it, and a copy of the message appears in the folder where you dropped it.

You can add and delete folders as needed, as well as any messages within the folders.

## Getting rid of junk e-mail

You can turn on Entourage's Junk Mail Filter to help you reduce the amount of junk e-mail—also known as spam—you receive in your Inbox. This feature scans incoming messages for material typically associated with spam. Any violators it finds are processed into the Junk E-mail folder. You can examine the messages later and decide whether they're worth reading. It also blocks embedded pictures.

To turn on the Junk Mail Filter, choose Tools ➪ Junk E-mail Protection. This opens the Junk E-mail Protection dialog box, as shown in Figure 25.31. The Junk E-mail Protection dialog box offers three tabs you can use to set up how you want to handle junk e-mail. The Level tab, shown in Figure 25.32, lets you set a protection level for the filter. You can choose from any of these levels of protection to apply:

- **None:** This option provides no junk e-mail protection.
- **Low:** This option catches only the most obvious spam e-mails.
- **High:** This option catches most spam, but sometimes legitimate messages are caught as well.
- **Exclusive:** This option delivers messages only from people in your Address Book, safe domains listed in the Safe Domains list, or addresses from the Mailing List Manager. All other messages are routed to the Junk E-Mail folder.

**FIGURE 25.32**

You can use the Junk E-mail Protection dialog box to set up junk e-mail options.

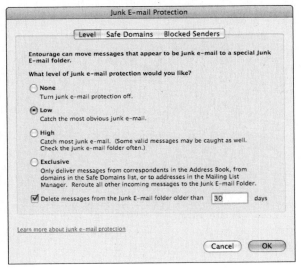

By default, the Junk filter is set to Low protection. You can choose to set a higher level of protection or turn the feature off entirely.

The Safe Domains tab, shown in Figure 25.33, lets you list all the domain names you trust for e-mail, such as your company's Web site, your banking institution, and so on. The domain name is always the part of an e-mail address that follows the @ sign. Just type in the domain name in the Safe Domains list box, and if you're adding more than one, separate them with commas.

The Blocked Senders tab, shown in Figure 25.34, lets you block e-mail messages. You can compile and maintain a list of specific addresses you do not want to receive e-mails from and make sure they are filtered into the Junk E-mail folder instead of the Inbox. As in the Safe Domains list box, just type the e-mail address. When adding more than one, be sure to separate them with commas.

You also can block a sender from the Inbox. Select the message you want to block from future e-mails, and choose Message ➪ Block Sender. Entourage automatically adds the e-mail address to the Blocked Senders list.

**FIGURE 25.33**

You can place trusted domain names in the Safe Domains list box, and Entourage knows to leave messages from these sources unfiltered.

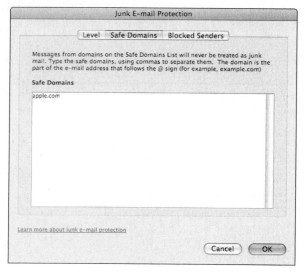

**FIGURE 25.34**

You can place unwanted e-mail addresses in the Blocked Senders list box, and Entourage blocks them from your Inbox.

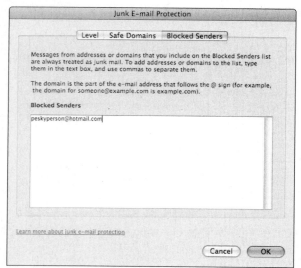

## Marking messages

You can mark your messages in the Inbox as read, unread, or junk. The marking tools are helpful in keeping track of which messages you've dealt with already and which ones you need to revisit again. Figure 25.35 shows a typical Inbox with both read and unread messages. You can label a message as junk and send it to the Junk E-mail folder. To mark a message, use any of these methods:

- To mark a message as read, choose Message ➪ Mark as Read.

- To mark a message as unread, choose Message ➪ Mark as Unread.

- To mark all messages as read, choose Message ➪ Mark All as Read.

 ■ To mark a message as a junk e-mail, choose Message ➪ Mark as Junk, or just click the Junk button on the Standard toolbar.

- To mark a message in the Junk E-mail folder as non-junk, choose Message ➪ Mark as Not Junk.

**FIGURE 25.35**

Unread messages appear in bold in the Inbox, while read messages are unbolded.

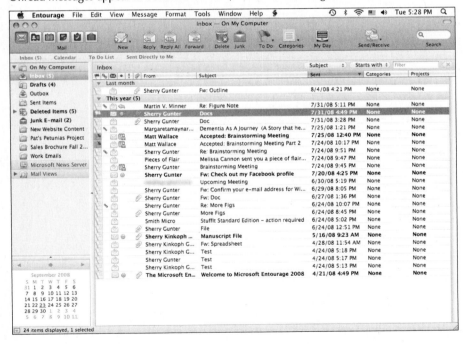

## Setting message rules

You can set up message rules to help you govern your e-mail messages. Message rules are simply filters you can apply to help sort and deal with your e-mails. For example, as you learned in the preceding section, you can set up a message rule to create an automatic response to any e-mail message you receive. By their very nature, rules or filters help you to file, answer, or remove e-mail messages based on their contents, subjects, senders, or sizes. Entourage's message rules are like having a personal secretary to sort through your mail. Message rules sort through your e-mails to organize them just the way you want, whether that means tossing out unwanted e-mail or filing company messages in a particular folder.

You can set up rules for any of your e-mail accounts and newsgroups. To set up a message rule, follow these steps:

1. **Click Tools ⇨ Rules.**

   The Rules window opens, as shown in Figure 25.36.

   If you're setting a specific type of rule based on a message, select the message first before opening the window. This fills in some pertinent information for you.

---
**FIGURE 25.36**

You can use the Rules window to create and manage message rules.

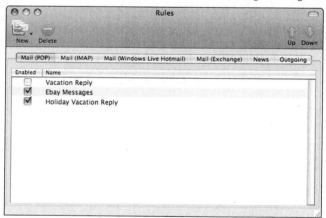

2. **Click the account type tab to which you want to write a rule.**

3. **Click the New button.**

   The Edit Rule dialog box opens, as shown in Figure 25.37.

4. **Type a name for the rule in the Rule name field.**

5. **Under the If settings, specify how you want Entourage to select messages to process.**

   For example, if you want Entourage to filter out messages from a particular person or company, click the Criterion button and use the From and Contains pop-up fields to specify an e-mail address.

   You can change the All messages pop-up field to specify another message aspect, such as content in the message body or e-mail size.

6. **Under the Then settings, specify how you want Entourage to proceed when a message meets your If criteria.**

   For example, if you want Entourage to move messages from your financial firm to a special folder, you can click the Change status pop-up field and choose Move message, and then in the second pop-up field, specify where you want the messages placed, such as a different folder.

**FIGURE 25.37**

Whip up new rules using the Edit Rule dialog box.

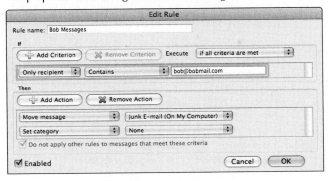

7. **Click OK to exit the Edit Rule window.**

   Entourage adds the rule to the list box, as shown in Figure 25.38. Leave the Enabled check box selected to turn the rule on now, or deselect the check box to turn the rule off until you need it later.

**FIGURE 25.38**

You can use the Rules window to control which rules are turned on or off.

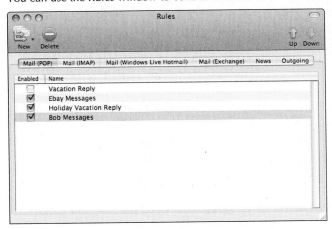

8. **Close the Rule window when finished.**

Entourage processes message rules based on their order in the Rules window list box. You can change the order around, if needed, using the Up and Down buttons in the upper-right corner of the window. You also can delete rules you no longer need; select the rule, and click the Delete button.

## Linking messages

You can link your Entourage e-mail messages to other Entourage features, such as a calendar event or a note. If you link to a calendar event, for example, Entourage adds a link in the calendar day that, when clicked, takes you to the related e-mail message. Entourage actually does linking automatically for some tasks, such as linking a message replay to the original message to provide a message history.

You can link messages in three ways:

- **Open Links:** This command opens the Links window, and you can create or remove links to new items or existing items, as well as open the item at the other end of the link.
- **Link to Existing:** This command creates a link to an existing Entourage item.
- **Link to New:** This command creates a link to a new Entourage item.

 To display the Links window to create and manage links, first select the message to which you want to assign a link. Next, choose Tools ➪ Open Links, or from the message window, click the Links button. The Links window appears, as shown in Figure 25.39. You can click the To New button to link to a new Entourage item or click the To Existing button to link to an existing item. The Links window keeps track of the links you assign to a message. You can use this same window to remove links you no longer want attached to the message.

---

**FIGURE 25.39**

You can link a message to other Entourage items via the Links window.

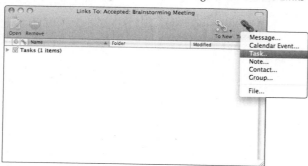

To link a message to an existing item directly, select the message in the Inbox, choose Tools ➪ Link to Existing ➪, and choose what Entourage feature to which you want to link. Depending on what you select, a Link window opens and you can select the item to which you want to link and click the Link button to create the link. In Figure 25.40, the message is linking to a task.

To link a message to a new item entirely, select the message in the Inbox, choose Tools ➪ Link to New ➪, and choose what Entourage feature to which you want to link. Depending on what you select, the appropriate window opens, and you can fill in the item details.

**FIGURE 25.40**

You can link a message to other existing Entourage items.

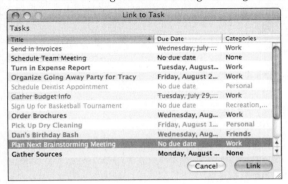

## Working with attachments

File attachments are files that come with e-mail messages. When you attach a file to an outgoing message, the file is uploaded to the server along with your e-mail. If someone sends you an attachment, you can download it onto your computer along with the message. File attachments are useful for sending along any kind of data that won't fit into an ordinary e-mail message. For example, you can send documents, spreadsheets, photographs, or sound files as attachments. File attachments take much longer to download. That's because they're usually much larger in size than the e-mail message itself.

### Receiving attachments

In your Inbox, messages including file attachments are marked with a tiny paper clip icon. When you open a message window that includes an attachment, the attachment appears in its own field, as shown in Figure 25.41.

You can select the attachment and perform one of these actions:

- **Open:** This command opens the attachment. If there's a corresponding program on your computer to view the file, it opens the file. You also can activate this option by simply double-clicking the file attachment name.

- **Save:** This command saves the attachment to a designated folder or drive.

- **Remove:** This command detaches the file and discards it.

You also can drag an attached file from the message window and drop it on the desktop or into another folder. From the Inbox view, Control+click a message with an attachment and choose Save Attachment from the pop-up menu. In addition, the Message menu offers a few attachment-related commands you can apply to a selected message in your Inbox: Save All Attachments, Remove All Attachments, or Remove Unsafe Attachments.

**FIGURE 25.41**

Attachments appear in their own field in the message window, and you can choose exactly how you want to deal with each one.

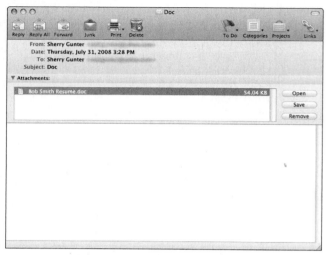

## Sending attachments

It's incredibly easy to attach a file to an e-mail message. Follow these steps to do so:

 **1. From the message window, click the Attach button in the window's toolbar.**

This opens the Choose Attachment dialog box, as shown in Figure 25.42.

**FIGURE 25.42**

The Choose Attachment dialog box lets you choose which file or files you want to attach to your outgoing message.

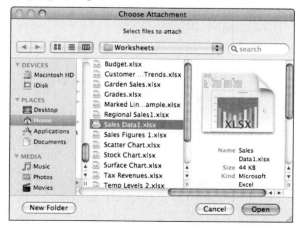

2. **Navigate to the file (or files) you want to attach, and select the filename.**
3. **Click Open.**

   Entourage adds the file to your message, as shown in Figure 25.43.
4. **Finish composing your message and send it on its way.**

**FIGURE 25.43**

File attachments are listed at the top of the message.

Attachments

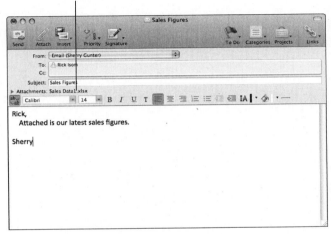

# Using the Address Book

You can use Entourage's Address Book feature to keep track of your contacts. A contact is usually a person, but sometimes a company. Acting like an electronic Rolodex, the Address Book lets you enter contact information such as names, phone numbers, addresses, and e-mail. After you've entered a contact, that person's information is always at your fingertips. For example, if you start a new e-mail message and type the first few letters of the person's name or e-mail address, Entourage pops open a tiny window of possible matches from your Address Book, and you can make your selection without needing to type the whole thing. This section explains how to add contacts and use the Address Book features.

## Attachment Won't Open?

Occasionally you'll encounter a file attachment that your computer cannot read. This can be caused by several factors. If the sender encoded or compressed the file in some way, you may need to decompress or unpack the file using a program like Stuffit Expander or something similar. If the file is from a PC user, the file may not open at all. If double-clicking an attachment doesn't open it, you can try dragging it to the program you think will read the file. For example, if the file uses a .doc file extension, you can drag it to Microsoft Word. If you still can't figure out how to open the file, contact the sender and have them resend it in a more universal file format.

## Introducing the Address Book

As shown in Figure 25.44, the Address Book's appearance closely resembles the Mail feature. Contacts appear in a list. Each column in the Address Book's main list pane tells something about the contact. The field headings at the top of the list describe each field in the contact entry.

To switch to the Address Book, you can use any of these methods:

- Click the Address Book button on the Standard toolbar.
- Choose View ⇨ Go To ⇨ Address Book.
- Press ⌘+2.

**FIGURE 25.44**

You can use the Address Book to store and manage contacts.

Click to view the
Address Book.

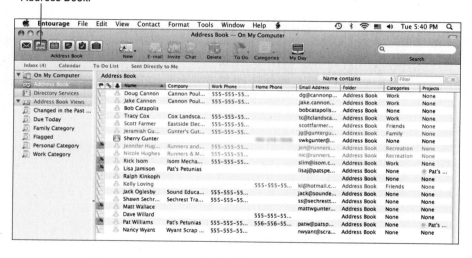

The main Address Book view displays three main panes: the Folders List pane, the mini calendar pane, and the main list pane for viewing contacts. The Address Book folder displays by default when you click the Address Book button. When you select a contact, the Preview Pane opens. This lower portion of the Address Book displays a detailed view of the contact's information, as shown in Figure 25.45.

The little icons next to the groups of information can do some pretty interesting things. Which icons appear in the Preview Pane depend on what information you've entered about the contact. For example, if you click the icon next to address information, a pop-up menu appears with options for showing the address on a map, gathering driving directions from home or work, or copying the name and address to the Clipboard so you can insert it somewhere else, like in a Word letter.

# Attachment Warnings!

Sometimes viruses and worms are sent as file attachments and spread around the Internet. Entourage warns you if it encounters such things when you attempt to open or save the attachment from the Entourage program window. This really isn't much of a problem for Mac users, thank goodness. To be on the safe side, if Entourage does warn you, you might as well remove the problem.

On the downside of this epidemic, however, is the inability to download any files ending in the .exe, .mpkg, or .webloc file extension. Entourage won't let you. But you can perform this workaround: Compress or archive the file before you attach it, and tell anyone sending you one of the forbidden file types to do the same.

**FIGURE 25.45**

You can use the Preview Pane to view details about a contact.

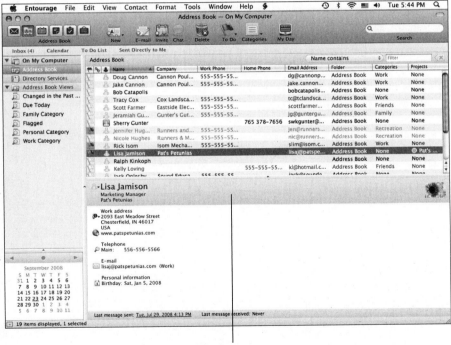

Preview pane

Here's a run-down of what each icon can do:

- **Address Actions:** Displays a pop-up menu with options for finding the address on a map, getting driving directions, or copying the info to the Clipboard.
- **Open Web Page:** Opens the associated Web page you entered for the contact.

- **Magnify Phone Number:** Displays a special magnified view box of the phone number, which is helpful if you're ready to make a call to the contact.
- **Send Mail:** Creates a new e-mail message addressed to the contact.
- **Add to Calendar:** Creates a new calendar event based on the contact's birthday or anniversary.

You can toggle the Preview Pane off or on by choosing View ➪ Preview Pane. To open any contact in its own window, double-click the contact in the list pane.

## Adding a contact

You can easily add contacts using the Create Contact form, a special dialog box with all kinds of fields for potential contact information, such as name and e-mail data, phone numbers, address, and more. The Create Contact form is an abbreviated form. You also can open the full-blown Contact window and find even more data fields you can fill in, such as birthday or anniversary dates, hobbies and interests, or even a field to add a photo of the contact. The Contact window offers seven different tabs full of data fields. Here's what you can find in each tab:

- **Summary:** Displays all the information about a contact.
- **Name & E-mail:** Displays fields for entering name and e-mail information, including multiple e-mails addresses, titles, nicknames, and so on. If a contact has multiple e-mail addresses, you can pick one to use as the default address.
- **Home:** Displays fields for entering a home address, telephone information, and Web page information.
- **Work:** Displays fields for entering a work address, telephone information, and Web page information.
- **Personal:** Displays fields for entering personal information, such as birth date, anniversary, spouse and children names, even a photo.
- **Other:** Displays a large field for entering note information about the contact.
- **Certificates:** Displays any encryption certificates for the contact.

Many of the tabs in the Contact window include customizing fields for storing additional information about the contact. The toolbar at the top of the window includes buttons for e-mailing, inviting, and chatting with the contact using Microsoft Messenger. The toolbar also has buttons for flagging a contact or assigning a category, project, or link.

To add a contact to your Address Book, follow these steps:

1. **Click the New button on the Standard toolbar, or choose File ➪ New ➪ Contact.**

   The Create Contact form opens, as shown in Figure 25.46.

2. **Fill in the pertinent contact fields as needed.**

   Optionally, you can assign the contact to a category or project using the Categories or Projects buttons.

3. **Click the More button.**

   Entourage opens the full Contact window, as shown in Figure 25.47.

4. **Click the tab you want to view, and fill in any additional information as needed.**

5. **Press ⌘+S to save the contact.**

6. **Close the window to return to the Address Book.**

   Entourage adds the contact to your Address Book list.

**FIGURE 25.46**

The abbreviated form contains basic contact information.

**FIGURE 25.47**

Open the full-blown Contact window if you want to fill in additional information. The tabs offer different kinds of information fields you can fill out for the contact.

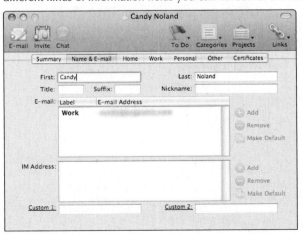

## Working with contacts

After you start adding contacts to your Address Book, you can work with them in various ways. Use any of these techniques:

- To make changes to an existing contact, double-click the contact name in the Address Book list pane to open the Contact window.

- You also can Control+click a contact and choose Open Contact.

- To remove a contact you no longer need, select it in the list pane and click the Delete button on the toolbar or press Delete. Entourage displays a warning box asking if you really want to delete the contact; click Delete.

- To e-mail a contact, select the name and click the E-mail button on the Standard toolbar to open a message window with the contact's e-mail address already filled in and ready to go.

- To send a contact an instant message, select the contact name and click the Chat button.

- To flag a contact and create a To Do list item, select the contact, click the To Do button, and choose a flag. Entourage immediately adds the contact to your To Do list.

- To print a contact, select it and choose File ➪ Print. This opens the Print dialog box, and you can change any print options before committing the contact information to paper.

- To view your Address Book while creating a new e-mail message, just click the Address Book button, as shown in Figure 25.48. From the Address pop-up window, double-click the name to add it to the To: field.

**FIGURE 25.48**

When creating a new e-mail, you can grab addresses from your Address Book.

Address Book button

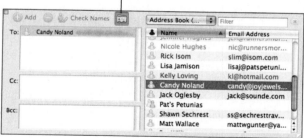

## Creating groups

You can use groups to manage related contacts in your Address Book. For example, you may group family members into one group and work associates into another. This makes it easy to send a group e-mail message to everyone in the group without having to enter each e-mail address individually. You can create as many groups as you like in the Address Book, and your contacts can appear in more than one group.

To create a group of related contacts, follow these steps:

1. **Select the contacts you want to group; to select multiple contacts, press and hold the ⌘ key while clicking contact names in the list pane.**
2. **Choose File ⇨ New ⇨ Group.**

   Entourage opens the Group window, as shown in Figure 25.49.

**FIGURE 25.49**

Use the Group window to create new groups.

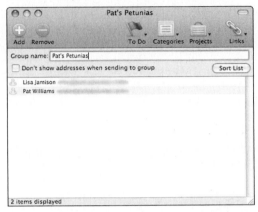

3. **Type a name for the group in the Group name box.**

   Optionally, you can click the Add button to add more names to the group or click the Remove button to remove a name from the list.

   You also can add names to the group list by dragging them from the Address Book list pane and dropping them in the Group window.

4. **Press ⌘+S or choose File ⇨ Save to save the list.**
5. **Close the window to return to the Address Book.**

   Entourage adds the group to the list pane.

To address an e-mail message to a group, click the Address Book button in the Address pop-up window that appears when you create a new e-mail message. Navigate to the group name, and select it to add it to the To: field.

## Importing and exporting contacts

You can import your contacts database from other sources to use in Entourage, as well as import any vCards people send you. vCards are the electronic version of a business card, containing pertinent information about the person. Some users include vCards with their e-mail messages. If you receive such a file attachment, you can add it to your Address Book. Entourage turns the information into a contact.

One way to import contacts is to use the Import Assistant. Choose File ⇨ Import, and walk through the Assistant steps to import data. Depending on your source program, you may need to import the data as an archive or import contacts from a text file, so you'll use different Assistant windows to walk through the procedure.

You also can export your Address Book to another program or archive file. Choose File ➪ Export. In the Export dialog box, choose how you want to export the data. The Export Assistant walks you through the steps to create an archive file or export the data in another format.

# Viewing Newsgroups

Newsgroups are Internet bulletin boards you can subscribe to and read the messages posted on the group. You can read these messages just like e-mail messages using Entourage Mail. Dating back to the 80s, newsgroups have been around a long time, and there's a group for every possible topic under the sun, from the weird to the mundane. Today, newsgroups don't always have a great reputation. Many of the groups, specifically groups in the ALT category, are known for distributing pirated software, music, and video files, as well as other disreputable things. Many Web servers won't let you connect to newsgroups for this reason. You'll need to check with your Internet Service Provider to find out what's allowed and what's not. The good news is that lots of useful information can be found in newsgroups, including tons of information about computers and programs.

## Setting up a news account

In order to access newsgroups, you need a news account. Your ISP may already offer such services. If not, you might try finding a news service on the Web. To set up a news account in Entourage, follow these steps:

1. **Choose Tools ➪ Accounts.**

    Entourage opens the Accounts window, shown in Figure 25.50.

2. **Click the New arrow button, and choose News from the pop-up menu.**

    The Account Setup Assistant opens, as shown in Figure 25.51.

3. **Click the Mail account pop-up menu, and select which account you want to use to post your newsgroup messages.**

    Optionally, type your organization in the Organization box.

---

**FIGURE 25.50**

Use the Accounts window to set up a news account.

4. **Click the right arrow button to continue.**

5. **Type the address of the news server, as shown in Figure 25.52.** You may need to check with your ISP to find out this information.

   Optionally, if the account requires an ID and password, click the My news server requires me to log on check box and fill in the appropriate information.

**FIGURE 25.51**

The Account Setup Assistant walks you through the steps for setting up a news account.

**FIGURE 25.52**

Type the address of your news server.

6. **Click the right arrow button to continue.**

7. **Type a name for the account in the Account name box, as shown in Figure 25.53.**

8. **Click the Finish button.**

   Entourage adds the new account to the Accounts window in the News tab.

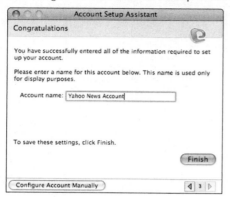

**FIGURE 25.53**

You can give the new account a unique name.

### Accessing newsgroups

You can access your news account through the Folders List pane in the Mail window. Simply click the newsgroup name. The first time you do, a prompt box appears, as shown in Figure 25.54, asking if you want to receive a list of newsgroups from the selected server. Click the Receive button, and then stand back and wait for the list of newsgroups to download. This process may take a few moments.

**FIGURE 25.54**

When you first open your news server, Entourage asks if you want to download the newsgroups.

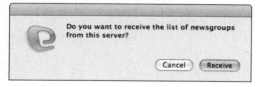

When the download is complete, the Mail window shows a list of newsgroups, as shown in Figure 25.55. In this example, the newsgroups are all dedicated to the subject of Microsoft. You can scroll through the list of newsgroups until you find one that interests you.

You may have so many newsgroups to choose from that it's overwhelming. To help you narrow your search, type a keyword in the Display newsgroups containing text box, located in the upper-right corner of the list pane, as shown in Figure 25.56. In this figure, I'm narrowing down the newsgroups to show only those related to Entourage. As soon as you type the keyword, the list is sorted, and any matches appear.

When you find a newsgroup you'd like to investigate, double-click the newsgroup name. Entourage then displays the individual messages in the group in a separate window.

## FIGURE 25.55

Newsgroups are listed in the list pane.

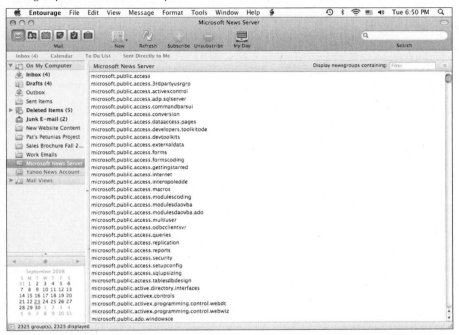

## FIGURE 25.56

Use the filter tool to narrow down your search for newsgroups.

Type a keyword.

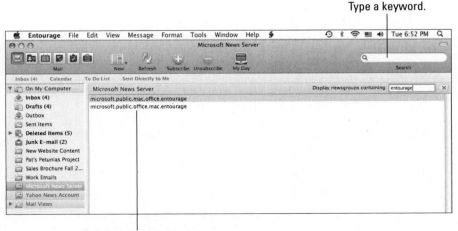

Matches are listed here.

To view any message in the group, simply double-click the message. Entourage opens the message in its own message window, just like your e-mail messages. Figure 25.57 shows an example. Like e-mail messages, you can choose to reply to the message, forward the message, print it out, and so forth. Also like e-mail messages, after you download messages from a group, you need to decide what to do with them. This is where your deletion skills really come in handy. You can use the same deletion techniques for deleting e-mail to delete newsgroup messages. You can close the newsgroup list pane to return to the main Mail window.

**FIGURE 25.57**

You can view individual newsgroup postings in separate message windows.

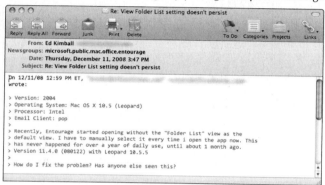

Meanwhile, back in the Mail window, here are a few tasks you can perform with your newsgroups list:

- You can choose to subscribe to a newsgroup to get regular updated messages downloaded into your list pane. To do so, click the newsgroup name and click the Subscribe button.
- You can easily unsubscribe again using the Unsubscribe button.
- Anytime you want to update the newsgroup listings, click the Refresh button.
- To return to your regular Inbox view, click the Inbox folder in the Folders List pane.

## Summary

In this chapter, you learned how to use both the Mail and Address Book tools in Entourage. I showed you how to create a new e-mail account using the same Setup Assistant you learned about in Chapter 24. You also learned the ins and outs of using e-mail. You learned how to send and receive e-mails, view and flag messages, set up automatic replies, and forward and reply to messages. You saw how easy it is to manage your messages by deleting and filing messages and sorting out junk e-mail. You also learned how to add signatures to your messages and work with file attachments.

This chapter also showed you how to use the Address Book to keep track of contacts in your personal and work life. You learned how to build a list of people and contact information and then use that same information to create e-mails, calendar events, and To Do tasks.

Lastly, you learned how to use the Mail tool to subscribe to Internet newsgroups, specialized groups focusing on a specific topic.

# Chapter 26

# Organizing Your Calendar

Like all busy people, your daily routine probably involves looking at a calendar of some sort, glancing at what your schedule holds for the day, and if you're really lucky, realizing it's your day off. Whether your calendar is on the wall, on your desk, in your personal organizer, or in your purse or briefcase, chances are good that you glance at it regularly. If you're reading this book, then you probably glance at your computer quite frequently as well. So why not combine the two and put your calendar on your computer? What—worried about computer crashes? I have one word for you, my friend—backups. Seriously, why not utilize your computer to keep track of your daily activities? It's easy, painless, and can even remind you about places you need to go, people you need to see, and things you need to do.

The Entourage Calendar tool can help automate how you record appointments and events, making recurring appointments a breeze. It can prompt you when an appointment approaches, making sure you don't forget it, and it can send e-mail invitations about the appointment to other people you're meeting with. In this chapter, you learn how to use the Entourage Calendar feature to keep track of your daily life, schedule and edit appointments and special events. You also learn how to import holidays, work with reminders and categories, juggle invitations, and print your schedule. Whew! With all we're going to cover, you should probably schedule a big block of time for it all. Go check your calendar to see if you're available, and then we'll get started.

## Working with the Calendar

The Entourage Calendar is a versatile feature that's easy to work with, and dare I say it, even kind of fun. You can use it to track your daily, weekly, and monthly schedule, adding appointments and events, and helping you balance and manage your daily routines. For example, if you're using Entourage at work, you can record appointments such as sales meetings, all-day conferences, and important deadlines. You also can keep track of personal appointments, such as a trip to the dentist or your children's soccer games. Acting just like a regular paper calendar, you can zip through the Calendar by date, week, or month, checking out the activities you have planned. Figure 26.1 shows an example of the Calendar showing the Month view.

 Are you ready to see your own calendar? Just click the Calendar button on the Standard toolbar. You also can choose View ⇨ Go To ⇨ Calendar. When you display the Calendar, a Calendar menu appears on the menu bar, featuring commands associated with the Calendar feature. The Standard toolbar also changes to show buttons for working with the Calendar. When you click another Entourage tool, such as Mail, the Calendar tools disappear.

## Using Calendar views

 The Entourage Calendar feature offers several ways to view your schedule. The quickest way to change views is to simply click the view button you want on the Standard toolbar. Anytime you want to jump back to the current day, click the Today button on the Standard toolbar. You can click the View Date button to open the View Date dialog box. The dialog box displays the current date, but you can specify another date and click OK, and Entourage displays the specified date in your calendar. The next sections show you in detail what you can expect to see in each view.

## FIGURE 26.1

You can use the Calendar feature in Entourage to keep your daily schedule organized.

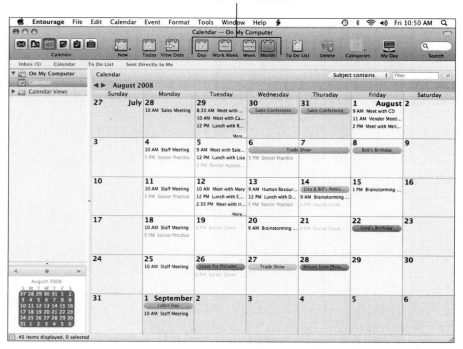

# Using the Mini Calendar

If the Folder List pane is displayed (the default pane on the left side of the program window), you can view the mini calendar in the bottom-left corner and see a monthly calendar. You can use this mini calendar to quickly navigate to a date just by clicking the date. You also can use the mini calendar's navigation buttons, left arrow and right arrow, to view other months. To view more than one month, you can drag the mini calendar's top border and display two or more months in the Folder List pane. The more you drag the edge upward, the more months you can view in the mini calendar. The current day is always shown in red with an underline. The mini calendar feature toggles on or off with a button in the bottom-left corner of the program window. Click the Show Mini Calendar button to display the calendar, or click the Hide Mini Calendar button to toggle the feature off again.

### Day view

When you click the Day view button, the Calendar displays a single day with hours shown in increments, as shown in Figure 26.2, and smaller dividers for half-hour increments. You can use the scroll bar to move up and down the day, starting with 12 AM at the top of the date and ending in 11:59 PM at the bottom of the date. You can click the navigation buttons at the top of the Day view to scroll between days. The current date always appears with a yellowish background. Any appointments you add appear as blue bars on the schedule. If the day has an all-day event assigned, the entire day appears shaded in blue, and the event is listed in the banner area at the top of the schedule.

**FIGURE 26.2**

The Day view shows your day in hour and half-hour increments.

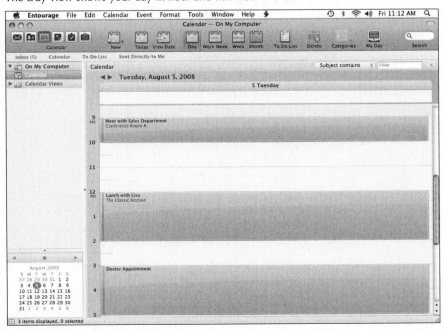

### Work Week view

 Click the Work Week view button to display your calendar as a typical work week, Monday through Friday. Figure 26.3 shows an example of the Work Week view. Like the Day view, the hours in each day of the week appear as increments with smaller dividers for half-hour increments. You can use the scroll bar to move up and down the day's schedule. You can click the navigation buttons at the top of the Work Week view to scroll between weeks. The current date is highlighted with a yellow background, and any days with scheduled appointments appear highlighted in blue. If the day has an all-day event assigned, the event is listed in the banner area at the top of the schedule. Depending on which category you assigned to the event, the entire day may appear shaded in a particular color denoting the category. For example, if you assigned the Family category to the event, the day is shaded in pink. If no category is assigned, the day is shaded in blue.

### Week view

 Click the Week view button to display your calendar as a full week, Sunday through Saturday. Figure 26.4 shows an example of the Week view. Just like the Day and Work Week views, the days are divided into hours, and you can scroll through the day using the scroll bar. Appointments appear highlighted in blue on the schedule. You can click the navigation buttons at the top of the Week view to scroll between weeks, but the current date always appears highlighted in yellow. If the day has an all-day event assigned, the entire day appears shaded in blue, which is the default color unless you assign a category to the event. Plus, the event is listed in the banner area at the top of the schedule.

---

**FIGURE 26.3**

The Work Week view shows your work week schedule, Monday through Friday.

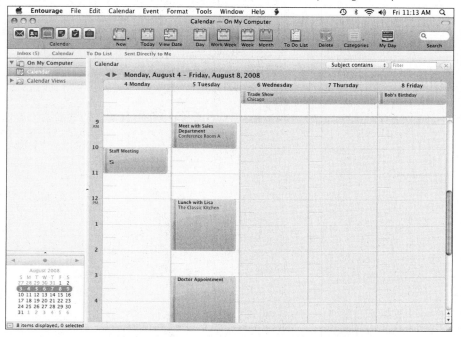

## Changing Your Work Week

Some people don't have regular five-day work weeks. If that's the case in your situation, you'll be happy to know you can change how the Work Week view displays days in the Calendar tool. To customize your work week, choose Entourage ➪ Preferences or press ⌘+,. This opens the Preferences dialog box. Under General Preferences, click the Calendar category. You can customize which days to include in your work week and even customize the work hours. Click OK to save your changes.

### Month view

 Click the Month view button to display your calendar as a full month of dates, as shown in Figure 26.5. The current date appears highlighted in yellow. You can click the navigation buttons at the top of the Month view to scroll between months. If the day has an all-day event assigned, a blue banner appears at the top of the date. If you've assigned a category to the event, the banner displays another color.

### List view

You can use the List view to display just your scheduled appointments and events, as shown in Figure 26.6. To view your list, choose Calendar ➪ List. You may prefer to use this view when you want to see your detailed appointments and events at a glance.

### FIGURE 26.4

The Week view shows your weekly schedule, Sunday through Saturday.

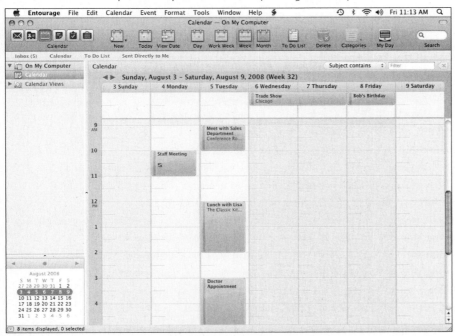

**FIGURE 26.5**

The Month view shows a full month's worth of days.

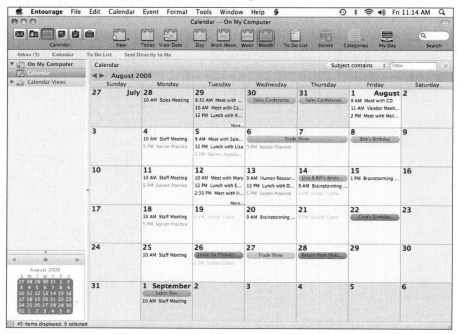

## Calendar views in the Folders List

You can use the Folders List pane to view filtered lists of events on your calendar, such as viewing all the monthly recurring appointments or all the family items on your schedule. To display the filtered Calendar Views in the Folders List, click the Expand arrow next to the Calendar Views heading, as shown in Figure 26.7. To see a particular filtered list, click the view name, such as Family Category or Next 7 Days. You can choose from the following filtered list views:

- **All Events:** Displays all the scheduled items in your calendar.
- **Family Category:** Displays only scheduled items assigned to the Family category.
- **Free Events:** Displays scheduled items you are free to attend.
- **Next 7 Days:** Displays all the scheduled items for the next seven days.
- **Personal Category:** Displays all the scheduled items to which the Personal category is assigned.
- **Recurring Monthly:** Displays all the recurring monthly items you have scheduled.
- **Recurring Weekly:** Displays all the recurring weekly items you have scheduled.
- **Recurring Yearly:** Displays all the recurring yearly items you have scheduled.
- **Tentative Events:** Displays all the invites you're tentatively attending.
- **Work Category:** Displays all the scheduled items to which the Work category is assigned.

To return to the regular Calendar view, click the Calendar heading in the Folders List pane.

## FIGURE 26.6

You can view a list of your appointments and events.

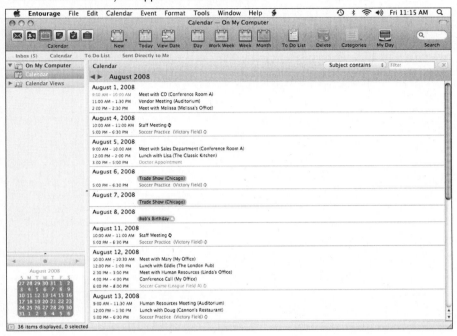

## FIGURE 26.7

You can filter your view of calendar items using the Folders List pane.

Click to return to
the Calendar.

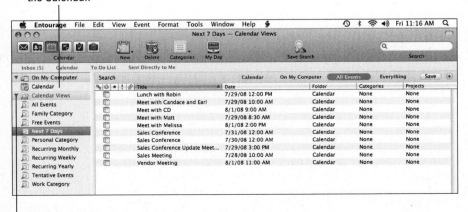

Click to expand
or collapse the list.

# Recording Appointments and All-day Events

The heart of the Calendar tool is the ability to manage appointments and all-day events. Regular, ordinary appointments are assigned to a time slot on your calendar. For example, you might schedule a meeting at 10:00 AM that lasts an hour. All-day events, on the other hand, occupy the whole day on your calendar. All-day events, such as birthdays, anniversaries, or conferences, don't require a specific time slot. As such, they appear as banners at the top of the schedule, and the entire day is shaded in a color depending on which category you assign. (You learn more about categories later in this chapter.) When it comes to appointments or all-day events, Entourage prefers to call everything "events." An event is basically any item you add to your schedule.

You're probably ready to start entering scheduled items onto your own calendar, so without further ado, the next sections show you how.

## Recording a time-slot appointment

When creating appointments, whether time-based or all-day, you can use the New Event window. This window contains all the necessary settings and options for creating and classifying a scheduled item in your calendar. How you get to the New Event window, is another story. Like everything else in Office, you can employ several different methods to summon the New Event window. All the methods below open the window:

- Double-click any date in the Month view.
- Double-click any time slot in the Work Week, Week, or Day view.
- Click the New button on the Standard toolbar.
- Right-click a time slot in your schedule, and click New Calendar Event, or ctrl+click if using a laptop trackpad.
- Choose File ➪ New ➪ Calendar Event.
- Press ⌘+N on the keyboard.
- In the Week, Work Week, or Day view, drag across the time slots on which you want to schedule an event and double-click the highlighted block of time.

The New Event window, shown in Figure 26.8, is basically a form you fill out to add the event to your schedule. It has its own toolbar, a set of options and fields for filling out, and a large blank area for holding notes you type or other items you paste into the area. You can press the Tab key to move from field to field in the form, filling out each area along the way. The top of the New Event window form lets you specify a name and location for the event. Whatever text you type into these fields appears in the Day, Work Week, and Week views on the calendar. In Month view, you see only the subject name and appointment start time. Assigning a title to your appointment using the Subject line can help you quickly see what sort of appointment it is, such as "Sales Meeting" or "Doctor Appointment." Because most appointments require a location of some sort, the Location field is useful for jotting down where the appointment takes place, such as "My Office," "Conference Room B," or "The Diner." If you don't require a location per se, you might jot down another type of note in the Location field, such as "Oceanic Flight 815" or "Corner of Elm & Main Street." If the location is not important, just leave the field blank.

You can use the Start and End fields and settings to specify when an appointment begins and ends by selecting a date, time, and duration. Depending on which method you used to display the New Event window, the start and end dates and times may already be filled in for you. You can change these settings as needed. You can type dates or times into the fields directly, or you can use the pop-up calendar or spinner arrows to change the display. When you click the pop-up calendar, you can click on a date or use the navigation arrows to scroll to another month. The pop-up calendar also has a Today button you can click to set the date to the current day.

Use the New Event window to schedule appointments in your calendar.

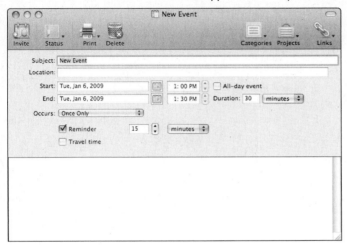

When editing the time settings for an appointment, you can click the spinner arrows to adjust the time or type a time into the field. You can adjust the settings by selecting the hour, minute, or AM/PM text you want to change and typing new values or clicking the spinner arrows. To the right of the time settings is a field for specifying a duration span for the appointment. You can specify the duration in minutes, hours, or days.

If you need to set a recurring appointment, you can use the Occurs pop-up menu to tell Entourage how often the appointment needs to be included in your calendar. By default, the Occurs option is set to Once Only. Based on what date you selected for the appointment, other options appear in the menu. For example, if you set the appointment on Monday, July 28, the Occurs pop-up menu displays Every Monday, Day 28 of Every Month, Every July 28, Every Day, Every Weekday, and Custom. If you activate the Custom command, a Recurring Event dialog box appears, and you can customize the event. Learn more about this option later in this section.

The remaining settings on the New Event window form are optional. For example, if you want Entourage to remind you about the appointment, activate the Reminder check box, or if you need to factor in travel time for the appointment, click the Travel time check box and specify how much time is required to get to the meeting. Lastly, you can add any notes about the appointment in the notes area. For example, you may want to add detailed driving directions, notes about what you want to accomplish at the meeting, or pasted items from other sources.

You can use the toolbar buttons at the top of the New Event window to assign a status level to the appointment, such as Busy, Free, or Tentative, assign a category, allocate a project to associate the appointment with, or link it to a contact or task. After you fill out the form, you must save it to add it to your calendar.

Follow these steps to fill out an appointment for a slot in your schedule:

1. **Open the New Event window (see the preceding bulleted list for methods you can use to display the window).**
2. **In the Subject line, type a name for the appointment.**

   As soon as you enter the text, the subject appears in the New Event window's title bar.

3. **In the Location line, type a location or other text to give you more detail about the appointment.**

4. **Specify a start date and time using the Start settings.**

   ■ You can click the pop-up calendar and click a date to specify a start date for the appointment, as shown in Figure 26.9.

**FIGURE 26.9**

You can click the pop-up calendar to set a date for the appointment.

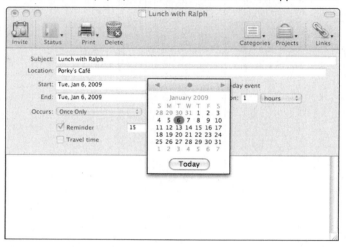

   ■ You can type in a time or use the spinner arrows to set a start time.

   The next section explains how to use the All-day event option.

5. **Specify an end date and time using the End settings.**

   ■ You can click the pop-up calendar to specify an end date.

   ■ You can type a time or use the spinner arrows to set an end time.

   ■ Optionally, you can specify a duration span for the appointment in the Duration field.

6. **Click the Occurs pop-up menu, and specify how often the appointment occurs in your schedule, as shown in Figure 26.10.** Once Only is the default selection. Learn more about setting recurring appointments later in this section.

7. **Click the Reminder check box to assign a reminder to the event.**

   The Reminder check box is activated by default. Deselect it if you don't want a reminder notice.

   Optionally, if the appointment requires travel time, click the Travel time check box and specify a travel time for getting to and from the appointment, as shown in Figure 26.11.

8. **Click in the notes field, and type any notes pertaining to the appointment.**

   Optionally, you can use the toolbar buttons to assign a status level, category, project, or link, invite others to the meeting, or print the details.

**9.** Press ⌘+S to save the appointment and close the New Event window. You also can click the Close button and click Save in the prompt box that appears.

Entourage adds the appointment to the calendar, as shown in Figure 26.12.

**FIGURE 26.10**

Use the Occurs pop-up menu to set a recurring event, if needed.

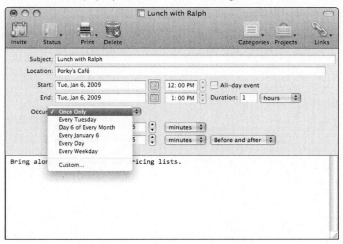

**FIGURE 26.11**

If you need to factor in travel time for the appointment, check the Travel time check box and adjust the settings that appear.

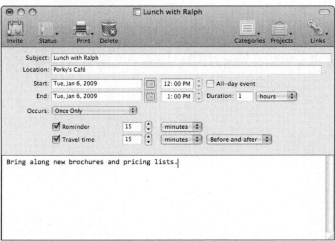

### FIGURE 26.12

After you create and save an appointment, it appears on your calendar.

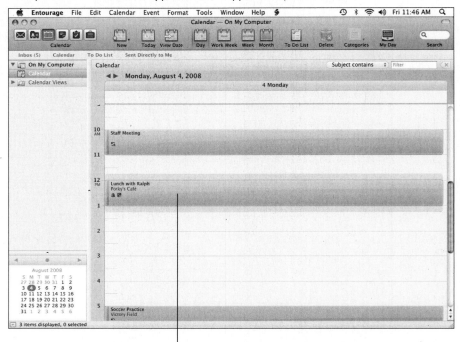

The new appointment

## Recording an all-day event

As mentioned previously, an all-day event lasts all day, so you don't need to specify a start and end time for the event. All you really need to do is activate the All-day event check box. When you activate this feature, all the time settings disappear in the New Event window. Follow the steps below to see how this works:

1. **Open the New Event window.**
2. **In the Subject line, type a name for the event.**
3. **In the Location line, type a location or other text to give more details about the appointment.**
4. **Click the All-day event check box, as shown in Figure 26.13.**
5. **Specify a start date.**
6. **Specify an end date.**
    - Optionally, click the Occurs pop-up menu and specify how often the event occurs in your schedule; Once Only is the default selection.
    - You can click the Reminder check box if you want to assign a reminder to the event. The Reminder check box is activated by default. Deselect it if you don't want a reminder notice.
    - Optionally, if the event requires travel time, click the Travel time check box and specify a travel time for getting to and from the event.

■ You can click in the notes field and type any notes pertaining to the event.

■ You can use the toolbar buttons to assign a status level, category, project, or link, invite others, or print the details about the event.

7. **Press ⌘+S to save the event and close the New Event window. You also can click the Close button and click Save in the prompt box that appears.**

Entourage adds the event to the calendar, as shown in Figure 26.14.

**FIGURE 26.13**

You can use the New Event window to create an all-day event for your calendar.

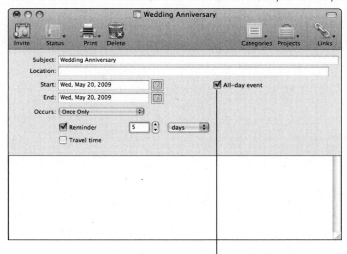

Select to set an all-day event.

**FIGURE 26.14**

Events appear as banners at the top of your schedule.

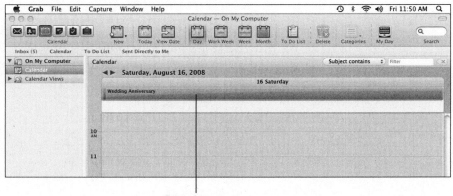

Event banner

## Recording a recurring event

Many people have schedules that involve recurring events, such as weekly staff meetings. You can use the New Event window to set up recurring appointments or all-day events in your calendar. For example, you may want to add your child's soccer practice times to your schedule that go on for a month or more, or you may want to show family member birthdays on a yearly basis. You can use the Recurring Event window to fine-tune the details about an appointment or event by setting a recurrence pattern. The dialog box offers four types of recurring events: Daily, Weekly, Monthly, and Yearly. After you make a selection, you can tell Entourage exactly how often the event recurs, such as every week on Tuesday. You also can designate an ending to the event; otherwise, it keeps showing up in your calendar for all eternity. For example, if it's a recurring soccer practice that lasts 10 weeks, you can tell Entourage to end the event after 10 occurrences. After you add a recurring event to your schedule, a tiny circling arrows icon appears with the event on the calendar.

The steps below show you how to set a custom recurring event:

1. **Open the New Event window.**
2. **Fill out the appointment or event details as described in the previous sets of steps.**
3. **Click the Occurs pop-up menu, and click Custom.**
   The Recurring Event dialog box opens, as shown in Figure 26.15.

### FIGURE 26.15

You can use the Recurring Event dialog box to customize a recurring appointment or all-day event.

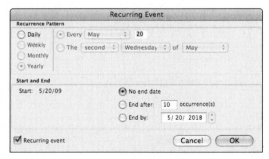

4. **Click the recurrence pattern you want to assign, and choose any accompanying details.**
5. **Specify an end date if you want the recurring event to end at some point.**
   Leave the Recurring event check box selected.
6. **Click OK.**
7. **Finish filling out the appointment or event details, and press ⌘+S to save the event and close the New Event window.** You also can click the Close button and click Save in the prompt box that appears.
   Entourage adds the recurring event to the calendar, as shown in Figure 26.16.

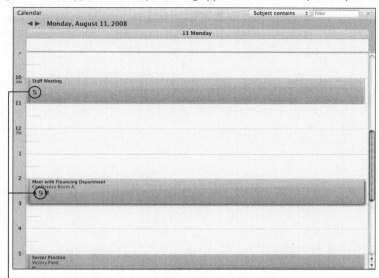

**FIGURE 26.16**

A recurring event icon appears with any recurring appointment or all-day event you set.

Recurring event icons

# Editing Calendar Items

Unless your calendar is set in stone, you'll probably want to make changes to it from time to time. Entourage makes it easy to edit your appointments and all-day events. You can make all kinds of edits to your appointments and events. For example, you can change the start time or end time for a time-slot appointment or turn an all-day event into a regular old appointment. You can adjust the duration of a meeting, assign a different category to the appointment, or move the event to another date entirely. You also can add or remove a reminder, add notes, or reassign the event to a project you're working on in the Microsoft Office Project Center. The next sections show you how easy it is to tweak your schedule.

## Editing events

Depending on the complexity of the changes you need to make, you can edit appointments and all-day events directly on your calendar, or you can reopen the Event window and work your magic. For example, perhaps you need to extend the timeframe for an appointment, or maybe you need to move it to another day. You can perform both types of edits without opening additional windows.

### Edit an appointment's timeframe

To edit the start or end time of an appointment, follow these steps:

1.  **Switch to the Day, Work Week, or Week view, and select the appointment you want to edit.**

2. **Move the mouse pointer over the border of the appointment until it becomes a double-sided arrow pointer.**

3. **Click and drag the border to adjust the time, as shown in Figure 26.17.**

   To start the appointment at an earlier time, drag the top border of the selected appointment. To change the end time, drag the bottom border of the appointment.

   When you release the button, the appointment is adjusted.

**FIGURE 26.17**

You can edit an appointment directly on your schedule.

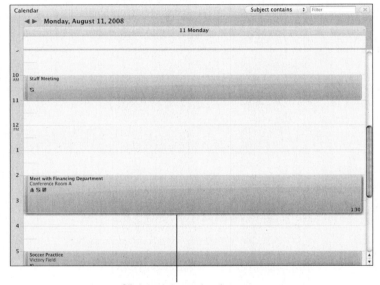

Click and drag a border
to change the time.

You also can edit timeframes in the Event, as you learn later in this section.

## Move an appointment

You can easily move an appointment from one spot to another or from one day to another on your calendar. You can use the drag-and-drop technique to move appointments or events.

To move an appointment, use these steps:

1. **Select the item you want to move.**

2. **Move the mouse pointer over the left border area of the appointment, and click and drag the appointment to a new location on the schedule, as shown in Figure 26.18.**

   As soon as you drop the appointment, Entourage sets the appointment in its new location.

**FIGURE 26.18**

You can edit an appointment directly on your schedule.

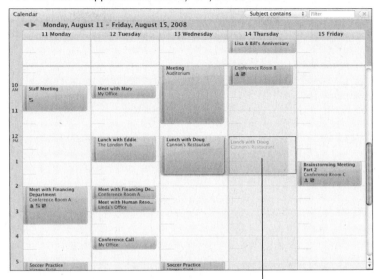

Drag and drop the appointment.

You can use any Calendar view to move appointment and events, but if you want to move an appointment to another day, you can't use the Day view. Switch to one of the other views to perform the drag-and-drop procedure. Here are a few more tips about moving events:

- If an all-day event spans two or more days, you can expand it further by dragging it across additional days in the Week, Work Week, or Month views.

- If you move a recurring event, the change is good only for the one event you moved. All the other events stay in place as originally set. To edit them all, use the Event window to make your changes to the date.

- To copy an event from one spot to another, press and hold the Option key while dragging the event.

- To quickly open the Event window at any time and change the date or time, Control+click and choose Open Event or double-click the event.

## Using the Event window to edit

For even more editing options, open the appointment's or all-day event's New Event window. Technically, it's not the New Event window anymore because it's already an existing event. I suppose we could call it the Old Event window, but that sounds demeaning. So we'll just call it the Event window. Follow these steps:

1. **Double-click the appointment or all-day event you want to edit.** You also can choose File ➪ Open Event, or Control+click and choose Open Event.

   The Event window opens.

2. **Make changes to the event as needed, such as setting new dates, times, or assigning any additional options.**

3. **When finished, press ⌘+S and close the window.**

## Deleting events

 It's easy to remove an appointment or event you no longer want on your calendar. You can select the event and press Del. Entourage displays a prompt box asking if you really want to permanently delete the item. Click the Delete button to finish the removal. You also can open the appointment or all-day event's Event window and click the Delete button on the toolbar. Here again, Entourage asks if you really want to delete the item, as shown in Figure 26.19. Click the Delete button, and the item is removed from your calendar. You also can Control+click and choose Delete Event to remove an appointment.

**FIGURE 26.19**

A prompt box appears when you try to delete an event.

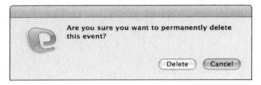

If you try to delete a recurring event, Entourage asks you to specify whether you're deleting a single occurrence or the entire series of recurring appointments.

# Working with Categories

You can use a color coding system to help you keep track of your scheduled items. For example, as you're glancing at your schedule in the Month view, it might help if you could tell which events are work-related and which events are personal. You can use Entourage categories to help make that distinction. By default, no category is assigned to new appointments and events, and any all-day events are shaded in blue on the calendar. If you assign the Family category to an item, Entourage color codes the item in pink on the schedule. Just by glancing at your calendar now, you can tell which events go with which part of your life.

Entourage offers nine preset categories you can assign:

- None
- Family
- Friends
- Holiday
- Junk
- Personal
- Recreation
- Travel
- Work

As you can see from the list, not all the categories fit events, but rather these categories are available throughout Entourage. For example, you probably wouldn't assign the Junk category to an event, but you would assign it to an e-mail message. You can assign these categories using the Categories button on the Standard toolbar, or the same button in the New Event or Event window. If you've already created the event, simply click it, click the Categories arrow button on the Standard toolbar, and make your selection. If you're in the middle of creating a new event, click the Categories arrow button in the New Event window and make your selection. If you click directly on the Categories button, the Assign Categories dialog box opens, as shown in Figure 26.20. Here, too, you can click a category and click OK to assign it to a selected event. Most users find that clicking the arrow button considerably speeds up the process versus having to open the dialog box.

**FIGURE 26.20**

Assign categories to your calendar events using the Assign Categories dialog box.

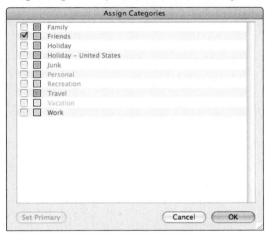

You can assign more than one category to an event. If you don't see a category you like, you can create your own and add it to the list. Follow these steps to create a custom category:

1. **Click an event on your calendar.**

   You also can access the Edit Categories window through the Event window.

2. **Click the Categories arrow button on the Standard toolbar or in the Event window.**

3. **Click Edit Categories.**

   The Categories window opens, as shown in Figure 26.21.

 4. **Click the New button.**

5. **Type a name for the category, and press Return.**

   Optionally, to change the color of the new category, click the color arrow and choose a new color.

6. **Close the window, and Entourage adds the new category to the drop-down list on the Categories button.**

---

**FIGURE 26.21**

Use the Categories window to add new categories to Entourage.

To remove a category, reopen the Categories window, select the category, and click the Delete button. You're prompted to confirm the deletion before making it final.

**NOTE** You can assign multiple categories to an event using the Assign Categories dialog box. Simply select all that apply. To control which category's color appears on your schedule, make that category your primary one by clicking the Set Primary button.

# Working with Reminders

You can use reminders in Entourage to help you remember upcoming events on your schedule. When you select the Reminder check box option, Entourage displays a pop-up alert box telling you that it's time for the event. Figure 26.22 shows an example of a reminder. When a reminder appears, you can tell it to go away or revisit you again shortly. You also can use them as shortcuts to view the appointment or all-day event.

**FIGURE 26.22**

Reminders appear as pop-up boxes on your screen.

Reminders are actually part of the Microsoft Office Reminders program, a small add-on program you can use with events or to-do items. The program is located in the Office subfolder located within the Microsoft Office 2008 folder. When an event or to-do item is due, the Office Reminders program pops into the Mac OS X Dock and then vanishes when you've told it what to do. The best thing about reminders and the Office Reminders program is that they work even when you're not using Entourage.

You can use the Event window to assign reminders to your events. To set one, simply check the Reminders check box in the Event window. After a reminder is assigned, a small bell-shaped icon appears with the event on your schedule.

**TIP** Not interested in reminders? You can turn the Office Reminders program off from within Entourage. Choose Entourage ➪ Turn Off Office Reminders. That's all there is to it. Use the same procedure to turn the feature back on again later.

When an event or task becomes due, the reminder prompt appears onscreen along with a chiming noise. Here's what you can do to respond to the reminder:

- You can click the Snooze button to make the reminder go away briefly, much like the snooze device on your alarm clock.
- You can click the Dismiss button to get rid of the reminder permanently.
- You can double-click the reminder to open the event window associated with the reminder.
- You can click the arrow on the Snooze button to view a pop-up menu of times when you want to be reminded again.

If your reminder prompt displays more than one item, you can double-click any item to open it. If you're using reminders for tasks, the reminder prompt also shows the due date for the task.

**TIP** If the reminder prompt's sound is too annoying, you can turn the sound off. Choose Entourage ➪ Preferences to open the Preferences dialog box. Under the General Preferences list, click the Notification category. Deselect the Reminder sound check box to turn the sound off, and click OK to save your changes.

# Adding Holidays

Your Entourage calendar does not show holidays, did you notice? Because most holidays are based mainly on religious and cultural beliefs, the programmers and developers at Microsoft decided its users would know best about which holidays they want installed. You can use the Import window to help you find the holidays you want to add to Entourage. When you add a set of holidays to your calendar, Entourage stores them in the Categories window. Follow these steps to add holidays:

1. **Choose File ➪ Import.**

   The Import window opens, as shown in Figure 26.23.
2. **Click the Holidays option.**
3. **Click the right arrow button to continue.**

   The Import Holidays page appears, as shown in Figure 26.24.
4. **Click the country or religion you want to import.** You can check more than one.
5. **Click the right arrow button to continue.**

   Entourage adds the holidays to your calendar and displays a prompt box.
6. **Click OK.**
7. **Click Finish.**

**FIGURE 26.23**

Use the Import window to import holidays.

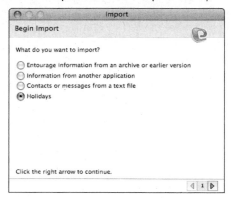

**FIGURE 26.24**

You can choose exactly which country or religion whose holidays you want to import.

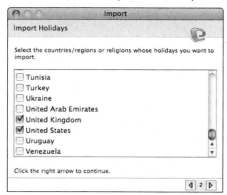

 Holidays appear as all-day events in your calendar, usually marked in red. You can edit the color using the Categories window. Choose Edit ⇨ Categories to open the window. Click the color icon next to the holiday set, and choose another color. You also can use this window to remove a holiday set from your calendar. Select the holiday set you want to delete, and click the Delete button.

# Working with Invitations

Here's something pretty amazing about Entourage: You can utilize the e-mailing abilities, your contacts database, and your calendar all together to send invitations about your scheduled events to other users. For example, if you have a sales meeting with Bob on Friday, and you know Bob's e-mail address or he's a contact in your Address Book, you can whip up an e-mail invitation to let Bob know about the meeting without leaving the Calendar tool. If Bob has Entourage or another program that supports the iCalendar data-exchange standard, he can receive your invitation, add it to his own calendar, and send back a response. Numerous e-mail and calendar programs support iCalendar today, including Entourage, Outlook, iCal, Lightning, and Sunbird. If Bob has an e-mail/calendar program that supports iCalendar, he can respond to your invitation by choosing to accept, decline, or accept tentatively. If Bob accepts your invitation, it's added to his calendar's schedule, and a response is e-mailed back to you. You can then use Entourage to track his response and the responses from any other invitees. If Bob doesn't have an e-mail program that supports iCalendar, he just gets a regular e-mail message with whatever note text you typed in the Event window. He'll have to e-mail you back, and you won't be able to track his response automatically.

## Creating an invite

An invite in Entourage is an event you add to your own calendar and invite others to do the same to their calendars. Just like a regular event, such as an appointment or all-day event, you fill out the Event window form specifying start and end dates and times, duration, location, and so on. Then you activate the Invite command, and Entourage displays an invite field box. Use this box to enter the e-mail addresses of the people you want to invite to your event. If these addresses are already in your Address Book, Entourage helps you fill them in as you're typing. You also can send invites to people not in your Address Book. After you finish entering e-mail addresses, the Event window adds them to the top of the form. Before sending the event as an e-mail, be sure to include an e-mail message. You do this by typing your message in the notes area of the form. Whatever you type in this area becomes the e-mail message the invitees see when they open the e-mail.

Follow these steps to send an event as an invite:

1. **Start and fill out a new event (see the steps in "Recording Appointments and All-day Events") using the New Event window.**

2. **Click the Invite button on the Event window's toolbar.**

   An invite field appears, as shown in Figure 26.25.

**FIGURE 26.25**

Use the invite field to enter e-mail addresses.

3. **Type the e-mail address of the person or persons you want to invite to the event.**

   If you start typing an address from your Address Book, Entourage automatically fills the rest in for you.

   You can continue adding more addresses as needed.

4. **Click the invite field's Close button (the tiny square in the top-right corner of the box), or click anywhere outside the invite field box.**

   Entourage adds the address, or addresses, to the top of the form, as shown in Figure 26.26.

**FIGURE 26.26**

Type an e-mail message in the notes area, and send the invitation.

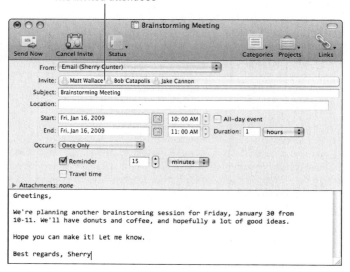

5. **Type an e-mail message to the recipients in the blank note area.**

6. **Click the Send Now button on the Event window's toolbar.**

Entourage closes the event, adds it to your schedule, and sends the e-mail invitation all at once.

You may notice after you add invitees to the Event window, two new buttons show up on the window's toolbar: Send Now and Cancel Invite. You obviously use the Send Now button to fire off the e-mail invitation. You can use the Cancel Invite button to cancel the invitations if they're sitting in your Outbox. If you've already sent them, activating the Cancel Invite button sends cancellation messages to your attendees.

## Receiving an invite

So what happens on the other end of the invitations you send from Entourage? You might be the recipient of such an event invitation yourself, so what do you do? If you or the recipient receives an invite, and the preferred e-mail/calendar program supports the iCalendar standard, three new buttons appear in the message window: Accept, Tentative, and Decline. Figure 26.27 shows a sample e-mail message window from Entourage showing the three buttons described. If the recipient is using Entourage, a yellow banner also appears at the top of the e-mail message with these same responses available as links. You or the other recipient can send back a response by clicking the appropriate button.

If you click the Accept button, Entourage adds the appointment to your calendar and sends back a response that can be tracked in the sender's program.

Regardless of which button or link you click, you're prompted to send a response, as shown in Figure 26.28. You can choose to send a response with or without comments, or you can choose not to send a response at all. Simply make your selection, and click OK.

The recipient of an invitation also can change his mind about attending at any time. All he has to do is reopen the original e-mail (if they still have it hanging around), choose another response option, and send it back to you.

## Tracking an invite

If you're the originator of an event invitation, you can track responses to your invite through the Calendar tool. When you open the e-mail response, a yellow banner at the top of the message window lists the response type: accepted, accepted tentatively, or declined. You can click the Show attendee status link to view a list box that tracks all the responses from everyone you've sent invitations to, as shown in Figure 26.29. The Attendee Status window lists everyone you've sent an invitation to and if applicable, shows their responses.

**FIGURE 26.27**

Invites to the event receive an e-mail message that looks like this one.

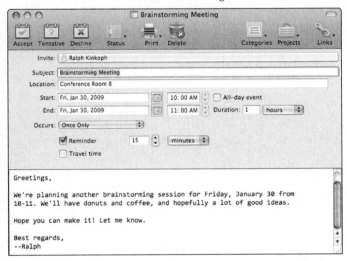

**FIGURE 26.28**

The recipient chooses how to respond to the invitation.

**FIGURE 26.29**

The Attendee Status window tracks responses to your invitations.

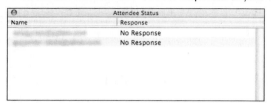

If the person you sent an invitation to does not have Entourage or an iCalendar-supported e-mail program, you receive a regular e-mail back with the person's response. You can open the Attendee Status window and manually specify whether the attendee has responded, accepted, tentatively accepted, or declined. Follow these steps to manually enter a response:

1. **Double-click the event on your calendar.**
2. **Click the View attendee status link.**

   This opens the Attendee Status window shown in Figure 26.29.
3. **Click the name of the person for whom you want to change the response.**

   A pop-up menu appears under the Response category.
4. **Click the pop-up menu, and choose a response, as shown in Figure 26.30.**

   The Response category now lists the new response.

**FIGURE 26.30**

Change the attendee's response using the pop-up menu.

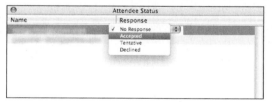

5. **Click the Close button to exit the window.**

You can revisit the Attendee Status list at any time to update the status of your attendee responses. If an attendee uses Entourage and makes a change to her response, the Attendee Status window automatically updates her status for you. If you make changes to the event's time or date, Entourage offers to send an update message to the invitees about the changes. You'll see a Send Update button you can click.

# Printing Calendar Items

You can print your schedule and take it with you. Using the Print dialog box, shown in Figure 26.31, you can specify what view you want to print and the start and end dates you want to include. You also can choose how you want the items to print or specify a form to print out on. When printing schedules, the following print options are geared toward calendar data:

- **Print:** Display the Print pop-up menu to choose what Calendar view you want to print: Day, Week, Work Week, or Month.

- **Start and End:** Use the Start and End pop-up menus to choose start and end dates for the printed schedule.

- **Layout:** Click the Layout button to view the Layout Options dialog box where you can choose to print tasks along with the events in your calendar and change the fonts and sizes used.

- **Form:** If you use a paper-based binder system, such as Franklin-Covey, Day Timer, or Day Runner, you can choose to match the layout for your planner.

**FIGURE 26.31**

You can print your schedule and specify what view to print.

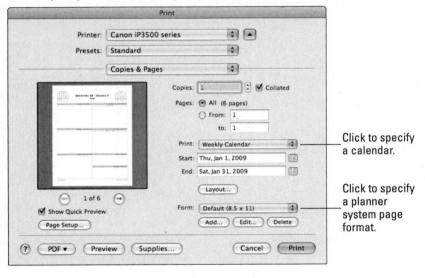

Click to specify a calendar.

Click to specify a planner system page format.

To print your schedule, follow these steps:

1. **Choose File ⇨ Print, or press ⌘+P.**

   The Print dialog box opens (refer to Figure 26.31).

2. **Click the Print pop-up menu, and choose a Calendar view.**

3. **Specify start and end dates for the schedule using the Start and End options.**

   Optionally, if you want to control which items are printed, change the font or font size, or include cut lines and holes for a binder page, click the Layout button and change the settings.

4. **If you want to specify a particular format for a planner system you're using, click the Form pop-up menu and select your planner system from the list.**

5. **Select any other printing options you deem necessary for your printout.**

6. The preview area shows an example of the printed page.

7. Click Print to print your schedule.

Obviously, you can use any of the other printing options in the Print dialog box to control the printed output, such as changing the printer used, printing more than one copy, and so on. Another useful tool to activate before printing is the Preview feature. Click the Preview button to see an exact preview of how your printed schedule pages will look. If you don't like what you see, you can fine-tune the settings or try another Calendar view before committing anything to paper.

# Summary

In this chapter, I introduced you to the Entourage Calendar tool, a helpful feature for keeping track of your busy schedule. You learned the various ways to view your calendar, how to record appointments and all-day events, and how to edit items in your schedule. You also learned how to assign categories to events, handle pop-up reminders, and add holidays to the Calendar tool. You learned how easy it is to invite other users to meetings and track their responses in Entourage. Lastly, you learned how to create a printout of your schedule.

# Chapter 27

# Tracking Tasks, Notes, and Projects

J ust how organized are you? Do people stop by your cubicle in awe of the neatness and efficiency, or do they step around your cubicle to avoid the heaping piles of stuff spilling out of your space? If you want to find something in your desk at home, will it take seconds to locate it, or will you spend at least a half-hour moving stuff around trying to find it? When it comes to tasks, notes, and projects, are you renowned for your organizational skills, or do you struggle to manage your bits of papers, sticky notes, and important items you've written down in marker on your own hand? Whether you're messy or neat, organized or disorganized, both types of people will find plenty to like about the Tasks, Notes, and Project Center tools in Entourage. Each of these tools can help you manage the things you need to accomplish at work or at home. For a quick look at all you need to accomplish for the day, you can summon the My Day tool and see your itinerary and goals at a glance without having to open the whole Entourage program window.

In this chapter, you learn how to use the Tasks tool to organize all kinds of tasks and other to-do things you need to keep track of and complete. You also learn how to use the Notes tool to quickly jot down notes you want to hold onto. This chapter also shows you how to manage large and small projects alike using the very powerful Project Center. Lastly, you learn how to make use of the handy My Day feature to view your day's itinerary at a glance. You'll see how easy it is to view all the important items you need to tackle for the day without having to deal with e-mail, tasks, and other distracting activities.

## Organizing Tasks

In Entourage, you can use the Tasks tool to create and manage your tasks at work, home, or school. Just what constitutes a task? A task can be any job, chore, action, errand, or situation you need to take care of in a timely fashion. A task can be a single item or part of a greater whole. A task can be as simple as a trip you need to make to the store or as complex as a multi-faceted project with lots of individual elements that need completing. The idea behind the Tasks tool is to give users a way to accomplish goals and objectives. By organizing the things you need to do in one handy place, Entourage can remind you about what needs to be done, show you what items you've already cared for, and generally keep you going in the right direction productivity-wise.

 To view the Tasks tool, click the Tasks button on the Standard toolbar. You also can choose View ➪ Go To ➪ Tasks. When you display the Tasks tool, two panes appear onscreen by default: the Folders List pane on the left and the Tasks pane in the center. The Standard toolbar changes as well, featuring commands associated with the Tasks feature. When you click another Entourage tool, such as Mail, the Tasks tool disappears. Figure 27.1 shows an example of the Tasks tool.

**FIGURE 27.1**

You can use the Tasks tool in Entourage to keep on top of things you need to do.

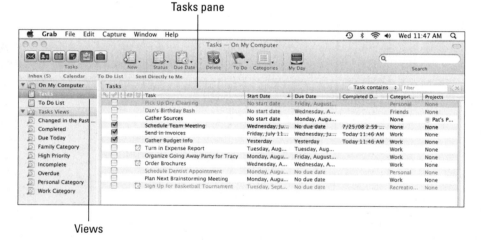

The large Tasks pane displays all the tasks you are tracking, along with tasks you've already completed. Columns in the list box help to organize, filter, and control the tasks you add to the list. The Tasks tool has two different views: Tasks and To Do List. Tasks view (refer to Figure 27.1) shows a list of all the tasks you have entered. The To Do List view, shown in Figure 27.2, looks much like the Tasks view, but it shows all the messages and contacts you've flagged and want to deal with at some point. When you flag a message or contact using the To Do button on the Standard toolbar, Entourage adds a little red flag icon to the message or contact. Entourage also automatically places the message or contact in the To Do List. Both the Tasks view and the To Do List can help you stay on top of things you need to take care of, gently reminding you when necessary.

You can use the Folders List pane to toggle back and forth between the two views. Click Tasks to view the Tasks pane, or click To Do List to view the To Do List pane. You can learn more about filtering each view coming up later this section.

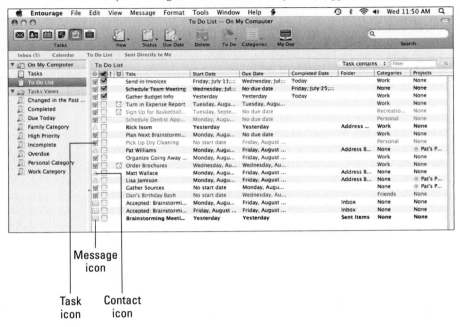

**FIGURE 27.2**

The To Do List shows you messages, contacts, and tasks you've flagged.

Message icon

Task icon | Contact icon

## Creating tasks

When creating tasks, you can use the New Task window, shown in Figure 27.3. This window contains all the necessary settings and options for creating, prioritizing, and classifying a task. You can find your way to the New Task window using several different methods as outlined below:

- Click the New button on the Standard toolbar.
- Choose File ⇨ New ⇨ Task.
- Press ⌘+N on the keyboard.
- Control+click a blank area on the Tasks list, and click New Task.

When you first open the window, it's untitled and full of blank fields, with the exception of the date fields. Entourage has filled in the date fields for you using the current date. Of course, you can change the date to whatever you want. The New Task window is essentially a form you fill out. It has its own toolbar, a set of options and fields for filling out details about the task, and a large blank area for holding notes you type or other items you paste into the area. You can press the Tab key to move from field to field in the form, filling out each area along the way.

**FIGURE 27.3**

Use the New Task window to add tasks to Entourage.

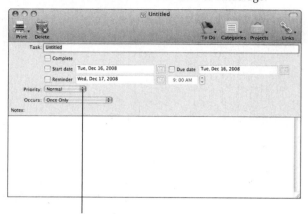

Priority level

The top of the New Task window form lets you specify a name for the task. Whatever text you type into this field appears as the task title. When assigning names, use labels that can help you quickly see what sort of task it is, such as "Gather Budget Info," "Take Out the Trash," or "Schedule Doctor Appointment." Just below the task name field are some important check boxes. If you're just starting a new task, you probably don't want to select the Complete check box, unless it's something important to a sequence of things to do and you just want to note that it's already done. The Start date check box, when activated, lets you specify a start date for the task, while the Due date check box lets you set a deadline for the task. By default, the current date appears in both fields unless you specify otherwise. If you want Entourage to remind you about the task, you can select the Reminder check box and specify a date.

Just below the check boxes, you can set a priority level for the task using the Priority pop-up menu. You can choose from Highest, High, Normal, Low, or Lowest priority levels. You also can make the task a recurring task using the Occurs pop-up menu. Recurring tasks work the same way as recurring events, which you learned about in Chapter 26. The final portion of the New Task window lets you type notes or paste other items to help you tackle the task. The window's toolbar displays tools for printing, deleting, assigning categories or projects, adding links, and flagging the task for the To Do List. For example, you might link a task to an e-mail message, a contact in your Address Book, or an event on your calendar.

Follow these steps to fill out a task:

1. **Open the New Task window (see the previous bulleted list for all the methods you can use to display the window).**

2. **In the Task name line, type a title for the task.**

   As soon as you enter the text, the name appears in the New Task window's title bar.

3. **Activate a check box option: Complete, Start date, Due date, and Reminder.**

   To specify a date, click the pop-up calendar or type a date, as shown in Figure 27.4.

   Optionally, if setting a reminder, you also can specify a time for the reminder alert message.

4. **Click the Priority pop-up menu to set a priority level for the task.**

## FIGURE 27.4

You can use the New Task window to set a start date, due date, and a reminder date for a task.

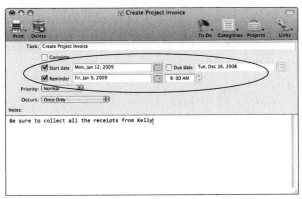

5. **Click the Occurs pop-up menu, and specify how often the task occurs.** Once Only is the default selection.

6. **Click in the Notes field, and type any notes pertaining to the task.**

   Optionally, you can use the toolbar buttons to flag the task; assign a category, project, or link; delete the task; or print the details. If you flag a task using the To Do button, Entourage also adds the task to the To Do List.

7. **Press ⌘+S to save the task and close the window.** You also can click the Close button, and click Save in the prompt box that appears.

   Entourage adds the task to the Tasks pane, as shown in Figure 27.5.

## FIGURE 27.5

After creating a task, Entourage adds it to your tasks list.

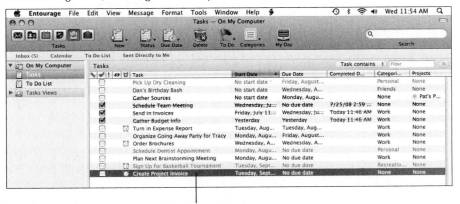

The new task

## Editing tasks

After you have a few tasks in your list, you can start working with them in various ways. You can check them off when they're completed, flag them with a priority level, add reminders, delete them, and more. You can change a task's details by using the toolbar buttons on the Standard toolbar or by reopening the Task window. The fastest way to edit a task is to select it in the list pane and click the appropriate toolbar button. Figure 27.6 shows the toolbar tools. Or, if applicable, you can edit the task directly in the list pane.

**FIGURE 27.6**

The Standard toolbar offers a variety of editing tools you can use to make changes to your tasks.

You can choose from the following toolbar actions and editing tips to manage your tasks:

- To assign a category, click the Categories button and choose a category. You can assign more than one category to a task.

- To set a priority level and flag a task for the To Do List, click the To Do button and make a selection.

- To change the status to Complete or Incomplete, click the Status button and make a selection.
- You also can click the check box for the task to add or remove a check mark and change the task's status.

- To change the due date, click the Due Date button and choose from Due Today or Due This Week. To set another date, open the Task window.

- To delete a task, click the Delete button. A prompt box asks you to confirm the deletion before permanently removing it from the list.
- You also can delete a task by pressing Delete or by choosing Edit ➪ Delete Task.
- To rename a task in the list, click to highlight the task name, then click again and type a new name, and press Return.
- To change a start date, due date, or completed date you've assigned, click the field twice and make your change by typing a date directly in the list.
- To change or add a category directly in the list, click the task's category field and make a choice from the pop-up menu.
- To change a project assigned to the task, click the task's project field and choose a project from the pop-up menu.

You can access all these commands on the shortcut menu. Control+click a task, and choose an action from the pop-up menu that appears. Figure 27.7 shows an example of just such a context menu. You also can access To Do, Categories, and Projects commands using the Edit menu.

**FIGURE 27.7**

You can use the context menu to work with tasks.

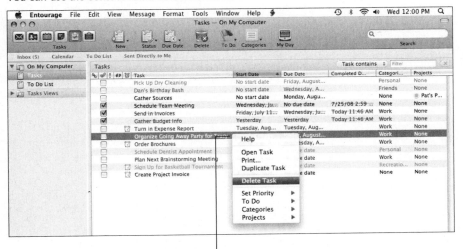

CTRL+Click a task to
view the context menu.

## Sorting and filtering tasks

You can sort and filter your task list and change how the tasks are arranged. For example, you may need to see all the tasks due today or glance at all the tasks you've completed so far. Sorting is just the process of rearranging the task records, while filtering is showing just the task records you want to see. If you're familiar with sorting and filtering techniques in other programs, such as database programs or spreadsheet programs like Excel, the same principles are used when sorting and filtering Entourage tasks.

Notice the Tasks view's list box pane is divided into many columns, as shown in Figure 27.8. You can use the headings at the top of the columns to sort the list. At the far left end of the columns, the headings are just icons. If you pause your mouse pointer over an icon, a ScreenTip shows the name of the heading. To sort the list based on a particular heading, just click the column heading. For example, if you click the Status icon, the list is sorted to show the completed items at the top of the list. Every time you click a column heading the list is sorted based on that particular heading. By default, the first click you make sorts the list in ascending order based on the heading. Click the column heading again to sort by descending order.

You can open a task's window at any time by double-clicking the task. In addition to the actions available on the Standard toolbar, the Tasks window lets you change the assigned links and projects; set a different start date, due date, and reminder date; and add notes about the task. Using this window, you have access to all the settings you used to first create the task.

**FIGURE 27.8**

Use the column headings in Tasks view to sort your tasks list.

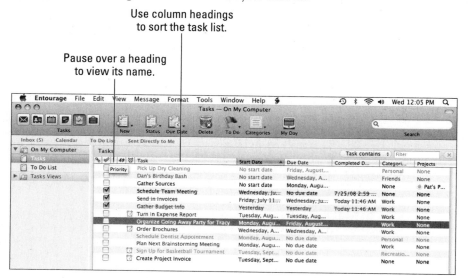

Table 27.1 defines each column, starting with the leftmost column and working across to the right. The column headings in Tasks view act as sort buttons when clicked, allowing you to rearrange your list in meaningful ways.

**TABLE 27.1**

## Tasks Columns

| Column Heading | Description |
|---|---|
| Links | Denotes any links you have assigned to the task. |
| Status | Denotes the task as completed with a check mark or uncompleted without a check mark. |
| Priority | Denotes the priority level assigned, such as Today, Tomorrow, or Next Week. The priority level you set flags the task and places it in the To Do List, too. |
| Recurring | Denotes the tasks as recurring or non-recurring. |
| Reminder | Denotes any reminders assigned. |
| Task Name | Lists assigned task names. |
| Start Date | Shows the assigned start date. |
| Due Date | Shows the assigned due date. |
| Completed Date | Shows the assigned completion date. |
| Categories | Displays assigned categories. |
| Projects | Displays assigned projects. |

You also can find sorting and filtering options on the View menu. For example, choose View➪Incomplete Tasks to view only the tasks you still have to do in your list. You also can use the View menu to filter completed tasks, tasks due today, or tasks due this week. To see the full task list again, choose View➪All Tasks.

If that wasn't enough sorting filtering options, you also can find more in the Folders List pane. The Tasks Views expand arrow (located to the left of the heading), when clicked, displays nine filtering categories: Changed in the Past 7 Days, Completed, Due Today, Family Category, High Priority, Incomplete, Overdue, Personal Category, and Work Category. Figure 27.9 shows the filters.

---

**FIGURE 27.9**

You can find more filters in the Tasks Views heading in the Folders List pane.

Click to return to
the full task list.

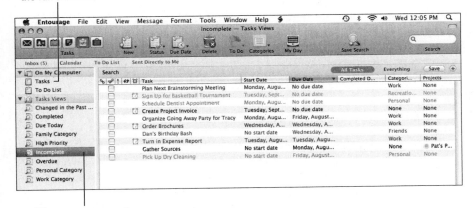

Filters you can apply

---

You can click the collapse arrow to hide the list again. To return to Tasks view, click the Tasks heading in the Folders List pane.

Just when you think you've exhausted all the possible sorts and filters you can apply to your tasks, there's one more feature I need to tell you about. You can use the filtering tools at the top of the Tasks view pane to perform more detailed filters on your list, as shown in Figure 27.10. You can click in the Filter field and type the text you want to use as a filter, such as a keyword from the note or task title, and then press Return, and Entourage filters the list based on your criteria. By default, the filter is set up to look through what the task contains. You can click the Task contains pop-up menu and filter by category or project, too.

## Handling reminders

Reminders help you remember upcoming tasks. When you activate the Reminder check box option in the Task window and the reminder date becomes due, Entourage displays a pop-up alert box reminding you about the task. After a reminder prompt appears, as shown in Figure 27.11, you can tell it to go away or revisit you again in a few minutes. You also can use reminders as shortcuts to view details about the task.

### FIGURE 27.10

You can create a custom filter using the Filter field at the top of the Tasks pane.

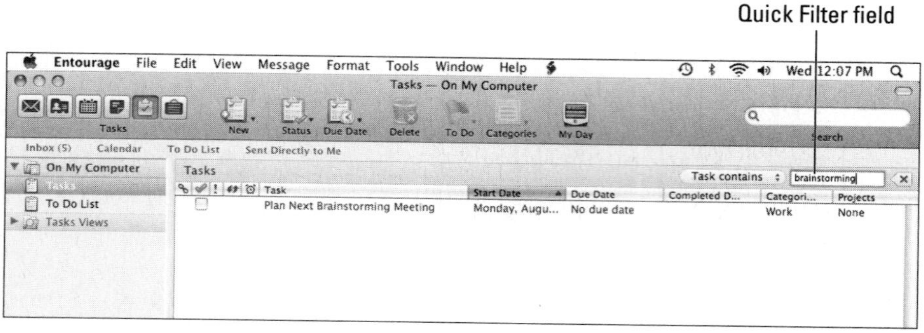

Quick Filter field

### FIGURE 27.11

Reminders appear as pop-up boxes on your screen.

You first learned about reminders in Chapter 26 when applying them to calendar events. As you learned then, reminders are part of the Microsoft Office Reminders program, a small add-on program you can use with events and tasks. When a task item is due, the Office Reminders program pops into the Mac OS X Dock, usually with a chiming noise, and then disappears when you've told it what to do. Reminders work even when you're not using Entourage.

You can use the Task window to assign reminders to your tasks. Just set one to check the Reminders check box in the Task window, and specify a date and time you want the reminder to sound off. After a reminder is assigned, a small alarm clock icon appears in the Reminders column in the task list.

To respond to the reminder when it appears on your screen, do any of these:

■ Click the Snooze button to make the reminder go away briefly, much like the snooze device on your alarm clock.

■ Click the Dismiss button to get rid of the reminder permanently.

■ Double-click the reminder to open the task window associated with the reminder.

■ Click the arrow end of the Snooze button to view a pop-up menu of times when you want to be reminded again.

If your reminder prompt displays more than one item, you can double-click any item to open it.

**TIP** Not interested in reminders? You can turn off the Office Reminders program from within Entourage. Choose Entourage ➪ Turn Off Office Reminders. You can use this same procedure to turn the feature back on again later.

# Working with the To Do List

As mentioned earlier in this chapter, any messages, contacts, or tasks you flag appear in a separate list called the To Do List, as shown in Figure 27.12. When in Tasks view, you can click the To Do List in the Folder List pane to view the flagged items.

Also like the Tasks pane view, the To Do List pane lists items in columnar format, with headings at the top of the pane. You can use the headings to sort the list. Pause your mouse pointer over a column heading icon to view a ScreenTip telling the name of the heading. To sort the list based on a particular heading, just click the column heading. Every time you click a column heading, the list is sorted based on the heading. One click sorts the list in ascending order, and a second click sorts by descending order. Table 27.2 defines each column heading, starting with the leftmost column heading.

**TABLE 27.2**

## To Do List Columns

| Column Heading | Description |
| --- | --- |
| Item Type | Denotes a message, contact, or task. |
| Status | Identifies the item as completed with a check mark or uncompleted without a check mark. |
| Priority | Denotes the priority level assigned, such as Today, Tomorrow, or Next Week. The priority level you set flags the item and places it in the To Do List, too. |
| Reminder | Denotes any reminders assigned to the item. |
| Title | Displays the name of the item. |
| Start Date | Shows the assigned start date. |
| Due Date | Shows the assigned due date. |
| Completed Date | Shows the assigned completion date. |
| Folder | Shows the assigned folder. |
| Categories | Displays any assigned categories. |
| Projects | Displays assigned projects. |

You can use the Quick Filter field at the top of the pane to filter the list based on any criteria you enter. For example, you might filter the list by all the items using the name Bob. You can filter the list by what the items contain or by category or project. You also can find filters listed in the View menu and can filter the list by Incomplete Items, Completed Items, Due Today, or Due This Week. To see all the items again after applying a filter, choose View ⇨ All To Do Items.

NOTE    The Expand All and Collapse All commands in the View menu control the filters listed in the Folders List pane. Learn more about using the Folders List pane in Chapter 25.

You can edit the To Do List just like you edit the Tasks list. Select the item you want to edit, and use the buttons on the Standard toolbar to make changes. You also can Control+click a selected item to view a shortcut menu of commands, or you can double-click the item to open its respective window and make changes to the settings there. Like the Tasks list, you also can make edits directly on the list. See the preceding section to learn the various ways you can change items in the list.

**FIGURE 27.12**

The To Do List shows a list of all the flagged items in Entourage, including messages, contacts, and tasks.

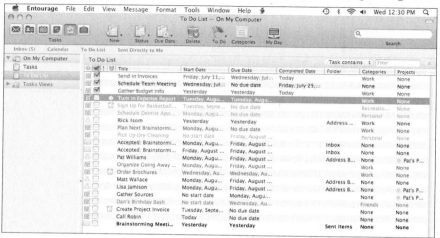

# Making Notes

You can use Notes view in Entourage to add and organize notes. Notes can be anything you want to jot down. Notes can be ideas you have about an upcoming project, creative endeavors such as poems and verse, random thoughts, organizational notes, driving directions, grocery lists, phone call information, anything you might ordinarily write down on a piece of paper. Entourage keeps a running list of the notes you add and displays them in a list box pane, shown in Figure 27.13. As you can see, notes are organized by details in the form of columns. The Notes tool keeps track of any links you assign to your notes, note titles, the dates you created or changed the note, and any categories or projects assigned to the notes.

 To view the Notes tool, click the Notes button on the Standard toolbar. You also can choose View ⇨ Go To ⇨ Notes. When you display the Notes tool, two panes appear onscreen by default: the Folders List pane on the left and the Notes pane in the center. The Standard toolbar changes as well, featuring commands associated with the Notes feature.

**FIGURE 27.13**

Use the Notes tool to collect notes of all kinds and organize them in one spot.

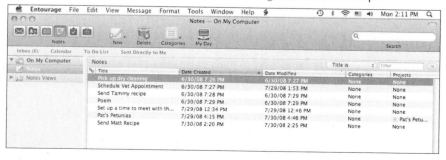

You can use the New Note window to create a note at any time. To open the window, use any of these methods:

- Click the New button on the Standard toolbar.
- Choose File ➪ New ➪ Note.
- Press ⌘+N on the keyboard.
- Control+click a blank area on the Notes list, and click New Note.

The New Note window, shown in Figure 27.14, looks very much like all the other windows you've used so far in Entourage to create messages, events, and tasks. The toolbar has a few buttons, a place to give the note a name, and a large open space to type your note or paste items. A formatting toolbar lets you format your note text, such as changing the font or font size.

Follow these steps to fill out a note:

1. **Open the New Note window (see the previous bulleted list for all the methods you can use to display the window).**

2. **In the Title field, type a title for the note.**

    As soon as you enter the text, the name appears in the New Note window's title bar.

3. **Click in the notes field, and type your note.** You also can paste items from other sources, such as a snippet of text from a Word document or e-mail message.

    - Optionally, you can use the toolbar buttons to print or delete the note and assign a category, project, or link.
    - Optionally, you can use the formatting tools to format your note text.
    - If you click the Insert button, you can insert a picture, background picture, sound clip, or movie clip into your note.

4. **Press ⌘+S to save the task and close the window.** You also can click the Close button and click Save in the prompt box that appears.

    Entourage adds the note to the Notes pane.

---

**FIGURE 27.14**

Use the New Note window to create a new note to add to Entourage.

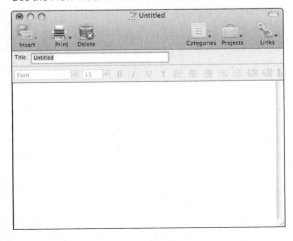

After you have some notes added to your list, you can edit them as needed. You can choose from the following toolbar actions and editing tips to help you manage your notes:

- Double-click any note item to reopen the Note window and make changes to the note's contents.

- You also can select any note in the list and assign another category or project to the note.

- To assign a category, click the Categories button and choose a category. You can assign more than one category to a note.

- You also can delete a note by clicking the Delete button on the Standard toolbar, pressing Delete, or choosing Edit ➪ Delete Note.

- To rename a note in the list, click to highlight the name, then click again and type a new name, and press Return.

- To change or add a category directly in the list, click the note's category field and choose from the pop-up menu.

- To change a project assigned to the task, click the note's project field and choose a project from the pop-up menu.

You can sort notes in the list using any of the column headings as filters. The Notes Views filters in the Folders List pane, shown in Figure 27.15, also has filters you can apply to the list: Changed in the Past 7 Days, Created in the Past 7 Days, Family Category, Personal Category, and Work Category. Click the Notes Views expand arrow button to expand the filter list, and click a filter. To return to the Notes pane, click Notes in the Folders List pane.

---

**FIGURE 27.15**

Use the Folders List pane's Notes Views to filter your notes.

Click to return to
the full Notes list.

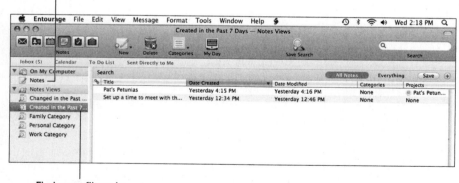

Find more filters in
Notes Views.

# Printing Tasks and Notes

You can print your tasks and notes and take them with you. Using the Print dialog box, shown in Figure 27.16, you can control which tasks and notes print, and how they are displayed on the printed page. You can activate the Print command from an opened Task or Note window using the Print button on the toolbar, or you can choose File ➪ Print. Either method opens the Print dialog box. If you select an item from the list before opening the Print dialog box, you can choose just to print the one item. For example, if you open the Task window for the item and activate the Print button, the Print dialog box shows just the one item for printing. If you use the Print command from the File menu, you can choose to print more than one task or note at a time.

**FIGURE 27.16**

You can use the Print dialog box to control how tasks or notes are printed.

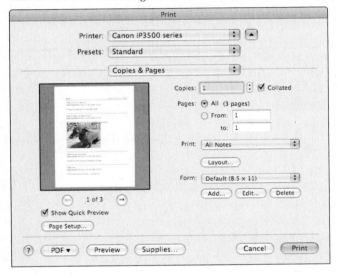

If you click the Layout button in the Print dialog box, the Print Layout dialog box opens, as shown in Figure 27.17. From here you can specify whether to print cut lines, page numbers, or pictures, and include any marks for holes if you're using a form and inserting it into a notebook planner system.

You can click the Preview button in the Print dialog box to open the Preview application, shown in Figure 27.18, and see what your notes or tasks will look like on the printed page. You can view different pages, zoom in, or zoom out. To exit Preview, choose Preview ➪ Quit Preview.

**FIGURE 27.17**

**FIGURE 27.17**

The Print Layout dialog box lets you determine what elements are printed.

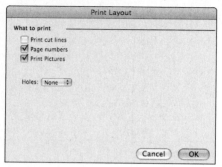

**FIGURE 27.18**

The Preview application lets you see what your tasks or notes will look like when printed.

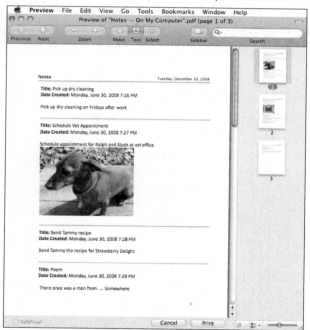

# Working with Projects

One of the best tools in Entourage is the Project Center. Few people make use of this powerful tool, but as you'll soon see, it can be a real lifesaver when it comes to organizing. The Project Center, shown in Figure 27.19, helps you to manage projects of any size, tracking all the various components that make up a project. By placing all the related items together, you can easily find out where you are with accomplishing your goals and completing the project. The Project Center works by creating a watch folder in which you can store everything related to the project, including e-mails, tasks, notes, contacts, and files.

 To view the Project Center, click the Project Center button on the Standard toolbar. You also can choose View ➪ Go To ➪ Project Center. When you display the Project Center, two panes appear onscreen by default: the Folders List pane on the left and the Projects pane in the center. The Standard toolbar changes as well, featuring commands associated with the feature.

What's so remarkable about the Project Center? Ordinarily, when you work with projects on your computer, the components are located in all kinds of different places. All the document files may be in the same folder, but e-mail messages are located somewhere else, a schedule in your calendar program in another location, and photos in a photo folder in a completely different location. The beauty of the Project Center is that it lets you bring everything together in one spot so you don't have to go searching elsewhere or trying to remember where you saved a file. This seriously cuts down on time spent looking for files and the possibility of losing something important in your growing file collections.

**FIGURE 27.19**

You can use the Project Center to manage projects large and small.

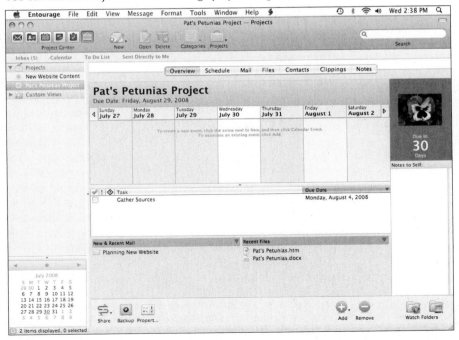

## Starting a new project

You can use the New Project Wizard to create new projects for the Project Center. The Wizard walks you through all the necessary steps using four pages or screens. To start a new project, follow these steps:

1. **Open the New Project Wizard by doing any of the following:**

   - Click the New button on the Standard toolbar.
   - Choose File ➪ New ➪ Project.
   - Press ⌘+N on the keyboard.
   - Control+click a blank area on the Projects area, and click New.

   The New Project Wizard appears, as shown in Figure 27.20. You can use the first page of the Wizard to assign a name, due date, picture, or color to the project.

**FIGURE 27.20**

The New Project Wizard helps you get started creating a new project.

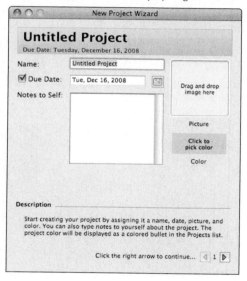

2. **Type a name for the project in the Name field.**

3. **If the project has a due date, click the Due Date check box and use the pop-up calendar to set a date.**

   Optionally, you can drag a picture into the Picture field to add an image to the project.

   Optionally, you can click the Color field and choose a color to associate with the project. A color can help you distinguish items in the project from other Project Center projects.

> **TIP** You can always revisit the properties you set in the Wizard dialog boxes and make changes later. To do so, just click the Properties button at the bottom of the selected project in the Project Center window. So if you decide to change a color later or add a picture, you can do so when you know what you want to assign.

4. **Click the right arrow button to continue.**

   The second Wizard page appears, as shown in Figure 27.21, with options for controlling where the project's watch folder is stored and which type of items you want to include in the project.

**FIGURE 27.21**

The second Wizard page helps you create a watch folder.

5. **Choose the type of watch folder you want to create.**

   To let Entourage create the folder, leave the Automatically create Project Watch Folders radio button selected. If you select this option, Entourage creates a folder based on the name you specified in Step 2. Watch folders that Entourage makes are stored in the Office Projects folder located in your Documents folder.

   To use an existing folder you've already started for a project, click the Manually set Project Watch Folders radio button and navigate to the folder you want to use.

6. **If you have an existing category or project you want to use for this new project, choose it from the Import items options.**

7. **Click the right arrow button to continue.**

   The third Wizard page appears, as shown in Figure 27.22, with options for setting message rules and adding the watch folder to your desktop.

8. **Under the Rules section, specify any e-mail message rules you want to apply.**

   If contacts from your Address Book are important to the project, you can include their e-mail messages in the watch folder by selecting the Associate e-mail from Project contacts check box. All e-mail from the contacts then becomes associated with the project.

   To associate any e-mail messages with subjects pertaining to your project, check the Associate e-mail with the following subjects check box and fill in the subject keywords.

**FIGURE 27.22**

The third Wizard page lets you specify any message rules.

Check the Don't apply other rules to these messages check box to disengage any rules you already have in effect for e-mail messages. When you activate this option, the rules don't apply to any e-mail associated with this project.

If you do want to keep your current rules in effect, check the Apply Rules to existing messages check box.

9. **Click the right arrow button to continue.**

   The last Wizard page appears, as shown in Figure 27.23, summarizing your choices.

10. **Click the right arrow button to continue.**

    Entourage creates the new project and displays it in the Project Center, as shown in Figure 27.24.

Congratulations! Your first project is added to the Project Center window and an alias to the Watch Folder is placed on your desktop. You're on your way to true organizing success. You no longer have any excuses about misplacing crucial elements to any project. You can keep everything in one spot and impress everyone who doesn't already know your secret organizational powers.

## Viewing projects in the Project Center

After you have a project in the Project Center window, you can use a variety of ways to look at the information you collect, find out how things are coming along, and add more items to the project When you open the Project Center window, two panes appear: the Folders List pane located on the left and the Projects pane located in the center. You can use the Folders List pane to change the view. To see all the projects you're working on, click the Projects folder heading on the Folders List pane or click the Expand Arrow icon to expand the list, as shown in Figure 27.25. When the Projects folder is highlighted, the Projects pane shows a list of every project you're tracking.

**FIGURE 27.23**

The fourth and final Wizard page summarizes your project settings.

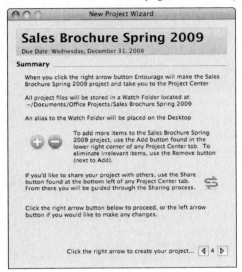

**FIGURE 27.24**

Entourage adds the new project to the Project Center.

**FIGURE 27.25**

You can use the Folders List pane to display a list of projects.

Click to view projects in
the Projects pane.

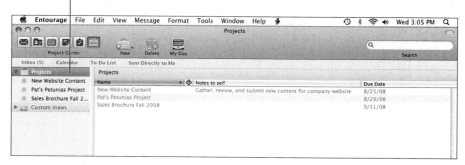

To view an individual project, click the project name in the Folders List pane or double-click the project name in the list box. As soon as you open the project, the Projects pane looks something like Figure 27.26. The title of the project appears at the top in the color you assigned during the New Project Wizard steps. Any picture you assigned appears as well. Every project has seven tabs: Overview, Schedule, Mail, Files, Contacts, Clippings, and Notes. You can click a tab to view its contents. The bottom-right corner of the pane displays icons for the Watch Folders you've created. You can drag and drop items into the Watch Folders as needed.

In some of the tab views, you can resize the panes to help you better see your project items. Move the mouse pointer over the border of a pane, and then click and drag to resize the pane.

Now let's look at what you can expect to find in each tab view of a project.

## Overview tab

The Overview tab, shown in Figure 27.26, gives you a quick overall look at a project, showing a seven-day calendar, a list of tasks, new and recent e-mail messages, and recent files. The tab also displays any associated picture and due date. This tab, displayed by default when you open a project in the Projects pane, is useful for catching up on where things are with a project, what's on the schedule, what tasks are listed to do, and recent work that's been done on the project. The bottom of the Overview tab view offers five different buttons:

- **Share:** Use this button to share the project with other users, allowing access to all the files and project information.

- **Backup:** Use this button to export your project items.

- **Properties:** Click this button to open the Project Properties dialog box, which shows the same Wizard screens you used to create the project, but this time in tabs. You can change the settings such as project name, assigned color, message rules, and more.

- **Add:** Click this button to add an event, task, message, file, contact, clipping, or note to the project.

- **Remove:** Click this button to remove the selected project item. This removes the item only from the project folder, not from its original location in Entourage or another source program.

The Projects area displays a work area for your project.

Click a project to view it
in the Projects pane.

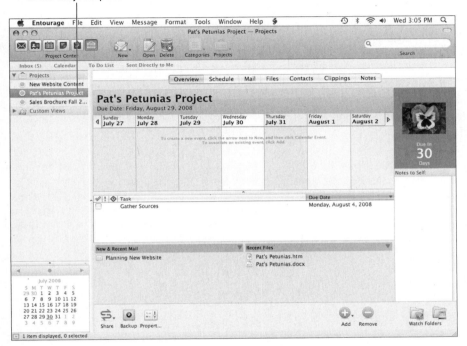

Several of these same buttons appear in the other six tabs. The Backup and Properties buttons are unique to the Overview tab.

### Schedule tab

The Schedule tab, shown in Figure 27.27, shows a larger view of your schedule, and anything related to the project appears on the calendar. None of the non-project related events appear, just the ones associated with the project. The same is true in the Tasks list pane located below the calendar. All the tasks you need to do for the project are displayed in the Tasks pane.

The Calendar pane works just like the regular Calendar tool in Entourage, but it's focused on the current project. You can view different months, weeks, or days. You can double-click an event to open the Event window. The Same is true for tasks: Double-click the task to open the Task window. Both the Calendar and Tasks panes have Quick Filter pop-up menus at the tops of the panes that you can use to filter the items shown.

**FIGURE 27.27**

Use the Schedule tab to hone in on events and tasks related to your project.

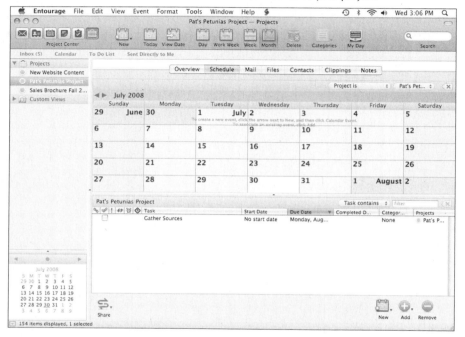

The Schedule tab offers four buttons at the bottom of the pane for working with the project events and tasks: Share, New, Add, and Remove. Use the Share button to share the items with other users. You can click the New button at the bottom of the pane to add a new event or task to the project. Click the Add button to add existing events or tasks. To remove an item, select it and click the Remove button.

### Mail tab

The Mail tab shows any e-mail messages associated with the project. To view a message, click it in the Mail pane, and the Preview pane shows you the contents. The Mail tab, shown in Figure 27.28, works like the regular Mail tool. You also can double-click a message to open the Message window. To sort the messages, use the column headings or filter the messages using the Quick Filter pop-up menus located at the top of the pane.

To add a new message, click the New button at the bottom of the pane. This opens a New Message window. If you want to associate an existing message with the project, click the Add button and choose the message. To remove a message from the project, select it and click the Remove button. Use the Share button to share the items with other users.

## FIGURE 27.28

Use the Mail tab to manage messages related to your project.

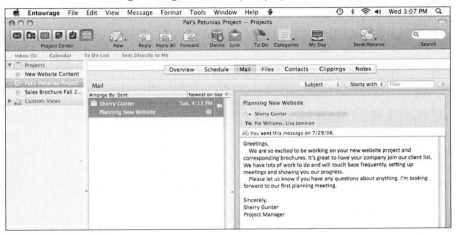

### Files tab

The Files tab, shown in Figure 27.29, keeps track of all the files you have associated with a project. Files can include documents, photographs, spreadsheets, and more. These are files stored in the Watch Folder for the project. You can include any type of file with a project, including other Office program files. When you created the project, an alias of the folder was added to your desktop. You can drag and drop files from your computer and place them in the desktop Watch Folder for the project.

## FIGURE 27.29

Use the Files tab to manage files related to your project.

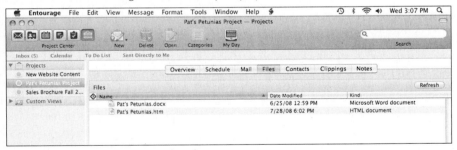

The buttons at the bottom of the pane allow you to share a file, send a file, add more files, or remove files. For example, to associate an existing file with the project, click the Add button and choose the file. To remove a file from the project, select it and click the Remove button.

## Contacts tab

The Contacts tab, shown in Figure 27.30, keeps track of any contacts associated with the project. If your project involves e-mailing the same people over and over again, add them to the Contacts tab for quick and easy access. You can associate contacts from your Address Book or add new contacts from scratch.

**FIGURE 27.30**

Use the Contacts tab to manage contacts related to your project.

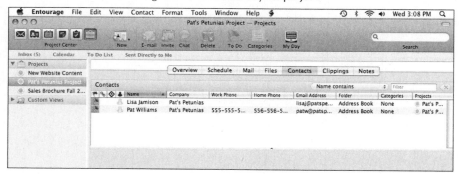

Look to the bottom of the pane for actions you can perform on your contacts. You can share them with others, contact someone via Microsoft Messenger, add new contacts or existing contacts, or remove contacts. For example, to add a new contact, click the New button at the bottom of the pane. This opens a New Contact window. Adding contacts from the Contacts tab works the same way as adding contacts using the Address Book tool.

### Clippings tab

You can use the Clippings tab, shown in Figure 27.31, to gather clippings from the Office Scrapbook feature that you want to associate with the project. Clippings are snippets of information and can include text and graphics. For example, if your project uses a logo, you might place it in the Scrapbook and then associate it with a new project you create. The buttons at the bottom of the pane allow you to share the clippings with others, add clippings, and remove clippings.

### Notes tab

Lastly, the Notes tab, shown in Figure 27.32, lets you view any notes associated with the project. You can sort and filter any notes you have listed in the pane, or use the buttons at the bottom to share notes, create brand new notes, turn existing notes into items associated with the project, or remove notes.

**FIGURE 27.31**

Use the Clippings tab to manage bits of Scrapbook text and graphics related to your project.

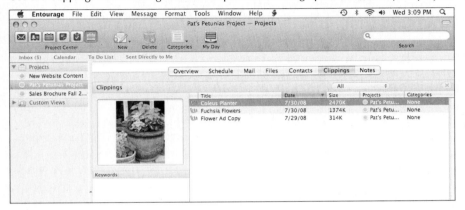

**FIGURE 27.32**

Use the Notes tab to manage notes related to your project.

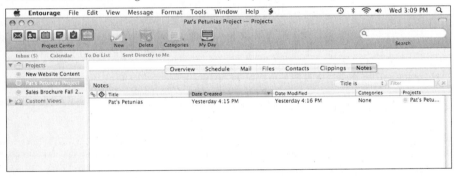

## Sharing projects

You can activate the Project Center's sharing feature and place the project on a server that others can access. This can make it really easy to collaborate on projects large and small. Sharing a project lets anyone involved view documents and notes, share e-mails, check the schedule, and more. You need a network server that everyone you're sharing the program with can access. You can use the Project Sharing Assistant, shown in Figure 27.33, to walk you through the setup using four screens. When you finish, Entourage moves all the elements associated with the project to the designated server.

The Project Sharing Assistant can walk you through the steps for setting up project sharing.

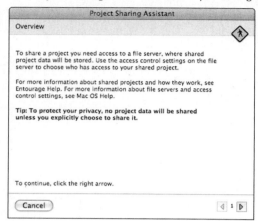

To share a project, follow these steps:

1. **Click the Share button on the project's Overview tab.**
2. **Click Start Sharing Project.**

   You also can choose File ⇨ Share a Project.

   The Project Sharing Assistant opens, as shown in Figure 27.33.

3. **The first screen of the assistant tells you how to share projects. Click the right arrow button to continue.**

   The second assistant screen opens, as shown in Figure 27.34.

The second Project Sharing Assistant screen allows you to specify an exact project.

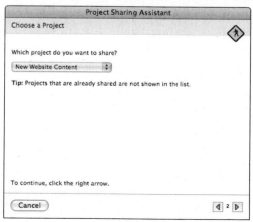

4. **Specify a project to share, if necessary.** Click the pop-up menu, and select the project. By default, the project you opened before starting Step 1 is displayed.

5. **Click the right arrow button to continue.**

   The third assistant screen opens, as shown in Figure 27.35.

**FIGURE 27.35**

Use the third Project Sharing Assistant screen to choose a server location for the project.

6. **Click the Choose button, and navigate to a server location for the shared project.**

   You can share projects on an HTTP DAV server, an Appleshare file server, or an iDisk.

7. **Click the right arrow button to continue.**

   The last assistant screen opens with a summary of the setup offering a few tips to read about.

8. **Click the Close button to finish the setup.**

   Entourage adds a small sharing icon next to the project name in the Overview tab.

**NOTE** If you choose to store the project on your computer, additional Project Sharing Assistant screens may appear. Fill in the information as requested.

Now that you've set up your project for sharing, you must alert your colleagues. You can click the Share button again and choose Invite people to join project. A prompt box appears asking if you want to create an e-mail. Click the Create E-Mail Invitation button. This opens a new Message window where you can invite others to join in the fun by entering e-mail addresses, typing a message, and sending out the invitation.

**NOTE** If you choose to store the project on your computer, you cannot e-mail invitations to other users. Instead, they'll have to subscribe using their Entourage window by choosing File ➪ Subscribe to Project.

To stop project sharing at any time, click the Share button and choose Stop Sharing Project. You also can select any item in the project and turn off sharing for that particular item. Click the Share button, and choose Do Not Share Item. To turn item-sharing back on again, click the Share button and choose Share Item.

## Backing up projects

To help you keep your project data safe, Entourage offers you a backup feature. When you activate this feature, Entourage creates an archive file using the .rge file extension. You can choose to import all or just certain items from your project.

Follow these steps to create a backup archive:

1. **Click the Backup button on the project's Overview tab.**

   The Export dialog box opens, as shown in Figure 27.36.

**FIGURE 27.36**

The Export dialog box walks you through the backup process.

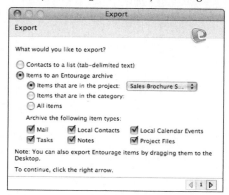

2. **Choose which items you want to include in the backup.**

3. **Click the right arrow button to continue.**

   The second Export screen asks you how you want to handle deleted items, as shown in Figure 27.37.

**FIGURE 27.37**

You can choose to keep even deleted items from Entourage archived in the original backup file, or you can remove them from the archive file as well.

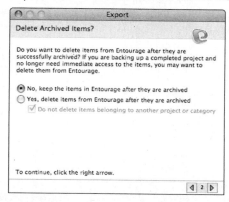

4. **Click the No, keep the items in Entourage after they are archived radio button.**

   If you want all the associated items removed from Entourage and kept only in the archive, you can select the Yes, delete items from Entourage after they are archived radio button.

5. **Click the right arrow button to continue.**

   The Save dialog box appears, as shown in Figure 27.38.

**FIGURE 27.38**

Give the archive file a unique name, and choose where you want to store it.

6. **Type a name for the archive if you want a different name than the project name, and choose a location for the file.**

7. **Click Save.**

   Entourage creates a backup archive file.

If you ever need to restore a project's backup file, just double-click the filename and follow the onscreen prompts.

## Using My Day

Have you ever wanted to check your tasks and appointments without having to open your personal information manager application? Well, now you can in Entourage 2008. The new My Day tool lets you look at your day's events and To Do List items without having to contend with the rest of your stuff. This lets you concentrate on what you need to attend to for the day without being distracted by e-mails, notes, and upcoming tasks and events. My Day is a mini-application, much like a widget, that works outside of Entourage, so you need not have Entourage open in order to view your current itinerary.

 To open the My Day tool, click the My Day button on the Standard toolbar or choose Window ➪ My Day. The My Day window opens, shown in Figure 27.39, looking very much like an electronic version of a PDA (personal digital assistant). The top section of the window shows the day's scheduled events, and the bottom section shows your To Do List tasks.

**FIGURE 27.39**

Use the new My Day tool to check your day's schedule and To Do List tasks.

Events

Tasks

Here's what you can do with the My Day window:

- To view an appointment's location, pause the mouse pointer over the event name.
- To open an event or task, double-click the item.
- To mark a To Do task as complete, click the check box in front of the task name.
- To add a new task to the list, click the New Task button in the bottom-left corner of the My Day window.
- To view another day's events and tasks, click the navigation arrow buttons at the top of the window. Click the left arrow to view the previous day, the right arrow to view the next day, and the middle button to view the current day.
- Click the scroll arrow buttons on either side of the timeline to change your view of the appointed time commitments.
- To set My Day preferences, such as showing the My Day window in the Dock, click the Preferences button located in the bottom-right corner of the window to open the General tab and change the settings as desired.
- To print the My Day items, click the Print button located at the bottom of the window.
- Use the window's Close, Minimize, and Zoom buttons to close, minimize, or enlarge the window.

# Summary

In this chapter, you learned all about using tasks and notes in Entourage. You learned how to create new tasks and keep them organized in the Tasks pane, and you learned how to turn tasks into important To Do List items. The only difference between tasks and To Do List tasks is that anything in the To Do List has been flagged as requiring attention. Unlike the Tasks pane, which contains nothing but tasks, the To Do List can include tasks, contacts, and messages. You also learned how to utilize the Notes feature to keep track of random thoughts, creative outbursts, or just plain notes about something. You learned how to print your tasks and notes to take them with you.

This chapter also introduced you to the power of the Project Center, Entourage's secret weapon for keeping all your projects and their components together in one tidy location. Last, but not least, you learned how to use the new My Day tool to view your day's schedule and tasks at a glance.

# Part VI

# Organizing Digital Media with Expression Media

# Chapter 28

# Introducing Expression Media

## IN THIS CHAPTER

Navigating the window

Using view modes

Setting annotations

Filtering views

Importing media files

Not very long ago, when film cameras ruled the photography world, photographers had to keep photos and negatives organized somehow. For home photographers, that usually meant a shoebox or three with several years of photographs organized somewhat haphazardly. Negatives, if kept, were even less organized. Home movies (on super-8 film or VHS tape) would be stored in their own shoeboxes. The digital age has provided some relief for this problem, but introduced some new challenges, too. Digital cameras have allowed photographers the freedom to take pictures without having to worry about the expense of film or developing, and digital video has given millions of people the ability to become amateur filmmakers in their own rights. The problem of cataloging all this stuff is still there, with file folders, CDs, and DVDs replacing the old shoebox. In addition, photographers need to be able to translate between media formats, browse instantly, and cross-reference files. Expression Media was created to try to help with these things.

Expression Media is what is known as a Digital Access Management (DAM) program. It can help you manage your digital media, including photos, videos, and even documents by storing thumbnails and references to them in files catalogs. Catalogs can reference files that don't live on your computer full time, so if you have an external hard disk, or photos stored on CDs or DVDs, you can use Expression Media to keep track of them. You can add a single file to multiple catalogs and assign keywords to make searching for them easier. Expression Media even lets you to do some simple editing, which can be helpful if you don't happen to have a full-blown image-editing program like Photoshop. It is also Web-friendly, in that it allows you to import media files from the Web and generate contact sheets and Web galleries.

Although Expression Media is new to the Office suite, it's not really a newcomer to the digital photography world. Expression Media started out as a program called iView Media Pro, available on both Windows and Mac OS X platforms since the 1990s. Microsoft purchased the company that created this package, iView Multimedia, in 2006 and soon after released Expression Media to be part of the Expression Studio suite on Windows and as a standalone application for the Mac.

The newest version of Expression Media, 2.0, is now part of the Office 2008 Special Media Edition as well as available standalone. In this chapter, we give you an introduction to Expression Media 2. You learn about the features of the program window and panels. You also learn how to import data from a variety of places, including files and folders on the hard drive, camera memory cards, and even the Web.

 **Microsoft has a 30-day trial version of Expression Media available for download at** www. microsoft.com/expression/products/purchase.aspx?key=media.

# Navigating the Expression Media Window

Expression Media's lineage isn't originally as a part of the Office package. This explains the fact that it doesn't share the Office look and feel as closely as the core applications such as Word, Excel, and PowerPoint do, and it doesn't always feel like an integrated part of the suite. That said, it's still an easy application to learn and use, as you will see after reading these chapters.

## Viewing the window parts

The interface for Expression Media includes many of the same standard features that most Mac applications have, including a title and menu bar and a program window with a toolbar, Status bar, and main document editing area.

The document type that Expression Media works with is called a catalog. Catalogs contain references that point to media files on your computer (and even on removable media or on the Web). The program window for Expression Media is geared toward helping you create, organize, and work with catalogs of your media files and for editing and viewing the actual contents of those media files.

Figure 28.1 shows the main program window of Expression Media 2 with an empty catalog.

### Title and menu bar

Expression Media, like most Mac programs, has a title and menu bar at the top of the screen. When the program is active, this bar shows the name of the program (Expression Media 2), along with items that make up the main menu categories. You can click any of the menu items to expand the menu to show related commands and submenus. Submenu items are identifiable by an arrow icon on the right, and selecting these items opens a new range of items. Menu items with ellipsis (three dots) at the end of the menu item open a dialog box when selected. Figure 28.2 shows the title and menu bar.

The program windows sit below the title and menu bar on the screen. A separate program window is displayed for each catalog that you have open. At the top of a program window are the program window controls and the catalog name. The program window controls, which are the three colored circle icons located at the far left side, allow you to close, minimize, and zoom the document window. (To learn more about how to use the program window controls, see Chapter 3.)

### Toolbar

Below the program window controls is the Expression Media toolbar, shown in Figure 28.3. This toolbar displays a row of tool icons for common tasks to be performed on media. To activate a feature or command, just click the associated icon. Unlike other Office programs, Expression Media does not have other toolbars, and the standard one does not change depending on context.

**FIGURE 28.1**

This is the main program window for Expression Media 2.

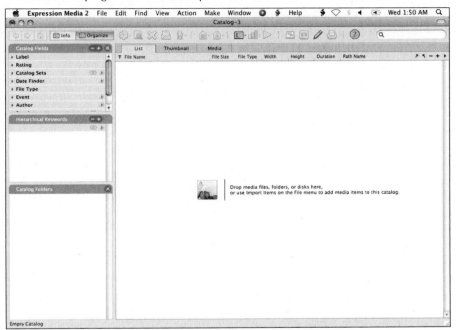

**FIGURE 28.2**

Expression Media's title and menu bar

**FIGURE 28.3**

The toolbar can be used to perform the most common actions on catalog and media files.

The Expression Media toolbar has some unique features geared toward its media-centric nature. On the right side of the toolbar is the search box, which lets you quickly find media files that match a name or keyword. To the left of the search box are the toolbar buttons, which are used to perform various common tasks with media files or catalogs. Finally, on the left side of the toolbar are tabs that you can use to select from the three view modes. The next section describes these three modes.

## View modes

The Expression Media program window can show three view modes: List view, Thumbnail view, and Media view. These three views let you switch among looking at the contents of the entire catalog, seeing thumbnail images of your media files, to viewing the media files themselves.

### List view

With List view, shown in Figure 28.4, you can see a hierarchical list of all the media files included in a catalog.

List view consists of a detailed listing of media files, arranged in a table form with columns giving you useful information about the files. Table 28.1 describes the columns shown in List view.

### FIGURE 28.4

List view shows you a list of all the files in a catalog, along with useful information about them.

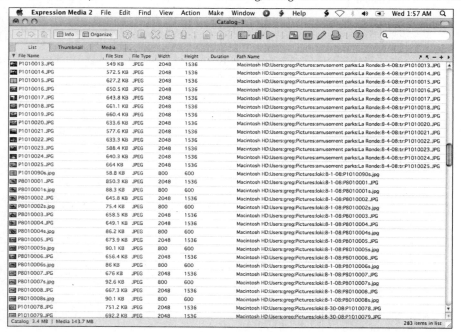

**TABLE 28.1**

# List View Columns

| Column Name | Description |
|---|---|
| File Name | The name of the media file. |
| File Size | The size of the file. This size is displayed in bytes, kilobytes (KB), megabytes (MB), or even gigabytes (GB), depending on the size. |
| File Type | The type of file it is (JPEG, PDF, QuickTime Movie, and so on). |
| Width | The width of the file. The default units are pixels; however, this can be changed in the Preferences dialog box to inches, centimeters, points, or picas. |
| Height | The height of the file. The default units are pixels; however, this can be changed in the Preferences dialog box to inches, centimeters, points, or picas. |
| Duration | The duration of play for movie files such as MPEGs, QuickTime MOV files, or even animated GIF images. |
| Path Name | The path to the image file. The path either starts at the local hard disk root or at the name of a removable disk. |

You can sort the files in List view by the values in any of the columns. Simply click the column heading, and the files are automatically sorted. Click the column header again to reverse the direction of the sort. Sorts also can be done using the View ⇨ Sort menu items, where many more options for sorting are available.

 **You can rearrange files in the list manually by dragging them to a new position in the list with the mouse. Clicking a column heading sorts them again.**

You can see more information about a particular file by pressing the Inspector key (by default, ?, although this can be changed in the Expression Media preferences on the General panel). You are shown a pop-up window that, depending on the type of file, gives you additional information, as shown in Figure 28.5. For example, video files such as MPEG or MOV files show the frame rate, running time, and information on the sound format. JPEG files show EXIF metadata, bit depth, the type of camera used to take the picture if this information is available.

## Thumbnail view

Like List view, Thumbnail view shows you all your files at a glance. Click the Thumbnail tab to activate this view. Instead of displaying image information in columns, this view displays small thumbnail versions of your files. The thumbnail images are created when you add a media file to the catalog and are quite a bit smaller than the full-sized images and videos. This handy feature helps you keep track of your images, videos, and other files, even if they are on removable drives or optical disks, because the thumbnail images are stored with the catalog and not with the original file. Figure 28.6 shows Thumbnail view.

**FIGURE 28.5**

The Inspector key can show you more information about a file at a glance.

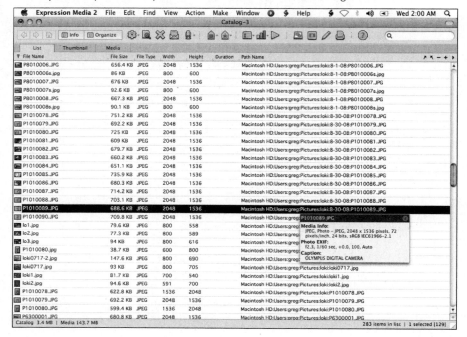

Thumbnail view is preferable over List view for browsing your files because you can see several images at a glance. This is useful if browsing over a large collection of images looking for just the right one.

> **NOTE** The Zoom In and Zoom Out functions help you switch between showing many thumbnails at once versus showing fewer, but larger views. Use the + and – buttons on the toolbar, choose View ⇨ Zoom In or View ⇨ Zoom Out, or press ⌘++ (plus) or ⌘+- (minus) to zoom in or out, respectively.

You can sort the files displayed in Thumbnail view just as you can in List view, by using the View ⇨ Sort submenu options. Files are displayed in order from left to right, from top to bottom.

**FIGURE 28.6**

Thumbnail view shows you small visual representations of your images.

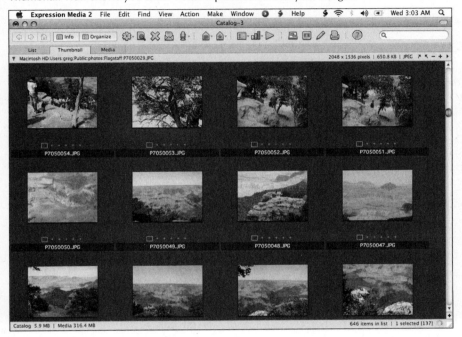

### Media view

While List view and Thumbnail view are useful for browsing the catalog contents, the actual meat and potatoes—viewing the full size content of your media files—is done in Media view, shown in Figure 28.7.

Media view is where Expression Media goes from being just a cataloging program to being a media viewing program as well. In Media view, you can see the full-sized photo, video, or even a representation of a document or HTML page from the catalog. You can activate Media view in several ways. Double-click a media file in List view or Thumbnail view to open the file in Media view, or simply select a file in one of the other views and click the Media button.

If the file is available on your system, it is loaded in Media view, where it can be manipulated (in the case of images) or played (in the case of audio/video files).

---

**FIGURE 28.7**

With Media view, you can see the full-sized file.

## Annotation panels

Info Aside from the information provided in the List, Thumbnail, and Media views, Expression Media also provides two annotation panels—the Info and Organize panels, accessible by buttons on the toolbar. These panels let you view information and metadata associated with an individual file, in the case of the Info panel, or with the entire catalog, in the case of the Organize panel.

## Info panel

The Info panel, shown in Figure 28.8, provides a way to see at a glance all the information and metadata associated with a particular media file. On this panel, you can see the file size and dimensions, timestamps, keywords, color depth and resolution, encoding type, photo EXIF (EXchangeable Image file Format), and more, depending on the type of file it is. To activate the Info panel, click the Info button on the toolbar.

On the top of the Info panel, the window shows a categorized collection of information about the currently selected file, organized in groups. The bottom contains a Caption section, which by default is also pulled from the file's metadata if available. You can enter a value to override this if you like.

Table 28.2 describes the groups that are presented in the Info panel.

**FIGURE 28.8**

You can use the Info panel to view metadata and stats for media files.

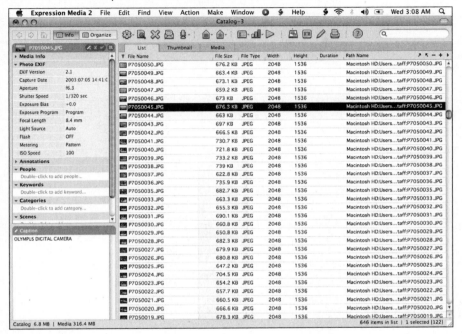

**TABLE 28.2**

# Info Panel Groups

| Category Name | Description |
| --- | --- |
| Media Info | This is the general group that contains most of the information about the media file. It displays the media type, file type, encoding, size, resolution, bit depth, color space, and more. For audio and video files, it shows information specific to that file type including duration, frame rate, audio channels, and more. |
| Photo EXIF | For digital photo files (JPEG, RAW), this group displays information about the photo, including aperture, exposure, shutter speed, focal length, and more. |
| Movie Tracks | For movie type files (MPEG, MOV, animated GIF files), this group shows information about video and audio tracks in the file, including encoding information, size, frame rate, and run time. |
| Annotations | This group provides a number of editable fields that can be used to identify your file in Expression Media. Fields you can add include author info, genre, title, ratings, credits, URL, and location. |

*continued*

**TABLE 28.2** *(continued)*

| Category Name | Description |
|---|---|
| People | This annotation group lets you add the names of people associated with the file. You can add names directly or double-click to activate a drop-down list to choose previously used names. Annotation groups can be used to organize or view files in the Organize panel. Use this to store the names of people shown in a photo or home video, for example, to make it easy to find pictures of them later. |
| Keywords | This annotation group lets you add keywords associated with the file. You can add keywords directly or double-click to activate a drop-down list to choose previously used names. |
| Categories | This annotation group lets you can define categories in which to organize your files. Examples of categories might include Vacation, Birthday Parties, Family, and so on. |
| Scenes | This annotation group is used to describe the scene of a photo. This is intended to specify one or more terms from the IPTC "Scene-NewsCodes" list; however, Expression Media allows for arbitrary values to be entered here. |
| Subject Codes | This annotation group is used to describe the subject code of a photo. This is intended to specify one or more terms from the IPTC "Subject-NewsCodes" list; however, Expression Media allows for arbitrary values to be entered here. |

**NOTE** **The IPTC (International Press Telecommunications Council) defined a set of metadata values that make up part of the XMP Core metadata standard. You can find more information regarding the IPTC NewsCodes at** www.iptc.org/NewsCodes**.**

The Info panel lets you decide which fields and groups to display. Click the Configure List button at the top right of the Info panel to open a submenu with commands for setting the configuration. Follow these steps to customize your Info panel display:

1. **Click the Configure List button at the upper-right corner of the Info panel.**

   The Configure List submenu opens, as shown in Figure 28.9.

2. **Choose Show/Hide Fields.**

   The Info: Show/Hide Fields dialog box appears, as shown in Figure 28.10.

3. **Uncheck the fields that you don't want shown on the Info panel.**

4. **Click the Close button on the dialog box's title bar.**

5. **Choose a save option from the Configure List submenu.**

   ■ Save this configuration as… lets you specify a name for the configuration that you can reload later.

   ■ Save as Default makes this the default configuration.

---

**FIGURE 28.9**

Use the Configure List submenu to customize your Info panel display.

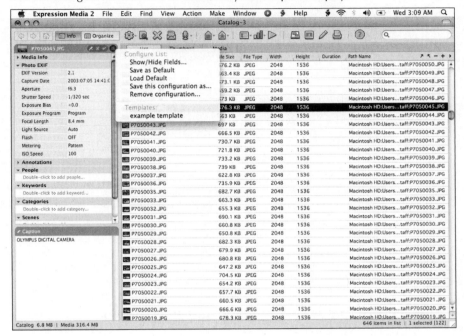

---

**FIGURE 28.10**

You can choose which fields you want to show or hide.

You also can save default values for your metadata as a metadata template, using a feature called Autofill. This lets you choose fields with entered values to save, so they can easily and efficiently be applied to other media files. Follow these steps to create a metadata template from the metadata entered for the current file:

1. **Click the Autofill button at the top of the Info panel.**

   The Autofill submenu opens, as shown in Figure 28.11.

**FIGURE 28.11**

You can save file metadata as a template, so it can be applied to other files.

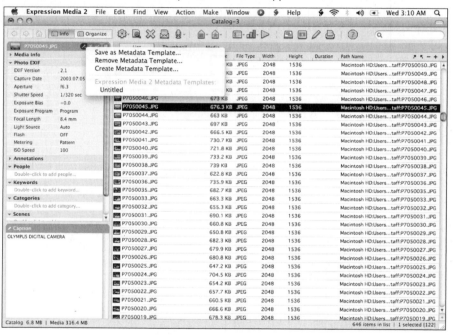

2. **Choose Save Metadata Template.**

   The Save Metadata Template dialog box appears, as shown in Figure 28.12.

3. **Uncheck the fields that you don't want to save as part of the template.**

4. **Click the Save button.**

5. **Enter a name for the template.**

   The template is saved and is now available as an option on the Autofill menu.

**FIGURE 28.12**

Choose metadata fields to include as part of the template.

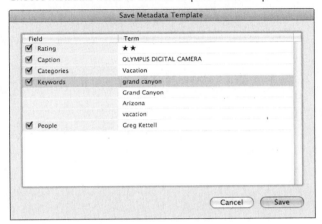

You can create a metadata template from scratch, as well. This allows you to enter values for all the fields that you want to include without needing to have these values already set for the current file. Follow these steps:

1. **Click the Autofill button at the top of the Info panel.**

   The Autofill submenu opens.

2. **Choose Create Metadata Template.**

   The Save Metadata Template dialog box appears, as shown in Figure 28.13. This time it includes all fields.

3. **Double-click a field, and enter a value.** Repeat for each value you want to add.

4. **Click the Save button.**

5. **Enter a name for the template.**

   The template is saved and is now available as an option on the Autofill menu.

**FIGURE 28.13**

You can create a metadata template from scratch.

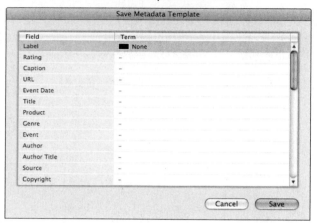

## Organize panel

 The Organize panel, shown in Figure 28.14, lets you take the individual metadata entered in the Info panel and use it to organize your catalog. You can use this panel to sort files based on metadata, group files together, or even filter the files shown based on specific metadata criteria. To activate the Organize panel, click the Organize button on the Expression Media toolbar. You may notice that you can only have either the Info panel or the Organize panel open at one time; opening one closes the other.

The Organize panel is arranged in three smaller panels: Catalog Fields, Hierarchical Keywords, and Catalog Folders. They are described here.

### Catalog Fields panel

The Catalog Fields section lets you filter your catalog's List view or Thumbnail view using the metadata fields that you entered on the Info panel. This panel shows a list of metadata groups that are expandable to show the individual metadata fields in that group. Each field shows a count of the number of media files with that particular metadata attribute.

The primary use of the Catalog Fields panel is to filter the media files in the catalog. You can do this by expanding the groups and clicking individual fields to select them. Select multiple fields by holding down the Option key as you click the selection dot to the right of the field.

You can customize the Catalog Fields display by choosing which fields to include in the display. Follow these steps to show or hide fields:

1. **Click the Configure List button at the top of the Catalog Fields panel.**
2. **Choose Show/Hide Fields from the drop-down menu.**

   The Organize: Show/Hide Fields dialog box is displayed, as shown in Figure 28.15.
3. **Check or uncheck the fields you want to show or hide.**

   The panel automatically updates in real time as you check or uncheck fields.
4. **Click the Close button at the top left of the dialog box.**

**FIGURE 28.14**

The Organize panel lets you group, sort, and filter your catalogs based on file metadata.

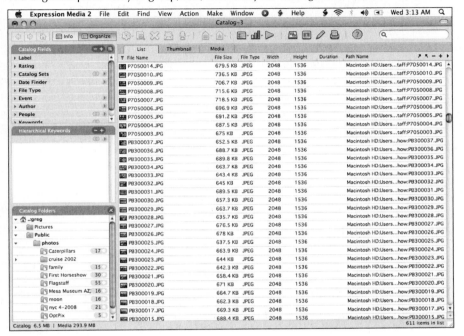

**FIGURE 28.15**

You can configure the Catalog Fields panel to display only fields that you are interested in.

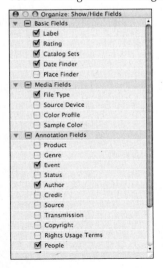

5. **If you want this to become the default view, choose Save as Default from the Configure List submenu.**

You can add new terms to fields that allow for custom values. Follow these steps to add a term:

1. **Click the Plus button at the top of the Catalog Fields panel.**

   The Add Term dialog box opens, as shown in Figure 28.16.

**FIGURE 28.16**

Add terms for customizable fields.

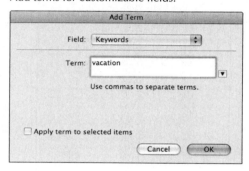

2. **Choose a field in the Field drop-down menu.**

   Fields that are hidden are not shown in this list.

3. **Enter a new value for this field.**

4. **Check the box if you want to apply this new keyword to any media files that might be selected in the List or Thumbnail views.**

5. **Click OK to add the term.**

You can use the Catalog Fields panel to apply fields to files en masse. Simply select all the files you want to assign a term to in List view or Thumbnail view, and drag them to the term that you would like to apply. You also can color-code your catalog files by dragging them to a color in the Label group.

### Hierarchical Keywords panel

The Hierarchical Keywords panel allows you not only to assign keywords to a file, but also to organize them into a nested hierarchy. For example, you could create a keyword called "vacation" for vacation photos, and add sub terms for your individual trips to "Europe," "Hawaii," and "Mexico," for example.

Do the following to add hierarchical keywords to your catalog:

1. **Click the plus sign button at the top of the Hierarchical Keywords panel.**

   The Add Keyword dialog box opens, as shown in Figure 28.17.

2. **Type the name of the keyword.**

3. **Use the Within menu to choose a parent keyword for this one.** Choose None if you want it to be at the top of the hierarchy. If this is the first keyword you are adding, None is the only option available.

4. **Check the box to apply this keyword to any files that you have selected in either List view or Thumbnail view.**

**FIGURE 28.17**

You can add hierarchical keywords to your media files, allowing you to organize your files.

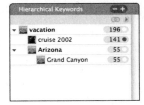

5. **Click OK to add the keyword.**

To apply keywords to media files, simply drag them to the keyword that you want to apply. All keywords higher than that one in the hierarchy are automatically applied to the file as well.

There are two options for filtering based on selected keywords. You can filter based on a union of selected keywords, which shows all files matching all selected keywords. Alternatively, you can choose to display an intersection of selected keywords, which shows only files matching all the selected keywords. Follow these steps to choose a filtering option:

1. **Click the arrow button at the top of the Hierarchical Keywords panel.**

   The submenu shown in Figure 28.18 appears.

**FIGURE 28.18**

You can choose a filtering option for selected hierarchical keywords.

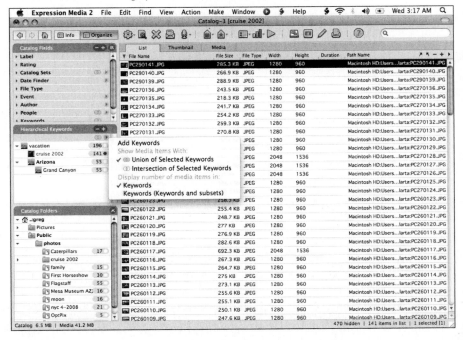

2. **Choose the filtering option that you want:**
   - Union of selected keywords filters the catalog to show media files that match any of the selected keywords.
   - Intersection of selected keywords filters the catalog to show media files that match all the selected keywords.

3. **Select multiple keywords by clicking them while holding down the Option key.**

4. **Right-click and choose Show Media Items.** All selected keywords show a green dot on the right to indicate that they are selected, and List view or Thumbnail view shows the filtered files.

### Catalog Folders panel

The Catalog Folders panel shows you all the folders that are included in the current catalog. This is displayed as a tree. If a folder contains subfolders, you can expand the list to show them as well, as shown in Figure 28.19.

**FIGURE 28.19**

Use the Catalog Folders panel to organize and update the catalog listing by folder.

If a folder contains cataloged media files, you see a count of the number of files on the right. You can click the dot in the oval surrounding this value to filter the display of the catalog to show only files in this particular folder.

You can enable catalog-wide folder watching to monitor folders that contain media in your catalog. You can either set up Expression Media to watch any number of folders and alert you when new media items appear in them, or have Expression Media automatically import any new items into your catalog.

Right-click a folder to display more options for a folder. Some of the more useful ones are described here:

- Show Media Files filters the List view display to show only files in this folder.
- Select Media Items selects all the media files in List view. You can then perform an action on all the files together.
- Update Folder Now automatically adds or removes files from the catalog that have been added or removed from the folder.
- Switch Auto-Update On instructs Expression Media to watch this folder for new or removed files and automatically updates the catalog accordingly.

Click the Catalog Folder Watching button to customize the display of the Catalog Folders panel:

- Choose a setting for Update Folders: Never, Every Minute, or Every 5 Minutes. This affects how often the Auto-Update option checks for changes.

- Check the Union of Folder Hierarchies item to have the file number displayed for each folder also include the files in subfolders and allow you to filter based on this.

- Check the Trim Folder Hierarchy item to filter the folder list to include only those folders currently in the catalog. This is the default setting. Uncheck this item to show all folders on the computer.

### Status bar

The Status bar is located at the bottom of the program window. This bar, shown in Figure 28.20, shows you some important statistical information about the catalog.

On the left of the Status bar, the size of the catalog file (including thumbnails) is shown. To the right of that, the total size of all the media files included in the catalog is displayed.

The right side of the Status bar shows you information on the number of files shown. If you have any files filtered using a metadata filter or a search filter, the number of hidden files is shown. The number of files that are currently visible follows. If you have any files selected, that number is displayed as well, with the file's position in the catalog list displayed if only a single file is selected.

---

**FIGURE 28.20**

The Status bar shows statistical information about the catalog.

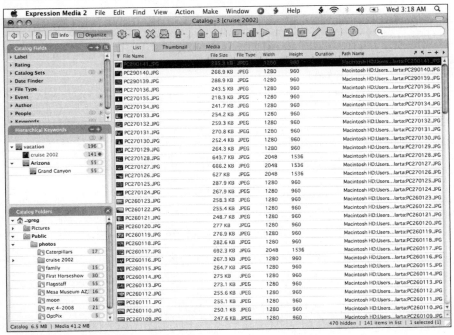

## Importing digital media

Naturally, an important part of organizing media into catalogs is letting the program know about the files to begin with. Expression Media's powerful media import facility helps you easily get the files you want into the catalog. You can import in a variety of ways, and you can choose from several different device types. This section explores these options.

### Importing from files or folders

Perhaps the most common place to import files from is your computer's hard drive. Expression Media gives you the flexibility to bring single files or entire folders into a catalog. Follow these steps to import a file or folder:

1. **Choose File ⇨ Import Items ⇨ From Files/Folders.**

   The Choose a media file or folder dialog box opens, as shown in Figure 28.21.

2. **Browse for the media file or folder that you want to import, and click it to select it.**

   Select multiple files or folders by holding down the Command key as you click.

   You can specify import criteria such as partial filename, size, or time last used.

3. **Click the Choose button to begin importing the file or folder.**

**FIGURE 28.21**

You can import individual media files or entire folders.

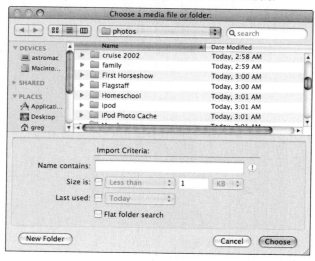

Another way to import files and folders into a catalog is to simply drag and drop them from the Finder onto the Expression Media Window.

## Importing catalogs

You can import directly from another Expression Media catalog. This automatically adds every file in a catalog to the current catalog, with the exception of files that are already common to both catalogs. This can be a great way to combine catalogs into a single one. Follow these steps to import a catalog:

1. **Choose File ➪ Import Items ➪ From Catalog File.**

   The Choose a catalog file dialog box opens, as shown in Figure 28.22.

2. **Browse for the catalog file (with an .ivc extension) that you want to import, and select it.**

3. **Click the Open button to begin importing the files.**

---

**FIGURE 28.22**

You can import entire catalogs of media files into the current one.

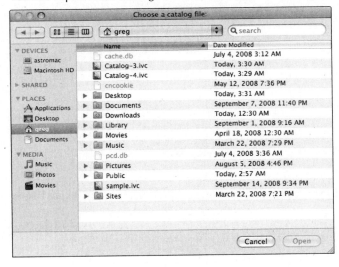

---

## Importing from the Spotlight feature

OS X has a powerful search capability built in called Spotlight that makes it easy to find files on your hard drive, based on their filenames or their contents. Expression Media has the ability to harness Spotlight to find files to import. To import from a spotlight search, do the following:

1. **Choose File ➪ Import Items ➪ From Spotlight Query.**

   The Run Spotlight Query dialog box opens, as shown in Figure 28.23.

2. **Type a word or phrase to search the hard drive.**

   Spotlight automatically finds files as you are typing, matching both filename and contents.

   Check the Add results to new catalog button to have Expression Media create a new catalog from the query.

3. Click the Import button to begin importing the files into the catalog.

 When you import using a Spotlight query, you have to import all the files that it finds. You cannot select individual files from the list.

---

**FIGURE 28.23**

Use the OS X Spotlight query to search for files to import.

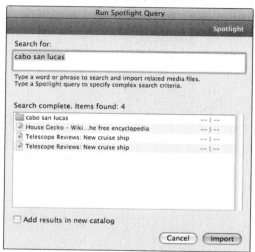

### Downloading and importing from cameras, removable disks, or memory cards

Expression Media not only knows how to retrieve files from your computer's hard drive, it also is adept at retrieving files from external media such as digital cameras, removable disks, or flash memory sticks and cards. To import from a removable disk or flash memory card, do the following:

1. **Attach the device to your computer.**
2. **Choose File ⇨ Import Items ⇨ From Disk.**

   The Download from Disk dialog box opens, as shown in Figure 28.24.
3. **Choose a source device from the Source list.**
4. **Click the Download list to open a tree view of the device's file system.**
5. **Locate and click the files or folders to select them for import.** Select multiple files or folders by holding down the Option button as you click.
6. **Click the Options button to set options for the import.**
7. **Choose a destination folder.** You can choose a folder using the following options:
   - **Download folder:** This places the file in the Expression Media 2 folder, located in your Documents folder.
   - **Today's folder:** Similar to the Download folder, this option lets Expression Media create another folder named after today's date in which to place the file.
   - **Original folder hierarchy:** The folders are copied directly from the source disk and placed in the download folder.

**FIGURE 28.24**

You can import directly from a camera, disk, or memory card.

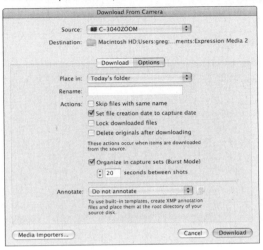

8. **Rename the file, if you like.** If you are importing multiple files, a sequential number is appended to the end of this filename.

9. **Choose an action to perform by checking one of the boxes.** Actions include skipping the importation of files with the same name, locking downloaded files, and deleting original files from the source device after downloading.

10. **Choose an annotation option.** You can use an annotation template to automatically assign metadata values to the file in the catalog.

11. **Click the Download button to begin downloading and importing the file.**

Importing from a camera is very similar to importing from a disk; however, you have some additional options:

■ The Download button shows thumbnails of the photos on the camera as opposed to the folder tree shown with a disk.

■ An Action is available that lets you have the downloaded photos use the capture date as provided by the camera for the file creation date.

■ If your camera supports a "burst mode" to rapidly take many pictures, you can have these bursts of files grouped automatically. Enter a time in seconds to determine whether pictures were captures using burst mode.

### Importing from the Web

You aren't limited to your own devices as a source for media files. In fact, there are no limits, because Expression Media can download media files directly from Web sites. There is one caveat, however; you can't just enter a URL for a Web site and have Expression Media download files from it. When using the Web import feature, you must specify a URL to the image file itself. Follow these steps to download and import media files from the Internet:

1.  Choose File ⇨ Import Items ⇨ From URL.

    The Download from URL dialog box opens, as shown in Figure 28.25.

**FIGURE 28.25**

You can download and import media files directly from a Web URL.

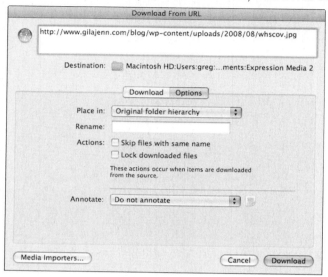

2.  **Click the Download button.**

3.  **Type the complete URL for an image that you want to download.** The URL for an image can be obtained from a Web browser.

    ■ If you use Safari, you can right-click an image and choose Copy Image Address.

    ■ If you use Firefox, right-click the image and choose Copy Image Location.

4.  **Click the Options button to set options for the import.**

5.  **Choose a destination folder.** You can choose a folder using the following options:

    ■ **Download folder:** This places the file in the Expression Media 2 folder, located in your Documents folder.

    ■ **Today's folder:** This is similar to the Download folder, but Expression Media creates another folder named after today's date to place the file in.

    ■ **Original folder hierarchy:** Folders are created in the download folder to match the structure of the folders from the original Web site.

6.  **Rename the file, if you like.** If you are importing multiple files, a sequential number is appended to the end of this filename.

7.  **Choose an action to perform by checking one of the boxes.** Two actions can be performed on Web imported images: You can skip the importation of files with the same name, and you can lock downloaded files.

8. **Choose an annotation option.** You can use an annotation template to automatically assign metadata values to the file in the catalog.

9. **Click the Download button to begin downloading and importing the file.**

Another way to import files from the Web is, in fact, the simplest. You can simply drag the file from the Web page onto the catalog you want to import it into, and the Download from URL dialog box opens automatically to let you specify the import options just as if you entered the URL by hand.

# Summary

In this chapter, you were introduced to the newest member of the Office 2008 suite. You learned that Expression Media is a Digital Access Management (DAM) program that can be used to catalog and organize the media files on your computer. Expression Media isn't limited to cataloging images; in fact, it is more than capable of recognizing a huge assortment of different file types, including images, PDF files, documents, audio and video files, HTML files, and more.

You learned that Expression Media lets you create catalogs, which are files that contain information about media files on your computer. Expression Media provides three different views for catalogs, ranging from the List view, which shows a listing of files in the catalog, to Thumbnail view, which shows small image representations of these files, and finally to Media view, which lets you view the media file in its full form.

You were shown how to annotate media files, by adding keywords and other identifying information. You saw how to control the display of files in the catalog by filtering based on folder, partial filename, and annotation terms. Finally, you learned about the various ways that Expression Media can import media files into catalogs, including downloading them from other devices such as a camera or the Internet.

# Chapter 29

# Working with Catalogs

The real power of Microsoft's Expression Media is its ability to catalog your digital media files. This cataloging process does not involve the actual original media files; rather, it stores links to the original files and creates a visual log of the data. This makes viewing your digital media content by thumbnail images easy. Because you aren't searching through the original files, the process is quick and painless. This then allows you to store your media files in multiple locations, yet still search through your inventory from a single spot. How handy is that?

To put it more succinctly, Expression Media is a visual database. Because Expression Media can work with more than 100 digital media file formats, you can easily create catalogs of everything you typically work with from digital cameras, CDs, DVDs, and the Internet. The realm of digital media includes photographs, music files, video files, PDF files, and so forth. You no longer have to worry about finding a photo or video clip among all the various folders, drives, or media storage devices associated with your computer. Instead, with a catalog of your content, you can quickly see what you have and find out where it's located. In this chapter, you learn how to create and work with Expression Media catalogs.

## Understanding Catalogs

A catalog in Expression Media is simply a collection of thumbnails of your digital media files; much like a folder stores actual files, a catalog stores thumbnails, which are links to the original files. Expression Media stores the digital media thumbnails and information about the media, such as its location. You can pretty much sum up Expression Media as being all about storing information, and information only. A catalog stores information about each file, and you can create as many catalogs as you want. A catalog can contain up to 128,000 files or up to 1.8GB of space.

**NOTE** We keep using the term "thumbnails" for pictures. In case you were wondering, *thumbnails* are reduced-sized versions of your photographs. The reduced size makes it easy to scan them at a glance to see what they are.

The beauty of Expression Media is that the original media files do not have to be present. For example, if you're storing your vacation photos on a CD, the CD does not have to be in your CD drive in order to view the images. When the images are added to a catalog in Expression Media, you can still view them as thumbnails. You cannot, however, view the images as larger sizes without access to the original files. There's always a catch, isn't there? Still, the ability to view all your photos without dragging out the original CD or DVD can be a big plus, allowing you to see what you have and help you label it for easy cataloging and locating. This also means that if you delete the original file, the catalog can't help you retrieve it. It can only remind you of the image you once had.

After you create a catalog, you can get down to the nitty-gritty business of adding captions, labels, and annotations, browsing through your media, and maybe even doing a little image-editing. You see, Expression Media not only helps you organize images and other digital media, it also features editing controls and features for creating slides shows and contact sheets. You need access to the original files in order to engage in any image editing techniques.

One of your biggest tasks with Expression Media is deciding how you want to catalog your digital media. Do you want to put everything into one big catalog, or do you want smaller subject-specific catalogs? Most users decide to catalog their media in one of these ways:

- **Chronologically:** You can organize your digital media by date and time.
- **By subject:** You can organize your media by subject matter, such as vacation, product pictures, or portraits.
- **By project:** You can organize your media by project name or type, such as sales presentation or client name.
- **By file type:** You can organize your media by file type, such as all your photo files in one catalog or all the music files together.

These are just a few ways. You can probably think of a few more.

## Saving a catalog

If you haven't imported your digital media yet, back up to Chapter 28 to learn how. When you're ready to commit your imported images to a catalog, follow these steps:

1. **Choose File ⇨ Save As.**

   The Save Catalog As dialog box appears, as shown in Figure 29.1.

2. **Type a name for the catalog in the Save As box.**

3. **Navigate to the folder or drive to which you want to store the file.**

   If the full Save window does not appear, click the Expand arrow button next to the Save As field.

4. **Click Save.**

   The photos are saved in the new catalog.

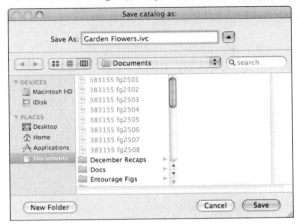

Use the Save Catalog As dialog box to save a catalog file.

Remember that the photos are just links to the original files. Saving the images in a catalog does not remove them from their original locations.

You also can create catalogs using files from within other catalogs. To do so, follow these steps:

1. **In Thumbnail view, select the images you want to move to a new catalog.**

   To select images in a group, click the first image, and press and hold the Shift key while clicking the last image in the group.

   To select non-contiguous images, click the first image, and press and hold the ⌘ key while clicking other images.

2. **Control+click one of the selected images, and choose Move to New Catalog.**

   Expression Media immediately moves the image to a new catalog.

   You can now save the new catalog file.

## Finding catalogs

You can access catalogs you save in numerous ways. You can quickly open a catalog you recently viewed using the Open Recent menu. Like the Open Recent menu in the other Office programs, this menu lets you view a list of recently used files. To view the menu, choose File ⇨ Open Recent and click the one you want to open it.

## Protecting Your Catalogs

**Y**ou can protect your catalogs from unauthorized viewing by assigning a password. When you attempt to view the catalog later, Expression Media prompts you for the password. To set a password, choose File ⇨ Catalog Info to open the catalog's Info dialog box. Click the Set Password button, and type a password. Whatever you do, remember it. If you lose it, you won't be able to access the catalog again.

You also can use the Catalog Finder, shown in Figure 29.2, to help you locate catalogs you stored with Expression Media. Follow these steps to use the Catalog Finder:

1. **Choose File ⇨ Open Recent ⇨ Catalog Finder.**

   This opens the Catalog Finder dialog box, shown in Figure 29.2.

---

**FIGURE 29.2**

You can use the Catalog Finder to look for catalogs on your hard drive and other storage devices.

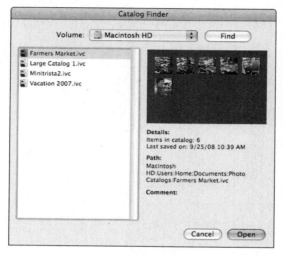

2. **Select the volume you want to search, such as your computer's hard drive, and click the Find button.**

   Expression Media immediately displays all the saved catalogs found within.

3. **To open a catalog, select it and click Open.**

# Viewing Catalogs

After you've imported some photos into Expression Media, you'll want to sort through the images and find the ones you want to keep and the ones you want to throw away, or you might want to catalog them all. As an efficient and versatile editing application, Expression Media allows you to look through your photos using the three view modes: List, Thumbnail, and Media. You learned about these modes in Chapter 28, but here's a refresher for you. List view displays a simple list of your images along with basic information about each. List view is useful for sorting or locating images, but it doesn't help you view them. To view images, use Thumbnail view, which displays thumbnails of your images as shown in Figure 29.3. To view a single image, use Media view. If you're just working on catalogs at the moment, Thumbnail view is the way to go.

**FIGURE 29.3**

Use Thumbnail view to peruse your imported images.

To open a catalog, choose File ⇨ Open Catalog. This displays the Choose a category file dialog box, which looks suspiciously like all the other Choose a File dialog boxes you've used in the past for opening every kind of Office file. Simply navigate to the catalog you want to view, and click the Open button. Once open, you can click the Thumbnail view tab to see thumbnails of the contents.

You can open multiple catalogs in Expression Media. To close a catalog at any time, click the window's Close button or choose File ⇨ Close.

Selecting media items in your catalogs is extremely easy:

- To select a single item, just click its thumbnail in Thumbnail view.
- To select adjacent items, click the first thumbnail, and then hold down the Shift key while clicking the last item in the group. Expression Media selects all the items in between.
- To select non-adjacent items, press and hold the ⌘ key while clicking thumbnails.
- To select everything, choose Edit ⇨ Select All.

Now that you know how to select items, you're ready to start performing all kinds of tasks in your catalog. You can do all kinds of things to your digital media items from Thumbnail view, including changing how the items appear in the view window. For example, you can use the tiny buttons on the tab's Header bar to view information about the selected thumbnail, as well as commands for rotating images and increasing or decreasing the size of the thumbnail display. Figure 29.4 points out these various buttons.

**FIGURE 29.4**

The Header bar in Thumbnail view shows information about the selected thumbnail as well as buttons to making the thumbnails appear larger or smaller in the window.

Here's what you can do in Thumbnail view:

- Depending on how many images are displayed in Thumbnail view, you can use the scroll bars on the right side of the view window to move your view up or down.
- To view information about a particular image, select it and click the Info button on the toolbar.
- To assign a color label to a selected image, click the Assign Label button and choose a color.
- To assign a rating, click the Rate Media button and choose a rating.
- To delete an image, click the Trash Selection button.
- To move an item, just drag it. You can drag items from one open catalog to another or drag them onto the desktop or into another folder.
- To invert the media in the catalog, click the Invert button, the tiny pyramid icon in the upper-left corner of the Thumbnail view window.
- To rotate a thumbnail, select it and click one of the Rotate buttons located at the top-right corner of the Thumbnail view window.

## Marking media

We touched briefly on assigning a color label or rating in the preceding bulleted list, but let's look at the various ways you can mark your digital media items in more depth. First, you may be wondering why you would want to mark your media items. Classifying your media is one of the important ways in which you can organize your digital photos and other media files, making them easier to locate and work with later. You can use various marking techniques to mark your favorites, rate them using stars, and label them using colors.

## Assigning a star rating

You can use a star-based rating system for ranking items in a catalog. Star rankings include one star to five stars, or you can apply no stars at all, which is the default setting. To rate an item, select it and use any of these methods:

- Click the Rate Media button on the toolbar, and choose a rating, as shown in Figure 29.5.
- Click and drag the item to the Rating section of the Catalog Fields, and drop it on the star rating you want to assign.
- Click the star rating bar directly below the thumbnail item to set the number of stars for the rating.
- Press Control+ and choose a number based on the star rankings (1 to 5), such as Control+5.

**FIGURE 29.5**

Apply a star ranking to rate your digital media items. To remove a rating, choose None from the Rate Media button's drop-down menu.

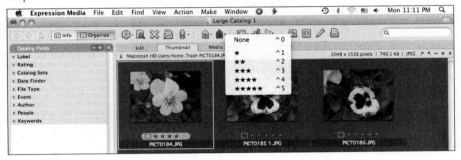

## Assigning a color label

Color labels are a great way to quickly apply a visual cue about a digital media item. It's up to you to decide what the color labels mean. For example, you may choose to mark questionable photos with a gray color label and the best photos with yellow. To apply a color label to a thumbnail item, select it and use any of these methods:

- Click the Assign Label button on the toolbar, and choose a label, as shown in Figure 29.6.
- Click and drag the item to the Label section of the Catalog Fields, and drop it on the color label you want to assign.
- Click the Color Label icon directly below the thumbnail, and select a color from the pop-up menu.
- Press a number key, 1 through 9, to assign a color.

You also can customize the labels by typing specific label names to go along with the colors. To do this, choose Expression Media ⇨ Preferences ⇨ Labels and Colors. This opens the Labels and Colors preferences dialog box where you can replace the color text labels with your own label text, as shown in Figure 29.7.

**FIGURE 29.6**

Use color labels to categorize your digital media items.

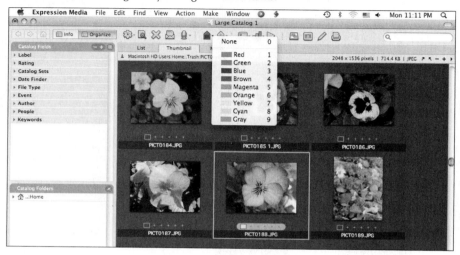

**FIGURE 29.7**

You can customize your color labels in this dialog box.

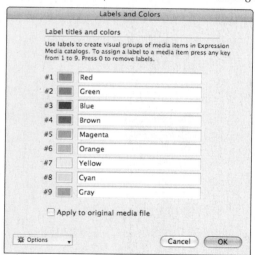

## Using the Light Table

Expression Media features a very nice tool for examining a single image or comparing several images. To view a single image, click it and choose View➪ Light Table, or click the View in Light Table button on the toolbar. You also can select which images you want to compare and then open them all onto the Light Table.

When you first open the feature, a list of keyboard shortcuts appears in a Shortcuts panel, as shown in Figure 29.8. Click the Close button to exit the Shortcuts panel. If you don't want to see the panel next time, just deselect the Always show this panel when entering Light Table check box at the bottom of the panel. If you close it and need help again later, Control+click anywhere in the window and choose Shortcuts.

The default display mode for the Light Table is to show a toolbar at the bottom of each image, as shown in Figure 29.9. If viewing more than one image, you can display the images in a grid layout, a landscape layout, or a portrait layout. To change the layout, press G, L, or P, the first letter of each layout style. You also can hide the toolbar at the bottom of each image by pressing T.

You can perform the following tasks in the Light Table mode:

- If the Light Table shows only one image, you can click the ↑ or ↓ buttons to move to the previous or next image in the catalog.
- To remove the selected image from the catalog, click the tiny icon showing a circle with a slash in the middle, and then click Move to Trash or Remove from Catalog.
- To label an image, click the Label icon and choose a new color label.
- To rate an image, click the Rating icon and choose a star rating.
- To rotate an image, click a Rotate icon left or right.
- To zoom an image in or out, click the Zoom icon and choose a zoom command from the pop-up menu.
- To exit the Light Table, click Esc.

Jump through the Shortcuts panel to get to the Light Table.

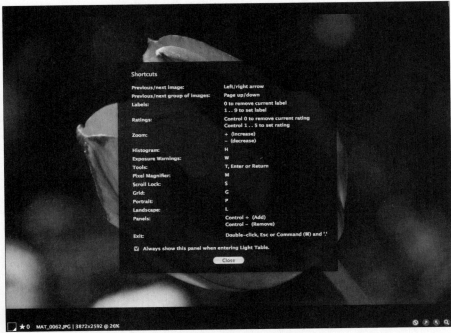

**FIGURE 29.9**

You can view a single image or multiple images using the Light Table.

# Organizing Catalogs

Acting as a window to your digital media files, you can perform a variety of tasks on your media items to help organize and categorize them. You can move them around in the catalog, rename files, filter them, and much more. This section shows you a few handy techniques to send you on your way to total organization, or at least a close facsimile.

## Moving media

You can move your media items around within Thumbnail view or List view to change the order in which they appear in a catalog. An easy way to move a selected image is to drag it to a new location and drop it. You also can use the View menu to move an item to a new location in the catalog, to the top of the catalog, to the bottom, or to a new catalog, or you can duplicate the same move you just performed on another item. Click the View menu, and choose a move option.

## File renaming

You can rename media items in your catalogs. Obviously, names are the best way to identify the content of your photos and other digital media. As your collection grows, however, naming can be a real chore. As you've probably already discovered, most cameras utilize a sequential naming system, such as pic010, pic011, pic012. This works well when you're moving items around, helping you to avoid any duplication.

To make the naming more useful, consider utilizing a sequential naming system that tells more about the image, such as who took it, the subject matter, the date, and the order. Here are some examples:

```
sarahj_080815_portrait_02
job016_20090514_005
williams_adams_wedding_090523_skg_120
```

To rename an item, click the filename and type a new name. Keep in mind that filenames are case sensitive, and you can choose to set lowercase, uppercase, or title case (first characters are capitalized).

## Batch renaming

Speaking of renaming, you can rename your catalog items in batches. This allows you to rename all the items in one fell swoop. You can use the Batch Rename dialog box to rename items by date, text, sequential numbering, and filename. To rename a batch of items, follow these steps:

1. **Select the media items you want to rename.**
2. **Choose Action ⇨ Batch Rename.**

   The Batch Rename dialog box opens, as shown in Figure 29.10.

**FIGURE 29.10**

Use the Batch Rename dialog box to rename media items in a batch.

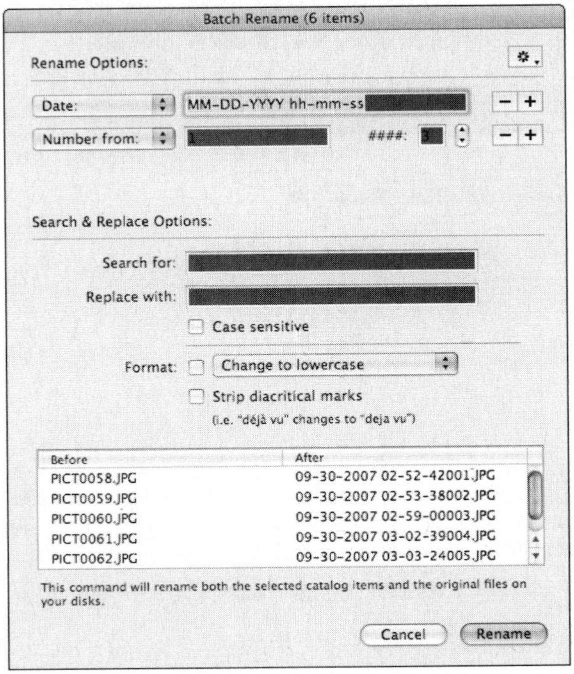

3. Under the Rename Options, click the first pop-up window and choose a function (Text, Date, Number from, or File name).

4. Click the tag field, and make any changes to the format as needed.

   Optionally, you can add an additional rename option field.

5. Click the Number from field, and define the starting increment for sequential numbering.

6. Click in the ### field, and specify the number of digits for the sequential numbering.

7. Click the Format check box and pop-up menu to define a format case: lowercase, upper-case, or title case.

   The Preview area shows what your numbering system looks like.

8. Click Rename to rename the files.

If you want to rename items by searching and replacing their filenames, you can engage the Search for and Replace with fields in the Batch Rename dialog box. This technique is similar to the Find and Replace commands found in Word.

## Searching through catalogs

You can easily conduct a search through your catalog to locate a specific media item. The quickest way to conduct a search is to click in the Search box on the toolbar, type the word or name you're looking for, and press Return.

For more detailed searches, use the Find dialog box, shown in Figure 29.11. It offers more options for searching, such as searching multiple catalogs, searching for specific elements in a media file, and specifying what to do after the item is found. To open the dialog box, choose Find ⇨ Find.

**FIGURE 29.11**

You can use the Find dialog box to conduct more detailed searches through your catalogs.

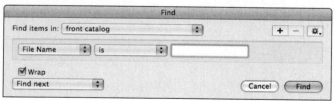

## Filtering catalogs

You can filter the way in which media items are displayed in Thumbnail or List views using the Catalog Fields in the Organize panel. Click the attribute field you want to use as a filter, and drill down to the data to filter by, such as an exact date or a specific file type, as shown in Figure 29.12. Using the Organize panel, you can choose to display items that match the attribute you specify and double-click the attribute.

You also can sort your catalog using the Sort button on the toolbar. Click the button, and choose a sort option.

**FIGURE 29.12**

Use the Organize panel to filter your catalogs by attributes.

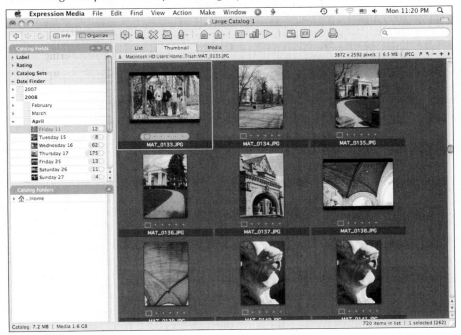

# Viewing Slide Shows

Expression Media offers a Slide Show feature that turns your photographs into a slide show with cut transitions and navigation buttons. You also can set slide show options to control how the show is presented.

To start a slide show from any catalog, use any of these methods:

- Click the Run Slide Show button on the toolbar.
- Choose Make ➪ Run Slide Show.
- From the Slide Show Options dialog box, click the Run Slide Show button.

To set options before running a show, open the Slide Show Options dialog box, shown in Figure 29.13. Choose Make ➪ Slide Show Options. You can set a duration for each slide, add a background color, choose transitions and scaling, specify a stage grid, and check playback options.

**FIGURE 29.13**

Use the Slide Show Options dialog box to set options for running a slide show.

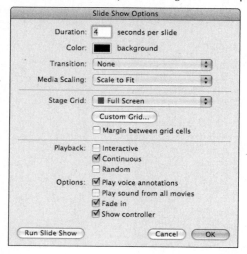

# Basic Image Editing Techniques

Expression Media offers some great image editing tools to edit your photographs. For example, you can tweak the color, sharpness, and brightness of an image, or remove red eye and crop out parts of the image you don't want to see. You can do all this through the Image Editor panel, as shown in Figure 29.14. When you select an image-editing filter from the panel, Expression Media automatically switches you to Media view so you can see the image more clearly.

When editing images, you are applying filter effects to the photo. You can apply multiple filters to a single image. To edit an image, select it in the catalog and follow these steps:

1. **Click the Image Editor button on the toolbar.**

   The Image Editor panel appears (refer to Figure 29.14).

2. **Click the filter you want to apply.**

   The filter's associated dialog box opens with additional settings you can adjust, as shown in Figure 29.15.

3. **Make any changes to the filter's options as needed.**

4. **To preview the filter effect, click the Preview check box.**

   A preview displays the edited effect as applied to the photo.

5. **To apply your changes to the image, click OK.**

6. **To keep your changes, click the Save button to open the Save dialog box and verify the Format.**

   To discard the changes, click Revert, and Expression Media loads the original image.

   To remove the last filter applied, click the Undo button.

7. **Click the panel's Close button to exit the Image Editor.**

**FIGURE 29.14**

**FIGURE 29.14**

Use the Image Editor panel to apply filters to your images.

**FIGURE 29.15**

Use the filter's dialog box to fine-tune the filter effect.

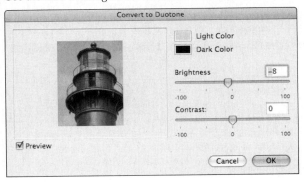

You'll want to experiment with the various filters found in the Image Editor panel to see what kind of edits you can make to your photographs.

## Printing Catalogs

You can print your images or your entire catalog in Expression Media. You can even create a contact sheet that prints thumbnails of your images just like they appear in Thumbnail view. The Print dialog box, shown in Figure 29.16, offers three printing options: Content List, Contact Sheet, and Media Sheet. Oddly enough, these three printing choices match the three view modes you use in Expression Media to view media items.

**FIGURE 29.16**

You can use the Print dialog box to set up how you want to print your media catalog items.

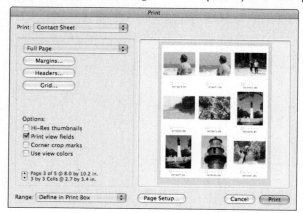

To print your catalog, follow these steps:

1. **Choose File ⇨ Print.**

   The Print dialog box opens (refer to Figure 29.16).

2. **Click the Print pop-up menu to select from Content List, Contact Sheet, or Media Sheet.**

   Depending on the option you select, different settings are displayed in the dialog box. For example, if you choose Contact Sheet, you can set high-resolution thumbnails, print view fields, and more. You also can control page margins, add headers, or change the layout grid.

3. **After you're happy with your print selections, click the Print button to commit the items to paper.**

## Summary

In this chapter, you learned how to tap into the power of cataloging digital media items in Expression Media. You learned how to save and open catalogs, how to move media items around in a catalog, and how to add labels and ratings to your items. You also learned how to view items, particularly using the Light Table feature.

This chapter also showed you how to rename images in batches, turn on the Slide Show feature, and print your catalogs. Along with all the organizing tools offered by Expression Media, you also learned how to utilize filters with the Image Editor panel to make changes to your photos.

# Part VII

# Working with Office Graphics and Web Features

# Chapter 30

# Adding Graphics

Now for some graphic talk. Just to keep things simple, think of the term graphics as meaning anything related to visual elements you add to your Office files. As such, this opens a whole wide world of possibilities, everything from simple shapes you draw in a worksheet to pre-drawn artwork you add to a Word document. Historically, the term graphics pertains to the art of drawing and printmaking. In the electronic realm, graphic objects include clip art, photographs, pictures, shapes, diagrams, and even text boxes—specialized boxes for holding text.

Although we've covered adding graphics in several places throughout the book so far, this chapter pulls all the how-to information into one spot. The various graphics features are available across the Office applications, so after you learn how to use a feature in one program, you can easily apply the same steps and commands in another program. As you can probably guess, graphics are not quite so important to Entourage as they are to the other Office programs. However, you can use a few graphics features in Entourage to add photos to your e-mail messages, for example. By and large, you'll mostly find yourself using graphics in Word, Excel, and PowerPoint.

When you insert a graphic object, such as clip art or a shape, you can move it around, copy it, resize it, and edit it to suit your project. When you select a graphic object, it's surrounded by selection handles, or tiny boxes on the corners and along the border. You can use these handles to manipulate the graphic object. Graphics are a great way to add a visual dynamic to any project. The information in this chapter shows you how to add every type of graphic element to your Office files.

## Working with Clip Art

Clip art is simply pre-drawn artwork. PowerPoint installs with a clip art collection, and you can find it in the Clip Gallery or access it through the Object Palette in the Toolbox. Plus, if you have an online connection, you can access even more clip art from the Microsoft Web site. In addition to drawn artwork, the Clip Gallery can also include photographs, sound, and video clips.

You can use clip art in various Office programs to illustrate your work or give your documents visual impact. You also can add your own clip art collections to the mix.

## Using the Clip Gallery

To find your way to the Clip Gallery, you can employ any of these methods, depending on which Office program you're using:

- Choose Insert ➪ Picture ➪ Clip Art.
- In PowerPoint, click the Picture button on the Standard toolbar and choose Clip Art.
- If the Drawing toolbar is displayed, you can click the Clip Art button.

You can use the Clip Gallery, shown in Figure 30.1, to search for a particular type of clip art or browse through the various categories to find something you want to use. To browse, choose a category and look through the artwork displayed in the Clips list box. The Category list on the left side of the gallery displays a variety of categories, each holding a collection of clip art related to the category name. When you find something you want to use, click it in the Clips pane and then click the Insert button, and it's added to your document. You also can just double-click the clip art to insert it immediately.

**FIGURE 30.1**

You can use the Clip Gallery to add clip art to your Office documents.

You can always preview clip art before inserting it. To do so, select it and click the Preview check box located just above the Insert button. When you activate this feature, it opens a larger preview window for getting a better view of the artwork, as shown in Figure 30.2. Deselect the check box again to close the Preview window.

**FIGURE 30.2**

Use the Preview window to check out the artwork before inserting it into an Office document.

If just browsing through clip art isn't producing what you want, you can conduct a search for a particular item by typing in a keyword or phrase in the Search field. As soon as you type in a keyword and press Return, the Clip Gallery displays any matching results. You can use the pop-up menu next to the Search field to return to previous searches you conducted.

The Show pop-up menu lets you control what types of clip art appear listed in the Gallery. For example, you may want to view all movie clips or all sound clips instead of pictures.

To check out detailed information about a piece of selected clip art, click the Properties button. The Properties dialog box opens, as shown in Figure 30.3. The Description tab gives you a description of the artwork and pertinent file information, such as size, dimensions, and location. You can use the Categories tab to assign the clip art to more than one category in the Gallery. You can use the Keywords tab to add or edit keywords associated with the artwork. The Preview button in the Properties dialog box works the same way as the Preview check box back in the Gallery. Click it to open a Preview window to better view the artwork.

You can change the categories listed in the Clip Gallery, add new ones, and delete ones you don't use. Simply click the Categories button to open the Categories dialog box, shown in Figure 30.4. To add a new category, such as a category for storing your own photographs, for example, click the New Category and type a name. To remove a category, select it and click the Delete button.

**FIGURE 30.3**

Look up detailed information about a piece of clip art using the Properties dialog box.

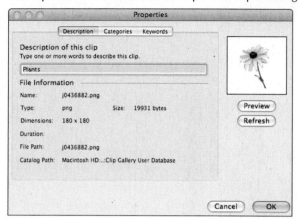

**FIGURE 30.4**

You can customize the Clip Gallery categories using the Categories dialog box.

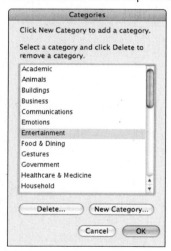

You can import a clip art collection from another source into the Clip Gallery. Just click on the Import button, to open the Import dialog box, shown in Figure 30.5. You can then navigate to the collection you want to use and choose to copy, move, or add an alias to the Clip Gallery.

**FIGURE 30.5**

You can use the Import dialog box to import a clip art collection into Office.

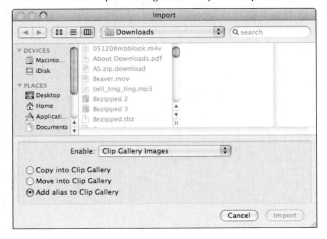

## Downloading more clip art

You can look for more clip art online and download artwork into the Clip Gallery using the Online button. Make sure you're connected to the Internet, and then follow these steps:

1. **Display the Clip Gallery.**
2. **Click the Online button, as shown in Figure 30.6.**

**FIGURE 30.6**

Use the Online button to access the Microsoft Clip Art Web site.

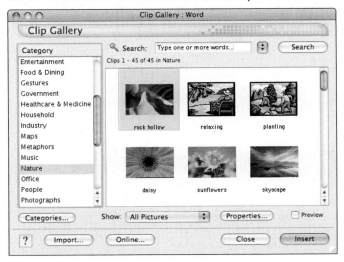

A prompt box appears, as shown in Figure 30.7, asking if it's okay to launch your default Web browser.

---

**FIGURE 30.7**

Click the Yes button to log onto the Microsoft Office Clip Art Web site.

3. **Click Yes.**

   Your default Web browser opens to the Microsoft Clip Art Web site.

4. **In the Clip Art search box, type a keyword or phrase for the type of clip art you want to find and press Return or click the Search button.** Figure 30.8 shows the results of a keyword search.

---

**FIGURE 30.8**

You can search for the type of art you want to find using keywords.

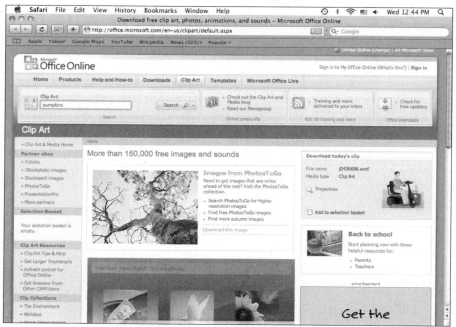

Any matching results appear on the page, as shown in Figure 30.9.

**FIGURE 30.9**

You can select which items you want to download.

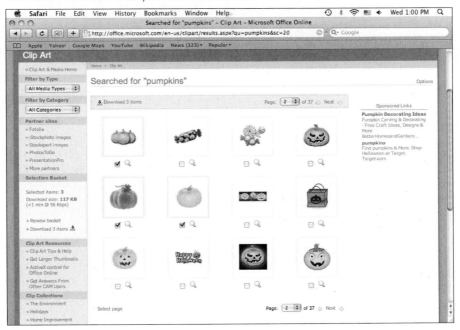

5. **Browse through the artwork, and check the boxes of the items you want to download.**

6. **When you're ready to download, click the Download link at the top of the window, as shown in Figure 30.9.**

   The Download page appears, as shown in Figure 30.10.

7. **Click the Download Now button.**

   Your selections are downloaded and added to the Downloads window, as shown in Figure 30.11.

8. **Double-click the clip art file.**

   The artwork is added to the Favorites category in the Clip Gallery, as shown in Figure 30.12. You can now use the clip art wherever you like.

 **Did you insert the wrong artwork? No problem, just activate the Undo command by pressing ⌘+Z.**

**FIGURE 30.10**

The next phase is the Download page.

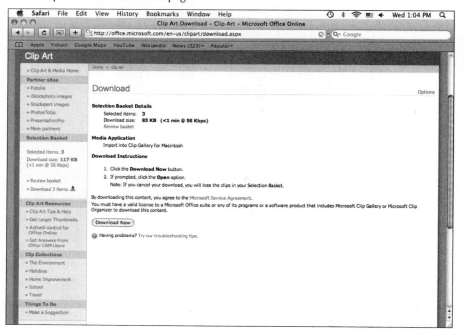

**FIGURE 30.11**

You can open the newly downloaded file from the Downloads window.

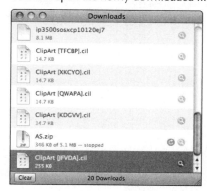

**FIGURE 30.12**

The newly added clip art appears in the Clip Gallery.

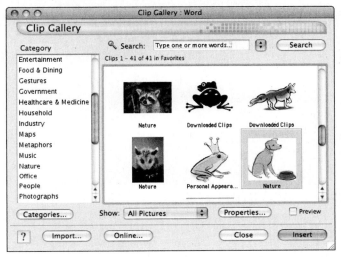

## Using the Object Palette

You can use the Object Palette to view and insert clip art. To display the palette, click the Toolbox button on the Standard toolbar, and then click the Object Palette button in the Toolbox. You can also get there by choosing View ➪ Toolbox ➪ Object Palette. The Object Palette, shown in Figure 30.13, has four tab buttons at the top for viewing Shapes, Clip Art, Symbols, and Photos. Click the Clip Art button to view a list of scrollable clip art, as shown in Figure 30.13.

To control what types of clip art appear in the list, click the All Images pop-up menu and choose a category or type. To adjust the size of the display, drag the Thumbnail Size slider.

When you find a piece of artwork you want to use, drag it onto the document. After it's inserted, you can resize, move, and format it as needed.

## Other Clips as Clip Art

When looking for clips in the Clip Gallery, you also encounter sound and video clips. Although these aren't very "graphic" in terms of visual impact, they can add dynamic properties to an Office project. The installed clip art collection doesn't offer much in terms of sound and video clips. However, you can find plenty of these online at the Microsoft Clip Art Web site.

You can use the Object Palette to insert clip art.

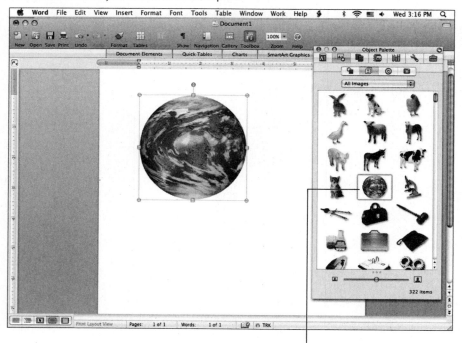

Drag the clip art onto the page.

# Adding Pictures

Another way to illustrate your work is to insert pictures, such as photographs or artwork you've created in another program. For most users, the term "pictures" means photos. There are two ways to insert pictures: using the Choose a Picture dialog box and using the Object Palette on the Toolbox. The Object Palette lists photos found on your computer; the Choose a Picture dialog box lets you insert picture files of any type.

## Choosing a picture

To insert a picture file, whether it's a photograph or another graphic file type, follow these steps:

1.  **Choose Insert ➪ Picture ➪ From File.**

    In PowerPoint, choose Insert ➪ Picture, or click the Picture button on the Standard toolbar and choose Insert Picture.

    The Choose a Picture dialog box opens, as shown in Figure 30.14.

**FIGURE 30.14**

You can insert picture files using the Choose a Picture dialog box.

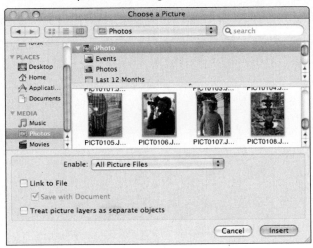

2. **Navigate to the folder or drive containing the file you want to insert.**

   Optionally, you can click the Enable pop-up menu to choose what kind of picture file types to display.

3. **Select the filename or thumbnail image.**

   You can click the Link to File check box to create a link between the source file and the document in which you are inserting the image. This way, any edits made to the original are reflected in the copy.

4. **Click Insert.**

   The picture is added to the document. You can now resize, move, or edit it as needed.

**NOTE** You can add a photograph or picture to an e-mail message in Entourage. Choose Message ➪ Insert ➪ Picture. This opens the same Choose a Picture dialog box described in the nearby steps.

## Using the Object Palette

You can use the Object Palette to view and insert pictures, specifically photographs from your Photos folder. Click the Toolbox button on the Standard toolbar to display the Toolbox, and then click the Object Palette button. You also can get there by choosing View ➪ Toolbox ➪ Object Palette. Of the four tab buttons on the palette, one is the Photos tab. Click it to view a list of photos, as shown in Figure 30.15.

You can adjust the size of the display by dragging the Thumbnail Size slider. You also can search for a particular photo based on its name or any keywords you assigned to the image. Click in the Search field, and type a keyword. As soon as you press Return, the palette displays any matches.

You can use the Object Palette to insert photographs.

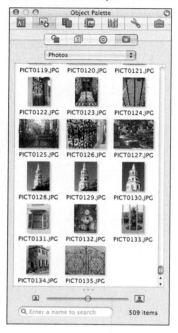

# Adding SmartArt Graphics

New to Office 2008, SmartArt graphics are handy pre-drawn artwork you can use to diagram processes, cycles, workflows, hierarchies, and relationships. For example, do you need to create a diagram showing your corporate structure? Easy! Peruse the SmartArt graphics to find just the right layout. At its very heart, SmartArt is a visual way of presenting data, such as a concept or idea.

The makers of Office have made it very convenient to find the SmartArt graphics by adding the feature to the Elements Gallery. Click the SmartArt Graphics tab on the Elements Gallery to view a list of all kinds of SmartArt, as shown in Figure 30.16. In Word or PowerPoint, you can display the Gallery by choosing Insert ➪ SmartArt Graphic.

You can add SmartArt graphics to diagram or explain relationships.

From the Gallery, click the artwork you want to insert. A Text Pane appears for you to enter the data to make the art, as shown in Figure 30.17, along with the layout you selected. You can type your text in the pane window or directly into the box. You can add more boxes, or shapes, to the layout by clicking the Add button in the Text Pane. To remove a shape, click the Remove button. You can reassign a selected shape by promoting or demoting it in the layout using the Promote or Demote buttons.

You can control the formatting of your SmartArt with a little help from the Formatting Palette. Located in the Toolbox, click the Formatting Palette, and then open the SmartArt Graphic Styles heading, as shown in Figure 30.18. You can experiment with the various controls to tailor your layout to suit your project.

**FIGURE 30.17**

Fill in the boxes with your own content.

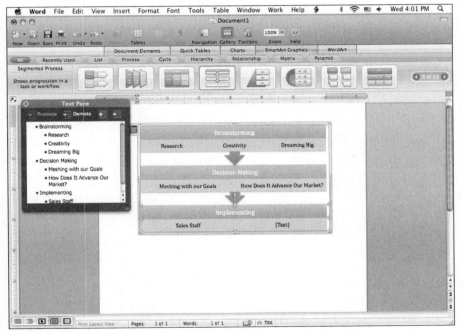

**FIGURE 30.18**

Use the panes in the Formatting Palette to make changes to SmartArt colors or styles.

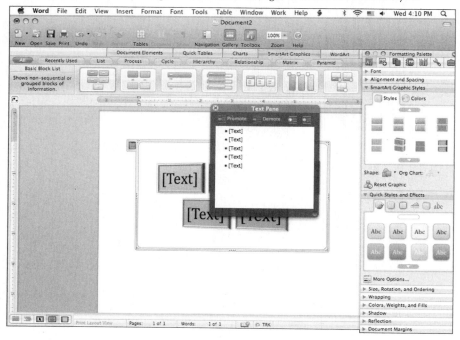

## Adding WordArt

Microsoft's WordArt feature has been around for a long time. You've probably seen it in previous versions of the Office programs. You'll be happy to know it's still around, featuring a few improvements. It's a handy little feature for turning text into artwork, which you can then manipulate like a graphic object.

You can find your way to the WordArt feature using the Elements Gallery in Word, PowerPoint, and Excel.

To add a WordArt object, follow these steps:

1. **Click the WordArt tab on the Elements Gallery, as shown in Figure 30.19.**

   You also can choose Insert ➪ WordArt (Word or PowerPoint), or Insert ➪ Picture ➪ WordArt (Excel).

**FIGURE 30.19**

You can find the WordArt feature on the Elements Gallery in Word, PowerPoint, and Excel.

2. **Peruse the styles, and click the one you want to use.**

A WordArt placeholder object appears in the document, as shown in Figure 30.20.

**FIGURE 30.20**

Behold, a WordArt object newly inserted.

3. **Double-click the WordArt object.**

The Edit WordArt dialog box appears, as shown in Figure 30.21.

4. **Type the text you want to use.**

The placeholder text is replaced with whatever you type.

Optionally, you can change the font, size, and style:

- Click the Font pop-up menu to choose a different font.
- Click the Size pop-up menu to choose another font size.
- Click the Bold or Italics button to change the text style.

5. **Click OK.**

The WordArt displays the new text, as shown in Figure 30.22.

You can move, resize, or change the WordArt object as needed. To return to the Edit WordArt dialog box at anytime, just double-click the object. You also can find formatting controls for editing your WordArt object in the WordArt pane located on the Formatting Palette in the Toolbox. You can use the tools in the WordArt pane to change the WordArt shape, change text height and position, and open the Format dialog box. You learn more about the Format dialog box later in this chapter.

**FIGURE 30.21**

Replace the placeholder text.

**FIGURE 30.22**

You can move or resize your new WordArt object just as you do any other graphic object in Office.

# Adding AutoShapes

In addition to clip art, SmartArt Graphics, and WordArt, you can draw shapes quite easily in your Office documents using Microsoft's AutoShapes. AutoShapes, like clip art and WordArt objects, are pre-drawn artwork that you can add and format as you like. For example, you can draw a perfect diamond shape or a starburst using AutoShapes.

You can use the Object Palette to view and insert AutoShapes. Click the Toolbox button on the Standard toolbar to display the Toolbox, and then click the Object Palette button. You also can get there by choosing View⇨Toolbox⇨Object Palette. Click the Shapes tab to view a list of shapes to choose from, shown in Figure 30.23. In addition to shapes, the AutoShapes list offers shapes for creating freehand line drawings and callout boxes on the document page.

You can adjust the size of the shapes display by dragging the Thumbnail Size slider. To control what types of shapes appear in the list, click the All Shapes pop-up menu and choose a category or type.

When you find a shape you like, click it. You can now draw it on the document page. Click and drag to create the shape, as shown in Figure 30.24.

---

**FIGURE 30.23**

You can use the Object Palette to insert AutoShapes.

Shapes tab button

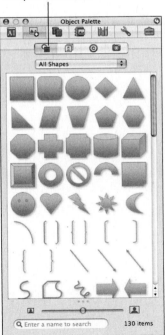

---

**FIGURE 30.24**

Click and drag on the document to draw your shape.

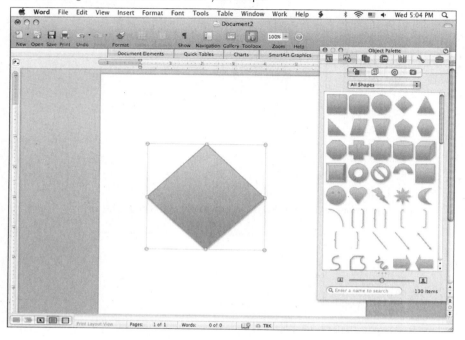

After creating a shape, you can switch over to the Formatting Palette in the Toolbox to find options for formatting the shape's color, line style, or transparency level.

## Adding Text Boxes

You may encounter occasions in which you'll need to place some text into some kind of "container" to keep it separate from other items in the document. For example, in Word, you might want to add a box of text in the middle of two columns to hold a quote. Text boxes allow you to add text and treat it as a separate element. Of course, in PowerPoint, text boxes are commonly used to hold slide text. In Word and Excel, however, they're not so commonplace.

To add a text box in Word or Excel, choose Insert ➪ Text Box. Click and drag on the document where you want the box to go. When you finish dragging, an empty text box appears, as shown in Figure 30.25. You can start typing your text and format the text to suit your project. The best thing about text boxes is that you can move them around and resize them as needed.

**FIGURE 30.25**

You can use text boxes as free-floating containers for text.

For additional text box controls, try the Text Box pane in the Formatting Palette in the Toolbox. Here you'll find text wrapping options, size options, and controls for setting the internal margins inside the text box. You also can find more formatting controls in the Format dialog box, which you learn about later in this chapter.

## Using the Drawing Toolbar

Word, Excel, and PowerPoint include a special toolbar full of tools for drawing and formatting your own shapes and artwork—the Drawing toolbar. To display this toolbar, choose View⇨Toolbars⇨Drawing. Shown in Figure 30.26, the toolbar varies slightly in each program, but it always includes tools for adding AutoShapes and inserting text boxes, WordArt, clip art, and pictures, as well as tools for creating freehand drawings. The Drawing toolbar appears anchored vertically by default on the left side of the program window.

**FIGURE 30.26**

The Drawing toolbar offers many of the same graphic object tools found elsewhere in your Office programs.

We've already covered how to add clip art, pictures, WordArt, AutoShapes, and text boxes, so let's look at how to draw lines and 3-D shapes.

To draw a line, click the Lines tool on the Drawing toolbar, and then click and drag on the document to create the line. If you want to draw a special kind of line, click the button's arrow icon and choose your line style, such as Freeform, Scribble, or Double Arrow, as shown in Figure 30.27.

If it's 3-D elements you're after, click the 3-D button and choose a style. Whatever style you choose is applied to the selected object on the document page, as shown in Figure 30.28.

**FIGURE 30.27**

In this example, I drew a scribble.

FIGURE 30.28

The scribble now has 3-D formatting applied.

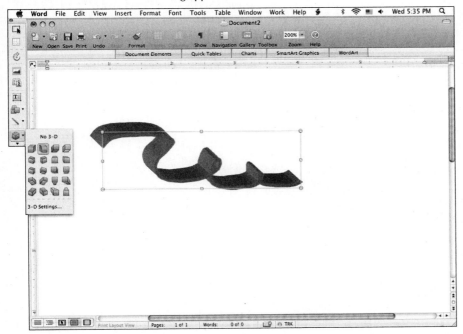

# Formatting Graphics

So, you've added a graphic object to your Office document. Now what? Is there anything else you can do with it? Yes, there's plenty. You can format it. Formatting can change the appearance of an object, whether it's a shape, clip art, photograph, text box, or WordArt object. For example, you may decide a piece of clip art needs a border around it, or perhaps a shape's color is not working with the rest of the project. You can make changes to the object's formatting attributes to edit its appearance, and as it turns out, the formatting options seem endless.

## Using the Formatting Palette

 Look to the Formatting Palette for many of the formatting tools you might apply to an object. For example, if you're working with an AutoShape, you can use the Size, Rotation, and Ordering pane, the Wrapping pane, the Colors, Weights, and Fills pane, or the Shadow pane to tweak the shape's appearance, as shown in Figure 30.29.

**FIGURE 30.29**

The Formatting Palette is packed with formatting tools for graphic objects.

The following sections offer a run-down of the panes and the types of tools you can find in them. Keep in mind that the panes vary based on the object you've selected onscreen.

## Size, Rotation, and Ordering

As you can tell by the title, this pane features tools for controlling the size of an object, rotation, and alignment of the object, and in the case of multiple objects, the order in which objects are stacked. Tools are grouped into two main categories: Size and Ordering. Among the Size tools are controls for height and width. As shown in Figure 30.30, the Height and Width boxes let you set a specific size for the object. You can lock the aspect ratio to keep the size aspect equal to the original height and width sizes.

FIGURE 30.30

The Size, Rotation, and Ordering pane

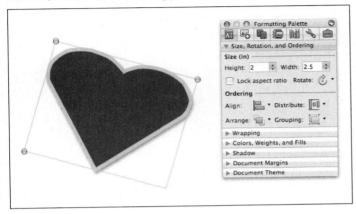

You also can rotate an object. You can choose a quick rotation option by clicking the Rotate pop-up menu. For example, you can rotate an object to the left, flip it vertically or horizontally, or rotate it freely in whatever direction you want. If you select the Free Rotate tool, you can drag an object's selection handle to rotate it.

The Ordering group of tools allows you to align selected objects, distribute them evenly, arrange them in stacking order, or turn multiple objects into a single group.

## Wrapping

The Wrapping pane, shown in Figure 30.31, offers tools for controlling how text flows around the selected object. You can choose from the following settings:

- **In Line with Text:** This option keeps the object on the same line as the text where it's placed. This is the default setting unless you specify otherwise.
- **Square:** This option keeps a nice square edge around the object and text wraps around all sides.
- **Tight:** This wraps text tightly to edge of object.
- **Behind Text:** Text wraps behind the object when you use this option.
- **In Front of Text:** Text wraps in front of the object with this option.
- **Top and Bottom:** This option wraps text around the top and bottom only.
- **Through:** This allows text to run through the object.
- **Edit Wrap Boundary:** This lets you set your own wrap boundaries based on edit points you can drag to adjust.

You can use the Wrap to command to control which sides of the object are wrapped, while the Distance from text settings let you set a precise measurement between the text wrapping and the object.

**FIGURE 30.31**

The Wrapping pane

## Colors, Weights, and Fills

The Colors, Weights, and Fills pane, shown in Figure 30.32, offers tools for setting a fill color and transparency and a line color and style. If your object is an AutoShape, for example, you can change the inside color and the outer border surrounding the shape. If your object is a piece of clip art or a photo, you can use the Line settings to add a border.

**FIGURE 30.32**

The Colors, Weights, and Fills pane

Under the Fill group, you can click the Color button and display a pop-up palette of colors from which you can choose. You can drag the Transparency slider to make the object transparent or opaque. Under the Line group, you can click the Color button to choose a line color, click the Style button to choose a style (line thickness), click the Dashed button to choose a dash style, or set your own line thickness in the Weight box. Like the fill color, you can drag the Transparency slider to make the object transparent.

### Shadow

The Shadow pane, shown in Figure 30.33, has tools for setting shadow effects. For example, if you're working with a shape, you can add a shadow to give the object some depth. Click the Shadow check box, then use the Angle tool to establish an angle for the shadow effect. You can choose a style, select a color, set a distance from shadow to object, or create a blur or transparency effect.

**FIGURE 30.33**

The Shadow pane

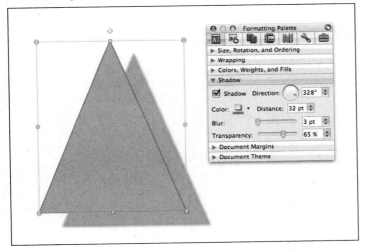

### Picture

If your object is a picture, you can use the Picture pane, shown in Figure 30.34, to apply formatting to the image. You can use the Recolor tool to change the coloring of the image, such as setting a sepia tone. You can crop out parts of the image using the Crop tool. Click the Crop button, and drag a crop handle on the image to crop it.

You can turn your image into an instant shape using the Shape tool. To remove parts of the image, use the Transparent Color tool. For example, if you want to keep the subject of the image only, you can click the Transparent Color tool on surrounding areas of the image to erase them, making the picture transparent in spots so you can see the background behind the picture.

Use the Brightness, Contrast, and Transparency sliders to adjust the image itself, such as changing its brightness level.

To replace the picture with another picture, click the Replace button. This opens the Choose a Picture dialog box, the same one you used to add the picture in the first place. The Effects and Format buttons open the Format dialog box, which contains more formatting controls for editing the picture.

**FIGURE 30.34**

The Picture pane

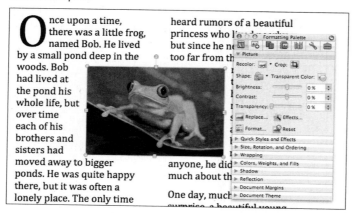

If you don't like all the changes you made using the Picture tools, you can click the Reset button to restore the original image.

## Quick Styles and Effects

You can use the Quick Styles and Effects pane to add all kinds of preset styles, shadows, glows, reflections, 3-D effects, and text transformations to your objects. Arranged in tabbed groups, you can click each style and effect to view a list of choices. For example, you can find some interesting borders for your photographs in the Quick Styles tab or add a color glow around an AutoShape. The pane, shown in Figure 30.35, lets you scroll through the various items and view a thumbnail of each. Click the More Options button to open the Format dialog box, where you can find even more settings to tweak the style's or effect's appearance.

**FIGURE 30.35**

The Quick Styles and Effects pane

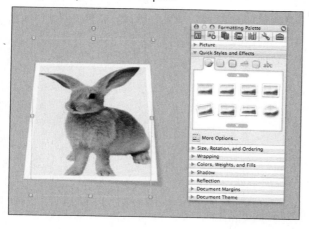

## Reflection

The Reflection pane, shown in Figure 30.36, creates the effect of a reflection for the selected object. This pane is available only for pictures and clip art. When the Reflection check box is selected, you can tweak the effect by adjusting the Transparency, Size, and Distance sliders.

**FIGURE 30.36**

The Reflection pane

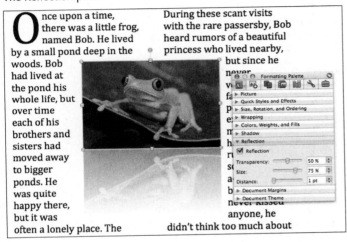

## Using the Format dialog box

You can use the object's associated Format dialog box to tailor the appearance of any object you place in a document. The dialog box offers additional tools not available in the Formatting Palette. To open the Format dialog box for any object, simply double-click the object. You also can select the object and choose Format ➪ and the object type, such as AutoShape or Picture. Depending on the object, the full name of the dialog box differs slightly, such as Format Picture or Format AutoShape, as shown in Figure 30.37.

**NOTE**   In the case of WordArt objects, you must click the Format WordArt button in the WordArt pane or choose Format ➪ WordArt to open the Format WordArt dialog box.

As you can see from the figure, the Format Picture dialog box is packed full of options. Organized into categories, you can click a category name to view associated options.

Now look at the Format Text Box dialog box shown in Figure 30.38. Instead of categories, the formatting options are arranged in tabs. The same is true of the Format AutoShape dialog box. Instead of clicking categories, you click a tab to view the associated options.

**FIGURE 30.37**

Every object has a Format dialog box you can use to edit the object.

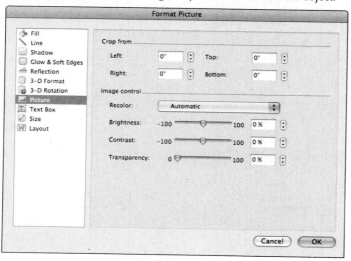

**FIGURE 30.38**

The Format Text Box dialog box arranges options in tabs.

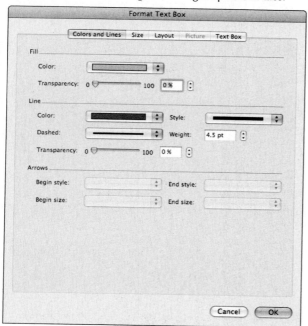

## Formatting options for pictures and clip art

The Format dialog box for clip art and picture objects share all the same categories and tabs. Many of the categories contain settings that are repeated from the Formatting Palette panes. However, some of the categories offer something not found on the Formatting Palette, such as the Gradient and Texture settings. For example, the Gradient tab is available in both the Fill and Line categories. As you peruse the Format categories, shown in Figure 30.39, you'll quickly notice that some categories have additional tabs with more controls, while other categories require only a single screen.

### FIGURE 30.39

The Format dialog box is the same for clip art and picture objects.

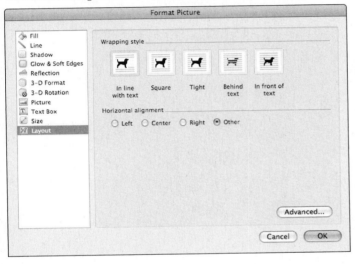

Here's a run-down of the Format categories:

- **Fill:** Find options for setting a fill color or using a gradient, picture, or texture as a fill.
- **Line:** This category offers controls for setting line color, styles and line thickness, or using a gradient effect as a line color.
- **Shadow:** Find options for setting shadow effects and controlling their style, color, size, blur, distance from the object, and transparency.
- **Glow & Soft Edges:** Add a glow or soft edge using these options, including setting a glow color and thickness.
- **Reflection:** Set a reflection effect with these settings, and control its transparency, size, and distance from the object.
- **3-D Format:** Fine-tune your 3-D effect by adjusting the bevel, depth, and surface controls.
- **3-D Rotation:** This category offers controls for rotating the 3-D effect.
- **Picture:** Find options for cropping and editing the image, including changing the brightness, contrast, and transparency.
- **Text Box:** Control the layout within a text box, including choosing alignment, setting internal margins, and fitting text within the text box shape.

- **Size:** Set precise height and width measurements, scale measurements, and rotation measurements using these options.

- **Layout:** Find wrapping controls and horizontal alignment settings in this category. For even more wrapping controls, click the Advanced button in this category to open the Advanced Layout dialog box containing more wrapping styles and settings.

A gradient effect is a blending of two or more colors to create a graduated appearance. To set a gradient fill effect, follow these steps:

1. **In the Format Picture dialog box, click the Fill category and then click the Gradient tab, as shown in Figure 30.40.**

**FIGURE 30.40**

You can set gradient effects for pictures and clip art objects.

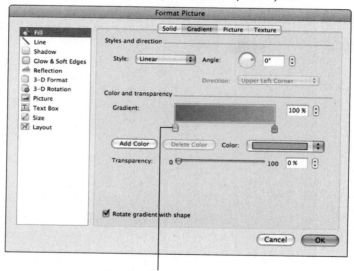

Set the gradient color.

2. **Click the Style pop-up menu, and choose a gradient: Linear, Radial, Rectangular, or Path.**

   Optionally, to adjust the angle of the blend, click the Angle option and drag it to a new setting or type a degree in the box; to adjust the gradient's direction, click the Direction pop-up menu and choose another direction.

3. **By default, the gradient effect is set to the one color and white; to change the colors of both settings, click the tiny icon under the Gradient preview and choose another color from the Color pop-up menu.** You can change the color of both icons.

   Optionally, to add more icons and color, click the Add Color button and repeat this step.

   Also optionally, you can change the transparency setting to make the effect more or less opaque.

4. **Click OK to apply the effect.**

 To undo a gradient effect, revisit the Format Picture dialog box and set the Style to None on the Gradient tab.

You can use the Texture tab to use a texture as a fill color. Shown in Figure 30.41, you can choose from a library of preset textures, and change the transparency setting to make the effect more or less opaque.

**FIGURE 30.41**

You can find texture effects only in the Format Picture dialog box.

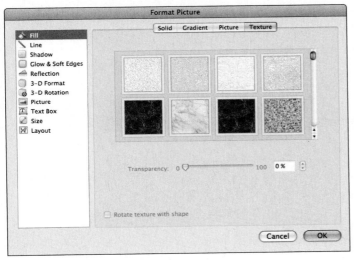

## Formatting options for shapes, text boxes, and WordArt objects

The formatting options for shapes, text boxes, and WordArt objects share all the same tabs in the Format dialog box, as shown in Figure 30.42. Like the Format Picture dialog box, many of the tab categories repeat settings found among the Formatting Palette panes. To view a tab, click it. Depending on the object you're currently working on, not all the tabs are available. For example, if you select a shape and open the Format AutoShape dialog box, the Picture and Text Box tabs are not available for selection.

Here's a run-down of the Format tabs:

- **Colors and Lines:** Find options for setting a fill color and transparency, line color and style, and arrows for lines.
- **Size:** This tab includes options for controlling the height, width, rotation, and scale of an object.
- **Layout:** Find wrapping controls and horizontal alignment settings in this tab. For even more wrapping controls, click the Advanced button to open the Advanced Layout dialog box containing more wrapping styles and settings.
- **Picture:** This tab has options for adding a picture as a background.
- **Text Box:** Find options for setting internal margins for text boxes.

**FIGURE 30.42**

The Format dialog box is the same for shapes, text boxes, and WordArt objects.

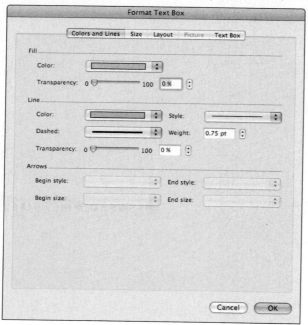

## Summary

In this chapter, you learned how to use graphic elements in your Office documents. You learned how to insert clip art from the Clip Gallery and the Object Palette. You also learned how to find more clip art online. You learned how to insert photographs, draw your own shapes and lines, turn text into a graphic with WordArt, and add text boxes to act as graphic objects.

After you've added a graphic object, you can find oodles of tools for formatting it the way you want. The Formatting Palette is a handy way to apply formatting to clip art, photos, shapes, text boxes, and WordArt objects. Depending on the object you select to edit, the palette displays different panes suited to the object. In addition, you can open the Format dialog box, a one-stop shop for all the formatting options and a few extra.

# Chapter 31

# Creating Web Content

The vast World Wide Web is a growing source of information—and sometimes misinformation. The amount of content available on the Web today is staggering, with more being added each day. For serious Web design, you need a specialized program, such as Dreamweaver or iWeb. However, for some simple Web content, you can turn any Microsoft Office document, spreadsheet, presentation, or calendar into a Web page that can be posted online.

In this chapter, you learn how to create simple Web pages and sites.

## Turning Office Files into Web Pages

Before you start creating Web pages, you might as well know what they're made of. *HTML,* which stands for Hypertext Markup Language, is the language you use to create documents comprised of text and coding that instruct a Web browser, such as Safari or Firefox, how to display the data. HTML documents are easily identified by their .html or.htm file extension. Because any browser can read an HTML document, you do not need a special platform to view the information. As a scripting language, HTML coding consists of tags, which are the individual instructions to the browser. Tags are surrounded by angle brackets, < >. HTML rules, called *syntax,* govern the way in which code is written. The most recent version of HTML is 4.01. This version allows for separate formatting instructions called cascading style sheets (CSS) and other presentation controls. By moving all the formatting controls to style sheets, HTML 4.01 frees up the Web developer to assign formatting not only to paragraphs of text, but also to the entire page or every page on a Web site. Moving all the formatting coding to a separate style sheet lets you more easily maintain other coding on the HTML document.

The World Wide Web Consortium, or W3C for short, is the governing body for setting HTML standards. This international group consists of the Web's founders and industry leaders, including companies like Microsoft. Web developers look to the W3C to establish standards and introduce new Web technologies. The W3C is responsible for maintaining and guiding all HTML standards. Not long ago, the W3C saw the need to an additional structure for HTML documents, so it introduced XML (Extensible Markup Language). XML is a meta-markup language for creating other languages; however, it is not as lenient as HTML, so the W3C rewrote HTML in XML and called it XHTML. XHTML has all the features of HTML but gains XML's power and flexibility. Although XHTML is technically an XML application, it closely copies much of HTML, so much so that many people view XHTML as a stricter version of HTML. With XHTML, the syntax is much stricter and the order of tags is strictly enforced. The XHMTL coding also requires all lowercase letters. The future of HTML lies in XHTML, but because so many pages are written in HTML and browser support is more common for HTML, HTML documents are not likely to go away for quite some time. If you do learn how to script in HTML, transitioning to XHTML is relatively easy, requiring only a dedication to detail when writing well-formed code.

Well, that was probably more than you wanted to know about HTML. What you really want to know is how to turn your Office documents into Web pages. The good news is that you don't have to know how to write HTML to make Web pages. For example, if you save a Word file as a Web page, Word takes care of the conversion process to turn your text into HTML. However, if you've created a complex document, the results may not turn out the way you want. Word tries to match the formatting with the closest equivalent Web formatting, but some text effects do not translate well. If your document is fairly simple in formatting and layout, the transition should be painless.

Of all the Office programs, Word is the most likely choice for creating Web pages, mainly because Web pages are content-based, which usually means text. So if you're just interested in whipping out a few content pages for the Web, you can use Word without many problems. You also can turn Excel data, PowerPoint slides, or an Entourage calendar into a Web page. Just remember, most Web developers will turn up their noses at your Office-content-turned-into-Web-pages. Why? When you convert an Office file into a Web page, gobs of behind-the-scenes coding and unnecessary computer instructions are included in the file. Why is this a problem, you might ask? Because it makes the pages slower to download into a browser window. In addition, the layout and formatting often don't translate well. As you know, the Internet is all about speed, so when you slow things down, it's frowned upon. If, however, you need to create a simple page, Office 2008 has the technology to do so.

If you get really serious about creating Web pages, your best bet is a proper Web-authoring program, such as Dreamweaver, GoLive, or RapidWeaver. But I'll leave that for another book to explain to you.

If you're creating a Web page from scratch, Word is the best application for the job. You can utilize a variety of Web page templates and themes or create your own from scratch. You also can turn an Excel worksheet into a Web page. This might be useful if you've got some important data or a chart you want to include on the company Web site, for example. You can do the same with a slide from a PowerPoint presentation. The only feature in Entourage that makes a good Web page is the Calendar tool. You can turn any day, week, or month into a Web page for posting. You might do this to share your schedule on the Web if you're doing a tour or traveling exhibition, or something along those lines. Remarkably, the process for turning any Office material into a Web page is the same in each program. You also can use the same previewing feature before committing your content into HTML format. The remaining sections show you how.

## A Word about Web Site Design

**W**hen you're considering creating your own Web page content, it's always a good idea to know how it's going to be used. For example, is the page part of a larger site, or is it a stand-alone page? In either scenario, you'll want to include links to other pages. Every Web site has a starting page, called a home page or index page. It's also quite common to see FAQs pages (frequently asked questions), contact pages (detailing how to contact the administrator or company), and other pages with content (such as photo galleries, articles, product lists, and so on). Are you designing one of these types of pages or another kind of page? What sorts of links does your page need—links to other pages on the site or links to other Web sites? Figuring out how your page fits into the site's design is an important part of the process, and it dictates what sort of content and formatting you'll include on the page.

# Previewing a Web Page

You can preview your HTML content before saving it to a file. Previewing can help you catch anything that needs to be changed first, especially before uploading the file to a server for Web display. Plus, if you've slaved over the process of creating a document that's Web-worthy, you most certainly want to preview how it will look in a browser before saving the file.

If you're using Word to create a Web page, you can use Word's Web Layout view to see what your page looks like. None of the other Office programs have a Web Layout view, just Word. Web Layout view is not one of the regular view buttons in the bottom-left corner. To access the feature, you must use the View menu; choose View ➪ Web Layout. Figure 31.1 shows an example of a Word document in Web Layout view.

If you'd rather use the real thing, you can activate the program's Web Page Preview command to get a quick peek at your work in your default Web browser. The Web Page Preview command is available in all the Office programs. To preview a document, choose File ➪ Web Page Preview. This command opens your default browser window and displays the document, worksheet, slide, or calendar. Exit the browser window to return to the program window you were using.

**FIGURE 31.1**

You can use Word's Web Layout view to get a feel for how your document will look in a Web browser.

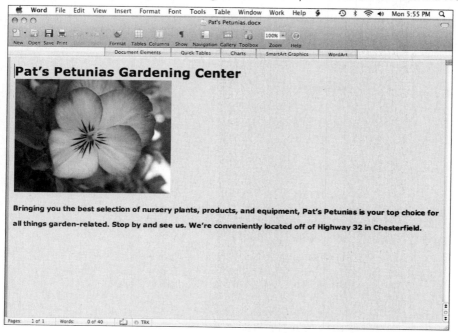

## Saving Content as a Web Page

Now that you've previewed the file, are you ready to turn it into a Web page? The process is as easy as saving any other Office file. In fact, the steps are the same in any program. Simply open the document, workbook, or presentation you want to turn into a Web page, or in the case of Entourage, the calendar view you want to turn into an HTML document. When you turn your Office content into a Web page, any pages in the file become Web pages. So if a slide show is ten slides long, the Save As Web Page command generates ten HTML pages, one for each slide. With this in mind, you definitely want to add some hyperlinks to link the pages and allow users to move back and forth between the content. Learn about adding hyperlinks later in this chapter.

Follow these steps to save your Office content as a Web page:

1. **Choose File ⇨ Save as Web Page.**

   The Save As Web Page dialog box opens, as shown in Figure 31.2.

2. **Type a name for the page in the Save As text box.**

   The .htm file extension is automatically added for you.

   Optionally, use the Where pop-up menu to save the file in another folder or drive.

**FIGURE 31.2**

Use the Save As Web Page dialog box to turn any document into a Web page.

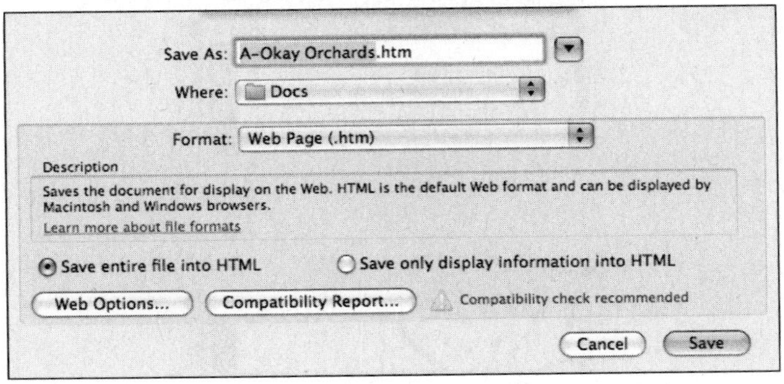

3. **Click the Save entire file into HTML radio button.**

   This option stores the file information for display on the Web and for display in Word. In the case of Word, this means that all the word processor elements, like headers and footers or page numbers, reappear when you open the document file in the Word program window again.

   If you select the Save only display information into HTML radio button, only the attributes viewable in a Web page are saved with the file. Word processor elements, like headers and footers, are not saved with the file. This option is good if you want a more compact file for downloading on the Web.

   Optionally, you can run the Compatibility Report feature if you're going to share the file with other users. It's not really necessary for creating a Web page.

4. **Click Save.**

   The file is saved as a Web page.

If you click the Options button in the Save As Web Page dialog box, the Web Options dialog box opens, as shown in Figure 31.3. This dialog box has four tabs of options: General, Files, Pictures, and Encoding. You can find fields for setting a page title and search engine keywords in the General tab. The Files tab has options for saving, which are essentially the same as the two radio buttons in the Save As Web Page dialog box. The Pictures tab has options for enabling PNG as the output format for your document's pictures. PNG is a universal Web page format for image files. The Pictures tab also has an option for setting the target monitor's screen size. Most users have their screens set to 1024×768, so this size is the default setting unless you choose another. Lastly, the Encoding tab lets you save the file in a foreign language browser format.

After you've created a Web page, you need to upload it to a hosting server so others can view your content. If you already have a Web site up and running, you probably know how to do this. If you're new to Web servers and hosts, you need to do some more research to find a site that will let you have some space to store your page and give it a URL others can find. Your Internet Service Provider (ISP) might offer such space, or you can sometimes find free hosting servers online. For a fee of $100 a year, you can have 10GB of Web storage space on your iDisk; see www.mac.com for more details.

**FIGURE 31.3**

The Web Options dialog box

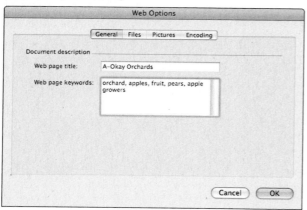

## Adding Hyperlinks

Hyperlinks, called *links* for short, are the links that allow you to jump from one HTML document to another. Links also can take you to movie clips, audio clips, and downloading activities. You also can link to e-mail addresses. Hyperlinks also have a use outside of Web pages. For example, you might use a hyperlink in a long document to jump to the end of the same document, or you might include a hyperlink that takes you to another file or folder on your computer. For the sake of this chapter's discussion, we're talking about links that help users navigate Web pages.

Hyperlinks are typically text and appear as blue underlined words or phrases on a Web page. Hyperlinks also can be graphical elements, such as buttons, shapes, icons, clip art, photos, or anything else that can be clicked in a Web page.

To add a hyperlink to a document, worksheet, or slide, use the Insert Hyperlink dialog box, shown in Figure 31.4. This dialog box features three tabs for each type of hyperlink you can create: Web Page, Document, and E-mail Address. For this task, we're focusing on the Web Page tab. When this tab is displayed, the very top of the dialog box shows fields for specifying the link's URL and the text to use for the link. If you've selected existing text to use as a hyperlink, it appears in the Display field. You can type different text, if desired. The Link to field is where you type the full URL for the Web page you want to link to. You don't need to type the http:// prefix; the Office program inserts that automatically for you.

URL stands for Uniform Resource Locator, in case you were wondering. Basically, it's an exact address or "resource" of a page on the Internet. Every page on the Web has an address. A URL typically contains a domain name or host name, which is the name of the server on which the resource is located. The name also may include a filename or other anchor reference to help identify a specific location for the file.

**FIGURE 31.4**

The Insert Hyperlink dialog box

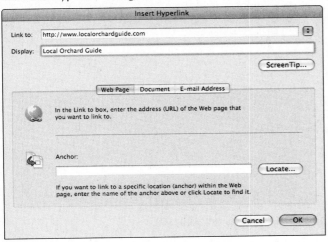

Follow these steps to insert a Web page hyperlink into a document, worksheet cell, or slide:

1. **Choose Insert ⇨ Hyperlink, or press ⌘+K.**

   The Insert Hyperlink dialog box opens (refer to Figure 31.4).

2. **Click the Web Page tab if it's not displayed already.**

3. **Click in the Link to field, and type in the URL for the Web page to which you want to link.**

4. **Click in the Display field, and type the text you want to use as your link text.**

   If you select the text in the document, worksheet cell, or slide before opening the dialog box, the Display field shows the selected text.

   Optionally, if you want the link to include a ScreenTip identifying it when the user moves the mouse pointer over the link, click the ScreenTip button and type some identifying text.

5. **Click OK.**

   The hyperlink is created in your document, worksheet cell, or slide. Figure 31.5 shows an example of a hyperlink in a Word document.

**NOTE** The Insert Hyperlink dialog box also has a setting for specifying an anchor point within a Web page to link to. The page must have HTML anchor tags or bookmarks in order for this feature to work.

If you can't remember the exact URL you want to link to, you can always drag it into your document, worksheet cell, or slide. Just open your browser, navigate to the page, select the URL, and drag it into the document, worksheet, or slide. This creates an instant link.

**FIGURE 31.5**

Hyperlinks appear as blue underlined text.

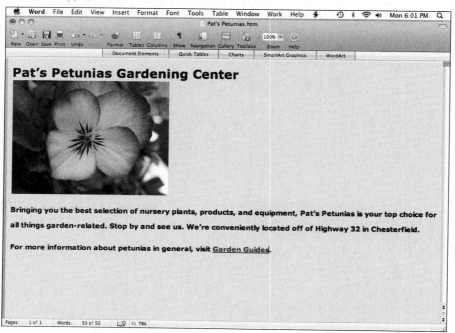

## Summary

In this chapter, you learned a little about how HTML documents work and how you can use Office to create your own Web page content. If you ever wanted to create Web pages, Word's the way to go to fully utilize all the text-based tools for creating content. You won't find the same features in Excel, PowerPoint, or Entourage. Obviously, it's far better to use a proper Web page design program for making Web pages, but Word can be a handy substitute for creating simple pages.

If you create any content for the Web, whether it's a document, worksheet, slide, or calendar, you should always preview it first and make sure it looks okay. You can use the Web Page Preview feature to quickly view your work in the default Web browser window. You also learned how to add hyperlinks to other Web pages in your documents, worksheet cells, or slides.

# Chapter 32

# Using Microsoft Messenger

**M**icrosoft Messenger is a communications resource you can use for instant messaging, file transfers, e-mailing, and more. As a counterpart to Windows Live Messenger, Microsoft Messenger for Mac lets you chat instantly with other users across platforms. You can chat with people using other messaging services, such as Yahoo! Messenger, AOL Instant Messenger, and iChat. Messenger is the perfect tool to connect live with friends, family, and coworkers in a variety of ways.

Connecting people live is a boon for companies, and it's great for personal use as well. For example, your office can conduct a live video conference with another office across the country, or your project team can talk live with each other from spots around the globe while you all examine the same document. Not only can you chat live, you can also use Messenger to swap Office documents, including Word reports, Excel charts, and PowerPoint slide shows.

In this chapter, you learn how to get started with Messenger by jumping through the setup steps to create an account. After you've established an account, you learn how to add contacts, send instant messages, send files, e-mail contacts, and tweak the preferences a bit to customize the program. This chapter focuses on using Messenger for personal messaging rather than corporate messaging; however, the techniques are the same in either setup.

## Setting Up Messenger

The Microsoft Messenger application comes with the Microsoft Office 2008 for Mac suite, regardless of which version you purchased. You probably installed it when you installed the other programs. If you didn't, you can go back and install it now that you need it. Revisit Chapter 2 to learn more about installing programs. Before you start using Messenger, you need to walk through the program's setup feature.

## What Is Windows Live ID?

**W**indows Live ID service lets you create one set of sign-in credentials to use everywhere you go among the Windows Live ID services. The services include MSN Messenger, MSN Hotmail, and MSN Music, just to name a few. Basically, anything featuring the Microsoft Passport Network or Windows Live ID icons or links can be accessed using your Windows Live ID. By using Windows Live ID, you can access all these services without needing to remember a bunch of separate names and passwords. If you happen to be using an MSN Hotmail account or an MSN.com account, you already have Windows Live ID credentials. Credentials are just your e-mail and password, by the way, lest you think they're some sort of important government papers or something. Best of all, it's free. The Web site stresses that you must be at least 18 to have an account, but children are allowed if they have the permission of their parents. I'm not sure how they plan to police this, but there you go. The bottom line is this: You can't use Messenger without the Windows Live ID.

Messenger offers two types of accounts: personal and corporate. You can create one or both. If you choose a personal account, you need to establish a Windows Live ID. The personal account works with the Windows Live Messenger service, connecting you to friends and family in your contacts list. You can sign up for a free Windows Live ID account. All you need is your e-mail address and a password. You can use a personal account to participate in instant message conversations with other users who also have instant messaging services.

If you choose a corporate account, it uses the Microsoft Office Live Communications Server service. You can use the corporate account to connect with colleagues in the same company or with associates in other locations. Like the personal account, you can chat instantly with users who have instant messaging services. When creating this type of account, you need to enter a User ID and password supplied by your network administrator.

In either case, you also need an Internet connection in order to connect with the outside world via Microsoft Messenger.

Follow these steps to walk through the setup process the first time you use Messenger:

1. **Open Messenger.**

   You can open Messenger from the Dock or use Finder to navigate to the program among the Microsoft Office applications. The Microsoft Messenger Setup Assistant opens, as shown in Figure 32.1.

2. **Click the Next button to continue.**

   The next screen, shown in Figure 32.2, lists the Terms of Use. Click Next to continue.

3. **In the prompt box that appears, as shown in Figure 32.3, click Accept to accept the Terms of Use and continue.**

   Next, the Version Check screen appears, as shown in Figure 32.4, and the Setup Assistant searches for any previous versions of the software.

## FIGURE 32.1

Here's the Welcome screen for the Microsoft Messenger Setup Assistant.

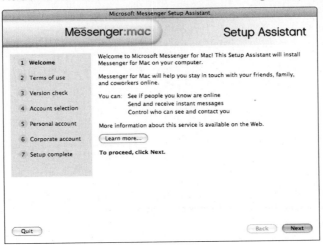

## FIGURE 32.2

You can read the Terms of Use document if you're feeling quite lawyerly.

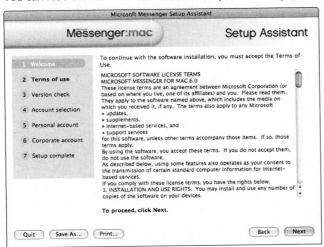

**FIGURE 32.3**

Click Accept if you agree with the Terms of Use.

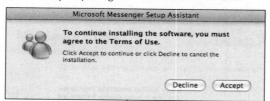

**FIGURE 32.4**

Setup Assistant checks your system for previous versions of the software.

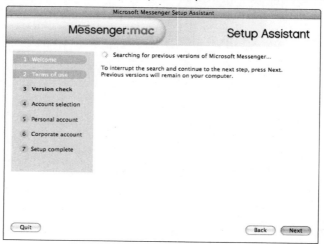

4. **Click Next when Setup is done searching.**

The Account Selection screen appears, as shown in Figure 32.5.

5. **Choose which type of account you want to create: Personal or Corporate.**

6. **Click Next to continue.**

Depending on which account type you selected, either the Personal Account or Corporate Account screen appears, as shown in Figure 32.6.

7. **For a personal account, type your e-mail and password if you already have a Windows Live ID.** If not, click the Create a Windows Live ID account button and follow the onscreen instructions.

 **NOTE** If you sign up for a new Windows Live ID account, keep in mind that extended characters, such as non-English characters, are not allowed for sign-in names or passwords.

**FIGURE 32.5**

Choose an account type from this screen.

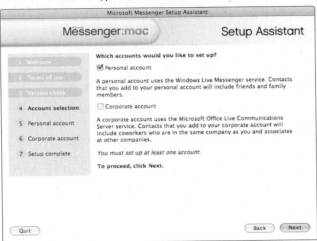

**FIGURE 32.6**

Enter your account information if you have a Windows Live ID account. If not, follow the links to set one up.

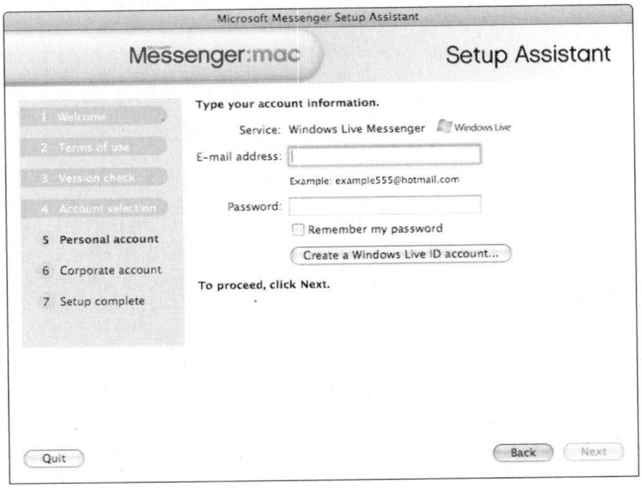

8. **Click Next to continue.**

   The last screen, shown in Figure 32.7, is the Setup Complete screen. This means you're at the end of the setup process.

---

**FIGURE 32.7**

On the last Setup Assistant screen, specify where you want to place Messenger and if you want it to start up as soon as you start your computer.

9. **Choose whether you want to include Messenger in the Dock or have it appear at startup.**
10. **Click Finish.**

When you finish using Setup Assistant, the Messenger application opens, and you're ready to sign on and start communicating.

**NOTE**  You can have more than one account with Messenger. For example, you may want both a personal and corporate account, or you might need an account for friends and another for family. If you have more than one account, you need to choose which one to use when you log in using Messenger. To create a new account, choose Messenger ⇨ Preferences to open the Preferences dialog box, and then click the Accounts icon. Click the Personal or Corporate tab, depending on the type of account you want to create, and click the Change button. You can then use the Settings dialog box to set up new sign-in information.

# Signing On and Out with Messenger

Whenever you're ready to start using Messenger, just open the program and log in using your Windows Live ID. After you install Messenger, an icon for the program is added to the Dock (if you selected that option when you stepped through Messenger's Setup Assistant). You also can launch Messenger using Finder; choose Finder ⇨ Open. Next choose Applications ⇨ Microsoft Office 2008, and double-click Microsoft Messenger. One of the other options during setup was a check box for starting Messenger whenever you start your Mac. If you opted to check this, Microsoft Messenger starts automatically for you, so you don't need to launch it.

Regardless of how you launch the program, you always arrive at a Contacts window of some sort. The Personal Contacts window is the starting point if you have a personal account. If you set up a corporate account instead, the Corporate Contacts window is the starting point. Figure 32.8 shows the Personal Contacts window. If the Personal Contacts window does not appear automatically for you when you open Messenger, just choose View⇨Personal Contact List (or Corporate Contact List if you're using a corporate account).

**FIGURE 32.8**

The Personal Contacts or Corporate Contacts window is the default starting point for your Messenger session.

From the Personal Contacts or Corporate Contacts window, you can click the Sign In button to sign in; this opens the Microsoft Messenger sign in window, as shown in Figure 32.9. If you want to sign in using another account, click the Sign in with a different account or change your status online link.

**FIGURE 32.9**

Sign in by entering your e-mail address and password.

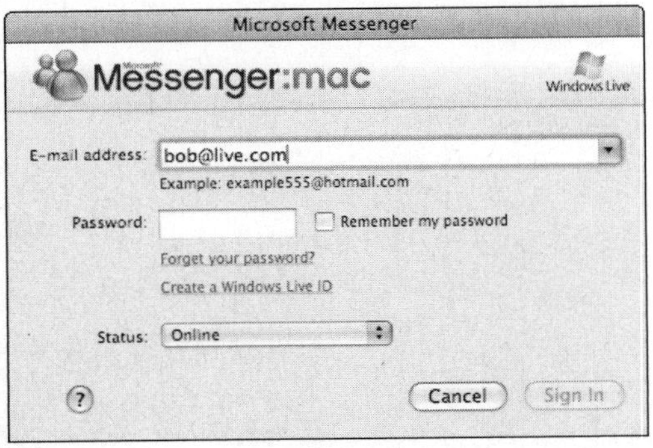

In the sign in window, type your e-mail address and the password you used to create your Windows Live ID account. If you check the Remember my password check box, you don't need to retype your password each time and can skip this dialog box entirely for your next session.

After you're logged in, the Personal Contacts window shows your status as Online next to your ID, as shown in Figure 32.10. The area below your ID info lists two categories: Online and Not Online. As you add friends, family, and coworkers to your contacts, the list shows who is online at the same time as you and who is not available.

**FIGURE 32.10**

When you're logged on, your Windows Live ID appears in the Personal Contacts or Corporate Contacts window.

**NOTE**   If for any reason you run into trouble signing in or need any assistance with Messenger, be sure to check out the Help files; choose Help ⇨ Help Topics. This opens your default Web browser and takes you to the online Help files where you can find some fairly decent Help topics, including one on troubleshooting.

To sign out when you finish using Messenger, choose Network ⇨ Sign Out. This doesn't log you off your Internet connection, nor does it close Microsoft Messenger. It simply takes you off the network, and you appear offline to others in your contacts list.

You can visit Messenger's Preferences dialog box and change any of your start up options, including whether you want Messenger to start up as soon as you start your computer. To find your way to preferences, choose Messenger ⇨ Preferences. This opens the Preferences dialog box. Click the General icon to find the Start preference, as shown in Figure 32.11. Here, you can control how Messenger starts and what sort of status to display if you're away from your computer for any amount of time or in the middle of working with lots of screens. Click OK to save any changes you make.

You can use the General preferences to control how Messenger starts up.

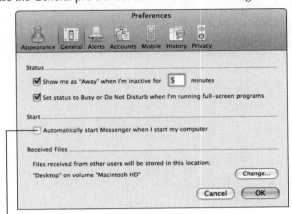

Deselect to turn off
Messenger at startup.

You also can use the Preferences dialog box to add a new account; choose Messenger ⇨ Preferences. Click the Accounts icon, and choose the Personal or Corporate tab, depending on the type of account you want to create. You can click the Change button to set up a new account with another e-mail and password.

# Working with the Personal Contacts Window

After you log in with Messenger, you're ready to start communicating. As mentioned earlier, the Personal Contacts or Corporate Contacts window (depending on which type of account you're using) is the jumping off point for your online session. From this little window, you can communicate with the outside world via your computer.

The Personal Contacts window (and the Corporate Contacts window as well) has a toolbar of buttons at the top and a list pane in the middle detailing who is online and who is not. Between the two areas sits a place with your name, online status, display picture, and personal message. The name is your display name, which is what other people see when you chat with them. To change the name, simply double-click the name and type another. To add a personal message, click the area where it says "Type a personal message," and type a message. You learn about changing your display picture and online status later in this chapter. For now, let's get right to those toolbar buttons you're dying to know about.

The buttons at the top of the window are the stalwart commands for communicating with Messenger. Table 32.1 explains what you can do with each button.

**TABLE 32.1**

## Contacts Window Buttons

| Button | Name | Description |
|--------|------|-------------|
| | Add | Click this button to add a contact. |
| | Send | Click this button to start chatting with someone from your contacts list online. |
| | Send File | Click this button to send a file to a contact. |
| | Page | Set up a pager address using this command, and send messages to mobile devices. |
| | Mail | Check your Windows Live Hotmail account using this command, and send and receive e-mail messages. |

Now that you know what the buttons do, you're probably ready to start communicating, right? Before you do, you need to establish who you're going to communicate with, and you do that by adding some contacts. The next section shows you how.

## Adding and deleting contacts

It's easy to add a contact to your Personal Contacts window. All you need is the person's e-mail address. Naturally, she needs to use an instant messaging service, too, such as AOL Instant Messenger (AIM), Yahoo! Messenger, or iChat. The nice thing about adding a contact is that you can invite her to sign up for instant messaging, if she doesn't have a service already.

To add a contact to Messenger, follow these steps:

 **1.** **Click the Add button in the Personal Contacts or Corporate Contacts window.**

The Add a Contact dialog box opens, as shown in Figure 32.12.

**2.** **Start by typing the person's e-mail address.**

If you need to invite this person to join you on Messenger, you can type a brief invitation. This is optional, of course.

If you want to include the person in your Entourage Address Book, click the check box and fill out the person's name and e-mail address. When prompted, allow Entourage to start in order to complete the task of creating the contact.

**3.** **Click Next to continue.**

Messenger adds the person to your contacts list and offers to e-mail her, as shown in Figure 32.13.

Optionally, you can click the Send Mail button to fire off an e-mail telling her how to download MSN Messenger.

## FIGURE 32.12

The only way you can send instant messages to anyone is to add her to your list of contacts, and you start with this screen.

## FIGURE 32.13

You can e-mail the person an invitation to chat with you on Messenger, if you want, or just continue plowing forward through the Contacts setup steps.

4. **If you're not e-mailing, just click Next to continue.**

The last Add a Contact screen appears, as shown in Figure 32.14.

**FIGURE 32.14**

When you're finished adding contacts, click the Finish button.

5. **Click Finish if you're finished; to keep adding contacts, click Next and repeat the steps again.**

When you finish adding a contact, the contact appears in the Personal Contacts or Corporate Contacts window. If you want to remove a contact from the list, click the name and press Delete, or choose Contact ➪ Delete. A prompt box appears warning you that you're about to remove a contact; click Delete to make it final. You also may notice that the prompt box warns you that you're still visible online to the contact even after you delete her and she can still e-mail you.

 If you want to stop someone from contacting you through Messenger, you need to block him; choose Contact ➪ Block to prevent the person from seeing your online status.

You can organize your contacts into groups in Messenger. For example, you may want to show family members together in one group, friends in another, and coworkers in yet another group. You can create your own groups to appear in the Personal Contacts or Corporate Contacts windows. To create a group, choose Contact ➪ Add a Group. Type a group name, and it's ready to go. You can drag and drop contacts from one group to another. To remove a group, select it and choose Contact ➪ Delete Group.

## Change your display picture

Messenger assigns a default picture to your profile, which you can view in the Personal Contacts or Corporate Contacts window or in the Conversation window when you're sending messages to others. You can change the default picture to something else. You can choose from a library of preset pictures or use one of your own pictures. Follow these steps:

1. **Choose Messenger ⇨ Preferences.**

   The Preferences dialog box opens.

2. **Click the Appearance icon.**

   The Appearance settings appear, as shown in Figure 32.15.

Use the Appearance settings to change your display name, picture, and font.

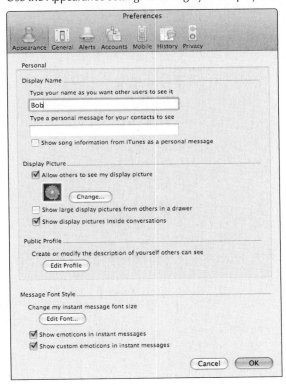

3. **Under the Display Picture area, click the Change button.**

   The Change Display Picture dialog box appears, as shown in Figure 32.16.

4. **Click the image you want to use.**

   To add your own, click the plus icon and choose a file.

5. **Click OK.**

   You're back in the Preferences dialog box.

   Optionally, you can turn off the picture display by deselecting the Allow others to see my display picture check box.

**FIGURE 32.16**

If you can't find a picture you like, you can use one of your own.

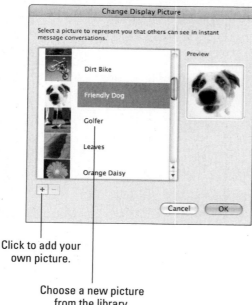

Click to add your
own picture.

Choose a new picture
from the library.

While chatting in an instant message window, Messenger puts the display picture in the window as well as in a drawer that slides out from the side of the window that shows larger versions of the image. To turn off the display, deselect the Show display pictures inside conversations check box. To turn off large pictures from others, deselect the Show large display pictures from others in a drawer check box.

6. **Click OK again to exit the Preferences dialog box.**

## Change your status and privacy settings

You can control your visibility online. Visibility is how others see you or don't see you in their Messenger windows. You also can change your status temporarily to show you're stepping away from the computer or going offline. To change the status, choose Network ⇨ My Status, and choose an option:

- Online
- Busy
- Be Right Back
- Away
- On the Phone
- Out to Lunch
- Appear Offline

You also can click the display picture in the Personal Contacts or Corporate Contacts window and choose a status setting from the pop-up menu, as shown in Figure 32.17.

**FIGURE 32.17**

If you can't find a picture you like, you can use one of your own.

Click to view a pop-up menu.

Whatever setting you choose is what others will see regarding your online status. The current status appears next to your username in the Personal Contacts or Corporate Contacts window, as well as any Conversation windows you have open.

To change your visibility and privacy settings, you can use the Preferences dialog box. The privacy settings keep track of who you allow to see you online and who you've blocked. These people are managed on an Allow List and a Block List. By default, only users on your Allow list can see your status and communicate with you. Anyone on your blocked list can't see your status or send you messages. To view the lists and change settings, follow these steps:

1. **Choose Messenger ➪ Preferences.**

   The Preferences dialog box opens.

2. **Click the Privacy icon.**

   The Privacy settings appear, as shown in Figure 32.18.

3. **Under the Visibility and Privacy area, choose how you want others to view your status:**

   - To block a user, select his name and click the Block button. Messenger adds him to the My Block List.

   - To unblock a person, select his name and click the Allow button.

   - To see who has added you to his contact list, click the View button.

4. **Click OK to exit the dialog box and save any changes you've made.**

**FIGURE 32.18**

Use the Privacy settings to change your visibility and privacy settings.

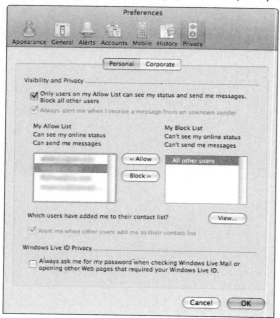

# Sending Instant Messages

As you're looking at your Personal Contacts window or your Corporate Contacts window, you can quickly see who's online and who's not. You can expand and collapse the Online and Not Online headings to view more or less of your contacts list. Click the arrow button in front of the heading to expand or collapse the list. To send an instant message to anyone on the list, follow these steps:

1. **Click the Send button.**

2. **Click the name of the person to whom you want to send a message.** You also can double-click the person's name.

   Messenger opens a Conversation window, as shown in Figure 32.19.

   The top of the window displays some important information about keeping you safe online, and the conversation takes place in the middle scrollable area.

3. **To converse, type your text in the bottom field (refer to Figure 32.19).**

   Optionally, you can click the Font button to change the font used in your text.

   Optionally, you also can click the Emoticon button to add emoticons to your text to express emotions.

**FIGURE 32.19**

Here's an example of a typical conversation window.

The contact's name

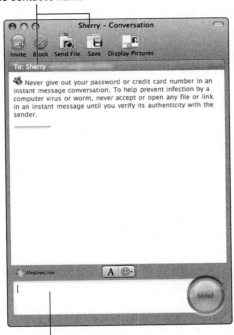

Type your message text.

4. **Click Send.**

The conversation appears in the scrollable pane, as shown in Figure 32.20.

What happens next is much like a tennis match, with conversation bouncing back and forth between both parties, each taking a turn to type and read, and type and read, and so forth.

5. **When your conversation is over, click the window's Close button.**

You also can change your status to show that you're stepping away from the computer or going offline. To change the status, choose Network ➪ My Status and choose an option. These tips and techniques can help you handle instant messages:

■ You can invite more than one person into your instant message conversation. Click the Invite button at the top of the Conversation window, and choose the contact name. If you select the Other option, you can invite someone via e-mail. You also can open more than one conversation window at a time.

■ To block the person from contacting you further, click the Block button.

■ To set the text size in your conversation window, click the Font pop-up menu and choose another font size from the Message Font dialog box that appears, shown in Figure 32.21. You also can set a font, color, bold or italic, and see a preview of the font and size.

**FIGURE 32.20**

As the conversation gets longer, you can use the scroll bar to view previous exchanges.

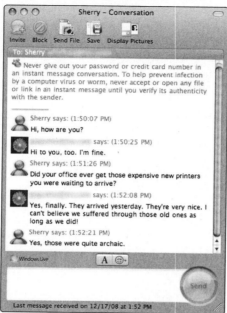

**FIGURE 32.21**

The Message Font dialog box allows you to change some font settings.

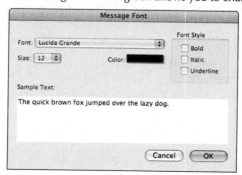

- Click the Emoticon button to view a pop-up menu of emoticons you can insert into your conversation text, as shown in Figure 32.22. To view more emoticons, click the Show more emoticons ellipsis at the bottom of the pop-up menu. This opens the Emoticon dialog box, and you can add more from the list.

## FIGURE 32.22

The Emoticon pop-up menu lets you choose emoticons to express emotions in your instant messages.

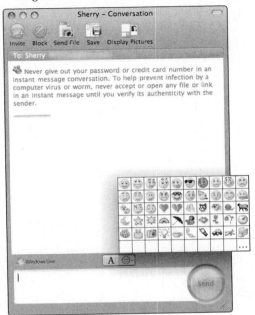

- You can click the Send File button to share a file with the person (learn more about this coming up next).

- Microsoft Messenger automatically checks your spelling as you type. To ignore a misspelling, press Control+click the word and select Ignore Spelling. To add the word to the dictionary, select Learn Spelling. To turn off the feature entirely, choose Edit ➪ Spelling and deselect the Check spelling as you type check box.

- To save your conversation in Messenger's Conversation History folder, click the Save button. You also can opt to save the conversation as a note in an Entourage project.

- To view a saved conversation, choose View ➪ Conversation History and click the All Archived Personal Messages folder or the All Archived Corporate Messages folder. Click the contact you want to view and the date the conversation occurred.

- Click the Display Pictures button to hide or display any profile picture associated with the conversant.

# Sending a File

You can send a file to share with the person you're exchanging messages with. For example, if you're chatting with your mom, you can share the latest photo of her grandson, or if you're chatting with a colleague, you can send a document file. File size is always a concern when transferring data across the Internet. The bigger the file, the longer it takes. Photo files are notoriously large, so you might want to compress it as much as you can before ever attempting to send it. When you send a file, Messenger prompts each user about the transfer. The person receiving it must accept the transfer. After she does, the transfer commences in earnest. Sadly, you can't keep chatting while transferring; you just have to be patient and wait till it's done. After the transfer is complete, you can start chatting again.

To send a file, follow these steps:

1. **Click the Send File button in the Personal Contacts or Corporate Contacts window, or click the Send File button in the Conversation window.**

    The Send File dialog box opens, as shown in Figure 32.23.

2. **Navigate to the file you want to transfer, and click the filename.**

3. **Click Choose.** You also can double-click the filename.

    Messenger displays a message about the transfer, as shown in Figure 32.24.

    As soon as the recipient accepts the transfer, the transfer begins. After the transfer is complete, Messenger lets both parties know, as shown in Figure 32.25.

To receive a file, follow these steps:

1. **When someone wants to send you a file, your conversation window looks like Figure 32.26.** Click Accept to start the transfer.

    A prompt box opens, as shown in Figure 32.27.

2. **Click OK if you trust the source of the file.** It's always a good idea to scan it with virus-protection software before opening the file.

    The file is transferred. Depending on the size, it may take awhile.

### FIGURE 32.23

Locate the file you want to send.

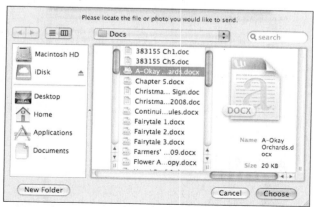

## FIGURE 32.24

Messages about the file transfer appear in the conversation window.

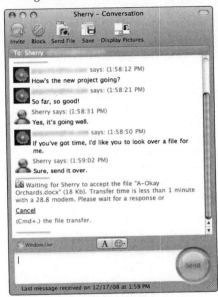

## FIGURE 32.25

Both parties are kept abreast of the transfer status.

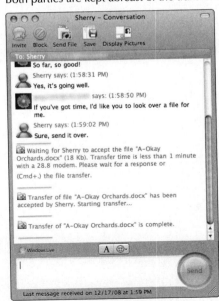

**FIGURE 32.26**

You can accept or decline a file transfer.

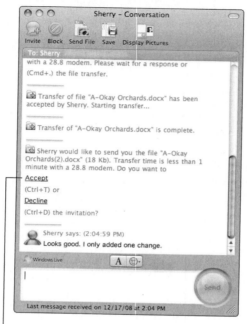

To receive a file,
click Accept.

**FIGURE 32.27**

Tell Microsoft whether you want to receive the file transfer.

# E-mailing from Messenger

Ideally, Entourage is the way to go when it comes to managing e-mail. However, Messenger and Windows
Live can help you e-mail, too. You can use MSN Hotmail on Windows Live to e-mail your contacts from
Messenger. To turn any contact into an instant e-mail, simply click the contact name in the Personal
Contacts or Corporate Contacts window. Next, choose Contact ⇨ Mail. This opens your default Web

browser to the MSN Hotmail page, as shown in Figure 32.28. The Web page is actually a form for creating an e-mail message, much like Entourage's message window. The contact's e-mail address is already filled in for you. All you have to do is type a subject title and a message. When your message is ready, click the Send button.

To check your Hotmail e-mail account at any time, click the Mail button on the Personal Contacts or Corporate Contacts window. This takes you to the Web site again to check your inbox.

**FIGURE 32.28**

Use your free MSN Hotmail account to e-mail contacts through Windows Live.

## Summary

In this chapter, you learned how to set up Microsoft Messenger so you can start sending instant messages your friends, family, and colleagues. The setup procedure walks you through each step for creating account using Windows Live. You can create a free Windows Live ID to use with any of the Windows Live services, including Messenger. Armed with an e-mail address and a password, you're ready to go. You can create a free e-mail address to use through Windows Live.

After you jumped through the hoops for setting up the program, you learned how to add contacts to Messenger and chat live using a conversation window. You also learned how to swap files using the transfer feature and even send e-mail through the MSN Hotmail site. You also learned how to customize various aspects of Messenger to change how others view you online.

# Part VIII

# Coordinating and Customizing Your Office

# Chapter 33

# Coordinating Projects

The very nature of a suite of programs like Microsoft Office 2008 for Mac is that they're designed to work together. Although each program has a unique purpose, you can use them together for even greater productivity. This concept really comes into play when you're working on projects. For example, maybe you've been asked to craft a detailed business proposal. The project may require documents from Word, spreadsheets from Excel, lots of communication through Entourage e-mails, and a slide show presentation in PowerPoint. As you work on the project each day, you need to create all these different kinds of files. That's where the Project Gallery can help. It's a jumping-off point for any kind of Office document you want to create.

With some projects, you end up accumulating lots of different notes and pieces of information before assembling a final product. You can use the Office Scrapbook feature to collect and store all the various pieces of information you want to use later to create a larger project.

In this chapter, you learn how to use both the Projects Gallery and the Scrapbook tool to help you coordinate projects big and small.

## Using the Projects Gallery

The Project Gallery acts like a lobby into the world of Office files. All you have to do is enter and choose which "office" you want to go into. Although we're talking about this feature way in the back of this book, you may have encountered it early on if your gallery is slated to appear by default. Whether it's opened by default or manually, you're presented with a lovely screen full of possibilities whenever you use the feature. Take a look at Figure 33.1. It shows an example of the Project Gallery that appears in Word. This feature is a launching pad for any new file you want to create based on which Office program you open. You simply choose which kind of file you want to create, and you're off and running.

**FIGURE 33.1**

The Project Gallery may appear by default, or you can activate it manually.

New tab appears
by default.

Documents

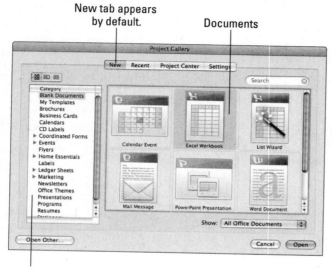

Templates list

To open the Project Gallery manually, choose File ➪ Project Gallery. This step works in any Office program. You also can launch the Project Gallery from the Dock. Just click the Microsoft Project Gallery icon.

**TIP**    **If your Project Gallery opens by default and you want to skip it, just press Esc or ⌘+. (period).**

## Creating a new project

When you first open the gallery, the New tab appears, displaying a plethora of file types you can create. The list box on the left offers an abundance of document ideas. Listing everything from blank documents to flyers to CD labels, you're bound to find something you need to create. This collection is actually a variety of templates. Here's a run-down of what templates you can expect to find:

- **Blank Documents:** This category not only includes blank Word, Excel, or PowerPoint documents, it also includes Entourage e-mails and events, a List Wizard, and Word Notebook or Publishing Layout documents. Needless to say, these are all blank and ready for you to fill out.

- **My Templates:** If you've saved any templates, they're listed in this category.

- **Brochures:** This category lists a variety of brochures you can whip up in Word.

- **Business Cards:** Choose from several professional-looking business card documents you can make in Word.

- **Calendars:** Choose from several attractive calendar documents you can create in Word's Print Layout view.

- **CD Labels:** You can create your own DVD or CD labels using these Word templates and use Avery brand stickers to print them out.

- **Coordinated Forms:** This category creates a variety of coordinated business forms and materials using Word, such as agendas, business cards, faxes, invoices, memos, and reports.

- **Events:** Find templates for creating awards, invitations, postcards, and posters in this category.

- **Flyers:** Choose from several flyer templates you can create in Word.

- **Home Essentials:** This category features Excel templates you can create to manage your household, including worksheets with finance tools, fundraising, graph paper, planners, and travel tools.

- **Labels:** Use the Mailing Label Wizard in this category to start your mass mailing projects.

- **Ledger Sheets:** This category contains Excel templates for making account sheets, budgets, invoices, lists, portfolios, and reports.

- **Marketing:** This category offers a slew of Word templates for marketing, including catalogs, menus, proposals, and signs.

- **Newsletters:** This category lists all kinds of newsletters you can create in Word.

- **Office Themes:** This category is full of PowerPoint presentation templates focusing on color.

- **Presentations:** This category is full of PowerPoint presentations, this time focusing on intent, such as photo albums, pitch book, and so on.

- **Programs:** The documents in this category let you whip up programs for your next recital, play, reunion, or other gathering.

- **Resumes:** Tailored to the job seeker, this category lists resumes.

- **Stationery:** Find letterhead, envelope templates, formal letter templates, and other office stationery items in this category.

> **TIP** You can create your own templates in any of the Office programs and add them to the list in the Project Gallery.

The templates are categorized, and some categories list more than one type to choose from. Categories with Expand Arrows in front of the category name can be expanded to show a larger list of specialized documents. Figure 33.2 shows the Marketing category expanded.

> **TIP** You can use the Expand Arrow to expand a category, and when it's expanded, a Collapse Arrow appears. Click the Collapse Arrow to collapse the list again.

**FIGURE 33.2**

You can expand a category to view more templates to choose from.

Click to expand.

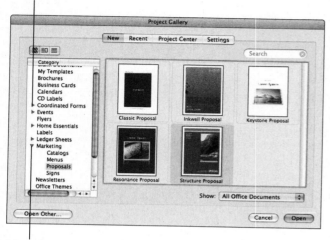

Click to collapse.

When you select a category from the list, icons representing different types of files appear in the center of the window. For example, when you expand the Marketing category and select Proposals, a preview of various types of proposals appears (refer to Figure 33.2). If you see one you like, click it and click the Open button to start creating the file. The template opens in the appropriate program window, and you can start replacing the placeholder text with your own text. In the case of a proposal, Word opens the proposal document you selected. Figure 33.3 shows an example of a proposal template in Word.

Meanwhile, back in the Project Gallery, you can tell the Project Gallery to show only certain Office files. Just click the Show pop-up menu, shown in Figure 33.4, and choose which file type you want to list. The All Office Documents option is selected by default, but you can choose to show just Word, Excel, PowerPoint, or Entourage documents.

If you can't find the document type you want to create, you might try a keyword search in the Search field. Click the field, type the word or phrase you want to search for, and then press Return. The Project Gallery lists any matches.

Or maybe you have other Office templates you want to use rather than the ones listed in the Project Gallery. If this is the case, you can click the Open Other button in the bottom-left corner of the gallery. This displays the Open dialog box, and you can navigate to the folder and file you want to use.

The splendor of the Project Gallery is this: You don't have to know what Office program you need to use to create the document. Office opens the appropriate program based on the template you choose. So if you're using Word, open the Project Gallery and choose to create a ledger sheet; Microsoft Excel opens automatically to help you start the project.

**FIGURE 33.3**

When a template opens, you can add your own text and save it using a unique filename.

Placeholder text

**FIGURE 33.4**

You can tell the Project Center which type of templates you want to view.

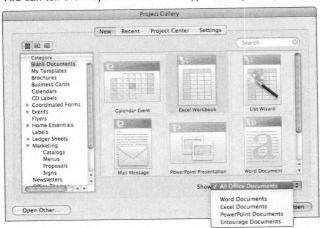

# On or Off?

If your Project Gallery launches by default every time you open a program, you may want to turn the feature off. On the other hand, maybe it's already off, and you'd really like to use it each time. No worries. You can change the launching action to suit your needs. Just open the Project Gallery, and click the Settings tab. Under the General settings, deselect the Show Project Gallery at startup check box. This turns the default launching of the gallery off. If you want to turn it on, just select the same check box.

## Opening recent projects

You can click the Recent tab in the Project Gallery to see a list of all the recent files you've worked on, as shown in Figure 33.5. The list box on the left lets you choose to view files from certain time periods. Click the Today category to see all the files you worked on today. Click the All category to view all the recent Office files you've dallied in. The buttons at the top of the list box let you control how the files are listed. You can choose to list them by icons, show details, or just as a list of filenames. Like the New tab, you can click the Show pop-up menu to control which Office files appear in the list.

### FIGURE 33.5

Use the Recent tab to open a recent file.

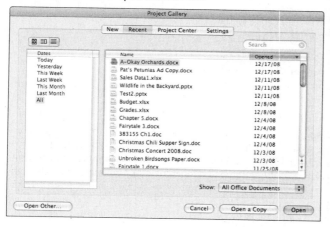

With the exception of Entourage, all the Office programs offer you a route to opening recent files within the program. Choose File ➪ Open Recent, and choose the one you want from the menu. The Project Gallery, however, gives you a chance to open any file, not just program-specific files.

## Using the Project Center

Click the Project Center tab in the Project Gallery to access all the ongoing projects you're working on through the Entourage Project Center tool, as shown in Figure 33.6. As you learned in Chapter 27, the Project Center is a very powerful tool for managing all the elements that go into a project, from messages to documents, from tasks to appointments. Basically anything associated with a project is managed in one central area. The Project Gallery works in cahoots with the Project Center to help you keep your projects organized. When you click the Project Center tab, a list of all your current projects appears on the left. You can click a project name to view its files. To open a file from the project, select it and click the Open button. You can then open any file and start working on it right away. You also can make a copy of the file to work on. Click the Open a Copy button to do so.

**FIGURE 33.6**

Use the Project Center tab to open file associated with a project.

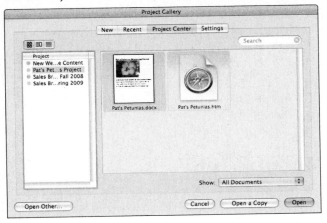

**CROSS-REF** See Chapter 27 to learn more about the Project Center tool.

## Customizing your settings

The last tab in the Project Gallery is the Settings tab, shown in Figure 33.7. As you can probably guess, this tab features all the ways you can control the gallery. This tab houses three main areas of preferences you can change: General, Documents and Wizards, and File Locations. Under the General area, you can control whether the gallery opens by default or specify a confirmation before opening other programs. You also can set the gallery to always open to a particular tab by clicking the Open on pop-up menu and choosing which tab you always want displayed. If you want to alter the number of recent files listed in the Recent tab, change the setting in the Show this number of recently opened files field.

The Documents and Wizards preferences let you select which types of documents and wizards are listed in the gallery. If you don't plan on using PowerPoint, for example, you can turn off the presentation files. Simply deselect any check boxes you don't want to see in the gallery. They're all selected by default unless you specify otherwise.

The File Locations preferences let you choose what templates are listed. By default, the User Templates that you installed with Office 2008 are displayed in the gallery. If you have another folder of templates you'd rather choose from, click the link and navigate to the folder. If you have any workgroup templates, you can add a link to them as well.

One last thing: If you make a bunch of changes to the preferences, you can always go back to the original settings by clicking the Restore Defaults button.

**FIGURE 33.7**

Use the Settings tab to set preferences regarding the Project Gallery.

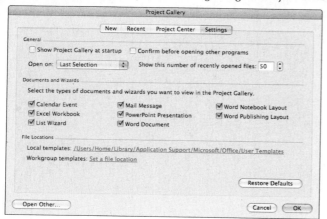

# Using the Office Scrapbook Tool

If you've ever jotted down a note, scribbled an idea, written down a quote, or typed a poem just for safekeeping, you'll find the Office Scrapbook tool useful. As part of the Office Toolbox, the Scrapbook is just as its name implies—a scrapbook of anything you collect and want to keep. Scrapbook items, called *clippings,* can be snippets of text from a Word document, a list of number data from Excel, a quote to use in a slide show, or a note you want to implement later into a message. Scrapbook items include text, graphics, even an entire file. For example, you might place a photo in the Scrapbook to use in an upcoming project, or you might want to grab a joke from an e-mail message to reuse it in a later message. The Scrapbook tool essentially acts as a compendium of electronic items you want to hang onto. It supports GIF, JPEG, PICT, PNG, BMP, PNTG, text, and Unicode text formats.

 To open the Scrapbook tool, you need to access the Toolbox. If you're using Word, Excel, or PowerPoint, click the Toolbox button on the Standard toolbar, and then click the Scrapbook button at the top of the Toolbox. You also can choose View ➪ Scrapbook. In Entourage, choose Tools ➪ Toolbox ➪ Scrapbook. The Scrapbook tool opens, as shown in Figure 33.8.

## Adding items to the Scrapbook

When you place items in the Scrapbook, they're copied and pasted, and the Preview window displays the clippings. The original data stays intact, unless you use the Cut command to remove it from its original location. To add any item to the Scrapbook, first select the text, graphic, or other data you want to copy. The quickest way to place it in the Scrapbook is to drag and drop it into the Scrapbook Palette. You also can use the Cut, Copy, and Paste commands to move data to the Scrapbook.

**FIGURE 33.8**

Behold, the Scrapbook tool, a handy feature for saving snippets of data.

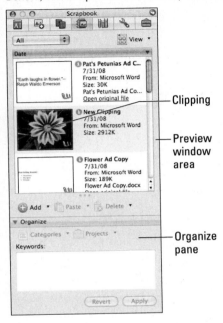

Clipping

Preview window area

Organize pane

In addition, you can use the Add button in the Scrapbook Palette to add items. Click the Add button to add the selected item immediately, or click the button's arrow icon to choose how you want to add an item. You can choose from four options:

- Click Add Selection to add the selected data.
- Click Add File to open the Choose a File dialog box, and select the file you want to add.
- Click Add from Clipboard to add any data you've cut or copied into the Clipboard.
- If you want to make sure you collect everything you're copying in a document, you can activate the Always Add Copy command. This means anything you cut or copy from here on out is added to the Scrapbook.

As your Scrapbook collection grows, you can scroll through the list to view various clippings. The clippings are arranged by date. You can collapse the Organize pane to view more clippings in the Preview window. Click the View button, as shown in Figure 33.9, to change how the items are listed. You can view them by List, Detail, or Large Preview views. Detail view is the default selection.

## FIGURE 33.9

You can control how items are listed in the Scrapbook using the View button.

You can use the pop-up filter menu at the top of the palette to filter clippings by creation date, project, category, originating program, item size, or keywords. Figure 33.10 shows the complete list of filtering options displayed when you click the pop-up menu.

## FIGURE 33.10

You can control how items are filtered in the list using the Quick Filter pop-up menu.

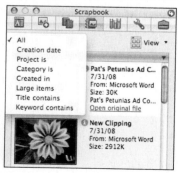

To edit the name of any clipping in the list, double-click the name field. Type a new name, and press Return. The Scrapbook now shows the new clipping name.

## Inserting items from the Scrapbook

 When you're ready to use an item from the Scrapbook, you can drag it from the Scrapbook and drop it where you want it to go. It's really that easy. You also can use the Paste button in the Scrapbook Palette. Click the Paste button to add the selected item immediately, or click the button's arrow icon to choose how you want to insert an item, as shown in Figure 33.11. You can choose from three options:

- Click Paste to paste the clipping just as you found it, original formatting and all.
- Click Paste as Plain Text to remove all the formatting and just paste the plain text.
- Click Paste as Picture to turn the clipping into an object that can be manipulated with any of the Office Picture tools.

**FIGURE 33.11**

To control how a clipping is pasted, click the Paste button's arrow icon and make a selection.

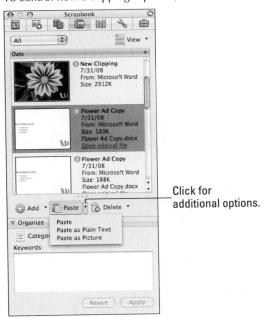

Click for additional options.

## Organizing the Scrapbook

You can use the Organize section at the bottom of the Scrapbook Palette to help organize your clippings. For example, you can assign keywords to a clipping that can help you search for it later. Simply select the clipping, and type the keywords you want to associate with the item in the Keywords box, as shown in Figure 33.12, then click the Apply button.

 You also can assign a category or project to a clipping. To assign a category, select the clipping and click the Categories button. This opens the Assign Categories dialog box where you can choose a category. For a faster assignment, just click the arrow icon next to the Category menu button and choose a category from the pop-up list. The same techniques work for assigning a project using the Project button.

**FIGURE 33.12**

Use the Organize pane to keep your clippings organized.

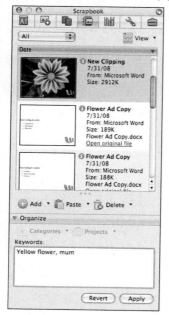

## Deleting clippings

You can easily remove a clipping you no longer want from the Scrapbook Palette. A prompt box appears warning you that the deletion is permanent. After you okay the removal, the clipping is gone forever. Use any of these methods to delete a clipping:

- Press the Delete key.
- Click the Delete button.
- Click the Delete button's arrow key, and choose Delete, as shown in Figure 33.13.
- Click the Delete button's arrow key, and choose Delete Visible or Delete All to remove every clipping listed.

---

**FIGURE 33.13**

Use the Delete button to remove clippings.

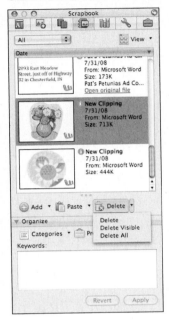

## Summary

In this chapter, you learned how easy it is to start any kind of document regardless of what program you're using. With help from the Project Center, you can quickly open a template and create a Word document, Excel spreadsheet, PowerPoint presentation, or Entourage message or event. In addition, the Project Center includes a few wizards to help you create lists and other custom documents. You also can use the Project Center to navigate to recent files or files associated with any projects you're managing using Entourage's Project Center tool.

This chapter also showed you how to use the Office Scrapbook tool to collect items from various Office programs and reuse again in later documents.

# Chapter 34

# Customizing Office

You can customize Microsoft Office 2008 for Mac to suit the way you work. Whether you're using Office at home, at work, or on the road, you can tailor the program settings to help you work more smoothly and efficiently. Most Office users never take advantage of the customizing options available and end up never discovering the hidden facets of tailoring the programs to make the most of their power and features. Lucky you, this chapter is about to show you how you can find all the options and settings you need to make Office work for you rather than you working with Office.

In this chapter, you learn about each program's preferences and see exactly what's available. You also learn how to customize toolbars and menus, and how to create your own toolbars and menus to use. We also briefly cover how to reassign the keyboard shortcut keys.

## IN THIS CHAPTER

**Using program Preferences to customize Office**

**Customizing toolbars**

**Customizing menus**

**Reassigning keyboard shortcut keys**

## Setting Program Preferences

Within each Office program, there's a behind-the-scenes command center for controlling how the program behaves. That command center is the Preferences dialog box. Depending on the program, the contents of the Preferences dialog box vary in options and appearance. For example, in Word, you find preferences for setting how you want data saved or how you want the spelling and grammar checker to behave. In Excel, you find settings for controlling the number of sheets in a workbook or how you want ToolTips displayed. The Preferences dialog box looks very similar in both Word and Excel, yet very different in PowerPoint and Entourage. Regardless of the varied options, the Preferences dialog box always works quietly in the background, as the bastion for program settings, and the path to reach it is the same in every program.

As far as knowing what settings to change, that's really up to you and what you need. The possibilities are vast, and it really depends on what you want to customize. No book can possibly tell you what preferences to set because they really are based on personal preference. Not every program feature has exhaustive settings you can fiddle with; many of the preferences categories feature only two or three settings you can change. Many of the settings are presented as check boxes or radio buttons you can click to turn the feature on or off. The good thing about the Preferences dialog box, however, is if you need help with identifying a preference setting, you can select it to reveal a description of the preference at the bottom of the dialog box. To help you a bit, however, we cover a few essentials, like how to set a different default file location, how to turn off onscreen elements, and a few of the other features.

## Setting Word preferences

To open the Preferences dialog box in Word, choose Word ➪ Preferences or ⌘+, (comma). Word preferences are grouped into sections, as you can see in Figure 34.1. The programmers tried to place all the various program options in logical groupings, but a programmer's logic may not always jive with everyday users. So to make sense of it all, here's a run-down of the main preference groups:

- **Authoring and Proofing Tools:** You'll find five distinct categories under this group: General, View, Edit, Spelling and Grammar, and AutoCorrect. These categories have settings pertaining to how you add and edit text in Word.

- **Output and Sharing:** This group includes categories related to producing output with your Word files. Categories include Save, Print, Compatibility, Track Changes, and Audio Notes.

- **Personal Settings:** Five more categories lurk under the umbrella of personal settings, which include options for specifying security settings and file locations. The categories include User Information, Security, Feedback, File Locations, and Gallery.

### FIGURE 34.1

You can use Word's Preferences dialog box to change how the program looks and feels, as well how some of the features work.

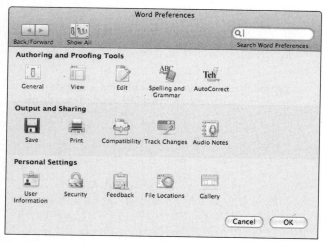

The toolbar at the top of the Preferences dialog box has navigation buttons for moving back and forth among the categories. Click the Back button to move to the previous screen you were viewing in the Preferences dialog box, or click the Forward button to move forward again after just pressing the Back button. Anytime you want to return to the main view of all the groupings, just click the Show All button.

You can use the Spotlight search tool to search for a specific feature in the Preferences dialog box, such as *scroll bar* or *password*. When you type a keyword in the Spotlight box, the location of the feature is literally spotlighted in the Preferences dialog box, and related matches appear below the Spotlight box, as shown in Figure 34.2.

**FIGURE 34.2**

The Spotlight tool can help you locate the preference setting you want to change.

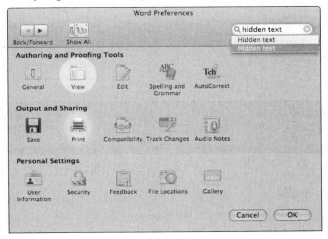

After making any changes to the preferences, you can click OK to exit the dialog box and apply the new settings. To exit without saving your changes, just click Cancel instead.

Now let's look at what kind of settings you can find within each category, starting with the Authoring and Proofing group.

### General

The General category, shown in Figure 34.3, offers a mishmash of options, many of them seemingly unrelated. For example, you can find settings in this group to control how many files appear listed on the Open Recent menu, whether you want to display the Project Gallery at startup, or what measurement units you want to use in the program. For example, if you want the Project Gallery window to pop up when you start Word, make sure this option is selected.

### View

The View category centers around things you view onscreen, such as the Status bar or scroll bars, or things like non-printing characters. You can turn elements on or off by checking or unchecking the check boxes. The Show group of elements includes settings for viewing comments or highlights. The Nonprinting group of elements includes settings for viewing paragraph marks, tab characters, and so on. The Window group of elements includes settings for viewing scroll bars, Status bar, or vertical ruler. For example, if you never look at the Status bar, you can turn it off and free up onscreen space in the work window. The same is true for scroll bars. Other features, such as Live Word Count, can secretly consume lots of CPU power in laptop computers, so turning it off can be a good thing.

**FIGURE 34.3**

Word's General preferences

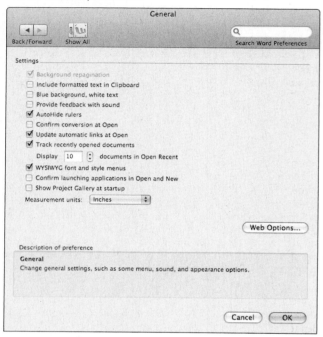

### Edit

The Edit settings include options related to entering data, such as click-and-type or drag-and-drop editing. Most of these options are turned on by default. You can enable or disable them using their check boxes. For example, if you don't want to be able to click anywhere in a document and start typing, you can turn off the click-and-type option.

### Spelling and Grammar

You can use the Spelling and Grammar preferences to turn the spell-check or grammar-check on or off, or control how the features work in Word. You can set both spelling and grammar features, change the associated dictionaries, and choose to check one without the other. You've probably already encountered Word's automatic spell-checking as you typed a document. It's turned on by default and checks your work as you type, underlining any misspellings. To turn off spell-checking, simply deselect the Check spelling as you type check box. To turn off grammar-checking, deselect the Check grammar as you type check box. You can always turn them back on later and check your document for errors. To learn more about Word's spelling and grammar features, see Chapter 11.

### AutoCorrect

You can use the AutoCorrect preferences to change how the AutoCorrect feature works in Word. As you may recall from Chapter 6, AutoCorrect automatically fixes your mistakes as you type. Some users think this is handy, but others don't like it at all. If you fall into the latter category, you can turn the feature off in the Preferences dialog box. Deselect the Automatically check spelling and formatting as you type check box. To learn more about using AutoCorrect, see Chapter 6.

# Setting a Default Font in Word

If you're looking through the Word Preferences options for something to help you change the font used for every file, stop looking. This is one preference you won't find in the Preferences dialog box. Instead, it's located in the Font dialog box. In Word, choose Format ⇨ Font. The Font dialog box opens with the Font tab displayed. Simply change the font, style, and size to the one you prefer, and click the Default button. Word displays a prompt box asking you if you really want to change the default font settings. Click Yes, and the deed is done. Any new documents you open automatically use the font, style, and size you specified unless you choose something else.

## Save

You'll find options for controlling how documents are saved in Word in the Save category of preferences. For example, you specify how often the AutoSave feature saves your data for recovery, specify a specific format for all your saved files, or choose whether to create backup copies every time. If you know you're always going to want to save your documents in another file format, say to pass along to people using older versions of Word, you can choose a different format in the preference settings. By default, Word is set up to save all your documents as .docx files whenever you open the Save As dialog box. This is the default Word 2008 file format. To change this file format in your preferences, click the Save Word files as pop-up menu and choose another file format. To learn more about how to save in Word, including how to use the AutoRecovery feature, see Chapter 5.

## Print

You can control some of the items printed with your documents with the settings in the Print category. You can choose to print drawing objects or hidden text. To learn more about printing in Word, see Chapter 11.

## Compatibility

When you are saving your documents into other formats, particularly earlier versions of Word, it's nice to be able to see what formatting or features you've included in your document that may not be read by earlier versions of Word. You can use the Compatibility tab to view recommended options for the format of your choice. This tab, in conjunction with the Compatibility feature found in the Save As dialog box, lets you view problem areas and make adjustments as needed. To learn more about using the Compatibility-checking feature, see Chapter 5.

## Track Changes

Back in Chapter 10, you learned how to track changes when a document is passed between two or more users for edits. You can use the Track Changes preferences to control the colors of edits made by each person. You can change the color of inserted text, deleted text, formatted text, changed lines, or comments. In other words, you can determine which color is associated with each person editing the document and how his or her edit marks appear. You also can control whether balloons are added or whether the author, time, and date stamp are included. To learn more about the Track Changes tool, see Chapter 10.

## Audio Notes

If you're using Notebook Layout view to add audio notes to a document, you can visit this category in the Preferences dialog box to control audio type, channels, sampling, and quality. Several audio options are available. To learn more about creating documents in Notebook Layout view, see Chapter 6.

### User Information

Word includes basic user information in the document properties for a file. You can change the user information and add additional, more detailed information to your properties. Using this category of preferences, you can set your name, company, address, phone number, and e-mail address. Keep in mind that this information is saved along with every file you create, which means it can be read by anyone viewing the file's properties. The information also is saved in your address book.

### Security

Security preferences allow you to assign a password to a document and remove any personal information associated with the file upon saving. To learn more about using passwords, see Chapter 5.

### Feedback

Here's an interesting category of preferences—this one's designed especially to collect information from you as a Microsoft customer. You had the option of okaying this data-collection program during installation and setup. If you opted out, you can opt back in. Or if you change your mind, you can opt out again. You can click the link in this screen to log onto the Microsoft Web site and learn more about the Customer Experience Improvement Program.

### File Locations

Whenever you open the Open and Save As dialog boxes, they automatically display default storage locations and search paths for documents, templates, and other projects you create in Word. You can change these default locations to other folders you use more frequently. For example, if you continually open a specific work folder every day to edit files, why not save yourself some steps and make it the default folder location for your files? You can adjust the location paths for documents, templates, clip art collections, and more using the settings in this category. To make a change, double-click the Location field or click the Modify button to navigate to a specific folder or file.

### Gallery

The last preferences tab in Word is the Gallery category. Use these settings to adjust how the Elements Gallery appears in Word. For example, you can change its color scheme and how it is displayed. To learn more about Word's Elements Gallery, see Chapter 5.

## Setting Excel preferences

Excel's Preferences dialog box looks much like Word's Preferences dialog box. Preferences are grouped into sections, as shown in Figure 34.4. You can click an icon to open the related settings. To display the Preferences dialog box in Excel, choose Excel ➪ Preferences or ⌘+, (comma). Here are the three main category groupings found in the Excel Preferences dialog box:

- **Authoring:** This group includes six distinct categories: General, View, Edit, AutoCorrect, Chart, and Color. These categories have settings pertaining to how you add and edit data in Excel and how you view elements in the program window.

- **Formulas and Lists:** This group lists categories for controlling how Excel performs functions, formulas, error-checking, and listing tasks. Categories include Calculation, Error Checking, Custom Lists, and AutoComplete.

- **Sharing and Privacy:** The five categories within this group include options for specifying security settings, compatibility settings, and how Excel saves data. The categories include Save, Compatibility, Security, Feedback, and Gallery.

**FIGURE 34.4**

Excel's Preferences dialog box is your one-stop shop for all program settings.

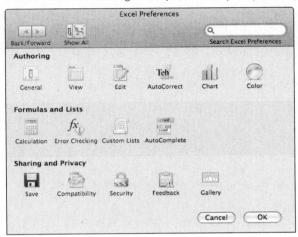

Just like the toolbar you learned about in the Word preferences, the toolbar at the top of the Excel Preferences dialog box has navigation buttons for moving back and forth among the categories. Click the Back button to move to the previous screen you were viewing in the Preferences dialog box, or click the Forward button to move forward again after just pressing the Back button. Anytime you want to return to the main view of all the groupings, click the Show All button.

To search for a specific feature in the Preferences dialog box, such as *scroll bar* or *password,* use the Spotlight search field. When you type a keyword in the Spotlight box, the location of the feature is literally spotlighted in the Preferences dialog box, and related matches appear below the Spotlight box.

When you finish adjusting your program settings, you can click OK to close the dialog box and apply the new settings. The next sections show you what you can expect to find in each Preferences category.

### General

The General category, shown in Figure 34.5, offers a mixed bag of options. For example, you can find settings to set up a specific file to open every time you start Excel. If you find yourself using the same workbook over and over again, why not make it your default file so it's always ready to go when you are? Look for the At startup, open all files in: field, and click the Select button. Navigate to the file you want to use as the default file and click Choose. Back in the Preferences dialog box, the file path appears in the field.

You can speed up your file-saving technique by establishing a default folder or drive that always appears listed first in the Save As dialog box. Click the Select button next to the Preferred file location: field, and choose another folder or drive. The next time you encounter the Save As dialog box, the new default folder location appears.

Another handy thing to look for in the General category is the Standard font and size settings. If you don't like the default font and size Excel assigns for every new workbook you create, change them to something more to your liking. Personally, I prefer a much larger font size so I can read my cell data more easily. To change the font, click the Standard font pop-up menu and choose another. To change the size, click the Size pop-up menu and choose another.

**FIGURE 34.5**

Excel's General preferences

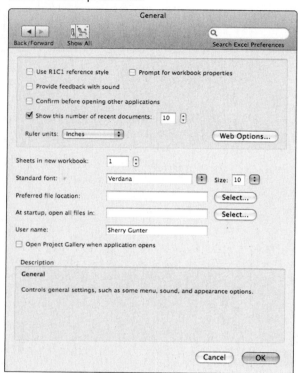

The General options also include settings for specifying ruler units, controlling the number of files listed in the Open Recent menu, and whether the Project Gallery opens at startup.

### View

Everything related to the appearance of program elements appears in the View category. You can turn program elements on or off by selecting or deselecting their check boxes. For example, you can turn the Formula bar or Status bar off or choose not to display comments or placeholders. You can turn off scroll bars, ScreenTips, row and columns headings, and so on.

### Edit

The Edit settings include options related to entering data into your worksheets. Here you find settings for controlling things like double-click editing, drag-and-drop editing, which direction to go when you press Return, and so on.

### AutoCorrect

Excel's AutoCorrect feature is turned on by default for automatically fixing typing errors. You can use the AutoCorrect preferences to change how the AutoCorrect feature works in Excel. You can turn the feature off entirely by deselecting the Replace text as you type check box. To learn more about using AutoCorrect in Excel, see Chapter 13.

### Chart

In The Chart category of preferences you can control how empty cells are plotted in a chart and turn off chart ScreenTips and data marker values.

### Color

You can change the color palette for your Excel workbooks using the settings found in the Color category.

### Calculation

The Calculation preferences let you control how Excel calculates your data. By default, Excel is set up to calculate your formulas and functions as soon as you enter them. You can set up Excel to calculate your data only upon your command. This can save some computer processing power. This category also offers options for calculating goal seeking or handling circular references.

### Error Checking

You can specify how you want Excel to conduct error-checking tasks using the preferences shown in the Error Checking category. You can check or uncheck which rules you want to apply, reset them when needed, and even specify which color is used when errors are flagged.

### Custom Lists

Excel's AutoFill feature, is handy for automatically filling in repetitive or sequential data, as you learned in Chapter 13. You can customize how this works using the options available in the Custom Lists category. The Custom lists box displays some default lists for entering days of the week and months of the year. You can add your own customized lists to the feature, such as Quarter 1, Quarter 2, and so on. You also can import a list from another source.

### AutoComplete

In Chapter 13, you learned about Excel's AutoComplete to help you fill in data more quickly as you type. You can control how this feature works using the settings in the AutoComplete preferences category. You also can turn the feature off entirely by deselecting the Enable AutoComplete for cell values check box.

### Save

The Save preferences allow you to save a preview picture of the workbook and set up AutoRecover to automatically save copies of your workbook as an AutoRecover file every few minutes. In case you experience a power outage or computer glitch of some sort, you can access the last AutoRecover file and recover your data.

### Compatibility

You can find settings for controlling compatibility issues in Excel under the Compatibility category. When you are saving your documents into other formats, particularly earlier versions of Excel, you can find out what formatting or features you've included in your document that may not be read by earlier versions of Excel. The Compatibility Report feature works inside the Save As dialog box to help you make sure your workbooks are compatible for other users.

### Security

Security preferences allow you to assign a password to a workbook to prevent unauthorized use or to prevent anyone from changing the workbook. You can choose to protect a single sheet in the workbook or the entire workbook.

### Feedback

The Feedback preferences are geared toward collecting information about your computer usage. If you opted not to disclose feedback, you can choose to participate again through this category. Click the link in the Feedback screen to log onto the Microsoft Web site and learn more about this program.

### Gallery

The final preferences category is the Gallery category. You can use these settings to adjust how the Elements Gallery appears in Excel. You can change how the feature opens, control its color scheme, and change how the feature is displayed.

## Setting PowerPoint preferences

The PowerPoint Preferences dialog box looks a bit different than the same dialog boxes in Word and Excel. Instead of icons listed as groups, the preferences categories are listed as icons at the top of the dialog box, as shown in Figure 34.6. Simply click the icon to reveal the related preferences.

When you finish adjusting your program settings, you can click OK to close the dialog box and apply the new settings. The next sections show you what you can expect to find in each Preferences category.

### General

The General category offers a variety of options that do not fit into other categories. The General options also include settings for setting Web and movie options, controlling the number of files listed in the Open Recent menu, and whether the Project Gallery opens at startup.

---

**FIGURE 34.6**

PowerPoint's General preferences

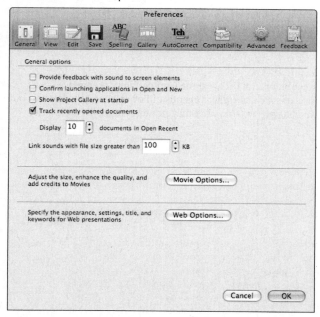

---

### View

The View preferences let you change a few ways in which PowerPoint displays the ruler, the default view for when you start presentations, and slide show navigation tools.

### Edit

The Edit settings include options related to entering text into your slides. Here you find preferences for cutting and pasting, text selection and editing, and how the Undo command tracks undos.

### Save

You find save options listed under the Save category. You can set up AutoRecover to automatically save copies of your presentation as an AutoRecover file every few minutes in case you experience a computer glitch. You also can set a default file format for presentations in conjunction with the Save As dialog box. You can find options for resolution settings when saving your slides as graphic files.

### Spelling

You can use the Spelling preferences to turn the spell-check on or off and control how the feature works in PowerPoint. The spell-check feature is turned on by default and checks your work as you type. To turn off spell-checking, simply deselect the Check spelling as you type check box.

### Gallery

Click the Gallery icon to view preferences for using the Elements Gallery in PowerPoint. The category offers the very same options as the Gallery category in Word and Excel.

### AutoCorrect

The AutoCorrect feature is turned on by default, which means it's always at work fixing common spelling mistakes as you type. You can control how the feature works using the Preferences dialog box. Click the AutoCorrect icon to view the options. To learn more about AutoCorrect, read about it in the Word section, in Chapter 6. The feature works the same in all the Office programs.

### Compatibility

The Compatibility Report tool, which appears in the Save As dialog box, can be controlled through the Preferences dialog box. Simply click the Compatibility icon to reveal the Compatibility preferences. As you're saving your presentations into other formats, such as earlier versions of PowerPoint, you can find out what formatting or features you've included in your presentation that may not be compatible with other versions of the program.

### Advanced

Although the Advanced preferences sound intimidating, the options within are not. Here you can set default locations for presentation files and associated files, and find fields for entering your name and initials to include as personal information.

### Feedback

The Feedback category lets you turn the Customer Experience Improvement Program on or off. This tool gathers information from your computer about the way in which you use hardware, software, and services. You may or may not want Microsoft to collect this information.

## Setting Entourage preferences

So far, we've examined the Word, Excel, and PowerPoint preferences. The Word and Excel preferences are presented in the same format. The PowerPoint preferences used a similar look and feel. The Entourage Preferences dialog box, shown in Figure 34.7, shows an entirely different presentation of options. Instead of icons or tabs, the preference categories are arranged as a list box on the left that you can click to view individual categories of settings.

When you finish adjusting your program settings, you can click OK to close the dialog box and apply the new settings. The next sections show you what's available among the Entourage settings.

### General

In Entourage, the General category of preferences, shown in Figure 34.7, includes an option for setting Entourage as your default e-mail client, settings for keyboard shortcuts, and the WYSIWYG (What You See Is What You Get) font menu. You can turn these various options on or off as needed.

**FIGURE 34.7**

Entourage's General preferences

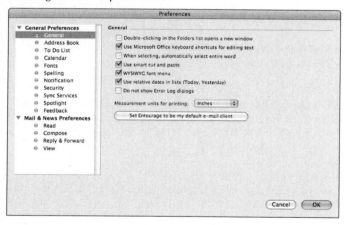

### Address Book

Display the Address Book preferences to change the default address or phone number formats and whether Entourage links contacts with messages. For example, you may want to list a default area code for all new contacts you create so that the number is already filled in for you whenever you start a new contact. Many countries use different addressing formats for mail. If your contacts are all from the United Kingdom, for example, you can set that country as your default address format style.

### To Do List

Edit the To Do List preferences by choosing a different due date or a default snooze time.

### Calendar

You can use the Calendar preferences to set the first day of the week, control which days constitute a work week, set work hours, set a default time zone, and control how reminders occur.

### Fonts

Use the Fonts preferences to set default fonts for list items, HTML messages, plain text messages, and printed items.

### Spelling

Like the other Office programs, Entourage includes a built-in spell-check feature that's turned on by default. You can specify how you want the feature to work using the Spelling category. You can use the Spelling preferences to turn spell-check on or off and control how the feature works. To turn off spell-checking, deselect the Check spelling as you type check box.

### Notification

Use the Notification preferences to change how Entourage alerts you to new message arrivals. You can set up Entourage to display alerts or set sounds for the various notification tasks.

### Security

You can use the Security category of the Preferences dialog box to set a few security options, such as warning before allowing external applications to send mail or access your address book, or HTML options, such as downloading pictures.

### Sync Services

Display the Sync Services preferences to synchronize Entourage with other features and applications, such as synchronizing Entourage events with iCal.

### Spotlight Services

The Spotlight Services category offers a few options for controlling how the Spotlight search tool works in Entourage.

### Feedback

The Feedback preferences let you turn the Customer Experience Improvement Program on or off. This tool gathers information from your computer about the way in which you use hardware, software, and services. You may or may not want Microsoft to collect this information. You can turn the feature on or off if you'd like.

### Read

You can find preferences for controlling how messages are read in Entourage using the Read category. You can choose what to do with messages upon reading them, determine how to mark them as read, and set a default character set.

### Compose

The Compose preferences help you set options for how you compose your messages, including attachments. You can find options for saving copies of sent messages, setting a default mail and news format, and applying any encoding or file compression.

### Reply & Forward

The Reply & Forward preferences include options for controlling whether the original message text is included in the reply, setting an attribution line at the top of the reply or forward, or using the default account to reply.

### View

Lastly, the View preferences let you control how messages appear, such as bold or in color, with or without pictures, and so on.

# Customizing Toolbars and Menus

One of the easiest ways to customize an Office program is to tweak its toolbars and menus. Each program comes with a default set of commands. The Microsoft designers and programmers tried to anticipate the ways in which most users would use the various commands and tools. As such, they've placed the most commonly used commands on toolbars and menus. These may or may not be the tools you prefer to access the most, or their arrangement may not particularly suit the way you work. For example, you may want a specialized menu with completely unrelated commands that you frequently use, or you may prefer an entirely different toolbar composition than what's available. Don't sweat it; change it! It's easy, and this section shows you how.

## Customizing toolbars

Every toolbar in the Office programs is customizable. You can move buttons around to change their order, delete buttons from a toolbar that you have no need for, or add buttons you do need but don't currently see anywhere else. You also can create an entirely new toolbar featuring just the tools you want to use, all conveniently located on one toolbar. For example, if you use lots of styles, why not place your favorites on a toolbar so you can access them with a single click? Your customization actions for toolbars and menus are done when you switch to Edit mode. This is accomplished through the Customize Toolbars and Menus dialog box. When you open this dialog box, your Office program makes all the toolbars and menus editable. This means you can make changes to them directly, or add new toolbars and menus. As soon as you close the Customize Toolbars and Menus dialog box, the customizing is over. You're back to the normal program screen.

When customizing toolbars, you can summon any existing toolbar and make changes to its buttons, or you can create a new toolbar and populate it with commands you use most frequently. The Customize Toolbars and Menus dialog box is divided into two tabs: Tools and Menus, and Commands. The Tools and Menus tab, shown in Figure 34.8, lists all the toolbars and menus found in the program. The Commands tab, shown in Figure 34.9, lists all the available commands found in the program.

## Viewing Toolbars

The Standard toolbar is a permanent part of your Office programs, but if you haven't already figured this out, you can use plenty of other toolbars to perform various tasks and activate commands. Depending on the task at hand, some toolbars pop up immediately as you're working. Other toolbars must be activated manually. The other toolbars can be turned on or off using the View menu. Choose View ➪ Toolbars ➪, and then choose the toolbar you want to view. A check mark next to the toolbar name means the toolbar is displayed; no check mark means the toolbar is turned off.

**FIGURE 34.8**

Use the Tools and Menus tab in the Customize Toolbars and Menus dialog box to view a list of all the toolbars and menus offered in the program.

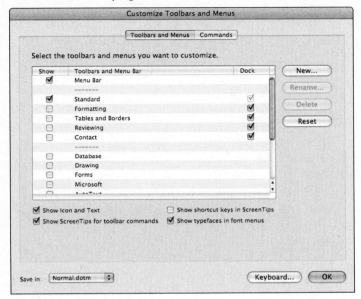

**FIGURE 34.9**

Use the Commands tab to view a list of all the commands offered in the program.

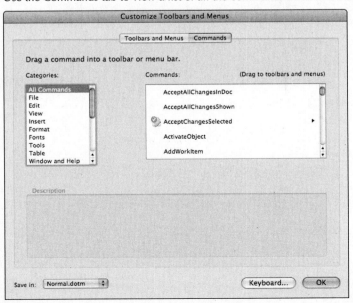

## Icons or Text?

When you add commands to a toolbar, they may or may not include an icon. Some commands are strictly text labels. You can take control over what icons or text labels are used with a little help from the Command Properties dialog box. Control+click the button and choose Properties to open the dialog box. You can choose a different button icon from the pop-up library, or you can design your own. You can even design a button in another program and copy and paste it into the Command Properties dialog box.

### Moving or deleting buttons

To move or delete a button from a toolbar, follow these steps:

1. **Choose View ➪ Customize Toolbars and Menus.**

   The Customize Toolbars and Menus dialog box appears (refer to Figure 34.8).

2. **Click the Toolbars and Menus tab.**

3. **Click the check box for the toolbar you want to edit.**

   A check mark in front of the toolbar name means the toolbar is displayed; no check mark means the toolbar is not displayed.

   If your toolbar already appears onscreen, such as the Standard toolbar, you do not need to turn it on; it's ready to edit now.

4. **To move a button, click and drag the button and drop it into a new location on the toolbar.**

5. **To delete a button, simply drag it off the toolbar or drag it onto another toolbar.**

6. **When you finish moving or deleting buttons, click the OK button to exit the dialog box and exit Edit mode.**

If you don't like all the changes you've made to a toolbar, you can restore it to its original appearance. Reopen the Customize Toolbars and Menus dialog box, and click the Toolbars and Menus tab. Next, click the toolbar you want to restore, and then click the Reset button. This restores it to the original Office settings.

### Adding buttons

To add a button to a toolbar, follow these steps:

1. **Choose View ➪ Customize Toolbars and Menus.**

   The Customize Toolbars and Menus dialog box opens.

2. **Click the Toolbars and Menus tab.**

3. **Select the toolbar you want to edit, if the toolbar isn't already displayed.**

4. **Click the Commands tab (refer to Figure 34.9).**

   A list of command categories appears, with commands grouped by menu, and the commands are listed on the right for each menu category.

5. **Peruse the commands until you find the one you want; select the command you want to add to the toolbar.**

6. **Click and drag the command from the dialog box, and drop it onto the toolbar where you want it to appear.**

   You can continue adding more buttons as needed.

7. **When you finish adding buttons, click the OK to exit the dialog box and exit Edit mode.**

# Moveable Toolbars

**D**id you know that the Office toolbars can be moved around onscreen? With the exception of the permanently docked Standard toolbar, you can move all the other toolbars around on the program window or dock them on the side of the window. To move a toolbar, essentially making it a floating toolbar, click and drag the toolbar's skinny little handle area at the far left end of the toolbar. If you drag a toolbar near the edge of the program window, it suddenly seems magnetized and wants to dock there. You also can resize a floating toolbar by dragging its bottom-right corner. When you move your mouse pointer over the corner, the arrow pointer takes the shape of a double-arrow pointer, which you can then click and drag to resize the toolbar.

### Creating a new toolbar

If customizing existing toolbars isn't floating your boat, you can design your own toolbar and fill it with the commands of your choice. For example, you might want a toolbar filled with buttons for copying and pasting data or inserting the current date and time. As the designer, you control exactly which buttons appear on the toolbar, and you can edit whenever you need to change it to suit your work needs.

To create a new toolbar populated with commands you use the most, follow these steps:

1. **Choose View ⇨ Customize Toolbars and Menus.**

   The Customize Toolbars and Menus dialog box opens.

2. **Click the Toolbars and Menus tab.**

3. **Click the New button.**

   The Add a Toolbar dialog box appears, as shown in Figure 34.10.

---

**FIGURE 34.10**
_____

You can give your new toolbar a distinct name.

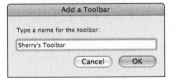

4. **Type a name for the new toolbar.**

5. **Click OK.**

6. **Click the Commands tab.**

7. **Locate the command you want to add to the toolbar, and then click and drag the command from the dialog box and drop it onto the toolbar where you want it to appear.**

   You can continue adding more buttons as needed, as shown in Figure 34.11.

8. **When you are finished building the new toolbar, click the OK to exit the dialog box and exit Edit mode.**

## FIGURE 34.11

When you create a new toolbar, you can choose whichever commands you want to appear on the toolbar.

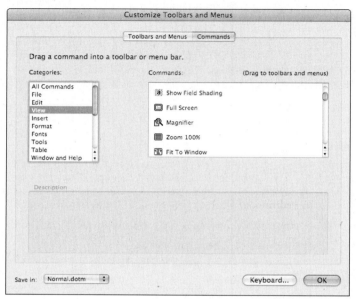

The new toolbar is added to the program's toolbar collection. To activate it at any time, visit the View menu and select it from the list of available toolbars.

## Customizing menus

Like the toolbars you learned about above, every menu in the Office programs is customizable. You can move menus around on the main menu bar, and you can move commands around, remove commands you never use, and add commands you want to use more often. You can use the Customize Toolbars and Menus dialog box to edit menus. The Tools and Menus tab in the dialog box lists all the toolbars and menus the program contains, and the Commands tab lists all the commands available. The commands are grouped by menu name.

### Removing menu commands

To remove a command from any menu, follow these steps:

1.  **Choose View ⇨ Customize Toolbars and Menus.**

    The Customize Toolbars and Menus dialog box opens, and an odd-looking menu bar appears at the top of the screen. This is a duplicate of the main menu bar, and any menu name you click opens to reveal a list of associated menu commands.

2.  **To remove a command, drag it off its respective menu.**

3.  **When you finish removing commands, click the OK button to exit the dialog box and exit Edit mode.**

You also can remove a menu. Just drag it off the duplicate menu bar.

If you ever need to restore your menus to their default state, open the Customize Toolbars and Menus dialog box, click the Toolbars and Menus tab, click Menu Bar, and then click the Reset button. This restores it to the original Office settings.

### Adding menu commands

To add a command to a menu, follow these steps:

1. **Choose View ⇨ Customize Toolbars and Menus.**

   The Customize Toolbars and Menus dialog box opens.

2. **Click the Commands tab, shown in Figure 34.12.**

3. **Locate and select the command you want to add.**

4. **Click and drag the command from the dialog box, and drag it over the menu where you want to insert it.**

   The menu opens (refer to Figure 34.12).

5. **Drop the command onto the menu where you want it to appear.**

   You can continue adding more commands as needed.

6. **When you finish editing menus, click the OK to exit the dialog box and exit Edit mode.**

While you have the Customize Toolbars and Menus open, you can change the order in which the menus appear on the menu bar. Simply drag a menu to a new location on the bar.

**FIGURE 34.12**

Customize an existing menu by adding or removing commands.

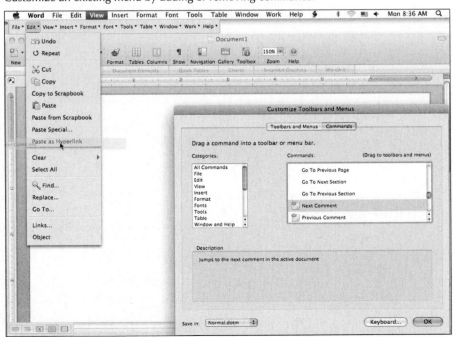

### Creating a new menu

To create a brand new menu and add it to the main menu bar, follow these steps:

1. **Choose View ⇨ Customize Toolbars and Menus.**

   The Customize Toolbars and Menus dialog box appears.

2. **Click the Commands tab.**

3. **Scroll to the bottom of the Categories list to select the New Menu command, as shown in Figure 34.13.**

---

**FIGURE 34.13**

To build a new menu, activate the New Menu option.

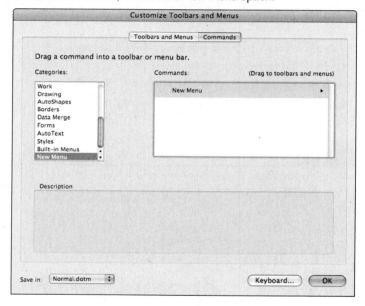

---

4. **Drag the command up to the duplicate menu, and place it where you want it to appear on the menu bar.**

5. **Control+click the new menu, and choose Properties, or just double-click the new menu.**

   The Command Properties dialog box opens, as shown in Figure 34.14.

6. **Type a name for the new menu in the Name field.**

7. **You can now populate the menu with the commands you want.** Using the Commands tab, you can drag commands onto the new menu.

8. **When you finish building the new menu, click the OK to exit the dialog box and exit Edit mode.**

**FIGURE 34.14**

Type a name for the new menu.

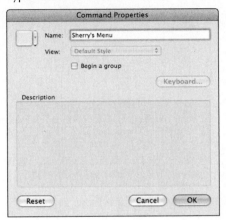

## Customizing Keyboard Shortcut Keys

Each Office program has keyboard shortcuts coded into the application for accessing common commands using the keyboard. Many users prefer to keep their fingers flying on the keyboard rather than clicking mouse buttons and moving the mouse around on a pad. If keyboard shortcut keys are your preferred method of assigning commands, you'll be delighted to know you can customize how they work in the Office programs. You can do this by reassigning the keys Microsoft has already assigned. In fact, sometimes the pre-assigned keyboard shortcut keys don't make much sense, and you may prefer another combination. You can reassign keys to your favorite commands easily. Now for the bad news—you can only do this in Word and Excel. You can customize keyboard shortcut keys for PowerPoint and Entourage; however, you have to go outside of the programs to do so—through System Preferences.

To reassign keyboard combinations in Word or Excel, start by opening the Customize Keyboard dialog box, shown in Figure 34.15, by choosing Tools⇨Customize Keyboard. This dialog box works very similarly to the one you used to customize toolbars and menus. You choose a category on the left and a command on the right. When you find a command you want to change, click the field labeled Press new shortcut key field and type the key combination you want to use. If the combination is already in use elsewhere, the dialog box tells you so. You can click the Assign button to reassign it anyway.

**FIGURE 34.15**

You can use the Customize Keyboard dialog box to reassign keyboard combination keys.

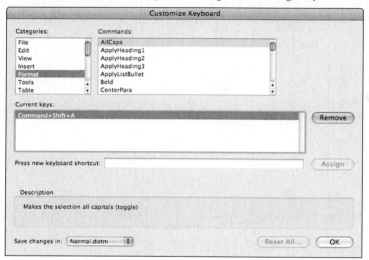

## Summary

In this chapter, you did a visual walk-through of all the preference settings for Word, Excel, PowerPoint, and Entourage. You also learned how to customize toolbars and menus to show only the commands you want by adding or subtracting commands. If adding or subtracting commands isn't enough, you were shown how to create a brand new toolbar and menu and populate it with commands you use the most. Lastly, you learned how to quickly reassign a keyboard shortcut key.

# Chapter 35

# Working with AppleScript

AppleScript is a scripting language built into Mac OS X to help users create instructions to tell the computer what to do without needing to use a mouse or keyboard. Granted, you're already doing that through commands, menus, clicking and dragging, and so on, but scripting is writing specific instructions tailor-made for your needs. For example, perhaps you have a folder filled with files you need to convert to another format. You can write a script that automatically converts the file formats for you, thus saving you oodles of time and effort ordinarily spent doing the task yourself, opening each file, going through the steps of saving them under another file format, and so on. That's just one tiny example of how you might use AppleScript. You can come up with literally hundreds of scripts to help make your own computer work easier.

If scripting isn't your thing, then you can skip all the programming language and use the Automator tool to whip up workflows for repetitive tasks. By using built-in actions, Automator lets you assemble a workflow step-by-step to instruct an Office program to handle tedious tasks while AppleScript works in the background.

In this chapter, you learn how to tap into the beauty of AppleScript by running some simple scripts in Office. You also learn how to use sample workflows and the Automator tool. In case you're keeping track, this is the last chapter—rejoice!

## IN THIS CHAPTER

Introducing AppleScript

Viewing the Script Editor window

Using Office scripts

Working with Automator

Using Office workflows

## What Is AppleScript?

AppleScript's been around awhile now, starting way back with a project called HyperCard. HyperCard made use of an English language-based scripting language known as HyperTalk. Apple engineers then utilized the scripting language in other applications and began placing it in System 7 in 1993 as an end-user l anguage for controlling applications and automating workflows. One of the very first major software applications to utilize AppleScript was QuarkXPress. This is worth mentioning because QuarkXPress is an extremely popular page-layout program used by large and small publishing companies to produce complex magazine and catalog layouts and other printed materials. Because QuarkXPress is one of the major forces in the worldwide publishing field, and therefore used

935

by a vast number of Mac users, its support of AppleScript was a considerable endorsement. In turn, AppleScript became widely adopted within the publishing industry, particularly in the Apple market, which continues to be the computer of choice in the creative marketplace today. With the move to Mac OS X, AppleScript continues to be a powerful tool for making your computer tasks more productive.

Most people never consider using scripts to control their computers. Because scripting is a programming language, most users think it's difficult and time-consuming and requires a certain level of knowledge. However, it's not as hard as it sounds, and you can use scripts to automate repetitive tasks, create shortcuts, or even build your own custom applications. Truth be told, much of what you do in the Microsoft Office programs is really AppleScript scripts at work behind the scenes. Individuals, professionals, businesses, and developers can find lots to like about AppleScript. For end users, AppleScript can help make easy work of seemingly daunting tasks like naming files or resetting preferences. For professionals and businesses, AppleScript can speed up data retrieval, schedule updates, manage files from remote servers, and more. AppleScript workflows provide accuracy, consistency, and speed, three overarching qualities for good business practices. For developers, AppleScript offers easy-to-use automation tools for creating applets, applications, and Automator actions. Since its introduction, AppleScript has been growing in popularity and usage, and with Mac OS X, numerous applications make use of its efficiency and effectiveness. Microsoft Office 2008 for Mac is no exception, and since Microsoft Office 2008 did away with VBA—Visual Basic for Applications—AppleScript is the only way to go now.

What's so interesting about AppleScript's scripts? The scripting language closely resembles English, and it's based on sentences and statements. When the computer's operating system reads these saved sentences and statements, which is called a *script,* it converts the instructions into Apple Event messages (messages sent from one Mac application to another) that tell the applications what to do. They call them scripts because, like a movie script or a script from a play, they are performed in the order in which they are written.

Messages and events are the underlying pillars of AppleScript. Applications perform tasks based on responses to events. The messages that applications send to each other are called *Apple events*. When an application receives a message about an event, it takes action based on the event. Actions can be anything from manipulating data to menu commands, and so forth. Every application you use on the Mac, from Finder to Office programs, responds to three basic Apple events: Open Application, Open Documents, and Quit Application. Most applications go far, far beyond just these three basics.

## What's a Workflow?

When talking about AppleScript, the term *workflow* seems to come up often. What exactly is a workflow anyway? For a lofty definition, a workflow is a repeatable pattern of activity utilized by a systematic organization of resources, an automation of a process in whole or part, during which information, documents, or tasks are passed from one spot to another for action according to procedural rules. For a more down-to-earth definition, a workflow is simply a sequence of operations. When it comes to scripting, a workflow is a way to make it easier for users to orchestrate a complex computer task from point A to point Z or wherever the task ends. The basic building blocks of a workflow are events, actions, conditions, and steps. Suppose your work team's job is to write, revise, and approve proposals. The proposals are stored in a document library. You might create a workflow that sends an e-mail notification that a new proposal has been added to the library, creates a task in the Entourage Tasks list, and when the document is reviewed, more actions are performed based on whether the document was approved or rejected. On a smaller scale, you might create your own workflow that takes a form letter you've drafted in Word and open it with details already filled in and addressed to an Entourage contact.

AppleScripts come in two flavors: applets or scripts. Applets, also called droplets, are by definition, small components that run in the context of a larger program, sort of like mini-programs within the major program. An applet becomes a droplet if users have to drag-and-drop files into it for launching.

Look at the following script:

```
activate application "Finder"
```

When activated, this line of script opens up the Finder window. That's all. No button pressing, no pulling down of menus and selecting commands. The Finder window just immediately opens. Let's see another one:

```
tell application "Finder" to open trash
```

This script tells Finder to open the Trash folder. As you can see, the scripting language is pretty straightforward. A single statement like the one above performs a simple task. Most tasks, however, require much longer statements than this one. Here's an example of a longer script:

```
tell application "Finder"
    if folder "Applications" of startup disk exists then
            return count files in folder "Applications" of startup disk
    else
            return 0
    end if
end tell
```

If you were to compile and execute this script, it returns the number of files—just the files, not the folders— found in the Applications folder on the current system disk. If it cannot find the folder, the script is instructed to return a count of zero. This script causes an Apple event to be sent to Finder, which in turn locates the Applications folder on the startup disk, counts the number of files it finds there, and returns the value. Pretty cool, eh?

## Viewing the Script Editor

You can use Mac's Script Editor, shown in Figure 35.1, for writing, editing, compiling, and running scripts. The Script Editor is part of your Mac OS X operating system. You can find it in the Applications folder located in the AppleScript application folder. To open Script Editor, double-click its name in the AppleScript folder window. When you first open the program, a blank script window appears. You can write only one script at a time in the Script Editor.

As you can see in Figure 35.1, the Script Editor window has a very simple interface with a large area for writing scripts. The top empty area is where you type scripts. The bottom area is the script description/result/event log area depending on what you're doing. Notice that the toolbar has only five buttons, and only four are active: Record, Stop, Run, and Compile are the active buttons you can use for building and editing your scripts.

**FIGURE 35.1**

The Script Editor lets you write, compile, and run AppleScript scripts.

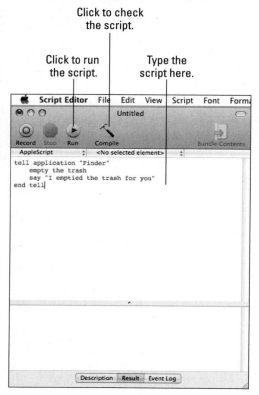

**Writing a script**

To get your feet wet in the pool of AppleScript, let's try typing a few scripts and see what they do. This will give you a little taste of programming and maybe inspire you to think of other things you can do with AppleScript. Follow these steps:

1. **Open the Script Editor; choose Applications ⇨ AppleScript ⇨ Script Editor.**

   This opens the Script Editor window (refer to Figure 35.1).

2. **In the blank area, type the following line of text, being sure to include all the punctuation you see, as shown in Figure 35.2:**

   say "this is a spoken sentence."

3. **Click the Run button on the toolbar.**

   If your volume is up a bit, you should hear your computer utter the line "this is a spoken sentence."

4. **To try another voice, add the following to the existing script, shown in Figure 35.3:**

   say "this is a spoken sentence." using "Fred"

**FIGURE 35.2**

You can type scripts in the upper area of the Script Editor window.

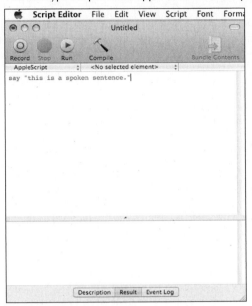

**FIGURE 35.3**

You can use this script to change the voice used to speak the text you type in the editor window.

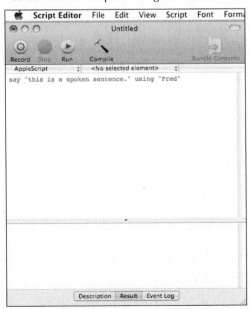

**5. Click Run.**

> This time the computer speaks the same sentence using another voice, which you defined as Fred. You also can try the voices Victoria, Cellos, or Zarvox.

One of the most used commands in AppleScript is "tell." This command lets you tell a specific application what to do. If you wanted to open Microsoft Excel in a script, for example, you'd type the following code:

```
tell application "Microsoft Excel" to activate
```

You can try this code in the Script Editor window, but be sure to erase the previous code you wrote. When you click the Run button after typing the activate Excel instruction code, the Microsoft Excel program opens. If you wanted the Excel window to close, you'd substitute "close" for "activate" in the script example above. As you can tell by the coding structure, AppleScript is very much like the English language. When writing scripts, you must act much like a boss or general, telling who is to perform a task and which task to perform. Here's another example of a script using Finder:

```
tell application "Finder"
  empty the trash
end tell
```

This script tells Finder to empty the trash. Notice the "end tell" instruction. Without this little code, Finder would keep emptying the trash.

## Compile a script

You can activate the Compile command to let the Script Editor check your script for any problems. Just click the Compile button. If you're using a laptop Mac, you can press Enter to the right of the spacebar, or the Enter key on the numerical keypad (Mac desktops) to compile a line of text while starting a new line of text in the script window. Although you do not have to compile a script before running it, the Script Editor does that as soon as you click the Run button, so it is best to compile your script often to check for errors. However, if you click the Compile button and you've written your script properly, the Script Editor formats your script in nice colors. Uncompiled text shows up in orange in the script window. If your script contains a mistake, an error message appears alerting you.

Here's one more fun little script example for you to try:

```
tell application "Finder"
  empty the trash
  say "I emptied the trash for you"
end tell
```

This script tells Finder to empty the trash folder and speak the statement. Anything between the tell and end tell parts of the script are called a *tell block*. All the instructions for the same application are coded within the tell block for that application.

## Saving a script

After you create a script you want to keep, you can save it using the Save dialog box shown in Figure 35.4. From the Script Editor window, choose File ⇨ Save to open the dialog box and give the file a name. By default, Script Editor saves the script in the script file format, and you can use the Script Editor whenever you want to run the script. There are other script formats you can choose. For example, if you save the script as an application, it has its own icon. You can double-click the icon to run the script.

**FIGURE 35.4**

You can save your scripts and give them unique names.

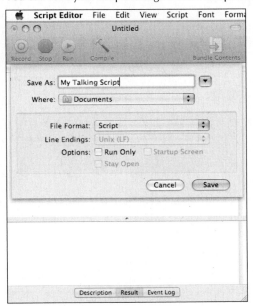

When you finish using the Script Editor window, close the window just like any other program window on your computer. Click the Close button, or choose Script Editor ⇨ Quit Script Editor. Although using the Script Editor in greater detail is beyond the scope of this book, you've at least had a little education about how it works. You can learn more about it from numerous other sources, including dozens of Web sites online. For the remainder of this chapter, we focus on ready-made scripts already available on Microsoft Office 2008 for Mac.

## Using Scripts in Office

So how do you know if you have any scripts in Office 2008 for Mac? Easy. Look on the program window's menu bar. At the far right end, just after the Help menu, you'll notice a funny-looking scroll icon. That's the Script menu, as shown in Figure 35.5. Word, Excel, PowerPoint, and Entourage all have such a menu. When you click it, the menu lists any available AppleScript scripts. The only Office program that actually has any scripts installed is Entourage.

You should be aware that the Script menu lists Automator workflows. Like AppleScript scripts, Apple Automator is used to create workflows for repetitive tasks, such as turning Word text to audio and sending it to your iPod. Every Office for Mac program features some sample Automator workflows you can explore. Learn more about these later in this chapter.

**FIGURE 35.5**

You can use the Script menu to view available AppleScript scripts in Word, Excel, PowerPoint, and Entourage.

Of course, you can add your own scripts to the Script menu at any time. Simply copy the script to the application's folder. For example, if you have a Word script you want to add, copy it to the /Document/ Microsoft User Data/Word Script Menu Items/ folder. This technique works only for compiled scripts, not applets.

> **TIP**    **Looking for more scripts? Go online! Type the keywords** *AppleScript Word* **or** *AppleScript Excel* **in your favorite search engine, such as Google or Yahoo!, and see what you can find. You also can find hundreds more online at sites that offer scripts, such as MacScripter** (http:// macscripter.net) **or Apple's own AppleScript site** (www.apple.com/applescript).

### Running scripts with keyboard shortcuts

After you add a script, you can assign a keyboard shortcut that you can use to quickly activate the script. Use Finder to locate the script, and add a backslash (\) followed by one or more modifier keys and a single character. For example, myscript\cf or myscript\msf. Use caution when assigning keyboard shortcuts. The Office programs do not check your keystrokes against the existing database of keyboard shortcuts already found within the programs (such as ⌘+P for Paste). If you choose one that's already in use, you end up with conflicting commands.

# Why Can't I Run VBA Scripts Anymore?

Office 2008 for Mac has done away with support for Visual Basic scripts and macros. Why did they do this? Although the intent for Office 2008 was universal application, the original Macintosh VBA Compiler was suited for earlier PowerPC-based Macs, not the new Intel-based Macs. In other words, the effort it would take to convert all the required coding was time-prohibitive. Instead, you must use AppleScript to write scripts. The good news is that everything you could do with VBA you can do with AppleScript. If you need some help migrating from VBA to AppleScript, an excellent source is Mactopia's (Microsoft) Web site (www.microsoft.com/mac), which includes AppleScript reference guides and a VBA to AppleScript guide.

Table 35.1 explains each modifier you can use with keyboard shortcut keys:

**TABLE 35.1**

## Script Modifiers

| Modifier Key | Letter Representing Modifier |
| --- | --- |
| Shift | S |
| Option | O |
| ⌘ | M |
| Control | C |

## Running an Entourage script

Because Entourage is the only Office program that comes with some existing scripts, let's find out how to use one. Entourage includes three scripts you can use to turn messages into events, notes, or tasks. Another script inserts a text file. One script opens an e-mail folder, and the last script saves the current selection as a document. For example, a colleague might e-mail you about an important trade show event coming up. You can turn the e-mail into an event on your calendar using a script. Or perhaps you want to save a block of selected text from an e-mail as a new document file for use later. You can turn the selection into a file using a script.

You can choose from the following scripts in Entourage:

- Create Event from Message
- Create Note from Message
- Create Task from Message
- Insert Text File
- Open E-mail Folder
- Save Selection

To practice using a script, let's perform the first one in the menu, turning a message into an event on your calendar. Follow these steps:

1. **Select the message in your Inbox or another e-mail folder that you want to turn into an event.**

2. **Choose Script ⇨ Create Event from Message, as shown in Figure 35.6.**

   Entourage opens the New Event window with the e-mail message's title in the Subject line and message body in the notes area, as shown in Figure 35.7.

3. **Fill out the remainder of the event form as needed, including location, start and end dates, reminders, and so on.**

4. **Save the event and exit the window.**

   Entourage adds the event to your calendar.

---

**FIGURE 35.6**

Use the Script menu to activate a script in Entourage.

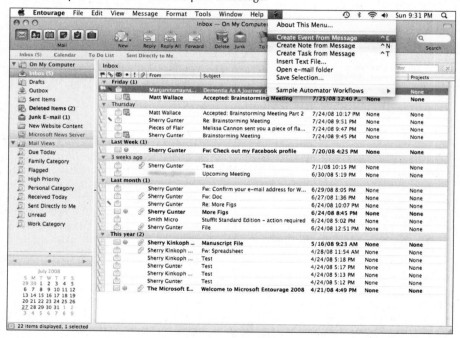

**FIGURE 35.7**

In this script, you're turning an e-mail message into an event.

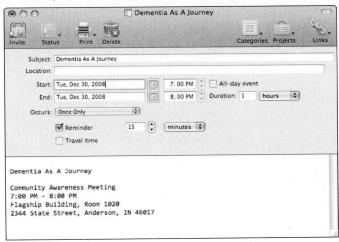

Now you can see how helpful it can be to come up with your own scripts to manage all kinds of tasks you perform not only in Entourage, but in all the Office programs.

## Using Automator workflows

Apple's Automator tool can help you create workflows for repetitive tasks you do using the Office programs. For example, you might use Automator to manipulate a large group of files, create a directory using contacts from your Address Book, collect your favorite images to send to iPhoto, and so on. Automator utilizes the power of AppleScript to give you a streamlined drag-and-drop (also called point-and-click) work platform for creating series of tasks without needing complex programming. As you learned previously, writing AppleScript involves typing statements that tell the computer what to do. Rather than having to build the script statements yourself, you can skip all the scripting and programming language and let Automator handle all the details. Automator works by letting you drag and drop commands, called *actions,* into a workflow that, when saved, tells programs what you want them to do.

Actions are the building blocks of workflows, and Automator comes with a library of preset actions and workflows you can use. Actions are any items that perform a single task, and each action is the equivalent of a single step in the process you're trying to create. You can combine actions in a series to create a workflow. Some actions are pretty straightforward, such as stopping an application, while others require user input or more information. When this is the case, a simple interface pops up for the user to enter information. The interface can be pop-up menus, check boxes, or buttons, just to name a few ways to collect user input. When you combine all these action steps, you're creating a workflow that executes each action in the order it was placed. After you've made a workflow, you can save it, reuse it, and share it with others. Any saved workflows you create can be run in the Automator window. You also can save workflows as standalone applications that can run on their own when activated. Quite simply, workflows are document files, and their entire goal is to help you accomplish a task.

### Viewing the Automator window

All the action—pun intended—surrounding Automator happens in the Automator program window. To find your way to Automator, go to the Applications folder and double-click Automator. When you first open Automator, you can start creating workflows right away using the Starting Points steps, shown in Figure 35.8. The Starting Points window walks you through the process of creating a workflow based on whatever type of goal you're trying to accomplish. Choose from Custom, Files & Folders, Music & Audio, Photos & Images, or Text. After you pick a type, you can specify the location of the content you want to use. After you make your selection and click the Choose button, you're off and running.

### FIGURE 35.8

The Starting Points steps can help you get started creating a workflow in Automator.

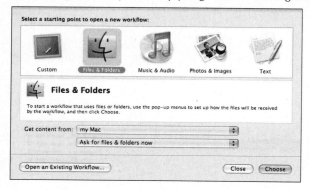

The Automator window, shown in Figure 35.8, is divided into sections. The far left has a paned section where you can select applications and actions. The larger main area is where you drag actions and order them for execution. This is where you create your workflow. The workflow shown in Figure 35.9 is one of Automator's sample workflows. The workflow is used to find a set of photographs, copy them, apply the Quartz Composition filter, and then preview the photo effects. As you can see in the figure, each step of the overall task is its own little box in the workflow. You can edit these action steps individually or reorder them depending on the workflow you're trying to create. To quit Automator at any time, click the Close button or choose Automator ➪ Quit Automator.

Sadly, we can't possibly cover everything you need to know about using Automator in this book. It's a vastly powerful tool, and it really requires its own book. However, you'll find plenty of help for using Automator in the program window's own Help files, as well as numerous sources online.

### Using Office Automator workflows

You'll be happy to know Microsoft Office 2008 for Mac comes with several Automator workflows you can try. Each Office program includes several workflows, and you can find them listed on the Script menu, as shown in Figure 35.9. The Script menu is the tiny scroll-shaped icon next to the Help menu on the menu bar. To activate a workflow and see how easy Automator is, let's try one of the sample workflows on some Excel data. You need to open Excel and select some data, and then you need to open Word. When you're ready, follow these steps:

1. **Select some data to copy in the Excel window.**

FIGURE 35.9

The Automator window in this example shows a Process Images workflow for applying a composition filter to a group of photographs.

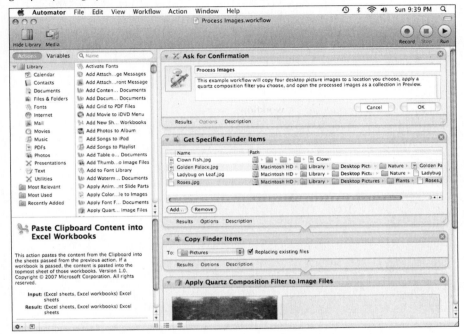

2. **Choose Script ➪ Sample Automator Workflows ➪ Send selected content to Word, as shown in Figure 35.10.**

FIGURE 35.10

You can use the Script menu to activate sample workflows.

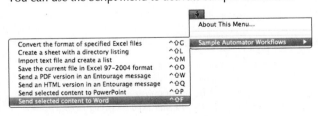

The selected data is immediately copied, Word opens to a blank document, and the data is pasted inside, as shown in Figure 35.11.

**FIGURE 35.11**

The selected Excel data is copied into Word in one fell swoop.

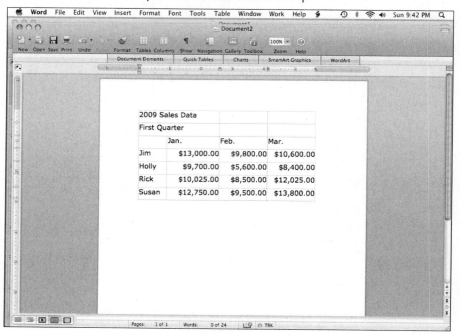

By skipping the normal copy-and-paste routine, this workflow has sped up the process of copying data. You can begin to see what enormous time-saving measures Automator workflows can achieve. You can open a sample Office workflow in the Automator window to view the actions that went into creating it, as shown in Figure 35.12. The sample workflows are found in the folder path Users ➪ Home ➪ Documents ➪ Microsoft User Data; choose the program's Script Menu Items you want to open, choose Sample Automator Workflows, and then select the workflow file.

For more information about Automator and workflows, be sure to check out the Automator Help files. You also can venture online and find help at the following sites:

- **Automator-Leopard** (`www.automator.us/leopard/index.html`): This site features training movies, podcasts, links, and more.
- **MacScripter** (`http://automatoractions.com/`): This site includes discussions and forums about Automator and actions, links, and lots of shared scripts.
- **Automator World** (`http://automatorworld.com/`): Find news and information about Automator on this site, plus hints and tips, and plenty of shared workflow documents.

**FIGURE 35.12**

You can examine any of the sample workflows using the Automator window to see how they were created.

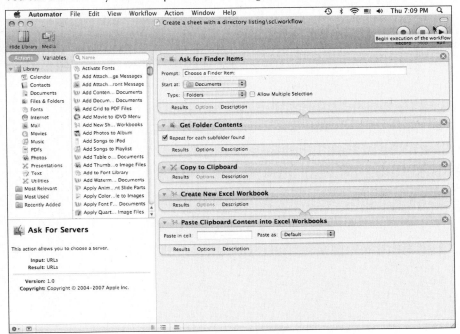

# Summary

In this chapter, we explored a little bit about the wide world of scripting. Scripting is a way of writing instructions that tell the computer what to do. You learned the basics about AppleScript and how to utilize the Script Editor window to write your own scripts. You also learned how to tap into several of the sample scripts that installed with Entourage.

You also were introduced to the world of workflows and automating repetitive tasks using Automator. The Automator tool is ideal for making quick work out of mind-numbing computer tasks, and each Microsoft Office program installs with a few workflows you can try.

Now that we've arrived at the last chapter, pat yourself on the back. You've thoroughly expanded your knowledge of the Microsoft Office 2008 programs, and we hope you've gained enough experience to move forward with mastering the ins and outs of one of the most popular software suites in the world. Good luck with all your Office projects now and in the future!

# Glossary

**absolute cell references**  An Excel cell reference that specifies the exact address of a cell. An absolute cell reference takes the form $A$1, $B$75, and so on.

**active cell**  The current cell in an Excel worksheet, surrounded by a dark border.

**active document**  The document window that is currently selected in your software window.

**active window**  In a multiple-window environment, the window that you are currently using or that is currently selected. Only one window can be active at a time.

**add-in**  A small program that can be installed to add commands and functions to a main program.

**Address Book**  An electronic equivalent of a contacts list or Rolodex. An integral part of Entourage, the Address Book organizes e-mail addresses, names, phone numbers, mailing addresses, and other contact information.

**alignment**  The way text or other document elements line up against the margins of a page, within the width of a column, within a text box, against tab stops, or in a worksheet cell.

**AppleScript**  A scripting language built into the Mac operating system for coding automated tasks, customizing routines, and speeding up workflow.

**applet**  Scripts written by other users; also called droplets.

**archiving**  The process of storing for future reference. You can archive old e-mail messages in Entourage and save them in a standard text-only .mbox file format.

**argument**  Information you supply a function for calculation. An argument can be a value, a reference, a name, a formula, or another function.

**attachment**  A complete file or item that is sent with an e-mail message or stored with a task entry in Entourage.

**auditing tools**  Excel tools for finding the root of formula errors.

**AutoCalculate**  An Excel feature that automatically calculates any selected cells.

**AutoCorrect**  A Word feature that corrects text or changes a string of characters to a word or phrase automatically.

**AutoFill**  An Excel feature that allows you to create a series of incremental or fixed values on a worksheet by dragging the fill handle with the mouse.

**AutoFit**  An Excel feature that helps you fit data into columns and rows.

**AutoFormat**  A feature found in Word and Excel that helps you quickly format your data based on preset formats.

**AutoMark**  A Word tool for marking and indexing lengthy documents using a two-column concordance style.

**Automator**  An easy way to automate tasks, such as file renaming, you perform repetitively using built-in actions to create workflows.

**AutoRecover**  An Office feature that allows you to easily recover data lost during a power outage or other mishap.

**AutoShape**  A collection of pre-drawn artwork installed with Office for adding shapes, arrows, flowchart objects, star and banner shapes, and other graphic objects to your Office files.

**AutoSum**  An Excel function for adding up a selected column or row of values.

**AutoText** A formatted block of boilerplate text that you can insert whenever you need it in Word.

**axes** Borders on the chart plot area that provide a frame of reference for measurement or comparison. On column charts, data values are plotted along the Y axis, and categories are plotted along the X axis.

**Bcc** Blind carbon copy. A copy of an e-mail message that you send without the primary recipient's knowledge.

**block quotes** A block of text set off with both a left and right indent from the margin, used for quoting other text or sources.

**boilerplate text** See *placeholder text*.

**bookmarks** Digital markers you can add to a document to help you return to a specific point or area.

**browser** A program for surfing the Internet, such as Safari or Firefox.

**Cc** Carbon copy. When you send an e-mail message, you can send a CC (copy) to other recipients.

**cell** The intersection of a column and a row.

**cell address** The location of a cell on an Excel sheet. This consists of a row address and a column address, such as F12, which indicates the intersection of column F and row 12. Also referred to as a *cell reference*.

**cell reference** The set of row and column coordinates that indentifies a cell location on a worksheet. Also referred to as a *cell address*.

**chart** A graphical representation of data, such as data in an Excel worksheet.

**chart area** The entire region surrounding the chart, just outside the plot area.

**chart type** The way chart data is displayed; column, bar, and pie are common chart types.

**circular reference** When you create a formula in Excel that refers to the cell containing the formula, creating an error.

**Citations** A specialized Toolbox palette for helping you refer to other sources, such as a book or article, in your Office documents.

**client** A program that receives data that is linked, copied, or embedded from another program.

**clip art** A pre-drawn illustration or graphics object you can insert into an Office file. Office comes with a collection of clip art files you can use to illustrate documents, worksheets, and presentations, called the Clip Gallery.

**Clip Gallery** A library of clip art graphics you can insert into your Office files.

**clippings** Snippets from documents, pictures, and other Office files you can store in the Office Scrapbook Palette to reuse again later, such as in a project.

**Close button** A tiny red circle button in the corner of a window that you can use to close the window.

**command** An instruction that tells the computer to carry out a task or perform an action.

**comment** Special text boxes used to add notes or a query within a document without adding the text directly into the document. Comments are commonly used with shared documents.

**Compatibility Report** An Office feature for checking backward compatibility with previous versions of Office, allowing you to fix any problems that may occur while saving files.

**conditional formatting** An Excel feature for formatting cells automatically when they reach a certain condition, such as turning the cell contents red when they reach a negative value.

**cursor** The flashing vertical line that shows where text is entered. Also called an *insertion point*.

**data** Information you type into a document, cell, or slide.

**data marker** A bar, area, dot, slice, or other symbol in a chart that represents a single data point or value originating from a worksheet cell. Related data markers in a chart comprise a data series.

**data point** An individual value, plotted in a chart, that originates from a single cell in a worksheet. Data points are represented by bars, columns, lines, pie or doughnut slices, dots, and various other shapes called data markers.

**data series** A group of related data points in a chart that originate from a single worksheet row or column. Each data series in a chart is distinguished by a unique color or pattern.

**data source** The underlying worksheet data that's displayed in a chart.

**data table** A range of cells used for analyzing data and outcomes.

**database** A computer program that specializes in organizing, storing, and retrieving data. The term also describes a collection of data.

**destination document** The document or file containing the data you link or embed from the source document.

**Document Map** A Word navigating pane for viewing just the headings in a document.

**drop caps** Extra large capitals that start the beginning of a chapter's first paragraph in books.

**Elements Gallery** A library of prebuilt elements such as title pages, tables, or ledgers that you can drop into your Office documents, worksheets, or presentations.

**embedded object** An object inserted from a source program into a destination document.

**encoding** The process of preparing a file attachment for opening in other programs when received as an e-mail.

**export** The process of converting and saving a file to be used in another program.

**extensions** The three- or four-letter suffix that follows a filename preceded by a dot, such as myfile.docx. File extensions tell what kind of file it is.

**field** In a list or database, a column of data that contains a particular type of information, such as Last Name or Phone Number. In a form, a field acts as a container for data entry.

**fill color** The color that appears behind text or a graphic.

**filters** A set of criteria you can apply to show specific items and hide all others.

**flagging** Marking an e-mail message with a visual symbol indicating some sort of follow-up or importance level.

**font** A typeface, such as Calibri, Cambria, or Arial.

**footers** Text that appears at the bottom of every printed page.

**format** To apply commands to data to change the way it looks or appears in a file. Formatting controls range from text formatting to formatting for objects such as graphics.

**formula** A sequence of values, cell references, names, functions, or mathematical operators that produces a new value from existing values. A formula always begins with an equal sign (=).

**function** A built-in formula that uses a series of values (arguments) to perform an operation and then returns the result of the operation.

**gradient** A color effect for creating the appearance of gradient changes from one end of a spectrum to the other in a fill color.

**group** To combine one or more objects to act as a single object, which you can then move and resize.

**gutter margin** The inner margin where pages attach to a spine. Gutter margins are usually much wider than outer margins.

**handouts** A PowerPoint feature that lets you create paper handouts to go along with the slide presentation.

**hanging indent** An indent that leaves the first line of a paragraph of text intact, but indents the rest of the paragraph.

**header** Text that appears at the top of every printed page.

**HTML** Stands for Hypertext Markup Language, a special format for Web pages.

**hyperlink** Colored, underlined text that you can click to open another file or go to a Web address.

**IMAP** The Internet Message Access Protocol, one of two popular standards for e-mail accounts.

**import** The process of converting and opening a file that was stored or created in another program.

**inline** An object that is placed with a line of text, behaving like a text character.

**insertion point** The flashing vertical line that shows where text is entered. Also called a *cursor*.

**iPhoto** An Apple software application for importing and organizing digital photos.

**iTunes** A digital media player application made by Apple, used for playing and organizing digital music and video files.

**junk mail** Unwanted or unsolicited e-mail.

**keyboard shortcuts** Keyboard combinations you can press to quickly activate a command rather than using the mouse to point and click.

**layering** The act of placing one object over another, such as a block of text over a graphic, creating a layered appearance. Also called *arranging*.

**layout** The arrangement of text, graphics, and other elements on a page.

**legend** A chart element that tells what each data series on a chart represents.

**ligatures** Pairs of letters that share common components when printed next to each other, such as ff or fi.

**line spacing** The amount of space between lines within a paragraph. The term leading (pronounced "ledding"), remaining from typesetting days, also refers to the amount of space between lines in a paragraph.

**linked object** To copy an object, such as a graphic or text, from one file to another or from one program to another so that a dependent relationship exists between the object and its source file. The dependent object also is updated whenever the data changes in the source object.

**macro** A set of stored automated commands that perform a common task.

**mail merge** The process of creating several identical documents, such as form letters or mailing labels, that each pull a different set of information, such as addresses, out of a database.

**mailing list** An electronic list for distributing information to many users at once. Also called an *e-mail list* or *e-list*.

**margin** The area surrounding the edge of a document page.

**Master Document** An organizational feature in Word for bringing together individual files to create one large document.

**Master Pages** A feature in Publishing Layout view in Word that contains all the objects you want to appear on every page in a printed document.

**merge** Combining two cells to create one cell in Word tables or Excel worksheets. In Word's Track Changes feature, merging changes from two or more different documents creates one document.

**My Day** An Entourage feature that works outside the program to show you important information about your schedule at a glance.

**Navigation Pane** A special pane in Word for helping you view and edit lengthy documents.

**nested formulas** An Excel formula that is used as an argument in another formula.

**nested tables** A table within another table.

**newsgroup** A repository of messages posted from users from different locations. Also called a *discussion group*.

**object** A table, chart, graphic, equation, or other form of information you create and edit. An object can be inserted, pasted, or copied into any file.

**palette** A box containing input choices you can select from for carrying out a specific feature or formatting task.

**PivotTable** A special Excel table that analyzes data from other lists and tables.

**placeholder text** Default text included to give you some ideas about content and the overall appearance of a document, presentation, or worksheet. Sometimes this text is nonsense text and is referred to as "Latin text" or "Greek text" because it can't be read.

**POP** The Post Office Protocol, one of two popular standards for e-mail accounts.

**Project Center** An Office tool for organizing and managing the various elements and parts of a project, ranging from notes and e-mails to documents and spreadsheets.

**Project Gallery** A library of templates you can use to quickly create Office files.

**precedents**  Cell references referred to in a formula.

**Quick Filter**  An Entourage function for helping you filter through e-mail folders to find an e-mail message.

**Quick Tables gallery**  Part of the new Elements Gallery that lists a variety of preformatted tables you can insert.

**range**  Two or more cells in an Excel worksheet.

**read-only files**  Files that can only be opened, not edited or changed in any way.

**record**  A single row in a database or list. The first row usually contains field names, and each additional row in the database is a record.

**reference**  The location of a cell or range of cells on a worksheet, indicated by column letter and row number.

**relative cell reference**  Specifies the location of a referenced cell in relation to the cell containing the reference. A relative reference in Excel takes the form of A4, C12, and so on.

**scenario**  A named set of input values that you can substitute in a worksheet model to perform a what-if analysis.

**Scrapbook**  An Office feature for collecting snippets of text, pictures, and other elements and keeping them in one location for later use. The Scrapbook feature is part of the new Toolbox collection of palettes.

**signatures**  Lines of text that appear at the bottom of every e-mail message you send or newsgroup message you post. Signatures can relay contact information, company information, or favorite quotes.

**slide master**  PowerPoint slides that allow you to control which elements appear on every slide in a presentation.

**Smart Button**  A button that appears in the Office programs right after you perform a certain task, such as pasting text. Smart Buttons, when clicked, display a pop-up menu of commands related to the task at hand.

**SmartArt**  A collection of graphics in the Office programs that you can use to illustrate processes, workflows, hierarchies, and other diagram illustrations.

**sort**  A method of organizing items in a database so you can find them more easily.

**spam**  Unsolicited e-mail. Also called *junk e-mail* or *bulk e-mail*.

**Spotlight search**  The Mac OS X search feature that allows you to search throughout all the Apple files to find results.

**styles**  A collection of formatting settings you can apply to text.

**tab-delimited**  A plain text document in which the information for each record appears on its own line with a tab between each field.

**task**  A to-do list item you add to Entourage to help you manage your things to do.

**template**  Predesigned documents, spreadsheets, or presentations you can use to create your own files.

**theme**  Custom color and font collections you can assign to your Office files.

**Toolbox**  A new Office window containing a collection of palettes of tools you commonly use.

**tracking**  A reviewing feature you can use when sharing Office files with colleagues to keep track of who adds what to the file content.

**transitions**  A slide show effect that determines how one slide advances to the next. Transition effects include fades, dissolves, and split screens.

**ungroup**  To separate grouped objects and return them to their individual elements.

**URL**  Uniform Resource Locator, a Web site address.

**watermark**  A faint design that appears behind text in a document.

**WordArt**  Pre-drawn text items that act as graphic objects you can place in your Office files.

**wrapping**  The way text flows around or through an object. For example, you can have a graphic object on the left side of the page and make text flow above, to the right of, and below the object.

**zoom**  To magnify your view of a document or to change the size of a window to full-screen or original size.

# Index

## SYMBOLS AND NUMERICS

# B

# N

# X